Wills From The Archdeaconry Of Suffolk:

1629–1636

Archdeaconry of Suffolk

Suffolk County, England

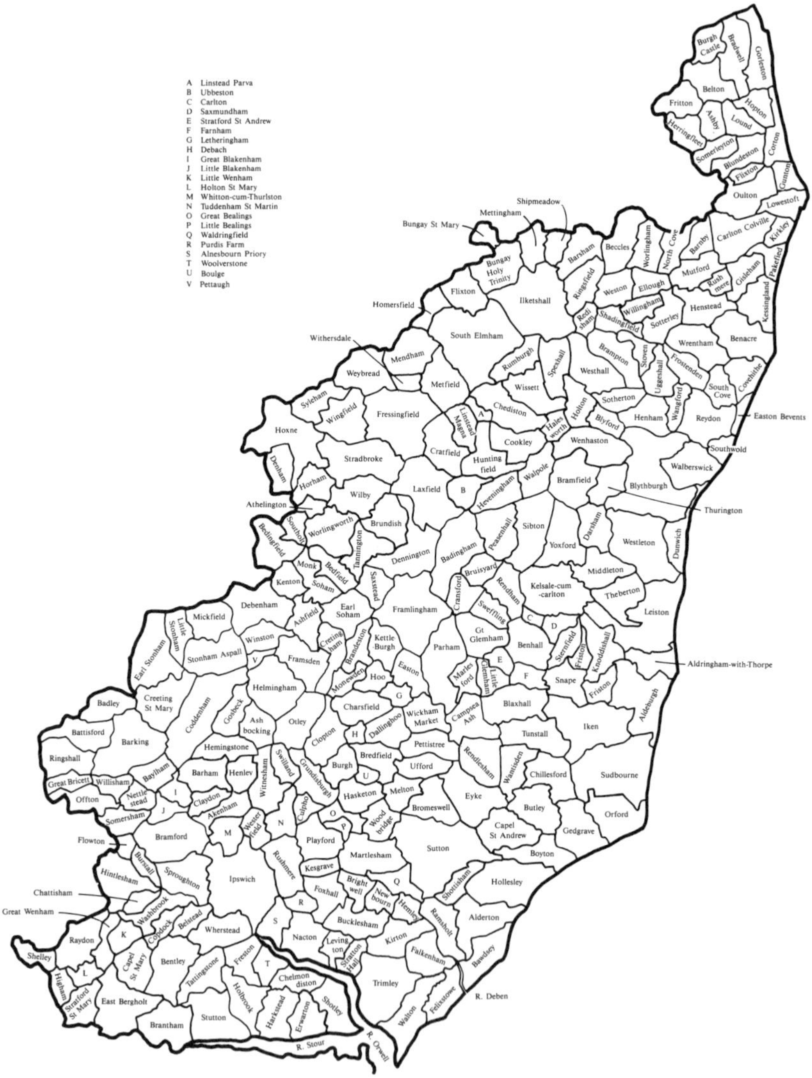

Wills From

The Archdeaconry Of Suffolk:

1629–1636

Abstracted by
Marion E. Allen
and
Nesta R. Evans

The Society gratefully acknowledges the support of
The John Brooks Threlfall Fund in publishing this volume.

New England Historic Genealogical Society
Boston
1986

Library of Congress Cataloging in Publication Data

Wills From The Archdeaconry Of Suffolk: 1629–1636

Includes index.
1. Suffolk—Genealogy. 2. Wills—England—Suffolk. I. Church of England. Archdeaconry of Suffolk. II. New England Historic Genealogical Society.
CS435.S7W55 1986 929'.34264 86-12547
ISBN 0-88082-017-9

Table of Contents

Acknowledgments

The New England Historic Genealogical Society would like to thank the compilers of this volume Marion E. Allen of Ipswich, Nesta Evans of Fressingfield and Richard B. Allnutt, also of Ipswich, for their valuable contribution to Suffolk history with the abstracting of the Wills from the Archdeaconry of Suffolk. Historians and genealogists on both sides of the Atlantic will find this new addition to published source records an invaluable tool for social and genealogical research.

The compilation of this volume could not have been accomplished without the financial support of the Society's John Brooks Threlfall Fund. This fund, created by John B. Threlfall of Madison, Wisconsin, an eminent genealogist in his own right, is also responsible for the publication of the *Essex Wills (England)* series, edited by F. G. Emmison, and a number of American projects including the *Vital Records of Charlestown, Massachusetts*.

In addition, the Society would also like to thank Dominique M. Pickett, the project editor, for handling the final production of the volume and indexes. Thanks also go to Rose A. R. Glass, Marian H. White, and Henry Hallowell for their assistance at various stages of production. We would also like to thank Dr. Ralph J. Crandall, the Society's Director, and Edward W. Hanson, Director of Publications, for their support of the expanded publications program over the past several years.

Introduction

This volume contains the 1091 surviving Wills proved in the Court of the Archdeacon of Suffolk during the calendar years 1629 to 1636 inclusive, which are old style years running from 25 March to 24 March. Wherever possible the register copies of Wills have been used, but the registers for 1632 and 1636 are lost. For these two years the original Wills have been abstracted. Occasionally in other years a will has survived in its original form and not as a register copy: these have also been abstracted.

The area covered by the Archdeaconry of Suffolk is roughly the same as that of the old county of East Suffolk, and the boundaries of its jurisdiction are marked on the map on the frontispiece. This map also shows the boundaries and names of all the parishes in East Suffolk to enable readers to find places mentioned in the text.

Until 1858 practically all Wills were proved in the ecclesiastical courts. In principle probate was granted by the archdeaconry court covering the area in which the testator's property lay, but if it came under the jurisdiction of more than one archdeaconry, then the Bishop's or Consistory Court was used. In the case of persons with property in more than one diocese probate was granted by the Court of the Archbishop of Canterbury, which covered the whole of the southern half of England. In practice these rules were not always followed, and many Wills were proved in a higher court than was strictly necessary. It is not always possible to explain why this took place, but geographical convenience and social aspirations are two factors which encouraged the proving of some Suffolk Wills in the Consistory Court of the Diocese of Norwich rather than in that of the local archdeaconry. For these wills T.F. Barton and M.A. Farrow, comps., *Index of Wills Proved in the Consistory Court of Norwich, 1604–1686* (Norfolk Record Society, 1958). Consistory court officials were to be found in a number of places in north Suffolk, and it was probably more convenient for executors in this part of the county to use their services rather than to travel to the Archdeacon's Court at Ipswich. Other Suffolk Wills are indexed in *Calendar of Wills at Ipswich 1440–1600* compiled by Frederick Arthur Crisp, *The Ipswich Probate Inventories 1583–1631*, volume 22 in the Suffolk Records Society's series edited by Michael Reed and the *Index of Probate Records of the Court Of The Archdeacon Of Suffolk, 1444–1700* issued by the British Record Society and edited by W.R. and R.K. Serjeant.

Generally speaking, Wills proved in the higher courts are those of the richer and more influential members of society. The corollary of this is that these people are under-represented in the Court whose Wills are published in this volume. It is yeomen, craftsmen and tradesmen who predominate, and the Wills of gentlemen, rich merchants and clergy are few in number.

It is impossible to say what proportion of the population made Wills in the early seventeenth century; estimates range from ten to twenty percent; nor how many of the Wills have survived. Equally no precise figures can be given for the size of the population of East Suffolk in the 1630s. In the year 1603 a return was made to the Bishop of Norwich of all communicants in his diocese. There were a total of 31,761 in the Archdeaconry of Suffolk, but this figure is defective as there are no returns for fifteen parishes, three of which are in Ipswich. Nevertheless, this figure can be used to give a rough estimate of the population at this date. It is usually assumed that there were 2.8 communicants per household, and that 40 percent of the population were children. On this basis, and making no allowance for the fifteen missing parishes, there were approximately 52,939 persons living in 11,343 households in the Archdeaconry of Suffolk in 1603. At this period Suffolk was one of the most densely populated and wealthy of English counties.

Legal Terms

It may be helpful to some readers to have explained certain legal terms which are used in some of the Wills. References to copyhold land are quite frequent. Land held by copyhold tenure depended on manorial custom and on the will of the lord of the manor; the tenant was protected not by statute law but by title written down in the manorial court rolls. In practice in seventeenth-century Suffolk most copyholds were of the kind known as copyhold of inheritance and which gave virtually as good security to the tenant as did freehold tenure. When copyhold property was sold or inherited the transfer was noted in the court rolls, and a copy of the entry was given to the new tenant: this constituted his title deed. It is not unusual to find a tenant 'surrendering' his copyhold property to 'the use' of his will to ensure that the land passes to his heir. Mention of this process appears in some of the Wills. In a number of the Wills reference is made to the dowry of the testator's wife. Alternative names for dowry are jointure or thirds. It was usual for the widow to have the right to one-third of her late husband's estate either during her own lifetime or until she remarried.

Finally in a handful of Wills, for instance that of Henry Lovedaye in Will 698, wardship is mentioned. On the death of a tenant-in-chief, that is one who held land directly from the Crown, and whose heir had not attained a majority (21 for boys and 14 for girls), the Crown was entitled to hold the land and draw its revenues until the heir came of age. This could be an useful source of income for the Crown, particularly so during the 1630s when Charles I was trying to rule without recourse to taxation which could be sanctioned only by Parliament. Wardships were often farmed out to the highest bidder, and this not infrequently led to abuses and mismanagement of estates.

Books in Wills

Bequests of Bibles are reasonably frequent, but it is much more unusual to find other books mentioned. Four of the Wills in this volume and three in the second volume include bequests of named books, and they are listed below just as they appear in the text. A brief note follows for the benefit of those readers who may wish to know more about these works and their authors.

1. William Cottwyn, yeoman of Woodbridge. Will: 662 *
   Mr. Perkins books

2. Edmund Ellitt, carpenter of Kessingland. **
   The Practice of Piety
   Josephus on the *Destruction of Jerusalem*
   A book called Admonition to the People of England
   Another called the Unburdening of a loaden conscience
3. Thomas Fenn, yeoman of Monk Soham. Will: 782 *
   Book called *Perdicall*
   Book called *Luther*
   Cooper on the Romans
   Dade on the Commandments
   Treatise of the Church
   The Way of Life
4. William Herringe, yeoman of Stradbroke. Will: 199 *
   A book called Hieron's works
   The Perkin's works
   Dr. Hill's works
   Mr. Ward's works
   Dr Preston's works in the three several books
   Sir Christopher Sibthorpe's works against the Papists
5. Samuel Lawrence the elder of Syleham. **
   Calvin's sermons of Job
   Mr Perkin's volume
   Erasmus on the Four Evangelists
   Thomas Adam's sermons
   Mr Parr's book of the Romans
   Mr Ward's sermons
   Mr Newton's work
   Mr Roger's sermons
6. William Martin, clerk of Cookley. Will: 941 *
   Downeham's *Christian Warfare*
   Mr Perkins *Six Principles*
   Mr Perkins *The Practice of Piety*
   John Calvin *The Institution of Christian Religion*
   Thesaurus Concionatorum
7. Roger Smallhead of Ufford. **
   Luther on the Galatians
   Physic books
   A trestise of the Pestilence
   One book called Dalton
   Mascall's book of cattle
   Dod on the commandments
   A Practical catechism
   The Grounds of Divinity
   Mr Perkin's works
   Treatise of God's Providence

*Wills in this volume (1629–1636)
**Wills in volume (1637–1640)

Almost all the books listed above are theological works, some by well known authors such as Calvin. The Mr Perkins mentioned in five of these Wills is William Perkins (1558–1602), who had a great reputation as a teacher at Cambridge and as a preacher. He was one of the most popular theological writers of his age. Like Perkins, all the others who could be traced were Puritan in their sympathies. Thomas Adams (fl. 1612–53) was a Puritan preacher, whose sermons were published in 1629. Gervase Babington's Works were published in 1613. William Cooper, whose *Three heavenly treatises upon the eighth chapter to the Romans* was published in 1609. Michael Dalton published *The Countrey Justice* in 1618, and Edward Dalton's *Doubting Downfall* appeared in 1621. The Dalton mentioned in Roger Smallhead's Will could be either of these. John Dod's (1545–1649) book *Puritan plaine and familiar Exposition of the Ten Commandments* appeared in 1604. John Downham or Downame (died 1652), was a Puritan divine and preacher. His *The Christian Warfare*, published 1604, is his best known work. Samuel Hieron (1576?–1617), a Puritan divine, had his Works published in 1614. Leonard Mascall (died 1589) was a translator and writer of books on husbandry and fishing. His book *The Firste Booke of Cattell* was published in 1587. Thomas Newton (1542–1607) was a poet, physician and divine. Elnatham Parr published *A Plain Exposition of Chapters of 8 to 12 of the Epistle to the Romans* in 1618 and of Chapters 13 to 16 in 1621. John Preston, D.D. (1587–1628), Cambridge don and Puritan divine, was chaplain to Charles I when he was Prince of Wales, and became Master of Emmanuel College, Cambridge. Richard Rogers' Sermons were published in 1611, but there are several authors with the name Rogers. Sir Christopher Sibthorpe (d. 1632), a Justice of the King's Bench in Ireland 1607–32 and Pamphleteer, published three tracts against Roman Catholics in 1622, 1625, and 1627. Mr Ward is probably Samuel Ward of Ipswich, who lived from 1577 to 1640. He was Town Preacher of Ipswich from 1603 to 1635. A collection of his sermons and treatises was published in 1627–8.

Sources: A. W. Pollard and G. R. Redgrave, *Short Title Catalogue of English Books 1475–1640*, (1926)
Dictionary of National Biography

Editorial Method

In abstracting the Wills published in this volume certain conventions have been followed, and these are set out here to aid the reader. Spelling of place and Christian names has been modernised, but surnames have been left in their original form. Archaic words are explained in the glossary, and a list of abbreviations used appears at the end of the introduction. In order to save space, and to avoid tedious repetition, certain frequently recurring and lengthy clauses have been abbreviated as follows. 'Benefit of survivorship' is used where provision is made for the eventuality of one or more of a number of legatees dying before inheriting. When authority is given to legatee(s) to enter property and/or distrain thereon to secure payment of a legacy, the phrase 'power of distraint' has been used. Lastly, use has been made of 'power reserved' when the Court has granted administration of an estate to one party, but has reserved the power to grant similar authority to another party if he or she applies for it. All details of bequests have been included, and appear in the order in which they are set down in the Wills, but religious preambles bequeathing testators' souls have been omitted. These last generally follow one of several standard formulae, and one is given here to indicate their content.

> I William Kettle of Beccles in the County of Suffolk yeoman being sicke in bodie but in good & perfect remembrance (thankes be given unto Almightie God therefore) doe ordeyne & make this my last will & testament in manner & forme following. First and principally I give and bequeath my sowle unto Allmightie God that gave it trusting asuredlie through the meritts of Jesus Christ to ryse agayne at the last daie to life everlasting.

Abbreviations in Wills

A	Administration act or bond
Admon.	Administration granted
als.	alias
bach.	bachelor
co.	county
esq.	esquire
exor(s).	executor(s)
exrx.	executrix
gent.	gentleman/woman
husb.	husbandman
(In.)	Inventory available
jnr.	junior
(N)	Nuncupative will
Pr.	Proved
R	Register copy is available
snr.	senior
W	The original will was used to make this abstract
(W)	The original will is available
W(R*)	The Wills are in the register but on damaged pages and can only be read completely in originals.
wid.	widow(er)
wit.	witness(es)
(X)	The person to whom is this mark is suffixed made his or her mark.
yeo.	yeoman

CHAPTER I

Abstracts of Wills Contained in Register No. 59 and/or File No. 65 of Wills Proved in the Court of the Archdeacon of Suffolk.

W(R) RALPH BLAXHALL of Bentley, husbandman (N). April 1629 (1)

All goods to CICELY READ of Bentley whom I appoint exrx., except 20s. owing from my brother SAMUEL of Bramford which I give him. Witnesses: Mrs ELIZABETH GOSNOLD, the wid. FORDE, THOMAS COE of Bentley. Pr. at Ipswich 30 May 1629.

W(R) THOMAS BISHOP (X) of Hemley. 7 March 1628/9 (2)

Sick. All goods bonds bills debts and duties due to me I give to TRYPHENA my wife and my daughter MARY COALE wife of PETER COALE of Felixstowe (and after her death to her children), by equal portions, all my debts being first paid and legacies given out, viz: to JOAN LINE of Woodbridge, wid., 10s. To THOMAS LAND of Falkenham 10s. To ROBERT DIDOM 5s. To JOHN LAUSON of Woodbridge, apprentice to WILLIAM DRIVER 20s. at age 24. These legacies to be paid within one half year of my decease. I appoint my said daughter sole exrx. Witnesses: GEORGE COULTON, WILLIAM [SHALE?] (X). His wife shall hold his farm in Hemley till Michaelmas, the profits being divided equally between his daughter and wife. And his meaning is that the goods be divided (the one parting and the other choosing) and then both join equally to make up the money for the above legacies. Pr. at Ipswich 3 June 1629. Admon. to MARY COLE daughter of deceased.

R(W) DOROTHY MIXTER (X) of Shotley, widow. 25 April 1628 (3)

To the poor of Shotley 30s. within 3 months. To THOMAS ADRYAN and EDWARD ADRYAN my nephews £5 each within 6 months with benefit of survivorship. To my kinswoman the wife of JOHN TOOLEY of Wivenhoe, co. Essex, £5 within 6 months. To MARY TOOLY and LAURENCE TOOLY, other 2 of her children, 20s. each within 6 months. To ELIZABETH KINGE my kinswoman £10 within 6 months, my best gown and best petticoat. To GRACE SMYTH and SUSAN SMYTH my kinswomen 50s. each within 6 months. To the Widow MYXTER, late wife of RICHARD MYXTER of Shotley 10s. within 6 months. To BRIDGET REYNOLDS my husband's kinswoman 10s. within 6 months. To ADAM ELLIS of Shotley 20s. at 21, failing him to the poor of Shotley, he to have the interest for said 20s. according to the king's majesty's allowance, till he be 21. To ELIZABETH WHITEHEAD my late servant 10s. within 6 months. To my servant SUSAN NUPORT 5s. To JOHN HAUELL of Chelmondiston, the writer hereof, 5s. To Mr CARTER, parson of Shotley, 10s. within 6 months on condition he preach one sermon at my burial. To my kinswoman the wife of JOHN TOOLY my cloak. Remainder of movables to be equally divided between my kinswomen aforementioned. I ordain JOHN COLE of Shotley my exor. and give him 20s. for his pains. Witnesses: JOHN HAUELL, SUSAN NEWPORT (X), ELIZABETH COOKE (X). Pr. at Ipswich 30 May 1629.

R(W) ELIAS READ (X) of Henley. 8 June 1629 (4)

Sick. To be buried in Henley churchyard. To my son ELLIS £20 at 22. To kinswoman AGNES WOLFE one calf. To my maid MATHEWE LORD 5s. My debts and funeral expenses paid, I give the rest of my goods to my wife AGNES whom I make with GEORGE SUGGETT exors. Witnesses: OLIVER KETTERIDGE (X), MICHAEL WOLFE (X), JOHN SIMPSON. Pr. at Ipswich 23 June 1629.

R(W) THOMAS SCOTCHMERE (X) of Earl Soham, yeoman. (5)
16 June 1629

Sick. Having formerly disposed of my lands, I give to THOMAS my eldest son the ceiled bedstead with the feather bed in the parlour wherein I lie, with the trundle bed under the same, and the flock bed thereon, and all the furniture belonging to same and used therewith except sheets; one glass keep, 1 table, 2 joined stools, 1 wicker chair, 1 great turned chair, 1 lesser turned chair, 1 coffer, 1 warming pan - these being now in the parlour; and the long table with the form and 1 cupboard and 1 little square table - these being in the hall; and 1 coffer on the hall chamber and 1 cheese-press, 1 salting trough, 1 milk tub, 1 standing churn the best, my best brass pot and best kettle, my lessest spit, the lessest dripping pan, 1 pair of querns, my cart tumbril, plough, harrows with all the plough and cart harness and furniture, with 1 coulter and 1 share. To PETER my son my ceiled bedstead standing on the east side of the hall chamber with the featherbed and flock bed thereon and the boulster and other furniture thereon used except sheets; 1 pillow and 1 pillowbere and 2 turned chairs in the hall, 1 joined stool, my best spit and dripping pan, a new coffer on the hall chamber, 1 brass pot in value next, the one kettle called the dish kettle being the lessest, the best candlestick, 1 other old kettle, 1 beer vessel next the best, the middle skillet. I give my corn on the chamber and on the ground to be equally divided among all my four sons THOMAS, PETER, ROBERT and JAMES. My cheese and butter to be equally divided between my four sons, and my hay among my three oldest sons THOMAS, PETER, and ROBERT. To ROBERT my son a joined bedstead, ceiled, standing on the west side of the hall chamber with a featherbed and flock bed lying thereon, with all the furniture therewith now used except sheets, with a pillow and pillowbere, 1 joined stool, 1 joined box, 1 cupboard table, 1 turned great chair, a lesser turned chair, 1 great joined chest in the parlour, 1 brass candlestick next the best, 1 kettle next the best, 1 pot posnet, the biggest skillet, 1 mortar of bell metal with a brass pestle, the lesser frying pan, 1 share, 1 coulter, 1 mattock, 1 spade, 1 hand-hook, 1 hatchet, the worst plough. To JAMES my son a livery bedstead standing on the chamber over the dairy, with the featherbed and other furniture belonging except sheets, with 1 pillow, 1 pillowbere, 1 hoop chair, 1 joined stool, 1 coffer on the hall chamber, 1 back turned chair, 1 little skillet, 1 brass candlestick, 1 little kettle. To THOMAS my son 2 trammels, 1 pair of cob irons, 1 fire shovel, 1 pair of tongs, 1 pair of bellows, 1 peel, 1 coal rake, 1 grindstone with the trough, 2 small joined stools, 1 pair of scales with the beam and weights, whereof 5 are leaden. Said son THOMAS shall pay his other three brothers out of the last gift and the best kettle 3s. 4d. each. To ROBERT my son all the debt which WILLIAM BARKER owes me being £40 "and so much at more", and £10 4s. which THOMAS TURNER owes me, and £10 8s. which NICHOLAS CARTER owes. To JAMES my son £21 10s. which JOHN TURNER owes and £21 12 s. which JAMES EADE owes, and £5 8s. which JOHN WAGE owes, and £26 13s. which THOMAS GOODALL owes, and 40s. which JOHN SHEPPARD of Creeting owes. To PETER my son £41 15s. which LAURENCE VINCENT owes. To my said 4 sons, 4 pairs of sheets equally divided. All my other linen, pewter, household stuff, implements and utensils of house and husbandry, and my wool and apparel to be equally divided among the four sons. To THOMAS my son my armour, my old mare with saddle, bridle, pommel and other riding furniture, and all my ladders, hay rakes, planks, boards and timber except one cart load of the last felling, which load I give to ROBERT my son. To THOMAS my son all my swine and poultry, paying my other three sons 15s. each; 2 of the best milch cows and 2 of the worst. To PETER my son 2 of the best milch cows and 2 of the worst after THOMAS has chosen. To ROBERT my son 3 cows - 2 of the best after this division and the worst. Sons THOMAS and PETER to be exors., to whom I give £8 12s. which my brother GILBERT SCATCHMER owes me and £4 7s. which JAMES SEAMAN owes, and any other debts not mentioned, and all ready money, towards burial charges, proving this will and paying debts. Witnesses: GILBERT CROTCHMERE, ROBERT DENNY, ROBERT SHEPPARD. Pr. at Earl Stonham 26 June 1629.

R(W) GEORGE SCARPE (X) of Brantham. 1 May 1629 (6)

To WILLIAM SCARPE my son 40s. at 21. To THOMAS SCARPE my son 40s. at 21. To MATTHEW SCARPE my son 40s. at 21. All other goods chattels and money to MARY my wife and sole exrx. Witnesses: THOMAS ROBBETT and ROBERT WYLYS. Pr. at Brantham 4 June 1629.

R(W) JOHN COCKER of Aldeburgh, housewright. (7)
10 January 1628/9

Sick. To be buried in churchyard of St. Peter, Aldeburgh. To FRANCES COCKER my wife my messuage wherein I dwell with yard and garden which lies between the house where I dwell and the house where HENRY KEMPSTER my son-in-law dwells, with the stead and part of the well and garden lying at the east end of the house; also with 1 pair of bedsteads standing in the hall chamber which should go with the house; also with free ingress to the other yard for passage to the seaside or for carts to bring firing and other provisions to the said FRANCES and her assigns, for her lifetime; also such household stuff as was hers before I married her, and all like movables which were PRUDENCE FAYCED's her mother; also half my household stuff for ever, all my wood and coal for firing, and 40s. To HENRY KEMPSTER and ROSE his wife my houses yards and staire ground unbequeathed, and those bequeathed to my wife after she shall have died -- to be held for the lifetime of said ROSE, and thereafter to the heirs of her body, for want of whom it shall be equally divided between THOMAS CROCKER, the son of my brother ROBERT, and the children of my sister ANN RICHES. Rest of household stuff to said HENRY and ROSE, they paying my debts legacies and burial charges. HENRY KEMPSTER to be sole exor. providing that if he defaults then FRANCES COCKER my wife shall take all the goods before given to him and ROSE, and also my year's profit from all my houses, yards and staire ground, and shall be sole exrx. Witnesses: JOHN COWBROGE and WILLIAM STEVENSONN. Pr. at Wickham 5 Aug. 1629.

R(W) MARY GARNETT (X), widow. 20 March 1626/7 (8)

Sick. To my brother JOHN FORD the £5 I lent him. To little JOHN BARNES a silver whistle. To my sister FORD, HENRY FORD's wife, my best gown. The residue to MARY FORD daughter of THOMAS FORD, to bring me to the ground and be my sole exrx. Witnesses: THOMAS KYRRE and EDMOND GREWE. Pr. at Ipswich 31 July 1629. Admon. to MARY FORD alias COOKE.

R(W) MARGERY BROWNE of Saxmundham, singlewoman. (9)
15 July 1629

Sick. To be buried in Benhall churchyard. I will there be a two penny dole at my burial. To the poor of Benhall 20s. within a month. To AGNES BROWNE my sister £18 in 6 years by even portions beginning at Michaelmas after my death; and my best coffer. To ELIZABETH my sister £20 within half a year and £14 more within 4 years, as it may arise out of the term mentioned in the will of THOMAS BROWNE my father, without any damage to the rest of my sisters; and my best bedstead, featherbed, boulster, coverlet, best blanket, a pillow, my great kettle, a little pan, 2 pair of sheets, 2 fine table napkins, my best table cloth, my best cushion. To MARGARET my sister £20 within half a year and £14 more within 4 years, as it may arise out of the term mentioned, without damage to the rest of my sisters; also my best featherbed, blue coverlet, a blanket, second best kettle, 2 pair sheets, 2 table napkins, best flannel petticoat. To BRIDGET my sister £20 within three quarters of a year and £10 more within 4 years as it may arise &c [as above]; also 2 pair sheets, 1 board cloth, 2 table napkins, 1 trunk. To JOHN GRIMSBY £7 10s. within 6 years, to JOHAS GRIMSBYE £7 10s. within 6 years, with benefit of survivorship. To MARGARET GAMAGE my god-daughter 10s. within half a year. To RICHARD BURWARD 5s. at Michaelmas and 5s. at Christmas after my death. To MARGARET HAUSE, wid., 1 ruff and my green saye apron. To MARY wife of JOHN PATCHELL my murrey coloured serge petticoat, best holland apron, best white coif, best double square. To MARY PATCHELL a white and black coif and a square. To BRIDGET BURWARD my old stuff gown. To ELIZABETH BROWNE daughter of JOHN BROWNE, my old serge gown. To ANN SMALLEDGE's daughter 20s. To ELIZABETH SIER a red carsey petticoat. The residue of chattels debts money plate jewels implements of household and household stuffs to be equally divided between my sisters ELIZABETH, MARGARET and BRIDGET. I ordain ROBERT RAMONT and JONAS WAITH exors. Witnesses: MARGERY BROWNE, GABRIEL REYE, JOHN PEACHELL. Pr. at Wickham 5 Aug. 1629.

R(W) WILLIAM RICHARDSON of Halesworth, yeoman. (10)
10 August 1629

To ELIZABETH my wife, for life, the messuage or tenement wherein I live, with the lands orchards meadows belonging, my horsemill with appurtenances in Halesworth, she maintaining all in good repair, and to enter immediately after my decease. After her death I give the same premises to PHILIP RICHARDSON my eldest son; also my land and pastures in Spexhall. To WILLIAM RICHARDSON my youngest son I give my messuage or tenement in Blyford at once after my death and £100 within 6 months. To SUSAN my daughter £120 at once. To ELIZABETH LEECE my daughter, wife of ROBERT LEECE, £20 within half a year. To said PHILIP my son £30. To ELIZABETH my wife 2 milch kine and the mare best; and half my corn, stuff and implements of household. The other half thereof to be divided equally between said WILLIAM my son and SUSAN my daughter, immediately. The which PHILIP my son and SUSAN my daughter I make exors. Witnesses: WILLIAM RICHARDSON, ROBERT LEECE (X), THOMAS FELLA with others. Pr. at Halesworth 20 Aug. 1629.

R(W) THOMASIN ANTLEBY of Kelsale, widow (N). (11)
6 September 1629

About two days before her death. All to THOMASIN my daughter who hath wrought and taken pains with me. Witnesses: the wife of EDWARD CAPP and the wife of [missing] MUSKETT and the wid. PEACHE. Pr. at Yoxford 15 Sept. 1629.

R(W) JEREMY BLYETH of Ipswich, clothier. 2 March 1628/9 (12)

Sick. To my nephew WILLIAM BUCKE in satisfaction of such moneys as were given him by JAMES BLYETH his grandfather now remaining in my hand £3; my gray mare with saddle and bridle, and my bible -- all forthwith, and 20s. within 6 months. To my mother ANN BLYTHE the use of £12, to be paid within a year, for life. Thereafter £6 to the three children of JAMES my deceased brother, viz. THOMAS, JOHN and JAMES; and £3 to JOHN BLYTH my nephew the eldest son of JOHN BLYTH my brother; and £3 to JAMES BLYTH son of HENRY BLYTH son of HENRY BLYTH my deceased brother -- with benefit of survivorship. Residue of goods and ready money to my wife MARY BLYTH, she to be sole exrx. My good friend Mr JOHN GOODWYN of Wherstead to be supervisor. Witnesses: WILLIAM VAUGHAN, JOHN BLYETH and EDMUND MYLES, notary public. Pr. at Ipswich 15 Aug. 1629.

R(W) MARGARET BENTLY (X), widow to SAMUEL BENTLEY of Somerleyton. 14 August 1629 (13)

Sick. To ELIZABETH PLAYFORD daughter of SIMON PLAYFORD of Corton, labourer, all apparel both linen and woolen, and 1 trundle bedstead with the natt, 1 featherbed, 2 pillows, 1 boulster, 3 coverings, 2 best platters, 1 salt cellar, 1 candlestick, 1 saucer, 1 new cushion, my best long belle and best brass pot, 1 great chest, 1 little chair and twistering wheel, 1 frying pan -- all these to be delivered to the hands of THOMAS RAYLTON of Corton, carpenter, as soon as I am dead, who shall keep them to the use of said ELIZABETH PLAYFORD till she be 21 or marry; which THOMAS RAYLTON I make supervisor. Failing the said ELIZABETH, all that I have given her I give to THOMAS RAYLTON, son of the said THOMAS RAYLTON. The rest of my movables I give to WILLIAM BENTLEY of Somerleyton, singleman, whom I make exor., he to deliver the goods given to ELIZABETH PLAYFORD within 5 days and prove my will within 20 days, failing which he shall have none of my goods, but they shall all go to the parties before-named. Witnesses: EDWARD MARTYN, THOMAS RAYLTON (X), THOMAS MARTYN (X). Pr. at Beccles 29 Aug. 1629.

R(W) HENRY COREWALLYS of Badingham, gentleman (N). 20 July 1629 (14)

Sick. To his mother for a remembrance 30s. To his sister FRANCES a piece to buy her a ring. To his brother CHARLES and sister BRIDGET for a remembrance 10s. each. To Mrs CATHERINE VAUGHAM 20s. To Mrs DOROTHY JEGGENS 10s. To his brother PHILIP 40s. to buy books. He named his wife sole exrx. and gave her all the rest of his goods. Witnesses: EDWARD MOULTON and [blank]. Pr. at Beccles 29 Aug. 1629 by oath of EDWARD MOULTON. Admon. granted to the relict JOAN.

R(W) FRANCES DENNY of Beccles, widow (N). 25 August 1628 (15)

To FRANCES DADE her daughter all her possessions whatsoever. Witnesses: MARGERY VYNIOR, wid., MARY wife of NICHOLAS PULHAM, and MARY wife of JOHN DADE, gent. Pr. at Beccles 26 Dec. 1628. Admon. to FRANCES DADE.

R(W) WILLIAM GRICE (X) of Beccles, butcher. 27 July 1629 (16)

Sick. To MARY my daughter £20 in 1 month, paid into the hand of friend ROBERT LONDON of Aldeby, co. Norfolk, to employ for said daughter till she be 21; failing her the £20 and the profit of it to be paid as to one half to my wife MARTHA and the other half between my brother NICHOLAS GRYSE and my sisters JOAN GRISE and ROSE PRYME. To the daughter of my brother JOHN GRYSE deceased £3, paid in 3 months to some able persons who shall undertake to bring up said child. To said brother NICHOLAS and my sister JOAN GRYSE 20s. each, paid in 3 months. The rest of chattels and implements and household goods to my wife MARTHA towards paying my debts and legacies and bringing up said daughter, and I make her sole exrx. Witnesses: ROBERT LONDON and WILLIAM BURDSEY. Pr. at Beccles 29 Aug. 1629.

R(W) GREGORY GLANDFELD of Kirketon [Kirkton] alias Shotley. 16 July 1629 (17)

Weak. To FRANCES my wife my tenement in Tattingston called Dowes, now in occupation of MICHAEL BENNETT, with all the houses, buildings, orchards, gardens and freehold lands late JOHN COKES, conveyed by said JOHN COKOS to STEPHEN GRANDFEILD as by his deed dated 20 Jan and 23rd year of queen Elizabeth [1581] appeareth, until my son JOHN be 21, after which the premises shall remain to said JOHN and his heirs. To said JOHN and his heirs one piece of meadow called Mill Meadow containing 3 roods 29 poles; and Poulters Field containing 3 1/2 acres; and Cherry Tree Field containing 1 1/2 acres and 26 poles. To FRANCES my wife my tenement "Wades" als "Waterhouse" in Tattingston with the orchard, garden and 1 rood of land used for a hop ground, in the occupation of JEWE AMYS, for her life, and thereafter to my daughter MARY and her heirs for ever. To said FRANCES my messuage or tenement in Shotley called "Upper House", now in occupation of MARY FOOKER with yards, garden and privilege of water, for life, and thereafter to the child my wife is conceived with, be it son or daughter, and its heirs for ever. If said son JOHN GRANDEFELD should die under 21, the tenement "Dowes" and the other lands bequeathed to him shall remain to the child my wife is conceived with if it be a son, and to his heirs, but if it be a daughter then to remain to MARY my daughter and her heirs. If my daughter MARY GRANDEFELD or the child my wife is conceived with should die before their ages of 21, the tenement bequeathed to MARY shall remain to the child and the tenement given to the child shall remain to MARY. I give said son JOHN GRANDEFELD £5, and my daughter MARY £5 and the child my wife is conceived with £5 -- all to be put out to their use within 6 months. I appoint my wife FRANCES sole exrx. Witnesses: THOMAS CARTER, HENRY ALLEN (X), THOMAS ARNOLD. Pr. at Ipswich 6 Aug. 1629.

R(W) EDWARD HACON of Oulton, singleman (N). 12 February 1628/29 (18)

To his sister-in-law, wife of JOHN HACON, 20s. and to her children 20s. each. To his sister HORSELLS children 20s. each. To his brother THOMAS HACON £5. To his brother JOHN his best suit. To BRIDGET STANTON and GRACE who did watch with him 5s. each. All the rest whatsoever he left to the disposition of

EDWARD HACON his father. Witnesses: JOHN CAPPS and CATHERINE the wife of JOHN HACON. Admon. issued at Lowestoft to EDWARD HACON, father of the deceased. 4 March 1628.

R(W) JOHN HUNT of Ipswich, clothier. 12 August 1629 (19)

Sick. To my daughter SUSAN HUNT £300 at 18, and out of the increase thereof my exor. is to pay my wife SUSAN £18 per annum during SUSAN's minority towards her good education so long as my said wife remain sole; and if she remarry I request my exors. to undertake the up-bringing of my daughter and to reserve to themselves the said yearly allowance of £18. If SUSAN die before 18 I will my exors. to pay the Bailiffs and Burgesses and Commonalty of the town of Ipswich, within 6 months of her death, £100 out of the £300, which I give them for ever to the following uses, viz. the £100 is to be lent out from time to time to 5 poor tradesmen of the parish of St Mary Elms during the term of 5 years, every of them entering into a bond to repay the same at the end of the 5 years and to pay to the churchwardens out of the increase after the rate of £4 for the hundred on every feast of St John the Apostle during the 5 years; and to buy smocks for the poor of the parish where most need shall be by the consent of the Bailiffs of the town. And I desire the said £200, residue of the £300, to be paid proportionally between MICHAEL OSBORNE and MARY OSBORNE, children of my said wife by her former husband, within 6 months of the death of my daughter SUSAN if my wife SUSAN shall then be dead also; during her life my wife shall have the benefit of it. To said wife SUSAN all household stuff in the house where I dwell. To my niece MARY CLEAVE £20 at 20. To my nephew EDWARD CLEAVE £5 at 24. To my sister MARY HUNT £10 in 6 months. To JAMES HUNT and RICHARD HUNT my 2 brothers £5 each in 6 months. To my sister REBECCA MARSH wife of HENRY MARSH £5 in 6 months. To JOHN CHAPMAN son of THOMAS CHAPMAN £5 in 3 months, he entering into a bond to repay that sum to my exors. at the end of 5 years. To ISAAC DAY and ISAAC GRENEWICH all goods and chattels and credits to discharge debts, legacies and funeral expenses, whom I appoint exors. To the churchwardens of the parish of St. Peter 20s. to distribute to the poor at Christmas next after my decease. Witnesses: LEONARD WOLLEY, PETER COALE, jnr. Codicil made same day: Whereas I JOHN HUNT before marriage with said SUSAN my wife entered into a bond to ISAAC GRENEWICH to pay the bequests given by the will of WILLIAM OSBORNE to MICHAEL OSBORNE, SUSAN OSBORNE and MARY OSBORNE, whereof my wife SUSAN is exrx., I therefore devise that my exors. shall within one year of my death pay my said wife SUSAN all sums of money being legacies of the said WILLIAM due to said MICHAEL, SUSAN and MARY at their several ages, which came into my hand by inter-marriage with SUSAN. Witnesses: as above. Pr. at Ipswich 18 Sept. 1629.

R(W) AUGUSTINE PARKER of Ipswich, mercer. 13 May 1629 (20)

Sick. To JOHN PARKER my brother my copyhold lands and tenements in Debenham in the occupation of SIMON BLOMFEILD, which late were lands of [missing] GORBOLD, to hold according to custom of the manor, on condition that he discharge my brother WILLIAM PARKER of £140, parcel of £200 which said WILLIAM is to pay JOHN at Michaelmas next by force of the will of WILLIAM PARKER my father deceased. If said JOHN refuse, then I give the same lands and tenements to the said WILLIAM my brother and his heirs. Also to JOHN PARKER my brother £250, of which £135 within 12 months and £100 in 18 months and £15 in 2 years; and my best black suit and black cloak and my white gelding. And if JOHN dies before receiving the £250 and having no issue, the unpaid portion shall be paid to my brother WILLIAM PARKER at the times JOHN would have had it. I forgive WILLIAM STYLES my father-in-law any unpaid sums of the agreement made on the marriage of his daughter MARGARET. To ALICE STREETE my sister and to SUSAN BROWSALL my sister £10 each within 12 months to buy a ring in remembrance of me. To WILLIAM UFFETT my cousin £5, to SUSAN UFFETT my kinswoman £5, to JOAN WARREN my kinswoman 40s., to THOMAS WARREN my kinsman 40s., to MARGARET WARREN my kinswoman 40s., to THOMASIN WARREN my kinswoman 40s. -- all to be paid within 2 years. To JOAN WILMONT my sister £50 within 18 months. To MARGERY SYMONDS my aunt, AUGUSTINE PARKER my nephew and SUSAN PARKER my niece, children of the said MARGARET, 20s. each in 18 months to buy a ring to wear in remembrance. To LIONEL WITHE my apprentice £30 in 12 months. To WILLIAM TYLER my uncle £20 in 2 years. To WILLIAM PARKER my brother £150 in 6 months if he shall discharge my exor. of £100 which I stand bound to NICHOLAS ROSE for him. To ELEAZAR PARKER, ELIZABETH PARKER, SUSAN PARKER, MARY PARKER, WILLIAM PARKER, AUGUSTINE PARKER, children of said WILLIAM PARKER my brother, £154 equally divided, to be paid to WILLIAM PARKER my brother to the use of the said children, whereof £32 in 18 months and £122 in 2 years, if the said WILLIAM shall become bound to my exors. in £300 with condition to pay said £154 to the children as they accomplish their ages of 21. To HENRY CHAPLYN my musket furnished and my hat and feather. To the poor of St Mary at Tower, Ipswich, £5 to be paid to the churchwardens in 2 years. All other goods, household stuff, plate, jewels, linen and debts I give to WILLIAM PARKER my brother, my debts and expenses of funeral and probate having been discharged. I make my friend JOHN BAKER sole exor., to whom £10 for his pains. He shall not take other benefit from my estate. Whatever arises to him therefrom as exor. shall be to my brother WILLIAM PARKER. Witnesses: THOMAS CUTLER, JOHN HARRYS and JOHN COLEMAN. Pr. at Ipswich 12 June 1629.

R(W) ALICE RAYNER alias DAY (X) of Coddenham, widow. (21)
29 March 1625

Weak. To ALICE BARKER my daughter the featherbed and flock bed whereon she lies with all the furniture belonging to same, and the posted bedstead in the same chamber next the hall with the stained cloth over it, 2 coffers that stand next the door in the same chamber, 2 of the chairs in the hall of the middle sort, 1 of the lesser kettles, 3 pewter dishes -- of each size one, 2 worser petticoats and a waistcoat. To JOHN BARKER £5 which was a legacy given him by his grandfather in his will. To ALICE COALE at 21 £10 on condition that her father JOHN COALE do not molest my exrx. The rest of goods and chattels to my daughter ANN DAY towards payment of debts and legacies, and I make her sole exrx. Published to be the last will of ALICE als. DAY this 31 March 1625 in presence of THOMAS ELRINGTON and DANIEL RICHER. Pr. at Ipswich 17 Sept. 1629.

R(W) MARTHA BLYTH of Waldringfield, widow (N). (22)
8 May 1629

All lands tenements and goods to RICHARD ROSE of the same, yeo., and his heirs for the bringing up of four children JOHN, ELIZABETH, MARTHA and MARY BLYTH, he to sell the same for this purpose. Any surplus to be divided equally between them at their ages of 21. Witnesses: JOHN GIRLINGE, GEORGE BENNETT (X). Pr. 2 June 1629. Admon. to RICHARD ROSE during minorities.

R(W) ROBERT CURSPE of Eyke, weaver. 22 June 1629 (23)

Very sick. To my son WILLIAM all the tools of my trade as weaver, and five pounds worth of yarn, half to be paid within 10 days and half at All Saints following; a flock bed standing upon the chamber with 1 coverlet, 2 sheets, the bedstead and boulster, all within 20 days. To ANN my wife one house freehold or tenement in Melton for life, and thereafter to my son-in-law THOMAS GILDERSLEVE and his wife, with power to sell at will giving five [sic] to JOHN CURPSE my grandchild at 21; £20 in money or, if she pleases, in household stuff brass pewter linen &c; and I make her joint exrx. with my son THOMAS GILDERSLEVE, paying half and taking half. To my son THOMAS GILDERSLEVE and his wife my colt at Faltenham. To ANN my wife, over and above the £20, the hempland in the meadow and all old hemp which she now has in custody. My son WILLIAM shall part with one pair of coomes unto my apprentice, my exor. paying him 10s. for them. To my son WILLIAM my best cloak. To my grandchild an old hutch and 2 sheets which were of PRUDENCE the wife of my son ROBERT. Witnesses: JOHN HARTE, JOHN BROWNE (X). Pr. 22 June 1629. Admon. to THOMAS GILDERSLEVE, the relict being present and declining.

R(W) GEORGE FREND of Little Blakenham, yeoman. (24)
24 March 1628/9

Aged but hale. To be buried at Lt. Blakenham. To JOHN FREND my eldest son all my lands and tenements with house barn garden and orchard in Little Blakenham and Somersham, charged to pay GEORGE, EDWARD, ROBERT, EDWARD and THOMAS FREND £40 equally divided within one year, and to ROBERT FREND £2 and EDWARD FREND £2, within one year, for the benefit of my grandchildren THOMAS son of ROBERT and MARY daughter of EDWARD. To THOMAS FREND my youngest son the best bed and boulster and bedstead wherein I lie, with the best coverlet, 1 pair sheets, 2 pillows, 2 pillowbeers, the cupboard in the parlour, the greatest kettle, 4 pewter dishes, 1 milch cow, all immediately after my death. To ROBERT FREND my son the cupboard in the hall and 2 pewter dishes. The milch cow, the biggest kettle save one, the chest, the long form and table in the hall which formerly I had once given to JOHN FREND my son, I will shall be equally divided among all my other sons. The residue of goods to be equally divided between my three sons GEORGE, EDWARD and ROBERT. I make JOHN my eldest son sole exor. provided he execute the will within 6 or 8 weeks, otherwise I make GEORGE FREND and EDWARD FREND joint exors. and give them all my lands and tenements to be sold and the money divided equally between my five sons within one year. Legatees to have power of distraint against JOHN FREND. Witnesses: RICHARD MICHELL, JOHN BOGAS, EDWARD ELLIOTT and ELLEN DAY (X). Pr. 22 June 1629.

R(W) THOMAS GIRLING now of Barnby. 5 August 1629 (25)

Revoking all former wills including one with my son JOHN. To the poor of Barnby 10s. at once. To my poor cousin WILLIAM GIRLING of Beccles 10s. at once, with whom my grandchild THOMAS is with to be taught his occupation so long as the said Mr GIRLING and ROBERT COOPER, grandfather also to my grandchildren, shall agree. I give my wife ANN GIRLING all my houses and lands in Barnby for life, and then to my said grandchild and his heirs so as he pay to his father, if alive, after the death of my wife £8 yearly, to be paid by his grandfather COOPER or his assigns, for life. For want of payment within 10 days of demand of a sum due my son may enter and receive the profits for life. If said grandchild should die without issue, then, after the death of his father also, all the said premises shall go to my other grandchild THOMAS GIRLING son of JOHN GIRLING, now of Pakefield, paying out of the profits to each of his two brethren £10 at 21, and to each of his three sisters £5 at 18, provided that said son THOMAS shall enjoy the premises for life if the said £8 be truly paid by him. As to my goods and writings, all were burnt except a featherbed and that poor stuff I have got since the burning which I will my old wife to have for life. I make my grandchild THOMAS GIRLING first named above sole exor., and entreat his grandfather ROBERT COOPER of Raveningham to be guardian and supervisor. Also I will that if JOHN [blank] and his wife will pay ROBERT COOPER £10 to use of his said grandchild to deliver them the lease they made to Mr CHESTEN with all other writings covering the same; and also if Sir HENRY JERNEGAN will pay to the said ROBERT COOPER £73 10s. to the use of my son THOMAS if he be living, then I will that Sir HENRY be acquitted of the execution of the judgement entered in Easter term, I take it in 8 James I [1611] and in roll number 312 or thereabouts: I never had but £40 of the judgment which came to above 9 score. I wrote this will with my own hand. Debts I owe now by speciality are but £10 upon a bill. Pr. 6 July 1629. Admon. To ROBERT COOPER, grandfather of the exor. THOMAS GIRLING, during the latter's minority.

R(W) WILLIAM WILKENSON (X) of Ipswich, yeoman. (26)
20 July 1629

Sick. To my wife ALICE 20s. in 6 months. To my son WILLIAM WILKENSON £60 at 21, failing whom £30 to my exor. for his own use and £30 equally divided between my other children then living. To my daughter ELIZABETH WILKENSON £40 at 21, failing whom £20 to my exor. and £20 equally divided between my other children. To my daughter KATHARINE WILKENSON £50 within 15 months, and 1 posted bedstead with the bed boulster coverlet and blankets as it now stands in the chamber over the parlour, and 1 drawing table in the parlour, 1 joined form, 3 joined stools, 1 joined back chair, and all linen given to her by her grandmother COLLER, and 1 chest where her linen now is. To my daughter ELIZABETH the trundle bedstead with the bed and other things belonging as it now stands in the parlour, to be delivered to her at 21, 6 silver spoons. To my daughter KATHARINE the smallest of my silver cups to be delivered immediately. To said son WILLIAM my great silver cup and 1 gilt silver spoon at 21. My son JOHN WILKENSON shall take care and charge and keep with all necessaries my said son WILLIAM and daughter ELIZABETH till each be 21, at his own cost. To my son JOHN WILKENSON all my unbequeathed goods, chattels, implements, stuff of household, debts, jewels, plate, corn and ready money, and I nominate him sole exor. Witnesses: WILLIAM SEEH, SAMUEL GREWE, NICHOLAS LOFTE, HENRY MUDD, ROBERT CLARKE. Pr. at Ipswich 17 Sept. 1629.

R(W) LAURENCE SHARP of Bramford, blacksmith. (27)
15 September 1629

Weak. To be buried in Bramford churchyard or at discretion of exrx. Whereas I have bargained and sold the house wherein I dwell with all the houses edifices yards gardens orchards and appurtenances belonging, and all the lands free and copy now or late in my own occupation to one JOHN COLE of Bramford, and have received of him £5 in part payment of four score and fifteen pounds, now, upon payment of 4 score and £10 on 29th September 1630 by said JOHN COALE, according to the agreement between us, to my wife MARGARET SHARPE or her assigns, my said wife and my friend ROGER ROSE of Bramford, yeo., or either of them shall have power to give an assurance to him the said JOHN COLE his heirs and assigns, in and of all the houses edifices [&c as above] and my wife shall deliver into the hands of SAMUEL BARKER of Newton near Stowmarket £29 of the said money by her received to the use of such legacies as I now appoint, viz. £5 each to his daughters SUSAN, MARGARET, and SARAH BARKER and £10 to his son JOSEPH BARKER; 40s. to ANN ROSE wife of NICHOLAS ROSE of Bawton* abovementioned, and 40s. to ANN ROSE the daughter of said ANN ROSE. But if JOHN COLE shall not pay the 4 score and £10 to my wife on 29 Sept 1630, then said MARGARET my wife shall have all the recited premises for life, and after her decease the abovementioned SAMUEL BARKER of Newton shall have power to sell and give an assurance of all the said houses [&c as above] and to pay

the aforesaid legacies. All else I give to MARGARET SHARPE my wife who I ordain sole exrx. Witnesses: DANIEL HERON and JOHN WATSON. Pr. 25 Sept. 1629.
[*Bawton has not been identified.]

R(W) WILLIAM SPRINGE (X) of Crowfield, gentleman. (28)
28 June 1628

Weak. To my cousin Mrs WINGFEILD £6 13s. 4d., and to DOROTHY WINGFEILD her daughter £10. To the rest of my cousin's children 20s. each. All the rest to my exor. towards funeral expenses and probate charges. I make my cousin HARBOTTLE WINGFIELD esq. sole exor. Witnesses: PETER SCOTCHMERE and ROBERT WITHIN (X) and ROBERT ARCHER. Pr. at Ipswich 10 Oct. 1629.

R(W) BENNETT ALDRED of St. Peter Ipswich, mariner. (29)
25 August 1629

Sick. My whole estate to my wife ANN ALDRED for life. To my son JOHN ALDRED that part of the hoy called the Pelycan of Ipswich and £10 for a stock, to have them after my wife's decease; to my daughter ANN ALDRED all the rest of my estate at her mother's discretion when she doth decease -- with benefit of survivorship. I appoint my wife sole exrx. and my friend DANIEL SNOWE supervisor. Witnesses: ISRAEL EXTON and EDWARD GOFFE. Pr. 9 Oct. 1629.

R(W) MARGARET BOND of Orford, widow. 8 June 1629 (30)

To MARGARET STYLES my grandchild my best posted bedstead standing in the parlour, 1 featherbed, 1 feather boulster, 2 pillows, 1 pair of blankets, 1 coverlet, my best brass pot, a mortar and pestle, 6 pairs of sheets, 2 board cloths, 2 long towels, 1 doz. napkins, 6 pieces of pewter, my best latten chafing dish, my great latten candlestick, a basin, my saddle cloth and bridle, and 40s. To MARGARET DRIVER my grandchild my other posted bedstead upon the parlour chamber, 1 featherbed, 1 feather boulster, 2 pillows, 1 pair of blankets, 1 coverlet -- at 21. To ALICE DRIVER my grandchild 2 pairs of sheets, 1/2 doz. napkins and 40s. at 21. To ELIZABETH STYLES my grandchild 2 pairs of sheets, 1/2 doz. napkins, a long board cloth and 40s. at 21. To SAMUEL DRIVER, JOHN DRIVER, GEORGE DRIVER my grandchildren, to every of them a pair of sheets and 40s. at 21. To JOHN STYLES my grandchild my best brass pot but one, a pair of sheets and 40s. at 21. To WILLIAM STYLES my grandchild 1 pair of sheets and 40s. at 21. To ANN STYLES, MARY STYLES and SARAH STYLES my grandchildren, to every of them 2 pairs of sheets and 1/2 doz. napkins and 40s. at 21. To SAMUEL DRIVER my son-in-law 10s. within a month. To ALLEN DUNNE my kinsman 10s. at 21. To JOAN DRIVER my daughter my best hat, my cloth gown, my new cloth petticoat and waistcoat, my green say apron and 3 pair sheets. To ELIZABETH STYLES my daughter my best stuff gown, my stuff petticoat, my best ruff and best smock. All the rest of my goods to be sold by my exor. towards the payment of debts and legacies. I nominate JOHN STYLES my son-in-law exor. Witnesses: TOBIAS COPPING and JOHN WHIDBYE. Pr. at Wickham 8 Oct. 1629.

R(W) WILLIAM CARVER of Fressingfield. 31 March 1628 (31)

To ANN my wife all goods and chattels on condition that she shall within one month become bound in the sum of £20 to JOHN WINCOPP of Heveningham, yeo, with the condition for payment at the church porch of Fressingfield to him of 40s. to the use of FRANCIS CARVER my son, and 40s. to the use of ELIZABETH CARVER my daughter, and 40s. to the use of ANN CARVER my daughter, and 40s to the use of RICHARD CARVER my son, at or before the day my wife shall chance to intermarry again. And if she enter into this bond I make her sole exrx. and the said JOHN WYNCOP supervisor. If she refuse I make JOHN WYNCOPP exor., and if he become exor. he shall pay to my 4 children 40s. each at 21, and in the mean-time pay them the yearly profit thereof -- with benefit of survivorship, and my wife shall have the rest of my goods, my debts and funeral expenses and other charges of my exor. first deducted. Witnesses: ROBERT PAGE (X), snr. and ROBERT PAGE jnr. Pr. at Yoxford 2 Nov. 1629. Admon. to exrx.

R(W) REYNOLD DOUZINE [DOWSING in margin] (N). (32)
About 4 September 1629

Delivered to GILBERT CORKER, parson of Sotterley and HENRY GOOCH of Rumburgh, blacksmith. I give to my wife all my goods and make her exrx. Pr. at Beccles 17 Oct. 1629. Admon. to the relict KATHARINE.

R(W) ELIZABETH DUKE of Benhall. 30 September 1629 (33)

Sick. To FRANCIS the son of my sister SMALEPEECE £100 within 6 months, put by the discretion of his father, and the same with its increase to be paid him at 18; failing him, to the next child that my sister shall bring forth. To my sister SMALEPEECE £15 in 6 months. To my cousin ANN WEBB £50 in 6 months. To my cousin ELIZABETH JERMYN £20 in 6 months. To Mrs TILLOTT £5 in 6 months. To my aunt GOODRICKE £10 in 6 months. To every of the servants of my brother DUKE which were with him at my coming from them 20s. apiece. To MARGARET my own maid 20s. To the poor of Benhall 10s. The rest of my estate to my brother EDWARD DUKE whom I make sole exor. Witnesses: LEONARD TILLOTT and MIRABEL PAMANT (X). Pr. at Ipswich 27 Oct. 1629.

R(W) MARY DAVY (X) of Benacre, widow. 9 October 1628 (34)

To THOMAS, ROBERT, JOHN, HENRY and GABRIEL my sons all my copyhold tenement 'Warnes' with the edifices belonging in

Benacre, with all lands and meadows belonging thereto in Wrentham and Benacre, containing by estimation 11 acres, to be sold by my exor. within a year, and the money that shall arise divided equally between said sons immediately, with benefit of survivorship. To ROBERT DAVY my son my cupboard of the wayncott, my table, the biggest kettle save one, a pot metal posnet, 3 pairs of finest sheets, 1 best pewter platter, 1 pewter basin, 1 salt, 2 porringers, my new gown cloth, my best chest with legs, my 2 forms, my gridiron. To JOHN DAVY my son 2 kettles with a trivet, 3 pairs of sheets, 2 pewter platters, 2 candlesticks, 1 scummer, 1 warming pan, 1 chest, 1 coffer. To GABRIEL my son my bed as it standeth with all that belongeth, 4 pairs of sheets, 1 box, 1 brass pot, 3 skillets, 2 pewter platters. All the rest to be sold by my exors. and the money to be theirs for defraying charges. I make ROBERT and JOHN my exors. Witnesses: ROBERT STANNARD, SUSAN BURTER and ROBERT REVE. Pr. 7 Nov. 1629.

R(W) MARK HARMAN of Sudbourn, yeoman. 23 May 1629 (35)

I give all the several closes and parcels of land marsh and meadow specially named to MARK GRYME the elder of Much Thay, co. Essex, yeo., to be sold within 2 years and the money thereof remain for the payment of legacies and debts. I will that close of arable called Harrie Hills in Sudbourn containing by estimation 12 acres; and 2 acres of arable adjoining on the east of Harrie Hills; and 1 pightle called Marsh Pightle containing by estimation 1 1/2 acres, one head abutting the way leading from Cows Well towards the marsh; and one marsh called Rushey Marsh containing by estimation 4 acres and join unto Anne Holmes Marsh towards the east; and one part of a marsh containing by estimation 2 1/2 acres and join unto the marsh aforesaid Ann Howes towards the east; and one little meadow called Hall Hill containing by estimation 3 acres -- all which are to be sold and are in Sudbourn. To MARK GRYME, the younger son of said MARK GRYME the elder, all my messuage or tenement called build house in Sudbourn, with all houses edifices yards orchards gardens and lands belonging thereto and used therewith not heretofore bequeathed, to hold to him and his heirs when he is 21, provided that MARY my wife shall have and enjoy, for her servants' and her own dwelling with her there during her natural life, the parlour and parlour chamber and garden and one turf house, parcel of the messuage or tenement aforesaid, and free liberty to bake in the oven belonging to the said messuage at all times convenient, together with free liberty of passage to and from the said parlour, parlour chamber, turf house and well and garden by the usual ways and passages, she committing no waste. If I should die before MARK GRYME jnr. is 21 the said MARK GRYME snr. shall take the profits of the lands &c given to MARK GRYME jnr. towards bringing him up, and shall pay the lords of whom these premises are held such fines as they will have for the admittance of MARK jnr. I give MARY my wife £8 per annum issuing out of all the lands and tenements bequeathed to MARK GRYME jnr., to be paid to her for life, she keeping herself a widow, at the 4 usual feasts or within 14 days thereafter, the first payment to be made on the next feast after my decease, with power of distraint. But if my wife should remarry she shall be debarred from any legacy under this will. To said MARY my wife while a widow, every year 1 coomb of wheat 1 coomb of rye 1 coomb of malt 2 loads of good wood, one of blocks and one of bond faggot wood, sized according to custom of the country; the corn to be delivered between Michaelmas and Christmas; 3 loads of flags to be delivered with the wood blocks between the feasts of the Nativity of John the Baptist [24 June] and Bartholomew the Apostle [24 Aug.]. To the said MARY all the household stuff and implements which shall be in the parlour chamber at my decease, and all the feather-beds boulsters coverlets blankets pillows, and all my brass pewter and linen for life and till she marry, and thereafter to said MARK GRYME jnr. MARY my wife shall within 6 months, upon reasonable request, release her interest of dower which she can or may have in any of the aforesaid lands and tenements demised in this will, to any person who shall have any right or title in them. If MARY should refuse to release her dower title she shall be barred from any benefit under this will. To ANN HOLDEN 1 milch cow or £3 10s. at her choice, within 6 months. To the poor of Sudbourne 20s. within a year. To MARY my wife all poultry. To said MARK GRYME snr. whom I nominate sole exor., all else. Witnesses: NATHANIEL SPARKHAWKE, ROBERT CLARKE, MARY CLARKE. Pr. at Ipswich 31 Oct. 1629.

R(W) SOPHONY SYMONDES of Winston, yeoman. (36)
23 October 1624

Aged and weak. To my wife ELIZABETH the tenement where I dwell with the houses yards gardens orchards lands meadows pastures feedings belonging in Winston and towns adjoining, for life. Thereafter, all these to HENRY SMYTH of Bramford, my sister ELIZABETH her son, and his heirs. To said wife ELIZABETH my cottage or tenement with yard and orchard belonging, which sometime was FRANCIS GYLES' and is now in tenure of LUKE LUFFE, for life; thereafter to remain to EMMA SMYTH my niece, sister unto said HENRY SMYTH, and to her heirs. To JOHN, AMY and JUDA STYMPSON, my brother EDMUND's children, 40s. each, to be paid by my nephew HENRY SMYTH out of my lands formerly given him, thus -- 40s. to JOHN 1 year after decease of my wife ELIZABETH, 40s. to AMY in 2 years and 40s. to JUDA in 3 years; with power of distraint if a payment in 20 days in arrears. To HENRY SMYTH my said nephew 1 feather-bed 1 feather boulster with bedstead and furniture as it stands in the parlour chamber, and one testament, and my wearing apparel unbequeathed. To my brother EDMUND STYMPSON my black horseman's coat. To KATHARINE, my nephew HENRY SMYTHE's wife, my bible. To HENRY SYMONDS aforesaid [sic.? in error for HENRY SYMONDS] my horse mill with all the furniture as it standith in the barn and one oaken ladder in the barn; my wife shall have the occupation and use of the mill and ladder at her pleasure for life. I ordain my said wife ELIZABETH sole exrx. Witnesses: JAMES WYTHE jnr., LUKE LUFFE (X). Pr. at Wickham 3 Nov. 1629.

R(W) WILLIAM SEWTER of Lowestoft, husbandman. (37)
20 August 1629

Sick. To be buried in said town. To my wife CECILIA SEWTER my house with appurtenances for life, she keeping it in sufficient repair; and after her decease to WILLIAM SEWTER my brother's son on condition that he pay to BRIDGET STEWARD within 1 year of my wife's decease 20s., and to HESTER NEWTON 20s. in 2 years, to BRIDGET SEWTER 20s. in 3 years, to FRANCIS SEWTER son of HENRY SEWTER 20s. in 4 years, to ANN STAMFORD daughter of BRIDGET STEWARD 20s. in 5 years, to ANNIS STAMFORD's eldest son now living 20s. in 6 years. Failing any of these, then WILLIAM SEWTER shall have that one's portion. The residue of my goods to my wife CECILIA, sole exrx. Should said WILLIAM SEWTER not pay that £6 he may be distrained upon. Witnesses: THOMAS POSSELL, MARK PAGE, THOMAS PACYE, JOHN COCKE the writer hereof. Pr. at Lowestoft 26 Aug. 1629.

R(W) JOHN SNELLING (X) of Ilketshall St. Laurence. (38)
21 September 1629

Sick. To AUSTEN BROWNE my house in Brampton with the yards and all commodities belonging, on condition that he hold my executor harmless from a bond wherein I stand bound with the said AUSTEN to FRANCIS ABSOLON of Brampton. All my moveable goods to MARY my wife on condition that she yield to AUSTEN BROWNE all her right or interest in my house above bequeathed within 2 months after the said bond shall have been discharged. I make her my exrx. Witnesses: THOMAS PAYNE and BENJAMIN COOPER (X). Pr. at Beccles 3 Oct. 1629.

R(W) ROBERT WARD of Needham Market, clothier. (39)
8 August 1629

Sick. To SARAH my wife my house and grounds freehold, now in occupation of me ROBERT WARD, HENRY BOSTON senior and DANIEL COLMAN, to hold to her and her assigns for life, maintaining all in good condition; and thereafter to my son ROBERT WARD and his heirs on condition that he pay my two daughters SARAH WARD and JOAN WARD £20 apiece thus -- £5 to SARAH within 1 year of decease of my wife, £5 to JOAN in 2 years, £5 to SARAH in 3 years, £5 to JOAN in 4 years, £5 to SARAH in 5 years, £5 to JOAN in 6 years, £5 to SARAH in 7 years, £5 to JOAN in 8 years, all payable by the said ROBERT or his heirs in the chapel porch of Needham Market; with power of distraint and benefit of survivorship. Whereas my son ROBERT will be heir to the pightle adjoining my back garden, being copyhold of the manor of Barking, and heir to the other house that DANIEL COLMAN now occupies or so much of it as is copyhold, and also so much of any other part of the houses or ground as is copyhold of the manors of Stonham and Barking, whether it be now in my occupation or that of HENRY BOSTON and DANIEL COLMAN abovesaid, which, if ROBERT my son or his exors. or assigns shall refuse, then all my freehold houses and grounds above-mentioned shall remain to my wife for life, and after her decease to my two daughters above-named and to their heirs. To SARAH my wife, for life, my best bedstead in the parlour, now in use of DONALD COLMAN, and my best feather-bed and boulster now in my own use, and after her decease I give them to my son ROBERT. The rest of my goods and chattels moveable and immoveable I give to SARAH my wife and I make her my sole exrx. Witnesses: RICHARD LOVE, HENRY BOSTON, DANIEL COLMAN, THOMAS WARD. Pr. at Ipswich 9 Oct. 1629.

R(W) THOMAS ROOMER [ROMER in margin] (X) of Bradwell, singleman. 27 April 1629 (40)

Sick. To THOMAS ELLIS of Ashby my late master £5 which he oweth me by his bill. To RICHARD ROOMER my brother £5 within 6 months; and £6 which should grow due to me from NICHOLAS ELLIS at the day of his marriage or of his death whichever first happen, being to be due to me from said NICHOLAS for a horse which he had of me; also all my apparel except my best cloak. To GEORGE ROOMER, son unto RICHARD ROOMER my brother, 40s. to be employed by my exors. to his use till he be 21. To MARY, wife of THOMAS ROOKINS of Lound, my sister, 20s. To ANN PALMER of Fritton, wid., my sister, 13s. To ELIZABETH COOKE and KATHARINE COOKE, my sisters, 20s. each. All these legacies to be paid within 6 months. To WILLIAM BULLWARD of Bradwell 20s. and my best cloak. To JOHN SHEPPARD my now master 20s.; to my dame his wife 10s. To MARY LUCAS 10s. To ELIZABETH SHEPPARD 20s. To ANN JARMAN of Thurleton, co. Norfolk, 22s. All these legacies to be paid within 6 months. To GRACE LEMMAN of Ashby, singlewoman, 10s. I will have a sermon preached at my funeral by whom my exors. think fit. All other goods and credits I give to THOMAS ELLYS of Ashby, my late master, whom I make my sole exor. To ANN ROOMER my sister £4 within 6 months. Witnesses: WILLIAM BULLARD (X) and ROBERT UNDERWOOD. Pr. at Ashby 10 Sept. 1629.

W(R) JOHN AWFEILD (X) of Westleton. 16 October 1626 (41)

Sick. To ROSE my wife all movables within and without. To ANN MYLLS my god-daughter 10s. within half a year. To AUSTEN AWFEILD my brother my doublet of leather, one pair of cloth breeches being my best except one, one coat, one pair of hose and shoes, and a hat at the disposing of my wife whom I ordain sole exrx. Witnesses: ROBERT BOUTHE, THOMAS ALBY, WILLIAM PEACOCK, JOHN ALBY. Pr. at Yoxford 2 Nov. 1629.

R(W) THOMASINE ADAMS of Snape, widow (N). died 9 October 1629 (42)

I give my two sisters ALICE wife of ROBERT RISBYE and ANN wife of HENRY PINCKINE all my moveable goods equally divided. Witnesses: ELIZABETH ADAMS (X), SUSAN ROGERS (X). Pr. At Saxmundham 2 Nov.

1629. These two witnesses appeared in person and swore with hand on gospel to the truth of the above. Admon. to ALICE wife of ROBERT RISBIE, sister of deceased.

R(W) WILLIAM BOWER of Stratford. 20 October 1629 (43)

Weak. To be buried in the churchyard of Stratford. To THOMAS BOWER of Hadleigh, tailor, my brother JOHN BOWER's son, 1s. To ELIZABETH BORAM my wife's brother's daughter, my bible in quarto with clasps and bosses. The rest of my goods I give to ALICE my wife, whom I make sole exrx. Witnesses: SAMUEL LINDSELL and ELIZABETH MITCHELSON (X). Pr. at Ipswich 26 Nov. 1629.

R(W) JOHN BROWNE of Falkenham, yeoman. 11 October 1629 (44)

Sick. To MARGARET my wife half my movables of all sorts and £10. The other half to JOHN BROWNE my son, the division to be in equal parts except that my biggest brass pot and piece I give to JOHN my son, and a feather-bed I give to PHOEBE my daughter which is the bed she usually lies on. To PHOEBE my daughter £40 within one year, together with my little house wherein ISAAC WRIGHT dwelt, called Baldeis with the little hempland adjoining; and £10 to be paid upon marriage, by my son JOHN, if she marry with consent of her mother; and a yearling calf which I bred. To my son-in-law ROBERT ALLEN of Kirkton that £40 which I lent him, provided that if his wife MARGARET my daughter die before him and without issue, the said ROBERT shall pay, of the said £40, £10 to my wife and other £10 to JOHN my son. I further give to MARGARET my daughter a two-year old bullock which her said husband ALLEN now pastureth. To the poor of Faltenham [Falkenham] 20s. to be delivered to THOMAS GOODAY and JOHN HART to be distributed within one month. To the poor of Kirton, to be delivered to my son-in-law ROBERT ALLEN, to be distributed as need requireth with the advice of the overseers there. To my sister KATHARINE MORRICE BLACKSALL 20s. within 1 month. To my god-child JOHN son of GEORGE PEARSEY 20s. to be paid when 16. To my cousin WILLIAM BROWNE of Falkenham 20s. in 1 month. To deaf JOHN BROWN/ 10s. To my kinswoman LETTICE WEBB I remit all her debt to me except her last year's rent. To NICHOLAS KEMPSTER my apprentice 20s. to be paid when he come out of apprenticeship on condition that he shall be willing to serve out his time with my wife or my son JOHN if she require it. To ANN my daughter-in-law the calf I bought of my son JOHN her husband. The rest of my goods and all my land free and copyhold I give to my son JOHN whom I make sole executor. Witnesses: EDMUND MAPLETOFF, JOHN HART and THOMAS GOODAY. Pr. at Ipswich 4 Nov. 1629

R(W) JOHN HELHOWSE.* [1629] (45)

Sick. To RICHARD PARRISH a bed ready furnished with a coverlet and a pair of sheets, and a table. To Mr CARTER, minister, one

half load of wood. To ROBERT ENGLISH 30s. To JOHN ENGLISH 15s. To WILLIAM HART 15s. To ELIZABETH ENGLISH 20s. To FRANCIS ENGLISH 10s. if it can be spared. To ELIZABETH ENGLISH the elder my ground. To JOHN BUSE 12d. To JOHN ENGLISH one danske chest. I ordain RICHARD CRESNOLD my sole exor. The legacies to be paid within 6 months of being demanded. Witnesses: JOHN ENGLISH (X), RICHARD CRESNOLD (X), JOHN ALDERMAN and JOHN COOKE (X). Pr. at Ipswich 26 April 1629.
[*This name does not appear in the printed index. The will is at folio 45v of Register 59.]

RW* THOMAS MEENE the elder of Weybread, yeoman. (46)
20 September 1629

To be buried in Weybread churchyard. To THOMAS MEENE, son of ROBERT MEENE my brother £15. To FRANCES MEENE, daughter of ROBERT my brother £5. To JOSEPH the son of HENRY MEENE my brother £5. To ELIZABETH daughter of HENRY my brother, now wife of one PREWNE, 50s. To SUSAN wife of JOHN SMYTH of Rougham, co. Suffolk, daughter of said HENRY my brother 20s. To the sons of EDMUND MEENE my brother -- THOMAS £3 6s. 8d., JOSEPH £5, JOHN £3 6s. 8d.; and to the daughters of said EDMUND -- ELIZABETH MEENE £3 6s. 8d., MARY MEENE 40s., REBECCA MEENE and ANN MEENE 50s. each. To the sons of my brother GREGORY MEENE -- WILLIAM £13 6s. 8d., RICHARD 50s., JOHN £5, SAMUEL 50s. To ANN LEESE daughter of NICHOLAS LEESE 30s. To HENRY the son of JOHAN LEESE my sister 40s., and to her son THOMAS £6 6s. 8d., and to her daughters LETTICE 10s. and AMY £3 6s. 8d. To RICHARD MEENE my brother £8. To GEORGE MEENE my brother £5. All these sums to be paid within a year of my decease, in the south porch of Weybread church. To THOMAS MEENE, HENRY MEENE and SAMUEL MEENE the sons of STEPHEN MEENE, late of Starston deceased, 40s. each to be paid at age 21 in the said place. To [missing] MEENE, son of THOMAS MEENE late of Wissett deceased, £5; and to [missing] MEENE the daughter of said THOMAS, 40s. at 21 to be paid in aforesaid place. To THOMAS MEENE son of GEORGE MEENE my brother £15 at age 36. To ABIGAIL MEENE daughter of said GEORGE £3. To MARY MEENE daughter of said GEORGE 40s. at age 30, at the place aforesaid. To GEORGE MEENE my brother 20s. per annum for life, the first payment at Michaelmas 2 years after my decease, with power of distraint. To JAMES MEENE my brother all my messuages, houses, lands and tenements in Weybread or elsewhere, to the only use of him and his heirs, whom I nominate sole exor. 20s. to be distributed among the poor of Weybread. To said JAMES MEENE my brother all my goods, chattels and household stuffs and implements for discharging funeral and other charges. Witnesses: SARAH FOX and JOHN BROWNE. Pr. at Beccles 17 Oct. 1629.
[*Original will checked re blanks in register copy.]

R(W) JOHN PAULL of Dennington, yeoman. 14 November 1628 (47)

Infirm through old age. To JOHN PAULL my son my messuage or tenement in Laxfield now or late in tenure of ROBERT BORRETT, and all my lands in Laxfield pertaining thereto, charged to pay to SAMUEL my son £40 in the south porch of Laxfield church by four annual portions of £10, beginning when he is 21. In case of default SAMUEL may enter the premises and receive the issues until he shall have received £50; thereafter JOHN shall re-enter and hold for ever; provided that if JOHN should die without lawful issue I give the lands and tenements to my son WILLIAM, subject to the aforesaid charge. To WILLIAM my son all my lands and tenements in Dennington called Tesards which I lately bought of RICHARD WODE, charged to pay to SAMUEL aforesaid £20 in the said porch in four portions of £5, beginning when he is 21. In case of default SAMUEL may enter and take the issues till he shall have received £30, after which WILLIAM shall hold the premises for ever; provided that if WILLIAM should die without lawful issue I will give all my lands in Dennington to the said SAMUEL on condition that he shall repay to my son JOHN the £40 which JOHN is to pay him under this will, payment to be made at JOHN's house in Laxfield. In case of default JOHN may enter and take the profits until he has received £40. To the said JOHN my son my posted bedstead standing in my parlour at Laxfield with its furniture, a trundle bed in the hall chamber in Dennington with its furniture, 2 feather-beds, 2 feather boulsters, 2 pillows of feathers, 1 down pillow, 2 coverings, 2 blankets, 2 pairs of sheets and all else belonging to the bedstead, 4 pairs of sheets of every sort, 2 long joined forms, my long table with the frame in my hall at Laxfield, my cupboard in my hall at Dennington, my best brass pot, 1 cauldron, 2 kettles -- one of the best and one of the second sort, my horse-mill and the stones and all the apparel and furniture belonging, all my glass and latterns [lanterns?] belonging to my houses in Laxfield, and all my boards and planks lying over my mill-house, one stone pot tipped with silver, 2 silver spoons, 2 of my best cushions, my best long diaper table-cloth, 2 diaper napkins, 4 hempen napkins, my double coffer, a little coffer wherein my writings lie, my best cob-irons, a fire-pan, a pair of tongs and a gridiron. To WILLIAM my son a bedstead with a half tester and a livery bedstead in the parlour at Dennington, 2 feather-beds, 2 feather boulsters, 2 feather pillows, 1 pillow of down, 2 pairs of sheets with all the apparel and furniture belonging, 4 pairs of sheets, my cupboard in the hall at Laxfield, my second brass pot, my second cauldron,2 kettles -- one best and one second best, 2 silver spoons, my long table with the frame, a long form standing in my parlour at Laxfield, my malt querns, 2 of my next cushions in value, my next cob-irons, a fire pan, a pair of tongs, my second gridiron, my short spit, my best long hempen table-cloth, 2 diaper napkins, my linen coffer and a coffer in the hall chamber in Dennington. To SAMUEL my son one posted bedstead in the hall chamber, one trundle bedstead on the vant ruff -- both in Dennington, 2 feather-beds, 2 feather boulsters, 2 pillows of feathers, 1 down pillow, 4 cushions of the worst sort, 2 pairs of sheets with all the apparel and furniture belonging to the said bedsteads, a livery table, 2 short forms in my hall at Dennington, a livery table in the shop chamber in Laxfield, 4 pairs of sheets, a little brass pot, a little cauldron, 2 kettles, 2 silver spoons, a pot tipped with silver, my long spit, a short diaper table-cloth, 2 diaper napkins, 3 hempen napkins, a long towel, my woolens coffer, a coffer in my closet -- all to be delivered to him at age 21. To said sons JOHN, WILLIAM and SAMUEL all my pewter linen and napery unbequeathed equally divided by two honest men. To the poor of Laxfield 20s. to be distributed by the minister, churchwardens and chief inhabitants. To MARY SHELDRAKE 20s. To my executors the residue equally divided. My sons JOHN PAULL and WILLIAM PAULL to be exors. and JOHN COCKE supervisor. Witnesses: JOHN PAULL, EDWARD NUNN, JOHN COCKE, THOMAS GIRLINGE. Pr. 2 Nov. 1629.

R(W) STEPHEN REMOULDS (X) of Ufford, husbandman. (48)
25 October 1629

Sick. I give my house and messuage with the hempland and yard to my son JOHN SMYTHE and my daughter ALICE SMYTH and to the longer liver of them, and after their deaths to ROBERT SMYTH the elder son of JOHN SMYTH my child; and if said ROBERT SMYTHE die before the age of 21 or without issue then it shall fall to JOHN SMYTH my other grandchild. I give my bedstead as it standeth at Ufford with feather-bed and boulster and pillow, and the long table in the hall and the biggest brass pot and biggest kettle to ROBERT SMYTH my grandchild. I give my bedstead which standeth at my son SMYTHES house in Eyke with my feather-bed, 1 boulster, 1 coverlet, and one little brass pot which is at my house in Ufford, and the biggest platter to THOMAS SMYTH my other grandchild. I give to JOHN SMYTH my grandchild my other great platter and a spit. I give to the children of MARGERY HAYNES my daughter £5 -- 20s. a year for 5 years beginning one year after my decease. The rest of my movables to ALICE my daughter and her husband whom I make exor. Witnesses: THOMAS WAYLAND, HUGH MARSH. Pr. at Wickham 25 Nov. 1629.

R(W) MARGARET SHARPE of Bramfield, widow. (49)
24 September 1629

Weak. To be buried in Bramfield churchyard. To the poor of Bramfield 5s. distributed at the day of my burial. To DORIS STUDD the bedstead in the parlour with the flock bed, 1 feather boulster, 1 pair of sheets, 1 pair of blankets, my best coverlet, my best stained cloth, my gown, 1 great kettle, 1 brass pot, 1 pillow and pillow-bier, 1 buffet stool, 1 pestle and mortar, 1 piece of pewter. To SARAH PARKE 1 flock bed, 1 flock boulster, 1 pair of sheets,1 pillow, 1 pillow-bier, 1 stained cloth. To AGNES NETHERGATE 1 great kettle, 1 coverlet, 1 chair. To THOMAS NETHERGATE the cupboard in the hall and 1 piece of pewter. To EDWARD NETHERGATE the younger 1 kettle and 1 piece of pewter. To RALPH STUDD the great table in the parlour with one pair of scales. To THOMAS STUDD 1 coverlet, 1 flock boulster and 1 stained cloth. To JOHN WATSON my late husband's best doublet and hose and 1 chair. To JOHN WATSON's wife 1 little brass pot, 1 kettle, 1 boulster. To MATHIE WATSON daughter of said JOHN WATSON and his wife 1 platter, 1 fruit dish, and 1 buffet stool.

To JAMES LADBROOKE 1 piece of pewter. To CHRISTOPHER ALDERMAN of Ipswich the halberd in the parlour with all my weights; and to SARAH ALDERMAN his wife my best pair of sheets with 1 pillow and 1 pillow-bier. To JUDITH SENDALL 1 boulster, 1 good pillow and 1 pillow-bier. All other goods and chattels to JUDITH SENDALL and ANN NETHERGATE, both of whom I nominate exrxs., discharging my legacies and debts and the debts of my deceased husband LAURENCE SHARPE and the probate of both wills and funeral expenses. I make CHRISTOPHER ALDERMAN and EDWARD NETHERGATE supervisors, allowing for their pains 1 feather-bed with 1 feather boulster to be sold and the money equally divided between them. Witnesses: DANIEL HERON and JOHN ALDERMAN. Pr. at Ipswich 26 Nov. 1629.

R(W) THOMAS WAKEFIELD of Beccles, tailor. (50)
22 January 1628/9

Weak. To RICHARD WAKEFEILD my son the messuage or tenement where I dwell with all the outhouses yards gardens and appurtenances lying in Beccles in or near Balligate Street. To FRANCIS WAKEFEILD my son £10. To CHRISTIAN my daughter the late wife of ROBERT KELL £4 -- 40s. within half a year and 40s. within 1 1/2 years. To MARY WAKEFEILD my daughter 1 posted bedstead cord and natt, 1 feather-bed, 2 feather boulsters, 2 feather pillows, 2 blankets, 2 coverlets, 1 table, 2 small forms, 2 buffet stools, 3 covered stools, 1 great chair and 1 small one, a couple of small chairs, a stander, 1/2 dozen cushions, a cupboard with the pewter and trenchers in the same, 1 pair of andirons, 1 danske chest as it standeth and a trundle bedstead as it standeth, 4 kettles, 1 brass pot, 1 skillet, 1 posnet, 1 frying pan, 1 warming pan, 3 candlesticks, a flat chest. To ELIZABETH the wife of JOHN HALTWAY 20s. To MARY WAKEFIELD my grandchild a great chest, a tipped pot and a silver spoon. All the rest of my movables to RICHARD WAKEFEILD my son whom I make sole exor. Witnesses: PHILIP SOOWTHALLS and ROBERT COBBE. Pr. at Beccles 10 Dec. 1629.

R(W) RICHARD MURELL (X) of Weybread. 6 November 1629 (51)

To MARY MURELL my sister 20s. To my four daughters all my pewter equally divided. The residue of movables to my two daughters TRYPHENA and LYDIA equally divided, and I appoint them exrxs., being persuaded that they will see my body decently buried and my will performed. Witnesses: RICHARD ALDOUS and JOHN TUTHILL. Pr. at Beccles 12 Dec. 1629.

R(W) WILLIAM ASHLEY of Woodbridge, grocer. (52)
18 December 1629

Sick. To HENRY LEAKE the eldest son of my brother-in-law HENRY LEAKE and of my sister his wife £50. To WILLIAM LEAKE another son of the same £20. To the three daughters of the same -- SUSAN, ROSE and MARGERY -- £10 apiece, all the said moneys to be paid at their several ages of 21 out of my personal estate, and to be employed by aforesaid HENRY LEAKE for the best advantage until payment be made; and the increase of the several moneys shall be severally paid to the children, with the principal sums, and with benefit of survivorship. To RICHARD MANN, an ancient servant unto my said brother LEAKE, £10; and to CLEMENT STYLES and ROBERT DENNEY, two other of his servants, 40s. apiece; and to ROSE YORKE and ELIZABETH SYMPSON, two maidservants of my said brother LEAKE, 20s. apiece; all these sums to be paid within 2 months out of my estate aforesaid. I make said HENRY LEAKE sole exor. and give him all my goods, ready money, and other estate whatsoever towards the payment of my debts and legacies, and the remainder to return to his own use. Witnesses: JEPTHA WALLER, EDWARD GOULDSTON and JOHN PARTRICH. Pr. at Ipswich 15 Jan. 1629/30.

R(W) JOHN BUCKNALL (X) of Dallinghoo, husbandman. (53)
7 July 1628

In health of body. To THOMAS BUCKNALL my son and to his heirs for ever all my messuage or tenement in Framlingham wherein JOHN AMYSON dwelleth, with all the houses, yards, gardens, orchards and appurtenances belonging, and all that meadow therewith used, containing 1 acre, in Framlingham. To KATHARINE my daughter the wife of THOMAS KEMPE 20s. to be paid within one year; and my bed boulster bedstead and coverlet and 2 blankets to be delivered presently after my decease. To MARGARET COATES my grandchild £20 at 21; if she die before 21 the £20 is to remain to my exor. To THOMAS my son the profits of all my lands and tenements in Winnycke in the counties of Huntingdon and Northampton, till Michaelmas after my decease. To WILLIAM BUCKNALL my son 20s. All the rest of my goods and chattels to said THOMAS BUCKNALL my son, and I make him sole exor. Witnesses: JOHN ROE, THOMAS PAYNE, MATTHEW DANBROOKE, and JOHN WATSON (X). Pr. at Wickham 14 Jan. 1629/30.

R(W) JOHN BUGG of Ipswich, ship carpenter. (54)
1 September 1628

In good health. To ALICE my wife all my messuage or tenement with its appurtenances which I purchased of EDMUND HUMFRIE, for her life; and thereafter to ELIZABETH my daughter, wife of THOMAS RANDALL, for life, she keeping the houses, buildings and pales belonging to said tenement in good reparation; and after her decease to ELIZABETH BUGG to hold to her and to the heirs of her body lawfully begotten; and, in default of such issue, the remainder thereof to JOHN HAYWARD my sister's son and his heirs. My grandchild ELIZABETH BUGG shall, within one year of decease of ELIZABETH my daughter if my wife be then dead, or else within one year after decease of my said wife, pay to BRIDGET her sister, out of the said tenement, 40s.; and, within the 2nd year after the decease of the last to die of said ALICE my wife and ELIZABETH my daughter, pay to my grandchild MARGARET BUGG 40s. All my goods and chattels -- my debts paid the probate of my will and burial expenses discharged -- I give to my said wife whom I make sole exrx. Witnesses: ROBERT HAMBYE, ANTHONY BLOMFEILD, WILLIAM CHAPLYN. Pr. at Ipswich 5 Jan. 1629/30.

R(W) ROBERT BUBDENSTON* [sic] of Needham Market, woolen weaver. 31 January 1624/5 (55)

Sick. To be buried in Barking churchyard. To THOMASIN my wife my cottage or tenement in Needham with a yard and appurtenances now in occupation of JOHN CANDLER and RICHARD COCKNELL, holden by copy of court roll of the manor of Barking, to be held for her life, she keeping the houses in good reparations; and after her decease to GEORGE BALDENSTON my youngest son. The cottage or tenement with appurtenances in Needham Market wherein I dwell, holden by copy of court roll of the same manor, shall be sold within 7 years by EDWARD TANNER the elder of Needham Market or his executors; in the meantime the rent of the first 2 years shall be bestowed in repairing the decays of the cottage, except for 13s. 4d. which I give to THOMASIN my wife after the 2 years expired; then, until it be sold, 10s. of the yearly rent is to be paid to ROGER BALDENSTON my eldest son, and 8s. to THOMAS BALDENSTON my son, and the rest (if any) to my wife. And after the cottage shall be sold £8 of the money arising shall be for the use of the children of ROGER BALDENSTON now living, to be paid at their ages of 23; and £6 for the use of THOMAS BALDENSTON, son of my son THOMAS, to be paid at 23. And my son ROGER shall have 10s. yearly of the profits of said £8 till his children attain said age; and my son THOMAS likewise to have 8s. of the profits of said £6 till his son attain said age. All the grandchildren to have benefit of survivorship. And if there arise more than £14 upon the sale, the overplus I give to my wife. The rest of my goods to THOMASIN my wife whom I make exrx. To said EDMUND TURNER and his exors. 20s. to be taken only of the sale of said cottage, for his pains. Witnesses: NICHOLAS BUBB, EDWARD TARVER and JOHN COOTES. Pr. at Ipswich 15 Jan. 1629/30.
[* Copyist's error for BALDENSTON.]

R(W) ROGER COLCHESTER of Barking, yeoman. 12 September 1629 (56)

Sick. To JOHN COLCHESTER of Barking my nephew, the son of THOMAS COLCHESTER my brother deceased, all my lease lands and tenements in Ringshall and Battisford, sometime Ellys, and my lease lands, sometime Prisons, in Ringshall now in occupation of WILLIAM BARNES to hold during the time yet to come specified in the leases after my decease. To said JOHN COLCHESTER my freehold called Lenses in Ringshall now in occupation of said BARNES, to hold for ever. To JOHN COLCHESTER of Battisford my nephew, the son of WILLIAM my brother deceased, my tenement and lands belonging in Battisford which I bought of WILLIAM my brother deceased, now in occupation of said JOHN and SAMUEL my nephews, except reserved out from said tenement the parlour with a going out into the garden, which SARAH my niece and sister to said JOHN shall have so long as she continue single, to be held (except as excepted) to him and his heirs immediately provided that he pay to his sister SARAH, out of said tenement and lands, £3 [yearly] by equal portions every quarter. To said SARAH my niece my 4 acres of land which I bought of Sir THOMAS BARKER in Battisford, to hold for ever. To ROBERT COLCHESTER of Barking my nephew, son of THOMAS my brother deceased, my tenement and land in Barking which I bought of STILES SOWGATE, to hold for ever. To WILLIAM COLCHESTER my nephew, son of WILLIAM COLCHESTER my brother deceased, my tenement in Needham Market with appurtenances and my meadow in Barking, late DRIVERS, lying in Greenstreet. To SAMUEL COLMAN my nephew £10 within 1 month. To JOHN COLMAN my nephew, £10 in 1/2 year. To DANIEL COLMAN my nephew £10 in 1/4 year. To MIRABEL COOLE my niece £5 in 1/4 year. To ANN IVES daughter of MIRABEL COOLE £5 at age 20. To ANN BARNES my niece £20 in 1/2 year. To ANN BENNYTT my niece £10 in 1/2 year. To LUCY MELLES £10 in 1/2 year. To RICHARD BREWES my nephew £10 in 1 month. To JOHN BREWES my nephew £10 in 1 month. To SUSAN GOODCHILD my niece £10 in 1 month. To THOMAS GOOD my nephew £8 in 1 month. To ELIZABETH COATES my nephew [sic] £10 in 1 month. To WILLIAM COLCHESTER the bedstead in my chamber at Needham which I gave him before. All the rest of my goods to ROBERT COLCHESTER and SIMON COLCHESTER my nephews whom I ordain exors. Witnesses: THOMAS LONE, JOHN COOTES, JOHN PULFORD. Pr. at Ipswich 16 Dec. 1629.

R(W) THOMAS CHAPMAN of South Cove, yeoman. (57)
17 October 1629

To the poor of South Cove 6s. 8d., of Reydon 10s., of Covehithe 10s., and of Easton 6s. 8d. To JOHN my son all my lands and tenements in Reydon, provided that my exor. shall be guardian to JOHN till he be 21 and shall use said lands and tenements and receive the profits towards the maintenance and bringing up of JOHN and of EUNICE my daughter, the said JOHN to be taught to read and write and the said EUNICE to be taught to read. If JOHN depart this life before 21 I give my said lands and tenements to EUNICE and her heirs, and I appoint my exors. to be her guardian till 21, and to employ the lands and take the profits for the maintenance of my said daughter. And I will that my exors. make true account unto JOHN my son and EUNICE my daughter of all the profits received, and they shall be allowed all expenses laid out by them about the maintenance of the children and for all such fines and rents as my lands shall be charged with, and for repairing said houses and all expenses; and the remainder shall be equally divided between my said children, with benefit of survivorship; and account shall be made within three months after my son JOHN accomplish 21 if he be living, but if dead, then account to be made to my daughter within three months after her age of 21. If both JOHN and EUNICE depart this life before 21 and before they have issue lawfully begotten, then I give all my lands and tenements to WILLIAM CHAPMAN eldest son of EDWARD CHAPMAN my brother, paying unto ELIZABETH and MARY his sisters £20 apiece at four equal payments in the next four years after WILLIAM shall enter my lands by virtue of my gift. To KATHARINE

FOX my servant 20s. To HENRY CHAPMAN my servant 20s. at age 21. After my legacies discharged, my debts paid, my funeral expenses and charge of my probate allowed out of my goods, then all the rest of my goods and chattels, ready money, plate, household stuff, corn cattle and movables shall remain to EUNICE, to be delivered to her at 21, if living, but if she be dead then I give all unto JOHN my son at age 21. I make DANIEL DEAVE the elder and FRANCIS MORSSE exors. Witnesses: ROBERT JULYANS (X) and ROBERT HOLLAND (X). Pr. at Yoxford 15 Dec. 1629.

R(W) WILLIAM CORNISH (X) of Laxfield, weaver. (58)
25 December 1628

Sick. To MARY my now wife my lands and tenements in Laxfield during her life, and after her decease unto my two sons ISAAC and DANIEL, the eldest and the youngest, and to their heirs. To MARY my wife all my goods and chattels within door and without, moneys in the house and any due to me, towards bringing up my children in the fear of God and in some lawful calling so far forth as God shall enable her, and I appoint MARY my wife wholely exrx. Witnesses: WILLIAM MELLING, SUSAN SMYTH (X), AMY MELLING (X). Pr. at Yoxford 13 Jan. 1629/30.

R(W) ROBERT COBB (X). 26 January 1629/30 (59)

To BLANCH COBB my wife all my goods and chattels, paying EDMUND TIDDEMAN £4 in Hallowmas day [1 Nov.] next; to JAMES TIDDEMAN £3 at Hallowmas next after that; to WILLIAM TIDDEMAN 40s. next Hallowmas after that; to NATHANIEL TIDDEMAN 20s. the Hallowmas after that. My wife to be sole exrx. Witnesses: LONE WINCKOP, RICHARD KNIGHTS, RICHARD GIRLING. Pr. at Yoxford 3 Feb. 1629/30.

R(W) ALICE EDMONDS of Northales (N). [1629?] (60)

To THOMAS CULLEN all her goods whatsoever to bring her to the ground in Christian manner. Witnesses: MARY WOODY, wid. and ELIZABETH DURRANT, singlewoman. Pr. at Beccles 19 Dec. 1629. Admon. to THOMAS CULLEN, general legatee.

R(W) THOMAS GILBERT of Orford, yeoman, (61)
one of the portmen of the said town. 11 November 1629

Sick. To SUSAN my wife £100 and all movables in the houses and yards now in my occupation. To MARGARET WOODD my wife's daughter £100. To WILLIAM GILBERT my uncle £10; to WILLIAM GILBERT his son £20. To KATHARINE PETLEY, wid., £4. To JAMES CORDY of Orford £3. To ANTHONY TAYLOR 20s. To all persons hereafter named and dwelling in Orford these sums of money viz: JOHN HARY 10s.; MARY BROWNE, JOHN GILBERT and ELIZABETH CORDY my god-children, to either of them 5s.; MARK MARSHALL 10s.; ROBERT TOOKELY all the debt he owe me (except my part of Coales); JOHN

GLOVER 10s; THOMAS BLANCHFLOWER 10s.; THOMAS BENNETT 10s.; the Widow GREENELIFFE 10s.; the Widow JESOPP 10s.; the Widow COSEN 20s.; JUDITH ELLIS 10s.; BOTOLF WRIGHT 5s.; HENRY WARNER 5s.; ROBERT PECKE 10s.; ROBERT SALTERNE 10s.; JOHN ROSE 10s.; JOHN GILLES 5s.;[blank] HASELL of Orford 10s.; ROBERT GILDINGWATER 10s.; MARY DUXE, widow, 10s.; Widow COE of Orford 10s.; ALICE EASTER 10s.; WILLIAM TOOKELY 10s.; PRUDENCE POTTER 10s.; JOHN WALKER, knacker, 10s.; ALICE TOWNES 5s.; Widow TISDALL of Orford 10s.; JOHN ESTROPPE 10s.; Widow GLEEDE of Orford 10s.; SIMON WINCKS of same 6s.; [blank] the wife of JOHN SPURDANCE of same 10s.; EDMUND MEEDE 10s.; RICHARD WHITLOCKE 5s.; HENRY NICHOLS 10s.; RALPH GARDNER 10s.; ROBERT WOLFE 10s.; RICHARD BARTON 10s.; JOHN WARREN 10s.; ROBERT HOULDYNG 10s.; the Widow PIGEON 10s.; BRIDGET VALE 10s.; FRANCIS COCKE 10s.; LEONARD GROBY 10s.; EDWARD RICHARDSON 10s.; mother HEATH, widow, 10s.; the wife of [blank] STEVENS 10s.; Widow SALTERNE 10s.; ROGER WOODWARD 10s.; DANIEL ELLYOTT 10s.; ELIZABETH WILKENSON 10s.; the wife of AMBROSE WARREN 10s.; JEREMY SHENE 10s.; ROBERT WARD 10s.; MARGARET TODD 10s.; ELIZABETH NOBBES 10s.; MARY FISHER 10s.; THOMAS LOWE 10s.; Widow TURNER 10s.; MARGARET wife of RICHARD HARVY 20s.; MARY wife of EDMUND JUDITH 20s.; THOMAS BOND 50s. which he doth owe me, so as he shall release my exrx. all such sums of money as I do owe unto him for ploughing, carting and other business; provided that if MARGARET WOOD, my wife's daughter, happen to die before the age of 21, then I give £40 of the said £100 to SUSAN my wife, and other £40, parcel of the said £100, to the said SUSAN, and the £20 residue of the said £100 I give to WILLIAM GILBERT my uncle and WILLIAM GILBERT his son and to the longer liver of them. To THOMAS BOND for making this will 10s. To THOMAS OSBORNE, clerk, now parson of Orford, NICHOLAS HASTLYN now mayor of Orford, RICHARD COPPING, JOHN COGGSHALL gent, NICHOLAS BEARMAN snr., FRANCIS MACE and ANTHONY CROSSE, now portmen of Orford, all my lands and tenements as well freehold as copyhold in Orford on both sides of Gropecunt Lane, to hold for ever provided that the profits arising thereof shall be to such uses and distributed yearly by the said donees in manner and form following: £3 amongst the poor of Orford on 2nd February, in money, corn or fuel, and the residue towards the payment of the lord's rents and repairing the houses and fences now or hereafter upon the said lands and tenements; and, as soon as any five of said donees be dead, that the other two or such of those two as shall be living shall convey all the said lands and tenements to the then parson of Orford and six other of the portmen of Orford and their heirs, the profits to be to such uses as abovesaid; and I will that this course of conveying the said lands and tenements shall be observed for ever. To ROBERT GYMSON of Aldeburgh my friend 20s. To FRANCIS PEIRSE of Orford 10s. To her that late was the Widow GENTRY, now married, 5s. To the poor of Orford £3 to be distributed by my exrx. at my burial. To the poor of Sudbourne 20s. My exrx. shall pay all aforesaid legacies within one year. I nominate SUSAN my wife sole exrx. and desire said THOMAS OSBORNE to be supervisor. Witnesses: EDMUND LEWES, THOMAS TOCKLEY and THOMAS BOND. Pr. at Wickham 16 Dec. 1629.

R(W) SUSAN HALLOWAY of Barking (N). [1629?] (62)

To ANN POSFORD wife of ROBERT POSFORD all her apparel except those which were then on her back. To SUSAN CUTBERT one piece of woolen cloth; to SARAH TAMPON one other piece. The rest of her goods to WILLIAM CUTBORE to pay debts and discharge her funerals. Witnesses: SIMON COULCHESTER. Pr. at Ipswich 16 Dec. 1629. Admon. to WILLIAM CUTBEARD.

R(W) WILLIAM JAMES of Ipswich, maltster. (63)
30 December 1629

The two tenements in Ipswich wherein my wife is joint purchaser with me I give absolutely to said wife ANN. To every of my four children SAMUEL, ANN, MARTHA and MARY £50 each at 21, with benefit of survivorship. The rest of my goods and household stuff I give to my wife ANN for the payment of my debts and performance of my will, and I make her sole exrx., and appoint PETER COALE of Ipswich, grocer, and RICHARD STUDD of the same, maltster, supervisors. My exrx. shall within one month enter into bond unto said supervisors in the sum of £200, conditioned for the performance of this will. And if she shall marry again, she and such party whom she marry shall, before their intermarriage, enter into bond unto my supervisors in the sum of £200 for the performance of so much as shall then rest unperformed. Witnesses: ROBERT HAMBY, HENRY FYRMYN and SAMUEL JAMES. Pr. at Ipswich 7 Jan. 1629/30.

R(W) ALICE LAUNE alias PALENT (X), widow. (64)
1 November 1629

Sick. To JOHN LAUNE als. PALENT my son and to DANIEL LAUNE als. PALENT my son and to ALICE LAUNE als. PALENT my daughter and to MARY LAUNE als. PALENT my daughter and to MARGERY LAUNE als. PALENT my daughter all my movable goods, equally divided by my exors., when they shall accomplish 21 years, with benefit of survivorship. I ordain to be my exor. JOHN ANDREWES of Worlingworth my brother-in-law; he shall enter into bond unto WILLIAM WATLING of Worlingworth, yeo., in double the value of all my movables when all my funeral and other charges be paid. Witnesses: ANN CRESNELL (X), BLITH ANDREWES (X) and WILLIAM WATLING. Pr. at Wickham 14 Jan. 1629/30.

R(W) ALICE LOWE (X) of Aldeburgh, widow. (65)
14 November 1629

To be buried in Aldeburgh churchyard. I give my house and tenement with yard as it is now parted in the occupation of JOHN PRUISE to MARY HOKER my daughter. All the rest of my houses and tenements to BENJAMIN HOKER my son and his heirs, paying to my two other daughters ALICE LOVE and AGNES LEVER £5 apiece within 3 months. To BENJAMIN my son one bed as it stands on the kitchen chamber, 1 long table with the stools and 1 cupboard as they stand in the kitchen. To MARY my daughter 1 bed as it stands in the hall chamber, 2 tables with the stools in the hall, 1 cupboard in the hall as it is now furnished. All the rest of my chattels shall be equally divided among my children after legacies and funeral charges be deducted. I ordain BENJAMIN HOKER my son and MARY HOKER my daughter exors. Witnesses: WILLIAM BRADLEY, JOHN BASE. Pr. at Aldeburgh 14 Dec. 1629. Admon. to BENJAMIN HOKER with power reserved.

R(W) JOHN MANING (X) of Flowton, yeoman. (66)
17 December 1629

Sick. To SARAH my daughter £50 at 21, which £50 JUDITH my wife whom I ordain sole exrx. shall pay to JACOB MANNINGE of Washbrook my brother and ADAM GOODALE of Flowton my son-in-law, by equal portions, as soon as she can conveniently, to the intent that they may pay the same to SARAH my daughter in manner aforesaid and also pay to JUDITH my wife during the nonage of the said SARAH yearly the sum of £3 for her better education and maintenance. And said JACOB MANNINGE shall lay in sufficient bond unto said ADAM GOODALL for the payment of £25, and ADAM GOODALL shall lay in sufficient bond unto JACOB MANNING for the payment of £25, and also to lay in sufficient bond to JUDITH my wife, each of them by themselves, that they shall yearly pay to JUDITH her exors. or assigns, during the nonage of SARAH, £3 -- each of them 30s. And if SARAH depart life before age 21, then the sum of £50 shall be equally divided among five of the youngest children of JUDITH my wife, viz. RICHARD, WILLIAM, ELIZABETH, ALICE, and MARY GOODALL. Also to my daughter SARAH my posted bedstead with all the furniture belonging, 2 chests and a box standing in my parlour, at age 21. The residue of goods, implements and household stuff to JUDITH my wife who I appoint sole exrx. I appoint my brother-in-law ROBERT WELHAM of Combs my supervisor. Witnesses: WILLIAM MANNINGE (X), JACOB MANNING (X), ADAM GOODALL and THOMAS BULL. Pr. at Ipswich 5 Feb. 1629/30.

R(W) ALEXANDER MAY of Walton, yeoman. 14 January 1629/30 (67)

In good health. To the poor of Walton 10s. To JOHN MAYE my brother my marsh called Little Marsh and the Whynny Close, containing together 18 acres in Walton, all which were given me by the will of JOHN MAYE my father, and I give them to my brother JOHN for the money I owe him and for £20 more to be paid to my brother ROGER for the use of my three sons hereafter named. To said JOHN MAY my brother the drift-way to and from the said marsh and Whynny Close. To ROGER MAY my brother all other lands and tenements together with the house, backhouse, barn, hay-houses, yards, garden and orchard belonging, given by the will of my father, as they are particularly expressed therein, upon condition that he pay, together with the £20 he shall receive from my brother JOHN, £280 to my three sons JOHN MAY, ALEXANDER MAY and ROGER MAY, to be equally divided when they are each 21, viz. £93 6s. 8d. to JOHN at 21, £93 6s. 8d. to ALEXANDER at 21 and £93 6s. 8d. to ROGER at 21, with benefit of survivorship. If all three should die then their portions shall remain to my exor. For want of payment of their portions my sons severally shall enter upon so much of the lands as their portions come to, to be laid out by two tenants unto them as they shall come to their several ages of 21. The residue of goods -- debts, legacies and funeral charges being discharged -- I give to my brother ROGER MAY to bring up my children and bestow some learning of them, whom I ordain sole exor. Witnesses: GEOFFERY TALBOTT, WALTER WISSOM (X), and ANN BETTS (X). Pr. at Ipswich 5 Feb. 1629/30.

R(W) EDMUND MAHEWE (X) senior of Gosbeck, yeoman. (68)
2 December 1629

Sick. To KATHARINE my wife the use for her life of one posted bedstead with all the furniture belonging as it stands in the low chamber, 1 square table, 1 great chair, 2 low stools, 1 cupboard, 1 brass pot, 4 pewter dishes, 1 trundle bedstead with the flock bed belonging, 2 pairs of sheets, 2 pillow-biers, 2 table cloths, 1 brewer's keeler, 1 little chair. After her death all the said household stuffs to my son WILLIAM MAHEWE. The residue of goods, chattels, stock, corn, grain and cattle I leave to WILLIAM my son towards the payment of my debts and performing my will and I make him sole exor. I make JOHN CHURCH snr. supervisor. Witnesses: WILLIAM STYLES, RICHARD DOWE, WILLIAM STUDD. Pr. at Ipswich 19 Jan. 1629/30.

W(R) SAMUEL OSBORNE of Ipswich, tanner. 26 November 1629 (69)

Somewhat sickly. To JOHN OSBORNE my brother my lands and tenements in Much Clafton [Great Clacton?] in Essex now in tenure of RICHARD COOLE. To my kinsman THOMAS OSBORNE, a shearman living in Haddye [Hadleigh?] in Suffolk, £20 within a year. To my kinsman JOHN DUNKON snr. dwelling in Mendlesham £20, which £20 he have in his hand, on condition that he pay my own mother the wife of THOMAS SHEPPARD 26s. 8d. every year during her life. To SAMUEL DUNKON son of ROBERT DUNKON of Ipswich £10 within a year. To SARAH DUNKON daughter of ROBERT DUNKON £5 within a year. To JOHN BEACH and SAMUEL BEACH the sons of my sister JOAN OSBORNE now the wife of JOHN BEACH 40s. apiece within a year. To SAMUEL WARD the Town Preacher at Ipswich 40s. within a year. To RICHARD RAINSFORD, minister of St. Helens in Ipswich 40s. within a year. To Widow GRENE of St. Helens in Ipswich 20s. within a month. To old GRAY 5s. and 15s. to be distributed to the poor of St. Helens. The rest of my goods, implements of household, movables, and money (my debts, funeral expenses and probate paid) I give to ROBERT DUNKON of Ipswich, tanner, and I make JOHN DUNKON snr. and ROBERT DUNKON of Ipswich my exors. Witnesses: FRANCIS DAWSON and MARTHA DUNKON (X). Pr. at Ipswich 17 Dec. 1629. Admon. to ROBERT DUNKON with power reserved.

R(W) JOHN PRIME of Halesworth, innholder. 14 November 1629 (70)

All that messuage or tenement and curtilage and one marsh adjoining called Chambers, with appurtenances, lying together in the suburbs of Dunwich, now in occupation of RICHARD LYATT, are to be sold towards payment of debts. To ALICE PRYME my daughter all those messuages or tenements wherein I dwell, with the yards gardens orchards and appurtenances belonging; also one meadow between the river on the north and the highway from Halesworth to Cheston [Chediston] on the south, and abutting Margeres Way to the west and a way now in tenure of GEORGE PRYME to the east, containing 4 1/2 acres; one close containing 1 1/2 acres between the way from Halesworth to Chediston on the north and lands of SPENCER REEVE now in occupation of JOHN CLARKE on the south, and one head abuts on the close of RICHARD WELTON to the west and the other on the said way to the east, the which meadow and close are holden by copy of court roll of the manor of Halesworth and are now in the occupation of said JOHN PRYME; 1 copper and guild set 1 mash vat 1 cooler 1 wort vat 1 underbecke 2 tables in the hall and 2 forms belonging and now in the brew-house -- all to be held to said ALICE and heirs lawfully begotten of her body -- provided that my exors. shall have the bringing up of ALICE till she be 20 and then she shall enter these gifts. Failing lawful issue of ALICE PRIME, these gifts shall remain to ROBERT PRIME the eldest son of my brother ROBERT PRIME and his heirs. If said ROBERT should live to enjoy the gifts given to ALICE he shall pay his 2 brothers JOHN PRYME and WILLIAM PRIME £20 to either of them, the first payment to be made JOHN PRIME within 2 years after the decease of ALICE, and the other £20 to WILLIAM within 4 years, with power for the two brothers to distrain. To ROBERT PRIME, JOHN PRIME and WILLIAM PRIME the 3 sons of my brother ROBERT PRIME, £10 apiece, viz. to ROBERT within 1 year after decease of my mother-in-law PRIME, the late wife of my father ROBERT PRIME, and to JOHN within 2 years and to WILLIAM within 3 years thereof, with benefit of survivorship. But if all decease before the £10 apiece be due, that £30 shall remain to my exors. And whereas my mother PRIME have one annuity of £6 p.a., I will that he that shall enjoy the gifts given to ALICE PRIME my daughter shall pay the said £6 out of the premisses aforesaid given to ALICE, all which payments are to be made in the south porch of the parish church of Halesworth. All my chattels, cattle, or implements of household stuff (except as excepted) shall be sold towards payment of debts and legacies. My exors shall be accountable to my daughter ALICE, when she is 20, for the overplus from these sales and the sale of my house at Dunwich, after debts and legacies have been paid and ALICE has been brought up to the age of 20. My exors. shall keep my tenements in sufficient reparations until then and make no strip or waste. To the poor of Halesworth 20s. I ordain WILLIAM SMYTH of Alderhallow in Suffolk and ROBERT HAWES of Woodbridge exors. and I give either of them £6 13s. 4d. for their pains. Witnesses: EDWARD FELMINGHAM, JOHN WILLS and me THOMAS SKARLETT. Pr. at Beccles 30 Jan. 1629/30. Admon. to WILLIAM SMYTH with power reserved.

R(W) MICHAEL QUINTIN senior of Stoke next Ipswich. (71)
11 December 1629

Sick. To MICHAEL QUINTIN my son and his heirs male my house and grounds in Hadleigh, now in tenure and occupation of one GARRARD. If said MICHAEL die without male issue I give said house to FERDINAND QUINTINE my grandchild, the son of FERDINAND QUINTINE my son. To MICHAEL QUINTIN, FERDINAND QUINTIN and ANN BACON the wife of ROBERT BACON, my sons and daughter, 40s. apiece within 14 days of my burial. To my 8 grandchildren now living £4 5s. apiece at age 21, viz. ANN, FERDINAND, FRANCIS and RUTH, children of FERDINAND my son, and ANN the daughter of SOLOMON my son, and JUDITH, ANN and JOHN the children of ROBERT BACON and ANN my daughter, with benefit of survivorship. The rest of my goods I give to SOLOMON QUINTIN my son, whom I appoint sole exor. To ANN FASTALL, wife of JOHN FASTALL of Bramford, 5s. To the poor of said parish of Stoke 20s. to be distributed within 1 week after my burial. To every one of my household servants 12d. Witnesses: GEORGE RIBBENS and ROBERT LORD. Pr. at Ipswich 19 Dec. 1629.

R(W) ALICE REUBEN of Felixstowe, widow. 7 December 1629 (72)

Weak. To my brother THOMAS WITHERS my house and land in Kirton on condition that he pay these legacies following: to my brother WILLIAM WITHERS 40s. within a year; to my sister late PHYLLIS WITHERS now wife of RALPH SPARLING 40s. within a year; to WILLIAM WITHERS the younger, son of WILLIAM WITHERS of Felixstowe 20s. at 21. Said WILLIAM and PHYLLIS to have power of distraint. I make THOMAS WITHERS my brother sole exor. I give to ANN WITHERS and THOMAS WITHERS, the children of WILLIAM WITHERS, 10s. each at 21. Witnesses: ALICE REUBEN (X), SIMON PETTEWARD and MARGARET TAME (X). Pr. at Ipswich 15 Jan. 1629/30.

R(W) HENRY SPARROW of Offton, yeoman. 20 October 1629 (73)

To the poor of Offton 20s. within a year. To MARY my wife £8 yearly for the term of her life, to be issuing out of all my freehold lands and paid half year and half year by equal portions. To HENRY SPARROW my son all my lands messuages and tenements free or copy in Offton and Little Bricett; and if he should die before 21, not having issue, I will said messuages and lands to ROBERT SPARROW my brother, paying out of the same to RICHARD SPARROW my brother £50 and to ANN BRABYE my sister the like sum and to JOAN BYLES my sister the like and to MARY ALEGOOD my sister £50 -- all which legacies to be paid out of my lands and tenements within one year after my said brother ROBERT SPARROW or his heirs shall happen to have the same by virtue of this will, but not otherwise; with power for legatees to distrain against ROBERT. To MARY my wife all movables she brought me and her cow and 1 feather-bed 1 flock bed 1 coverlet 2 blankets 1 pair of sheets 1 other bedstead as it stands in the house of EDMUND GOODALL in Willisham; also £5 to be paid out of my stock within 2 months; and so much of my butter and cheese and corn as will keep her and my son with one servant until new come again. And if my wife shall please to dwell in my said house wherein I now dwell she shall have it before any other, giving for it as any other will and 20s. less yearly, so long as she please to have it or therein to dwell. To HENRY SPARROW my son all my linen together with 1 silver cup which Mr BUCKENHAM gave him, all which are to be kept for my son till he be 21. My exors. shall have the disposing of my said messuage lands and tenements, with the putting out of such portions as shall be raised out of my said lands yearly, as well as the profits thereof as also out of the sale of my goods, until the said HENRY my son shall be 21. My exors. shall yearly allow so much as shall be thought fit for bringing up said son and maintaining him in learning during his minority, and during his minority shall pay to MARY my wife the annuity of £8, given her by this will, paid half year and half year at my mansion where I now dwell, in lieu and recompense of her dower or thirds in any of my said lands. And I desire her to be careful in bringing up my said son in learning and in the fear of God, and that she be a mother to him. All my movables personal and real are to be sold towards payment of debts and expenses, and the overplus thereof, with the profits of my said messuages lands and tenements, shall be employed for said HENRY my son until his age of 21, and immediately after that my exors. shall yield unto him a perfect account of the profits and the overplus, and deliver to him all such goods as they think fitting to be preserved for his use and which may be kept without loss on them. My exors. shall pay BRABYE, my sister's daughter, 40s. at 21. I make ROBERT SPARROW of Colchester, my brother, PHILIP BRABYE and THOMAS BILES, my brothers-in-law, my exors.; and my father-in-law WILLIAM STRUTT supervisor, entreating him to see this will performed and to be a help unto my son in seeing him to be brought up in learning and good education. Witnesses: CHRISTOPHER BEALE, ANDREW RUDLAND (X), and NICHOLAS KYRKEY. Pr. at Ipswich 5 Feb. 1629/30.

R(W) ELLEN STORER of Laxfield, widow. 14 May 1629 (74)

To JOHN BORRETT jnr. of Laxfield, yeo., my copyhold messuage and tenement with a yard and orchard in Badingham, on condition that he pay all my legacies hereafter declared. To ELIZABETH BORRETT, KATHARINE BORRETT and MARY BORRETT, daughters of said JOHN, 30s. and my best chest my keep my desk my 2 best cushions and my little box, equally divided. To SAMUEL BORRETT son of said JOHN BORRETT 10s. To WILLIAM BURGES of Gillingham 20s. and my 2 best gowns 2 best petticoats and my warming pan. To FRANCIS CARFFE of Stradbroke 20s., 1 chest with the cover broken and plated with iron, and a little pewter dish. To GILLIAN WYARD, wife of ROBERT WYARD of Laxfield, my cloak. These legacies to be paid and the goods delivered within half a year of my decease. The rest of my goods and chattels I give to said JOHN BORRETT, whom I make exor. Witnesses: WILLIAM GODBOLD and WILLIAM PAYNE. Pr. at Yoxford 13 Jan. 1629/30.

R(W) ROBERT WRIGHT senior (X) of Stradbroke, yeoman. (75)
22 January 1627/8

To my wife THOMASIN all my movable goods and chattels upon condition that she shall pay ALICE my daughter £12 which I owe to be paid on reasonable demand. To ALICE my daughter £8, 1 feather-bed with all things belonging, at the discretion of THOMASIN my wife. To ELIZABETH KYAN my daughter £5. To RICHARD KYAN my grandchild 40s. To ANN KYAN my grandchild £3. To RICHARD GRENELING my landlord for my love towards him 20s. All these legacies to be paid within one year of the decease of THOMASIN my wife, for my wife shall have the profit of all my aforesaid legacies. I make THOMASIN my wife and GEORGE PULHAM my brother-in-law my exors., and for his pains I give him 20s. And I desire RICHARD GRENELING my landlord to be my Supervisor. Witnesses: FR. GODFREY, RICHARD GIRLING, SAMUEL LAWRENCE. Pr. at Beccles 21 Jan. 1629/30.

R(W) ROSE WYTHE (X) of Framsden, widow. 20 January 1626/7 (76)

To FRANCES FENN wife of THOMAS FENN, my daughter, and to ANN BARBER wife of GEOFFREY BARBER, my daughter, and to DOROTHY JACKSON wife of GEORGE JACKSON, my daughter, all my goods equally divided between them and delivered within one month of my decease; and all debts due to me at my death also equally divided. I make THOMAS FENN, GEOFFREY BARBER and GEORGE JACKSON, my sons-in-law, exors. Witnesses: ABIGAIL GOODINGE (X), ELIZABETH LOWNDES (X) and GEORGE RUSSELL. Pr. at Wickham 16 Dec. 1629. Admon. to GEOF. BARBER and GEO. JACKSON with power reserved.

R(W) ELIZABETH BADSON, singlewoman (N). (77)
[blank] October 1629

On the day of her death she left to her brother BADSON's children, of Shipmeadow, 20s apiece. To THOMAS BATSON son of PAUL BATSON 20s. To every of the children of her brother a coif, a forehead cloth and a singleband. The rest of her estate she gave to PAUL BADSON and his wife to bring her to the ground. Witnesses: MARY EDWARDS and ELIZABETH RANDALL. Pr. at Beccles 6 Oct. 1629. Admon. to PAUL BADSON and his wife, general legatees.

R(W) WILLIAM BAKER of Uggeshall, yeoman. 10 May 1628 (78)

Sick. All goods chattels messuages lands and tenements as well freehold as copyhold lying in Uggeshall or elsewhere (except one little piece of ground called the Hardewe lying in Nether Green containing 1/2 rood) I give to NICHOLAS BAKER my son. I give the said little piece to JANE now wife of said NICHOLAS. To THOMAS MAY of Beccles my son-in-law £5 within half a year. NICHOLAS my son shall (in consideration of the gift of said lands), within one month of my decease, convey all that messuage or tenement with orchard and garden of said NICHOLAS BAKER, situate in Beccles, to said THOMAS MAY. I make NICHOLAS my son exor. Witnesses: FRANCIS MORSE, JOHN FOXLEY, DANIEL DEANE jnr. Pr. at Beccles 18 April 1629.

W(R) RICHARD BURGES of Beccles. 17 March 1629/30 (79)

To be buried in the parish church of Beccles. To RICHARD and THOMAS my 2 sons my house in Beccles, to be sold and equally divided. To PRISCILLA my daughter my miele at Southcove. My household stuff to be sold to pay debts, and the remainder to be equally divided between my 2 sons RICHARD and THOMAS. Witnesses: PETER BURROWE (X), JOSEPH DIX, ELIZABETH DOWE (X). Pr. 22 March 1629/30. Admon. to RICHARD BURGES, son of deceased.

R(W) GILES BORRETT senior of Stradbroke, yeoman. 1 April 1629 (80)

ALICE my wife shall have my messuage or tenement in Stradbroke called Brockes, wherein HUGH WRIGHT inhabiteth, with all the lands and hereditaments belonging, late Brocke's, to hold during her life in augmentation and further satisfaction of all right of jointure or dower in any of my lands or tenements whereof I have been seised of any estate of inheritance any time during the coverture between us, doing no estripment or waste, and keeping the houses in good reparations, and discharging all rents due, provided that it may be lawful for said ALICE and her assigns to take sufficient hedge-bote for maintenance of the premises in hedging and fencing, and sufficient timber for maintenance of the houses and buildings. Unto GILES BORRETT my son all my messuage or tenement aforesaid and all said lands and tenements as well freehold and charter-hold as customary and copyhold to the said tenement belonging, and all my messuage or tenement in Stradbroke called Harvies wherein I do now inhabit, and all my lands tenements meadows pastures feedings and hereditaments in Stradbroke as well freehold as copyhold to the said tenement belonging, which I lately purchased of JOHN HARVY and ROBERT HARVY deceased, and he to enter the same presently after the decease of said ALICE; also all my grounds called Impayes with 18 acres of land or pasture to the same adjoining, in Stradbroke, which I lately had by the gift and devise of GEOFFERY BORRETT my father deceased, and to enter the same presently after my decease, to have and hold in lieu and full satisfaction of the use and occupation of a certain pightle I have had and occupied ever since the same was by my appointment assured unto the said GILES my son or his heirs by WILLIAM GIRLING esq. now deceased. To JOHN BORRETT one other of my sons and his heirs all my meadow and the pightle adjoining in Stradbroke, nigh Barlowe Bridge, which I lately purchased of GEOFFERY CLOWTING my brother-in-law, and one piece of copyhold land in Laxfield containing 1/2 rood called Sabins Yard, with a ditch which I hold by copy of court roll of the manor of Studhawe in Laxfield, and he to enter the same presently after my decease, to hold to said JOHN and his heirs for ever. To the said NICHOLAS my son and his heirs all my messuage or tenement in Athelington wherein THOMAS JESOPP inhabiteth, and all my lands tenements meadows pastures feeding and other hereditaments in Athelington and Worlingworth to the said messuage pertaining, which I lately purchased of EDWARD HARPER; and all my grounds in Stradbroke lying nigh to the vicarage, called Clowtings, with a cottage thereon; and all my messuage or tenement in Stradbroke wherein ANTHONY BORRETT now inhabiteth with all the yards orchards gardens and a pightle adjoining; and all my shop or house in Stradbroke and my candle-house salt-house and shop in the end thereof, now in the farm or occupation of EDWARD BORRETT or his assigns; and all my lands and tenements in Stradbroke which I lately purchased of GILES BANNOCKE alias BARBER, to hold to said NICHOLAS my son his heirs and assigns for ever, and he to enter the same presently after my decease. To the said NICHOLAS the title in the term of years which I hold by lease for divers years yet to come of certain grounds in Syleham called Grampitts, to hold after my decease during the whole term of years then to come and in as ample manner and form as I myself now hold the same by virtue of the said lease. To ELIZABETH CLOWTING my sister the wife of said GEOFFERY CLOWTING one annuity of 30s. to be paid at the usual feasts of the Annunciation and of St. Michael by even portions, the first payment to begin at either of said feasts which shall first happen after my decease. To said ALICE my wife £100 of money or so many of my goods plate chattels and credit as shall amount to said sum at a reasonable price and at her choice, to be paid or delivered with 14 days after my decease discharged of all former rights and properties. Said ALICE shall have the use of my copper as it hangeth in my tenement Harvies, and of my horse-mill there with the mill-stones and furniture belonging, during her life. After her decease the same shall remain with my said tenement. I forgive to GILES BORRETT my son all such sums of money as he owe unto me or as I have paid for him to any person. I give the children of GEORGE BORRETT my nephew (MARY the wife of GEORGE FOSTER only excepted) £5 to be paid within 5 years, equally divided between them. To every of the daughters of EDWARD BORRETT my brother late deceased, and to JOHN COLBY my godson, the son of JOHN COLBY, 40s apiece, to be paid to them or their exors. and assigns within 2 years after my decease. To GILES BORRETT my grandchild and godson, son of JOHN BORRETT my son, £10. To WILLIAM COPLAND my grandchild and godson, son of THOMAS COPLAND my son-in-law, £20 to be paid to them or their exors. or assigns within 4 years; to GILES CLOWTING my nephew £5, and to GILES his son my godson 33s. 4d.; to WILLIAM CLOWTING, HENRY CLOWTING, THOMAS CLOWTING, CICELY YOUNGEMAN the wife of THOMAS YOUNGEMAN, ALICE CLOWTING and KATHARINE RISING, widow -- the sons and daughters of said GEOFFREY CLOWTING -- £3 6s. 8d.; to every of my now servants 10s. to be paid to them or their exors. or assigns within one year. To GILES BANNOCKE alias BARBOR the younger my godson 20s. presently after my decease. To the poor of Stradbroke £3 6s. 8d.; and of Fressingfield 30s.; and of Laxfield 20s.; and of Wingfield 15s.; and of Hoxne 10s.; and of Horham 15s.; and of Wilby 10s.; and of Syleham 5s.; and of Denham

5s.; and of Athelington 5s. to be distributed presently after my decease at the discretion of the minister and churchwardens and chief inhabitants where most need shall happen to be. My exors. shall receive my debts and pay my debts and bring me honestly to the ground in Christian burial. The residue of my goods chattels implements corn hay swine poultry utensils unbequeathed shall be sold towards the payment of debts and legacies. I give to said GILES and NICHOLAS the surplus of all receipts which shall come into the hands of my exors. (my debts legacies etc. being paid) equally to be parted between them. I make the said GILES BORRETT and JOHN BORRETT and NICHOLAS BORRETT my sons exors., unto whom I give for their pains to every of them £5, and I appoint said GEORGE BORRETT my nephew and FRANCIS SANDCROFT the younger supervisors of this will, whom I also give for their pains either of them 20s. Witnesses: JOHN BORRETT, GILES BORRETT, ROBERT OFFOODE. Pr. at Yoxford 17 March 1629/30.

R(W) JOHN BORRETT of Laxfield, yeoman. 20 October 1627 (81)

In good health. DOROTHY my wife shall have the use of my parlour chamber and vanx ruffs over the same, parcel of the messuage or tenement wherein I dwell, with the garden and new orchard lying at the west end of said parlour, to hold for a place of residence during her life if she keep herself unmarried, with liberty of ingress egress regress ingate and outgate for her and her friends servants and family, but not otherwise. To FRANCIS BORRETT my eldest son all that messuage wherein I dwell in Laxfield with all my lands and tenements in Laxfield now in occupation of HENRY BORRETT of the demise of me, excepting out of this my gift to FRANCIS one close in Laxfield called Surrs and one other close called Long Pightle. To DOROTHY BORRETT my wife during her life (in satisfaction and in lieu of such title to dower as she may claim in the said messuage lands and tenements given to FRANCIS) one annuity of £20, issuing out of the said premises, to be paid to her by my said son FRANCIS yearly at the south porch of the parish church of Laxfield on 1st January, 25th March, 24th June and 29th September by equal portions, the first payment to be made on that of the said days which shall happen first after my decease, with power for DOROTHY to distrain if payment is behind in the space of 10 days or, if it is behind 40 days, to re-enter and occupy the whole premises. To ROBERT BORRETT my son the said Surrs Close and Long Pightle and one other close containing 6 acres in the occupation of the said ROBERT in Laxfield, called Broadoak, and one other pightle in Laxfield on the west of the market-way containing 2 acres and now in occupation of said ROBERT. To DOROTHY my wife (in lieu of thirds or dower in the aforesaid closes and pightles bequeathed to ROBERT) an annuity of £5 issuing out of the said two closes and two pightles, to be paid by the said ROBERT yearly at the south porch of the parish church of Laxfield, on the said 1 Jan., 25 March, 24 June and 29 Sept. by even portions, with power to distrain if payment is 10 days behind, or, if 40 days behind to occupy till arrears plus a penalty of 10s. be paid. To said son FRANCIS the long table in the hall, the iron at the stock of the kitchen chimney and the cob-irons there, the bedstead and bed whereon I usually lie with all the bedding boulster blankets and coverlet, with 2 pillows 2 pillow-biers 2 pairs of sheets a pair of andirons a pair of tongs and the fry-pan in the parlour; and all the timber plank and board in or about my said messuage; my horse-mill and roan gelding. To SAMUEL my son one of my sets of silver buttons; my other set of silver buttons I give to my son ROBERT. I make DOROTHY my wife and my son ROBERT BORRETT exors. Read sealed subscribed and published by the testator in the presence of LAURENCE LOMAX and GEORGE DUNSTON; altered and now published in the presence of THOMAS GREENE, FRANCIS VERDEN, FRANCIS SANDCROFT. Pr. at Yoxford 17 March 1629/30.

R(W) ROBERT COWELL (X) of Leiston. 29 December 1629 (82)

To THOMASIN my wife my best bed and bedstead with the boulster coverlets blankets and all things belonging unto it now; all my linen with a great chest that was her mother's and a pair of bellows; 1 cow to choose from my dairy. The rest of my goods and movables (my debts being paid and burial expenses and charges of this my will discharged) I give to my wife and 5 children WILLIAM, ROBERT, JOHN, THOMAS, and ARTHUR equally divided. I make JONAS PERMAN and WILLIAM COWELL my brother exors. Witnesses: GEORGE JERMY and WILLIAM GARRARD (X). Memorandum my will is that my 4 grandchildren have every one a lamb to be chosen out of my flock at Lammas day next, and that the child wherewith my daughter-in-law the wife of JOHN my son goeth hath one. Wit. GEORGE JERMY, WILLIAM GARRARD (X). Pr. at Yoxford 25 Feb. 1629/30.

R(W) NICHOLAS CORBETT of Kessingland, bachelor (N). (83)
ca. 22 March 1628/9

Did about 2 or 3 days before New Year's day, in the year 1628, make his will. He gave to ELIZABETH PALMER his mother-in-law, GEORGE CORBETT his brother and ELIZABETH CORBETT his sister his movable goods rights and credits to be parted amongst them. Witnesses: JOHN WEBSTER and FRANCIS WEBSTER. Admon. 20 March 1629/30.

R(W) JOHN COVE (X) of Great Redisham, thaxter. (84)
2 June 1629 Codicil 10 January 1629/30

Sick. To ROBERT COVE my godson the son of ROBERT COVE my brother late deceased £5 and a posted bedstead; to WILLIAM COVE another of the sons of said ROBERT my brother 40s., 1 coffer and 1 pair of sheets -- all to be delivered within 1 year; to JAMES COVE, MARY COVE, ALICE COVE, FRANCIS COVE and SIBYL COVE, 5 other children of said ROBERT deceased 40s. apiece to be paid as aforesaid. All these gifts of money to be subject to benefit of survivorship. To WILLIAM NICHOLLS my godson, son of ALICE

NICHOLLS widow my sister, a bed and bedstead as it standeth full furnished, and £5. To ANN NICHOLLS one of the daughters of said ALICE 1 feather-bed, 1 joined chest and £5 to be paid within a year. To GEORGE NICHOLLS and ALICE NICHOLLS, 2 other children of said ALICE, 40s. apiece to be paid as aforesaid. To ELIZABETH COVE, ROBERT COVE, MIRABEL COVE, WILLIAM COVE, MARY COVE and [blank] COVE, the 6 children of WILLIAM COVE my brother, 40s. apiece, which sum amounting to £12 shall be delivered to my supervisor within a year, to be employed to the use of the said children till their several ages of 21, with benefit of survivorship. To WILLIAM NICHOLLS son of the aforenamed WILLIAM NICHOLLS being my godson 1 cupboard and £5. To my said sister ALICE NICHOLLS 1 warming pan and 1 buffet stool, and my exor. shall put out £14 during the life of said ALICE and the profit thereof arising every year shall be paid to her towards their maintenance. To WILLIAM COVE my brother all my part in a pair of mustard querns, my part in the great skoales, and my part in a four-quarter cheese vat and breede to it. I nominate said WILLIAM NICHOLLS my kinsman sole exor. and JOHN LONE of Worlingham, my kinsman, supervisor. I give him 40s. for his pains. My exor. shall within 1 year after the death of my said sister ALICE NICHOLLS distribute the said £14, as also the price of my goods and chattels not bequeathed (my funeral charges and legacies first being taken out) among the parties hereafter named, by equal portions, viz. ROBERT, JAMES and WILLIAM , sons of said ROBERT COVE my brother deceased, the said 6 children of my said brother WILLIAM COVE, and WILLIAM NICHOLLS my exor. and WILLIAM his son, or so many of them as shall be living. Witnesses: WILLIAM LONE the writer, THOMAS FOLKARD (X), WILLIAM DAWSON. Pr. 10 Jan. 1629/30. Codicil: My supervisor shall within one month after he shall have received of my exor. that £12 (to be disposed unto the 6 children of WILLIAM CAVE) give his bond to my exor. to pay him 12d. in the pound yearly for so much money as shall remain in his hands during any of the children's minorities. And if my supervisor shall refuse to give such bond my exor., shall upon request to him made by my supervisor enter unto my said supervisor a bond with a surety for the payment of the children's portions and 12d. in the pound yearly unto my supervisor as an increase of the said children's portions during the minority of them. Witnesses: JOHN ELLES, WILLIAM ELLIS, HENRY GARROD. Pr. at Beccles 1 March 1629/30.

R(W) MARGERY GILDE (X) of Ilketshall, widow (N). (85)
24 January 1628/9

To my son JOHN GILD all my apparel linen and woolen except such particulars as I have disposed to others, which particulars I have acquainted my friend Mr GOLDING and ELIZABETH his wife, and it is my will they shall more plainly say which they are. All the rest of my goods unbequeathed after what I name, in my house or without, and money by bonds or ready money I give to my 2 sons JOHN and SAMUEL, equally divided, whom I nominate exors. Witnesses: WILLIAM GOULDING, PETER FASSETT. Unto CHRISTIAN WARNE a cloth petticoat, a waistcoat and a green apron. To SUSAN the wife of HENRY WELTON a russet petticoat and a russet waistcoat. To ELIZABETH wife of WILLIAM GOLDING her best ruff and coif. Pr. at Beccles 18 March 1629/30. Admon. to JOHN GILD with power reserved for SAMUEL GYLD.

R(W) WILLIAM GODBOLD senior of Worlingworth, yeoman. (86)
12 April 1629

Aged and sickly. If WILLIAM GODBOLD my son, upon reasonable request to him made by my son ROBERT GODBOLD after my decease, shall remise and quitclaim to ROBERT and his heirs all right that said WILLIAM may have in those lands and tenements which I by this will shall give to said ROBERT GODBOLD in present possession; and if said WILLIAM shall also on like request deliver to the exor. of this will one deed thereby releasing to my exor. all manner of accounts legacies debts duties and personal demands whatsoever, then I give to said son WILLIAM and heirs of his body lawfully begotten all my messuages lands tenements and hereditaments which, or the reversion or remainder of which, I had of the bargain sale feoffment grant and confirmation of my said son WILLIAM, situate in Worlingworth Allington [Athelington] Hoxne Weston and Brampton in Suffolk. The remainder of all the said premises I give to my said son ROBERT and the heirs of his body lawfully begotten, and for want of such issue the remainder to the right heirs of said WILLIAM for ever. Also, on the same conditions, I give my said son WILLIAM my brewing copper, horse-mill, the great bedstead in my parlour with the bedding thereon as it is now furnished, and the long table in my hall. But if my said son WILLIAM shall refuse releases as aforesaid, or if he or any other person claiming by or under him shall do any act to frustrate my last will he shall take no benefit by this will and then I do devise all the aforesaid messuages &c to my said son ROBERT and the heirs of his body lawfully begotten, the remainder to the right heirs of me the said WILLIAM. If JOHN GODBOLD my son shall upon request by my exor. make a general release to him of all personal actions legacies &c then I give my said son JOHN during his life all my houses lands meadows pastures tenements and hereditaments free and copy which I purchased of NICHOLAS BALDRY and JOHN DOWSING, and my close called Jernegans containing 12 acres lying in Worlingworth and Allington, the remainder after his death I give to the first-begotten son of said JOHN and the heirs of his body lawfully begotten, the remainder to the second son of said JOHN and his like heirs, the remainder to the third son of said JOHN and his like heirs, the remainder to the fourth son of said JOHN and his like heirs, the remainder to the fifth son &c, the remainder to the sixth son &c, the remainder to ROBERT GODBOLD my son and the heirs &c.&c, the remainder to my right heirs for ever. But if my said son JOHN, being requested, shall not make such a general release, then my said son JOHN shall take no benefit of this will and my demise to him made, with all such remainders as thereupon depend shall be void, and then I do demise all the last-mentioned houses &c unto the said ROBERT GODBOLD my son and the heirs of his body &c, remainder thereof to my said son WILLIAM GODBOLD and the heirs &c&c, the remainder to the right heirs of me the said WILLIAM for ever. I give to my said son ROBERT the heirs &c my close called Sallowfield containing 18 acres and my houses lands and tenements as well freehold as copyhold being in or extending into Allington and Hoxne or towns adjoining which I purchased of FRANCIS KENT (excepting the aforesaid close called Mansafeild). And all my other lands tenements &c not formerly bequeathed, with all appurtenances, and remainder of all the aforesaid houses closes land and tenements last bequeathed I give to said JOHN GODBOLD my son and the heirs &c, remainder to my son WILLIAM and his heirs for ever. To my servant ALICE MAYHEWE 20s. The rest of my personal estate goods corn cattle chattels and debts I give to said son ROBERT towards payment of debts and performance of this will, whereof I make him sole exor. Witnesses: LAURENCE LOMAX, GEORGE DUNSTON, FRANCIS CHENEY. Pr. at Yoxford 25 Feb. 1629/30.

R(W) JANE HOLMES of Sudbourne, widow. 10 June 1625 (87)

To ANN BALDREE of Sudbourne, widow, £3 to be paid within 2 years, and my saye apron and my best hat. To LAURENCE BALDREE snr. of Sudbourne £3 to be paid within 2 years. To ELIZABETH CROSSE of Iken my kinswoman 9s. to be paid within 2 1/2 years. To ELIZABETH TINDALL of Dunstall my kinswoman £3 to be paid within 3 years, 20s. a year till all be paid, and my workinday apparel and 1 cupboard. To MARY PEIRSON my kinswoman 30s. within 2 years. To LAURENCE BALDREE jnr. 10s. to buy him a spoon. All the rest of my movables I give to ROBERT SILLETT jnr. to be delivered presently after my decease. Witnesses: JANE HOWES, ROBERT SILLETT. Pr. 25 Feb. 1629/30 at Yoxford. Admon. of the goods of JANE HOMES to ROBERT SILLET, general legatee.

R(W) JOHN LONE of Sandcroft [South Elmham St. Cross], bachelor. 7 October 1629 (88)

I give the reversion of my tenements with all lands belonging being in South Elmham or elsewhere to RICHARD LONE my brother and his heirs for ever; he shall pay out of the said lands and tenements to JAMES LONE my brother £4 within 2 years after the said ROBERT shall have possessed my lands, with power for JAMES to distrain. To JAMES LONE my said brother, ELIZABETH WHITINGE MARY ELMER and SARAH LONE my living sisters, the legacy of £10 given to me by JAMES BRAME my uncle late of St. Margaret South Elmham; likewise the £10 which was give me by the will of JOHN BRAME my uncle late of St. Margaret South Elmham which is to be paid within 8 years of the decease of said JOHN BRAME; the which £20 is to be equally divided among them. I appoint RICHARD LONE my brother sole exor. Witnesses: JOHN NEWSON, JOHN GOWING. Pr. at Beccles 6 March 1629/30.

W. ROSE ALDES (X)(N). 10 March[blank] (89)

A note of certain commodities which ROSE ALDUS did distribute the 10 March before us whose names are under-written: To her cousin ESTHER HAWES of Sutton one ewe and 10s. and a coffer. To ROBERT BRIKWELL his daughter one sheep and 20s. To ROBERT BRIKWELL 20s. being in the hands of WILLIAM FOXE, and all her other things to pay for keeping her in her sickness and to bring her body decently to the ground. Witnesses: RICHARD HOWSEN, ROBERT FERMAN, JOHN ARCHER. Pr. at Wickham 23 Sept. 1630. Admon. to ROBERT BRIGHTWELL.

W. THOMASIN ANTLEBY of Kelsale, widow (N). (90)
6 September 1629

About two days before her death she gave all that she had to her daughter THOMASIN "who hath wrought and taken paynes with me for it". Witnesses: The wife of EDWARD CAPP, the wife of[missing] MUSKET and the Widow PEACHE. Pr. at Yoxford 15 Sept. 1629. Admon. to THOMASIN, daughter of deceased.

W(R) LAURENCE NEWSONN (X) of Stradbroke, yeoman. (91)
25 January 1629/30

Sick. My debts FRANCES my wife should pay out of my movables and the remainder take for her use for the term of her life, and after her decease to be equally divided among my children. My lands I give to my wife until my son WILLIAM shall come to 24 years, to bring up my children, giving unto my son WILLIAM in the meantime 40s. a year. To my son WILLIAM and his heirs all my houses and the 2 pightles next the way, the home close, the middle close, the new laid close, the grove and the close next the new laid close -- to enter at age 24, paying unto his mother £6 a year for life. To ALICE my daughter £20 at age 24; to ANN my daughter £20 at 24; to FRANCES my daughter £20 at 24; to ROBERT my son £30 at 22 -- all which sums my son WILLIAM shall pay, and in default my son LAURENCE shall take the lands and pay the legacies, provided that if any of the four children, ALICE ANN, FRANCES and ROBERT, shall die before the ages specified, not having issue, their portion shall be equally divided among the other three. To LAURENCE my son and his heirs Wood Close, the long meadow abutting upon lands of THOMAS CARVER to the east, and one pightle abutting upon the king's highway to the west and the land of GILES BORRETT towards the south; paying to his mother £4 per year for life, and to ALICE my daughter £10 at age 26, and to ANN my daughter £10 at 24, and to ROBERT my son £15 at 22 -- all which sums my son LAURENCE shall pay, and if he or his exors. shall refuse, then my son ROBERT shall take the land and pay them, provided that if any of the said ALICE ANN FRANCES or ROBERT shall die before the ages specified, not having issue, their portion shall be shared among the other three. I make my wife sole exrx. Witnesses: JOHN HERING, HENRY BULLEN, WILLIAM

HERING (X), WILLIAM THROWER. Pr. at Yoxford 17 March 1629.

R(W) ANTHONY PAYNE of Kirton, husbandman. (92)
5 February 1629/30

Sick. To be buried in Kirton churchyard. To ANN my wife all the estate she brought me at marriage; and if she be with child I will bequeath it half the residue of my estate, and my son ANTHONY the other half, to be equally divided within 6 months of my decease. If ANN be not with child, she and her children (if she wish) shall continue with my son ANTHONY and take her diet with him till Lady Day or Michaelmas next at her choice. To said ANN £5 within one year; and whereas I sold a cow of hers, I give her instead one black three-yearling bullock, to be had immediately. To ANTHONY my son the bed and bedstead that I lie on with all that belongs to it; and all movables in that little chamber except one box and one coffer of my said wife. My linen is to be divided so that my wife takes what was hers and ANTHONY takes what was mine. My son ANTHONY to be sole exor. Witnesses: ALLEN CONE and THOMAS WOODWARD. Pr. 27 Feb. 1629/30.

W(R) ALICE SHIPMAN (X) of Sizewell, widow. (93)
11 January 1629/30

Sick. To FRANCIS SHIPMAN my son and his heirs all my houses and lands in Sizewell and Leiston. To WILLIAM SHIPMAN my son £10 to be paid by FRANCIS within one year. To BRIDGET WELLES my daughter 40s. a year to be paid by FRANCIS, during her life, at the two feasts of Michaelmas and Lady Day 20s. at every feast. To my grandchildren ALICE CORDWALL and ISABEL CORDWALL, BRIDGET CORDWALL, ELIZABETH CORDWALL, and WILLIAM MILLS £4 apiece to be paid by FRANCIS my son within 2 years and then put out by FRANCIS SHIPMAN my son to the best profit, to be received at their several ages of 21. The rest I give to FRANCIS my son, paying all charges and bringing my body to the ground, and I nominate him sole exor. Witnesses: RICHARD SPALDING, JOHN FISKE (X). Pr. at Yoxford 25 Feb. 1629/30.

R(W) MARY SHELDRAKE of Nacton (N). [no date] (94)

About one month before her death, by her will, gave the parishioners of Nacton, in respect that they should relieve her during her life, all her goods for the use of the poor of the parish. Witnesses: THOMAS KINGSTIE and ROBERT BAKER. Admon. to WILLIAM BOWLES and EDWARD CAPPS, Overseers of the Poor of the parish of Nacton. 27 Feb. 1629/30.

R(W) ROBERT SHERINGTON of Westleton (N). (95)
January 1629/30

To ROBERT SHERINGTON his son £60, parcel of a sum of money due to him from JOHN HADNAN of Westleton, payable within 3 months of the death of JOAN SHERINGTON his mother, by indenture. All the rest he gave to MARY his wife towards payment of debts and funeral expenses. Witnesses: FRANCIS SEAMAN and SUSAN DODD the maid-servant of the said FRANCIS. Pr. at Yoxford 25 Feb. 1629/30. Admon. to relict.

R(W) ROBERT WINCKE senior of Bungay, linen weaver. (96)
20 June 1628

Weak of body by constitution of nature. As to my messuages tenements houses and buildings in Bungay, and all my transitory goods, I give to ROBERT WINCKE my son and his heirs and assigns my hall house with all the rooms therein, and part of the shop in the yard to the same hall belonging, as the same are now in occupation of said ROBERT WINCKE in Bungay, on condition that they shall pay to THOMAS WYNCKE my son or his assigns, from out my said house and part of my shop, every year during his life 40s., by 10s. every quarter, beginning within a quarter of a year of my decease, and in case of default THOMAS may enter the premises and take the profits until he shall have been fully paid. To said THOMAS WINCKE I give my fire house and chamber over the same wherein he now dwelleth, to hold for life; and after his decease I give the same to ROBERT WINCKE my son for ever. To MARY my now wife and her assigns, for her life, my house wherein LAURENCE CLEMENCE, glover, now dwelleth in Bungay, on condition that neither she nor her assigns make any claim of jointure or dower in any of my messuages lands or tenements in Bungay or trouble my aforesaid children for any such; and if she should do so she shall be void of all such demise of my house as in my will I have given. After my wife's decease I give my said house to said ROBERT my son for ever. To said ROBERT I give one obligation wherein EDWARD AGGES standeth bound for payment of £13 14s.; and my mortar of bell metal the pestle to it and the stock it standeth in, together with my great frame table standing in my hall house, my bench there also standing, my great chest standing in the hall chamber, and my great brass pot which was mine own before I was married to my said wife. To my son THOMAS my loom now standing in the said shop. To my son ROBERT all my bedding and bedstead now standing in the hall chamber. The residue of all my household stuff implements and utensils I give to MARY my wife. I ordain said ROBERT WINCKE sole exor. Witnesses: JOHN HOULDER, HENRY CUNNINGHAM, and me THOMAS FRANKLYN the writer. Pr. at Beccles 30 Jan. 1629/30.

R(W) ROBERT WRETTS of Saxtead, cordwainer. 16 May 1627 (97)

I give all my tenement wherein I dwell, with an orchard adjoining, which I bought of ROGER HOWELL and MARGARET his wife, as it is now enclosed, containing 1/2 rood more or less with appurtenances situate in Saxtead, after the decease of my wife, to ANDREW WRETTS my son and his heirs for ever. The said MARGARET shall have the use and occupation of all my goods and household stuff during her life, and after her death all my household stuff shall remain to FRANCIS WRETTS my son and MARGERY WRETTS my daughter, to be equally divided. I make ANDREW WRETTS my son sole exor. Witnesses: GEORGE RUSSELL, JOAN RUSSELL, and THOMAS RUSSELL. Pr. at Wickham 18 March 1629/30.

R(W) GEORGE YOUNGES of Rushmere, singleman. (98)
14 January 1629/30

Sick. To the poor of Rushmere 10s. to be distributed at my burial at the discretion of the churchwardens. To MARY the now wife of EDMUND COOPER, my aunt, 2 sheep after they have been clipped. To JOHN CROSSE of Rushmere my new suit of apparel. To my uncle JOHN COOKE of Rushmere my other apparel. To WILLIAM JOHNSON of Rushmere 2 grey mares and 1 colt and 6 coombs of oats which now lieth at my grandmother's in the hall chamber, and 8 bushels of brank which lieth at the house of EDMUND COOPER aforesaid. To said WILLIAM JOHNSON my hay and tares lying in the barn, and 3 acres of rye now in the ground, on condition that he give to JOAN YOUNGES and DOROTHY YOUNGES my sisters 20s. at age 21. Whereas THOMAS DAMARON of Rushmere the elder oweth me 37s., I will that WILLIAM JOHNSON shall receive it and pay it to JOAN YOUNGS and DOROTHY YOUNGS abovesaid at age 21, divided part and part alike. To WILLIAM JOHNSON abovesaid my harness harrows ploughs with all things belonging thereunto. Whereas THOMAS MINTER of Wethersfield owe me 8s. for rent, I give it to WILLIAM JOHNSON. Whereas I have a field called Shrip Close lying in Rushmere of the Widow DANES and ROBERT COOKE, and the rent is paid unto them till Michaelmas next, I will that WILLIAM JOHNSON shall enjoy the same till Michaelmas next. Whereas I hire of GEORGE COOKE of Rushmere 2 closes called Judasses lying in Rushmere I will that WILLIAM JOHNSON shall enjoy the same until Michaelmas next, paying the rent of £3 -- 30s. at Lady Day and 30s. at Michaelmas. Whereas I hire of ROBERT FULLER of Playford part of the warren in Playford I will that WILLIAM JOHNSON shall enjoy the same till Michaelmas next, paying the rent of 50s. -- 25s. at Lady Day and 25s. at Michaelmas. I give WILLIAM JOHNSON 1 1/2 bushels of barley which lieth at the house of EDMUND COOPER. Whereas I have 3 score sheep I will that WILLIAM JOHNSON shall sell them at Michaelmas next and the money that shall arise he shall pay to DOROTHY and JOAN YOUNGS my sisters when they come to the age of 21, part and part alike; and if either die before 21 the older liver shall enjoy all the portions before bequeathed. WILLIAM JOHNSON shall be at the charge of my burial, and my sole exor. Witnesses: THOMAS RUNTUR (X), WILLIAM PRESTON, GEORGE YOUNGES (X). Pr. at Ipswich 27 Feb. 1629/30.

R(W) GEORGE DOWE of Brandeston, yeoman. (99)
23 December 1629/30

In reasonable health. To be buried in Brandeston churchyard. To GEORGE DOWE my eldest son my houses lands tenements and hereditaments free and copy, with appurtenances, in Brandeston and Kettleburgh or elsewhere in Suffolk, upon payment of such debts and legacies hereafter set down, viz: I give to EDEN DOWE my eldest daughter £40, £20 within one year and the other £20 within 2 years; to ELIZABETH DOWE my daughter £40, £20 within 3 years and other £20 within 4 years, and 10s. a year till she shall receive the first payment of her portion aforesaid; to WILLIAM DOWE my son £40, £20 within 5 years and other £20 within 6 years, and 20s. a year till he shall receive the first payment of his portion; to THOMAS DOWE my youngest son 4 score pounds, £20 within 7 years and so forth every year till £80 be paid. And my said son GEORGE shall provide said son THOMAS with sufficient meat drink apparel lodging and washing with convenient schooling and all other things necessary during his childhood, that is until he reach 16 years, and thereafter, instead of the allowance of meat apparel etc., GEORGE shall pay THOMAS 40s. per annum until he shall receive the first payment of his portion of £80 -- all which payments to be paid at the now mansion house of the said GEORGE DOWE in Brandeston. If any son or daughter die before they have their legacy then that portion shall first be paid to their issue, if any, equally divided, or otherwise to the rest of the legatees equally divided. Legatees to have power to distrain upon GEORGE in case of default. To my daughter EDEN the great chest in the loue [low?] chamber which was given her by my daughter BRIDGET deceased, another chest standing in the same chamber and my great brass kettle, one of my feather-beds in the parlour chamber, which she shall choose, together with the bed-stead bolster blankets and all other things to the same bed belonging (the coverlet only excepted), the cupboard standing in the hall, and she shall enjoy her heifer and calf; but if my son GEORGE will pay her 20s. he is to have the calf. To my daughter ELIZABETH the white coffer in the parlour chamber and one flock bed and bedstead with all the furniture belonging, standing in the hall chamber. To WILLIAM my son one little flock bed and a trundle bed with the furniture belonging in the hall chamber together with the long cupboard and little square table given him by his sister BRIDGET deceased. To my son THOMAS one bedstead standing in the parlour and the feather-bed thereupon according as his sister BRIDGET deceased did give unto him and all furniture to the same bed and bedstead belonging; the table as it stands in the parlour; and one mare colt. Whereas I have a bearing cloth kerchief and furniture of all sorts of child-bed and christening linen, my will is that all my said children shall have title and interest therein to be used at such times as any of them shall have need and use for that purpose of child-bearing or christening, to be in the meantime in the custody of my son GEORGE. And if he shall deny any his brothers and sisters the use thereof he shall lose his interest use and possession thereof, that possession then to be with EDENY my daughter. All the rest of my goods and chattels I give to GEORGE DOWE my son whom I make sole exor. I desire my friend Mr ANTHONY STARLING of Brandeston to be my supervisor of my will, to be aiding my exor. in the preformance thereof and the rest of my children that all of them may have their portions with quiet and according to brotherly love; and for his pains therein my son GEORGE shall give him 20s. And if I happen to die between Michaelmas and May Day then my children shall remain in my house and have meat drink and lodging till May Day next following; and if I die between May Day and Michaelmas they shall so remain and have meat drink and lodging for 6 weeks after my decease, and then depart, unless they shall otherwise agree. If my son GEORGE do give any money binding forth my son WILLIAM an apprentice, then that same money shall be abated to GEORGE out of the first payment of the portion to be paid to WILLIAM, provided that such bonding forth and money given shall be first with the consent of my supervisor. If any controversy shall arise amongst my children about any bequest it shall be decided by my supervisor. Witnesses: FRANCIS KENT, THOMAS WADE, ANTHONY GODBOULD. Pr. at Wickham 18 March 1629/30.

R(W) WILLIAM GLOVER of Campsea Ash. 23 October 1628 (100)

To ELIZABETH GLOVER my wife, for life, in recompense as well for her jointure of £50 per annum, before marriage agreed upon and accordingly performed, as in lieu of any dower she may demand in or out of any my manors lands tenements or hereditaments, all my manor of Ashmore Hall with appurtenances in Suffolk, and all my messuages lands tenements meadows pastures feedings ways commons and hereditaments lying between the king's highway leading from Hacheston to Rendlesham on the east, and the lands of JOHN BRAME in part and the lands of JOHN BULL in part on the west, and between the lands of JOHN GRENE in part and lands of JOHN BULL in part and the old river in part on the south, and the way called Fullstaie Way on the north, with appurtenances, in Ash aforesaid and Hacheston, 2 pieces of land, parcel of the demesne of this manor, lying in Church Close, only excepted. Also to said wife an annuity of £10 yearly for life issuing out of my messuage called the Dairy House, being in the site of the manor of Bawdsey Butley alias Glovers in Bawdsey, Suffolk, and all my marsh called the Isle of Oxney, and my rectory and parsonage of Bawdsey with all the tithes glebe lands profits and commodities belonging, with the appurtenances, in Bawdsey, and paid at the two usual feasts viz. the Annunciation of the Blessed Virgin Mary and St. Michael, by equal portions, payment to begin at whichever of the said feasts shall first happen after my decease, with power of distraint. To said wife 1 bedstead 1 feather-bed whereon she usually lieth with bolster coverlet blankets and other furniture belonging, 1 livery bedstead 1 feather-bed bolster coverlet and blankets meet for her maid, 4 pairs of sheets 1 pair pillow-biers 2 square board cloths 1 dozen napkins 2 towels 1 chest meet to lay her linen in 1 chair 2 stools 1 little table 1 washing basin half a dozen pewter and 1 silver spoon provided that if said ELIZABETH my wife or any person for her and by her consent shall hereafter by any means get any jointure or dower out of any of my manor lands etc., other than by this will given, then the gift of this manor of Ashmoore Hall the messuages lands etc. and the said annuity and every gift in this my will given to said wife to cease and be void; and then I will that the rents and profits of said manor and lands and the said annuity shall be during her life equally divided between such persons as shall sustain any loss in or out of the said lands to him or them assured or hereby devised. I give, after decease of said ELIZABETH my wife, all that other my aforesaid messuages lands and tenements meadows pastures feedings fishing commons and hereditaments in Ash and Hacheston, to my said wife devised for life, to WILLIAM GLOVER my son for life, and after his decease to WILLIAM GLOVER my grandchild, son of said son WILLIAM, and to his heirs male of his body lawfully begotten, and for want of such issue male unto the 2nd 3rd and 4th son of the said WILLIAM successively by seniority, if he happen to have any 2nd 3rd or 4th son, and to the heirs male of their bodies lawfully begotten, failing them I bequeath said manor and premises to my son THOMAS GLOVER and his heirs male for ever. And whereas by my indenture tripartite dated 15th April 1619 between me WILLIAM GLOVER of the first part and said WILLIAM GLOVER my son and ANN his wife of the second part and SAMUEL BLENNERHASSET, THOMAS CORNEWALLYS, both deceased, and THOMAS WARD esq. and THOMAS SHAWE deceased of the third part, I have conveyed and estated to stand seised of and in my capital messuage wherein I now dwell and of and in divers other messuages lands etc. in the said indenture expressed, to the use of myself for life without impeachment of waste, and after my decease to the use of my said son WILLIAM for the term of his life and after his decease to the use of the first begotten son of said WILLIAM and to the heirs male of such son lawfully to be begotten, with divers sundry other remainders over as by the said indentures more fully appeareth, I hereby ratify and approve said indentures and devise the said capital messuage and all other the lands and tenements therein contained and mentioned to be conveyed and assured unto my said son WILLIAM for the term of his life and to such other persons as therein mentioned and to such uses and estates as by the same indenture are expressed, desiring notwithstanding that my son WILLIAM and such other persons as shall by virtue of said conveyance or otherwise be interested in my said capital messuage quietly to permit my said wife to have during her life those rooms which be in the pile of my capital messuage next the garden where she now lodgeth, with liberty of ingress and egress for her and her assigns. Also I desire that my said son WILLIAM and his heirs or assigns shall deliver to my wife sufficient fire-bote for her fuel to be spent there during her life and continuance there. To my friend Mr HUMFRY RANT esq. my son-in-law THOMAS DENNEY and ROBERT LONDON, towards payment of my debts and performance of this will, all my manor of Frostenden and all my lands and tenements rents services meadows pastures feedings commons waste and other privileges and hereditaments with their appurtenances in Frostenden, Covehithe alias Northales, Uggeshall, Stoven, Wangford, Southwold, Brampton, Beccles and other towns adjoining in Suffolk, and all my advowson of the church of Frostenden, to hold for four years after my decease, the rents and profits thereof arising for the first two years to be employed towards the payment of my debts and legacies, and the rents and profits for the other two years to be employed for raising and payment of these several sums following viz: to ANN GLOVER eldest daughter of my son WILLIAM 200 marks; to my said grandchild WILLIAM GLOVER £100; and the residue of the said issues with reasonable deduction of all such costs as paid HUMFRY RANT, THOMAS DENNEY and ROBERT LONDON shall sustain touching the same, to be paid to my exors., all which payments to be made within 3 months after the end of said four years. And the said HUMFRY RANT, THOMAS DENNEY and ROBERT LONDON or their exors. or assigns shall yearly during the said term of 4 years, out of the issues of said manor lands and premises, pay my said grandchild WILLIAM GLOVER £20 towards his maintenance and education, which yearly sum of £20 I will my cousin ANN WARD, in respect of her love and entire affection to my grandchild shall have the disposing for the first year. And from immediately after the end of the said term of 4 years I devise the said manor of Frostenden lands tenements and other premises aforesaid unto my said grandchild WILLIAM GLOVER and to the heirs male of his body lawfully begotten, and for want of such issue to the 2nd 3rd and 4th son of my said son WILLIAM GLOVER and to the heirs male of their bodies lawfully begotten successively as they shall be of age and seniority. And, for default of such issue, unto my said son WILLIAM GLOVER for life, and after his decease to my son THOMAS GLOVER and his heirs male for ever. My cousin ANN WARDE shall have the use of all the rooms in the little new brick building at the south-west corner of my garden in Frostenden and her dwelling there with liberty of ingress egress and regress at all times, and sufficient fire-bote for her expenses there so long as she keep herself sole, any gift of the said manor and other premises to the contrary in any wise notwithstanding. I give my said son WILLIAM GLOVER and the heirs male of his body lawfully begotten all my manor called the Dairy House, being the site of the manor of Bawdsey Butley alias Glovers with appurtenances in Bawdsey; and also my manor and signory of Bawdsey Butley alias Glovers with appurtenances, and all my moiety of the fishing, wreck of sea, groundage and other realties and privileges of said manor; and also my marsh called Oxney Marsh or the isle of Oxney; also my rectory and parsonage of Bawdsey with all the tithes glebe lands profits and commodities belonging with appurtenances in Bawdsey, and for default of such issue male of my said son WILLIAM I give the said manor marsh tithes and premises last-mentioned to my said son THOMAS GLOVER and his heirs male for ever. I give to my said son WILLIAM GLOVER and my grandchild WILLIAM his son and to their heirs male for ever those my messuages lands tenements meadows marshes pastures feedings and hereditaments with appurtenances in Alderton and Bawdsey now in occupation of ROBERT CHANDLER or his assigns, not formerly conveyed and assured to my son HENRY GLOVER. I give said son THOMAS £40 per annum for life, to be issuing out of my messuage called Dairy House and my march called Oxney marsh or the isle of Oxney and all my rectory and parsonage of Bawdsey and all the tithes glebe lands and other profits and commodities belonging with appurtenances in Bawdsey, at the 2 usual feasts viz: St. Michael the Archangel and the Annunciation of the Blessed Virgin Mary by equal portions, the first payment to begin at which of the feasts shall first happen after my decease, with power of distraint. I give to ANN GLOVER, daughter of my son JOHN GLOVER deceased 100 marks at her age of 21 if then living, provided that if said ANN or any person for her make any claim to any my manor lands tenements or hereditaments then the legacy shall be void. I give more to my cousin ANN WARD £30 to be paid within 6 months, and 1 feather-bed bolster pillows blankets white rug with the curtains and vallance and other furniture belonging which she useth to lie upon at Frostenden, and 2 pair sheets 1 pair pillow-biers 1 chair 2 stools a livery cupboard and 2 best milch cows. To my daughter ELIZABETH MORSE 100 marks to be paid into the hands of my friends WILLIAM GOODWYN and ROBERT LONDON within 1 year, to be employed towards the maintenance of my said daughter during the life of her husband THOMAS MORSE; and if my said daughter happen to survive her said husband, then it is to be paid to her within 3 months after his death. And if my said daughter die without issue of her body living then I will that WILLIAM GOODWYN and ROBERT LONDON shall repay the said 100 marks to ANN GLOVER, daughter of my son WILLIAM GLOVER if she be living, and if she be dead then to be paid to my exors. within 6 months after the death of said ELIZABETH MORSE without issue. To my said son WILLIAM GLOVER my silver salt, 6 of my best feather-beds with their furnitures, all my tables stools forms and chairs livery cupboards, my coppers brewing and dairy vessels which shall be at the time of my death at my house in Ash, not formerly given to any other person. And if said WILLIAM shall not suffer the tenants and farmers to hold and enjoy after my decease all such lands and tenements as is formerly conveyed unto him during such term and under such yearly rent as I have or shall devise the same for, then my devise of my said goods and chattels shall be void. To my said grandchild WILLIAM GLOVER 1 silver-gilt bowl 2 lesser beer bowls 6 silver spoons 1 silver salt 2 of my best bedsteads 2 feather-beds and all other their furniture 2 other bedsteads 2 feather-beds with their furniture 1 down bed and furniture, my coppers and all my brewing and dairy vessels, my long table in the hall with all other my tables forms stools livery cupboards and chairs, all which plate and goods are now standing in my house in Frostenden. To the poor of Frostenden 40s., the poor of Alderton 10s., and of Bawdsey 10s. To my nephew HUMPFRY RANT, my daughter ELIZABETH MORSE, my son-in-law THOMAS DENNEY, my daughter ANN his wife, my daughter-in-law ANN GLOVER the wife of my son WILLIAM, my son HENRY GLOVER, the said WILLIAM GOODWYN, my said cousin ANN WARD and ROBERT LONDON, to every of them 20s. apiece to buy them rings to wear in remembrance of me; or otherwise I will that my exor. do buy them rings of that value and give every of them one ring. To every of the children of my daughter ANN DENNEY at their several ages of 18 £3 6s. 8d. to buy a piece of plate to keep in remembrance of me. To my cousin JOHN HALL and to WILLIAM MANSHIPP 20s. apiece. To every of my servants dwelling with me at the time of my decease 10s. And whereas TOBIAS DOWNING late took to him and his heirs, of the surrender of CHRISTOPHER CHILDRONS, one parcel of marsh or fen ground with the gardens 9alled Southdoles containing by estimation 12 acres, holden by copy of court roll of the manor of Frostenden, which said premises the said TOBIAS had only in trust for the use of me and my heirs and assigns, now I hereby limit and appoint that the said marsh should be sold by my exor. within one year towards the payment of debts and legacies, and I appoint said TOBY DOWNING that he do upon request surrender said premises with the appurtenances according to the custom of the said manor of Frostenden to the use of such person as my said exor. shall name. The residue of my goods household stuff debts chattels and ready money and plate not formerly bequeathed I give to my exor. towards payment of debts and legacies and performance of this will and I make my son WILLIAM GLOVER and my grandchild WILLIAM GLOVER exors., and I make my said nephew HUMPFRY RANT and ROBERT LONDON supervisors of the same and I give either of them for their pains 40s. apiece. Witnesses: ROBERT LONDON, THOMAS PEARSE (X), WILLIAM FARRER, WILLIAM BLOMFEILD, WILLIAM MANCHIPP (X), EDWARD MANTHORPE. Pr. at Beccles 13 March 1629/30. Admon. to WILLIAM GLOVER, son of deceased, with power reserved for WILLIAM GLOVER, another exor.

R(W) JOHN CAROTHERS (X) of Culpho. 17 May 1629 (101)

Sick. To be buried in Culpho churchyard. To JOHN CAROTHERS my son £4, to WILLIAM CAROTHERS my son £4; to THOMAS CAROTHERS my son £4 when he is 24 and in the meantime my exors. shall put the £4 in some sufficient man's hand and take bond of him to pay said THOMAS or his assigns 5s. yearly for the use of it till he accomplish 24 years, and if he depart his life before he receive the said portion, the same shall be equally divided among the rest of my children then living. To my sons JOHN CAROTHERS and WILLIAM CAROTHERS all my bonds and bills and money owing me. To ELIZABETH CAROTHERS my daughter £3 within one half year after my decease. To ANN CAROTHERS my daughter £3 within 1/2 year. To MARGARET CAROTHERS my daughter £3 within 1/2 year. I nominate my two sons JOHN and WILLIAM CAROTHERS my exors. to take money due to me, they to pay themselves the legacies I have given them and all other legacies. The rest of my goods and household stuff to be sold, and the money arising I will to pay my debts and bear my funeral charges, and the overplus to be divided equally among my two daughters ANN and MARGARET CAROTHERS, provided my will is to except out of the said household stuff my brass pot, which I give to JOHN my son, to be delivered immediately after my decease. Witnesses: PHILIP REYNOLDS (X) and EDWARD LEACHE. Pr. at Ipswich 6 Aug. 1629.

R(W) THOMAS YOUNGE of Orford, sailor (N). [no date] (102)

A day or two before his death did bequeath all his goods and chattels and debts and all that he had to JOSINE his wife, THOMAS YOUNGES and JOHN YOUNGES his sons, to be equally divided, there being then and there present ELIZABETH SPOONER wid., JOHN HATCH and GEORGE MAYES. Admon. to JOSINE, relict of deceased, 27 Feb. 1629/30.

R(W) THOMAS BRADSHAWE of Framsden, yeoman. 4 July 1624 (103)

Sick. To MARGARET my wife all my movable goods and chattels, my living cattle only excepted, immediately after my decease, for ever. And to the said MARGARET my freehold lands in Framsden, Pettaugh and Winston, together with one piece of copyhold land containing 1 acre 1 rood, holden of the manor of Abbots Hall in Pettaugh which I lately purchased of JOHN BRADSHAW my brother, all which my said wife shall have and hold immediately after my decease, during her life. To WILLIAM BRADSHAWE of Norwich my nephew all my said freehold and the piece of copyhold, to have immediately after the decease of said MARGARET my wife, to hold to him and his heirs for ever on condition that he pay within one year after the decease of said MARGARET to every one of the children of said MARGARET which she had by WILLIAM HANWORTH her former husband, my late predecessor, which shall then be living £5 apiece, paid in the church porch of Framsden. To JOHN BRADSHAWE of London, my nephew, my tenement in Pulham St. Mary Magdalen in Norfolk, together with all houses and edifices to the same belonging; and also my lands both free and copy belonging to the said tenement lying in Pulham, he to have and hold the same immediately after the decease of said MARGARET, for life, and after the decease of him I give the said tenement and lands with their appurtenances to JOHN BRADSHAWE the younger, my godson, the eldest son of said JOHN BRADSHAWE my nephew, he the said JOHN BRADSHAWE the younger to hold the last described premises to him and his heirs for ever. In case my copyhold tenement in Framsden wherein I now dwell and the copyhold lands thereunto belonging do hereafter either by law or custom of the manor of Framsden (whereof they are holden) descend and come to JOHN BRADSHAWE my nephew, and not unto GEOFFREY BRADSHAWE my nephew, youngest brother of said JOHN, then I will that said GEOFFREY shall have my said tenement and lands in Pulham aforesaid, in such manner as they were before devised to JOHN BRADSHAWE my nephew, he the said GEOFFREY to have and hold said tenement and lands on condition that he shall pay to my said godson, JOHN BRADSHAWE the younger £100, to be paid by £10 yearly, the first payment to be made within one year after the said GEOFFREY shall enter the tenement and lands at Pulham, and the payments shall be tendered in the porch of the church of Pulham St. Mary Magdalen. To MARGARET my wife, who I ordain exrx., all my living cattle (before excepted) towards the payment of my debts and funeral charges. Witnesses: PETER BLOMEFEILD and BARNABY GREENE. Pr. at Ipswich 3 April 1630.

R(W) STEPHEN GARDNER of Southwold, mariner. (104)
2 December 1629

Sick and weak. To MARY my wife during her life all my messuages houses lands and tenements, and after her death to MARY GARDNER my daughter if she be living at the time of the death of my said wife; but if she die before said wife then I give them all to my wife her heirs and assigns for ever. To said MARY my wife all my household stuff and implements of household and shipping goods and chattels, after my debts paid and funeral charges disbursed, and I do make her my sole exrx. Witnesses: THOMAS WAREN jnr. and AUGUSTINE WARD and ISAAC DAMERELL. Pr. at Beccles 3 April 1630.

R(W) MARY MUNSON of Worlingworth, widow. 8 December 1617 (105)

To my brother-in-law RICHARD ALDIS and ROBERT his son all my lands holden by lease and houses lying in Bedfield, on condition that they pay all legacies hereafter appointed. To ROBERT MAYHEW my sister's son £100 within 2 years. To MARGARET MAYHEW, MARGERY MAYHEW and ANN MAYHEW, sisters of said ROBERT, unto either of them £5 to be paid within one year after my decease. To MARY ALDIS daughter of my sister MARGARET £20 at 21 years. To JOHN GLOVER and to his sister, children of my sister BRIDGET, to either of them £5 to be paid within 3 years. To JOHN PAGE the elder of Worlingworth and to his wife in regard of their pains and their children's taken about me in my sickness and other kindnesses that I have found at their hands £100 to be paid within 1 year. If RICHARD ALDIS and ROBERT his son shall be sued or molested in regard to the tenure title and occupation of my lands formerly recited, then they to whom I have given my legacies shall bear some part of the charge according to their proportion. To the poor of Bedfield 20s., to the poor of Worlingworth 20s. The rest of my movable goods I give to my exors. to see my body buried. To JOHN EDWARDS my godson 10s. I appoint JOHN PAGE the elder and RICHARD ALDIS my brother-in-law to be my exors. Witnesses: JOHN PAGE jnr., HENRY PAGE, BENJAMIN PAGE 4 June 1624. Memorandum the day and year above-said the said MARY MUNSON did confirm this to be her last will in the presence of us HENRY PAGE, BENJAMIN PAGE. Pr. at Stradbroke 5 April 1630.

R(W) RICHARD BROWNE of Bungay, labourer. (106)
13 February 1629/30

To DOROTHY BROWNE my wife all my goods bonds bills money chattels implements and household stuff, on condition that she or her exors. shall pay all gifts and legacies which I shall hereafter demise. To DOROTHY BROWNE my daughter £10 to be paid at the day of the death or the day of the marriage of said DOROTHEY BROWNE my wife, whichever shall first happen; to ELIZABETH BROWNE my daughter £10 to be paid in like manner; to MARGARET BROWNE my daughter £10 to be paid in like manner; in case any of them die without lawful issue before she shall have received her legacy it shall remain to the survivors to be equally divided. I nominate DOROTHY BROWNE my wife sole exrx. Witnesses: RICHARD NUN, WILLIAM TANNER (X). Pr. at Beccles 5 April 1630.

R(W) GEORGE SAYER of Mettingham, yeoman. 24 February * (107)

Sick. To be buried at the parish of St. Johns. To kinswoman KATHERINE GOOCH of St. Margarets and to MARY GOOCH her daughter to either of them 1 pair sheets of the best sort and a piece of gold of 22s. To GEORGE BURTON of Norwich, my son, 1 little feather-bed and bolster and a pair of blankets a pair of sheets and a coverlet, 1 brazen posnet, a press a chest and a piece of gold of 22s. To THOMAS BURTON my son-in-law 1 pair sheets. To the Widow BURTON my daughter-in-law a pair sheets. To my nephew MICHAEL SAYER 1 feather-bed 2 bolsters 1 pair blankets a coverlet and bedstead and 2 pair sheets. To my brother JOHN SAYER 1 piece of gold of 22s. The rest of my goods chattels implements of household and ready money and debts I give to TIMOTHY SAYER and NICHOLAS SAYER whom I make exors. Witnesses: ROBERT GARNER (X). Pr. at Bungay 6 April 1630. [* No year is given in the register copy, and the head of the original will is defective.]

R(W) RICHARD SILOME of Northales alias Covehithe, mariner. 1 May 1629 (108)

My house I give to him to whom by rights it shall descend after my decease. To PRISCILLA my wife all my movable goods and chattels towards payments of my debts and funeral charges, and I ordain her exrx. Witnesses: JOHN GOODWYN and JAMES CUNNINGHAM, the writer. Pr. at Beccles 10 April 1630.

R(W) WILLIAM ELLIS of Stratford, yeoman. 6 November 1628 (109)

To the poor of the parish where I now dwell 20s. to be distributed at the discretion of my exor. within 3 months. To WILLIAM ELLIS my eldest son and his heirs my parcel of land called Churchfield in East Bergholt on condition that they pay to my daughters MARY ELLIS and MARTHA ELLIS or their assigns £10 apiece within 2 years of the decease of my wife MARY ELLIS, at the mansion house where I now dwell in Stratford, with power of distraint. To MARY my wife her heirs and assigns my parcels of land or pasture called Fishers in the parishes of Stratford and Holton, on condition that they shall dispose of the same towards paying my debts and legacies, and the remainder thereof shall be equally divided among my children. To WILLIAM my son and his heirs and assigns my parcel of land called Long Davies in Stratford and Holton containing 8 acres more or less, lying between the highway leading from Holton to East Bergholt to the east and Gravel Pit field in part and Johnswent field in part to the west, and one head abutteth upon a way tending towards Syrells Hall towards the north on condition that they shall pay unto REBECCA ELLIS my daughter £30 within 1 year after decease of MARY my wife, at the house where I now dwell, with power of distraint. To JOHN ELLIS my youngest son and his heirs the parcel of ground called Crossfield upon which the tenement or dwelling-house wherein JOHN PASKALL now dwelleth hath been of late builded, in Stratford, one head thereof abutting on the king's highway which leadeth from Stratford church towards Ipswich to the north, even at the four way leete commonly called the Four Sisters; yet WILLIAM my son shall have the one half of the rent thereof after my son JOHN hath accomplished his age of 14 years until his full age of 21 years. To WILLIAM my son the joined bedstead in the parlour, the feather-bed and other furniture belonging, and the cupboard in the parlour, the little table, the long table in the hall, a joined form and 3 joined stools, 1 chest in which my writings lie, and my great brass pot. To MARY ELLIS my daughter the joined bedstead that standeth in the kitchen cellar and the feather-bed and other furniture to the same belonging, one chest -- the next in goodness, and 4 pieces of pewter. To MARTHA ELLIS my daughter a trundle bedstead with a bed and other furniture belonging, 4 pieces of pewter of the best and 1 trunk and 1 chest. But MARY ELLIS my wife shall have the use of all my household stuff during her life. The rest of my goods chattels and cattle I leave to my executrix towards the paying of my debts and legacies; any remainder after my debts paid, after the decease of my wife, shall be equally divided among my children. I appoint MARY my wife sole executrix, desiring that she will use her diligence and care therein and be very careful that there be no waste nor estripment made upon my lands. I appoint ALLEN HAM my brother-in-law to be my overseer and supervisor of this will. Witnesses: ROBERT CLOVER, HENRY LIBBIS (X), ALLIN HAM. Pr. at Ipswich 16 April 1630.

R(W) ELIZABETH BEDINGFIELD (X) of Earl Soham, widow. (110)
26 February 1629/30

To the poor of East Bergholt £20, of which £10 to be distributed within 1 month and the rest within half a year. To RICHARD WEBSTER and ROBERT GOBBET my servants £20 apiece within 1/2 year. To JOHN JONES and KATHERINE HARGRAVE my late servants £6 13s. 4d. apiece within 1 year. To WILLIAM SEAGAR and ANN SMITH my late servants £3 6s. 8d. within 1 year. To HENRY CHURCH and JOHN WOODS my servants £5 apiece within 1 year. To ROBERT DAVIE £5 within 1 year. To all my other servants and boys 40s. apiece within 1 year. To ELIZABETH SMITHE daughter of DANIEL SMITH of Cretingham £10 within 1/2 year. To ELIZABETH LACY daughter of WILLIAM LACY late of Earl Soham £5 within 1/2 year. To JOHN BETTS son of MICHAEL BETTS of Framsden £5 within 1/2 year. To SARAH ALDRICH my chamber-maid 40s. within 1/2 year. To REBECCA BARBER and ANN HAWKE my servants £5 apiece. To said REBECCA BARBER and ANN HAWKE 1 feather-bed apiece with all the furniture belonging as they now stand upon the chamber called the maids' chamber. To all my other maid-servants 40s. apiece within 1/2 year. To JOHN TWINLEY, JOHN BUTCHER, PHILIP BOONE and WILLIAM RUSSELL my late servants 40s. apiece within 1/2 year. To ELIZABETH BULLS, wid., my late servant £20, and to THOMAS BALLS her son 40s. within 1/2 year. To my worshipful good friend JOHN SCRIVENER and to loving cousin WILLIAM DADE esq. to either of them 1 gold ring. To Mrs WINGFIELD wife of HARBOTTELL WINGFIELD of Crowfield esq. my best gown together with the whole suit thereunto belonging. To

RICHARD CLARKE my physician 40s. To Mrs ELIZABETH BOWMAN 40s. To SARAH PARTICH 40s. The rest of my movable goods chattels cattles corn grain household stuff ready money plate jewels chains and other goods I give to GEORGE RUSSELL of Cretingham and DANIEL SMITH of the same, whom I make exors., they paying my debts and legacies and causing me to be decently buried and my funeral executed according to my calling. After the payment of my debts and legacies and funeral expenses the overplus shall be equally divided between said GEORGE RUSSELL and DANIEL SMITH. Witnesses: RICHARD GOLLIS, clerk, ROBERT GOBBET, RICHARD WEBSTER (X). On 20 April 1630. Admon. to JOHN SCRIVENER and WILLIAM DADE esqs. creditors, the executors having renounced duty through THOMAS FASTOLF, Notary Public, their Proctor. [A copy of the instrument by which the executors appointed THOMAS FASTOLFE, EDWARD TROTT and EDMUND MYLES, Notaries Public, to be their Proctors jointly and severally, dated 1 April 1630, is appended to the copy of the will in the register.]

R(W) JEREMY WILSON of Theberton. 23 October 1626 (111)

To HENRY WILSON and BENJAMIN WILSON my sons all my lands tenements and hereditaments, free and copy, in Theberton to hold to them and their heirs and assigns for ever, to be equally divided between them. To JOHN WILSON my son £10 to be paid at Michaelmas next after my decease; and 2 pewter dishes 1 pewter platter and 1 pair sheets. To THOMAS WILSON my son £26 13s. 4d. at his age of 24. To MARY my wife £27 10s. within 1 year, provided she shall on reasonable demand within 3 months of my decease release to said HENRY and BENJAMIN WILSON my sons all right of dower in every of said lands and tenements; otherwise the gift shall be void and I give the £27 10s. to said HENRY and BENJAMIN to be equally divided. The rest of my goods I give to HENRY and BENJAMIN towards payment of debts and legacies funeral expenses and probate, and any overplus I give to my exors. equally divided, and I nominate said HENRY and BENJAMIN exors. Witnesses: THOMAS LONDON and THOMAS EADE. Pr. at Yoxford 3 May 1630.

W(R) ROBERT SPACHIT (X) senior of Rumburgh, yeoman. (112)
17 April 1629

To be buried in Rumburgh churchyard. To MARGARET SPACHIT my wife 40s. yearly for life out of the tenement and lands I now occupy and dwell in, 20s. within half a year, and half a year after that another 20s., and so yearly during her life. To ELIZABETH SPACHIT my daughter £10, 50s. within 2 years and within 2 years after that other 50s., and so every 2 years 50s. till the £10 be fully paid. To MARY SPACHET my daughter £10, [50s.] within 3 years after my decease, and within 5 years after it other 50s., and so every 2 years till the £10 be fully paid. To ANN SPACHET my daughter £4 viz. within 9 years of my decease 10s. and so 10s. yearly till the £4 be paid, provided that if my daughter ANN shall challenge my promise of any debt due from me then the gift to be void and they [sic] to have no part thereof. To JOHN SPACHIT my son all my tenement and lands that I hold by copy of court roll of the manor of Wesell on condition that he perform this my will; and if he refuse then ELIZABETH and MARY my said 2 daughters shall have said tenement and lands, paying to JOHN my son £20 as he should have done to them. To JOHN SPACHET my son all my goods and chattels and household stuff on condition that he shall be at the charge of my funeral expenses and probate of this will. I make ELIZABETH SPACHIT and MARY SPACHIT my daughters exrxs., and for the help of them I intreat JOHN ELME and JOHN BALLS my supervisors. Witnesses: JOHN BALLS and THOMAS BALLS. Pr. at Beccles 6 May 1630. Admon. to JOHN SPACHET, son of deceased, ELIZABETH and MARY SPATCHETT having appeared in person and renounced executorship.

R(W) EDMUND LEAGUY of Wherstead, yeoman. (113)
11 December 1629

Sick. To my son EDMUND LEAGUY my messuage and tenement wherein I dwell in Wherstead and Freston, with all lands pastures feedings and hereditaments with appurtenances belonging, to hold when he attains the age of 21, and thenceforth to him and heirs of his body lawfully to be begotten; and for default of such issue I bequeath the premises aforesaid to STEPHEN LEAGUY my second son at 21 and to heirs of his body lawfully begotten if he should die before then; and for default of lawful issue of STEPHEN I bequeath the same premises to RICHARD my third son and the heirs of his body lawfully to be begotten, for ever. To my said son STEPHEN LEAGUY my messuage or tenement called Brownes in Wherstead with all the lands etc. belonging, to have at the age of 21; and if he die before 21 or without lawful issue I bequeath the same to EDMUND LEAGUY my son and the heirs of his body lawfully to be begotten, he to enter at such time as my son STEPHEN should have done if he had lived. To my son RICHARD LEAGUY 3 score pounds at age 20. To the child with which ANN my wife is now great withall 3 score pounds at age 20; andif it do not live to 20 years then I give that sum to RICHARD LEAGUY my son to be paid at such time as the child should have been 20. If said son RICHARD shall die before 20 without receipt of his legacy of 3 score pounds I bequeath that sum to the child with which my wife now is, to be paid at age 20. And if both RICHARD and the said child die before 20 then I bequeath the legacies made to them to my son STEPHEN. To my wife ANN LEAGUY, towards her own maintenance and the education and good bringing up of all my said children with meat drink and apparel, £30 yearly taken by my exors. out of the yearly profits rents and revenues of all my said messuages tenements etc. aforementioned, and paid quarterly until STEPHEN LEAGUY my son shall accomplish or should have accomplished full age of 21. Further to said ANN, after STEPHEN shall or should be 21, the thirds of all my lands herein mentioned, in the name of dower by law due and accustomed, for life. To said ANN one half of all my household stuff, viz. bedding brass pewter linen woolen and utensils now in my house (my plate only excepted) to be divided and delivered to her within 1 month. To my said wife 12 good and able cart loads of one-bind wood for firing, yearly till my son STEPHEN shall or should have accomplished his age of 21, or otherwise the sum of £4 16s. in lieu thereof, which of them my exors. shall see fit. And my wife shall have the use of the hall and parlour of the messuage wherein I dwell and of the 2 chambers over the same by the space of three months after my decease, and then to depart out of the same, leaving them to the use of my exors. to dispose at their will, provided that if at any time during the minority of any of my said children my wife shall refuse to maintain and educate all my children in decent manner and putting them to school then it shall be lawful for my exors. to withhold the said annuity of £30, allowing her only the thirds of my said lands for dower, and the bequest of the annuity and loads of wood or money in lieu to be frustrate. I appoint my friends and kinsmen RICHARD GOODING and JOHN GOODING of Wherstead, gent., exors., to whom I bequeath all the profits rents and revenues of all my messuages lands tenements and hereditaments, they not cutting or felling any timber thereupon but for the necessary use in and about my said houses during the minority of my children, together with all my other goods chattels household stuff plate corn cattle and whatsoever else not formerly bequeathed, towards the payment of debts and legacies and probate of my will and the bringing of my body to the ground and the performance of my will. Witnesses: EDMUND LEAGUY (X), DOROTHY WORLICH (X), EDMUND MYLES, Notary Public. Pr. at Ipswich 5 May 1630.

W(R) MARGARET WHIGHTHEAD of Lowestoft, widow. (114)
29 April 1630

Sick. All my copyhold houses and lands in the town of Lowestoft I bequeath to my son WILLIAM WHIGHTHEAD and his heirs on condition that he pay to my son ROBERT WHIGHTHEAD 20s. within 1 year and so every year succeeding 20s. until £10 shall be to him paid; and to my daughter RUTH £10 viz. £6 within one year and 20s. each succeeding year till £10 be paid. But if he fail in payment of the said sums given to ROBERT and RUTH then I give said houses and lands to my said daughter RUTH WHIGHTHEAD and her heirs on condition that she shall pay to my son ROBERT WHIGHTHEAD £10, viz. 20s. within 1 year after my decease and 20s. each succeeding year till the said £10 be paid -- or otherwise 20s. a year for so many years as shall be left unpaid by my said son WILLIAM until said £10 be fully paid, provided that my son ROBERT WHIGHTHEAD shall have his free dwelling for life in the little tenement next adjoining that tenement which I lately sold unto Mrs THACKSTER, wid. To my daughter RUTH my bedstead with feather-bed transoms coverings and all things belonging to it as it stands; and all my linen and woolen, a table, a form, a chest, a kettle and certain keelers. The rest of my goods cattles debts rights and chattels I give to my son WILLIAM WHIGHTHEAD whom I make sole exor. Witnesses: JOHN [MUNNES?] (X), JAMES SMITER (X), and me JOHN WILD the writer. Pr. at Beccles 15 May 1630.

R(W) WILLIAM ALDOUS of St. James Southelmham, yeoman. (115)
20 October 1622

Sick. To MAUD my wife my little tenement in Cratfield with the yard belonging, containing 1 1/2 roods, which I purchased of JOHN ALDOUS my brother, for ever; and all my other lands and tenements in Cratfield for life, she keeping my houses in good reparation, committing no waste on the premises, and paying to ELIZABETH my mother £10 per annum according to the tenor of the will of ROBERT ALDOUS deceased my father. And after her decease I will the same shall remain to the child she is now with if it be a man child, and to his heirs for ever. I will that if SARAH my daughter and the child my wife is now with shall die before the age of 20 without issue lawfully begotten I devise my lands and tenements last recited to GREGORY ALDOUS my brother and to his heirs for ever, upon condition that he or his heirs shall, in the porch of the parish church of Cratfield, pay to SAMUEL ALDOUS my brother £20 upon the Michaelmas day 12 months after entry into my said lands and tenements by virtue of this will, and and to RICHARD ALDOUS my brother £20 on the Michaelmas 2 years after entry, and to JAMES ALDOUS my brother £20 on the Michaelmas day 3 years after entry, and to ELIZABETH COOKE my sister £20 on the Michaelmas day in the 5th year after entry. And if GREGORY my brother or his heirs default, then I devise my said lands and tenements to the use of the said SAMUEL, RICHARD, JAMES and ELIZABETH for ever. To MAUD my wife all my goods and chattels and household stuff and implements money and plate and other utensils, towards the payment of my debts burial expenses and the probate of this will, and I make her my sole exrx. Witnesses: JOHN PULHAM, GREGORY PULHAM. Pr. at Beccles 22 May 1630.

R(W) GEOFFREY CHAPMAN of Cookley, yeoman. (116)
14 January 1629/30

To JUDITH my wife my posted bed in the parlour with the feather-bed and bolster with a coverlet and blanket curtains and all other furniture belonging and all my feather pillows. To JOHN CHAPMAN my eldest son my long table standing in my parlour with the 2 forms belonging; my livery cupboard and 1 turned back chair, 2 buffet stools and my wicker chair. To GEOFFERY CHAPMAN my son my table in the hall with the form belonging and 1 turned chair in my parlour; 1 livery bedstead. To my daughter ANN 1 posted bedstead in my little chamber with a feather-bed 1 bolster and all the furniture belonging; 1 little table and 1 joined chair. To ELIZABETH my daughter 1 heifer of 2 year old 1 livery bedstead 1 feather-bed 1 feather bolster and all the furniture belonging and 1 chair. All these shall be delivered to each of them immediately after my decease. To ELIZABETH my daughter and her assigns £10 to be taken out of my goods and chattels which I appoint to be sold immediately after the decease of my wife JUDITH. To every of my grandchildren being now born £10 apiece, taken out of my goods to be sold. The rest of my movable goods bills bonds and specialties I give to JUDITH my wife towards the maintenance of her living, she to have them for the term of her life, and after her decease shall be sold and the money thereof divided equally among my 4 children JOHN CHAPMAN GEOFFERY CHAPMAN ANN CHAPMAN and MARY CHAPMAN provided that JUDITH my wife shall maintain and employ said movable goods and farr furth and honestly as she may for the benefit and behoof of my said children, so to be had after her decease. I make JUDITH my wife sole executrix and nominate my brother-in-law THOMAS SCALDING and aforesaid JOHN CHAPMAN my eldest son to be supervisors, and to said THOMAS SCALDING I give for his pains 10s., desiring him to be aiding my exrx. in my burial and the probate of this will. Witnesses: GEOFFERY CHAPMAN (X), RICHARD ALLGAR (X) and THOMAS FELLA. Pr. at Yoxford 14 April 1630.

R(W) RICHARD VALENTINE of Woodbridge, yeoman. (117)
6 February 1629/30

Sick. To be buried in Woodbridge churchyard. To THOMAS my son at age 21, £20. To RICHARD my son £20 at 21. To FRANCES my daughter £20 at 21. To JOAN my daughter £20 at 21. To ELIZABETH my daughter £20. To each of the 3 said daughters, in each of the three years before each of them be 21, 30s. each. If any of them die before receiving, the survivors to share equally in that portion. All my household stuff to be sold and the proceeds together with my ready money shall be used to pay legacies and funeral charges and to bring up my son RICHARD and my daughters JOAN and ELIZABETH till each is old enough to be put out to service. GEOFFERY SALE of Woodbridge, yeo., to be sole exor. Witnesses: JOHN WILKENKON, WILLIAM ROGER, JOHN WARREN, THOMAS VALENTINE. Pr. at Wickham 14 April 1630.

W(R)(A) THOMAS WRIGHT (X) of Beccles, yeoman. (118)
15 December 1628

Sick. To HENRY my son and his assigns for life my close in Beccles near Engate Field which I purchased of WILLIAM GOODWYN and my messuage or tenement belonging thereto situate in Redenhall in Norfolk; and after the decease of said HENRY I devise the premises above-mentioned to the heirs of his body lawfully begotten to be begotten. Then I give all the said premises to PETER BARRET my son-in-law and MARY his wife and to the heirs of the said MARY for ever. To said HENRY my son 2 pots tipped with silver, a silver cup, 10 silver spoons, a livery bedstead cord and natt, a feather-bed, feather bolster, a pair of blankets, a coverlet, my gold ring with a seal, all my wearing apparel and £250. To said PETER BARRET my son-in-law and MARY his wife and to the heirs of said MARY for ever all my lands which I hold by [copy] of court roll of the manor of Beccles, late by me purchased of THOMAS FLETCHE, gent, and also 1 close being freehold in Beccles near to Ridgebone Hill which I late purchased of NICHOLAS LOCKINGTON, gent. To said MARY my daughter 4 silver spoons a silver salt, a posted bedstead cord and natt with the 2 feather-beds 2 bolsters, blankets and coverlets, as they now stand in the parlour next the street of my dwelling house in Beccles, and £250. PHOEBE my now wife shall have and enjoy to the only use of said PHOEBE and her assigns during her life my messuage or tenement wherein I dwell in Beccles with the garden and orchards adjoining, she paying to our lord the king and his successors 4d. for the task hereafter to be due out of the same premises, committing neither estrip nor waste upon the premises, but keeping the same under reasonable reparations. To said PHOEBE my posted bedstead cord and natt 1 down bed 2 feather bolsters 2 pillows 2 blankets 1 coverlet the curtain and valance to the same belonging, as they stand in the chamber where I now lie; 1 deep silver cup for beer 6 silver spoons a pot tipped with silver a trundle bedstead and £10, she to have all the movables for life and entering a bond to pay my exors. for the delivery of said movables to my children after her decease. And after her decease, to be equally divided between them, provided that if said PHOEBE upon reasonable request at the charges of my children shall refuse to release all such estate of her dower or thirds as she might have in any of my messuages lands or tenements by this will devised to either of my said children, within 30 days after such request, all the bequests given by me in this will to said PHOEBE shall be void. To PETER BARRET and MARY his wife and the heirs of said MARY for ever my messuage or tenement with the houses yards gardens and orchards belonging, before given in this will to said PHOEBE, they to enter the same immediately after the death of said PHOEBE or of her such refusal to release her right of dower. To Mr THOMAS DAYNES, clerk, as a gratuity to preach a sermon at my burial 20s. To Mr JOHN VAUGHAN, parson, 10s. To the children of JOHN DAVISON 40s., to be equally divided among all of them. To THOMAS COLEMAN my late servant 10s. To ANN COUSWELL my sister 20s. To MARGERY GREENE my sister-in-law 20s. To every such servant as shall dwell with me at my death 10s. To the poor of Beccles £3 to be distributed by the churchwardens and overseers where most need be. To said PETER BARRET and MARY his wife all such messuages and lands which I hold by lease of any manner of person. To the said HENRY all my horses and carts with the furniture belonging. To the same HENRY WRIGHT my son all the remainder of that bargain of woods and timber which I lately bought of Mr TOOGOOD and ROBERT MANN as the same now is about Redisham Corner, provided that if HENRY PARKER shall be aiding my son HENRY in selling the said woods and timber in husbandly manner HENRY shall give to the use of HENRY PARKER 40s. out of the profits for his pains. The residue of my goods chattels implements of household and my debts which I shall owe, my funeral expenses and probate of this will excepted, I give to HENRY my son and PETER BARRET my son-in-law to be equally divided, and I make my friends NICHOLAS BRADLEY of Beccles and HENRY PARKER of the same exors., and bequeath to either of them 40s. over and above such charges as either of them shall be at in proving this will. And I entreat Mr THOMAS DAINES to be my supervisor and give hime for his pains 40s. Witnesses: RO. COBBE, THOMAS GOSLINGE, JOHN ALARDES, JOHN RUSSELLS (X). On 10 April 1630 NICHOLAS BRADLIE and HENRY PARKER attended in person and renounced executorship, and admon. was granted to PETER BARRETT and MARY his wife and HENRY WRIGHT, son of deceased.

W(R) PETER WRIGHT of Homersfield (N). [no date] (119)

All that he had to MARGARET his wife during her life and then to be equally divided between his children PETER, JOHN, HENRY and OLIVE WRIGHT. Witnesses: THOMAS LOVECK and ROGER COGSWELL. Admon. to MARGARET WRIGHTE, relict, and PETER and JOHN WRIGHTE, sons of deceased, 4 May 1630.

W(R) THOMAS ELLIOT (X) of Needham, glazier. 9 April 1630 (120)

Sick. To ELIZABETH my wife my tenement or cottage with the houses rooms yards and appurtenances belonging in Needham wherein I dwell, and after her decease to that child that she now is withall, and to their heirs for ever. If the child shall not live to enjoy and dispose of the premises itself, then they shall remain to my right heirs. All my working stuff and tools of my trade of glazing I give to THOMAS ELLIOTT my father. And if the aforesaid child shall not live to enjoy the premises, then my brother WILLIAM ELLIOT shall sell my said tenement or cottage after my wife's and supposed child's decease and divide the money thereof equally between himself and my three sisters ELIZABETH, CECILY and ANN ELLIOTT and their heirs. Which, if my brother refuse or leave undone, then the cottage &c shall remain to my three sisters and their heirs for ever. The rest of my goods I give to my wife ELIZABETH whom I make my exrx., to pay my debts but especially 40s. to my half-sister MARY, she having no specialty for it. Witnesses: JO. ROE, writer hereof, DANIEL BONNET, ROBERT DRAPER (X). Pr. 13 May 1630.

W(R) JOHN CLUBBE of Horham, yeoman. 30 July 1625 (121)

To MARGARET my wife one annuity of £10 issuing out of my messuage or tenement wherein I dwell and out of all my lands tenements meadows pastures steadings and hereditaments called Jerningham Great Close, now divided into divers closes, which I lately bought of RICHARD GOLDSMITH and Mr HENRY GOLDSMITH his brother, situate in Horham, to be paid to her for life at the feasts of the Annunciation and of St. Michael by equal portions, or within 10 days thereafter, in the porch of the parish church of Horham, in full lieu and satisfaction of all dower or thirds in any of my lands and tenements [with power of distraint]. To said MARGARET another annuity of £5 issuing out of the lands and tenements that I do hereafter in this will devise to JOHN CLUBBE my son, to be paid for life if she keep herself a widow, to be paid upon the same feasts or within 10 days thereafter, by equal portions, in the porch of said church, in lieu of dower or thirds in my lands in Horham [with power of distraint]. To said MARGARET the bedstead and bed in the hall chamber which we now use to lie on with the furniture belonging. And said MARGARET shall have her dwelling occupy and use the parlour at the messuage wherein I now dwell, with liberty to brew bake and wash in the backhouse there, and liberty to place her wood in the yard, and liberty of ingress and egress to and from the premises and the waters and garden, and to have delivered to her at or near the parlour every year 4 loads of good firewood, so long as she keep herself a widow and claim no dower. To ELIZABETH CLUBBE my daughter her heirs and assigns for ever, my little tenement or messuage wherein ROBERT MAYHEW now dwelleth, with all the lands pastures feedings and hereditaments now in farm and occupation of ROBERT MAIOR under my demise, provided that if she or her heirs shall sell the same, then they shall sell it to JOHN my son and his heirs for the sum of 100 marks if the said JOHN or his heirs will accept; otherwise she to be at liberty to sell to whom she will. My two closes called Buckinghams shall be sold within a year by my exor. and one or two other persons whom ANN, ALICE or SUSAN my daughters shall name, and the money thereof shall be equally parted among my three daughters, they to have the use of the closes until the sale thereof. If not sold within one year, then I give the said closes to the said daughters for ever. To DENNY CLUBBE my son his heirs and assigns my capital messuage wherein I now inhabit, with all the houses buildings barns stables yards orchards moats and grounds adjoining other than such part as I have given to MARGARET my wife so long as she keep herself a widow, and all those lands and tenements which I lately purchased of said EDMUND GOLDSMITH and HENRY GOLDSMITH, called Jerninghams Great Closes, the said DENNY and his heirs paying my debts and such sums of money as I have herein bequeathed to any person, limited to be issuing out of those lands &c so purchased. To said DENNY my son my best cupboard, my table standing in the hall with the form belonging, my brewing copper, my mill with all the furniture belonging, my cart and biggest tumbril buck and all my ploughs and trace, also the coffer wherein my evidences are, he giving to the rest of my children their several evidences to whom they shall belong and that appertain to their several lands &c. To JOHN CLUBBE my son his heirs and assigns for ever my copyhold and customary lands and tenements which I hold of EDWARD COAKE knight, late lord Chief Justice of the King's Bench, as of his manor of Horham Jerninghams, except one pightle called Colts pightle and my house wherein my father did dwell at the time of his decease, with the lands and gardens belonging, the said JOHN paying all such sums as I have bequeathed and appointed the same to be paid. And DENNY CLUBBE my son shall at the time of his decease devise to JOHN CLUBBE, son of said DENNY, my grandchild and godson, and to his heirs, discharged of all encumbrances done by the said DENNY and his wife's dower therein only excepted, all my said capital messuage wherein I now dwell and all the lands &c given by me to said DENNY, or the most part thereof, which if the said DENNY shall not do then I devise to the said JOHN CLUBBE his son £400 to be issuing out of my lands &c hereinbefore bequeathed to DENNY, to be paid in the porch of the parish church of Horham, viz. within one half year after the decease of DENNY my son £100 if said JOHN CLUBBE or any issue of his body lawfully begotten shall then be living, and so every year £100 until the £400 be fully paid, with power for JOHN to distrain upon the lands &c which I lately purchased of EDMUND and HENRY GOLDSMITH, herein devised to DENNY my son, until my grandchild shall have been paid twice so much money as shall be unpaid contrary to my intent. To

JOHN CLUBB my son my copper in the house called the candle house, and my other tumbrel with all things belonging, my cheese press and salting tray at my house wherein WILLIAM MAYHEW dwelleth, and all my board lying there, all my tools in my shop, my table in my parlour where I dwell, 2 forms in my parlour chamber and my square table in the hall there, and my musket furnished. To ALICE CLUBB my daughter my bedstead with curtains standing in the parlour chamber, a feather-bed and bolster and a coverlet belonging thereto. The residue of my bedding shall be equally divided among ANN, ALICE and SUSAN my daughters. All the rest of my brass and pewter and the rest of my household stuff within my insett houses shall be equally divided among my wife and four daughters. To ALICE my daughter or her assigns £10 to be paid within 10 years of my decease, if she or any issue of her body lawfully begotten be then living, out of all my lands &c bequeathed to my son DENNY [with power of distraint]. The residue of my goods and chattels I give to DENNY CLUBBE my son whom I make my sole exor. If said DENNY shall refuse to take upon him the execution of this will or shall not within 2 months after my decease prove the same in the office of the spiritual court, then I will disclaim said DENNY to be my exor. or to have anything to do with this will, and then I will that all the bequests herein given to him and his heirs shall be frustrate, and then I ordain JOHN CLUBBE my son my sole exor., and that he shall have all those lands &c which I have before given to DENNY during the term of 100 years from thenceforth towards the payment of my debts and legacies, and then also do I devise all goods and chattels and legacies before given to DENNY unto said JOHN my son towards the executing of this will. To ROBERT CLUBBE my grandchild, son of WILLIAM my son, £5 at 21; and to every one of the rest of my son WILLIAM's children 20s. at their several ages of 21; and to MARGARET CLUBB my grandchild, daughter of DENNY my son 20s. at 21. Witnesses: THOMAS COOKE of Eye, cordwainer and JOHN KEWE the writer. Pr. at Wickham 27 May 1630.

R(W) BARTHOLOMEW TALBOTT of Walton, gentleman. (122)
15 April 1625

Sick. To be buried in Walton churchyard. To the poor of Walton 40s. to be paid within 1 month. To GEOFFERY TALBOTE the house and hempland that I bought of CHARLES BARNES with the ground belonging, and the piece of ground which I bought late of Mr SCRUTTEN joining to Mr PETTEWARD's vicarage and the piece of ground at the vicarage gate and Priors Close, and all those pickells lying between the lands of THOMAS BOYTON and his own house where he dwelleth, to enter the Michaelmas twelve months after my wife's decease. To WILLIAM GLOVER my house in Ipswich wherein CHARLES SMITH dwelleth to make sale of it within 3 months after my decease; also one piece of freehold land lying in Felixstowe joining to MICHAEL MARSHLANDS land, to make sale of the same as soon as he can. To THOMAS ROE my russet suit with cloak jerkin and hose, with my sealed ring and one of my biggest silver bowls. To ANN ROE my 2 silver hatched bowls and half a dozen silver spoons where she will choose. To MARRIAN TALBOT my house and hempland wherein WILLIAM HEAD now dwelleth to enter upon presently after my decease. All the rest of my movable goods utensils money plate and household stuff I give to WILLIAM GLOVER and ANN ROE. My lands unbequeathed I give to MARY my wife during her life and the Michaelmas after. My corn cattle and all such things I give to WILLIAM GLOVER and ANN ROE towards the payments of my debts and legacies. To JOSEPH SCOTT 20s. to be paid within 3 months. I nominate WILLIAM GLOVER and ANN ROE my exors. After the death of MARY my wife those lands to her bequeathed shall go to JOHN TALBOTT the grandchild of JOHN TALBOTT late of Wanesden [Wantisden] deceased, to him and his heirs for ever. Witnesses: ROGER BARNS and JOHN SCOTT. Pr. at Ipswich 28 May 1630. Admon. to WILLIAM GLOVER with power reserved for ANN ROE.

W(R) CLEMENT TURNER (X) of Spexhall, yeoman. 10 July 1627 (123)

To THOMAS TURNER my son £5 to be paid by JANE my wife within 4 years in the south porch of the parish church of Spexhall. To JANE my wife the use of all my movable goods and chattels during her life so long as she keep herself unmarried; and after her decease these goods shall be divided equally, by 3 honest neighbors dwelling in Spexhall, into 3 parts; and 2 of the 3 parts I give to FRANCIS TURNER my son and the other third to MARY CRISPE my daughter. If JANE shall marry again I will that 10 days before the solemnisation of her marriage all the said goods appointed unto JANE, after the £5 given to my son THOMAS be thereof taken out and my funeral expenses probate of this will and my debts and legacies all paid, shall be equally divided by my supervisor and 2 other honest neighbors, or by two of them, into three parts whereof I give to JANE my wife one part, and the other 2 parts shall likewise be divided into 3 parts, and 2 of these three I give to FRANCIS TURNER my son, and the third to MARY CRISPE my daughter, provided that JANE my wife shall within one month after my decease become bound unto my supervisor in the penal sum of 200 marks to maintain all my goods, in the will appointed to her to have to her use for her life, so far forth as by any means she may, conveniently making use thereof, to preserve the same. And if said JANE should marry again, then 10 days before the solemnisation of her marriage she shall help to set forth all my said goods &c to be divided as above, provided further that if she shall refuse or do not become bound as above specified the all legacies unto her shall be void, and all my goods, after the £5 taken and funeral expenses probate debts and legacies paid, shall be divided as aforesaid within 6 weeks after my decease, and after the division thereof JANE my wife shall have one part of the three and the other two parts shall be divided into three, whereof FRANCIS my son shall have two parts and MARY my daughter the other part. Now for the true love that always have been between me and JANE my wife I appoint her to be exrx. to the will desiring her that she will "see the same performed soe farr forth as in her lyeth." And I nominate ROBERT TURROULD of Spexhall the elder to be supervisor, and I give him for his pains one piece of gold of 11s. to be paid to him by JANE my wife. Witnesses: ROBERT MIGHELLS and ROGER MIGHELLS. Pr. 25 May 1630.

W(R) THOMAS RAWLINGE of Frostenden, yeoman. 7 April 1630 (124)

To my daughter SARAH all my free lands and tenements which I hold of the manor of Frostenden in Northales alias Covehithe and in Haverland Field in Wrentham, to hold to her and her assigns so that they do pay unto KATHERINE my wife yearly, during the life of LUCY RAWLINGE my aunt, towards her maintenance (whom I have commended to the care of my said wife) 30s. upon the usual feast days of St. Michael and of the Annunciation, by even portions. To the said KATHERINE my freehold lands and tenements (late JOHN RAWLINGES, my father) situate in Wrentham between the king's highway leading from Southwold to Beccles in part on the east part and the lands of Mr RICHARD GARRARD the elder on the part of the west, and do abut upon a little green or common toward the south, and the lands of FRANCIS BREWSTER esq. towards the north, containing together in divers enclosures, by estimation, 10 acres of land and pasture, to hold to said KATHERINE and her assigns during her life; also all my free lands and tenements in Haverland Field which I hold of Mr BREWSTER, during her life; and all my goods chattels money plate and jewels; and I appoint her exrx. Witnesses: THOMAS JONES, THOMAS MORSE, MARY STEDMAN (X). Pr. at Frostenden 9 June 1630.

W(R) WILLIAM ELLES of Bedfield, yeoman. 15 April 1630 (125)

To JOHN ELLES my brother and JANE BURCH my sister my tenement called Osbornes wherein I dwell, with all the lands and tenements belonging lying in Bedfield, to hold to said JOHN and JANE and the longer lived of them on condition that they quietly agree together, but if there be disagreement between them, then JANE my sister shall have the tenement to her own proper use during her life on condition that she pay said JOHN my brother £5 yearly, by equal portions at the Annunciation and the feast of St. Michael [with power of distraint for JOHN]. If JANE die before JOHN he shall have all my said lands during his life, and after the decease of JOHN my brother and JANE my sister I give the tenement called Osbernes with the lands belonging to WILLIAM ELLES, the son of THOMAS ELLES my brother deceased, and to his assigns for 4 years, without doing strip or waste, and after the 4 years I give the same to GEORGE BURCH the elder, son of the said JANE, during his life on condition that he or his executors pay NICHOLAS BURCH, son of said JANE, £10 -- £5 within 1 year after the term of 4 years limited unto WILLIAM ELLES my kinsman be expired, and the other £5 within 2 years next after that term. After decease of said GEORGE BURCH the elder I give said lands &c to GEORGE BURCH the younger, son of said GEORGE, and to his heirs for ever. To GEORGE BURCH the younger my posted bedstead in the parlour, my down bed and bolster, 1 blanket and 1 pair sheets and 1 pillow with 1 burditt coverlet, all which shall remain in the custody of said JANE BURCH his grandmother, to her use during her life. To

NICHOLAS BURCH 1 trundle bedstead in the chamber, 1 pair sheets 1 blanket 1 coverlet. To JANE BURCH my sister 1 brass pot 1 great brass kettle and a little spit. To ROBERT CATCHPOL my kinsman 40s. to be divided and bestowed upon his children. To said WILLIAM ELLES my brother's son £20 within 1 year. To MARGARET DANIELL now wife to LIONEL NICKOLES 40s. To SUSAN DANIEL now wife of WILLIAM LINGE 20s. To SITH DANIELL and EDITH DANIEL my kinswomen, to each 20s. To THOMAS VIRGOO 40s. To MICHAEL VERGO my kinsman £10. To PARNEL ELLIS my kinswoman 20s. To MARY ELLIS my kinswoman 40s. To PRUDENCE ELLES my brother's daughter 20s. To JOSIAS DENNY 20s. To MARY DENNY now wife of SIMON PENNY 40s. To PRUDENCE ALLEN and ELIZABETH ALLEN to either of them 20s. To THOMAS LARKE, ELLES LARKE, MARY LARKE, SARAH LARKE and PHILIP LARKE, to every of them 20s. To THOMAS ELLES son of THOMAS my deceased brother 10s. To MARGERY his sister the wife of ROBERT LYON 20s.; to ELIZABETH his sister 20s. To said NICHOLAS BURCH my sister's son 5s. To THOMAS DENNY my kinsman 20s. To KATHERINE his sister 10s. To MARY BEMOND daughter of HENRY BEAMOND 10s. To KATHERINE FULKARD my apprentice 20s. All these legacies to be paid within one half year of my decease. To my brother JOHN ELLIS my horseman's coat and the best of my two heiffers. All the rest of my cows, my corn on the chamber or elsewhere, and all my hay shall be divided equally between JOHN ELLIS my brother and JANE BURCH my sister. To the poor of Bedfield 20s. within 1 year. The rest of my movables to my exors. towards the payment of such charges as shall be due for performing and proving this will, and I make JOAN BURCH my sister and GEORGE BURCH the elder, her son, my exors. And I appoint TIMOTHY BOWMAN, parson of Bedfield, to be supervisor and give him for his pains 5s. Witnesses: TIMOTHY BOWMAN, RICHARD GIRLING, WILLIAM TITLEY, LAURENCE MAYHEW. Pr. at Wickham 27 May 1630.

R(W) JOHN FISH senior of Badingham, yeoman. (126)
30 September 1626

Sick. To PLEASANCE my wife, in consideration that she shall not claim any dower out of my lands and tenements, an annuity of 20 marks to be paid by LAURENCE, WILLIAM and GEORGE my sons, at the usual feasts viz. Christmas and the Annunciation, by equal portions, at the porch of Framlingham parish church, the first payment to be on the first feast after my decease, of which annuity LAURENCE shall pay £4 10s., WILLIAM £4 10s. and GEORGE £4 6s. 8d.; and if any of my sons make default any legacy given to him shall be given to said PLEASANCE. To PLEASANCE my best feather-bed bolster and pillows with the coverings and bedstead belonging, now standing in the hall in the house where I dwell; and all my linen and 1 chest and a coffer which were her own before I married her; a new brass kettle which was bought last, 2 pewter dishes, a pair of tongs and a firepan. To JOHN my son and his heirs for ever all my houses lands meadows pastures feedings and hereditaments in Framlingham, Snape and Sweffling (one tenement in Framlingham late of JOHN PAGES excepted), provided that if he should die without issue of his body lawfully begotten all the said houses &c remain to my sons LAURENCE, WILLIAM and

GEORGE and their heirs for ever, equally divided, provided that if JOHN shall endeavor to make sale or convey away any of said messuages &c shall devised to him, then that devise shall be void and all the messuages &c shall descend to the rest of my sons and their heirs to be equally divided, provided that if PLEASANCE my wife shall claim dower out of any of my said lands I will that the annuity of 20 marks granted to her shall cease. Whereas there are lands in Framlingham of EDMUND DURRANTS, and also lands in Peasenhall of REGINALD ROWSE, gent, which were mortgaged to me, and lands of said REGINALD ROWSE are now forfeited for want of payment of certain sums, my will is that the said REGINALD his exors. or administrators shall within one year after my decease discharge to my exors. all such sums as are specified in the mortgage, together with all interest due, then my son JOHN shall reassure all the said lands back again to REGINALD ROWSE and his heirs, and if he shall refuse so to do then the devise of my messuages &c made to him shall be void and then I give the same to LAURENCE, WILLIAM, GEORGE and their heirs. Whereas certain copyhold lands in Framlingham of the said EDMUND DURRANT are mortgaged to me by conditional surrender, and the money for which the same are mortgaged is not yet payable, I will that if it be not paid at the days and place expressed, yet if the said EDMUND DURRANT shall pay within one year after such sums as shall then be due, with interest, then EDMUND DURRANT shall have such lands reassured again unto him by GEORGE my son upon reasonable request, or else said GEORGE shall lose all benefit by my will and all legacies to him shall remain to LAURENCE and WILLIAM my sons. And if those lands are not redeemed within 1 year then I devise all the same copyhold lands and tenements to LAURENCE, WILLIAM and GEORGE my sons. I give the said WILLIAM my copyhold tenement in Framlingham, late JOHN PAGE's; and to LAURENCE all my lease or term of years yet to come specified in the original lease assigned by Mr FULLER. To MARY CULLINGTON my servant £5 to be paid within a fortnight. All my household stuff cattle corn and such money as shall be upon any of the mortgages aforesaid, all my debts being paid, I give to said LAURENCE, WILLIAM and GEORGE my sons, equally divided, and I make them exors. I ordain my friend THOMAS ALLEXANDER of Framlingham, gent., my supervisor. Witnesses: ROBERT CAPON, THOMAS ALLEXANDER. Pr. at Yoxford 26 May 1630.

R(W) THOMAS GOSLING of Wilby, husbandman. 1 May 1630 (127)

To be buried in Wilby. To ROSE my wife during her life the profits arising on that piece of ground inclosure or yard, with appurtenances, formerly belonging to the messuage or tenement thereon wherein I dwell, all which I give after my wife's decease to my 2 sons THOMAS and JOHN for ever on condition that during the life of ROSE their mother my son JOHN and his assigns shall [allow] the said ROSE or her assigns to have at all convenient times free access and use of the oven that is in that part of the house that is his, and that she shall suffer her son JOHN and his assigns to have right and liberties for the convenient setting of his wood and fuel in the yards, and for ingress and regress to the water and to that part of the house and shop that are his; and that my son THOMAS and his assigns, after his mother's decease shall have like access and use of the oven; and after her decease my 2 sons shall have interest and right to the said ground and yards equally dividing the yearly profit thereof; and if either shall refuse to perform these conditions, either towards their mother or towards one another, he shall put himself quite out from all the aforesaid right to the premises, and the right to stand wholly good to his brother and his heirs for ever. To my son THOMAS my malt querns after my wife's decease, enjoining him to suffer his brother JOHN to have the use of them at all convenient times; and 1 feather-bed with the furniture as it is standing in the hall chamber. To my son JOHN my cheese press after my wife's decease. To my daughter MARGARET 1 new feather-bed with all that belongs, with the trundle bed on which it lieth in the hall chamber. All my other goods movables and chattels I give to ROSE my wife for maintenance of herself and the bringing up and disposing of my children till they attain the age of 21; and then if she and they shall so agree to be divided among them at their discretion, by the advice of 2 honest neighbors. I appoint ROSE sole exrx. Witnesses: JOSEPH FLETCHER and THOMAS CLOUTING. Pr. at Yoxford 6 May 1630.

R(W) JAMES MASTERSON of Wickham, carpenter. 22 April 1630 (128)

Sick. I devise all that part of my tenement wherein JOHN SYMONDS now dwelleth, situate in Wickham Market, as the same now is in the tenure of JOHN SYMONDS or his assigns (one stable only excepted) to be sold by THOMAS MASTERSON my brother or his heirs within a year, and the money thereof arising to be bestowed toward the payment of my debts and performance of my will; the profits arising before it be sold, taken by said THOMAS, should be accounted assets remaining in his hand towards the payment of my debts. To the said THOMAS MASTERSON I give all the rest of my lands and tenements in Wickham for ever, on condition that he shall pay to JAMES MASTERSON my father and ELIZABETH my mother and to the longer lived of them 30s. yearly for life, to be paid on the feast of the Annunciation and the feast of St. Michael by equal portions, the first payment to be made on the first of said feast days that shall happen after my decease, every payment to be made in the porch of the parish church of Hacheston. If payment be unpaid in whole or in part 14 days after any feast day I will give all the houses and lands last-devised to the said JAMES MASTERSON my father and ELIZABETH my mother to hold during the lives of them, and after their decease I give the same to said THOMAS MASTERSON my brother and his heirs for ever without condition. To said JAMES MASTERSON my father all my apparel (except my cloak and my best doublet which I give to said THOMAS my brother). To ELIZABETH MASTERSON my sister £5 within 1 year. To said THOMAS MASTERSON my brother all my goods and chattels not formerly bequeathed towards the payment of my debts and the performance of this will and I nominate him sole exor. Witnesses: JOHN STYLES, THOMAS HARRISON, ROBERT WARD and JOHN HUNT. Pr. at Wickham 27 May 1630.

R(W) THOMAS ROOKE (X) of Badingham, singleman. (129)
1 April 1630

To be buried in Badingham churchyard. To REGINALD ROOKE my brother all my lands and tenements and hereditaments in Badingham (except my piece of meadow or pasture at the upper end of my lands whose west head abutteth upon the lands of ROBERT SPARHAM and containeth by estimation 1 acre and 1 rood) to hold for life and after his decease I give same to THOMAS ROOKE my nephew and godson, son of said REGINALD and his heirs for ever. I give my piece of meadow aforesaid to REGINALD ROOKE my brother and his assigns during the term of his life, paying all my debts and also paying to ROBERT ROOKE my nephew, son of said REGINALD, £5 at 21, in the south porch of the parish church of Badingham. And after the decease of said REGINALD I give said piece to THOMAS ROOKE my nephew, paying to REGINALD ROOKE my nephew, son of said REGINALD, £5 at 21 at the place aforesaid if said REGINALD my brother shall not then be living; but if he shall be living then the said REGINALD my nephew shall not have his legacy of £5 until 6 months after said THOMAS my nephew or his heirs shall be possessed of said piece of meadow by force of this will. If the said REGINALD my brother shall depart this life before ROBERT my nephew shall have accomplished his age of 21, then THOMAS my nephew and his heirs and assigns shall pay said ROBERT his legacy of £5 in such manner as my brother should have done in case he had lived; provided that if REGINALD my brother shall not within 3 years after my decease have paid all my debts or shall fail in the payment of said £5 to ROBERT, then it shall be lawful for ROBERT or his assigns to enter the said piece and enjoy it during the term of the life of REGINALD my brother, paying so much of my debts as shall be unsatisfied at the time of his entry, and provided also that if THOMAS my nephew shall make default of the legacy of £5 to ROBERT, then I will that ROBERT his heirs and assigns shall have that piece of meadow, paying to my nephew REGINALD his legacy of £5 in the manner aforesaid. To the said THOMAS ROOKE my nephew my cupboard, framed table, joined form with 2 buffet stools, new joined chest and turned chair. To the said ROBERT and REGINALD ROOKE my nephews my half dozen pewter porringers to be divided betwixt them. More to REGINALD one of my great wrought pewter dishes. To ROBERT ROOKE my brother my cloak and second suit of apparel viz. my doublet and hose, and my best hanging of stained cloth. To my sister-in-law my brother ROBERT's wife my desk and bible. To EDMUND ROOKE my nephew my posted bedstead with a matt and line, the teston and other hanging of stained cloth belonging to it, with the feather-bed and bolster, a coverlet and a pair of blankets which were my father's. To JOHN ROOKE my nephew my other great wrought charger. To ALICE ROOKE my niece my great pewter platter which is plain. All which legacies unto my brother ROBERT ROOKE's children shall be delivered to said ROBERT my brother to their several uses within one month of my decease. To MARTHA ROOKE my niece my livery bedstead that is now broken, with a matt and line, my feather-bed and bolster that was my uncle ANTHONY PYE's with 2 coverlets belonging, a pillow 3 blankets 2 pair sheets my belt of linsey-wolsey, my black coffer as it standeth and my other coffer and a stool now standing in the work house, 2 pewter dishes, a brass pot with a pair of pot-hooks, a skillet, a pair of bellows, and my best stained cloth that was my uncle's and now in my own room -- all which shall be delivered within one month. My goods and chattels unbequeathed I give to said REGINALD ROOKE my brother towards my burial expenses and probate of this will, and I nominate him sole exor. Witnesses: FRANCIS WARD, ROBERT ROOKE, EDWARD MOULTON. Pr. at Yoxford 26 May 1630.

W(R) ROGER ANDROUSE (X) of Stradbroke, husbandman. (130)
24 April 1630

To MARY my daughter the posted bedstead with the bed and all other things belonging as it now stands on the buttery chamber. To MARY the daughter of my daughter the cupboard and the long table in the hall, only her father to have the use of it until she shall come to have use for it herself. To ALICE READ the daughter of my daughter one chest and one cupboard table and one desk all standing in the hall, only her father and mother to use them until she shall have use for them herself. To FRANCES my wife the bed whereon I now lie in the hall as it stand, and all other movables and money that is due unto me, indoors and without, I give unto my wife and I ordain her sole exrx. to pay my debts and burial charges. Witnesses: ROBERT READ (X), WILLIAM THROWER. Pr. at Yoxford 26 May 1630.

W(R) WILLIAM MURRELL (X) of Trimley St. Martin, yeoman. (131)
19 April 1630

Sick. To MARY MURRELL my daughter my house and a little hempland belonging thereto called Little Londen in Trimley St. Martin, for term of her life, she to enter the Michaelmas after my decease. To ANN MURRELL my wife all my freehold land in Trimley St. Martin and one other piece of freehold land lying in Leston Close in Trimley St. Mary which my brother EDMUND MURRELL purchased of one master THOMAS LAMBE, gent.,and abuttelling the lands of Sir JOHN BARKER, knight and baronet, to her and her heirs for ever. If my daughter MARY shall die my wife ANN shall have the said house and hempland. More to my daughter MARY MURRELL a feather-bed and all that thereunto belongeth, and a brass pot, a copper kettle, a little table and 2 little stools. To ALICE MURRELL a brazen candlestick and a little firkin. To ANN MURRELL my wife all the rest of my goods to pay my debts, and I nominate her to be exrx. Witnesses: NICHOLAS BETT, JOHN WYETHE and PHILIP PLOYSE. Pr. at Ipswich 28 May 1630.

R(W) ROSE TAVENDER (X) of Iken, widow. 25 April 1630 (132)

Sick. To JOAN my daughter my lands and tenements in Iken on condition that she choose WALTER ASHLEY of Aldeburgh to be her guardian, and him to receive the profits thereof and employ the same towards the bringing of her up until her age of 21. And JOAN shall pay to JOHN TAVENDER my son £10 within 1 year after her age of 21, which £10 I give him on condition that he make no claim upon the house which I sold DRAKE of Thorpe. If JOAN die before her age of 21 I give the said lands &c to JOHN my son and his heirs for ever; and if he shall die before 21 my lands &c shall be sold and the money divided between MARY KNIGHTS daughter of PETER KNIGHTS and JOHN WILLIAM the son of RICHARD WILLIAM late of Butley. To JOHN my son 1 bible. To WALTER ASHLEY all my goods and chattels towards payment of debts funeral charges and probate, the remainder to be employed towards bringing up my daughter JOAN, and I appoint said WALTER ASHLEY exor. Witnesses: JOHN BRALE, MARY WILBY, ANN HALFE. Pr. at Wickham 27 May 1630.

W(R) NICHOLAS INUSFER (X) of Easton, husbandman. (133)
27 May 1630

To MARGARET my wife one tenement in Rumburgh street, one yard being new built called Roulenes, being estimated 10 or 12 perches, with appurtenances, freely as her proper own to sell after my decease. And if my wife MARGARET do spare anything when God shall call her out of this tenement I will have her bestow it upon my kindred where most need is. Also to MARGARET my wife all my movable goods bedding brass pewter linen and woolen whatsoever. I appoint JOHN AYSON my kinsman in Easton Bavent my supervisor and give him for his pains 10s. Witnesses: PHILIP SEAMAN, JOHN AYTON (X). Pr. at Beccles 29 June 1630.

R(W) JOHN ARCHER of Tunstall, yeoman. 10 June 1630 (134)

To ELIZABETH ARCHER my daughter £40 at her age of 21. To AGNES ARCHER my daughter £40 at 21. To said daughter ELIZABETH 15s. yearly till she be 21. To said daughter AGNES 20s. yearly till she be 21. To the poor of Tunstall 20s. within 2 months of my decease. The rest of my goods and chattels corn household stuff utensils of husbandry I give to JOHN ARCHER my son whom I nominate exor. Witnesses: RICHARD LANGLIE, ALEXANDER RENELL, JOHN OSBORNE, EDWARD COULDS. I do annex this bequest viz. to AGNES ARCHER my wife £10 to be paid within 1 year. Witnesses: JOHN ARCHER, RICHARD LANGLYN, JOHN OSBORNE, EDMUND COULDS, ALEXANDER RENELL. Pr. at Wickham 17 June 1630.

R(W) ROGER BLOMFIELD (X) of Stonhal Aspall, yeoman. (135)
20 May 1630

Aged and weak. Whereas I have heretofore made such provision for my wife and children by assurance done in my lifetime as myself have thought fit and proportionable according to my ability, I hereby ratify the same. And whereas I have by a deed dated 18 Oct. 1622 given unto JOHN GOSLIN and to ELIZABETH my daughter, wife of said JOHN GOSLING, all my goods and chattels as well within the house real as personal, with the exception of some particular things as in the deed appeareth, intending then, as I still do intend, my wife during her life to have the use and profit and occupation and decrease of all my said goods and chattels, as well those given to the said JOHN GOSLING and ELIZABETH his wife, as also those others that are excepted, and whereas since that time the property of my goods given to the said JOHN GOSLING and ELIZABETH his wife especially my cattle hath been altered, now my will is and I do hereby give to JOHN BLOMFIELD my son, in performance of my former agreement and promise, all those parcels of goods particularly excepted in the said deeds, my wife to have the use of them in her life; also to said JOHN GOSLING and ELIZABETH his wife all other my goods and chattels, my wife likewise to have the use of them during her life, provided that my wife whom I have appointed sole exrx. shall pay herself out of such of my goods as have been renewed or altered since the day of the date of the said deed her reasonable costs and charges to be expended about my burial and the proving of this will. Witnesses: JOHN TRIPP (X), MARY PATTLE (X), ROBERT SHIPPE. Pr. at Mickfield, 21 June 1630.

R(W) THOMAS BOBBETT of Melton, weaver. 14 May 1630 (136)

Sick. To KATHARINE my wife all my houses and lands in Melton, Asketon [Hasketon], Bredfield and Ufford for her life-time, charged to bring up my children in learning and good education and to pay to my son THOMAS BOBBET, at age 21, 40s. a year; and to my daughter ELIZABETH, at 18 years, 20s. a year; and to the landlord his rents. If KATHARINE should not maintain the houses and lands in good condition the gift to her shall be void. After the decease of KATHARINE I give the said lands and houses to my son THOMAS BOBBET, charged to pay to my daughter ELIZABETH £10, half within 3 years of enjoying the said property and half the next year. Should THOMAS die before he is 21 I leave the said property to ELIZABETH. To THOMAS my son the bedstead in the parlour with all its furnishings, my bible, my book of MARTIN LUTHES, 1 gript kettle, 6 pewter platters and 1 skillet, my great chest in the parlour, 1 little table. To my daughter ELIZABETH a bedstead in the shop chamber with all things belonging, 1 table, 1 keep, 1 chest in the said chamber, 1 cupboard in the hall, 1 brass pot, 1 great pan, 1 little kettle, 6 pewter platters or dishes, 1 skillet. All the rest of my goods I give to KATHARINE my wife, she to be sole exrx. If she should die before my children THOMAS and ELIZABETH be 21, then my cousins ROBERT MATHEWES of Sutton and GEOFFERY BROWNE of Debach shall be guardians till THOMAS be 21 and ELIZABETH 18. Witnesses: WILLIAM PRATT, doctor of Melton and FRANCIS BETTES (X). Pr. 19 June 1630.

R(W) GEORGE GRICE (X) of Halesworth, armourer. 24 May 1630 (137)

To be buried in Halesworth churchyard. My lands and houses yards gardens in Halesworth shall be sold so soon as convenient and one half of the money thereof I give to JOHN GRICE and RICHARD GRICE my sons, equally divided, and the other half shall be equally divided between MARGARET, STEPHANIE and ELIZABETH my 3 daughters and ELIZABETH COOPER my grandchild, immediately after the sale. Immediately after my decease my exors. shall sell all my movable goods and stuff of household; and one half of the money thereof coming I give to JOHN and RICHARD my sons, equally divided, and out of the other half I give 40s. equally divided among all the children of STEPHEN THORNMAN, and 20s. to JOHN GARDNER son of CLEMENT GARDNER, and the rest of that half shall be equally divided among my 3 daughters MARGARET, STEPHANIE and ELIZABETH and also ELIZABETH COOPAR my grandchild, without fraud or delay. More to said JOHN GARDNER, my brass pot. I make said JOHN GRICE and RICHARD GRICE my sons exors. Witnesses: THOMAS FELLA, JOHN MAPES, GEORGE PORTER, RICHARD ROOSETER. Pr. at Halesworth 11 June 1630.

R(W) DOROTHY TISDALL of Orford (N). [no date] (138)

To AGNES SWEETEMAN a petitcoat, a hat, half of her wearing linen and 2 hens. All the rest of her goods to JOHN ESTROPP in regard of the charges which he had been at in the keeping and maintaining of her. Witnesses: ELIZABETH wife of THOMAS TOOKELY, ALICE wife of GEORGE DIGGS. Admon. issued at Wickham to JOHN ESTROPP, general legatee 27 May 1630.

R(W) THOMAS CAMPELL of Shotley, yeoman. 18 June 1630 (139)

To MARY BROOKE my daughter-in-law £5 to be paid at New-year's Day come twelvemonth. To my nephew EDMUND CAMPELL £5; to THOMAS CAMPELL his brother £3; to ELIZABETH CAMPELL their sister 20s., to be paid to each of them at the feast aforesaid. To my nephew ANTHONY CAMPELL 40s.; to JANE CAMPELL his sister 40s.; to GRISELDA CAMPELL another sister 40s., to be paid to each of them at the same feast. To my nephew RICHARD CALEY 40s. and to every of his sisters 20s. apiece, to be paid at the said feast. To my son-in-law JOHN PODD £5 and to his son THOMAS PODD 20s. and to his daughter SUSAN PODD 20s., to be paid to the said JOHN PODD at the feast aforesaid. To EDWARD CHERILL £5; to SARAH CHERILL his daughter £5, to be paid to said EDWARD at the feast aforesaid. To ANN FREEMAN daughter of JOHN FREEMAN 50s. and to MARTHA FREEMAN, sister of ANN, 50s., to be paid to said JOHN FREEMAN at the feast aforesaid. To SARAH COCK my daughter-in-law £5 to be paid at the feast aforesaid. To ALICE SMITH daughter of JOHN SMITH 20s. to be paid to said JOHN SMITH at the day aforesaid. To the poor of Shotley £6 to be paid to the minister and churchwardens for the time being, and by them to be distributed thus -- at Candlemas next 40s, at Candlemas come twelvemonth 40s., and at Candlemas 1632 40s. I give £10 to be paid at New-year's Day come twelvemonth to the minister and churchwardens for the time being, and by them to be lent out for 3 years to some young beginner in Shotley that is godly and provident, he laying in security to pay it again at the 3 years' end to said minister and churchwardens, and then they to lend it to some other young beginner, and so to remain for ever lent out by 3 years successively to some young beginner in Shotley, he laying in security as aforesaid. To the poor of Chempton [Chelmondiston] 20s. to be paid within one month of my decease; and to the poor of Erwarton 20s. to be paid within one month of my decease. To my cousin ANDREWES a fat wether to make merry with his neighbours, and to Mr THOMAS CARTER, rector of Shotley another fat wether, the best they can find, to make merry with his neighbours. To MARGARET my wife £40. I nominate said MARGARET and JOHN WRIGHT my son-in-law executors to see my body decently disposed, and all my goods unbequeathed (my funeral and probate charges discharged) I give to the said MARGARET and JOHN to be equally parted. Postscript: I give Sir JOHN FELTON 20s. to be paid at the feast of St. Michael next ensuing the date abovewritten. Witnesses: to will and postscript THOMAS CARTER, JOHN COLE, GEORGE WHITTOCK. Pr. at Ipswich 3 July 1630.

R(W) EDWARD CLEMENTS of Ipswich, clothworker. (140)
23 July 1630

Sick. Whereas ROBERT KNAP of Ipswich, merchant, stand bound by one obligation unto me in the sum of £120 which have been long due, now said ROBERT KNAPPE his heirs and executors shall be freely acquitted from said obligation upon condition that said ROBERT KNAPPE together with SAMUEL KNAPPE his son shall within one month after my decease become bound by obligation in the sum of £160 unto my wife MARY CLEMENTS with condition for the payment of £10 yearly to her during the term of her life, £5 every half year. And if ROBERT KNAPPE and SAMUEL KNAPP, or either of them, shall refuse to become bound, then the said obligation shall stand and remain in force to the use of my exor. And my exor. shall within 2 months after my decease, instead of ROBERT KNAPP's bond, become bound with one sufficient security in £160 to my wife, with the condition of the payment of £10 yearly for life, £5 every half year. To MARY KNAPP and ELIZABETH KNAPP daughters of ROBERT KNAPP, and to the daughter of SAMUEL KNAPP my silver cup and 11 silver spoons and 3 tipped pots, equally divided, after my wife's decease. To GEORGE ABBOTT of St. Clements my best laced ruff. To WILLIAM BOYCOTT my stiletto with the knives and bodkin. To my servant JOHN WATSON my blue cloak and to JOHN PRESSON my old cloak. To ANN DAMMERON wife of EDMUND DAMMERON one coloured embroidered stuff petticoat. To EDWARD ASTON £20 within 2 months after my decease. To my brother JOHN CLEMENTS £5 within 6 months. To my wife such necessary household stuff and implements as she shall think fit to take to use the same during her life, and after her decease I give the same to my exor. To my friend AMBROSE EVERED of Glemsford, clothier, all my goods chattels and implements stuff of household debts ready money not heretofore given, and I nominate him sole exor. Witnesses: CHRISTOPHER WILKINSON, JAMES SMITH, ROBERT CLARKE. Pr. at Ipswich 28 July 1630.

R(W) THOMAS GOODALL of Earl Soham, gentleman. (141)
13 November 1629

Whereas MARTHA my wife and THOMAS my eldest son were by conveyance made upon my marriage with the said MARTHA formerly provided for, and as yet no provision made for some other of my children, now I do give all my close containing by estimation 5 acres which my late father purchased of JOHN COOKE, then of Creeting, unto MARTHA my eldest daughter and her heirs upon condition that if the said THOMAS my son his heirs or assigns shall pay £30 at my mansion house in Earl Stonham as followeth, viz. to the said MARTHA my daughter at 19 years if she be living -- and if she be dead then to 2 other of my daughters equally between them, that is to ELIZABETH and MARY or such of them as be living, at such time and place as MARTHA should have received the same -- that then the gift of the said close to MARTHA to be void, and then the close shall remain unto THOMAS my son and his heirs. I give my close called Wheatfield containing by estimation [blank] acres unto MARY my said daughter and her heirs, on condition that if the said THOMAS his heirs or assigns shall pay £100 at my mansion house to MARY my daughter at age 19 if living -- and if she die before, then equally unto MARTHA and ELIZABETH or the survivor of them at such time and place as the said MARY should have had the same -- that then after such payment the gift of Wheatfield close to said MARY to be void, and then the same shall remain to THOMAS my son and his heirs for ever. I give to said MARTHA my daughter £60 at her age of 19 if living, and if she die before then the same shall be paid to ELIZABETH and MARY my other 2 daughters or the survivor of them at such time as the said MARTHA should have received the same. To my friends, viz. my brother FENTON and his wife and my brother GRIMWOOD and his wife and my two brothers EDMUND and JOHN GOODALL, my aunt STUBBS my brother HARRISON and his wife and my sister EDWARDS, WILLIAM BLOMEFIELD of Little Stonham and his wife and to every of them 10s. to buy rings in remembrance of me. MARTHA my wife shall have the education and bringing up of my 2 sons JOHN and EDMUND and of MARTHA, ELIZABETH and MARY my 3 daughters in the fear of God and with meat and drink apparel and learning meet for their degree and capacities until they attain their several respective ages of [blank] years if they will so long be ruled by her, and the better to enable her to pay my debts and legacies and perform this will I give her all my movables except only one lease made unto me of the tenement Reves in Earl Stonham, with all the lands belonging sometime holden by copy of the manor of Earl Stonham for the term of 40 years from the feast of St. Michael next after the date of said lease bearing date 6th April 1627, which lease taketh no effect till the feast of St. Michael 1637 by reason of a former lease thereof made by GEORGE HARYSON late of Little Stonham, gent, unto THOMAS BROMYLE then of Earl Stonham for the term of 25 years, which lease still in being and endeth not until the feast of St. Michael 1637. The said MARTHA and her assigns shall have and enjoy all the said lands and tenements so demised as aforesaid during the term of 4 years immediately ensuing from the expiration of the former recited lease made unto THOMAS BROMLY; and I give the remainder of the said term of 40 years after the end of the said term of 4 years to my 2 sons JOHN and EDMUND. I nominate the said MARTHA my sole exrx., paying my debts and legacies and seeing my body decently buried. [No witnesses are named.] Pr. at Ipswich 30 July 1630. [The blanks indicated above occur in both the file copy and the register copy of the will.]

R(W) RACHEL SCRUTTON (X) of Ipswich, widow. (142)
19 April 1630

To my daughter JUDITH CRANE in satisfaction of all such sums of money due unto her from me, 4 score pounds to be paid within one month of my decease. Whereas JOHN CRANE my son hath mortgaged a certain meadow in Stoke next Ipswich, near Handford bridge, containing by estimation 5 roods, which is forfeited to me, I give the same piece to said JOHN on condition that he or his heirs do pay to my daughter JUDITH 4 score pounds as aforesaid and every other legacy herein mentioned; and if JOHN or his heirs refuse to pay said sum to my daughter then I give the same piece of meadow unto her and her heirs for ever, and then my daughter to have only in money £50, to be paid by my exor. To my son THOMAS SCRUTTON the messuage wherein WILLIAM HUNTING and NICHOLAS HUDSON dwell, situate in Walton, to have with all the lands appertaining, on condition that he shall within one month after he has attained the age of 21 make sale and deliver to my exor. an absolute acquittance of all demands due from me unto him, unto the time of the making thereof, or until the accomplishment of his said age. But if he shall refuse and not deliver such an acquittance then the same messuage or tenement with appurtenancies I give to my son JOHN CRANE and his heirs for ever, provided that if he shall refuse to accept the execution of this will then my other exor. hereafter named shall take the profits and revenues of the same messuage until such time as my debts and legacies be paid. I give my daughter ANN my riding suit and furniture; all the rest of my apparel both linen and woolen I give to my 3 daughters RACHEL, ANN and JUDITH equally to be parted among them. To my grandchild JOHN CRANE my silver and gilt salt cellar, and to my grandchild FRANCES SCRUTTON my great silver can with a cover. All the rest of my household plate and stuff I give to my son JOHN CRANE and to ANN CRANE and JUDITH CRANE and THOMAS SCRUTTON equally to be parted among them. To the poor of Stoke next Ipswich 20s.; the poor of the parish of St. Margaret 10s. My exor. shall have the education and bringing up of my son THOMAS until he shall be 21, and in the meantime my exor. to receive the profits of all the lands and tenements bequeathed to him. All the rest of my movable goods and chattels debts and ready money, my debts and legacies being discharged and probate of this will defrayed, I give to JOHN CRANE my son whom I make exor. provided that he shall forthwith after my decease, and before he shall intermeddle with any of my movables, enter into bond in the penal sum of £300 unto JOHN DEYNES of Coddenham my brother, with condition underwritten for the sure payment of all my aforesaid legacies and the true performance of this will, the which if he shall refuse then I give all the legacies herein bequeathed to my son JOHN unto JOHN DEYNES my brother, and then the said JOHN DEYNES to be sole exor. Witnesses: WILLIAM SEELI, MARY WALKER (X), and EDMUND MYLES, notary public. Pr. at Ipswich 30 July 1630.

R(W) ROBERT JUDYE (X) senior of Henstead, yeoman. (143)
16 May 1628

To be buried in Henstead churchyard. To ROBERT JUDYE my kinsman my houses lands and tenements in Wrentham during the life of said ROBERT; and until the Michaelmas next after his decease unto the exors. of said ROBERT, on condition that he shall keep said houses in good order during his life and that his exors. shall leave them in sufficient reparations; and at the Michaelmas after decease of said ROBERT JUDYE I give all the said houses &c to ROBERT JUDYE the son of NICHOLAS JUDY and his heirs for ever. To NICHOLAS JUDYE my kinsman all my lands and grounds in Benacre, provided that it shall be lawful for said ROBERT JUDYE my kinsman to take and have convenient timber for needful reparations for my houses at Wrentham, formerly given unto him for term of his life, out of my grounds at Benacre formerly given to NICHOLAS JUDYE and his heirs. To ELIZABETH JUDYE daughter of NICHOLAS JUDYE 1 bed 1 bolster 1 covering 2 blankets 2 pair sheets 1 great chest in the chamber 1 coffer 2 small chairs 1 pillow to be delivered to her presently after my decease, provided that if said ELIZABETH shall depart this life before she shall have received these legacies then they shall be given unto SUSAN her sister. The rest of my goods and chattels ready money and implements of household I give to ROBERT JUDYE my kinsman whom I make sole exor. Witnesses: THOMAS ALDRED and RA. TURNER. Pr. at Beccles 24 July 1630.

R(W) EDMUND PEITE (X) of Preston. 1 May 1629 (144)

Sick. To my eldest son THOMAS my best doublet and breeches to be delivered to him within one month of my decease. To my wife SARAH PEIT all my movable goods and chatells towards the maintenance of herself, the discharging of my debts and bringing up of my children. I nominate my wife exrx. Witnesses: EDWARD LANGLY, EMMY BIRDE (X). Pr. at Ipswich 9 July 1630.

R(W) JOHN SYMONS (X) of Dunwich. 2 January 1629/30 (145)

Sick. To my friend ROBERT PAKE the pastor of this place, to the end he may certify himself, a certain sum of money which I owe him by bond, and also upon confidence that he will be careful to get in such moneys as are coming unto me, and to pay my debts and in hope that he will stand my good friend to supply and relieve any wants during the time of my sickness, and I make said ROBERT PAKE exor., entreating him to give somewhat of my estate unto MARY PREMUTT, widow, and to ANN SYMONS my brother's daughter or to one of them if any such shall be left and remaining after payment of my debts and other necessary things discharged. Witnesses: PHILIP KNIGHTS, ANTHONY RISBIE (X), JOHN REDWELL (X). Pr. at Yoxford 7 July 1630.

R(W) ROBERT ALDOWES senior of Fressingfield. 1 June 1628 (146)

To JAMES ALDOWES my son my messuage or tenement with appurtenancies in Fressingfield wherein I now inhabit, and all the lands and tenements being freehold in Fressingfield to the said messuage appertaining, to enter within 40 days of my decease, to hold to him and his exors. or assigns during the term of 3 score years, upon condition that he or they shall pay unto ANN ALDOWES my daughter her exors. or assigns at the south porch of the parish church of Fressingfield £100 within one year after my decease; and if the said JAMES his heirs or assigns shall default payment then the said lands &c shall remain to the said ANN for ever. But if he or they shall truly pay the £100 in the manner limited then I will give all my said lands &c to JAMES my son and his heirs and assigns for ever. My daughter ANN shall, upon receipt of the said sum, deliver to JAMES his heirs exors. or assigns a writing acknowledging receipt. To the said JAMES and his heirs all my lands and tenements being copyhold in Fressingfield and Stradbroke to hold to him and his heirs for ever, and he to enter the same within 40 days after my decease. The said ANN shall have the use of all my said lands and tenements as well freehold as copyhold from after my decease until the end of the said 40 days and the revenue thereof arising in the meantime, doing no estripment or waste, and discharging all the rents due for the premises during the same time. To the said ANN all my goods and chattels movable and not movable, plate household stuff corn cattle hay swine poultry bedding linen brass pewter dairy vessels implements and utensils of what nature condition or quality soever they be, the same to be taken by her presently after my decease. To ANN ALDRED my kinswoman 40s. to be paid within one year after my decease. I constitute JAMES ALDOWES my son sole exor., and JOHN ALDOWES my brother supervisor, to whom 10s. for his pains, to be paid presently after my decease. Witnesses: JOHN ALDOWES, NATHAN ALDOWES, FR. SANDCROFT. Memo the words of the second and third side blotted out before the sealing hereof in the presence of JAMES ALDOWES, NATHAN ALDOWES, JOHN ALDOWES. Pr. at Beccles 10 Aug. 1630.

R(W) WILLIAM SPINCKE of Capel. 23 April 1630 (147)

Sick. I give all my lands and tenements in Capel to ELIZABETH my wife during her life, and out of the profits of them she may have wherewith to keep herself and my two children. When my son JOHN shall be 21 ELIZABETH shall give him yearly £4, viz. 40s. each half year. To my daughter ELIZABETH 3 score pounds to be paid within one month after she shall accomplish her age of 20 years. After the decease of ELIZABETH my wife all my lands and houses shall be my son JOHN's, to whom I give them with this condition -- that one year after my decease, if he be living and doth possess my said houses and lands, that he pay my daughter ELIZABETH £20, and for default of payment ELIZABETH shall have that house and tenement with the land thereto belonging upon Capel Green wherewith dwelleth the widow WOODDURE, for ever. If both my children die without issue of their body lawfully begotten living, then I bequeath all my said lands &c to ELIZABETH my wife absolutely. To the poor of Butley 6s. 8d. to be divided by the churchwardens where most necessary. To the poor of Capel 6s. 8d. to be distributed by my exor. where most necessary. The rest of my goods I give to my wife whom I make exrx. Witnesses: EDWARD OLIVER, THOMAS FENER. Pr. at Wickham 8 July 1630.

W(R) ELIZABETH BUCKENHAM of Dunwich St. Peters, singleman (N). [no date] (148)

To MARY CRISPE and ELIZABETH CRISPE the children of THOMAS CRISPE all her sheep except one which she gave to her goddaughter, the daughter of one AYERS. All the rest of her goods and estate she bequeathed to the said children of THOMAS CRISPE, affirming that she had got her estate in the house of THOMAS CRISPE and ROGER CRISPE his father, and therefore she would leave it to the said children. Witnesses: SUSAN BIRKETT and ELIZABETH the wife of THOMAS CRISPE. At Beccles on 2 Oct. 1630. Admon. to EDWARD ODIERNE of Dunwich during the minority of MARY CRISPE and ELIZABETH CRISPE. [But see also the immediately following will.]

W(R) ELIZABETH BUCKENHAM of Dunwich, singlewoman (N). 26 September 1630 (149)

To RICHARD BUCKENHAM her kinsman 20s. All the rest of her goods and chattels ready money and debts she gave to JOHN BUCKENHAM of Ipswich shoemaker, her kinsman, excepting 2 lambs which she gave to 2 of her godchildren, 1 to LAUNCE REVE and 1 to SUSAN DARKETT, and she named said JOHN BUCKENHAM sole exor. Witnesses: ELIZABETH DENERELL wid. and MARY EYRES wid. Pr. at Ipswich 4 Oct 1630. [But see also the immediately preceeding will.]

A. ELIZABETH BUCKENHAM of Dunwich St. Peter, singlewoman. 2 October 1630 (150)

Administration of the goods mentioned in her nuncupative will annexed was issued to EDWARD ODIERNE during the minority of MARY CRISPE and ELIZABETH CRISPE the natural and lawful children of the deceased.

W(R) ROBERT BLOSSE (X) of Raydon, yeoman. 24 July 1630 (151)

Weak. To THOMAS BLOSSE my son my house called Cockrells with the cistern and all the houses barns stables gardens orchards and lands in Raydon or elsewhere, and to the heirs of his body lawfully begotten. If THOMAS die without a surviving child then I give said houses and lands to my son EDMUND and the heirs of his body lawfully begotten, and if he shall die without a child surviving then I give the lands to my son PETER and the heirs of his body lawfully begotten, and if he die without a child surviving I give them to my daughters ANN and MARY and to their heirs for ever. Neither my son THOMAS nor any one else for him shall enter upon my house or lands until Michaelmas next. To my son THOMAS £10 and my best cloak jerkin doublet and breeches. To my daughter the wife of THOMAS my son the coloured stuff gown which was my late wife's. To my son EDMUND my houses and the grounds belonging which I bought of HENRY HADLOCK, lying in Raydon, and if he die without heir of his body or heir surviving, then I give it to my son PETER; and if he die without heir of his body or heir surviving, then I give it to my son THOMAS for ever. To my son EDMUND £40 and my riding coat and 1 suit of clothes, the best next that I gave my son THOMAS. To my son PETER £40 and my other riding coat and one suit of clothes, the best next that I gave my son EDMUND. To my daughter ANN STEPHENS £15. To ANN STEPHENS my goddaughter and grandchild £5. To the 2 children of my son-in-law SAMUEL STEPHENS £5, viz. 50s. to his son and 50s. to his daughter, to be paid to SAMUEL STEPHENS within 2 months after my death to the benefit of his children; provided that if he live to enjoy the legacies to his children he shall enter bond to my exor. for to repay the legacy to his children when they be 21; and if my daughter ANN survive her husband SAMUEL, he dying before the receipt of his children's legacies, then she shall receive the legacies bequeathed to her children and enter into such bond as her husband is before enjoined. If my daughter ANN STEPHENS die before the payment of the legacy of £10 before bequeathed to her, notwithstanding it shall be paid to him as a legacy which I gave unto both or either of them. More to my daughter ANN STEPHENS 1 cloth gown and a russet petticoat with 3 laces which were belonging to my late wife. To my daughter MARY £35 and my late wife's her mother's wearing linen; and MARY shall give to my son THOMAS BLOSSE's wife a ruff that was my wife's and 1 shift of head-linen; also MARY shall give to my daughter ANN STEPHENS one ruff that was my wife's and 1 shift of head-linen. More to my daughter MARY, my late wife's black stuff gown and the murrey cloth petticoat. I will the legacies shall be paid within 2 months after my decease. To the poor of Raydon 40s. to be distributed at the discretion of my exor. the Sabbath after my burial. To my pastor and friend Mr FRANCIS QUARLES 2 two-and-twenty shilling pieces. I give one two-and-twenty shilling piece to my friend and exor. ROBERT PLAMPINE of Raydon whom I desire to undertake the trust I commit unto him for the good of my children. My exor. shall pay such debts as I shall owe and he shall enter upon my houses and lands &c at my death and use them with the benefit thereof until Michaelmas next ensuing, and to be countable for the profits to the performance of this will. The rest of my goods and chattels leases money furniture of household with all debts or surplus which my exor. shall receive shall be employed to the payment of my debts and charges arising about the performance and probate of this will and my funeral expenses, if my said goods shall thereto extend; but if they will not, then there shall be a proportionable abatement made out of the legacies unto my children. But if my goods and chattels amount to more than is before bequeathed, legacies performed and debts paid, the overplus shall accrue to my sons EDMUND and PETER to be shared between them. I ordain my friend ROBERT PAMPLINE of Raydon my sole exor. Witnesses: FRANCIS QUARLES, SAMUEL APPLETON, EDWARD GLANDFIELD. Pr. at Ipswich 31 Aug. 1630.

W(R) RICHARD EMANS of Walberswick (N). [no date] (152)

About a week before his death gave to ELIZABETH his wife and HENRY SIER his son-in-law all his goods to be equally divided. Witnesses: LAURENCE WINCOPP and THOMAS [?ERICE or ?ERNE]. Pr. at Yoxford 28 July 1630. Admon. to ELIZABETH the relict and JOHN SCIER, general legatees.

R(W) JOHN COWBRIDGE of Aldeburgh, tailor (N). (153)
20 July 1630

Sick. All movable goods chattels and utensils of household stuff to LUKE COWBRIDGE my son. My debts to be paid out of my goods and the remainder put to the best use for my son LUKE. Witnesses: ELIZABETH USHER (X) the wife of RICHARD USHER and JOAN CUTTING wid. Pr. at Yoxford 20 Sept. 1630. Admon. to JOHN HARRISON during the minority of LUKE COWBRIDGE.

R(W) JEREMY FISKE of Laxfield, yeoman. (154)
22 August 1630

Sick. To be buried in Laxfield churchyard. To JOHN COCK the eldest son of PETER COCK my son-in-law all my messuage or tenement in Titteshall, Norfolk, as well freehold as copyhold with all the land to the same belonging, now in the tenure or occupation of one LOTER. To ANN COCK daughter of said PETER COCK my messuage or tenement with appurtenances now in tenure or occupation of WILLIAM SMITH; and the said ANN shall pay her sister ELIZABETH COCK £10 presently after my decease. To PETER COCK the son of PETER COCK aforesaid my messuage or tenement with appurtenances as well freehold as copyhold in Laxfield, with all the lands and tenements belonging, now in the tenure of me, the lands and tenements called Craiches only excepted. To JEREMY COCK the son of PETER COCK my son-in-law all my messuage or tenement with appurtenances called Craiches and Vaces in Dennington and Laxfield, with all the lands and tenements belonging, now in the tenure or occupation of me. TO MARGARET RACKHAM my servant the house called Copphall with the yards &c belonging, now in the occupation of JAMES DALLINGER. To ALICE COCK daughter of said PETER COCK £10 to be paid by my exor. immediately after my decease. To MARY COCK daughter of said PETER COCK £10 to be paid likewise. I make JOHN COCK son of PETER COCK my son-in-law sole exor of my will, hoping that he will perform the same and take my debts and pay my debts and bring my body in decent order to the ground. I ordain PETER COCK to be supervisor. All the rest of my goods unbequeathed I give to my exor. Witness: JOHN COCKE. Pr. at Stradbroke 15 Sept. 1630.

R(W) MARGERY GOODWINGE of St. Margarets Ipswich, widow (N). 31 July 1630 (155)

I give the £10 that GRYMEWOOD of Aldham near Hadleigh owe me to my son-in-law TASTER. The £10 which ANTHONY KIRRICH owe me I do give £5 thereof to his wife and the other £5 shall be bestowed upon my burial. I give the eldest daughter of my son JOHN GOODING of Hadleigh £7 which ROBERT MOORE of Nettlestead oweth me. The £3 which JOHN WENNELL of Barham oweth me I will be divided between my 4 daughters to buy them rings. I nominate WILLIAM GOODING my son to be my exor. and he shall deliver to ALICE BEARD wife of ROBERT BEARD 40s., 1 coverlet and my best hat. All other movable goods to be equally divided between my 2 sons. Witnesses: ANTHONY AYLEMER, EDWARD DAYNES. Pr. at Ipswich 24 Sept. 1630.

R(W) ROBERT GEYTON of Easton, yeoman. 11 June 1630 (156)

So much of my movables as will amount to the payment of my debts to be sold by my exor. and my creditors all satisfied and the charges about my burial be discharged, and all the rest I give to my exors. whom I do nominate MARGARET my wife and ROBERT the elder my son, to be equally divided between them. Witnesses: WILLIAM MORGAN, STEPHEN PARKER, JOAN GOARE. Pr. at Wickham 23 Sept. 1630.

R(W) MARGERY KERICH of Saxtead, widow (N). [blank] May 1630 (157)

Sick. I give all my coffers and linen in them to the children of THOMAS KERICH my son. Witnesses: PHILIP RUMSEY and WILLIAM REVANS. Pr. 26 May 1630. Admon. to THOMAS KERICH, son of testator.

R(W) GREGORY NOTTINGHAM of Alderton (N). 1 September 1630 (158)

Sick. To MARGARET my wife all the household stuff which was hers before our inter-marriage, and the use of all my linen pewter and brass and other household stuff during her life, and after her decease I give the same unto such of my children as shall be then living, to be equally divided. To my said wife 4 cows and 1 horse, she to make her choice, and all my hemp and swine and poultry, and as much corn as shall serve for her expense for 1 year, and £10. To my son GREGORY at the age of 21; to my son JOHN £40 at 21; to my 3 daughters ROSE, MARGARET and MARY £20 apiece at 21, with benefit of survivorship. To my daughter-in-law ANN BEECH £5 at 21. If my stock shall amount to more than I have bequeathed (my debts paid) the money so arising to be equally divided between the said children, but if my stock shall not so much arise as I have bequeathed then there shall be an equal and proportionable abatement of their legacies. My white suckling colt to JOHN FINCH my nephew. And my goods shall be sold and my debts paid and the money arising put out to the best profit for the use of my said children. I entreat my brothers GEOFFERY HAUGHFEN and JOHN ARMIGER to have the ordering and disposing of them. I desire my brother JOHN FINCH and JOHN HARRISON to be aiding my said brothers in the advancement of the sale of my goods. Witnesses: JOHN ARMIGER, GEOFFERY HAUGHFEN, URSULA ARMIGER and MARGARET the relict. Pr. at Wickham 23 Sept. 1630. Admon. to GEOFFERY HAUGHFEN and JOHN ARMIGER.

R(W) KATHARINE POLEY of Fressingfield, spinster (X). (159)
9 November 1629

10s. to be paid for the preaching of a sermon at my burial. To ROSE BROWNE of Chatfield [recte Cratfield?] singlewoman 20s. to be paid within 28 days after my decease in the south porch of the church in Fressingfield. To the poor of Fressingfield £3, viz. 20s. within 1 year and 20s. yearly till £3 be paid. Residue of my movable goods and chattels to mine exor. towards paying my debts, proving this will and discharging my burial rites. I nominate SIMON BARBOR the elder of Fressingfield sole exor., and in case he should not within 1 month prove my will then I nominate SIMON BARBER the younger my sole exor. Witnesses: JOHN BARBER and ROBERT GODFREY. Pr. at Flixton 30 Aug. 1630.

R(W) JOAN PAYNE of Ufford, widow. 23 April 1627 (160)

To GEOFFERY GOOCH my kinsman 20s. to be paid within 3 months. To MARY BATE my kinswoman and goddaughter my bed I lie on and bedstead as it standeth and my cupboard in the hall. The rest of my goods and chattels household stuff money and all that I have whatsoever to the said MARY BATE and JANE BATE and ANN BATE and JOHN BATE my kinswomen and kinsman, the son and daughters of JOHN BATE and CECILIA BATE my brother-in-law and my sister, equally divided. I make said JOHN BATE and CECILIA BATE co-exors. Witnesses: WILLIAM PEMBERTON and TRANT THOMAS. Pr. at Wiskham 23 Sept. 1630. Admon. to JOHN BATE with power reserved for CECILIA BATE.

W(R) ERASMUS READ (X) of Burgh Castle, husbandman. (161)
26 August 1630

To my son ERASMUS READ my house and ground with all appurtenances belonging within one year, on condition that he quietly permit my now wife to dwell in the little backhouse and give her half the profits which shall arise out of the grounds yearly during her life, and then to remain wholly to him and his heirs. If ERASMUS depart this life without heirs male of his body lawfully begotten then my said house &c shall go to my son ANTHONY READ and his heirs, he performing the same condition and paying those legacies which shall be left unpaid at the death of my son ERASMUS. To my son ANTHONY a little chest immediately after the decease of my wife. To my son EDMUND READ £3 to be paid by ERASMUS within 4 years. To my son WILLIAM £3 to be paid by ERASMUS within 6 years. To my son JOHN £3 to be paid by ERASMUS within 8 years. To my daughter ALICE a trundle bed as it standeth to have it presently after the decease of my wife. But if my son ERASMUS will give her 20s. he shall have the cupboard. Whatsoever I have not bequeathed I give to my exrx. whom I ordain my wife. For her assistance I entreat my brother WILLIAM NEWTON to be supervisor. Witnesses: CHRISTOPHER RISING (X), WILLIAM NEWTON (X), EDWARD REVE (X). Pr. at Beccles 17 Dec. 1630.

W(R) JOHN TOCKLEY of Cransford. [no date] (162)

To THOMAS TOCKLEY my son my horse-mill at Cransford with all other my goods at that house. To ELIZABETH my wife my great chest in the parlour where I now dwell with a box upon my parlour chamber. To ANN GILLIONS my wife's daughter a posted bedstead now standing upon the shop chamber. To my son THOMAS my lease at Darsham with all my tools. I give my wife in the same house the parlour with the shop chamber for her dwelling whilst the Michaelmas 12-month after my death. The lands I do dwell in should be occupied by my son and wife to the best advantage whilst Michaelmas, and then out of my goods all my debts to be paid except £10 which is a legacy which my land at Cransford stands bound for, and that shall be my son's debt alone. The remainder of my goods, my debts being taken away, shall be divided equally between my son and my wife and my wife's daughter. To RICHARD GILLIANS all my wearing apparel except my best cloak. I ordain my son THOMAS my sole exor. Witnesses: ROBERT BARFAT and EDMUND WEEDINGES. Pr. at Yoxford 28 July 1630.

R(W) GILES WRIGHT of Bedingfield (N). (163)
Wednesday 4 August 1630

Sick. All that I have to MARGARET my wife. Witnesses: Mr JOHN COTTESFORD, clerk, and MARGARET ALLAM, wid. Admon. to relict 9 Aug. 1630.

R(W) JOAN WOLNOUGH of Fressingfield, widow. 27 April 1625 (164)

Sick. To my son THOMAS WOLNOUGH the trundle bed in the parlour chamber, the oldest feather-bed pillow and pillowbier, the best transom or bolster in the parlour, 1 blanket there in the parlour and a coverlet in the parlour chamber, a pair of my best sheets, a table in the parlour chamber, an old chair in the hall, 2 buffet stools the biggest being in the parlour and a lesser standing in the parlour chamber, the newest chair, 2 cushions, the best old blanket of the three, a plate in the parlour for a candle stick. To MARGARET WOLNOUGH wife of my said son THOMAS my new undercoat with my cloak, 2 milk bowls in the dairy, an old coffer upon the parlour chamber. To WILLIAM RICHARDSON my son-in-law the bedstead with the hangings standing in the parlour, the new feather-bed in the little chamber with the old bolster there, 2 pillows, 2 milk bowls in the dairy, a kettle, a new chair, 3 buffet stools, a new flesh-tub, a new ale vessel. To SARAH RICHARDSON my daughter the newest coffer in the parlour chamber with all that is within it, my gown, my blue petticoat. To my son JOHN the cupboard in the hall with a table there. To my son SIMON a pair of sheets. To my daughter LYDIA my stammel petticoat. All the bequests to be delivered presently after my decease. I nominate THOMAS WOLNOUGH my said son sole exor. to pay my debts and receive my debts and bring my body to the ground, discharging my funeral expenses. Witnesses: EDWARD PETTEFER and ROBERT GODFERY. Pr. at Ipswich 25 Aug. 1630.

R(W) ROBERT BISHOPP of Yoxford (N). August 1630 (165)

Sick. All the goods which I have to ELIZABETH my wife whom I appoint my exrx., except 40s. which I give to REYNOLD BISHOPP of Peasenhall my nephew, and 20s. to my kinsman JOHN BISHOPP, both to be paid by her within a year after my decease. Witnesses: THOMAS BLOCK, clerk, and JOHN FOX, gent. Pr. at Yoxford 22 Sept. 1630.

R(W) KATHARINE EBBES of Dunwich, widow. 1 May 1629 (166)

Weak. To JOHN EBBS my son or his heirs all my messuage or tenement in which I dwell. To JAMES EBBS son of said JOHN EBBS the long table in the hall with the great cupboard in the parlour. To PRUDENCE my daughter, the now wife of MICHAEL HARMON, my messuage or tenement wherein THOMAS CROSSE and the widow NEWSON now dwell, with the orchards gardens yards and well belonging, situate in St. James Street in Dunwich, which I purchased of JOHN HILL, to hold from the day of my death for her life, she keeping the same in good tenentable reparations; and after her decease I give the same to EDMUND TOOKLIE my grandchild, he paying within 6 months after he shall enjoy the same 20s. to WALTER WARD's eldest son, being grandchild's child, and 20s. to said WALTER WARD's eldest daughter. And if EDMUND TOOKLY die without issue then I give said messuage or tenement to MARY EBBS and ELIZABETH EBBS and their heirs forever. To MARY EBBS and ELIZABETH EBBS my grandchildren, my pightle of lands in Milgate street which I lately purchased of WILLIAM BULBROKE, to hold to them and the issue of their bodies lawfully begotten, provided they pay to PRUDENCE my daughter 14s. a year for life, 7s. every half year, to begin within 6 months of my decease; and for default of such payment I give the pightle to my said daughter and her heirs until she be paid the 14s. yearly. And if the said MARY or ELIZABETH shall sell either of their parts my desire is the one should buy the other's part and have it 10s.

better cheap than a stranger. To SUSAN wife of WILLIAM FARROW my grandchild my lesser cupboard standing in the hall where I dwell, and my reed coffer in the chamber, and 1 new blanket, all to be given him presently after my decease. If said SUSAN die before she receive my gift then all the aforesaid things shall remain to her eldest daughter living. To JOHN EBBS the eldest son of my son JOHN 1 great brass cauldron to be delivered presently after my decease. To the eldest son of WALTER WARD 1 brass pot, 1 pair sheets, 1 candlestick, immediately after my decease. To JAMES WARD my grandchild 40s. and 1 feather transom, six weeks after my burial. To EDMUND WARD my grandchild £3, 1 candlestick, 1 pair sheets, 1 pewter platter and a feather pillow, all within six weeks of my burial. To MICHAEL WARD my grandchild £12 within 1 month. To ELIZABETH EBBS my grandchild 1 chest of joiner's work, 1 feather-bed next the best, 1 new blanket, 1 great chafing dish, 1 candlestick, 1 short joined form, 2 silver spoons, 1 long fustian pillow, 1 livery bedstead termined with the half-head, 1 joined stool 1 pewter platter 1 trundle bedstead clasped with iron, all presently after my decease. To KATARINE PEEKE my kinswoman 1 black petticoat. To MARY EBBS my grandchild my greater chair and 1 tipped pot and the keep which hang in the hall in which I now dwell; also my posted bedstead in the hall with the curtain and curtain rods and one settle to it belonging; also my best feather bolster 1 flock bed my best pair of blankets, being blue and white, 1 great brass pot with a broken verge, 1 dansk chest standing upon the chamber over the parlour, 1 joined form 1 child's chair, my best covering of white and blue, 1 great brazen mortar and pestle, 2 pair sheets 2 silver spoons my best trundle bedstead 1 great kettle 1 little square table standing in the hall 3 buffet stools standing in the hall 2 great pewter platters my best transom 1 long board cloth stitched at one of the ends thereof. To my 2 grandchildren MARY EBBS and ELIZABETH EBBS my coffer of linen standing at my chamber door, to be equally divided, with benefit of survivorship. To my grandchild ELIZABETH EBBS 1 great brass pot 2 buffet stools 1 coverlet of a green colour. More to WALTER WARD's daughter my grandchild's daughter 1 little brass pot 1 pair sheets at 21. All the rest of my goods and chattels household stuff and implements plate jewels ready money bonds bills &c I give to JOHN EBBS my son and MARY EBBS my grandchild presently after my decease, paying my debts and discharging my funeral expenses and performing this will so fare forth as on their part is to be performed and done. I make my said son JOHN EBBS and MARY EBBS my grandchild exors., and my grandchild THOMAS TOOKLY supervisor, for whose pains I bequeath 5s. Witnesses: NICHOLAS ELLIS, WILLIAM BIRD, and JOHN LING snr. Pr. at Yoxford 22 Sept. 1630. Admon. to JOHN EBBS with power reserved for MARY EBBS.

W(R) ROSE ALDES (X)(N). 10 March [missing] (167)

To her cousin ESTHER HAWES of Sutton one ewe and 10s. and a coffer. To ROBERT BRIGHTWELL's daughter one sheep and 10s. To ROBERT BRIGHTWELL 20s. being in the hands of WILLIAM FOXE, and all her other things to pay for keeping her in her sickness and to bring her body decently to the ground. Witnesses: RICHARD HOUSDEN, ROBERT FERMAN, JOHN ARCHER. Pr. at Wickham 23 Sept. 1630. Admon. to said ROBERT.

R(W) JOHN BEALE of Thorpe, yeoman. 1 June 1620 (168)

Sick. To MARGARET BEALE my wife all my goods and chattels and implements of household for ever, and all my houses and lands in Thorpe during her life. After her decease I give my said houses and lands to ANN BEALE my daughter and her heirs for ever, on condition that she pay to FRANCES BEALE her sister £30 within 1 month after FRANCES shall be 21; and if ANN shall refuse, then I give all the said houses and lands, after the decease of my wife, to FRANCES BEALE my daughter for ever, on condition that she pay to ANN her sister £30 within one month after FRANCES shall have the houses and lands; and if FRANCES shall refuse to pay the £30 then the said houses &c shall remain to the said ANN and FRANCES to be equally divided between them and their heirs. I ordain MARGARET BEALE my wife sole exrx. Witnesses: RICHARD POOTIE, WILLIAM MILLS (X). The said JOHN BEALE did surrender all his houses and lands in Thorpe into the hands of the lord of the manor this 15 June 1630, by the hands of JOHN MILLS, copyhold tenant of this manor, in the presence of JOHN CLARKE a like tenant, to the use of his last will. Pr. at Yoxford 22 Sept. 1630.

W(R) EDWARD BRAME (X) of North Cove, yeoman. (169)
20 March 1627/8

To WILLIAM BRAME son of PETER BRAME my brother £4; to THOMAS son of said PETER £4; to ROGER son of said PETER £4; to MARGERY BRAME daughter of said PETER £4; to KATHARINE HAWKER wife of FRANCIS HAWKER, one of the daughters of said PETER, one pair of sheets worth 6s. 8d. -- all to be paid within one year after my decease, with benefit of survivorship. To REYNOLD BRAME son of JOHN BRAME my brother 20s.; to BENJAMIN son of said JOHN 20s.; to RICHARD son of said JOHN 30s.; to JOHN son of said JOHN 40s. -- all to be paid within one year of my death; to EDWARD son of said JOHN 40s. at 21; to BRIDGET and MARY BRAME, daughters of said JOHN, 20s. apiece within a year after my death; with benefit of survivorship among all JOHN's children. To MARGARET daughter of NATHAN FISK 20s. at 21. To ANN MARTINER 20s. and 1 pair sheets within 1 year after my death. Into the hands of the churchwardens of Beccles 20s. to be distributed among the poor. To the poor of North Cove 8s. To the repairs of North Cove church 6s. 8d. within half a year of my decease. To the town of Barnby 5s. To 4 several men that shall bear me to my burial 12d. apiece. To Mr ROBERT REYNER, minister of North Cove 20s. for his pains to be taken in preaching a sermon at my burial. To MARGARET SAWKER daughter of FRANCIS SAWKER 20s. at 21. To WILLIAM BRAME, THOMAS BRAME, ROBERT BRAME, ROGER BRAME, KATHARINE SAWKER now wife of FRANCIS SAWKER, MARGERY BRAME, the children of my brother PETER £20 equally divided, with benefit of survivorship, within one month of my wife's decease. The rest of my movable goods and chattels

I give to my wife whom I make sole exrx. I appoint JOHN LONE of North Cove, gent., supervisor and give him for his pains 10s. Witnesses: ROBERT REYNER, ROGER RICCARD (X), RICHARD SMITH and me JOHN LONE. Pr. 15 Oct. 1630.

R(W) WILLIAM COORY of Beccles, clockmaker. 29 July 1630 (170)

All my movable goods and chattels to be inventoried and prised, and one half thereof I give to ELIZABETH COORY my wife, and the residue, my funeral charges being paid, I give to my 3 daughters MARGARET, MARY and ELIZABETH COORY, equally divided; and sufficient bond to be entered by my exors. within one month of my decease, to every one of my three daughters for the payment of their portions within 3 months of my decease, at the now dwelling house of me the said WILLIAM COORY in Beccles. I ordain ELIZABETH COORY my wife and my cousin JOHN COORY of Bramerton [co. Norfolk], merchant, son of ROBERT COORY, exors., and I give said JOHN 20s. for his pains to make him a ring. Witnesses: THOMAS DAYNES, THOMAS MARTYN, ROBERT HAWES. Pr. at Beccles 9 Sept. 1630. Admon. to relict with power reserved for JOHN CORY.

R(W) RICHARD DUGDELL senior (X) of Aldeburgh, tailor. (171)
22 August 1630

Sick. To be buried in Aldeburgh churchyard. To ALICE DUGDELL my wife my copyhold house or tenement where I dwell, with the yards, for life. To RICHARD DUGDELL my son the said house &c after my wife's decease with this condition, that he pay MARGARET DUGDELL my daughter £6 by 40s. a year after the decease of said ALICE, in the south porch of the parish church of Aldeburgh. And for want of none to re-enter into the said house or tenement as her own estate and her heirs for ever, and if RICHARD shall have no heirs, then to be equally sold and divided between my three children. All movable goods and chattels after the decease of said wife shall be equally divided between three of my children KATHARINE, NICHOLAS and MARGARET. I nominate ALICE DUGDELL my wife my exrx. Witnesses: THOMAS TIRNALLE and WILLIAM SHIPMAN. Pr. at Yoxford 22 Sept. 1630.

R(W) HENRY FALE (X) of Bruisyard, husbandman. (172)
11 July 1629

To ALICE FALE my wife all my houses lands goods and household stuffs in Bruisyard in her lifetime; and thereafter to my two daughters ALICE FALE and MARGERY FALE, charged to pay within one year of my wife's death to ISABEL my daughter, the wife of ROBERT BROWNE £20. If my said lands be sold, then if either daughter is able to buy the other's part, the buyer shall have it for 40s. with the price that someone else would pay. ALICE FALE my wife and ALICE FALE my daughter to be exrx. Witnesses: THOMASIN GARDINER and EDMUND GARDINER. Pr. 22 Sept. 1630.

W(R) ROBERT GOODING of Ipswich. 22 July 1630 (173)

To KEBELLA HUMPHRY my daughter the wife of HENRY HUMPHRY during her life those two houses or tenements in St. Margaret's in Ipswich with the yards and gardens, now in the occupation of WILLIAM CORTNALL and ROBERT WEBBER, and after her decease I give to HENRY HUMPHRY their son and his daughter for ever that house &c wherein said WILLIAM CORTNALL doth dwell, and likewise after her decease I give ROBERT HUMPHRY their son that house &c wherein ROBERT WEBBER doth dwell. And if either brother depart this life before his mother, the surviving brother shall have both houses. To EDMUND GOODING my son all my books of physic and surgery, and all my shop stuff and instruments of surgery on condition that he pay my son JOHN £10 within 3 months and other £10 within 6 months of my decease. The books and shop stuff and instruments shall remain with my exrx. till said son EDMUND shall have paid the money or renewed his bond to his brother JOHN for the payment. In case my son EDMUND fail to pay the money or give surety for the same, then I give the books shop stuff and instruments to my son JOHN. All other goods and chattels I give to MARGARET my wife whom I appoint sole exrx. Witnesses: SAMUEL SAMWATHS, HENRY SHIRMAN, ROBERT BURMAN. Codicil: I give KEBELLA my daughter one half of that stock in place of them that I excepted the time of my marriage. Pr. Ipswich 24 Sept. 1630.

R(W) GEORGE HARTLEY alias WHISTLE of Ipswich, cooper. (174)
10 July 1630

To my sister ALICE DEBNAM 2s. and to her son JOHN 2s. To my wife MARY my tenement with house and yards in the parish of St. Mary Quay now in the occupation of EDWARD FIELD mariner, between the tenements and yards of EDWARD DEBNAM in the north and the south, for life. And I appoint her sole exrx. to whom I give all the rest of my goods. Witnesses: PHILIP BROWNE, EDWARD DEBNAM (X). Pr. at Ipswich 24 Sept. 1630.

R(W) HENRY HAYLE of Framsden, singleman. 20 July1630 (175)

Sick. To RICHARD HAYLE my brother all my lands tenements meadows pastures and feedings with appurtenances in Framsden now in the occupation of PHILIP ALDRICH, as well freehold as copyhold, on condition that the said RICHARD shall pay to my four sisters £20 apiece, the eldest sisters to have their gifts within one year and the two youngest within two years of my decease, with power of distraint in case of default. To HENRY BLOMEFEILD my godchild 40s., and to my cousin ROBERT BLOMEFIELD 20s. to be paid within three years after my decease. To the said RICHARD HAYLE all my goods and chattels and apparel, and I nominate him sole exor. Witnesses: THOMAS HEARING, NATHANIEL BOWMAN. Codicil: 23 July 1630. £3 to be paid to the churchwardens and overseers of Framsden to the use of the poor, within one year of my decease. Witnesses: [the same as above]. Pr. at Ipswich 24 Sept. 1630.

R(W) KATHARINE KING of Marlesford, widow (N). 16 October 1630 (176)

Being sick upon her bed took her daughter MARGERY the widow of THOMAS PECKETT by the hand and said "MARGERY I give ye all my movable goods; nobody shall have a pennyworth from ye" -- or words to that effect. Witness: JOAN REVE (X). Pr. at Wickham 13 Oct. 1630.

R(W) ROBERT KNAPP of Needham Market, yeoman. 31 July 1630 (177)

Sick. To ROBERT KNAPPE my son and his heirs for ever, at his age of 21, all my tenements both free and copyhold in Needham Market, Barking and Darmsden, holden of the manor of Barking with Needham, in my own occupation, and JOAN my wife shall enjoy the same and take the rents and profits during the minority of my son, she keeping the same in good reparations, and allowing my son ROBERT £20 per annum for his maintenance and schooling until he shall be fitting to go to the university of Cambridge and then allow him £30 p.a. till his age of 21. I will my wife to raise and allow every year after my decease out of my said lands £10 until ROBERT shall be 21, towards a stock to be paid to him at 21. To JOAN my wife when ROBERT shall or should attain the age of 21 £50 a year for life, which I wish my son ROBERT shall pay unto her half year and half year by equal portions, with power of distraint. If ROBERT should die before his age of 21 without issue of his body then I give all my lands and tenements aforesaid to JOAN my wife, upon condition that she pay my three brothers JOHN KNAPP, EDWARD KNAPP and EDMUND KNAPP £50 apiece, by £50 per annum, the first £50 to JOHN KNAPP within one year after she shall enjoy the lands, and £50 to EDWARD 2 years after, and £50 to EDMUND within 3 years after, with benefit of survivorship; and then after the death of JOAN my wife I give the lands &c to EDMUND my brother and his heirs for ever on condition that he shall pay to JOHN KNAPP and EDWARD KNAPP, his brothers, £200 each to be paid by £50 p.a. after EDMUND shall enjoy the same, with power of distraint. And if the said EDMUND happen to die before he shall enjoy said lands, then I give them to EDWARD KNAPP and his heirs upon the same condition. JOAN my wife shall pay three parts of the fine divided into four parts for the admittance to his copyhold lands of the manor of Barking cum Needham when the said ROBERT shall be admitted. To ROBERT KNAPP my son, at 21, all my lease lands which I hold of the chapter of Ely, containing about 36 acres of land meadow and pasture in Bosmere, together with the lease of all my right therein during the remaining number of years; and JOAN my wife shall take the benefit rents and profits of the same lease lands until ROBERT attain 21 years. Whereas ROBERT KNAPP my father holdeth certain lease lands of the Dean and Chapter of Ely which by his last will, dated 12 May 1618, he did demise unto his three youngest sons JOHN, EDWARD and EDMUND, which lease after the death of my father I did receive and take in my own name from the Dean and Chapter, as by the said lease appeareth, now I give to JOHN, EDWARD and EDMUND my brothers the said lease mentioned in the will of my father. To SUSAN KNAPP my sister £10 to be paid within 3 years after my decease. To my sister MARY KNAPP 20s. to buy her a ring. To my friend Mr FLECHER, minister of Barking, 20s. for a funeral sermon. To the poor of Needham Market Barking and Darmsden £5 to be distributed at my burial by my exor. The rest of my goods and chattels I give to JOAN my wife whom I make sole exrx. on condition that she enter into bond of £500 unto Mr EDWARD CORDINALL, my friend and cousin, within one month after my decease, to see this will performed; and if she refuse her executorship shall be void and I make my son ROBERT exor. Witnesses: EDWARD CORDINALL, ROBERT NEWTON, ALDRIAN ALDRICH. Pr. at Ipswich 9 Oct. 1630.

W(R) WILLIAM MASSY alias CANDELER. 16 August 1630 (178)

To MARGERY my wife both my houses and lands belonging unto them by the name of Renhamfild on condition that she maintain them in sufficient reparations. If said MARGERY shall chance to put away MARGARET my daughter then I give to MARGARET my new house and 20s. a year during said MARGARET's life; further I condition that MARGERY my wife shall sell one close lying between ROBERT EADE's close and my own, by estimation 3 acres; further if MARGERY shall put away MARGARET then I give her one trundle bed as it stand. To my son WILLIAM my old tenement where I now dwell after the decease of my wife, upon condition that he pay 20s. a year to said MARGARET so long as she live. And WILLIAM shall give to FRANCES my daughter £6 within one year after my wife's decease. Further to MARGERY my wife all my movables with the said close to pay my debts. To MARGARET aforesaid my new house so long as she live, with ingress egress and regress at all times, and after her decease to my son WILLIAM also with half the ditch. I make my wife sole exrx. and said ROBERT EADE supervisor. If my wife refuse to prove my will then I make my supervisor sole exor. Witnesses: DANIEL HARBEN and FRANCIS MILES (X). Pr. at Yoxford 22 Sept. 1630.

R(W) OLIVER MYNTER of Rendlesham, yeoman. 14 May 1627 (179)

Sick. All my goods and chattels shall be prised, out of which my debts and proving this testament shall be taken. Of the remainder I give one half to ELIZABETH my wife and the other half or the value thereof my exor. shall use to the best benefit he can towards bringing up my son JOHN MYNTER until he come to the age of 21, and then I give to my said son the aforesaid moiety to be paid to him by my exor. at the age of 22, or sooner at the discretion of my exor. If JOHN my son should die before he is 21 then I give the said half that he should have had to ELIZABETH my wife to be paid to her at such time as JOHN should accomplish the age of 21. To the poor of Rendlesham 5s. within one month of my decease. To my brother-in-law HENRY TOWNERAWE £10 for his pains in seeing my will performed and I make him sole exor. Witnesses:

REGINALD BUCKNAN (X), EDMUND POPE (X). Pr. at Ipswich 12 Oct. 1630.

R(W) JOHN MEADOWE of Washbrook, yeoman. 19 August 1630 (180)

Not well. To JOHN MEADOWE my son my messuage or tenement in Washbrook wherein I dwell, with the houses buildings barns stables yards orchards gardens land and tenements meadows pastures and feedings belonging, with their appurtenances, lying in Washbrook Great Wenham Little Wenham and Chattisham in the tenure or occupation of me or of my assigns, to hold to him and to the heirs of his body lawfully begotten forever, presently after my decease. To the said JOHN my long table standing in my hall. To the 3 children of my brother GEOFFERY MEADOWE the several sums of 30s. To the poor of Washbrook 20s. to be distributed equally by the churchwardens. My son JOHN shall pay to his sister MARGARET £20 within 1 year after my decease out of the profits of said lands and tenements, at the church porch of Washbrook; and shall pay to my other daughter, his sister, JOAN MEADOWE £20 within 3 years at the said porch. To JOAN my wife an annuity of £15 a year out of my said lands in lieu of her thirds or dower, to be paid quarterly. All other goods chattels household stuff corn cattle money and debts (my debts and legacies and my funeral charges and probate of this will paid) I give in the following manner: all said goods &c (excepting 10 coombs of wheat and 5 coombs of barley and all my cheese, which I give my wife) shall be within 6 days after my decease equally divided in 3 parts by my exors, and JOAN my wife to have one part during her life and after her decease that her part shall remain to my 2 daughters MARGARET and JOAN MEADOWE to be equally divided between them, provided that if the said JOAN my wife shall after my decease happen to marry, then I will that the third part devised unto her shall be frustrate and I give her part to my 2 daughters, they to have the said goods presently after her marriage; and the other two parts I give to the said MARGARET and JOAN to be equally divided by my exors. I nominate GEOFFERY MEADOWE my brother and JOAN my wife exors. and JACOB MANNING the elder of Washbrook supervisor. Memorandum that before the sealing hereof the testator JOHN MEADOWE willed that if his son JOHN MEADOWE died without heir lawfully begotten then the messuage and lands should be divided equally between the two daughters MARGARET and JOAN; and he willed to FRANCIS SUGDEN at 21 a sum of 30s.; and if his son JOHN should fail in the payment of their legacies of £20 apiece that his sisters may enter the premises to hold until the legacies be paid. Witnesses: JACOB MANNING (X), THOMAS DENTON. Pr. at Ipswich 8 Oct. 1630.

R(W) JOHN PODD senior of Capel, husbandman. (181)
4 October 1626

To ANN my wife all the household which she had when I came to her; and one cow. To ROBERT my son 12d. To my two sons JOHN jnr. and JOHN snr. all goods and chattels unbequeathed, my funeral my debts and my legacies being discharged. The rest of my goods to be equally divided between these two sons and their children. JOHN PODD the younger shall have my other son JOHN's part in his hands to pay to him and his child by equal portions yearly every year within 10 years after my decease. I appoint as exors. JOHN PODD jnr. and Mr WILLIAM BAYNUM of Studley. Witness: HENRY KING (X). Admon. to JOHN POD, WILLIAM BAYNUM renouncing.

R(W) THOMAS ROWE of Shotley, yeoman. 29 May1629 (182)

Sick. To the poor of Shotley 20s. where most need is, at the discretion of my exors., within 3 months. To THOMAS ROWE my son, after the decease of EDITH my wife, my lands and tenements and their appurtenances lying in Capel, called Knebins, which I lately purchased of EDITH MOYSE, widow, one of the daughters of JOHN BUNN late of Holbrook, deceased, and of her three daughters and their husbands, to hold to said THOMAS my son and heirs of his body lawfully begotten, for ever; and for want of such issue I bequeath the same to WILLIAM WIGGIN my son-in-law and heirs of his body lawfully begotten; and for want of such issue I bequeath them to EDITH my wife and her heirs for ever. EDITH my wife shall bring up THOMAS my son to school until he shall be fitting to be put to an apprentice. My wife shall bind my said son apprentice to some trade such as he shall best like. To the said THOMAS ROWE my son £30 at his age of 24. My wife shall make no strip nor waste of any wood or timber upon my lands, but shall as often as need shall require amend and keep the lands, and tenements and houses thereto belonging, in good tenant-like reparations, which if my wife shall not perform my supervisor shall enter into the aforesaid lands and tenements and take the benefit until the said houses be repaired as before. To WILLIAM WIGGIN my son-in-law £50 to be paid out of my said lands and tenements, £10 yearly, the first payment to begin within one year and a half after the decease of EDITH my wife, with power of distraint. The remainder of my goods and chattels, my debts and legacies and funeral charges with the probate of this will discharged, and all other ecclesiastical duties born and deducted, I give to EDITH my wife, and I make her and NATHANIEL HEDGE my brother-in-law exors.; and I make CHRISTOPHER ROWE my brother supervisor. Witnesses: JOHN HAVELL the wr.iter and JOHN GREENE (X) and EDITH MOYSE (X). Pr. at Ipswich 11 Oct. 1630.

W(R) THOMAS RANNALES (X) of Walberswick, limeburner. (183)
16 February 1629/30

Sick. To be buried in the churchyard of Walberswick. To KATHARINE REYNOLDS my daughter-in-law all my houses yards sheds limekiln stables with their appurtenances holden of Sir ROBERT BROOKE, for the term of her life, and thereafter to my grandchildren viz. THOMAS REYNALLS, ABRAHAM REYNALLS and their heirs for ever, to be equally divided among them. To KATHARINE REYNALLS all my movable goods and debts duties bonds bills or anything coming to me for any matter; and the moveable goods to be sold by my exrx. to the payment of my debts within two years of my decease. To ROSE my wife 10s. to be paid within 10 days by my exrx.; and 1 kettle 1 stond 1 skillet 1 keller 1 roast-iron 1 little chair 1 cover, also a bundle of towne. I make KATHARINE REYNALLS my sole exrx. Witnesses: GEORGE RANOULDS, JOHN BARWICK, JOHN FEARMES. Pr. at Yoxford 22 Sept. 1630.

R(W) ELIZABETH SMITH of Southelmham St. George, widow. (184)
31 March 1629

Sick. To be buried in the churchyard of Southelmham St. George. My movable goods and apparel, as well linen as woolen, (except one cupboard) with the debts to me owing I give wholly to JOHN SISSAM my son-in-law, he paying all legacies hereafter bequeathed. To the five children of JOHN SMITH of St. George abovesaid, my son, namely to JOHN, NICHOLAS, HENRY, ANDREW and RICHARD 40s. apiece as they attain 21 years. My daughter SISSAM shall have the excepted cupboard during her life, and after her decease I give it to ELIZABETH her daughter. I nominate said JOHN SISSAM my son-in-law sole exor., charged with my burial. Witnesses: JAMES GODBOLD, WILLIAM NORMAN. Pr. at Beccles 21 Oct. 1630.

W(R)(A) ELIZABETH TOMSON* of Rumburgh, widow (N). (185)
[no date]

In the space of one week before her death declared her will, viz. She gave all her goods and estate to BRIDGET WALES the wife of NICHOLAS WALES, and MARY the wife of THOMAS DRAPER, her daughters. Witnesses: ANN BATTELIE wid., ISABEL ODBIE and MARY UTTING. Admon. to THOMAS DRAPER and MARY his wife, daughter of deceased, 20 Nov. 1630.
[*The register copy of this will incorrectly gives the name of the testator as ELIZABETH TEASON, but the probate note in the register refers to the goods of ELIZABETH TOMSON, and that is the name that is given in the volume wherein grants of administration are recorded.]

R(W) JOAN ALDRED of Bruisyard, widow. 25 March 1626 (186)

To THOMAS ALDRED my son all my movable goods now in his custody. To THOMAS COLMAN my son-in-law all my moveables in his house and custody except one bond. To said THOMAS COLMAN the use money arising of the said excepted bond and the quarterly annuity which I am to have of WILLIAM HURRELL during my life. To EMMA MALING and WILLIAM MALING my grandchildren, out of the said bond, £10 to be paid by my exor. by even and equal portions. To the three daughters of THOMAS ALDRED my son, out of the said bond, £10 to be paid in like manner. To the three children of THOMAS COLMAN my son-in-law, out of the said bond, £10 to be paid in like manner. The remainder of the excepted bond (the charges of my burial and the probate of this will deducted) I give to THOMAS ALDRED, my son, and to THOMAS COLMAN my son-in-law whom I make exors., provided that if either exor. refuse to prove this will then he shall have no part of the remainder of the bond and I give the same wholly to the other exor. Read sealed and delivered into the hands of JANE COLMAN my daughter. Witnesses: HENRY CANNAP, JOHN HELWES and WILLIAM HARDING (X). Pr. at Yoxford 24 Nov. 1630.

R(W) WILLIAM BRAME of Kessingland, carpenter. (187)
16 December 1630

Sick. To be buried in the churchyard of Kessingland. To UNICE my wife my freehold tenement with the orchard and hempland belonging, wherein GEORGE ELLIS dwelleth, during term of her life. After her decease I bequeath the same to the child my wife is now with, if it be a man child; and if it be not, then the tenement &c shall be equally divided between my daughters then living. My wife shall maintain the tenement in good reparations during her tenure. To my said wife my copyhold tenement with the yard belonging, during her life, towards the bringing up of my children, she keeping the same in good reparations; and after her decease the said tenement and yard shall be equally parted among my daughters then living. My wife shall not take neither father mother brother nor sister not to dwell in either of the said houses at any time during her said term; if she do, her gifts to be void, and the benefit of them to be to my children. All my horse beasts and neat beasts to be sold towards the payment of my debts. The rest of my movable goods I give unto my wife towards the payment of debts and I make her sole exrx. Witnesses: WILLIAM CAPON (X), THOMAS PAYNE. Pr. at Beccles 3 Jan. 1630/1.

R(W) WILLIAM BROWNE (X) senior of Sweffling, yeoman. (188)
18 November 1630

Sick. To DIANA my wife all my goods household stuff and implements of household, paying my debts (except my long table frame and form in the hall -- all which DIANA shall have during term of her life, and after her decease I give them to THOMAS BROWNE my eldest son, paying to said DIANA 5s. within one year after my decease for these same). To the said DIANA all my houses lands meadows pastures yards orchards, with appurtenances, except my little house shop and shop chamber now in occupation of my son WILLIAM, to hold for life, and after her decease THOMAS BROWNE my eldest son shall have all my said houses and lands &c, except before excepted, paying to NICHOLAS BROWNE my son £10 within two years after the decease of DIANA my wife; also paying my son ROBERT BROWNE £10 within three years after her decease; also paying to MARGARET my daughter £5 within four years after DIANA's decease; also paying to my daughter ANN BROWNE £10 within five years of DIANA's decease. All which legacies, which I have here given unto the said NICHOLAS, ROBERT, MARGARET and ANN shall be in full discharge of all legacies given either of them by the will of ROBERT BROWNE my brother deceased; and if any of them shall be not contented with such legacies as I have given them in this will, but shall molest or trouble DIANA my wife for any legacy given them by said ROBERT my brother, then their legacies by me herein given shall be void. To EDWARD BROWNE my youngest son £5 and to DIANA BROWNE my youngest daughter £5, to be paid to them by THOMAS my son within six years after the decease of DIANA my wife. If THOMAS shall refuse to pay any of the legacies by me given to any of my sons and daughters, whom he shall refuse shall have power of distraint. WILLIAM BROWNE my son shall have my little house wherein he now dwelleth, with the shop and shop chamber, with the appurtenances, as he now hath, with free ingress egress and regress to and from the same for WILLIAM and his assigns during the life of DIANA my wife, WILLIAM paying her 20s. yearly at the feasts of the Annunciation and of St. Michael, by even portions. And after the decease of DIANA, WILLIAM shall have the little house shop and shop chamber &c for life. After his decease I will give the little shop &c to THOMAS my son and his heirs for ever. I nominate DIANA my wife sole exrx. Witnesses: RICHARD SHALDRACKE and LAURENCE PELLS. Pr. at Yoxford 24 Nov. 1630.

W(R) EDMUND BEAGLE of Southwold (N). [no date] (189)

On the day before his death gave to FRANCIS BEAGLEY his brother his cloak, paying 12s. to HENRY BLAKES. All the rest of his goods he gave to PHOEBE the wife of HENRY BLAKES, his sister. Witnesses: JOHN JURDON and the wife of THOMAS ELLIOT. Admon. to PHOEBE wife of HENRY BLAKES 24 Nov. 1630.

W(R) MARGERY BURRWOOD (X) of Aldeburgh, spinster. (190)
8 July 1630

To my brother BURRWOOD £4 the which he hath already in his hand, which was due unto me for my father's gift. To my brother EDWARD 20s. To JOHN BURWOOD £5. To ROSE SHRIMPER my sister £5. To ALICE my sister my murrey coat and my best ruff. To ALICE BURRWOOD my mother one pair of sheets. To ALICE MAYNE my best apron. The rest of my movable goods to be equally divided between my brothers and sisters. I make JOHN BURRWOOD my brother sole exor. Witnesses: SUSAN RANOLDS (X), JOHN THOMPSON and PHOEBE HIRSSEN. Pr. at Yoxford 24 Nov. 1630.

R(W) ANTHONY CHAPMAN of Benacre (N). [no date] (191)

Sick. About 2 or 3 days before his death willed all his goods, after his debts funeral expenses probate of this will and other necessary charges deducted, to be equally divided between KATHARINE CHAPMAN his wife and AGNES CHAPMAN his daughter and the child that KATHARINE his wife is now conceived, in case she be with child; otherwise to be equally divided between KATHARINE and AGNES, and the other part which shall become due to AGNES to be employed for her bringing up until her age of 17 or 18, and then the remainder of her part not spent about her bringing up to be paid to her if she be of capacity and understanding and ability to govern it; otherwise to remain then to her further provision. If the said AGNES should die before her portion shall be spent about her bringing up, then he willed £3, part thereof, to ELIZABETH HARRIS his half-sister and to THOMAS HARRIS and WILLIAM HARRIS the two children of THOMAS HARRIS, to every of them 20s.; and the remainder of her portion to his wife KATHARINE whom he nominated exrx. Witnesses: THOMAS HARRIS, THOMAS WOLNOUGHE and JOHN AYTON and one HARPER of Southwold. Pr. at Beccles 21 Dec. 1630.

R(W) ANN CROWE of Dunwich, widow. 16 July 1621 (192)

To be buried in the churchyard of All Saints, Dunwich near my late husband WILLIAM CROWE. To WILLIAM CROWE my son my tenement with appurtenances in Dunwich which WILLIAM CROWE my late husband and I purchased jointly of NICHOLAS RUDDS the elder of Dunwich, fisherman, deceased, upon condition that the said WILLIAM my son his heirs and exors. do pay £5 to my son EDWARD CROWE within three quarters of a year after my decease, at my tenement before-given, and £5 to URSULA my daughter the wife of THOMAS STRAFORD within one year and a half at the place aforesaid, and to five of the children of HENRY HUGMAN which he have by his wife ALICE my daughter, to each of them 3s. 4d., to be paid within one year, and to my four daughters ANN wife of JOHN GOSLYNE, ELIZABETH wife of LUKE SHERINGTON, CECILY wife of RICHARD THIXON and URSULA wife of THOMAS STRATFORD all my wearing apparel both linen and woollen to be equally divided in four parts and delivered to them presently after my decease. And if any of my said children shall happen to come and dwell with me in my said tenement, wherein myself do dwell, given to my son WILLIAM, and in the same tenement to remain dwelling with me until it shall please God to take me, then I will he or she shall have and occupy my said house, keeping it in good repair, for the space of one half year after my decease, peaceably and without denial of my son WILLIAM his heirs exors. or assigns, freely and without paying anything therefore, together also with one half of the crop that shall then happen to arise and come of the yard belonging to said tenement. All the rest of my goods chattels household stuff and implements of household, bills, bonds and ready money shall remain unto my six children WILLIAM CROWE, EDWARD CROWE, ANN wife of JOHN GOSLEYNE, ELIZABETH wife of LUKE SHIRINGTON, CECILY the wife of RICHARD THIXTON and URSULA the now wife of THOMAS STRATFORD, and be divided into six equal parts by three or four of the chief inhabitants of Dunwich within eight days after my decease, and presently delivered to the six children. And if any of them depart this life before the receipt of their portion, that portion shall remain to the children of him or her so de-ceased. I ordain RICHARD CROWE my son my sole exor. to execute this will and pay my debts and legacies and funeral expenses and probate of this will, and to prove this will within one month. And if he refuse executorship then he shall lose the benefit hereof, and all my gifts herein made to him shall be frustrate, and I ordain EDWARD my son exor., he to have my said tenement on condition that he pay to the said WILLIAM £5 within six months and pay all other legacies and perform all other things in this will which WILLIAM should have done if he had not refused. Witnesses: JOHN HURSTELOR (X) and JOHN REYNOLDS, the writer hereof. Pr. at Beccles 26 Nov. 1630.

W(R) RICHARD CURTICE of Darsham, husbandman. (193)
22 November 1630

To THOMAS my eldest son £45 to be paid within one year of my decease in the porch of the parish church of Darsham. To RICHARD my youngest son £45 within two years paid at the place aforesaid. If THOMAS die before he is to receive his portion, without issue lawfully begotten, the same shall be paid to RICHARD my son and his heirs within two years of my decease at the place aforesaid. If RICHARD depart this life before he is to receive his legacy, without issue lawfully begotten, my son THOMAS shall have the legacy bequeathed to RICHARD at such time and place as RICHARD should have received the same. If both sons depart this life before either of them shall have had their several legacies, without issue of either of their bodies lawfully begotten, then the one half of such legacies unpaid shall remain to ANTHONIA my wife and her heirs for ever; the other half shall be equally divided between RICHARD CURTICE, son of RICHARD CURTICE late of Hazelwood my brother deceased, and the five children of NEALE HALL of Holton, widow, my sister, or so many of them as shall be living two years after my decease. To the said RICHARD my nephew £5. To MARY wife of PAUL HALL of Gisleham, my sister, 20s. To MARY CURTICE daughter of ANN CURTICE my late sister deceased 5s. All the sums to be paid within one year after my decease. All the rest of my goods cattle chattels and ready money household stuff utensils bills bonds debts and duties unbequeathed I give to ANTHONIA my wife to pay my debts and legacies, and for her maintenance. If it shall appear at the inventory-making unto my supervisor and such as shall be appointed to apprise my said goods that the same will not amount to the sum of forty pounds and five over, besides all my debts legacies and funeral charges, to remain and come to ANTHONIA for her portion, then that £5 shall be abated out of the legacies to my two sons, out of either of their portions 50s. Any such goods as my wife shall put to sale my sons or either of them shall have any such goods before any other, they giving as much for the same as any other will give. I make my wife sole exrx. and my neighbour and friend JOHN MOLL of Middleton, yeoman, my supervisor. My exrx. shall enter into one obligation of £100 unto my supervisor with condition to prove and perform this will. Witnesses: EDWARD ELLIS, ANN ALLEN (X) and JOHN MOLL. Pr. at Yoxford 13 Dec. 1630.

W(R) ISAAC DILLISTON of Hopton. [no date] (194)

All the corn which is in Hopton or elsewhere is to be brought to the barn at Hoblande Hall except the crop which shall be then growing in the mill hill close and in the lower part of 18-acres, the which I give to my brother-in-law HENRY PEAD. All my corn and cattle to be sold to pay my landlord WILLIAM VEISIE esquire. The residue which remains when he is paid my wife may have so long as she live, she to pay thereout such debts as shall be lawfully demanded, and after her decease if she do not marry she shall leave £20 to JOHN PEAD her brother and £20 to ISAAC HOWE my sister's son; but if she marry she shall only leave £20 to ISAAC HOWE, and her husband shall be bound for the payment thereof. To my maid JOAN ROSE one heifer of two years old and the vantage. Also to ESTHER, the child which I have brought up, all the household stuff lying within the chamber where I lie at my decease, the same to be delivered to her after the decease of ESTHER my wife, whom I make exrx. Witnesses: JOHN RICHMOND, RICHARD CLISEN (X). Pr. at Beccles 22 Jan. 1630/1.

R(W) WILLIAM GODBOLD of Dennington, husbandman. (195)
14 October 1630

To ANN my daughter all my lands and tenements with appurtenances in Fressingfield, paying out of same to ELIZABETH my wife during term of her life one annuity of £3 on the feast days of the Annunciation and of St. Michael or within 6 days thereafter, by equal portions, at my messuage in Fressingfield, payment to begin at which of the feasts shall first happen after my decease, with power of distraint for ELIZABETH if ANN make default, provided the annuity shall be in consideration that ELIZABETH shall not claim or have any dower out of any of my lands and tenements aforesaid. All my goods chattels household stuff and implements of household (my debts burial expenses and probate of my will discharged) shall be equally divided between my wife ELIZABETH and ANN my daughter. I nominate my wife and ANN my daughter exrx. Witnesses: JOHN MULLINER and EDWARD MOULTON. Pr. at Yoxford 24 Nov. 1630.

R(W) JOHN GODARD of Kirton, yeoman. 25 March 1629 (196)

Sick. Whereas I lent unto WILLIAM BACON of Ashbocking, husb., 4 score pounds, as in a deed appeareth bearing date 20 Dec 1627, my son RICHARD GODARD shall have £40 thereof, with the use, to be paid him at the age of 21 by my exor.; to my daughter ELIZABETH £30 being another part of the 4 score pounds, to be paid to her with the profit that shall be growing thereof, to be paid by my exor. at her age of 21 or day of marriage; the residue of the 4 score pounds with the interest that is and shall be due hereafter by virtue of the aforesaid deed and a certain bond I give, with the profits thereof and 16s. more to be paid out of my other goods, unto my daughter MARY by my exor. at 21 or marriage -- with benefit of survivorship. And if all my three children die before marriage or without issue lawfully begotten I give all the portions to these parties following, viz: To THOMAS GODARD, NICHOLAS GODARD, and THOMAS PARKER, equally divided. To my daughter ELIZABETH a pair of bedsteads now in the parlour together with a down pillow 2 blankets a covering 1 coarse sheet 1 holland sheet 1 holland pillow-bier thereunto belonging, and my great brass pot, to be delivered to her presently after my decease. To MARY my youngest daughter 1 livery bedstead whereon I lie as it standeth furnished in the little chamber. To RICHARD my son 1 trundle bedstead as it standeth furnished in the little chamber together with a boarded posted bed as it standeth upon the chamber furnished. To my daughter ELIZABETH my cupboard in the hall and to my daughter MARY my press in the parlour. To RICHARD my son my square tub in the parlour and a cupboard in the buttery. Concerning my goods and cattles unbequeathed and my corn and other movables, my exor. shall make sale of them as they see fitting and shall discharge such charges as they shall be liable unto for bringing my body to the ground, and the rest to be divided among my children by equal portions, and so to the only use and behoof of my said children until their day of marriage or age of 21 years. I nominate RICHARD COBBALD and SAMUEL REVITT and ROBERT ALLIN exors., and I give to RICHARD COBBALD and SAMUEL REVITT 20s. apiece for their pains. ROBERT ALLIN shall have 10s. Witnesses: ALLEN CONE, THOMAS PAGE(X), THOMAS ELMES (X). Pr. at Ipswich 6 Nov. 1630. ROBERT ALLIN renounced; admon. to RICHARD COBBALD with power reserved for SAMUEL REVIT.

R(W) JOHN HUBBARD of Aldeburgh, beer-brewer (N). (197)
5 January 1630/1

Lying sick upon his death-bed. To SUSAN HUBBARD his daughter 1 posted bedstead as it standeth in the parlour chamber. To EMMA HUBBARD his other daughter the posted bedstead with all things as it standeth in the hall chamber. All the rest of his goods and chattels to JUDITH HUBBARD his wife towards the payment of debts and bringing up his daughters. He made his wife exrx. Witnesses: MARY HUBBARD, wid., JOHN BALDEN and JOHN SMYTH. Pr. at Yoxford 12 Jan. 1630/1.

W(R) THOMAS HOWSON senior (X) of Reydon. (198)
11 January 1629/30

Whereas I have formerly paid to ANN GUNNE, late of Hadleigh and now of Ipswich, widow, for the debt of my son THOMAS HOWSON jnr. £5 of principal and 50s. at least for the use thereof 7 or 8 years, which I forgive to the said THOMAS, I desire my exor. to deliver unto him the said obligation to be cancelled. Whereas there are other specialties of his in my hands and that he owes other sums, I appoint that upon that day month after my burial THOMAS and my exor. shall meet at Hadleigh and discharge each other. If THOMAS should refuse to meet and give acquitance, then I leave my exors. free to recover such moneys as are due. To my said son THOMAS I give one Iron Pitch for a hop ground. And whereas I have in my keeping ROSE JASTLING my grandchild, and there are ANN and PHILIP JASTLING my grandchildren, I leave them to the care of my exors. to do what they conveniently can to see them well brought up. The residue of my goods I give to GRACE my wife and MARY JASTLING my grandchild, to be equally divided, and I appoint them exors. Witnesses: ROBERT NUTTON, DANIEL RAY. Pr. 19 Nov. 1630.

W(R) WILLIAM HERRINGE of Stradbroke, yeoman. (199)
10 October 1630

JOAN my now wife shall have the use and occupation of all my messuages lands tenements meadows, pastures and feedings, with appurtenances, either copy or freehold, in Stradbroke where I now dwell, to hold until WILLIAM my son shall accomplish his full age of 24, committing no estripment or waste, keeping the houses in good reparations, discharging the rent payable out of the premises, and performing this will. JOAN shall likewise have the use and occupation of all my messuages lands &c which I lately purchased of EDMUND POLEY esq. in Wingfield, to hold until JAMES my second son shall accomplish his age of 24, she committing no waste, maintaining my house in good reparations paying all rents and performing this will, provided that it shall be lawful for JOAN to take competent fire-bote and hedge-bote to be spent upon the aforesaid premises and not elsewhere. All my messuages houses lands &c wherein I dwell in Wingfield, late my father's, after that WILLIAM my son shall have accomplished his age of 24, shall wholly remain to him and his heirs for ever, paying out of the premises aforesaid to JOAN my wife every year £5 at the two usual feasts, viz. St. Michael the Archangel and St. Mary the Virgin by equal portions, the first payment to begin at the first feast aforesaid which shall happen after my decease, with power of distraint if a sum be unpaid 40 days after either feast. To JAMES my second son at his age of 24 all my messuages houses lands &c both copy and freehold lying in Stradbroke which I lately purchased of EDMUND POLEY esq., to hold to him and his heirs and assigns for ever, yielding to JOAN my wife yearly £4 at the south porch of the parish church of Stradbroke upon the two usual feasts &c (as above) and with power of distraint (as above). To ANN my daughter £30, £10 every year till £30 be paid, payment to begin within one year after my decease. To JOHN my son £30 to be paid at his age of 22 at the place aforesaid. To THOMAS my son £20 to be paid at his age of 21 at the place aforesaid, provided that if THOMAS decease before his age of 21 then I give that £20 to ANN my daughter and JOHN my son, equally divided, to be paid at such days and place as THOMAS would have received the same. All which sums bequeathed to ANN, JOHN and THOMAS shall be paid by JOAN my wife her exors. or assigns out of the revenues of my lands and tenements aforesaid until the said WILLIAM and JAMES shall have accomplished their several ages aforesaid. And the annuity of £5 per year out of my lands and tenements wherein I do now dwell, and the annuity of £4 out of the lands &c purchased of EDMUND POLEY esq., formerly demised unto JOAN my wife, shall be in lieu of such title of dower or thirds or other demand payable to JOAN out of my aforesaid lands &c. If she or any other in her name shall implead either of my sons their heirs or exors. for any dower out of the said messuages &c then the annuities shall cease and be void. If JAMES my son shall decease before 21 without issue of his body lawfully begotten I will give the aforesaid lands and tenements called Deys to JOHN my third son for ever, to enter into the same when the said JAMES my son should have entered, paying to ANN my daughter £10 within 2 years after his lawful entry, and £10 more within 2 years of entry, and £10 more unto my son THOMAS within 4 years of entry. To the said THOMAS £5 to be paid by WILLIAM my son at his age of 21, with power of distraint against WILLIAM or the owners for the time being of the lands called Deyes. To ANN my daughter a bedstead with turned posts at the feet, a featherbed a bolster a pillow a blanket and a bind cover, as it standeth in the hall chamber, and a book called Hieron's Works. To WILLIAM my son the framed table in the hall and the Perkin's Works in one volume. To my son JAMES Mr Babington's Works. To my son JOHN Doctor Hill's Works and Mr Ward's Works. To my son THOMAS Doctor Preston's, in three several books, and Sir Christopher Sibthorpe's Works against the papists. I nominate JOAN my wife sole exrx. to take my debts and bring my body to the ground. I will that JOAN my wife, before any marriage to be solemnised between her and any person, she shall enter into bond to my supervisor in the penal sum of £100 with condition for the performance of this testament, and if she shall refuse her aforesaid annuities shall cease and be void. JOAN at her own cost shall educate and provide for my two youngest sons JOHN and THOMAS, and in her discretion bind them as apprentices till their several ages of 21 at the least. To the poor of Stradbroke 20s. to be disposed by the advice of Mr BACKE, the churchwardens and my brother-in-law JAMES ALDOUS, whom I nominate supervisor. The rest of my movables I give to my exrx. for the payment of debts, the bringing up of my children and discharging funeral expenses. Witnesses: WILLIAM BROWNINGE, RICHARD ALDOUS, HENRY BULLEN. Pr. at Wilby 1 Nov. 1630.

R(W)(A) JOHN JACOO (X) of Witnesham, husbandman. (200)
28 May 1621

To be buried in the churchyard of Witnesham. To my wife all my lands free and copy in Witnesham for term of her life, and after her to my son JOHN, paying my debts and legacies. To my son HENRY JACOO my house and ground in Ufford. To my eldest daughter MARY JACOO £20 upon consideration of a gift her grandmother gave her to be paid at the age of 30 years. To my daughter ELIZABETH JACOO £15 to be paid at the age of 30 years. To my daughter URSULA £15 at 30 years. And MARY shall have her £20 at 3 several pays, that is to say 20 nobles a year. My other 2 daughters shall have their portions paid in 4 years, ELIZABETH £7 10s. a year to be paid in 2 years; and after URSULA £15 in 2 years i.e. £7 10s. a year. My wife and my son shall be exors. and ROBERT POOPE my supervisor; and if he shall refuse then RICHARD CUDBARD shall be. To URSULA my wife all my movable goods during her

life, and after her decease to my children part and part alike. Witnesses: THOMAS HUTCHINSON, ROBERT MEDOWE and LAMBERT NOLLOTH. Pr. 4 Nov. 1630.
[The entry in the Administrations book adds nothing to this bare date.]

W(R) BARTHOLOMEW KETTEL (X) of Pettaugh, labourer. (201)
19 March 1609/10 Codicil 14 September 1617

Sick. To be buried in the churchyard of Pettaugh. To WILLIAM KETTELL my oldest son my chief house wherein I now dwell, and the yards and orchards used thereto, and a little shop built upon the premises; and the lower pightle and a way out of the said yards through my upper pightle into the lower for cart and drift. To BARTHOLOMEW my younger son the house wherein Widow WALTON now dwellethand the pightle wherein it standeth lying on the king's highway upon the south and upon lands in occupation of HENRY SHARPE on the west and north part, and upon the lower pightle and the churchyard on the east. To JOAN my wife all my movable goods during her life, provided if she shall marry again then she shall lay in good and sufficient bond unto THOMAS KETTELL my brother, husbandman, dwelling in Langham, Suffolk, and unto JOHN HAYLE of Pettaugh, linen-weaver, for the giving of the said movable goods after her life endeth unto WILLIAM and BARTHOLOMEW KETTELL my sons, to be equally divided, with benefit of survivorship, as well in movables as in land. I make JOAN my wife exrx. and my brother THOMAS KETTELL of Langham and JOHN HAYLE of Pettaugh overseers and supervisors. Memo that the 14th Sept. 1617 this will was confirmed sealed and delivered in the presence of these persons who have subscribed their names, before which sealing the testator gave more to BARTHOLOMEW KETTELL one piece of ground employed to hops, lying within and at the upper part of the orchard before given to WILLIAM KETTELL his eldest son, with so much ground more as is now dooled out by JOHN HAYLE, lying in the orchard given to WILLIAM KETTELL, to be fenced out at the costs of BARTHOLOMEW KETTELL. Witnesses: GEORGE BURROUGH parson of Pettaugh, JOHN HAYLE, ALICE WALTON (X), wid. This will was confirmed and ratified on 14th Sept. 1617 in the presence of ROBERT DOWE (X) and RICHARD WYLY. Pr. at Ipswich 4 Nov. 1630. Because JOHN KETTLE named as exor. died before the testator admon. was issued to WILLIAM KETTELL, son of the deceased.

R(A) ELIZABETH KERICH of Claydon, widow (N). (202)
19 October 1630

To ANTHONY KERICH my son my best bed with the bedstead thereto. My other bed to SUSAN LOCKWOOD my daughter. To my grandchild ANN KERICH one cow. To CHRISTOPHER KERICH my son one coverlet. The rest of my goods and chattels to be divided equally between my children. Witnesses: Mr NORTON, clerk, parson of Claydon, ELIZABETH wife of OLIVER KERICH and ELIZABETH FENNOR. Pr. 3 Oct. 1630. Admon. to OLIVER KERICH the sons [sic] of deceased.

[recte OLIVER, GEORGE and CHRISTOPHER KERICH -- as recorded in the Liber Admon.]

R(W) AUDRY KNYVET of Sotherton, widow. 14 December 1626 (203)

In health. To my son EDMUND BONAN my basin and ewer of silver, one bed tester of needlework wrought with coloured silks with a feather-bed and my best counterpane, of all which he shall have the use during his life, and after his decease they shall all descend unto his eldest son which shall be at the time of his death, and so successively to the eldest heirs of the family in memory of me and my love to them. To said son EDMUND BOHAN my windmill with all the gear thereto which is built upon my jointure at Brampton. To my 5 daughters FRANCES, MURIEL, ELIZABETH, MARY and ABIGAIL and my daughter-in-law Mrs MARY BOHAN, wife to my son HUMPHRY BOHAN, one barred chest of linen. And all the rest of my plate to be equally divided between my said 5 daughters and my daughter-in-law by the discretion of my exor. To said son HUMPHRY BOHAN my messuage or tenement in Sotherton together with all the houses and buildings belonging and all my lands freehold or copyhold in Sotherton, Henham, Blyford, Brampton or any other town adjoining which I now have or may have by any means or title, either in my own occupation or of any other person by assignment, with their appurtenances, all which said copyhold lands I have surrendered into the hands of the lords of the manors whereof they be holden, to the use of this will, to have immediately after my decease and to hold to him and his heirs for ever. To said son HUMPHRY, towards the payment of such fines as shall grow due upon the taking up of the said several copyhold lands, my coach and coach-horses with their harness. To the poor of the parishes near and adjoining £10 to be distributed at the discretion of my exor. The residue of all my goods chattels household stuff ready money debts owing me and all other utensils I give to my said son HUMPHRY BOHAN towards payment of my debts, discharging my funeral expenses and probate of my will, whom I constitute my sole exor. Witnesses: THOMAS HAMMANT, WILLIAM TOLLIFER (X). Pr. at Beccles 18 Dec. 1630.

R(W) FRANCIS KIRBY of Blythburgh, blacksmith. 4 June 1628 (204)

Sick. To ANN my wife all my lands and tenements with their appurtenances to hold to her and her assigns during her life according to the custom of the manor of which the same been holden, and after her decease they shall descend unto WILLIAM KIRBY the son of JOHN KIRBY my brother and his heirs, so that my said brother JOHN and his heirs do at all times keep harmless and indemnified ANN my wife and her exors. from all manner of customs and demands which shall arise by reason of any obligation or bills of debt wherein I stand bound together with the said JOHN KIRBY. If the said JOHN KIRBY and his heirs or exors. shall not fulfill this condition then all my said lands and tenements shall descend to BEIGHTON JONES and his heirs, the son of my sister ELIZABETH, wife of THOMAS JONES of Frostenden, so that the said

BEIGHTON JONES his heirs and exors. shall perform the said condition. To RICHARD LONE son of my sister ANN the wife of THOMAS UTTING, clerk, £5. To ELIZABETH JONES my goddaughter, daughter of said THOMAS JONES, £5. The residue of my goods and chattels I give to ANN my wife and constitute her my sole exrx. Witnesses: THOMAS JONES, HENRY CROFFOOTE, GEORGE BILBE. Pr. at Yoxford 13 Dec. 1630.

R(W) EDMUND LEWES of Orford, yeoman. 11 November 1630 (205)

Sick. If MARGARET my wife be now with child I give my said wife one messuage or tenement called STEVEN MARGETS and one close in the occupation of STEVEN ARCHER or his assigns, also one barn and one close called Downefield with divers other lands now in the occupation of THOMAS BLOWERS or his assigns, all which premises lie in Hollesley, Alderton and Shottisham, until the said child shall come to the age of 21, towards the education and bringing up of the child. And if the child shall accomplish the age of 21, then I give all the said lands and tenements to the child and heirs of the child for ever. And if the child shall depart this life before the age of 21 I give the said lands and tenements to my wife and her assigns until WILLIAM LEWES my son shall come to his full age of 21, towards the bringing up and education of the said WILLIAM, and then I bequeath the said lands &c to WILLIAM and his heirs for ever. I give the residue of my lands and tenements in Hollesley Alderton and Shottisham to MARGARET my wife and her assigns until the said WILLIAM shall come to his age of 21, and thenceforth unto said WILLIAM and his heirs for ever. I give all my lands and tenements and lease lands in Orford to MARGARET my wife and her assigns until ELIZABETH my daughter shall come to her age of 21 years, towards the education and bringing up of the said ELIZABETH, and then unto ELIZABETH and her heirs for ever. To the churchwardens and overseers of the poor of Orford £4 to be distributed among the poor of Orford at the burial of me. To the churchwardens and overseers of Hollesley 40s. to be paid to them within half a year and distributed among the poor. To THOMAS BOND snr. my loving friend 20s. I nominate MARGARET my true and loving wife sole exrx. Witnesses: TOBIAS COPPING, THOMAS TOCKLEY, WILLIAM BLANCHFLOWER (X), THOMAS BOND. Pr. 14 Dec. 1630.

R(W) JOHN MARGETS (X) of Bawdsey, yeoman. 6 October 1630 (206)

Sick. To JOHN MARGETS my son and his heirs all my messuages lands tenements and hereditaments in Hollesley on condition that he and his heirs or assigns shall pay to BRIDGET MARGETS my daughter and her assigns £20 and to KATHARINE MARGETS my daughter £20 in the manner following -- to BRIDGET first £6 13s. 4d. within one year after JOHN my son shall accomplish his age of 22, and the next year after to KATHARINE £6 13s. 4d., and within the third year again to BRIDGET £6 13s. 4d., and within the fourth year again to KATHARINE £6 13s. 4d., and within the fifth year to BRIDGET £6 13s. 4d. and the sixth year to KATHARINE £6 13s. 4d., with benefit of survivorship. Every payment aforesaid shall be paid at the south porch of the church of Bawdsey. If JOHN or his exors. make default in part or in whole I do give all my said messuages &c to my said daughters BRIDGET and KATHARINE and their heirs for ever. If JOHN shall die without heir of his body lawfully begotten I bequeath all the said messuages &c formerly given to JOHN unto THOMAS MARGETS my son and his heirs for ever, paying unto BRIDGET and KATHARINE the several legacies given unto them in such manner as JOHN should have paid them and under such condition of forfeiture. And to THOMAS my son and GEORGE MARGETS my son and their heirs all my lands and tenements &c (lands assured to EMMA my now wife for a jointure excepted) in Bawdsey, to be equally divided between them, with benefit of survivorship. I give such messuages tenements lands and hereditaments as my wife hath assurance of for the term of her life, in Bawdsey, to my said sons THOMAS and GEORGE and their heirs equally to be divided after the decease of my wife, with benefit of survivorship. To BRIDGET and KATHARINE and their assigns for ever all my goods chattels household stuffs and implements, to have them presently after the day of marriage of my said wife after my decease, or the day of her death, which shall first happen after my decease. To EMMA my wife all my messuages tenements &c formerly mentioned in this will towards bringing up my said sons and daughters so long as she keep herself a widow, and also the use of my goods and chattels so long as she keep herself a widow towards the bringing up of my sons and daughters; during the time she shall possess the said goods &c she shall not alien sell waste or convey cattles chattels &c to the hindrance of my said daughters. Presently after the marriage of my said wife my exor. shall take into his hands all the said goods and chattels in the occupation of EMMA my wife or her assigns, to the use of my said daughters and their assigns. I nominate my brother-in-law THOMAS COWPER of Bricett, yeoman executor, to see my body interred and my debts paid and to receive debts to me due, to prove this will and prise my goods at a rateable value and perform all other things in this will to be executed. Towards his pains and travail herein to be taken I do give him 10s. to be paid presently after my decease, also my funeral charges and charges of probate and for the inventories shall be paid unto him presently after my decease out of my goods and chattels, any gift formerly of them made to the contrary notwithstanding. Witnesses: THOMAS BUTTELL (X) and RICHARD SMYTER. Pr. in the parish church of Wickham on 5 Nov. 1630. Admon. to the relict EMMA, the named exor., THOMAS COOPER, having renounced duty and sworn upon the gospels that he will not intermeddle in the goods of the deceased.

R(W) HENRY MUNNIS alias MELLS of East Bergholt, husbandman. 21 September 1626 (207

Sick. To ELIZABETH MUNNIS als. MELLIS my wife £10 towards the bringing up of WILLIAM MUNNIS my youngest son, to be paid to her 10s. within half a year after my decease and so after every half year until the £10 be paid. My exor. shall deliver yearly for 4 years next after my decease 2 bushels of rye towards the bringing up of WILLIAM. To said wife ELIZABETH and to JOHN MUNNIS, DAVID MUNNIS and HENRY MUNNIS, my three sons, and to ANN PEACOCK my daughter all my household stuff, equally divided by 3 or 4 honest indifferent men. My son HENRY MUNNIS shall choose the first part where he thinketh good, and after him ELIZABETH my wife shall choose the second part, and the other three parts shall be divided by lot. To WILLIAM MUNNIS my youngest son 40s. at age 21. Remainder of my goods and chattels, my debts paid my funeral expenses and other charges discharged, probate of my will paid, I give to HENRY MUNNIS my son whom I make exor. ELIZABETH my wife shall have and enjoy all that her household stuff which was her own when I did marry her. I make my well-beloved in Christ CHRISTOPHER LEWIS of East Bergholt my supervisor. Witnesses: ANTHONY BUNNE, JOHN STEVENSONNE and ANTHONY BUNNE (X). Pr. 8 Nov. 1630, when HENRY MUNNES als. MELLES of Dedham, Essex, exor., appeared in person and renounced executorship. Admon. to JOHN MUNNES als. MELLES of Kersey, Suffolk.

R(W) JOHN NOBLET (X) of Monk Soham, singleman. (208)
8 November 1630

Very sick. To JOAN my sister wife of ROBERT SALLOWES £14, £7 within one year and the other £7 within 5 years of my decease. To ELIZABETH NOBLET my sister £14, £7 within 2 years and the other £7 within 6 years. To ROBERT NOBLET my brother £14, £7 within 3 years and the other £7 within 7 years. To FYNETT my sister wife of JOHN MAYHEW £10, £5 within 4 years, and other £5 within 8 years. To WILLIAM NOBLET my brother £14, £7 within 9 years and other £7 within 10 years of my decease. To JOHN NEWSON of Earl Soham 30s. to be paid within 2 days of my decease. To JOHN SUTTON of Kettleburgh 34s. within 4 years. To THOMAS KASBY of Kettleburgh 34s. within 5 years. To MARGARET JENKINSON of Kettleburgh 10s. within half a year after my decease. To THOMAS SMITH of Earl Soham 20s. within 1 year. To ISAAC BLYRES of Monk Soham 15s. within 2 years. All these payments to be made at the now dwelling house of JOHN MAYHEW in Bedfield. To said JOHN MAYHEW all my lands holden by copy of court roll of the manor of Kenton Hall cum Sudden Hall, to hold to him his heirs and assigns for ever at the will of the lord according to the custom of the manor, to pay all my debts and legacies and bring my body in decent and Christian manner to the ground, provided that if ANTHONY NOBLET my brother and his heirs and assigns shall permit the said JOHN MAYHEW to take the yearly rent and profit of all the rest of my lands and tenements holden of the manor of Framsden together with the rent and profits of said lands holden of the manor of Kenton Hall cum Sudden Hall to his and their only use towards the payment of my debts and legacies until the said ANTHONY NOBLET shall accomplish his age of 21, and shall then give bond to said JOHN MAYHEW his heirs or assigns for the payment of all those legacies which shall then be behind or unpaid, then I will that all of the said lands and tenements as well the lands holden of the manor of Framsden also the lands holden of the manor of Kenton Hall cum Sudden Hall shall be and remain unto the said ANTHONY NOBLET my brother and his heirs and assigns for ever. I make said JOHN MAYHEW sole exor. To the poor in Monk Soham 10s. within 3 months of my decease. Witnesses: ANN MAYHEW and JOHN MAYHEW. Pr. at Wickham 13 Jan. 1630/31.

R(W) ELIAS PROW of Woodbridge, tailor. 30 October 1630 (209)

Sick. To ELIZABETH my wife all my goods and chattels and household stuffs and implements on condition that she shall not convey or purloin any of the said goods in her lifetime to any kindred or other person, which goods &c are set down in writing in an inventory bearing the date hereof, without the consent of my 2 exors. I make WILLIAM PROW of Hemley and JOHN PROW of Sutton my exors. To JOHN PROW my exor. one feather-bed with all things to the same belonging, presently after my said wife's decease. To WILLIAM PROW also one feather-bed with all things belonging, standing in the chamber, also 1 cupboard in the hall. To PATHEM the wife of WILLIAM BRIDGES 1 seege chair or chair of easement. If the wife of WILLIAM BRIDGES shall depart this life before her brother JOHN, then the said JOHN to have the chair. Witnesses: ROWLAND LATHAM (X), JOHN SMITH, FAITH LATHAM (X). Pr. at Ipswich 15 Dec. 1630.

R(W) THOMAS PREST (X) of Lound, husbandman. (210)
10 November 1630

Very sick. To ROBERT PREST my youngest son my houses lands and tenements in Lound which late I purchased of JOHN BLYTH, with all the lands both free and copy belonging, after the decease of my wife ELIZABETH who shall have them during her life, and after her decease to the said ROBERT and his heirs for ever except such as shall hereafter be mentioned, which I will shall be sold towards the payment of my debts, viz. the acre called Hurne and the half-acre lying in Hopton field. To ELIZABETH my daughter £9 to be paid by said ROBERT, £5 within one year of the decease of my wife and £4 such time 12 months after. To MARY my daughter £9 to be paid by ROBERT, £5 within 3 years of decease of said wife and £4 12 months after, with power of distraint. To ELIZABETH my wife my land in Corton field called Steeplerent acre during her life, and after her decease I give the same to HENRY my son and his heirs for ever. My other lands in Corton shall be sold towards payment of my debts. All which land bequeathed for payment of debts my exors. shall make sale thereof so soon as maybe after my decease. All my movable goods credits chattels household stuff and implements I give to ELIZABETH my wife towards the bringing up of my children. And if my wife depart this life before my children be grown up to some discretion to shift in this world my other exor. shall have the use of all my houses lands and tenements before bequeathed unto my son ROBERT until he shall come to his age of 16 years, and then to enter the same and begin his payments within one year after to his sisters. I make ELIZABETH my wife and ROBERT PREST my brother exors. Witnesses:

THOMAS ELLES, ROBERT UNDERWOOD. A postscript and addition to this my testament: I give to BENJAMIN my eldest son £5 to be paid by my son ROBERT, and in regard to the small portion I give him he shall have the same within the first year after the decease of my wife, and my daughters not to have any until a year after he be paid, and for default he to have liberty to distrain. Witnesses: THOMAS STARES and me ROBERT UNDERWOOD. Pr. at Lowestoft 8 Dec. 1630.

R(W) JOAN POWES (X) of Aldeburgh, widow. 13 August 1630 (211)

My debts and funeral charges shall be paid by my exors. and the remainder of my goods and chattels shall be equally divided between my 2 daughters EMMA DUX and JOAN DUX. I appoint my daughter EMMA DUX exrx. Witnesses: THOMAS FISKE, THOMAS BOONE, SUSAN SHANKE (X). Pr. at Yoxford 2 Nov. 1630.

R(W) ROBERT PAGE (X) of South Cove, husbandman. (212)
10 December 1630

Sick. To be buried in the churchyard of South Cove. To MARGARET my wife all my movable goods on condition that she pay to WILLIAM SMYTH of Sutton, my brother-in-law, £40 within 6 months after my decease. Upon receipt thereof WILLIAM SMYTH or his executors shall become bound unto FRANCIS PAGE my only son in the penal sum of 4 score pounds for the payment of the said sum to the said FRANCIS if he shall accomplish his age of 21, or otherwise to the benefit of the said WILLIAM SMYTH and his heirs for ever, provided that the said WILLIAM his executors and assigns shall every year of 3 years after my decease pay unto MARGARET my wife £3 towards the maintenance of FRANCIS my son, the first payment to begin within one month after my decease. FRANCIS my son shall give notice unto the said WILLIAM SMYTH his executors or assigns at the now mansion house of the said WILLIAM situated in Stoven 20 days after he shall accomplish his age of 21. To MARGARET my wife my tenement with appurtenances in Easton during the term she shall keep herself a widow, she keeping the houses in tenantable reparations; but if she shall marry then I give the tenement with the lands and appurtenances to my son FRANCIS, then presently to enter the same to his use, and she shall have no benefit of thirds in the same, for if she make entry of them then my former gifts unto her shall be void. But if my son depart this life before the age of 21, then I give the fee simple estate thereof to MARGARET my wife. I make said MARGARET sole exrx. Witnesses: WILLIAM SMYTH, JOHN COLBECKE, clerk. Pr. at Beccles 31 Dec. 1630.

R(W) WILLIAM PEIRSE* of South Cove, yeoman. (213)
1 February 1626/7

Whole in body. To be buried in South Cove churchyard. To KATHARINE my wife all my tenements and lands which lie about the homestall, which are five parcels of fen ground called summer fen ground, to hold with other their premises during her life, provide that she make no strip or waste but keep my houses and tenements in sufficient reparations and my lands well fenced and ditched. To the said KATHARINE the thirds of all the lands of my son ROBERT PEIRSE; 2 bedsteads 2 feather-beds transoms and other furniture unto them belonging as they now stand in the hall and parlour; 1 cupboard 1 table 3 buffet stools 2 chairs 2 cushions 2 coffers 1 chest 1 keep a warming-pan a brass pot a posnet a skillet a spit a dripping pan 6 pewter dishes 2 andirons a pair of tongs a roastiron a hake 3 milk bowls and all her linen and woolen 2 kettles and all other things being of small value; 2 cows at her choice of the best, 1 hog, all the fowls, all my hemp; all such provision of victuals viz. rye wheat malt butter cheese beef pork and all else necessary to the maintenance of my house which shall be unspent in my house at the day of my death. To THOMAS PEIRSE my son all my lands in South Cove in the north field both free and copy containing by estimation 8 acres; 2 acres in Cove Common being copyhold holden of Mr THOMAS PRESTON, with my part in the grove or wood, and 1 pightle called Stoneland pightle in the south field to hold for ever; 1 bay nag or horse a saddle a bridle boots and spurs a calf a year old 2 theaves or sheep. To THOMAS PEIRSE my son and [deleted] PERSE my daughter shall find unto KATHARINE my wife and lay in at her house in Cove bread corn and ale-corn for one whole year when they shall be thereto demanded. To ROBERT PEIRSE my son all my copyhold lands holden of the manor of Frostenden to hold for ever provided that he shall not trouble my exor. to take away any of the crop which shall be growing upon said lands at the time of my death, but shall be content to take the yearly rent for them for one year next after my decease, and then to hold the lands for ever. If ROBERT shall refuse so to do then my son THOMAS PEIRSE shall have my said copy lands for ever. To ELIZABETH PEIRSE my daughter £50, £10 within 1 year after my wife's decease and £10 yearly till the £50 be satisfied. To MARY PEIRSE my daughter £50, by £10 a year, the first payment within one year after my wife's decease. To ELIZABETH PEIRSE my daughter 1 milch cow 2 sheep. To MARY my daughter 1 calf 2 sheep. To my son ROBERT PEIRSE all my messuage lands and tenements except such lands and part of a grove bequeathed to my son THOMAS PEIRSE provided that the said ROBERT PEIRSE and his executors shall pay to ELIZABETH my daughter £50 and £50 to MARY my daughter in the manner above specified. If ROBERT shall refuse, then THOMAS shall have the said messuage lands &c, he and his executors to pay the legacies to ELIZABETH and MARY as specified. And if THOMAS shall refuse then my daughters ELIZABETH and MARY shall have the said messuage and lands &c equally divided. To ROBERT my son all the rents due from Mr RICHARD GARRARD of Southwold unto me, which is one penny per annum, and the rents due from WILLIAM BARBER, which is 10d. per annum, and to hold these yearly rents hereafter. To all my godchildren who are males 2s. 6d. within 6 months of my decease. To THOMASINE PAGE 2s. 6d. within one month. The rest of my goods and chattels, my debts and funeral expenses discharged, I give to THOMAS PEIRSE, ELIZABETH PEIRSE and MARY PEIRSE, my sons and daughters, to be equally divided. I make THOMAS PEIRSE my son

and [MARY deleted] PEIRSE my daughter joint executors. Witnesses: HENRY SPORNE, WILLIAM PEIRSE and me JAMES CUNNINGHAM. Pr. at Beccles 11 Jan. 1630/1.
[*The name is spelled PEARCE in the original will.]

R(W) HUGH STACEY (X) of Blythburgh, shoemaker. (214)
2 August 1630

To my son HUGH STACEY now dwelling in Walberswick all my movable goods and chattels unbequeathed heretofore absolutely and presently after my decease upon condition that he pay all my debts and provide that my body be decently and comely brought to the ground. Witnesses: JOHN PALMER, HENRY GREEN, WILLIAM CHARROLD. Pr. at Yoxford 24 Nov. 1630.

W(R) MARGERY SMETHE (X) of Bramford. 13 December 1626 (215)

To be buried in Bramford churchyard. To JOHN SMETHE the son of HENRY SMETHE my bed as it standeth with all things thereon, the covering only excepted. To JINE SMETHE the coverlet that lie on my bed, my best petticoat, a ruff, 2 coyes one quarter a pillow-bier, my biggest bowl, my biggest kettle, a tub a tramell a pair of pot-hooks a roast-iron a pail a tow-comb a coffer. To ALEXANDER COLE 10s. to be paid to JOHN COLE his father, to his use. The rest of my goods to HENRY SMETHE whom I make sole exor. Witnesses: ROGER RAFE, GEORGE CUDBARD (X). Pr. at Ipswich 9 July 1630.

R(W) RICHARD SHEPPARD of Wenhaston (N). 6 December 1630 (216)

To ALICE his wife all his goods. Witnesses: REGINALD LESSEY and SUSAN BENNUCLE. Pr. 6 Dec. 1630.

R(W) WILLIAM SMALLEHEDGE (X) of Eyke, yeoman. (217)
21 September 1628

To ELIZABETH SMALEHEDGE my wife all my movable goods and chattels comprised in an inventory hereafter following viz. 3 feather-beds 3 feather bolsters 4 pillows 3 blankets 3 coverlets 2 other bedsteads with joined heads and hangings to them, with 3 lines and 3 matts, 2 trundle bedsteads 2 flock beds 2 coverlets 2 matts and lines, 1 cupboard 1 long table 1 form 3 joined stools 2 small tables 6 chairs 2 keeps 1 warming-pan, 3 chests with 8 pair sheets 2 board cloths 6 tablenapkins 4 pillow-biers 4 towels 4 brass kettles 1 cauldron 1 copper 2 skillets 4 brass pots 16 pieces pewter 3 salts 4 brazen candlesticks 1 brass mortar and pestel 2 cob-irons 2 pair tongs 2 fire-pans 2 hakes 1 roast-iron 3 spits 1 trivet 1 frying-pan 3 beer vessels 3 brewing tubs 2 keelers 3 milk bowls 1 cheese press 3 cheese vats and 2 breads 1 chair 1 salting tray and salting-trough 1 moulding board 1 pair malt querns a wicker chair 1 boarded hogs' cote 1 milch cow 2

shoats 2 coombs of barley 1 coomb of brank 1 load of hay 2 remble of hemp 2 loads of blocks; one half year's rent due out of the house and lands at Ufford wherein ROGER SMALHEDGE my son doth dwell, if it be due to me at the day of my death. In witness that this deed of gift made at Eyke the day and year abovesaid I have with my own hands delivered one piece of pewter before given, being part of the goods aforesaid, unto ELIZABETH SMALHEDGE my wife in the presence of these whose names are hereunto subscribed: JOHN NEWMAN, JOHN SMALLEDGE, HENRY WAISTHE. Admon. to ELIZABETH SMALLEDGE the relict, 14 Dec. 1630.
[Note: This document is in the form of a deed of gift, rather than of a will.]

R(W) THOMAS SIEDGWEEKES (X) of Walton, husbandman. (218)
3 November 1630

Sick. To the poor of Walton 10s. presently after my decease. To JOHN FROST and FRANCIS HUMFREY of Walton, my executors, 15s. apiece for their pains. To THOMAS SEIGWEEKES my only son all my goods and chattels, my debts legacies and funerals being discharged. All my goods and chattels shall be sold by my exors. and the money arising shall be improved to the good of my son, to be paid to him at his age of 21. My exors. shall bring up my son to school until he be fit to be an apprentice and then to put him out to whatever trade he shall have most mind. I make JOHN FROSTE and FRANCIS HUMFREY my exors. and SIMON PETTEWARD of Walton, clerk, my supervisor; and my exors. shall enter to him into bond within one month after my decease, of three score pounds, for the performance of this will. Witnesses: SIMON PETTEWARD, MARGARET HUMFREY (X), ELIZABETH MARTYN (X). Pr. at Ipswich 26 Nov. 1630.

R(W) JOHN SOUNDS of Brantham, husbandman. 16 October 1630 (219)

Sick. To be buried at the discretion of ALICE my wife whom I make exrx. To the poor of Brantham 10s. to be distributed by the discretion of my exrx. where most need shall require within one month of my decease. To JOHN my son my parcel of lands called Stonelands in Bromely Parva, Essex, containing by estimation 10 acres, so soon as he shall attain the age of 21; all my other lands and tenements called Russells in Bromly Parva to ALICE my wife during her life, and after her decease to BENJAMIN SOUNDS my son; with benefit of survivorship. My wife shall make no strip nor waste but shall keep the aforesaid messuage in good sort during her life. To HELEN SOUNDS and ELIZABETH SOUNDS my daughters £40 at their several ages of 21 or day of marriage, with benefit of survivorship if either should die without issue before her legacy be due. To HELEN WILES my sister 10s. per annum for life at two several payments every year by equal portions. I make ALICE my wife sole exrx. and give her the rest of my goods towards bringing up my children and paying my debts and legacies, desiring her to have especial care in bringing them up in the fear of God. Witnesses: JOHN RAND, THOMAS ROLFE, JOHN HAVELL snr. Pr. at Ipswich 20 Nov. 1630.

R(W) JOHN TUTTELL of Framsden, tailor. 10 October 1630 (220)

Weak and aged. To JOHN TUTTELL my son which I had by my first wife my house and tenement wherein I now dwell with all my lands meadows pastures tenements and hereditaments as well free as copy, on condition that he pay to ANN my wife, JOHN my youngest son and ANN my daughter and SAMUEL my eldest son the several sums that I shall hereafter limit: to ANN my wife £25, of which £20 within 6 months and £5 within 2 years of my decease, both payments to be made in the south porch of Framsden church, which sum of £25 I give in full satisfaction of her jointure and all such title of dower as the said ANN, by one indenture made 1 Oct. 1621 upon consideration of marriage, or by any other means, may claim out of my lands tenements &c; to my eldest son SAMUEL £15, £10 within 4 months and £5 within one year of my decease, to be paid at the place aforesaid; to JOHN my youngest son 50s. when he is 14, to be paid at that place; to ANN my daughter 50s. when she is 15, at the same place. To ANN my wife all my household stuff, chattels and implements of household, and I nominate her and the said JOHN TUTTELL, my son by my first wife, exors. Witnesses: NATHANIEL BOWMAN and LEONARD COALE. Pr. at Ipswich 16 Nov. 1630.

R(W) THOMAS WATSON of Somersham, yeoman. 3 September 1628 (221)

Whole but aged. To be buried in Somersham churchyard. To JOHN WATSON my second son my dwelling house with orchard and garden barn and stable, one piece of land called Halls, with one little close being between Halls and the barn; 2 pieces of land called Churchfield and Peasefield with the piece of freehold, sometime Courtnalls, after the decease of my wife, on condition that he shall pay to THOMAS WATSON my eldest son £20 within 4 years of the decease of JOAN my wife, £5 the first year after, £5 the second year, £5 the third year and £5 the fourth year, with power of distraint. To RALPH my youngest son the tenement called Needs, one piece of land called the Little Pightle in Somersham, one piece called Barnards in Little Blakenham, after the decease of my wife, on condition that he pay to THOMAS my eldest son £20 within four years after the decease of JOAN my wife, £5 the first year, £5 the second, £5 the third and £5 the fourth year after her decease, with power of distraint. I will that the footpath that now lieth in the meadow being part of the tenement called NEEDS shall be free to JOHN WATSON my second son and his heirs and assigns as a footpath for ingress egress and regress for ever. To JOHN WATSON the best feather-bed and bolster, 2 feather pillows, the bedstead as it now standeth with the best covering, the best pair sheets, the great table in the hall, all these after the decease of my wife; in the meantime the best bedstead and great table in the hall are not to be removed from where they now stand. The portion of any son dying shall be equally divided among the others living. To THOMASINE HARVIE my grandchild 20s. at age 21. To JOAN my wife all my lands during widowhood, paying to every child 20s. apiece yearly. If she marry she shall pay every of my sons 40s. yearly. To JOAN my wife all my movable goods except the goods formerly given, and I make her sole exrx. Witnesses: NICHOLAS MICHELL, clerk, JOHN BOGAS, WILLIAM TORBOLD (X). Pr. at Ipswich 23 Oct. 1630.

R(W) JOHN WATLINGE (X) of Wenhaston, butcher. (222)
20 November 1630

To ANN my wife all my goods and chattels towards the maintenance and bringing up of all my children till their several ages of 21, and also shall pay such portions to every one of my children at 21 as shall be thought meet and fitting by my kinsman THOMAS WATLING, so as it do not amount to above £10 apiece, provided that my said wife shall, within 10 days after my decease, enter into one obligation in the penal sum of £200 unto my said kinsman THOMAS WATLING with condition that she shall perform this will. I make said ANN sole exrx. Witnesses: JOSEPH THETFORD, EDMUND WATLING, SUSAN FOX (X). Pr. at Yoxford 13 Dec. 1630.

R(W) WILLIAM WARNER (X) of Petistree, husbandman. (223)
22 November 1630

To ANN my wife £10 within one month after my decease, and she shall carry away all such household stuff as she brought to me at the time of our marriage. Also to the said ANN 13s. 4d. yearly for life, to be paid by KINBOROUGH my daughter out of my house and lands in Pettistree at the two feasts of Saint Michael and the Annunciation of Our Lady by equal portions, the first payment to begin at either of the feasts which shall first happen after my decease. To KINBOROUGH my daughter all my houses and lands as well freehold as copy in Pettistree for ever; and 2 cows, one black and the other brown. To BRIDGET REYNOLDS my daughter now wife of THOMAS REYNOLDS all my money obligations bills debts, except one obligation wherein Mr ROBERT LANE of Campsea Abbey standeth indebted to me which shall be paid into the hands of my exor. until BRIDGET REYNOLDS my grandchild shall accomplish the age of 21 and then the said £20 to be paid to her, and in the meantime my exor. shall pay to BRIDGET REYNOLDS my daughter for the use of the said £20, 26s. 8d. yearly towards the education of the said child, and if BRIDGET my grandchild depart this life before the age of 21 the £20 is to be paid to my daughter BRIDGET REYNOLDS within 3 months of the decease of the said grandchild. To BRIDGET REYNOLDS my daughter 2 cows, one white and another red. All my hemp to be equally divided into three parts whereof ANN my wife to have one part and my two daughters the other two. The rest of my goods shall be equally divided between my two daughters. I make [blank] WAYLOND of Petistree sole exor., with power to sell so much of my goods as shall pay to my wife the

£10, and I give him 20s. towards his pains, and all his necessary charges about my will. Witnesses: ROBERT LANE, FRANCIS BARNES (X), ROBERT BAUDWELL. Pr. at Wickham 14 Dec. 1630.

R(W) MARGARET YOUNGS (X) late wife of CHRISTOPHERYOUNGS (224) deceased, of Southwold. 27 October 1630

For the house and lands I dwell in I desire it may be divided among my children according to my husband's will. For all my household stuff money plate chattels, my will is that my debts and funeral charges being paid, the remainder to be equally divided between my six children JOHN, JOSEPH, CHRISTOPHER, MARY, MARGARET, MARTHA, or so many as shall be alive at my decease. I ordain my two sons JOHN and JOSEPH YOUNGS my exors. Witnesses: REYNOLD HOXTON, WILLIAM RAINBOROW, ANNIS GY, wid. (X). Pr. at Beccles 8 Jan. 1630/1.

R(W) SIMON FISHER of Lowestoft, yeoman. 8 January 1630/1 (225)

Sick. To FAITH my wife and RICHARD FISHER my son all my goods and chattels and bedding with all my debts due to me, to be equally divided between them, whom I make exors, charging them to pay all my debts. Witnesses: MARK PACYE and me MAPLIZDEN. Pr. at Beccles 26 Jan. 1630/1.

R(W) ELIZABETH GROOME (X) of Mendham, widow. (226) 29 December 1630

To THOMAS CROWE my son-in-law's children WILLIAM CROWE 3s. 4d., MARGARET CROWE 3s. 4d. To FINETE GROOME daughter of NICHOLAS GROOME 3s. 4d. To ROBERT ROPE's son ROBERT ROPE, my son-in-law's child, 3s. 4d. To ROBERT BARBERE my son-in-law's child ROBERT BARBER 3s. 4d. To JOHN RUSHMER son of JOHN RUSHMER 3s. 4d. To ELIAS DAYE 10s. To the poor of Mendham 10s. To JOHN RUSHMER the elder 5s. To JOAN READE and MARY RICHARDSON, ANN CARTER, FRANCIS BOWLES and CHRISTOPHER FROST 12d. apiece. As to the rest of my goods; provided that my exor. shall receive the money which is due to me by bonds (that was an annuity from PETER GROOME my husband, lately deceased, and this money to be received from my sons and sons-in-law within two months after my death) he shall bear all charges of my burial and this will, and the remainder to be divided equally between my sons and sons-in-law WILLIAM GROOME, THOMAS GROOME, JOHN TUTTELL, THOMAS CROW, ROBERT BARBER, ROBERT ROOPE; the children of my son TENSULETH GROOME, lately deceased, should have that part that he should have had equally divided between them viz. PETER, THOMAS, and JOHN GROOME. A sum of £10 15s. due to me from JOHN MANNING's heirs for 2 years' board is to be divided equally between my sons and sons-in-law above-mentioned. These legacies are to be paid within half a year of my decease. I constitute JOHN TUTTELL my son-in-law sole exor. and THOMAS GROOME my son supervisor. Witnesses: ROBERT BABERE, ANN GROOME (X), ELIZABETH TUTTLLIE (X) and me JOHN RUSHMEERE. Pr at Beccles 15 Jan. 1630/1.

R(W) MARY BROWNE of Brundish (N). [no date] (227)

To RICHARD BROWNE her son 1 coomb of wheat and 6 bushels of malt. All her linen to be equally divided between ANN BROWNE, MARY BROWNE and ALICE SPARKE her daughters. To ALICE SPARKE a chest and a desk. Witnesses: RICHARD BROWNE and ALICE SPARKE. Admon. to RICHARD BROWNE 2 Nov. 1630.

R(W) ANN BIRDE (X) of Baylham, widow. 4 November 1630 (228)

To my son JOSEPH 30s. To my son HENRY BIRD £5 within one year; if he die before then it shall be equally divided between my sons NATHANIEL and DAVID. To my sons NATHANIEL and DAVID BIRD £20 apiece within one year after my death if they then be 21. If they die before then it shall be equally divided among the rest of my children. To my daughter ANN GRAMES £30 within one year of my death if she outlive her husband ROBERT GRAMES, but during his life the £30 shall remain in the hands of my exor. to be employed for the use of the said ANN GRAMES, but if she die before him it shall be equally divided among the rest of my children. To my daughter SUSAN £30 at marriage or within one month after, but if she live a singlewoman then shall receive the use of it every year by the appointment of my exor., and when she dies it shall be equally divided among my children that survive. To my daughter FRANCES £30 to be paid at marriage or within one month after provided that she shall not marry nor be contracted to any man without approbation of my exor. If she shall bestow herself contrary to this my desire then she shall only receive the use of the £30 during her life, and the principal sum remaining after her death shall be equally divided among the rest of my children. If I die before my two sons NATHANIEL and DAVID BIRD have served out the time of their apprenticeships their portions shall rest in the hands of my exor. until that time be accomplished and half a year after, and in the best manner to be improved by my exors. And the use and benefit thereof shall also accrue for increasing their portions and, at the time appointed, shall be paid to them. The residue of my goods (my debts and funeral expenses and probate paid) to be bestowed at the discretion of my exors. I ordain my two sons JOHN BIRD and SAMUEL BIRD exors. and give JOHN BIRD 30s. and SAMUEL BIRD £20 for their pains. Witnesses: WILLIAM BOWTELL, WILLIAM MANNING (X). Pr. at Ipswich 14 Jan. 1630/1. Admon. to JOHN BIRD with power reserved for SAMUEL.

R(W) MATTHEW BITTON of Dunwich, mariner. (229)
16 January 1630/1

To FINITE my wife my mansion house wherein I now dwell with the houses yards lands feedings and appurtenances during her life, and thereafter to WILLIAM BITTON my son and his heirs for ever, and he shall pay £20 within two years after his entry by the death of my wife as followeth: to MARGERY my daughter £8, to FINITE my daughter £6, to SUSAN my daughter £6. I give my other house called Coppins with the yards gardens &c in Dunwich to FINITE my wife and her heirs to be sold for the payment of my debts. To my three daughters FINITE, SUSAN and MARGERY 2 herring nets ready newed for the seas, to be delivered to them when they accomplish their several ages of 16. All other goods and chattels within the house or pertaining to the sea I give to FINITE my wife, whom I ordain executrix, and I name my bretheren-by-law JOHN ROBSON jnr. and NICHOLAS RUDDES to be supervisors, and give them for their pains 20s. To reparation of the church and chancel of St. Peter in Dunwich 20s. to be paid within one year after my decease to the churchwardens. Witnesses: THOMAS PEARCE, NICHOLAS RUDES. Pr. at Yoxford 3 Feb. 1630/1.

R(W) THOMAS GILMORE of East Bergholt, gentleman. (230)
14 October 1630

Sick. To my daughter ELIZABETH and her husband DANIEL RAYE £50 to be paid to either of them, £25 within 6 months and the other £25 within one year of my death, at the south porch of the parish church of East Bergholt. To said DANIEL RAYE my bay mare or my black nag at his choice. To SUSAN GILMORE my youngest daughter £250 to be paid in the south porch of the church, £100 within 1 month after she attain the age of 21 and £100 more one month after she attain the age of 22, and £50 after she attain 23 years. RALPH GILMORE my son and heir apparent shall, at his own cost, in meet decent and comely manner, as well with diet and apparel as with other necessaries, educate maintain and bring up SUSAN my daughter until her age of 21. To the said SUSAN the bedstead whereon I do usually lay, 2 feather-beds 2 feather bolsters 2 feather pillows a pair of blankets used to the bed 2 coverlets 20 pieces of pewter great and small 1 brass pot 1 brass kettle 2 pair sheets, but not of the coarser sorts, to be delivered to her within 1 month after she attain the age of 21. The rest of my goods chattels and personal estate I give to my exors. towards the satisfaction of the legacies given in this will. To the said RALPH GILMORE my son all those my three parts (into 4 parts divided) in East Bergholt called Flatford Mill and the land whereupon the same is situate, containing by estimation half an acre, with every of their appurtenances; and my 3 closes copyhold lying next the rectory lands of East Bergholt, called Webbers, containing by estimation 4 acres, with their appurtenances, to hold to himself and his heirs and assigns on condition that within 3 months after my death he prove and undertake the performance of this will, and he or his exors. or assigns shall pay the said SUSAN or her exors. the £250 afore-mentioned and shall satisfy to my daughter ELIZABETH and her husband the said sum of £50, and shall discharge all sums of money as my son-in-law DANIEL RAYE standeth now engaged with or for me unto Mr SALTER, Mr BRETTEN, Mr NORWICH, Mr EDWARD CLARKE and the inhabitants of the town of East Bergholt, by any bond wherein I am principally and first named. If my son RALPH or his heirs exors. or assigns fail in the due proof and just performance of any part of this will, then it shall be lawful for said DANIEL RAYE his exors. and assigns to make sale of my aforesaid water-mill and my copyhold lands, and with the money thereof coming to pay all legacies and debts as shall then be unpaid, and instead the aforesaid RALPH my son whom I hereafter name my sole exor. I then constitute the said DANIEL RAYE the sole exor. to see the will performed; and if after the payment of the £250 to SUSAN and the £50 to ELIZABETH wife of DANIEL RAYE and after payment of my debts there shall remain any overplus from the sale it shall be divided equally between my 2 daughters. I further give to said RALPH GILMORE my son all the rest of my lands and tenements for ever. To my dear and beloved friend ANN SAYER of Pulham St. Mary the Virgin, widow, my bay gelding whereon I do usually ride, to be delivered presently after my death and £5 within 6 months after. To Doctor JAMES, minister of East Bergholt 40s. within 1 year. To the poorest of East Bergholt £4 within 6 months. To the poorest of Eastborough, Norfolk, 40s. within 1 year. I make said RALPH GILMORE my son sole exor. Witnesses: LAURENCE MAIHEW, THOMAS MILLES (X), THOMAS SHALLES (X). Pr. at Ipswich 8 Jan. 1630/31.

R(W) WILLIAM HEMPSON (X) of Baylham, husbandman. (231
20 November 1630

Sick. To WILLIAM HEMPSON my son 12d. To WILLIAM HEMPSON son of the said WILLIAM 12d. To MARY HEMPSON daughter of my son WILLIAM 2s. 6d. To ROBERT HEMPSON my son 12d. To ANTHONY HEMPSON 30s. to be paid half a year after my death. The residue of all goods and chattels, my debts funeral expenses and probate of my will being discharged, I give my exors. I make ANN my wife sole exrx. Witnesses: ABIGAIL RUDLAND and ROBERT HEMPSON. Pr. at Ipswich 14 Jan. 1630/31.

R(W) ELIZABETH PERRESON of Beccles, widow. (232
29 December 1630

Sick. To my son JOHN PERISON's 4 children MARGARET, FRANCIS, MARY and LUCY PERISON 5s. each within one year after my decease. To EDMUND, JOHN and ROBERT PERISON my grandchildren, the sons of ROBERT PERISON, 20s. to be equally divided, within one year after my decease. To my son ROBERT PERISON my little table and the form to it, as it is in the chamber on the shop. To MARGARET NUSSEY daughter of NICHOLAS NUSSEY my son-in-law my bedstead full furnished as it is in the same chamber. To HENRY NUSSEY my grandchild, son of said NICHOLAS NUSSEY, my great chest standing in the same chamber. All my brass and pewter to my son-in-law's children NICHOLAS NUSSEY, viz. MARGARET, HENRY, FRANCIS and MARY, equally divided. The rest of my goods to my son-in-law NICHOLAS NUSSEY and MARGARET my daughter, nominating him sole exor. Witnesses: JOSEPH HORBORE, ALICE HARBOR (X), ROBERT HARBOR. Pr. at Beccles 10 Jan. 1630/1.

W(R) HENRY PINCKNEY of Snape, yeoman. (233)
15 December 1630

To be buried in the parish where he dies. To ANN PINCKNEY my wife my copyhold lands which late I purchased of EDMUND KING, now dwelling in Badingham, until HENRY PINCKNEY my son accomplish his age of 21, and then I give to HENRY my son all those copyhold lands lying in Snape, provided that if HENRY depart this life before the age of 21 I give them to ANN my wife for ever. To MARIA my daughter £10 at 15 years of age, one feather-bed with all its appurtenances as it standeth in the parlour chamber. All my other goods and chattels to ANN my wife and I appoint her sole exrx. If she refuse to perform the will then HENRY my son and MARY my daughter shall have all my lands and movable goods and money equally divided. Witnesses: NICHOLAS KING, GEORGE PERSE, FRANCIS WICE (X), ROBERT STANNARD. Pr. at Saxmundham 12 Jan. 1630/1.

R(W) SARAH SPAULDING (X) of Friston, widow. (234)
4 January 1627/8

To be buried in the town where she dies. To JOHN SPALDING my eldest son all my houses and lands in Friston on condition that he pay to SARAH PETERSON my eldest daughter 10s. yearly for life, to be paid at two terms by equal portions, viz. at the Annunciation and the feast of St. Michael, and on condition that he suffer SARAH my daughter to dwell in this my said house, with free ingress until the feast of St. Michael next ensuing. To my 3 sons JOHN my eldest, THOMAS my second and ROBERT my youngest £3 10s. apiece to be paid on 20th October 1628. To my 3 daughters, SARAH my eldest, ELIZABETH my second and MARY my youngest £3 10s. apiece to be paid on the 20th Oct. 1628. To THOMAS my second son my flock bed with the posted bedstead, a pair of sheets 1 blanket 1 pillow my biggest brass pot 1 coffer and the keep in the hall, immediately after my decease. To ROBERT my youngest son my best feather-bed with the trundle bedstead 1 pair sheets 1 pillow-bier and the green coverlet and the coffer which was my mother's, my least brass pot and biggest brass skillet. To JOHN SPALDING the eldest son of my eldest son the deep platter of pewter. To SARAH my daughter the middle kettle with the iron band, the broad pewter platter, the little pewter pot and all my apparel. To ELIZABETH my second daughter one kettle, the spit and the dripping pan, the little black coffer, a pewter candlestick, a great pewter platter and a saucer, 1 pair sheets and 4 pillows. To MARY my youngest daughter my other feather-bed and blankets, a pair of sheets, one pillow-bier, my hutch standing in the hall, my biggest brass kettle, my little bread platter and the table in the hall. To ELIZABETH PETERSON my grandchild my little brass kettle. To WILLIAM BATTELLED my son-in-law the bond of £10 8s. 4d. which he is indebted unto me. I have entreated NICHOLAS KING and THOMAS REEVE of Friston to be my exors. and I give them 10s. apiece for their pains, provided that if my exors. cannot receive this money, which I have given unto my children by this will, within the time appointed which is due by bonds, then my exors.

shall sustain no loss but that my children shall stay for the receipt thereof until payment be made by the creditors [sic.]unto my exors. Witnesses: JOHN GOOSE, THOMAS ASHKETS. Pr. 12 Jan. 1630.

W(R) WILLIAM SMITH of Freston, clerk. 29 October 1629 (235)

To ANN my wife that house and tenement wherein I do now dwell with the yards orchards and gardens belonging, as also my lands in Freston for ever. To ROBERT my son all such of my goods as he was possessed of before the day of the date hereof; and 10s. to be paid within 6 months after my decease. To DORCAS my daughter 1 feather-bed and bolster whereon my two daughters MARY and ELIZABETH doth now lie with the coverlets and blankets now used therewith and all such movable goods of mine as she was possessed of before the date hereof. All other moveables I give to ANN my wife whom I appoint sole exrx. Witnesses: SAMUEL SAMWAYES, ROBERT BURMAN. Pr. at Ipswich 14 Jan. 1630/1.

R(W)(A) THOMASINE WARNER of Theberton, widow (N). 6 January 1630/1 (236)

To JOHN WARNER her son all her goods whatsoever for the payment of her debts and discharging her funerals, excepting 1 feather-bed which she gave to WILLIAM DOWE on condition that he pay the said JOHN WARNER £4 17s. which he stands indebted to her. Witnesses: WILLIAM REINOLDS and ALICE FISKE. Pr. 3 Feb. 1630/1. Admon. to JOHN WARNER. [But the Act Book records that admon. was issued to WILLIAM REINOLDS during minority of JOHN WARNER.]

R(W) NICHOLAS ROW (X) of Middleton. 18 December 1630 (237)

To ELIZABETH now wife of NICHOLAS HELLWYS and to MARY ROW my two daughters, equally divided, my cottage or tenement and piece of land thereto adjoining in Middleton and Fordley, on condition that they and their heirs and assigns permit ALICE my wife and her assigns to occupy my said tenement and land and have the profits thereof during her life; otherwise I give the said tenement &c to ALICE and her heirs for ever. To said MARY my daughter my best cupboard, best posted bedstead, feather-bed feather bolster 2 pillows, my birded coverlet, 2 pair best sheets, best brass pot and kettle, trundle bedstead and the matt and line used to the said posted bedstead. The rest of my goods and chattels I give to ALICE my wife and her assigns during her life, and after her decease I give the same to ELIZABETH my daughter. I make said ALICE sole exrx. Witnesses: JOAN FLATMAN (X), THOMAS EADE. Pr. at Yoxford 3 Feb. 1630/1.

R(W) WILLIAM BAZELIE of Shaddingfield (N). (238)
7 November 1630

To THOMAS WILDES, his wife's son, all his apparel. The rest of his goods to KATHARINE his wife whom he made exrx. Witnesses: JOAN wife of WILLIAM CLARKE and ANN wife of EDWARD BURWELL. Pr. at Beccles 8 Jan. 1630/1.

W(R) MARY CLAYDEN (X) of Southwold, widow. (239)
21 December 1630

To my daughter MARY my best gown and 2 silver spoons. To my daughter SUSAN a livery bedstead and feather-bed bolster blanket coverlet and 2 pillows as it stands in the entry chamber, 6 pair sheets, the long table in the hall and the form there, a great chair a hoop chair a back chair, 2 candlesticks the middle brass pot 2 kettles -- one pieced kettle, the other a little kettle without pieces -- and another little pieced kettle, half the 13 [deleted] pewter dishes and platters and half the stone platters, the cupboard in the parlour and the biggest tipped pot, 4 silver spoons, my heifer, my livery bedstead and feather-bed bolster blanket and coverlet in the parlour chamber. To my daughter SARAH the other half of my 13 dishes and platters and the other half of the stone platters, and the bedstead feather-beds coverlets table "ches" stools keep and all that is in the parlour except the cupboard before bequeathed, the 2 little tables and 3 chairs in the hall, 2 brass pots 2 kettles -- the biggest that I have and another -- a brass posnet, a chest upon the parlour chamber with all that is in it, the cupboard in the hall, my cow. To ROBERT CORSE 4 herring nets, 9 skors as they come from the sea and all my part of the calfer. The rest of my movable goods money plate chattels and cattles shall be equally divided between my 2 daughters SUSAN and SARAH, my debts and funeral charges first paid. I ordain my daughter SARAH my exrx. Witnesses: REYNOLDS HOXTON the elder, JOHN JACKSON (X), MARGARET JACKSON (X), ELIZABETH CEOLET. Pr. at Southwold 2 Feb. 1630/1.

W(R) JONAS BLOBOLD (X) of Dunwich, merchant. (240)
20 October 1627

Sick. To ANN my wife 2 closes lately purchased of Mr WILLIAM BUD, and a little pightle lying in Dunwich right against the house late of Mr JOHN HARPER deceased, she to have them presently after my decease during the time of her widowhood; and after, the said 3 pieces of land shall remain to JONAS BLOBOLD my son during his life; and after the decease of JONAS to TIMOTHY BLOBOLD the son of the said JONAS and heirs of his body lawfully begotten; and for default of such heirs of said TIMOTHY the 3 pieces shall remain to the rest of the children of said JONAS my son. To JONAS my son my house with the yard belonging which late I purchases of WILLIAM GYLES, and my tackle house which I lately purchase of BUSHE and CHILSTON, as they lie in Dunwich, and he to have them during his life and to enter them presently after my decease. And after the decease of said JONAS my son the said house last before to him given shall remain unto RICHARD his son and my grandchild, and to the heirs of his body lawfully begotten. And for default of such heirs the houses I bought of GYLES and BUSH and CHILSTON shall remain to the rest of the children of JONAS my son. To the said JONAS £6 presently after my decease, for part whereof there is in my hand his bill for the payment thereof, which bill I will shall be delivered to him by my exrx. To said JONAS £5 within one year after my decease, and upon receipt thereof my said son shall give out of it as my gift unto ELIZABETH daughter to the said JONAS 40s. which shall be put forth to her best benefit according to law and equity. I give more to the said JONAS my horseman's coat which was his brother's, presently after my decease. To ANN BLOBALD, DOROTHY BLOBALD and FRANCES BLOBALD, daughters of WILLIAM BLOBALD my son deceased, £12 to be paid presently after my decease by the mother FRANCES BLOBALD the late wife of WILLIAM BLOBALD deceased according to the tenor of certain bonds in that behalf made by WILLIAM my son deceased, and so to be paid equally divided between them three; EDMUND HAMOND of Ufford, merchant, shall receive the said money for the children and have the ordering thereof for the good of the children till they come to their several ages of 21 or day of marriage, with benefit of survivorship. To SIMON COLLET one heale net and 3 lines to be delivered presently after my decease. The rest of my goods and chattels implements of household bills and bonds I give to ANN my wife, she to have them presently after my decease, paying my debts and funeral expenses and probate of this will, and performing the same, and I make her sole exrx., and I constitute GEORGE DENNY of Westleton, yeoman, my supervisor to assist my exrx. Witnesses to the will or interlinings therein: THOMAS BREWSTER (X), LYDIA COWELL (X), JOHN REYNOLDS the writer and THOMAS PEARCE. Pr. at Yoxford 3 Feb. 1630/1.

R(W) THOMAS BENNES of Kelsale, husbandman. 6 October 1630 (241)

Sick. To AGNES BENNES my daughter £20 when 21. The rest of my movables bills bonds money &c to ALICE my wife whom I make exrx., she paying my debts, performing this will and bringing my body decently to the ground. Witnesses: JOHN SAUNDERS, clerk, WILLIAM REYNOLDS (X), LAURENCE SHANKE. Pr. at Yoxford 3 Feb. 1630/1.

R(W) ROBERT GOODWYN of Fressingfield, yeoman. (242)
6 January 1630/1

MARIAN my wife shall have the use and occupation of my parlour where I now dwell, with free ingate and outgate from the premises to the orchard and all my lands and tenements for any necessary use for her and her assigns, as also a convenient place to set a wood-stack nigh to the parlour, together with the liberty to use the water and watering adjoining. It shall be lawful for MARIAN yearly to store fell and take upon any my lands 3 loads of wood to be burnt upon the premises during the term of her life if she shall there like to dwell. To said MARIAN £10 in lieu of such dower or thirds she may claim out of my lands, to be paid yearly during her life at Michaelmas and the Annunciation of Mary the Virgin by equal portions, with power of distraint, if any payment shall be behind by the space of 40 days, in all my lands in Fressingfield and Metfield. To said MARIAN my linen and napkins. To JOHN GOODWYN my son all my messuages houses lands tenements meadows pastures feedings in Fressingfield and Metfield. To my son JAMES £40; to my son ROBERT £40; to FAITH my daughter £40; to ANN my daughter, the wife of WILLIAM SMETH, £20 -- all to be paid within 6 months of my decease, with benefit of survivorship if any die without heir of their body lawfully begotten. To WILLIAM SMETH my grandchild the son of WILLIAM SMYTH my son-in-law £10 at his age of 21. To JAMES GOODWYN my son £10 within one year of the decease of my wife MARIAN; to FAITH my daughter £10 within 2 years and to ROBERT my son £10 within 3 years of the decease of said MARIAN; with power of distraint if any sums be behind and unpaid by the space of 40 days. To MARIAN my wife the bed bedstead feather-bed 2 bolsters 2 blankets 2 coverings and 2 pillows as they stand in the parlour; my best little brass pot and posnet, a brass kettle -- the best save two, 8 pieces of pewter at her choice, 1 washing bowl at her choice, a washing tub at her choice, a little table standing in the hall, 1 chest with linen in the parlour chamber. My wife MARIAN shall have the use of all my movable goods in the parlour as also free liberty and use of my mill also of the oven to bake and use all of my houses for any necessary use during her life, both for her and her assigns such as shall remain with her during her widowhood, as also some of my beer vessels and a convenient roomth to set her beer or drink, and some trifling necessaries in other of my houses if she shall desire the same. To JAMES GOODWYN my son and ROBERT my son either of them a bedstead a feather-bed bolsters blankets and all other necessaries to them belonging at either of their choice, as they stand in the buttery chamber, the said JAMES to choose first. To FAITH my daughter a posted bedstead as it stand in the parlour chamber, a feather-bed bolster covering blankets and all other necessaries thereupon commonly used, which I usually lie upon. The residue of my movable goods and chattels I bequeath to JOHN GOODWYN my son towards payment of my debts and legacies and the bringing of my body to the ground in Christian burial, and I nominate said JOHN GOODWYN sole exor., and if he shall not prove this will within one month after my decease then I nominate JAMES my son sole exor., and if he shall not take upon him the probate within one month after that then I nominate ROBERT my son sole exor. Witnesses: JAMES GOODWYN (X), ALICE FOSTER (X), WILLIAM BROWNING. Pr. at Beccles 24 Feb. 1630/1.

R(W) HENRY LAWE senior of Framlingham, husbandman. (243)
11 January 1630/1

To HENRY LAWE jnr. my sole son, my freehold tenement Coleshall in Framlingham, presently after my decease; all my movable goods chattels bills and bonds of debts now within the room and lodging place where I do now lie, or elsewhere after my decease. To

LAURENCE HABBERGHAM of Framlingham one skep of bees. To ELIZABETH GODDARD my daughter the wife of JOHN GODDARD one other skep of bees, to take them at their pleasure now by my lifetime or presently after my decease. The rest of my bees remaining, with all the profits, I bequeath to my son HENRY LAWE provided that parcel of the aforesaid bequeathed goods and chattels are to be sold by my exor. for satisfaction of my debts and funeral expeenses. I make RICHARD SPARHAUKE of Framlingham, cordwainer, my sole exor. and my friend in Christ WOLFRAME DOWSINGE my supervisor to oversee that my exor. shall make true account of his executorship. Witnesses: THOMAS BUDD, SUSANNAH MORRIS, JOHN MORRIS. Pr. at Wickham 4 Feb. 1630/1.

W(R) ANTHONY MATSOME (X) of Stratford, husbandman. (244)
29 May 1628

Weak. To be buried in Stratford churchyard. To RACHEL my wife my now dwelling house in Stratford during her life, with the yards and orchard belonging, provided she keep the same in good reparation upon her own cost; and after her decease I give the same to my son ANTHONY MATSOME. To said ANTHONY my house yard and other appurtenances in Polstead, now in occupation of WILLIAM BRUCE and THOMAS BUTCHER, but for charge of it till he come to the age of 21 my will is that for the first two years my wife RACHEL shall have it towards the bringing of him up, but afterwards it shall be kept for him by somebody that he shall make choice of for his guardian till he become 21, to make him a stock. To my son ANTHONY MATSOME 1 flock bed 2 bolsters 2 coverlets 1 blanket 1 bedstead, all which I now do lie upon; 4 of my best hutches 1 long table and form 1 great brass kettle 2 pieces of pewter 1 pot, all which shall be kept for him by his mother till he be 21, provided she do not marry again. But if she do, then all my said movables she shall presently deliver into the hands of him whom my son ANTHONY shall appoint, to be kept for his use afterwards. The rest of my goods and chattels I give my wife RACHEL desiring that she would remember my son ANTHONY to bestow some of them upon him when it please God that she shall die, which RACHEL my wife I make sole exrx. Witnesses: SA. LINDSELL, ROBERT BRAGGE. Pr. at Ipswich 5 Feb. 1630/1.

R(W) ROBERT NEWMAN of Walpole (N). 15 January 1630/1 (245)

Died 18 Jan. 1630/1. Within the space of 3 days before his death, by will, gave to JOHN NEWMAN his son all his goods for the payment of his debts. Witnesses: WILLIAM CARY, SAMUEL GREENE. Pr. at Yoxford 3 Feb. 1630/1.

R(W) RICHARD SMYTH (X) of Hollesley. 23 December 1630 (246)

To ANN my wife the little tenement wherein I now dwell, with the houses buildings orchards yards lands pastures and feedings belonging, together with all my movables chattels moneys and household stuff within the town of Hollesley or otherwhere, during her life. To WILLIAM SMYTH my eldest son the little tenement wherein I live after the decease of ANN my wife, with all the houses &c in the possession of me in Hollesley on condition that he pay to his two sisters and two brothers each of them £5 within one year after the decease of my wife ANN, viz. to my daughter FRANCES, now married to THOMAS BUTTALL in Norfolk, my son RICHARD, my son CHARLES and my daughter MARY. To my son RICHARD £10 to be paid out of my movables within 1 year after decease of my wife. To my son CHARLES £10 to be paid out of my moveables within 1 year after decease of my wife. To my daughter MARY £20 within 1 year after decease of my wife. If either FRANCES or RICHARD die before the time expired in which they should have the legacy then that legacy shall be equally divided between my son CHARLES and my daughter MARY SMYTH; and if either shall die the survivor to be heir of the other. I make my wife ANN sole exrx. Witnesses: THOMAS WARREN, JOHN BALTON, NATHANIEL SADLING. Note that whereas I have ordained my son WILLIAM SMYTH to pay £5 unto each of my other children, if he deny the payment then I ordain my son CHARLES to enter upon the lands and pay the legacies. Pr. at Wickham 4 Feb. 1630/1.

R(W) ANNA MAIOR of Ipswich, widow. 27 December 1630 (247)

Sick. To my son THOMAS MAIOR £5 within 1 year after my decease; and all the benefit which shall be due to him by virtue of an indenture made between me of the one part and THOMAS JESOPP my father of the other part bearing date 19th April 1625. And my said father shall have the education and bringing up of my son until his age of 21, and to have a competent allowance for the same out of his portion and the profits thereof. To my son JOSHUA MAIOR £5 to be paid out of the obligation I had of WILLIAM COOKE and also all such benefit due unto him by virtue of the same indenture; and out of the same there shall be bestowed a competent portion of money towards the binding out of him to be an apprentice as my exor. shall think fit; and my bible, my coffer that is in the chamber over the hall of my dwelling house. I appoint my daughter HANNAH to pay my son JOSHUA 50s. towards his apparelling and binding out. I appoint my friend Mr RICHARD REYNSFORD, minister of the parish of St. Helen in Ipswich to be guardian to my son JOSHUA till his age of 21 to receive said benefit due to him and the said legacy of £5 and 50s. to be paid by the said HANNAH for the use of the said JOSHUA. To Mr REYNSFORD 12s. towards his pains in the execution of the trust in him reposed for his aid. To my daughter HANNAH and her heirs for ever my tenement in Botesdale now in the occupation of NICHOLAS DOWE or his assigns; and the remainder and benefit of the sums of money mentioned in the said indenture which is in my power to dispose of in this my will; and all my goods and chattels unbequeathed, my funeral expenses and probate of this will discharged. To my cousin WILLIAM CHENERY 12s. and I appoint him guardian to my daughter HANNAH, and I appoint my daughter HANNAH MAIOR to be exor. of this will. Witnesses: ANNA REYNOLDS (X), RICHARD REYNSFORD, KATHARINE SAMELL (X). Pr. at Ipswich 25 Jan. 1630/1.

W(R) THOMAS MANTHORPE (X) of Beccles, sherman. (248)
2 July 1627

Old and sickly. HENRY MANTHORPE my son shall have my house or tenement with the yards belonging, now in my occupation in Beccles, on condition that he pay all such debts as I owe upon the day of my death and pay GRACE my daughter, the now wife of ROBERT RYSING, SUSAN my daughter the now wife of WILLIAM WINTER, LETTICE MANTHORPE my daughter, MARGARET MANTHORPE my daughter, MARTHA MANTHORPE my daughter, and MARY my daughter, to every of them, at the north porch of the parish church of Beccles, within one year after his entry into possession of the premises, £5, provided that ALICE my wife shall occupy and enjoy all my said house during her life, she keeping the same in reasonable reparations. And after her death the said HENRY to enter the same upon the performance of the payments above specified, and not before. If HENRY or his exors. make default in payment of any of my debts or legacies, then at the expiration of one year after the death of the said ALICE my wife my said house or tenement or woods above specified shall be sold by my supervisor at the best price he can reasonably get and as soon as conveniently may be, and the money thereof arising my supervisor shall pay unto all my sons and my six daughters above named within the said church porch, by even portions, with benefit of survivorship. All my movable goods and chattels to ALICE my wife whom I appoint sole exrx. And I appoint my friend HENRY NUSSEY of Beccles supervisor, and I give him for his pains 10s. above his charge to be expended about the performance of the contents above expressed. Witnesses: ROBERT COBBE, JOHN RABARDES and EDMUND PEIRSON (X). Pr. at Beccles 19 Feb. 1630/1.

W(R) ELIZABETH NEWSON (X) of Leiston, widow. (249)
11 January 1630

Weak. My houses lands tenements and hereditaments bond and free, with their appurtenances, in Knodishall to REBECCA and SARAH my youngest daughters, equally divided. My other tenement lying in Aldeburgh, with appurtenances, wherein [blank] STYLES, to be sold within 1 year after my decease and the money divided into 3 parts, one part to ELIZABETH my daughter, another part to ALICE my daughter, and the other to REBECCA and SARAH my two youngest daughters, which money to be paid to my said children as they shall be of age to give my exor. a discharge. And whereas there is an agreement made between me and my three eldest daughters that the goods which were late my husband's, who being deceased, should be equally divided into six parts, one part to me and the other to my five daughters, my will is that my part together with all the other goods belonging to me I bequeath to my two youngest daughters REBECCA and SARAH NEWSON. I will that my exor. take all those my goods lands and tenements before-mentioned into his possession to be employed to the bringing up of my two youngest daughters, as also for paying such fines reparations and necessary charges imposed on my exor. by virtue of this will. I make EDMUND EWYN my friend, the elder, of Yoxford, yeo., sole exor. Witnesses: JOHN GORIEL, JOHN BRIDGES. Pr. 21 Feb. 1630/1.

R(W) ROBERT AYTON of Kessingland, fisherman (N). (250)
[no date]

Sick. His house in Kessingland should be sold and the money accruing go towards the payment of his debts, and the remainder he gave to his brother JOHN AYTON towards the education of his children and he nominated the said JOHN AYTEN his brother sole exor. desiring him to have a care and respect unto his children. Witnesses: CHRISTOPHER WATSON, JOHN LOUND, ADAM BURGES. Pr. at Beccles 19 Feb. 1630/1.

R(W) HUMPHREY CROSWELL of Blundeston, husbandman. (251)
17 February 1630/1

Sick. To be buried in Blundeston churchyard. All my lands and tenements in Blundeston and Corton to my eldest son RICHARD CROSWELL. All my movable goods as corn cattle household stuff to my son THOMAS CROSWELL, provided that he shall give out of my movables a feather-bed and a bolster with a posted bedstead to my son WILLIAM; and to my daughter ELIZABETH WARNES he must give a feather-bed a bolster and a posted bedstead, and to my son RICHARD CROSWELL the joined cupboard as it standeth in the hall. To ROBERT CROSWELL my grandchild the son of RICHARD CROSWELL my son £5, £3 thereof to be paid by THOMAS 3 years after my decease unto my son RICHARD to the use of ROBERT, and the other 40s. to be paid by my son WILLIAM 3 years after my decease to my son RICHARD to the use of ROBERT; and my son RICHARD to pay the said £5 with the full use thereof unto my grandchild ROBERT at the age of 21. But in case my grandchild ROBERT shall die before the time THOMAS and WILLIAM is to pay this money to their brother, then it shall be lawful for them to dispose of the several sums of £3 and 40s. as they see most fitting. And if ROBERT CROSWELL shall die after the money be paid to my son RICHARD and before ROBERT be 21, then it shall be lawful for my son RICHARD to dispose of the said £5 as he please. I make my son THOMAS CROSWELL my sole exor. Witnesses: JAMES ROBINSON, RO. GROSSE, WILLIAM WOODS, ROBERT UNDERWOOD. Pr. at Beccles 26 Feb. 1630/1.

R(W) THOMAS PEVERELL of Kessingland (N). [no date] (252)

To ELIZABETH his wife all his goods during her life, and after her death the same to be divided equally between MARY and

ELIZABETH his children. Witnesses: JOHN PEASE, clerk, and ELIZABETH the relict of deceased, and his children. Pr. at Beccles 26 Feb. 1630/1.

W(R) JAMES RIPINGE (X) of Benacre, husbandman. (253)
2 April 1627

To LETTICE my wife all that household stuff she did bring with her at the time of her widowhood which shall be remaining at the time of my decease, excepting 1 brass pot; and £6 viz. 20s. 12 months after my decease and so 20s. a year till £6 be paid; and if LETTICE depart this life before the legacy be totally paid, the part unpaid shall cease. To ELIZABETH RIPING my daughter all my household stuff corn cattle chattels implements utensils within and without the house, also to take my debts and pay my debts. If LETTICE my wife shall molest strive or contend with my exrx. the said ELIZABETH RIPING for any part of my movable goods which I have bequeathed to my said daughter, then the legacy of £6 given to LETTICE shall be void. Of this will I make ELIZABETH RIPING my daughter sole exrx. and HENRY BOONEFELLOW of Knodishall, cooper, supervisor; and I give him for his pains 10s. to be paid within 3 months after my decease. Witnesses: EDWARD DINNINGTON and me MYLES BRISSTELD the writer, HENRY BONFIELD. Pr. at Beccles 5 March 1630/1. Admon. to ELIZABETH GIBBINS alias RIPINGE, daughter of deceased.

R(W) THOMAS WHITTWELL (X) of Gorleston, carpenter. (254)
14 February 1630/1

Sick. To be buried in Gorleston churchyard. To ANN WHITTWELL my daughter part of my tenement in Gorleston which late I purchased of RALPH BOSSELL, viz. those rooms which late were in occupation of JOHN HACKER called the kitchen and the shop, together with that part of the yard containing the full passage from the door to the well and from the well towards the south, square with her said house, together with free use of the well, she paying my son JOHN WHITTWELL one shilling yearly towards the slitt of the stops and ropes, the said JOHN keeping the same well in fitting reparations to draw water at. All the aforesaid premises to be held to her during her life, and after her decease to my son JOHN and his heirs, provided that my son JOHN and his assigns or servants or tenants shall have liberty at all convenient times to make use of the oven in the rooms of my daughter or her assigns. The other part of my tenement with the grounds and other appurtenances belonging I give to JOHN my son, on condition that he shall keep it in good reparations and pay to my daughter ANN £3 yearly during her life at the usual four seasons viz. the feasts of St. Michael, the birth of Our Lord, the Annunciation of the Virgin Mary and St. John the Baptist, by even portions, the first payment to begin at the first of the feasts which shall happen after my decease, with power of distraint. To my daughter 10s. to be paid by my exor. within 8 days of my decease. To my son JOHN my 2 best bedsteads with the feather-beds and all the furniture belonging as they now stand, 2 best tables 2 best chests 2 carpets 2 cupboards my tipped pot and 6 silver spoons. To ANN my daughter my 2 other bedsteads and all the furniture to them belonging as they stand, my frame table on the chamber and 4 chests, my cloak, my mortar and pestle. All other household stuff and implements to be equally divided between my said son and daughter, my son to divide them and my daughter to make choice first which part she shall have. In regard that I know that my daughter is weak in capacity for bestowing herself in marriage, that she shall take her brother's advice in bestowing herself, but if she wilfully bestow herself contrary to her brother's mind, he showing just reasons to the contrary, then my son shall detain and keep back half the yearly payments in this will bequeathed. All other goods and credits and cattles and chattels and working tools I give unto JOHN my son whom I ordain sole exor., to take my debts and pay my debts and perform this will. If it happen that my son depart this life before proving my will, ANN my daughter shall be my exor. and I nominate NATHANIEL HARDEN my brother-in-law to be supervisor, and for his pains I give him 10s. to be paid within one month after this will shall be proved. Witnesses: THOMAS STARES (X), HENRY WARRANT (X) and me ROBERT UNDERWOOD. Pr. at Beccles 9 March 1630/1.

W(R) FRANCIS HALTWAY of Beccles, yeoman. (255)
3 January 1630/1

Sick. To the poor of Beccles £5 to be distributed with the direction of Mr DEYNES and the overseers of the poor. To AUDREY HALTWAY my kinswoman, daughter of WILLIAM HALTWAY my deceased brother, £10 within 2 years. To EDWARD FULLER snr. of Norwich, my kinsman, £3 within a year. To JOHN FULLER his son £5 in 2 years. To MARY LEA my kinswoman, wife of RICHARD LEA of Norwich, 20s. in a year. To BRIDGET FOSTER my kinswoman, wife of RICHARD FOSTER of Norwich 20s. in a year. To ROBERT HOLTWAY snr. of Lowestoft 30s. in a year. To [blank] HALTWAY, widow, now or late of Ellingham, Norfolk, 20s. in a year. To [blank] late the wife of THOMAS HOLTWAY, my kinsman, late of Hopton, 20s. in a year. To MARY, sister of THOMAS HOLTWAY, 20s. in a year. To Mr DEYNES of Beccles, ISAAC COWARD snr., ROGER BROWNE and JOHN SEAMAN of Sotterly 10s. each. To PETER DISBONET snr. of Beccles 20s. in a year and a gray coat which I did buy of him. To ALICE BORRET, servant of said PETER, 20s. To [blank] BORRET, widow, of Norwich, mother of the said ALICE, and to ANN BORRET her daughter 5s. each. To WILLIAM FISHER of Wenhaston, 20s. in a year. To SIMON HOLTWAY son of JOHN HOLTWAY deceased 20s. in a year. To GRACE MORSE of Blythburgh, late the wife of EDWARD MORSE deceased, 20s. in a year. To FRANCIS ANTHONY late of Sotterley and to SUSANNAH and FRANCES his daughters, 15s. each in a year. To HELEN ANTHONY one other daughter of said FRANCIS 15s. in a year, and also one chest. And I make ELIZABETH WATLYN my sister exrx., to whom I give the residue. Witnesses: WILLIAM LEGATE and EDWARD DENNINGTON. Pr. at Beccles [No date given, probably Feb. 1630/1].

R(W) HENRY BENNETT (X) of Helmingham, yeoman. (256)
20 January 1630/1

Sick. To ANN my wife £20 within one year after my decease, on condition she doth not challenge or take any of the goods that were and are mine before I married her, but only such goods as I shall name and give unto her in this will. To my said wife 1 coomb of wheat 2 coombs of malt a quarter of my best cheese and half a firkin of butter presently after my decease. To HENRY BENNETT my son all my goods and movables chattels cattle implements of household corn ready money and debts owing to me, by specialty or without, presently after my decease, all which said goods and chattels whatsoever before given to my son I will shall presently after my decease be ordered sold or otherwise disposed of to the use of my said son, by my executor, in such manner as he shall think meet; and my exor. shall, out of the money of the sale, pay such legacies of money to my first wife's children as I stand bound to pay by bond, and I will that those three children of my first wife shall have every of them a feather-bed and all that is expressed in the said bond for them to have therewith, to be delivered within three months after my decease. Notwithstanding my present gift of goods to my said son presently after my decease, yet my will is that my exor. shall, if he shall live until my said son come to his age of 21, have the whole ordering and disposing of all my goods to the use of my said son and also the ordering and bringing up of my son (at his charge) till his age aforesaid, allowing himself sufficiently out of the use of my said goods for the maintenance of my son till his age of 21, and all such charge as he shall necessarily expend about proving my will and my burial charges, and at my said son's said age, to yield up to my son and his heirs the whole remainder. If my son shall depart this life before 21 I give all these goods given to my son to JOHN BAYGYTT and ANN BAYGYT my first wife's children, to be equally divided between them within half a year after the decease of said son. I nominate JOHN HARWYNE of Hellingham the elder my exor. Witnesses: THOMAS [?HARALD], WILLIAM ROE (X), THOMAS BEANE (X), BAR. RUSSELL. Pr. at Ipswich 23 Feb. 1630/1.

R(W) WILLIAM BENDS (X) of Thorington, husbandman. (257)
7 February 1630/1

To ELIZABETH my wife all my goods and chattels movable and immovable excepting 1 flock bed which I give unto THOMAS BROWNE of Sibton, shoemaker. I make ELIZABETH my wife sole exrx. Witnesses: HARBORNE FELTHAM, RICHARD ALDUS and FRANCIS SEPENES. Pr. at Yoxford 27 Feb. 1630/1.

R(W) MARGARET BERRIE of Ash, widow (N). [no date] (258)

A few days before her death. MARY the wife of HENRY FACON shall be at the charge of my burial and pay my debts out of my goods. The remainder I give unto DOROTHY CLARE my grandchild, which the said MARY shall deliver unto DOROTHY at her age of 16, and in the meantime she to keep the overplus of my goods or deliver the same to Mr HUBBALD of Rendlesham, to be kept for my grandchild -- the one of them to keep the goods and the other a note of them. Admon. issued at Wickham to MARY wife of HENRY HACON, nearest relative, 2 Feb. 1630/1.

R(W) JOHN BACKLER of Ipswich, carpenter. (259)
21 January 1630/1

Weak. To JOHN BACKLER my son part of my messuage or tenement in the parish of St. Peter and St. Augustine in Ipswich and in Stoke near Ipswich, now in possession of GEORGE HAMLIN, that is to say the entry, the parlour, the kitchen with chambers on them, the slaughter-house, the coal-house, the close or orchard belonging thereto, and part of the yard to be taken out from the west side of the entry right up to the orchard. To ANN BACKLER and ABIGAIL BACKLER my daughters the other part of my tenement from the entry westward, that is to say the hall, the two butteries with the chambers and garrets over them, with the rest of the yard; and also my tenement now in possession of FRANCIS SMYTH, both lying in the parish of St. Peters and St. Augustines in Ipswich and in Stoke near Ipswich, with the yards and all the houses thereto belonging, to be equally divided between them. My son JOHN BACKLER shall have free ingress and egress to and from the pump yard for him and whosoever he shall appoint to use the pump therein for the benefit of his house. If any of my children die without issue the part of him shall be equally divided between my other children that survive. My wife MARGARET BACKLER shall take the profits of my tenements aforesaid towards the bringing up of my children, keeping my tenements in good reparations until my son shall come to the age of 21 and my daughter to the age of 20, and after they come to such ages she to enjoy the one half of the profits of my said messuage or tenement during her life. The rest of my goods and chattels I give to MARGARET my wife, paying my debts and discharging my funeral, whom I make sole exrx. If it happen that my movables besides my household stuff and tools will not amount to the payment of my debts, my tenement where FRANCIS SMYTH now dwelleth shall be sold towards the payment. And if it be sold my son JOHN BACKLER shall pay unto his two sisters £10 apiece within 2 years after he have possession of the lands and tenements bequeathed to him. Witnesses: NICHOLAS BEARDE, JOHN WITTOM. Pr. at Ipswich 23 Feb. 1630/1.

W(R) JUDITH CHAPMAN (X) of Heveningham, widow. (260)
24 January 1630/1

To GEOFFREY CHAPMAN my son my feather-bed that my husband gave me by will. To ANN CHAPMAN 40s. the bedstead was sold for which my husband also gave me. To MARY CHAPMAN my daughter the coverlet and blanket which my husband did give me by his will. To ELIZABETH MILLER the wife of SIMON MILLER my curtains that also my husband did give me. I give 4 pillows to my son JOHN, and to my three daughters one of them apiece, all presently to be delivered after my death. The rest of my goods and chattels, bills bonds and specialties which are mine by the gift of GEOFFREY CHAPMAN my husband late deceased I give to be equally divided by my exor. and supervisor unto my children now living according to the bequest of my husband as in his will more plainly appears viz. £10 to ELIZABETH my daughter, and the rest to the rest of my children equally divided. I appoint THOMAS SKOLDING my brother exor. and ROBERT MOLLING my brother supervisor. Witnesses: WILLIAM PAYNE, ANN SMYTH (X), wid. Pr. at Yoxford 21 Feb. 1630/1.

R(W)(A) JOAN CURTIS of Little Glemham, widow (N). (261)
[no date]

Not long before her death bequeathed unto FRANCES KING her grandchild 1 feather-bed a feather bolster 2 feather pillows 1 blanket 1 coverlet and the coffer with certain linen and other things in it as it stand; of which coffer she delivered the key to the said FRANCES before her death. Witnesses: EDITH KING and MARY CURTIS the wife of MATTHEW CURTIS. Admon. to JOHN KING of Benhall, father of the said FRANCES, during her minority.

R(W) ELIZABETH COOKE (X) of Rushmere, widow. (262)
21 February 1630/1

Sick. To JOHN COOKE my son £8 within 3 months after my decease. To GEORGE COOKE my son £8 within 3 months after my decease. To MARGARET HALLIBROAD my daughter £8 within 3 months after my decease. To MARY COOPER my daughter £8 within 3 months after my decease. To JOAN FROST my daughter £8 within 3 months after my decease. To ANN ASHFORD my daughter £8 within 3 months after my decease. To JOHN FROST my grandchild the best of my two bullocks which are now at my daughter ASHFORD's, 1 kettle, 1 blanket, which are now in the possession of my kinsman WILLIAM JOHNSON, and the said bullocks to be delivered to her or her assigns presently after my decease. To MARGARET ARROLD my grandchild 1 other bullock at my son ASHFORD's to be delivered presently after my decease. To my 4 fore-named daughters all my household stuff and implements of household, equally divided, within one week of my decease. All my movable goods and chattels not bequeathed I give to my two sons and four daughters, equally divided between them, within one year and a half after my decease, my funeral charges first taken out. To ELIZABETH FROST my grandchild 20s. within 3 months after my decease. To GEORGE COOKE the son of GEORGE COOKE 1 colt now at ASHFORD, to be delivered presently after my decease. To the poor of Rushmere 6s. 8d. to be distributed at the day of my burial. I nominate RICHARD MERVIN my brother sole exor. and give him 40s. for his pains. Witnesses: THOMAR LONGE (X), MARGERY SONDERS (X), WILLIAM FRISTON. Pr. at Ipswich 17 March 1630/1. Admon. to RICHARD MARVEN.

R(W) JOHN DEEKS of Offton, husbandman. 15 March 1629/30 (263)

In good health. I give the messuage or tenement and lands thereto belonging wherein I do now dwell in Offton to WILLIAM DEEKS my son and his heirs on condition that he give HENRY DEEKS my son £10; and ANN MOYSES my daughter £3 and ABIGAIL DEEKS my daughter £5 and JOHN MOYSES and ANN MOYSES, the children of ANN MOYSES, 40s. apiece; and ELIZABETH DEEKS my daughter 20s. yearly during her life -- all these sums issuing out of my said messuage and lands in the manner following, viz. to the said HENRY my son his heirs and exors. £5 within 2 years after my decease, and the like sum within 3 years next after the first day of payment; and to ANN MOYSES my daughter £3 within 1 year after my decease; and to ABIGAIL my daughter £5 in 4 years after my decease; to JOHN MOYSES and ANN MOYSES, my daughter ANN MOYSES' children, 40s. at their several ages of 21, i.e. 20s. apiece with benefit of survivorship; and to ELIZABETH DEEKS and her assigns the said 20s. yearly, the first day of payment to begin at the first next usual feast day that shall come after my decease 5s., and so quarterly the same to be paid always upon the usual four feast days -- all these payments to be made in the church porch of Offton, with power of distraint against the said WILLIAM DEEKS in case of default. To ABIGAIL DEEKS my daughter 1 feather-bed with 1 coverlet with 1 little coverlet lying under it 1 blanket 2 bolsters 1 pair sheets with the bedstead as it standeth in the lower bedchamber in my house; and her dwelling in my said messuage, together with all the profits arising in my said lands until Michaelmas day next following my decease, she committing no strip nor waste. To ELIZABETH DEEKS my daughter 1 flock bed 1 coverlet 1 blanket 2 bolsters 1 pair sheets with the bedstead as it standeth in the lower chamber. The residue of my movable goods shall be equally divided among all my children. I ordain WILLIAM DEEKS my son sole exor. Witnesses: ARTHUR POWELL, CHRISTOPHER BEALE. Pr. at Ipswich 19 Feb. 1630/1.

R(W) THOMAS DYE of Benhall, yeoman. 3 March 1630/1 (264)

To be buried in Benhall churchyard. To THOMAS DYE my son ISAAC's eldest son the house where I now dwell with all the appurtenances thereto and the field grounds and closes lying in Benhall and Saxmundham when he shall attain the age of 21, excepting one acre lying in the heather field of Benhall which I reserve and bequeath to THEOPHILUS DYE my son ISAAC's youngest child, and my youngest grandchild, when he attain the age of 21; and my little house in Benhall wherein THOMAS SAYER now dwelleth, with all that belongs to it, as the pickell, the hempland and the piece of land towards the Parkeward, between 2 pieces of land in the use and occupation of goodman GRINSBYE the younger of Benhall and which he now hireth of me, when the said THEOPHILUS shall accomplish the age of 21; also a brass pot. To the said THOMAS DYE the table in the hall and the great chest, provided that if either the said THOMAS DYE or THEOPHILUS DYE shall depart this life before the age of 21, whichever shall survive shall enjoy the deceased brother's portion, his house and land and whatsoever else I gave in this will. If both happen to die before the age of 21 then I bequeath my two houses and my lands in Benhall and Saxmundham to ELIZABETH DYE and SUSAN DYE the two daughters of my son ISAAC DYE, late of Benhall deceased. Further to the said ELIZABETH DYE my bedstead and bed as it standeth, and unto her sister SUSAN a cupboard table and a kettle. I will my cow and 10 sheep to be sold to the utmost price that can be made, to be raised for a stock for the use and behoof ELLEN DYE the daughter of my eldest son THOMAS DYE, the which stock to be paid to her at the day of her marriage or age of 21, whichever come first. To her sister MARY DYE, youngest daughter of my son THOMAS, £3 to be paid in the said form. SUSAN DYE my daughter-in-law, late wife of ISAAC DYE deceased, whom I make exrx., shall have all the benefit and profit arising of my houses and lands aforesaid during the minority of the said THOMAS DYE and THEOPHILUS DYE for the education and maintenance of them and of her other children and the rest of the family. And when the said THOMAS and THEOPHILUS shall be at full age, then THOMAS shall pay to his mother 40s. a year during her life, and her dwelling in the parlour and half a bushel of hemp seed sowing in the best of the hemp yard yearly and 1 coomb of wheat and 1 coomb of barley yearly; and the said THEOPHILUS 20s. a year in like manner and a coomb of rye. To my daughter-in-law SUSAN the yard at this side the pond next the house for to set her wood and broom, and to have free egress and regress to come in with her horse and cart and for to bake in the oven. And she shall cut wood for her fire but not to make any strip or waste, and to go to the well for water. And if any of my grandchildren shall refuse to pay the yearly sums aforesaid then I will that my daughter SUSAN shall enter either of their lands or possessions and them to occupy until she be fully satisfied. Witnesses: THOMAS TAYLOR the writer, THOMAS HIMS, JOHN BIRLINGHAM. Pr. at Benhall 16 March 1630/1.

R(W) NICHOLAS FISKE senior of Laxfield, yeoman. (265)
4 July 1621

ELIZABETH my wife shall have the use of my posted bedstead as it standeth belonging to the messuage or tenement wherein I do now inhabit, with the feather-bed apparel and furniture thereto belonging for the term of her life, and after her decease I give the same unto JOHN FISKE my son. To NICHOLAS FISKE my son my posted bedstead whereon he usually lieth with the feather-bed furniture and apparel thereunto belonging, to be delivered to him presently after my decease. My exor. shall receive my debts and pay my debts and bring me honestly to the ground. The rest of my goods and chattels as well movable as not movables, household stuff cattle debts duties implements and utensils whatsoever yet unbequeathed I give unto the said JOHN FISKE my son towards the payment of my debts and legacies and the performance of my will, and I constitute the said JOHN my sole exor. Witnesses: JEREM. FYSKE, JOHN BORRET, JOHN ETANNAREY, FR. SANDCROFT. Pr. at Yoxford 5 Mar 1630/1.

R(W) JOHN HERRING (X) of Easton, yeoman. (266)
16 September 1628

All my lands and tenements to WILLIAM my son and his heirs for ever. To EDITH my daughter now the wife of ROBERT ALLEN £55 within 2 years of my decease. To ELIZABETH my daughter £75 within 2 years of my decease; and my little bedstead upon the hall chamber as it standeth furnished with coverings blankets bolsters and pillows, together with 2 pair sheets and 2 pillow-biers. To ELIZABETH ALLEN my grandchild £5 at her age of 21. To JOYCE ALLEN my grandchild 40s. at 21. To ROBERT ALLEN my grandchild 40s. at 21. To JOHN ALLEN 40s. at 21. To ELIZABETH my said daughter my virginals. To every one of my servants 6s. 8d. The rest of my goods unbequeathed I give to WILLIAM my said son whom I make sole exor. Witnesses: DANIEL DEANE and WILLIAM LANGTON. Pr. at Wickham 16 March 1630/1.

R(W) ROBERT MUTTET (X) of Darmsden, husbandman. (267)
6 March 1630/1

Sick. To ROBERT MUTTET my son £10 at his age of 16; to MARY MUTTET my daughter £10 at the age of 16; to ELIZABETH MUTTET my daughter £10 at the age of 16; with benefit of survivorship. The rest of my goods and chattels I give to ELIZABETH MUTTET my wife whom I make sole exrx., paying my debts and entering bond of £100 to THOMAS LONE of Needham within one month after my decease for the performance of this will; and if she refuse so to do I will that THOMAS LONE shall be exor. to pay such legacies to my children as my wife should have done, and he to have all the rest of my goods and chattels, paying my debts and performing this will. Witnesses: THOMAS LONE, ROSE CATTON (X), THOMAS INNALL. Pr. at Ipswich 19 March 1630/1.

W(R) MARGARET POTTER (X) late wife of WILLIAM P.,widow. (268)
25 November 1631 [sic].

Sick. To LIONEL DENNY of Otley, tailor, my kinsman, one suit of apparel laid with gold lace and £3 to be paid at the feast of St. John the Baptist next after my decease. To FRANCES DENNEY and ANN DENNEY the two sisters of LIONEL DENNY aforesaid £3 equally divided within 6 months after my decease. To FRANCES STEBIN and ELIZABETH STEBIN my two grandchildren my box and my new chest as they stand in the hall with those goods which be in them, equally divided between them by their mother. All my other movable goods and chattels bills bonds and debts to me due I give unto ALEXANDER STEYNER my son-in-law to pay my debts and perform my legacies and I appoint him sole exor. Witnesses: AMBROSE FLEET, JANE FLEETE, SUSAN SMYTH (X). Pr. at Wickham 16 March 1630/1.

R(W) EDITH ROWE (X) of Kirton alias Shotley, widow. (269)
8 January 1630/1

Weak. To the poor of Kirton 20s. to be distributed where most need is on the day of my burial by my exor. WILLIAM LEWING shall have the bringing up of my son THOMAS ROWE to school until such time as he shall be fit to be bound out apprentice to some trade that he shall best like; and I allow him £12 a year out of my lands in copyhold for his maintenance. For the residue of the revenues of the said lands he shall be accountable to my said son when he shall come to the age to have his lands. To WILLIAM WIGGEN and THOMAS ROWE my two sons £50 apiece to be paid when my son THOMAS ROWE shall accomplish his age of 24 years. £40 of the said legacy shall be taken out of my movable goods. If any of my children depart this life before the said legacies be due the survivor to have his part, provided that if I depart not this world upon this sickness which I now have my gift of £50 apiece to my sons shall be void. I give to WILLIAM LEWING a certain extent laid out of certain lands in Erwarton, late WILLIAM LAYES, which is the sum of £4 p.a. for the term of 12 years, and I nominate the said WILLIAM LEWING exor. upon condition that he shall duly execute the last will of my late husband THOMAS ROWE deceased, and also this will. And if THOMAS ROWE my son shall mislike of his keeping and schooling by my exor., then my two sisters MARY and MARGARET shall have power to keep my said son to school and my exor. to pay unto them the said £12 p.a. towards his maintenance. The rest of my farm moveable goods as corn cattles chattels debts implements of husbandry and household stuff, my debts and legacies being paid and funeral expenses discharged, I give to WILLIAM LEWING. And my exor. shall immediately after my decease enter into bond to my supervisor of this will in the sum of £500 for the performance of the same. And I appoint ISAAC GOODWIN my brother-in-law to be supervisor. Witnesses: JOHN GREENE (X), MARGARET EDWARDS (X), JOHN BROTHERTON. Pr. at Ipswich 29 Jan. 1630/1.

R(W) EDMUND ROWE of Saxmundham, labourer or husbandman. (270)
9 January 1630/1

Sick. To ALICE my wife all my lands both free and copy with all my houses messuages &c with all their appurtenances during her life to bring up the child that she is now withall, if it shall please God to give it life in this world. After her decease I give to the said child all the foresaid lands and tenements, and the heirs of the same child, for ever, provided if so be the child die before ALICE my wife then she shall have and enjoy all my lands and tenements for ever. Item, to ALICE my wife all my movable goods and chattels, and I ordain said ALICE sole exrx. Witnesses: NICHOLAS PERSKE, THOMAS ALDUS. Pr. at Saxmundham 15 March 1630/1.

W(R) JOHN SAVAGE (X) of Debenham, carpenter. (271)
21 August 1630

To MARGARET my wife all those movable goods household stuff and utensils of husbandry as were hers in her widowhood when I married with her. To said MARGARET 6 milch cows, she to take her choice; my bulting hutch the lesser milk tub 4 keelers of the best 1 eared keeler 1 churn and the milk bowls 4 cheese vats the best, my two biggest kettles brass pot skillet 4 milk pails to be taken indifferently, my cheese-press at Wetheringsett, my bedstead and 1 feather-bed in the parlour with the cord matt coverlet and 1 feather boulster 2 feather pillows with the biers, my best chair my cupboard keep with the little table it standeth on, my 2 glass keeps in the parlour, 1 little back chair my best chest 2 boxes in the parlour 1 little table in the buttery, 1 beer vessel 1 beer stool 1 large joined stool 6 other stools, all her own apparel and all my linen. I nominate ROBERT my son sole exor. to whom I give all other my good and chattels debts due unto me ready money household stuff tools implements of house and husbandry corn cattle hay and all other my goods towards the charges of my burial, the proving of my will and the payment of my debts. Witnesses: ROBERT SHEPPAR senior, PHOEBE BORE (X), ALICE CALLINDER (X). Pr. at Ipswich 17 March 1630/1.

W(R) WILLIAM SPARROW of Ringshall. 27 April 1629 (272)

Sick. To be buried in the churchyard of Ringshall near unto the place where THOMAZIN SPARROW my wife was buried. To the poor in the town of Ringshall and the poor resorting to my burial 40s. to be distributed part upon the day of my burial and the rest within 1 year after my decease at the discretion of my exor. To THOMAS SPARROW my nephew which was the son of EDMUND SPARROW my brother all my lands and tenements both free and bond in the parishes and fields of Wantisden and Ringshall and Combs, presently after my decease, he yielding and paying all such sums of money to such persons at such days and times as in this my testament hereafter shall be expressed. THOMAS SPARROW my nephew his heirs or assigns shall pay out of my lands afore-given him to SARAH NORRIS his sister £30 in the form following, viz: within 2 years after my decease £10; and the 3rd year another £10, and the 4th year another £10; and they shall pay out of my lands aforesaid unto the 2 daughters of RALPH SPARROW my nephew, deceased, £10--£5 apiece, to be paid within 6 years after my decease; and shall pay out of the said lands unto GRACE COULMAN my niece the wife of DANIEL COULMAN £10 to be paid the 7th year after my decease; and to LEONARD SPARROW my nephew which was the son of ROBERT my brother £10 within 8 years of my decease; and to ROBERT SPARROW my nephew which was the son of ROBERT SPARROW my brother £6 13s. 4d. within 9 years after my decease; and to JOHN SPARROW my nephew which was the son of ROBERT my brother £6 13s. 4d. within 10 years of my decease; and to GRACE COULMAN my niece the wife of JOHN COULMAN £5 within 11 years of my decease; and to ROBERT DENNEY the younger which was my wife's grandchild £5 within 12 years after my decease, if he be then living, and likewise to have a great brass pot which was his grandfather's and 2 gowns 1 stamell petticoat, 1 cloak and 1 waistcoat which was his grandmothers at the time aforesaid, if he be then living; and to THOMAS POOLE which was the grandchild of KATHARINE POOLE my sister 20s., and likewise to the 2 daughters which were the daughters of THOMAS POOLE my nephew, sisters to the said THOMAS, now living, 40s. apiece, and likewise to EDMUND SPARROW my nephew which was the son of EDMUND my brother, £5 -- to be paid to the parties above within 13 years next after my decease. To SARAH NORRIS my niece my chest which my wives ould gowne is in, one little posnet 1 kettle and 1 platter. To MARY NORRIS the daughter of SARAH NORRIS my niece my little coffer which I myself do use, 1 little posnet 1 kettle 1 platter. If THOMAS SPARROW his heirs and assigns shall fail in payment of any of the above sums of money, the party not being paid shall enter into the lands and tenements given unto THOMAS SPARROW, and them to possess until fully satisfied. The rest of my goods and chattels I give to THOMAS SPARROW, he bringing my body honestly to the ground and performing this will, and I make said THOMAS my sole exor. Witnesses: WILLIAM WHITE the elder, WILLIAM WHIT the younger (X) and WILLIAM LANKSOND (X). Pr. at Ipswich 23 Feb. 1630/1.

W(R) ANN SPRING of Ipswich, widow. 27 December 1630 (273)

Sick. To be buried in the church of Wattisham. To WILLIAM HAYLE son of my son-in-law RICHARD HAYLE of Ipswich, merchant, £15 to be paid at his age of 21. To ROBERT HAYLE , JOHN HAYLE, RICHARD HAYLE, MARY HAYLE and ANN HAYLE, the sons and daughters of my said son-in-law RICHARD HAYLE, to every of them £5 to be paid at their several ages of 21, with benefit of survivorship. To JOHN BALL son of[missing] BALL of Hitcham £15 to be paid at his age of 24. To THOMAS BALL, ELIZABETH BALL, EDWARD BALL, BRIDGET BALL, the sons and daughters of my son-in-law JOHN BALL, to every of them £5 to be paid as they shall accomplish their ages of 21, with benefit of survivorship. To my son ROBERT SPRINGE £40 provided that he pay unto one STEPHEN KEMBALL £10 which I undertook for the said ROBERT, and that he pay to my exor. £10 more, and if the said ROBERT shall fail to pay either sum, so much thereof of default shall be made shall be deducted out of the said £40 by my exor. for his own use. To WILLIAM SPRING my godson £10 at his age of 21. To JOHN SPRING, BRIDGET SPRING and SUSAN SPRING sisters of the said WILLIAM SPRING, to every of them £5 as they shall accomplish their several ages of 21, with benefit of survivorship among the children of the said ROBERT SPRING. The legacy to ROBERT SPRING my son shall be paid within one year of my decease. To my son JOHN SPRING £10 to be paid within 1 year after my decease; and to his daughter ANN SPRING £5 at 21. To my son THOMAS SPRING £5 within 1 year after my decease. To MORDENT SPRINGE and THOMAS SPRINGE the sons of the said THOMAS, to each of them £5 at 21, with benefit of survivorship. Whereas my son JOHN BALLE oweth unto me £20 principal debt upon a bond, I forgive him the said debt and will that the bond be delivered to him to be cancelled after my decease, provided that if he do not make my daughter, his wife, assurance during her life of lands and tenements in Suffolk of the clear yearly value of £6 within 3 months after my decease the said legacy of £20 to him shall be void, and my exor. shall retain the said bond for his own use. To Mr POWELL, minister of Wattisham, 20s. and to the poor of the same town 20s. For the raising of a sum of money for the payment of the aforesaid legacies I give to the said RICHARD HAYLE my son-in-law and his heirs and assigns all my lands and tenements and hereditaments holden by copy of court roll of the manor of Chelsworth to the intent that he and his heirs or assigns shall as soon as they conveniently can after my decease within one year bargain and sell in fee simple estate the same lands and tenements and hereditaments and therewith pay the legacies aforesaid. The rest of my goods and chattels, my debts funeral expenses and probate of this will discharged, I give to the said RICHARD HAYLE my son-in-law, and make him sole exor. Witnesses: THOMAS LARTER, RICHARD PEICE (X). Pr. at Ipswich 17 March 1630/1.

R(W) ROBERT WARD (X) of Wickham Market, labourer. (274)
22 January 1630

Sick. To MARGARET WARD my wife my house and lands in Wickham Market during her life, and after her decease to ROBERT my eldest son and his heirs for ever. All the rest of my movable goods and household stuff to MARGARET my wife and her heirs towards the payment of my debts, bringing up my children and funeral charges, whom I ordain sole exrx. Witnesses: JOHN MARTYN, FRANCIS HAYLE, SAMUEL FORS (X). Pr. 21 Feb. 1630/1. [Place where proved is not stated]

R(W) THOMAS WILSON (X) senior of Beccles, blacksmith. (275)
27 August 1624

To be buried in Beccles churchyard. To THOMAS WILSON my kinsman my house and houses with appurtenances thereto belonging, that is my hall parlour and milkhouse with my orchard hempland and gardens, my household stuff and tools that I use of smithcraft, with iron both wrought and unwrought, and all my cattle, to pay out of them these legacies as followeth: to CHRISTOPHER WILSON 3 score pounds, to be paid at the years of one and twenty £20, at 22 £20, and at 23 other £20, provided that if he shall not hold himself contented at this my gift, but shall contend in law against the said THOMAS WILSON, then I give nothing to him out of my goods but what he can receive by law. To my brother's children in the North Country £12, when they come to demand it, amongst them. To the poor of Beccles £3. To CHRISTOPHER ALLARD 20s. To my maid THOMASIN CHAPMAN 40s. To JOHN DAVISON £3 [provided] that if the said THOMAS WILSON shall die without issue lawfully begotten of his body then I will that CHRISTOPHER WILSON have the house with the appurtenances. And if the said CHRISTOPHER die without issue I will that the nearest of the kindred shall possess it. And I make THOMAS WILSON sole exor. of this will and WILLIAM RUSSELLS the elder my supervisor, giving him 20s. for his pains. To my god-children so many as are living 5s. apiece. Witnesses: CHRISTOPHER BALLARD, JOHN DAVISON the writer. Pr. at Beccles 5 March 1630/1.

R(W) JAMES HARLWYNE of Ringshall, yeoman. (276)
18 February 1630/1

Sick. To ELIZABETH my wife my tenement houses lands and all the appurtenances, in Ringshall, which were given unto me by my father JAMES HARLWYNE of Ringshall late deceased, and also one other close field which I lately purchased of ROBERT HARLWYNE of Ringshall, during the term of 3 score years if she shall so long live, and after her decease to JAMES HARLWYNE my son and his heirs for ever, provided that my wife shall commit no waste upon the premises by pulling down of the houses or stubbing up of the timber trees fit for to grow for timber, but shall maintain the houses in good condition. To my exor. my tenement houses &c in Ringshall which I lately purchased of STEPHEN HOULT of Great Bricett for the term of 22 years next after my decease towards the payment of my debts and maintaining my mother KATHARINE HARLWYNE, and after the end of the term of 22 years to DANIEL my son and his heirs for ever. I give my tenement houses and lands with all appurtenances, both free and bond, lying in the parish of Barking to my exor. towards paying my debts, to be sold by my exor. to the best advantage. To THOMASIN HARLWYNE my daughter £100 of goods and money, to be paid out of my tenement and lands which I purchased of STEPHEN HALT aforesaid, and before by me bequeathed to my exor. for the term of 22 years, within 12 years next after my decease. And if my exor. shall neglect to pay to my said daughter her said portion of £100 then my said daughter shall enter upon my said tenement and lands and take the rents &c till she be satisfied and paid her £100, provided that if my daughter die before she receive her portion it shall be equally divided between my two sons JAMES and DANIEL, provided that if either depart this life without issue of their body lawfully begotten his portion shall remain to him surviving. To ELIZABETH BRAND my best bed standing in the parlour where I now do lie, furnished as it stand, and also my table in the hall and one of my cupboards standing in my parlour and she to take her choice of the same. My wife shall have the custody of my two sons to educate and bring up, also the custody of my daughter. All the rest of my goods and chattels household stuff and implements of household I give unto my exor. and, my debts being paid and legacies performed and my funeral charges defrayed and my will proved, the superplusage, if any, shall remain to my two sons to be equally divided between them, and I appoint ELIZABETH my wife and DANIEL PULFORD my brother my exors. Witnesses: WILLIAM KEBLE, JAMES LADBROOKE. Pr. at Ipswich 17 March 1630/1. Admon. to DANIEL PULFORD, the other exrx. renouncing.

W(R) ROBERT MANINGE of Walton, yeoman. 9 December 1630 (277)

To the poor of Walton £3 distributed by the consent of my exor. by the churchwardens and overseers within one month after my decease. To my daughter ELIZABETH MANINGE my messuage or tenement in Bromeswell with the lands pastures meadows feedings and hereditaments belonging, now in the tenure of [blank] GIRLING or his assigns. To said ELIZABETH £50 to be paid within 1 year of my decease; a posted bedstead 1 feather-bed with all the furniture belonging as it standeth in the little parlour. To my daughter SUSAN my two tenements in Eyk wherein JOHN STUD and [blank] DUNN now dwell, with all the lands &c belonging in the occupation of said JOHN STUD and [blank] DUNN or either of them or of their assigns. My son ROBERT MANINGE shall be guardian of the said SUSAN my daughter and take the benefit and profit of the foresaid 2 tenements lands &c until SUSAN shall accomplish her age of 18 years, and with the said profits shall educate and bring up my said daughter in the fear of God during the said term; and at her age of 18 years shall become countable unto said SUSAN concerning the profits which he shall have received for the same, and also pay so much or such overplus as shall remain in his hands more than for her necessary maintenance during the foresaid term. To the said SUSAN £100 which shall be paid to SUSAN her heirs or assigns when she shall or should have accomplished the age of 21; one bedstead one feather-bed with all the furniture belonging as it standeth in the parlour chamber. To ELIZABETH the wife of THOMAS BOYTON 40s. to be paid within 3 months after my decease. To ROBERT MANNING my son and his heirs for ever all my other lands and tenements. The rest of my goods and movables, plate, ready money leases or other personal estate I give to aforesaid ROBERT my son upon condition that he shall pay my debts and legacies and perform my will, and I make him sole exor. I further give ROBERT MANINGE the son of ROBERT MANNING of Woodbridge my godson £3 6s. 8d. to be paid when he shall accomplish his age of 21. Likewise to ROBERT MANNING the son of THOMAS MANNING my godson 20s. to be paid within one year after my decease. Witnesses: HENRY TOWNERAWE, WILLIAM GARRARD (X). Pr. at Ipswich 23 Feb. 1630/1.

R(W) PRISCILLA SILEHAM of Covehithe, widow (N). (278)
12 March 1630/1

All her goods whatsoever to the 3 children of her husband THOMAS BONER, viz. to ANN BONER, PLESANCE BONER and FRANCIS BONER, they to have her goods towards the payment of her debts and funeral expenses. Witnesses: NICHOLAS MYEHAELLS, ANN JESOP. Pr. at Beccles 12 March 1630/1. Admon. to FRANCIS BONER.

R(W) THOMAS HERING of Holbrook, yeoman. (279)
20 January 1622/3

ROBERT DOVE shall have all my messuages lands and tenements in Helmingham and Ashbocking. To my master and my lady each of them a pair of gloves of 10s. a pair. To Mistress DOROTHY JACKSON 10s. To EDWARD SMYTH of Holbrook 10s. To THOMAS TURNER and his wife 5s. apiece. To THOMAS TURNER his son 5s. To CECILY GLOVER 5s. To CHRISTIAN RAYNBURD 5s. To ANN WALLER 5s. To ANN WYARD wife of JOHN WYARD of Hoo 5s. To WILLIAM GIRLING and his wife 10s. apiece. To ROBERT GIRLING his son 30s. To WILLIAM GURLING 10s. To ROSE GIRLING the daughter of WILLIAM GIRLING the elder 20s. To the poor of Helmingham £10 to remain for a stock, and the use thereof to be given to the poor, and the £10 of money to be kept by the churchwardens and overseers of Helmingham from one to another for ever. To ELIZABETH DOVE my sister's daughter £400 to be paid when she is 21, and in the meantime to pay the said ELIZABETH yearly after my decease £20 until she be 21; if she marry against the exor.'s and supervisor's will and without their consent and be not married to one that have 4 score pounds a year in his own hand in free lands to make her a jointure, as the exor. and supervisor shall think fitting, then ROBERT DOVE my sister's son shall have the £400, and to pay her £20 a year so long as she shall live. To Mr LAISTER £10 to get the monies into my exor.'s hand that the bonds doth make mention of; he shall not have the £10 before the money be paid to my exor. which the aforesaid bonds do make mention of. To CHRISTOPHER FOSDOCK of Debenham 20s. To ELIZABETH FOSDOCK 20s. To LAWRENCE FOSDOCK 20s.; and the rest that is overplus I give to ROBERT DOVE my sister's son. ROBERT DOVE my brother and ROBERT DOVE his son shall be my exors. To ROBERT DOVE my brother £10. Mr WILLIAM HERING of Easton shall be my supervisor. To said WILLIAM HERING for his pains £3. To the poor of Holbrook £5 to remain and continue as a stock, and the use and profit thereof to be given to the poor, and the foresaid stock of £5 shall remain to be kept by the churchwardens and overseers from one to another for ever. To EDENY ALLEN of Helmingham one pair of gloves of 10s. To ELIZABETH HERING and KATHARINE her sister 10s. apiece. Witnesses: WILLIAM GURLING, THOMAS TURNER. Pr. at Ipswich 29 Jan. 1630/1. Admon. to ROBERT DOVE jnr., ROBERT DOVE snr., the other exor., renouncing.

R(W) JOHN BATEMAN of Peasenhall, singleman. 6 August 1630 (280

Sick. To be buried at Badingham. To the 3 children of my brother PHILIP BOOTEMAN deceased £6 to be paid out of my movable goods when they shall accomplish their several ages of 21, with benefit of survivorship. To AGNES PAYNE of Peasenhall, widow, £5 to be paid within a quarter of a year after my decease; also my "hagg sow," my best coverlet and a hatchet. To STEPHEN NORTON, vicar of Sibton, £8 to be paid out of my moveable goods within a quarter of a year after my decease for preaching at my funeral in Badingham. To 12 men £4 within one month after my decease, to carry me to Badingham church, the men to be appointed by me, if not, by my exor. To my exor. 30s. to set up two posts at the ends of my grave, with a rail over it that I am the last of ten of the BOOTEMANs buried in Badingham. To SIMON BAULDRY 6s. 8d. to make my grave where I did appoint him, next unto my brother FRANCIS. To JOAN SMYTH, widow, £5 within one year after my decease. To MARY PEIRCE, servant with WILLIAM DRAKE of Peasenhall £10 when she shall have accomplished her age of 21. To ELIZABETH CHILDRAKE 40s., JANE COLLEN servant with WILLIAM DRAKE 40s., JOHN BARBER servant with WILLIAM DRAKE 40s. REYNOLD BUSHOPP of Peasenhall 40s. -- to be paid out of my moveable goods within one year after my decease. To AGNES PEARSE, widow, 10s. within one month after my decease. To NICHOLAS BARFOOTE £7. All the brass and pewter and the rest of my movable goods unbequeathed (all my legacies debts funeral charges expenses about the probate of this will and all other expenses taken out) I give unto AGNES AUSTINE dwelling with the Widow PAYNE in Peasenhall, to be paid within one year and a half after my decease. If it happen that AGNES die within a year and a half of my decease and shall not come to those goods given her in this will then all so given her shall be equally divided amongst the 3 children of my brother PHILIP BOTEMAN deceased when they shall accomplish their several ages of 21. I make NICHOLAS BARFOOTE of Peasenhall the elder sole exor. and I appoint him to provide no other provision for the company at my funeral (before they go to church) but beer and cakes; and when they come back again five messe of meat to be provided for the company which I have appointed. Witnesses: ELIZABETH BARFOOTE (X), NICHOLAS BARFOOTE. Pr. at Yoxford 22 Sept. 1630.

R(W) RICHARD LYST of Bedingfield, yeoman. (281)
2 November 1630

To ANTHONY LYST of Debenham. butcher, all my lands tenements &c. in Bedingfield upon condition that he tender unto my supervisors a sufficient obligation at or in the now dwelling house of one of them within one month after my decease, whereby said ANTHONY LYST and his heirs shall be bound in double of the value of the legacies hereafter by me bequeathed, with the condition for the payment and performance of all the gifts and legacies by me bequeathed, to be paid in the churchyard of Bedingfield in manner and form following, and upon condition that he and his heirs and assigns permit EDWARD LYST my brother and ELLEN his wife and the longer lived of either of them to hold their dwelling in the house wherein they now dwell, freely with[out] paying anything for the same; and if said ANTHONY shall not tender aforesaid obligation I give all my lands and tenements &c unto my supervisors to hold for ever, performing and paying in manner and form aforesaid all the legacies hereafter specified: To ALICE TUMNER wife of CHRISTOPHER TUMNER one annuity of 40s. to be paid yearly during her life at two several days, viz. Michaelmas and Our Lady, 20s. on either day, the first payment to begin the feast day which shall first happen after my decease; to said ALICE TUMNER 1 feather-bed 1 bolster 1 pair sheets to be delivered within 1 month of my decease if she demand the same; to EDMUND TUMNER the son of said CHRISTOPHER £6 13s. 4d.; to MIRABEL CROPLEY wife of MICHAEL CROPLEY of Gosbeck, yeoman, 1 feather-bed bolster and a pair sheets to be delivered within 1 month after my decease if she demand same; to JOHN CROPLEY son of said MICHAEL CROPLEY £6, and to ROBERT, MICHAEL and WILLIAM CROPLEY, 3 other children of said MICHAEL, to either of them £6 13s. 4d.; and to

SUSAN and MARGARET CROPLY , 2 other daughters of said MICHAEL CROPLEY the elder, to either of them £6 13s. 4d. to be paid as they shall accomplish their several ages of 21; to GEORGE SIMPSON son of DANIEL SIMPSON 20s.; to JAMES LYST son of WILLIAM LYST deceased 30s.; to ELIZABETH BEALE wife of JOHN BEALE, clerk, 13s. 4d.; to ANN HULKES 40s.; MARY and ANN HULKS sisters of said ELIZABETH 13s. 4d. either of them; SIBLEY MANN 10s.; ROSE MANN 20s.; MARGARET MEEKS 20s.; ELIZABETH CLARKE wife of THOMAS CLARKE 20s.; ELIZABETH MURTOUN daughter of JOHN MURTOUN, feltmaker, 20s.; RICHARD LYST of Cretingham, tailor 40s. and to JANE his wife £3; to FRANCIS WADE, widow, 20s.; to FRANCIS MORE son of FRANCIS MOORE 3s. 4d. -- all which legacies shall be paid to as many of them as shall be living at the end of 2 years next after my decease and of full age of 21, by the said ANTHONY his exors. or assigns, within the church porch of Bedingfield, every one of them giving a lawful acquittance for the sum, but if any of them die before the legacy become due, his part shall remain unto ANTHONY LYST his exors and assigns. To EDWARD BARKER late of Bedingfield, clerk, to either of them 5s, at their ages of 21 if they be living, else not. To JOHN MURTON the elder £10 within 2 years after my decease, but if he die, to his children. To GEORGE FENN son of ROBERT FENN of Kenton £3 6s. 8d. at his age of 21, and if he die to his brother and sister to be equally divided. To JANE TAYLOR 20s. and to JOAN THATCHER 20s. within 2 years after my decease if they be living. To ELIZABETH TORBOLD wife of ROBERT TORBOLD £6 13s. 4d. within 2 years after my decease if she be living. To the township of Bedingfield £5 to be paid into the hands of the churchwardens and overseers within 2 years after my decease, to be employed to the benefit of the poor of the parish according as my friend PHILIP BENNINGFIELD esq. shall think fit. To the poor of Kenton 20s. All which legacies shall be paid by the aforesaid ANTHONY in manner and form aforesaid. I give all my other goods chattels &c not formerly bequeathed to ROBERT FENN of Kenton, yeoman, paying such legacies as are heretofore [sic] named viz. to MICHAEL CROPLY the elder £6 13s. 4d., CHRISTOPHER TUMNER £5, ELIZABETH TORBOLD the wife of ROBERT TORBOLD £12, and unto her child £8, to WILLIAM LYST son of CHRISTOPHER LYST 40s. and to every of his other children 13s. 4d., to KATHARINE WARD daughter of WILLIAM WARD £12 and every one of his other children 20s. at their ages of 21, to GODFREY WOOD 20s. at age 21, to FRANCIS MORE £5 within 2 years after my decease and to every of his children 20s. at age 21. I make ROBERT FENN sole exor. I nominate my friend WILLIAM DRANE of Kenton, yeoman, and THOMAS EASSON of the same supervisors and give them for their pains 10s. apiece to be paid by the aforesaid ANTHONY within one month after my decease. Witnesses: JOHN PUNCHARD, JEREMY PUNCHARD. Postscript: I give to EDWARD LYST my brother £5 to be paid within one year after my decease, SUSAN WHITTE 40s. to be paid within one year. Pr. at Ipswich 13 Nov. 1630.

R(W) THOMAS IRESON alias POMFRET of Bungay, shoemaker. (282)
23 March 1629/30

Sick. All my goods rights credits debts, upon bond or otherwise, chattels &c to SUSAN POMFRET my wife whom I name sole exrx. Witnesses: CHRISTOPHER SMYTH, ELEAZAR SHRENE. Pr. at Bungay 16 July 1630.

R(W) JOHN HEARING of Mendham, gentleman. 15 August 1630 (283)

To FRANCES my wife my capital messuage in Mendham wherein I dwell with all the lands hereunto occupied by EDWARD NEECH, of the demise of me the said JOHN HERING, known as 'Sibles Hills,' containing 4 acres, adjoining lands in my occupation called 'The Wynnes'; also the meadow called 'Damage Fenn' in Mendham, to be held by her for life so long as she resides there and makes no claim for any annuity or dower out of any other property and maintains the premises in good repair, taking upon the freehold premises sufficient timber &c for the purpose without committing any waste, and sufficient cart-wood, plough-wood, gate-wood, pale-wood and fire-wood as necessary during her residence. After her decease or discontinuance of abode or breach of above-mentioned conditions I give the same premises to my exors. until WILLIAM HERRING my son is 21, that they may pay out of the profits £40 yearly to my wife for life by our equal portions at the usual four feasts <u>viz.</u> Christmas, Annunciation, John the Baptist and Michaelmas, in the south porch of Mendham church, she claiming no other interest out of other lands of mine. And when WILLIAM is 21, my wife being dead or non-resident or in breech of conditions, I give the messuage and premises to WILLIAM HEARING for ever, charged to pay that £40 per annum to the said FRANCES , with power for her to distrain. To the said FRANCES I give also my coach, which lately I made for her, and 2 of my best geldings, and all the implements of household, household stuffs, jewels and plate that were hers in her widowhood before she married me. The rest of my goods shall be inventoried and valued, and said FRANCES shall have the use of them so long as she remains resident, including the use of goods elsewhere than at the said messuage, and of my cattle, provided that she gives my exors. security that she or her exors. will redeliver everything or the value thereof to my exors. within one month of her decease or her being no longer resident or her making default in maintenance of the premises. Goods thus redelivered are to be used to pay debts and legacies. To JOHN HEARING my eldest son my capital messuage in Yaxham, Norfolk, with the lands and tenements belonging; and my messuages and tenements in Mendham, Metfield and Withersdale which I bought of JOHN PALMER, THOMAS BOTEWRIGHT, BRYAN FOX and JOHN FOX, excepting one piece of meadow in Mendham called 'Trapp,' containing 1 acre, which I bought of said JOHN FOX and lies between 'Maunday Meadow' on the east and 'Reads Fen' on the west -- to be held for ever, charged to pay to THOMAS HEARING gent., my kinsman, and ELIZABETH his wife such annuities and rent charges as I the elder JOHN HERRING have assured to them, as they become due; and charged also to preserve, defend and keep harmless the messuage and premises devised to my wife and all other my messuages, lands &c other than those thus devised to said JOHN; charged also to pay to LAWRENCE HERRING, son of GEORGE HERING my brother deceased, £200 as and when I have bound myself to do, and the annuities I have granted him for non-payment of the said £200; charged also to keep harmless the personal estate of my exors. and my messuages and lands other than those devised to said JOHN and the occupiers of them. My exors. are to have the use of all the messuages and lands that were MARY's, my former wife, until WILLIAM HERRING my son be 21, to use for his education; and if his capacity shall not attain to learning, then to bring him up in some other virtuous and godly course of life "as his apprehension and capacity will most fitly serve for;" and out of the same revenues to pay debts not paid from my personal estate, and legacies under this will; any residue shall be paid to WILLIAM within 6 months of his reaching 21, or failing him, to the said JOHN at the same date that WILLIAM would have been paid. The stock of goods that my wife is to have the use of, or the money in lieu thereof (my son WILLIAM having attained the age of 21) is to be divided equally between my sons JOHN and WILLIAM or the survivor of them. And after WILLIAM is 21 I devise as well as my messuages and lands and all the messuages &c late of said MARY my deceased wife, whereof I have appointed my exors. shall have the use during the minority of WILLIAM , also the capital messuage &c devised unto FRANCES my wife (she being deceased or not resident) unto the said WILLIAM HERRING my son to hold for ever. My son JOHN shall give facilities to other parties concerned in administering the estates, so that the interests of all can be ascertained in detail. Likewise WILLIAM is to be equally co-operative. I have a special care that this will should be performed without any pretence of title by one to another's estate. JOHN my son and his heirs shall at all times convenient, upon reasonable request and at the cost of my wife for her estate, and of my exors. for their estate, and of my son WILLIAM for his etstae, procure every act in the law for the perfecting of their several estates in the lands and tenements given them and the extinguishment of any claim therein by the said JOHN. If JOHN shall refuse, whoever is thus refused shall enter into the premisses bequeathed to JOHN and enjoy them until JOHN do perform such acts. Likewise my son WILLIAM after he shall have attained 21 years, and after JOHN shall have performed to WILLIAM acts as aforesaid, shall, upon like request by and at the costs of JOHN perform unto JOHN every act required in law for establishing the right of JOHN in the premises devised to him, so as the title given to WILLIAM in any such lands &c be not thereby disabled. If WILLIAM shall refuse, JOHN may enter the premises given to WILLIAM and enjoy them until WILLIAM perform such acts. And as I have a special care that the annuities I have tied myself to pay to the said THOMAS HEARING and ELIZABETH his wife and the said LAURENCE HEARING should be paid by JOHN my son, for which I have charged my lands, so as there shall be no cause of suit for the non-payment, I charge my son JOHN that he do pay the same as due, whereby my exor. may not be hindered in the performance of my will, nor my personal estate questioned for the same, nor yet the premises devised unto my wife and to WILLIAM charged therewith.

If JOHN do default in payment of the annuities whereby my exors. as for my personal estate may be sued, or the premises bequeathed to my wife and my exors. and to WILLIAM my son may be charged thereto, or any distress thereupon taken or any other action against my wife my exors. my son WILLIAM or the farmers or occupiers of the same be brought, then any one of them so charged may enter upon every freehold messuage lands etc. bequeathed to JOHN, and may occupy them until satisfied and paid, together with their costs. I ordain THOMAS FRESTON of Mendham, gent., and ANTHONY GRENLING of Stradbroke, my friends, exors., and give each of them £10 for their pains; and I appoint ROBERT HARPER of Mendham supervisor and give him £5. Witnesses: THOMAS WALES, JOHN WISEMAN. Pr. 18 Jan. 1630/1 at Mendham. Admon. to THOMAS FRESTON, the other exor. declining.

CHAPTER II

Abstracts of Wills Contained in the Will Register for 1631 and File Number 67 of Wills Proved in the Court of the Archdeacon of Suffolk. [The Wills do not appear in strict chronological order in the gatherings, and so do not appear in these abstracts, in strict date order.]

R(W) WILLIAM HADENHAM the elder of Darsham. 3 April 1631 (284)

To HENRY HADNHAM, second son, all lands, tenements purchased by testator from JEREMY BARBER of Westleton, merchant, i.e. one close in Westleton called Penies (12 acres), one close in Westleton called Willowes (3 acres), one close in Westleton called Gelcroftes in three pieces (5 acres), one close in Westleton called Colines (3 acres). To WILLIAM HADENHAM, eldest son of testator, residue of lands in Darsham and Westleton, both free and copyhold, provided he pay to testator's widow ANNE £10 p.a. on the usual feasts of the Annunciation, Nativity of St. John Baptist, Christmas, and Michaelmas, or within 10 days; first payment to be made on the first of the feasts after testator's death; all payments to be made at the church porch of Darsham. To wife ANNE, the parlour in testator's house; also the lower little room on the north side of the entry between parlour and hall; use and benefit of the well, liberty of backhouse and oven for baking, washing, and brewing; as much fruit pears and apples from the yards and the orchard about the house. Son WILLIAM to provide and store her firewood. Also to ANNE all chattels etc. needed to furnish the parlour. Son WILLIAM to provide her with all she require for bread and beer to deliver the same. To daughter MARY, married to RICHARD MOLLETT, £3 p.a. to be paid by her brother WILLIAM, until her daughter ELIZABETH MOLLETT reach 21, payable on Lady Day and Michaelmas, equal installments, at Darsham church porch. To niece ELIZABETH MOLLETT, when 21, £20 to be paid by WILLIAM HADENHAM; if she die before 21, then sum to be equally divided between surviving children of MARY and RICHARD MOLLETT. To MARY MOLLETT, daughter of testator, when ELIZABETH MOLLETT is 21, 30 shillings p.a. payable by WILLIAM HADENHAM. WILLIAM HADENHAM also to pay for the apprenticing of WILLIAM MOLLETT, testator's grandson and godchild, £3 6. 8 when he reach 14. To HENRY HADENHAM, second son, 1/4 of fruit on the trees standing in the east side of the foot path between testator's two houses; also posted bedstead, one feather bed, one feather bolster, one pair of blankets, one coverlet, three pair of sheets, one feather pillow, one brass pot, six pewter platters, the best cauldron, one brass pan, the old sorrell gelding with all his tackles and working equipment, and his own cows and sheep. HENRY to pay to his mother ANNE HADENHAM 40s. p.a. at Lady Day and Michaelmas equally, at Darsham church porch. To grandchild ELIZABETH SAYER, 30s., within 3 yrs. of testator's death. To grandchild MARY SAWER, 30s. within 4 yrs. of testator's death. To grandchild JOHN MOLLETT, 20s. within 5 yrs. of testator's death. To grandchild ROBERT MOLLETT, 20s. within 6 yrs. of testator's death. To son-in-law RICHARD MOLLETT, £10, payable by WILLIAM HADENHAM. To son WILLIAM HADENHAM residue of goods, stock, etc. Son WILLIAM HADENHAM sole executor. Written in the parlour; Witnesses WILLIAM HARTE, EZECHIELL BACKLER, JOHN WOODCOCK, WILLIAM HADENHAM. Pr. at Yoxford 22 March 1631/2.

R(W) THOMAS LOVE (X) of Kessingland, yeoman. (285)
10 October 1628

Sick; to be buried in Kessingland churchyard. To wife ANNE, all land in Kessingland for life. To son THOMAS, one piece land (5 1/2 acres) in Kessingland between land of RICHARD LUICE, clerk (W). copyhold of THOMAS LOVE (E); one piece land (7 acre, 1 rood) between lands of THOMAS PECK and THOMAS LOVE (W) and THOMAS LOVE (E); one piece (2 1/2a) between lands of WILLIAM CAPON (W), THOMAS LOVE (E); one piece of marsh (3a). These to pass to him on death of ANNE LOVE, if THOMAS pay to sisters MARY and ANNE LOVE, £8 each -- MARY to receive £4 within 3 yrs. of mother's death, and £4 within 4 yrs. of mother's death; ANNE to have £4 within 5 yrs. of mother's death, & £4 in 6 yrs. of Mother's death. To son JOHN, two pieces copyhold land containing 2 1/2 a in the Millmount close between lands of THOMAS LOVE (W) WILLIAM LOVE (E) one head abuts on Millmount(N); 1a. copyhold in the Eastfield between Mrs DARLEY (W), Mr HEYWARD (E); 1 1/2a freeland between WILLIAM CAPON (E) and JAMES BARNES (W); these to come on death of ANNE. To wife ANNE all goods, etc.; she to pay £16 to MARY LOVE within 6 yrs. of testator's death, and to pay £14 to ANNE LOVE within 10 yrs. of testator's death, with benefit of survivorship. ANNE to be sole executor; brother WILLIAM LOVE to be supervisor, and to receive 10s. for his pains. To the poor of Kessingland 10s., paid on day of his burial. Witnesses WALTER HUNT (X), THOMAS PAYNE. Pr. at Beccles 10 March 1631/2.

R(W) ROBERT PAYNE of Bungay St. Mary, yeoman. (286)
13 December 1631

Weak of body, by constitution of nature. To wife MARGARET, all goods, etc. for life. MARGARET to be sole executor. Witnesses: HENRY CUNNINGHAM, THOMAS FRANCKLYN. Pr. at Yoxford 21 February 1631/2.

R(W) ROGER RICCARDE of North Cove, yeoman. (287)
18 January 1629/30

To wife MARGARET, three of best young cattle (neate) in the dairy herd chosen within one month of testator's decease; and three more out of the herd after the executors have chosen theirs; also one heifer; also £20 to be paid within one month of testator's decease; also one half posted bedstead, a feather bed, two pillows, two pillow beares and all things pertaining to the bed as it stands in the hall; one framed table, one great back chair and four other chairs, two forms and one dresser also standing in the hall; also one trundle bedstead, a feather bed and all things belonging to it standing in the hall chamber; one formed chest, one new keep in the parlour and one desk in the parlour; also the best great kettle, one little kettle, six pewter dishes, one pewter basin, one double pewter salt in the buttery; also half of all dairy vessels except the cheese press in the dairy -- to go to executors and the other half of the dairy vessels -- if executors quarrel, then supervisor to determine. Also to wife, ten pair of sheets of her own choosing, the best board cloth, six table napkins, and one little cheese press standing in the shop. To daughter MARY RICCARD £30 when 19 or on her marriage; to daughter MARGARET £30 when 19 or on her marriage; to son THOMAS £40 when 21, with benefit of survivorship. Executors to enter into bond of £200 with supervisor to pay the legacies, and also to pay MARGARET, testator's wife, £8 p.a. out of the use of £100 to pay for education and upkeep of children; £8 to be paid on the feasts of Lady Day and Michaelmas; if executors refuse the bond, then MARGARET to be sole executrix. To daughter MARY, one two yearlin heifer. To son THOMAS one ambling mare colt. Wife and executor to live together until Michaelmas after testator's death. To daughter ANNE, wife of JOHN COLMAN, 20s. To sister-in-law THOMAZINE BRIGGS 5s. To the poor of Northcove parish 5s. To son MATTHEW RICCARD, sole executor, residue of goods, etc. To brother ROBERT MANN, supervisor, 10s. Witnesses JOHN LOVE, FRANCES LOVE; signatories ELIZABETH CHAPMAN, THOMAS CRISPE. Pr. at Beccles 10 March 1631/2.

W. WILLIAM BEETS of Wheatacre All Saints (Norfolk). (288)
6 September 1631

To the poor of Wheatacre 25s. To servant JOHN GILBERT 10s. To Widow LADELOW 10s. To wife KATHERINE BEETS residue; wife, sole executrix. Witnesses CHRISTOPHER MILLS, clerk, WILLIAM LONDON; Item; in the afternoon after he had made his will, he changed his bequest to the Widow LADELOW; now 5s. to the widow, and 5s. to the poor of Burgh St. Peter (Norfolk). Pr. at Beccles 10 Sept. 1631.

R(W) ROBERT ROBERSON of South Elmham All Hallows, yeoman. (289)
29 June 1631

Sick. To wife MARGERY, for life, all land, free and copyhold held of Peasenhall manor in Peasenhall. On death land to be sold by exec. in fulfillment of legacies. To daughters ELIZABETH and FRANCIS £100 each from the sale, within one month of sale; to son JAMES the remainder of the sale money; these legacies in full satisfaction of legacies to them from grandfather BOWD and uncle DAWSON. To daughter AMY £30 within one year of testator's decease in full satisfaction of legacies from grandfather and uncle. To son JAMES residue of land, goods etc. To JAMES, AMY and FRANCIS a bed, fully furnished, as they stand -- JAMES to have the bed he sleeps in, AMY the bed in the parlour FRANCIS the one in the chamber. To wife MARGERY the posted bedstead fully furnished in the parlour, a green rug, rest of the movables. MARGERY to be exec., with friend STEPHEN LILLY of Metfield. To STEPHEN LILLY of Metfield, yeoman, 40s. Witnesses: JOHN SAGER, WILLIAM BALLS and others [unspecified]. Pr. at Beccles 16 Sept. 1631.

R(W) AGNES SPARKE (X) of Peasenhall, widow. (290)
9 March 1626/7

To son JOHN GRENNE, £10 to be paid as 40s. a year, 1st payment 1 yr. after A.S. death. To son THOMAS GRENNE £7 to be paid 40s. a year, in 2 years after A.S. death. To daughter ALICE SEARLES £8 to be paid in 2 years after A.S. death. To daughter AGNES MILLER £6 to be paid in 2 years after A.S. death. To daughter ELIZABETH PAYNE £5 to be paid within 2 years after A.S. death. To grandchild MARY DENNY £6 to be paid within 2 years after A.S. death. To ELIZABETH JELLY £6 to be paid within 2 years after A.S. death. To EME GREENE, daughter of THOMAS, 40s. within 2 years after A.S. death. To ELIZABETH and HENRY GREENE, children of THOMAS, 40s. each in 2 years after A.S. death. To RICHARD SARLES £4 within 2 years after A.S. death. To ANTHONY SEARLES, son of RICHARD, 40s. within 2 years of A.S. death. To ELIZABETH KIDMER, daughter of testator, 40s. within 2 years of A.S. death. To ANTHONY, THOMAS, GEORGE, & EDWARD GREENE, sons of JOHN GREENE, 40s. each within 2 years of A.S. death. To CONSTANCE GREENE, daughter of JOHN GREENE, 20s. in 2 yrs. after A.S. death. To PHILIP MILLER, son of ANNE MILLER, 40s. within 2 yrs. of A.S. death. To RICHARD MILLER, son of ANNE, 20s. within 2 yrs. of A.S. death. To MARGARET NEALE and ELIZABETH KIDMAN 20s. each within 2 yrs. of A.S. death. To son HENRY GREENE all goods etc., to pay legacies. Any child/kin unsatisfied with legacy and complains thereof, to loose the money -- money then to go to exec. HENRY GREENE, son, haberdasher of London, executor. Witnesses: EDWARD BOOTHE, THOMAS CULLINGTON, THOMAS GREEN of Knodishall, son. Pr. at Yoxford 22 March 1631/2.

R(W) BARTHOLOMEW WAYE of East Bergholt (N). (291)
[blank] March 1631

To son MICHAEL loom with all tackle, bed as it stands, great brass pot, a brass kettle, three pewter plates of the best, 40s., the cupboard in the hall all on his marriage, or on the day of his mother's remarriage or death, whichever first. To daughter MARY, 40s., two pewter platters, iron pot, brass kettle, trundle bed as it stands in her chamber. To daughter SUSAN, 20s., iron pot, brass kettle, two pewter dishes, trundle bed as it stands. To daughter ANNE, 5s., and all his clothes, save cloak and coat. To son SICKLMER 5s., and to his daughter 5s. All gifts to remain with testator's wife until she remarry or die, save for legacies to MICHAEL on his marriage. Pr. at Ipswich 24 March 1631. Admon. to wife.

R(W) THOMAS WILSON of Weston. 7 October 1631 (292

To GABRIEL BATEMAN of Knodishall, son-in-law £3 and a set of silver buttons, in 1 yr. of testator's decease. To son-in-law MATTHEW PLAYTERS of Kessingland £4 within 1 yr. of T.W. death. To granddaughter ALICE PLAYTERS, £4 on 21; if die before legacy to grandson THOMAS PLAYTERS when 21. To son-in-law EUSEBIUS UTTING of Weston, all household goods etc., already in his possession, save a bond of £10 of EDMUND GILBERT. To the poor of Henstead 10s. within 1 month of decease. To son-in-law EDMUND GILBERT, all household goods etc. already in possession, and the £10 bond previously mentioned. EDMUND GILBERT sole exec. Witnesses: THOMAS UTTING, FRANCIS ISACK, STEPHEN ANDREWS, T. WILLSON. Pr. at Beccles 3 March 1631/2.

R(W) ELIZABETH WELCH of Covehithe, widow. 6 March 1631/2 (293

To son WILLIAM WELCH £5; one long legged brass pot, when 21; exec. to bring him up and use profits from rent to maintain son, and the house. To daughter JOAN GOOSE £20 within 1 yr. of E.W. death; one cow called JOAN's cow; the profit from £20 to maintain her; 20s. to exec. to pay for JOAN to be taught to read and sew. To son JOHN GOOSE, £10 within 3 yrs. of E.W. death; all tools for the carpenter's trade. To daughter MARY GOOSE, a black heifer with a pie on her forehead. To son JAMES GOOSE a grey hobble mare, to son JOHN GOOSE a heifer. All brass and pewter (save WILLIAM WELCH's legacy) to be equally divided between MARY, JAMES, JOHN & JOAN. To JOHN YONGS, minister, 20s. Benefit of survivorship to her children by JAMES GOOSE. Sole exec. ROBERT DARLEY of Wrentham, to whom £4 and one fowling piece; also control over JOAN GOOSE and WILLIAM WELCH. Witnesses JOHN YONGS, JOHN FAYRCHILDE, MARGARET ELDER. Pr. at Beccles 18 Feb. 1631/2.

R(W) JOHN WELTON of Metfield (N). March 1631 (294

Sick. To wife ELIZABETH, all goods, etc. (save tools) for life. To son JOHN, all tools, the bed he sleeps on and all belonging to it, table & three buffet stools. To daughter ANNE, cupboard, a keep, a chest. Remainder of goods, on death of wife, to be equally divided between JOHN & ANNE. Witnesses: THOMAS ALLDOUS, GEORGE WELTON, ELIZABETH WELTON. Pr. 8 March 1631/32.

W. JEREMY CLARKE of Blythburgh, yeoman. 1 February 1631 (295

Sick; to be buried in Blythburgh church yard. To wife JOAN, all goods etc., in his houses. To son ROBERT, £20 on death of mother. To son JEREMY, £10 on death of mother. To son MICHAEL £10 on death of mother. To son JOHN, £10 on death of mother. To daughter SARA £10 on death of mother. To daughter KATHERINE £10 on death of mother. To daughter JOAN £10 on death of mother. Sole executrix wife JOAN. Witnesses: WILLIAM RIVETT (X), DOROTHY THARSTON (X), THOMAS DURRANT. Pr. at Yoxford 22 Feb.

1631/2.

R(W) JAMES WALLER of Ramsholt, gentleman. (296)
27 February 1631

Sick; to be buried in Ramsholt church. To wife DOROTHY, all lands, goods, etc. for life, then to pass to daughter DOROTHY. To sister MARY, annuity of £7. Witnesses: WILLIAM AUSTEN, JOHN JACKSON, DANIEL AUSTEN, WILLIAM FOSTER (X). Pr. at Ipswich 13 March 1631/2.

R(W) SUSAN WALL (X) of Aldeburgh, widow. (297)
20 September 1631

To grandchild ROGER YAXLEY, son of ROBERT YAXLEY, testator's son-in-law, £4 when 21. To grandchild ROBERT YAXLEY, as above, £4 when 21. To grandchild SUSAN YAXLEY, as above, £10 when 21 or on marriage. To grandchild SARA YAXLEY, as above, £10 when 21 or on marriage. Benefit of survivorship. To WILLIAM HYNDES, EDWARD HYNDES, JOHN HYNDES, sons of WILLIAM HINDES, deceased, of Aldeburgh, 6s.8d. each when they reach 21. To grandson ROGER YAXLEY, best Dansk (Danzig) chest. To ELIZABETH CARABLE of Aldeburgh widow, 10s. on testator's death. Residue of goods, etc., to be equally divided among grandchildren. To MARGARET LOWE of Aldeburgh, widow 20s. on testator's death. ROBERT YAXLEY sole exec. Witnesses: JOHN WALL, snr., THOMAS BOONE. Pr. at Yoxford 22 Feb. 1631/2.

R(W) RICHARD DENNY of Beccles, gentleman. (298)
24 September 1631

Sick. To wife ALICE, all lands, free and copy, in Beccles and Wangford Hundred, for life if she remain widow, to provide for education etc. of children; void on remarriage. To son RICHARD, on mother's death or remarriage, house, barns, stables occupied by testator, and pightle behind the house; moiety of well in Seaman's tenement. To son JOHN, three tenements near Fayer close lane, with gardens, orchards, etc., and Broome pightle. To son WILLIAM, Seaman's tenement, with all buildings, & moiety of well; one enclosure with barn, part of White cross close. To son ROBERT, tenement occupied by WILLIAM CASON, with yards etc., with liberty of access to the well, and liberty of passage through Seaman's tenement to reach the back lane; also one pightle lying next to Swynes green, late part of White cross close; also pightle with barn at Pyes mill; also lease of the long meadow part of Beccles fen. To daughters HESTER & FRANCES tenement where NICHOLLS lives. To wife, sole executrix, all goods not devised previously. Witnesses: JOHN DADE, HENRY PARKER, MARGERY VYNES. Pr. at Beccles 22 Nov. 1631.

R(W) JOAN HARRYSON (X) of Belton, widow. (299)
25 September 1631

To be buried at Belton as close as possible to her children buried there. To eldest son NICHOLAS HARRYSON, all movable goods, save weaving clothes which are divided equally between JERONOMY, wife of son JOHN HARRISON, and daughter BRIDGET COLL. NICHOLAS HARRYSON sole exec. Witnesses: EDWARD WATTSON, WILLIAM SPRINT (X). Pr. at Beccles 25 Feb. 1631/2.

R(W) JOHN HUGGEN (X) of Capel. 5 May 1631 (300)

Sick. To eldest brother WALTER HUGGIN of Capel, £10 bond held by ROBERT WEBBER of Melton, husbandman. Also all wearing clothes, hoes, and shoes; pair of twill slaies to weave, chest with contents. WALTER to be sole executor. Witnesses: THOMAS JOHNSON, JOHN NUSON (X), JOHN BETTS (X). Pr. at Butley 19 July 1631.

R(W) ROBERT RICHMAN (X) of Ipswich, baker. (301)
10 January 1629

To be buried in St. Matthews, Ipswich. To eldest son ROBERT, all houses etc., in Brook Street, Ipswich, save two tenements -- one occupied by EDWARD SUGDEN, which is to be given to testator's daughter CHRISTIAN, and a tenement occupied by ELIZABETH SHUCKFORD to be given to testator's second daughter SARA RICHMAN. ROBERT to have his legacy if he pave the piece of yard between the stables and the tenement in the tenement which CHRISTIAN is to inherit; also ROBERT when he is 24, has the Brook Street lands if he pays MARGARET, his mother, an annuity of £7, payable in the South porch of St. Matthew's church by equal parts on Lady Day and Michaelmas; MARGARET has power of entry and distraint if default made. To son SAMUEL, when 14, tenement in St. Matthews parish, if pay annuity of 40s. to mother MARGARET. If die, benefit of survivorship to brother ROBERT. To daughter MARGARET, tenement in St. Matthews parish occupied by JOHN BAKER, the cobbler, if on age of 18 pay annuity to mother of 20s.; benefit of survivorship to brother SAMUEL, then to brother ROBERT. Residue of goods equally divided between children. To the poor of St. Matthews the profits from rent of a house in St. Matthews parish not exceeding 6s. 8d. p.a. To JOHN WALDEGRAVE, the younger, son of WALDGRAVE of Baddingham 20s. within 1 yr. of testator's decease. To JUDITH WALDEGRAVE, daughter of WALDGRAVE of Baddingham, 10s. within 1 yr. of decease. To GEORGE FENN, the younger, of Holbrook, 20s., within 1 yr. of R.R. decease. Exec.: JOHN WALDEGRAVE, the elder, wife MARGARET RICHMAN. Witnesses: MARY WALDEGRAVE, the elder (X), MARY WALDEGRAVE, jnr. EDMUND GARDYNER. Pr. at Ipswich 4 Nov. 1631 granted to MARGARET RICHMAN, and at Yoxford on 2 Nov. 1631 granted to JOHN WALDEGRAVE.

R(W) NICHOLAS WOOLNOUGH of Ipswich, apothecary. (302)
1 October 1631

Weak and sick. To aunt ALICE JAMES, widow, of Woodbridge, rent of messuage in Woodbridge, of £5 p.a. for life. To kinsman WILLIAM JAMES, sailor, of Woodbridge, £30 in 6 months of N.W. death. To kinsman JOHN JAMES, apothecary, of Ipswich £150 in 6 months of N. W. death. To kinswoman ALICE BEAREMAN, wife of THOMAS BEAREMAN of Woodbridge, linen draper, messuage in Woodbridge; also all household goods etc. To THOMAS & WILLIAM BEAREMAN, sons of ALICE, £10 each when 21. To WILLIAM WATERS of Woodbridge £10 in 6 months after N.W. death. To RICHARD & JONAS WATERS, brothers of WILLIAM, £10 each when 21. To poor of St. Margaret's parish Ipswich £3 & poor of Woodbridge £5. To minister who preaches at his burial 30s. Exec.: THOMAS BEAREMAN of Woodbridge; Witnesses: EDWARD MAYHEW, jnr., ROBERT MARYOTT. Pr. Wickham Market, 30 Nov. 1631.

R(W) THOMAS STARES of Lound, yeoman. 9 August 1631 (303)

Very sick; to be buried at Hopton church. To wife MARTHA, for life, tenement in Lound; on her death or remarriage then nephew WILLIAM FAYREWETHER,to have the same, paying to MARTHA on her marriage an annuity of £10 payable equally on Lady Day and Michaelmas. If WILLIAM die before inheriting, benefit of survivorship to brother BARTHOLOMEW FAYREWETHER on same conditions. To nephew EDWARD FAIREWETHER, lands in Flixton, if pay to JOAN HUNT, testator's sister £5 within 1 yr. of T.S. death; also to pay £5 each to three sons of JOAN HUNT -- 1st son to have £5 within 1 yr. of T.S. death; 2nd son £5 in 3 yrs., 3rd son £5 in 4 yrs. Also EDWARD to pay to his brother JOHN FAYREWEATHER 40s. a year within 1 yr. of gift to JOAN HUNT's 3rd son's gift. Power to enter and distrain to the HUNT's, if default of payment. To nephew EDWARD PEEDE, lands in Corton, if he pay JOAN HUNT £5 within 1 yr. of T.S. death, and £5 to each of her three daughters; £5 to the 1st within 2 yrs., £5 to the 2nd in 3 yrs., £5 to the 3rd in 4 yrs. of T.S. death. Also EDWARD to pay to his brother RICHARD PEEDE £10 -- £5 within 5 yrs. of T.S. decease, and £5 within 6 yrs. of same. Power to HUNT's and RICHARD to enter and distrain if default. To nephew WILLIAM FAIREWETHER, lands in Hopton and Brotherton, provided he pay his brother BARTHOLOMEW FAIREWETHER £20, £5 within 1 year of decease, and £5 a year thereafter for the next 3 yrs. Also WILLIAM to pay to THOMAS PEEDE, testator's nephew, £5 in 5 yrs. after T.S. death, and to HENRY PEEDE £5 in 6 yrs. after T.S. death and to their half brother JOHN PEEDE £5 in 7 yrs. Power to enter and distrain on default to the PEEDE's. Also if WILLIAM die on his sailing voyages then benefit of survivorship to BARTHOLOMEW FAIREWETHER. To wife MARTHA, all stock and goods, save one Danske chest and a desk; all farm implements; wife to pay to testator's sister MARGARET PEEDE £10 -- £5 within 1 month, and £5 within 1 yr. of testator's death. To poor of Lound and Hopton 20s. each. To JOHN STARES of Corton, tenant, 40s. within 1 yr. of decease of T.S. Residue of all lands and goods to nephew

EDWARD PEEDE, sole executor. Witnesses: THOMAS BUGGE (X), ROBERT UNDERWOOD. Pr. at Beccles 23 Aug. 1631.

R(W) ROBERT DAVY of Aldringham, yeoman. 21 May 1631 (304)

Sick. To the five children of his daughter CICELY, late wife of JOHN TAYLOR, £10 within 4 yrs. of testator's decease; equally divided. To grandson ROBERT DAVY, son of SIMON DAVY, £10 within 1 yr. of R.D. death. To granddaughter ELIZABETH DAVY, daughter of WILLIAM DAVY, £10 in 1 yr of R.D. death. To rest of grandchildren £5 each within 1 yr. of R.D. death. To daughter ELIZABETH DAVY all goods specified in an inventory. Residue of goods to SIMON DAVY, MARY HERRINGTON, ALICE BURWOOD, & ELIZABETH DAVY to be equally divided; but SIMON DAVY & MARY HERRINGTON to have sufficient goods, to enable them to pay exec. 12d. every year until ELIZABETH DAVY reach 21 to pay for her education; also ALICE BURWOOD to give £15 for ELIZABETH DAVY. To ROBERT DAVY, sole executor, 20s. to buy a ring. Witnesses: EDWARD LOFTS, WILLIAM MILLS, ROBERT DAVY. Note that testator acknowledges a debt of £14 to his son ROBERT DAVY who is to be reimbursed. Pr. at Yoxford 22 Feb. 1631/2.

R(W) WILLIAM ANDERSON of Dunwich, mariner. 7 May 1630 (305)

To brother ASLAKE house & lands in Dunwich if he pays to JOHN, ROBERT, MARY, SUSAN, & ELIZABETH ANDERSON, children of W.A.'s brother ROBERT, £5 each on their 21st birthdays; to be paid in the S. porch of St. Peter's church Dunwich. To the poor of Dunwich 20s. within 6 months of W.A.'s death. ASLAKE ANDERSON to pay his daughter MARY £10 within 1 yr. of W.A.'s death. ASLAKE to have residue of goods, and appointed sole executor. Witnesses: MARY NOLLOTH (X), THOMAS HERFORD. Pr. at Yoxford 14 Dec. 1631.

R(W) JEAN HUNT of Burgh, widow. 18 September 1631 (306)

To daughter ANN HUNT best chest, and contents, in parlour. To grandchildren MARTHA & ELIZABETH, daughters of WILLIAM HUNT, 20s. each in 1 yr. J.H. death. To daughter ANNE all apparrell, linen and woollen. To the poor of Burgh 5s. To son WILLIAM and daughter ANNE residue of goods, equally divided. Sole exec. ANNE HUNT; supervisor FRANCIS LANGLY. Witnesses: JOHN WELLS, SAMUEL BOWLES. Pr. at Burgh 1 March 1631/2.

R(W) JOHN HACHER of Cransford, yeoman. (307)
10 February 1631/32

To be buried in Cransford churchyard. To eldest son JEREMY HACHER £18 on 21st birthday. To son JOHN HACHER £16 on 21st birthday. To sons GEORGE, RICHARD, MICHAEL, & WILLIAM HACHER 20 marks each on 21st birthdays. To daughter JOANNE HACHER £10 on 21st birthday. All these bequests with benefit of survivorship.

Wife DIANE HACHER sole exec. and residue of estate; power to wife to bind sons as apprentice and deduct the fee from the son's legacy. Witnesses: WILLIAM MOASE, EDMUND WEEDINGS. Pr. at Wickham Market 23 Feb. 1631/2.

R(W) GEORGE GYLLIANS (X) of Sotherton, yeoman. (308)
14 November 1630

To wife MARGARET, all goods, if pay to son-in-law GEORGE SEPPIN £30 bond. To daughters ALICE DOWSEING & ELIZABETH SEPPENNE 5s. each. If testator die without children by MARGARET his wife, then MARGARET to be bound to testator's son ROBERT GYLLANS in £20, payable within 1 month of her death. Wife to be sole executor. Witnesses: HUMFREY BOHUN, snr., DOROTHY CRETING (X), JOHN LEESE. Pr. at Beccles 11 Feb. 1631/2.

R(W) FAITH GOODWIN(X) of Freesingfield. 6 March1631 (309)

To mother, £10, part of £40 which testator's brother JOHN has the administration of. To brother ROBERT, £10 part of the above mentioned £40. To brother JOHN, £5 and to brother JAMES £5, part of the above mentioned £40. To sister MARY, wife of ROBERT SWATTMAN £5, part of the £40. To sister ANNE, wife of WILLIAM SMITH, £5, part of the £40. To brother ROBERT, bed in the parlour chamber with everything relating to it; also a box, with contents. To mother cupboard in the hall, with contents; coffer in the chamber. To brother JAMES's wife, table in the chamber, waistcoat with lace on it. To Goodwife FOX of Metfield, green cloak, mulberry coloured (murrie) waistcoat, green stiff petticoat. To JOSEPH GOODWIN's wife, new cloth petticoat with two laces. To ELIZABETH HAZELL, servant to JAMES GOODWIN, red under petticoat, 2 old petticoat. To sisters MARY & ANNE, pair of sheets each. To brother ROBERT residue of linen and contents of the coffer devised to mother; also residue of all goods. ROBERT to be sole executor. Witnesses: JAMES FALE, SARA GOODWIN (X), JOSHUA GOODWIN. Pr. at Yoxford 22 March 1631/2.

R(W) FRANCIS EMMS of Little Glemham. 4 January 1631/2 (310)

To his master THOMAS MORTYMER all his goods, to bury him. Witnesses: JOHN WEBSTER (X), JOHN BUSHE, FRANCIS MORTYMER (X). Pr. at Wickham Market 12 Jan. 1631/2.

R(W) PLEASANCE FISHE of Framlingham, widow (N). (311)
[blank] January 1631/2

Made about two weeks before her death. To servant MARY CULLINGTON, pair of sheets, a small light chest for clothes (hutch) and a petticoat. To servant ANNE AMIE, one petticoat. To daughter-in-law ELIZABETH, wife of GEORGE FISHE, all ready money. To son GEORGE FISHE, residue of goods. Witnesses: ELIZABETH WRIGHT (X), ANNE AMIE (X). Pr. at Wickham Market 12 Jan. 1631/2.

R(W) EDWARD DRAX (X) of Thorpehithe, yeoman. 2 April 1630 (312)

Sick. To son EDWARD DRAX, and daughters ALICE & MARY all sea craft to be sold by HENRY CLARKE & JONAS PERRYMAN; profits to be equally divided between them. To son EDWARD, best suit of clothes. To wife EMMA, tenement late TAVERNERS, for life; then to son MATTHEW. Residue of goods to wife to provide for his children. Wife sole executor of goods, save the sea craft. Witnesses: MICHAEL CANNAPP, JONAS PERRYMAN (X), HENRY CLARKE (X), MARIA LIST. Note, that EDWARD DRAX surrendered copyhold into court's hands -- MICHAEL CANNAPP, & JONAS PERRYMAN witnessed this surrender. Pr. at Yoxford 21 Feb. 1631/2.

R(W) GILBERT CHAPMAN of Southelmham St. James (N). (313)
[blank] March 1631

Sick. To wife MARY, all goods. Witnesses: SAMUEL KNAPP (X) clerk, NICHOLAS CATTLYN (X). Pr. at Bungay 1 March 1631/2.

R(W) MARY CORWEN of Southwold, widow (N). (314)
[blank] March 1631

Sick. To son-in-law HENRY REEDE, all goods. Witnesses: PHILIP SEAMAN (X), WILLIAM GODDINS. Pr. at Yoxford 23 March 1631.

R(W) JOHN COLEBY of Kirkley, yeoman. 4 April 1630 (315)

To the poor of Kirkley 3s. 4d. To the poor of Pakefield 6s. 8d. To wife REBECCA, for life, all houses, and lands in Pakefield, Kirkley, Carlton Colville in the half hundred of Mutford. On her death to be divided as follows: To eldest son THOMAS COLBY, all lands occupied by SAMUEL FISHER, ploughwright, of which 5 acres were bought from the coheirs of THOMAS WIGG, in the south field of Pakefield; also 1/2 acre land at the south end of Westwins in Lawses grove near the packway, and 1 acre bond land lying at the south end of Pakefield parish late NATHANIEL COLBY -- testator's father; also three pieces of fen, one piece purchased from EDWARD HUBBERT, other two pieces bought from the heirs of RICHARD DAY of Pakefield, lying together in Kirkley between a packway on the east leading to Lowestoft, and the common of Carlton Colville on the west; provided THOMAS pay to ROBERT COLBY, ALICE COLEBY, RUTH COLEBY & MARY COLEBY, the children of NATHANIEL COLEBY, son of the testator, and to granddaughter SUSAN FOWLER, £5 each, the first payment to be made within 2 yrs. of THOMAS inheriting the land. Power to enter and distrain if default. To son NATHANIEL COLEBY, all lands bought from JOHN FENN, where testator now lives, and two pieces enclosed land in Kirkley bought from JAMES

RIPENG and his daughter ELIZABETH of Benacre, which lands abutts on Saltergate way on the south, and on the lands of THOMAS FOWLER on the north; also two pieces heath doles late the testator's father, in Kirkley heath. To son JOHN COLEBY, all houses and lands bought from the coheirs of THOMAS WIGG, with pightel late BRISTOWE's, late HENRY RICHARDS; the camping close, the pightle at the chancel's end (late NATHANIEL COLEBY's) 1/2 acre late WILLIAM NEWMAN's. To daughter ALICE COLEBY £40; £20 within 1 yr. of J.C. death, £20 in 2 yrs. To son THOMAS COLEBY, all his right in the fisher boat jointly owned by the testator and THOMAS, with all warrops, tackle, etc., provided THOMAS will take on winter fishing 8 herring nets each holding 2 dole; also 12 mackerel netts each holding 3 dole; and for the North Seas 2 herring nets -- all these nets to be placed for testator's wife REBECCA, for her life. Also to son THOMAS, the smallest farry boat with 4 oars, one prop anchor, and one prop provided when he fish for spratts then one dole of spratt nets for REBECCA, and if the boat use flewes nets (a herring net) then 1/2 dole for REBECCA. To son NATHANIEL COLBY, a line boat with all tackle and oars, provided he gives to REBECCA one dole of flewe nets and a mand (1,000) lines with hooks. To youngest son JOHN COLEBY, a fishing boat built by JOHN BARKER, with all tackle provided he gives 10 nets each holding 2 1/2 doles herring in winter fishing, and 14 mackerel nets containing 3 1/2 doles, for REBECCA -- she to repair the boat; also to son JOHN 1/3 part of the North seas caravell of which NATHANIEL owns 1/2. To son NATHANIEL further 1/6 part of the North sea caravelle of which he already owns 1/2, provided he carry 1/2 a dole of herring nets for North seas fishing, and 2 dole of herring nets in winter fishing for the use of his mother; mother to repair the ship. Also to son NATHANIEL the brewing copper in the backhouse, and the malt mill in the flag house, on the death of REBECCA, provided he let brothers and sister have access to the copper and malt mill -- they to provide 12d. each to the repair of same. To wife REBECCA £10, to be paid by JOHN COLEBY within 6 months of testator's decease, power to distrain on caravell boat if default; also to wife, 30 deep sea herring nets chosen from his stock, all to hold 7 1/2 doles each; also 42 mackerell nets each holding 10 1/2 doles. Residue of deep sea nets and mackerel nets to be equally divided between sons THOMAS, NATHANIEL, & JOHN. If any son at sea on testator's death, then profits of that voyage to REBECCA. To wife REBECCA, heath doles from ground belonging to THOMAS COLEBY in Carlton heath; also 2,000 flaggs for fire, two loads of bond wood also from Carlton heath. Residue of goods to REBECCA, she to be sole executrix, provided she enter into bond of £200 with her sons within 2 months after testator's decease to pay legacies etc. Sons to be supervisors of will. Witnesses: WILLIAM GIRLING the elder, JOHN ARTIS. Pr. at Beccles 18 Feb. 1631.

R(W) JOHN COOKE of Wingfield, yeoman. 20 October 1629 (316)

To wife MARGARET, all land, both free and copyhold and leasehold in Wingfield, provided she keep the property in good repair; MARGARET to take all wood she need for her firing, for fencing and for repairs to property. On her death the property to pass to testator's son ROBERT COOKE, provided ROBERT pay within one year of MARGARET's death £10 to be equally divided between testator's grandchildren -- ROBERT ALDRICH, GILES, ROBERT, FRANCIS, THOMAS, MARY, JOHN, WILLIAM, HENRY, and ALICE PRETTY. Proviso also, that if MARGARET re-marry, then son ROBERT is to enter the land immediately on the remarriage, and has to pay to MARGARET, quarterly at the south porch of the church at Wingfield, £5 in equal payments, the first payment to begin on the first quarter day coming after the remarriage. Power given to MARGARET to enter the property and distrain if default of payment. To son ROBERT, the long table and cupboard in the hall, the feather bed in the parlour and all things pertaining to it, and the brass cauldron in the buttery. To servant MARY HENDRY, 10s. in the quarter year after testator's death. To the poor of Wingfield, 20s. to be paid on the first Sunday after testator's death. To wife MARGARET residue of all goods to pay debts, funeral and probate expenses, and legacies specified in the will. Wife to be sole executrix, with son ROBERT as supervisor. Witnesses: THOMAS WRITHOCK, ELIZABETH FULCHER (X). Pr. at Wingfield 12 March 1631/2.

R(W) JEREMY CLARKE of Blythburgh, yeoman. (317)
1 February 1631/2

Sick; to be buried in Blythburgh church, or church yard. To wife JOAN, all movables, goods, and house. To son ROBERT, £20, payable on death of testator's wife. To sons JEREMY, MICHAEL, and JOHN, £10 each on death of testator's wife. To daughters SARA, KATHERIN, and JOAN, £10 each on death of testator's wife. Wife JOAN to be sole executrix; to pay all debts, funeral expenses, legacies, and probate costs. Witnesses: WILLIAM RIVETT (X), DOROTHY THURSTON (X). Pr. at Yoxford 22 Feb. 1631/2.

R(W) THOMAS BURFORD of Walberswick, merchant. (318)
28 November 1631

To wife FRANCES, for life, an annuity of £15, payable in equal installments, on Lady Day, and Michaelmas; this to be given in lieu of her dower. Provision for her to reclaim dower if default made in payment of annuity. To son THOMAS, and his heirs, all lands in Raydon, Wangford and Walberswick, except for tenement, late ROBERT SMITH's where the Widow FENN lives; this tenement to pass to testator's daughter ELIZABETH. To daughter ELIZABETH £40 within 3 months of testator's death. To daughter MARGERY. £60, within 3 months of testator's death. To daughter SUSAN, £100 within 3 months of testator's death. To daughter MARY, £100 on her 21 birthday or her marriage. To daughter FRANCES £100 on her 21 birthday or her marriage. Proviso, that if daughters MARY & FRANCES die before their 21 birthday or marriage, then benefit of survivorship to their sisters, legacy(ies) to be equally divided between sisters. Proviso also, that MARY & FRANCES to receive £6 each annually until 21 or marriage, towards their maintenance.

To wife FRANCES, £40 and one of the best milk cows; all beds, bedding and other household stuff which are in the south parlour of the house the testator lives in in Walberswick; also all linnen. Son THOMAS BURFORD to be sole executor, but as he is under 17, then WILLIAM CANHAM, the elder, of Lowestoft, testator's cousin, to act on THOMAS's behalf. WILLIAM to receive £10 for this task of supervision. Witnesses: EDWARD BURFORD, THOMAS CANHAM, WILLIAM CANHAM, WILLIAM BUCKENHAM, BENJAMIN BUCKENHAM. Grant to WILLIAM CANHAM to act on behalf of THOMAS BURFORD with regard to this will, made at Lowestoft on 7 March 1631. Pr. at Lowestoft 17 Jan. 1637.

R(W) WILLIAM BLOCK of Yoxford, yeoman. 13 February 1631/2 (319)

To wife MARY, in lieu of dower, for life, lands and tenements in Peasenhall, except for 2 closes called Further Closes, containing 14 acres, which lie against Heveningham lane. MARY to keep all houses and fences in the properties in good repair; she to take enough wood for her use, and stakes for fencing; the farmers/occupiers of closes not to take more than 4 loads of wood, and only necessary fencing materials of wood and bushes. MARY to bring up at her own cost their daughter ALICE until she reach 21 or marriage; MARY also to provide for their son STEPHEN, until he reach 21, partly at her own cost, and partly from the profits of land devised to her; MARY also to provide for sons EDWARD & THOMAS until they come of age to inherit lands devised to them by this will. Proviso, that if MARY re-marry, and her second husband refuses to provide for, or neglects, the upbringing and welfare of testator's children ALICE, EDWARD, THOMAS, & STEPHEN, then testator's brother THOMAS BLOCK, and testator's son JOHN BLOCK, to provide for these children at their or one's discretion, out of some reasonable part of land devised to MARY to provide for these children in accordance with testator's wishes as made plain by him to his wife. To son JOHN BLOCK, and his heirs, the two closes mentioned above in the bequest made to MARY, viz. Further closes, lying against Heveningham land; also all lands previously bequeathed, on the death of MARY. If JOHN has no heirs, then lands to pass to son EDWARD, and in default of heirs from EDWARD, then lands to pass to son THOMAS, and in default of heirs from THOMAS, then lands to pass to son STEPHEN. If no male heirs then lands to pass to testator's three daughters, and their heirs. Son JOHN BLOCK, or his heirs, to pay to testator's son STEPHEN, £20, at the porch of Yoxford church within two years after JOHN inherits his lands; if default made of all or part of £20, then STEPHEN to have power to enter and hold lands until default is made good. Proviso, that if STEPHEN die before 21 unmarried without issue, then the £20 legacy to be equally divided between testator's daughters, they to have similar power of entry to lands if default made in payment of legacy. Proviso, that if wife MARY die before ALICE or STEPHEN reach 18, then JOHN or his heirs are to pay to ALICE in Yoxford church 40s. a year from the death of MARY until ALICE reaches 18; and to pay to STEPHEN in Yoxford church porch £4 a year by the space of two years next after the death of MARY, and after the said two years to pay yearly to STEPHEN or his assignes 20s. until STEPHEN reach 18. If default made, then STEPHEN & ALICE have power to enter lands in Peasenhall given to JOHN and to distrain for the default, and for arrears and for a further 20s. in the name of compensation [nomine pene], and to keep the distress until fully satisfied. Son JOHN BLOCK, or heirs, to pay at Yoxford church porch to ALICE when 21 £40; if default made then ALICE to have power of entry into the two closes, and to hold the same until full satisfaction is made of the legacy, together with all damages sustained by the default. JOHN BLOCK also, on the death of mother MARY, to pay in Yoxford church porch, yearly, an annuity of £3 to testator's daughter ELIZABETH, the wife of EDMUND MILLS, on Lady Day and Michaelmas, by equal portions. If default then ELIZABETH to have power to enter into all/part of lands in Peasenhall devised to JOHN, and to distrain for the annuity/arrears and to impound or detain any goods to the value of the annuity/arrears, until she be fully satisfied for the annuity, arrears, and all damages sustained in the name of compensation [nomine pene]. JOHN BLOCK or heirs to pay at Yoxford church porch to THOMAS MILLS, testator's grandson, son of EDMUND MILLS and ELIZABETH, £40 out of the lands in Peasenhall, within one year after the death of ELIZABETH if THOMAS is 21; if under 21 then JOHN BLOCK to convey and assure some house or lands, void of incumbrances, to the value of £40, to the said THOMAS. If default, power to enter and enjoy any part of lands devised to JOHN, and to hold until legacy, and arrears and damages sustained in default, be fully satisfied. To daughter MARY, wife of NICHOLAS BEAUMONT, all lands called Mills and the meadow adjoining it in Yoxford; to hold for 4 years after testator's decease; after the 4 years, land to pass to testator's sons EDWARD & THOMAS. If MARY or heirs commit any waste, or take more than 2 loads of wood a year then MARY forfeits the remainder of term, and EDWARD & THOMAS enter land immediately. To daughter MARY, all copyhold land and tenements in Yoxford, on death of testator for 4 years; land then to pass to testator's son STEPHEN BLOCK. Son JOHN BLOCK to permit MARY, testator's daughter, to have the ground called Mills with adjoining meadow, for the 4 year term, and on reasonable request made thereon, respectively release to MARY and EDWARD & THOMAS, all his rights to the ground; otherwise on the death of testator's wife, MARY, the daughter, shall have all copyhold lands from the manor of Sibton for the 4 year term, and that after the end of this term then the lands held from Sibton manor to pass to testator's sons EDWARD & THOMAS. Wife MARY, to pay, on testator's death, to daughter ELIZABETH, the wife of EDMUND MILLS, yearly, for the term of her life 40s., payable on Lady Day and Michaelmas, at Yoxford church porch by equal installments; if default then ELIZABETH to have power to enter lands given to MARY, testator's wife, and to distrain for the default, until fully recompensed for default, arrears, and compensation for damage sustained. To wife MARY, all personal estate to pay a debt of £26 due to the five children of JOHN HALL of Yoxford, due to be paid by testator as executor of the will of KATHERINE FALE; wife to pay all other debts, funeral and probate expenses. The residue of his personal estate, on the death of wife MARY, to be equally divided amongst his children, excepting son JOHN. Proviso, that if wife MARY remarry, then ten days before her marriage, MARY to enter into a bond of £100 with testator's brother THOMAS BLOCK for the performance of this will. If she refuse the bond, then wife to forfeit all benefits to herself devised by the will, and testator's brother THOMAS to have the benefits and performance of the will. MARY to be sole executrix; brother THOMAS BLOCK to be supervisor. Witnesses: THOMAS BLOCK, JEFFREY BLOCK, JAMES BISHOP, BENJAMIN BUCKENHAM. Pr. at Yoxford 22 March 1631/2.

R(W) ROBERT BETTS of Wantisden, husbandman. (320)
19 January 1631/2.

Sick; to be buried in Wantisden parish church. To Mrs ROBLETT of Wantisden £5 within 6 months of testator's death. To MARIAN ROBLETT £5 within 6 months of testator's death. To BENJAMIN ROBLETT 40s. within 1 year of testator's death. To the wife of PHILIP QUINTON £5 within 3 months of testator's death. To the Widow MARRIOTT, £5 within 3 months of testator's death. To ROBERT BICKERS of Beccles 40s. within 1 year of testator's death. To JOHN STUDD of Eyke husbandman 10s. within 1 month of testator's death. Residue of goods to ROBERT CORBOLD of Wantisden, who was appointed exec. Witnesses: NATHANIEL FERION; JOHN HARVY. Pr. at Wickham Market 23 March 1631/2.

R(W) NICHOLAS BUGG of Needham Market, husbandman. (321)
3 March 1631

To wife MARY BUGG, for life, all houses and property in Needham Market, and all movable goods. To daughter MARGARET, my parlour with the chamber over it, with the yard and part of the well belonging to it on the death of her mother MARY. To daughter ELIZABETH, all other houses and yards adjoining the parlour already devised, on the death of her mother MARY. To daughter MARGARET, all my movable goods as they stand in the parlour already devised on the death of her mother MARY. To daughter ELIZABETH, all movables standing in the part of the house already given to her on death of her mother MARY. Wife to pay all debts, funeral expenses and probate charges; to be sole executrix. Witnesses: HENRY SAVAGE, PETER WARDEN, ROBERT ELLIS, and WILLIAM BROWN. Pr. at Gipping 24 March 1631.

R(W) JOHN BETTS of Blundeston, husbandman. 15 June 1630 (322)

Sick. To wife MARGARET, all goods and chattels, provided that within 3 months after testator's death pass and present assurance of lands in Oulton which she and testator were joint purchasors, to daughters MARY and ANNE, and their heirs. If wife fail to do this then lands given to MARGARET to be equally divided between MARGARET, MARY & ANNE. MARGARET to be sole executrix. Witnesses: JOHN CAPS, GEORGE HALSE, knight. Pr. at Lowestoft 7 March 1631/2.

R(W) JOHN ALDOUS of Fordeley, yeoman. [no date] (323)

To wife MARGERY, all copyhold lands and tenements held of the manor of Whittingham with Wakelyn in Fressingfield, occupied by WILLIAM LEVITT or his assigns, containing 20 acres. This to her for life provided she keep all in good and tenant like repair, and on her death to lands to pass to testator's son JOHN and his heirs, provided he pay to his own daughters FRANCES & BRIDGETT or their assigns, £160 -- namely to FRANCES ALDOUS £80 when she reach 21, and £80 to BRIDGETT ALDOUS when she reach 21. Payments to be made in the south porch of Cookley church. If default in legacy then FRANCES & BRIDGETT each to have half of the said copyhold lands. If these girls die without heirs before reaching 21 then their legacy to be void. Further proviso that if MARGERY ALDOUS be still alive when her granddaughters FRANCES & BRIDGETT reach 21 then the granddaughters to wait for their legacy until MARGERY's death and a further 6 months. To wife MARGERY all goods, chattels, money and movables towards the meeting of all debts, paying funeral expenses and probate charges. Wife to be sole executrix and she to give poor of Middleton with Fordeley 10s. Witnesses: JOHN WOODCOCK, WILLIAM WHINCOPP. Pr. at Yoxford 22 Feb. 1631. [This will has no date either in the original will or in registered copy; also initially the registered copy had wife's name down as MARGARET, subsequently crossed out, and the error noted in the register's margin.]

R(W) MARY UNKETEL of Theberton, singlewoman (N). 13 June 1631 (324)

All goods to nephew ROBERT GOODWIN. Witnesses: AGNES BAKER, the wife of JOHN BAKER, ANNE RUSSELL, widow. Probate granted to nephew ROBERT GOODWIN at Yoxford 2 Nov. 1631.

R(W) THOMAS WAYLAND of Bromeswell, yeoman. 11 December 1631 (325)

Sick. To grandchild THOMAS WAYLAND my biggest brass pot. To wife [name not given] one cow bought from WILLIAM PITT, and all cheese and butter; my little hen, and one hog; 4 keelers [shallow tubs in which milk is set to cool], 3 tubs, 2 cheese vats, 1 cheese-brig [crossed bars of wood, resting across the cream pan to support the skimming bowl], 1 wicker chair; 2 chests -- one like a church chest, the other the biggest standing in my parlour; all hemp, and all wood in the yard and out houses; all goods as were hers before marriage. To son JOHN WAYLAND, all lands and tenements, both free and copyhold, late WILLIAM WAYLAND's, called Taylor's, also one rood of ground lying between Foxborough and Brightwell purchased from JEFFREY PELLS. To son THOMAS WAYLAND, and male heirs, tenement called Smallhead, with all houses barns etc., provided THOMAS pay his mother £5 yearly, by quarterly payments of 25s. To son-in-law WILLIAM PITT £20 within 1 year of testator's death; but if he (WILLIAM PITT) does not satisfy a bond entered into by testator and WILLIAM PITT to LAURENCE SCOTTSON of Sutton, the legacy to be void. Testator's wife is to deliver to executor of the will a bond wherein the testator was bound to his wife for payment of £20; this bond to be cancelled as soon as the executor enters into bond with the testator's wife, in £100, for the payment of £5 a year. If testator's wife refuse to deliver the original bond then legacies given to her to be void. To son JOHN WAYLAND, one standing bed and bedstead in testator's parlour, with one feather bed and feather bolster; one flock bed, one feather pillow, one covering, three blankets, one pair of sheets. To son THOMAS WAYLAND residue of goods, chattels etc.; he to be executor. Witnesses: GERVASE HUBBALD, ROBERT MARSH, LAURENCE PELLS. Pr. at Wickham Market 1 Feb. 1631/2.

R(W) SYBIL WINSTON of Wrentham, widow (N). 15 August 1631 (326)

To son ROBERT GEORGE all goods. JOHN GEORGE, executor. Witnesses: WILLIAM GRUDGEFIELD, gent.; SUSAN OWEN, the wife of THOMAS ROUS. Pr. at Beccles 20 Jan. 1631/2.

R(W) HENRY WHITLOCK of Pirlston alias Billingford (Norfolk), yeoman. 20 May 1628 (327)

Aged and weak in body. To daughter ANNE ASHWELL, for life, messuage and lands in Billingford and Osmondstone alias Skole; after her death lands to pass to testator's two grandchildren ELIZABETH & ANNE ASHWELL, daughters of ANNE ASHWELL, provided they maintain and keep testator's wife MARGARET for life and provide with sufficient meat, drink, and clothes. Also to pay to testator's daughter MARY, provided she remain unmarried, £5 a year for life, at Lady Day and Michaelmas by equal portions at Billingford church porch, and also to allow her to live peacefully in testator's parlour with yard with convenient access to the well, and also to have half a hundredweight of wood delivered and stacked for her every year. To wife MARGARET, the benefit and use of all movable goods and household stuff and stock, for life; these to pass on her death to testator's son-in-law NICHOLAS ASHWELL and his wife ANNE, provided they allow to MARY WHITLOCK half the household goods, provided she remain unmarried. Proviso, that MARY WHITLOCK to loose all her legacies if she marry. Executor to have all ready money, to pay debts, funeral expenses and probate charges, and to give 10s. to the poor. Residue of money after these charges met to be equally divided between MARGARET WHITLOCK, ANNE ASHWELL, & MARY WHITLOCK. MARGARET WHITLOCK & NICHOLAS ASHWELL to be executors. Witnesses: JOHN ASHWELL, the elder (X); JOHN ASHWELL the younger (X); WILLIAM WHITTON. Pr. at Wickham Market 1 Feb. 1631/2.

R(W) RICHARD PIGEON of St. Margaret's South Elmham, yeoman. 21 January 1631 (328)

Sick. To be buried in the churchyard of St. Margaret's Southelmham. To wife MARYAN, for life, the use and occupation of two chambers, namely the chamber over the hall, and the one over the kitchen; also the use of the kitchen and the oven in the kitchen. To daughter JUDITH and heirs, all lands and tenements, save one piece called Colshill, provided JUDITH pay testator's wife £5 a year from the profits of these lands -- the first 50s. to be paid within 6 months of testator's death. MARYAN also to receive yearly a hundredweight of wood worth 20s., to be laid out in the yard. All wood and timber now cut to be equally divided between JUDITH & MARYAN. To wife MARYAN, one cow called Munn, to be kept on the land given to daughter JUDITH; six sheep to be equally shared between JUDITH & MARYAN -- MARYAN to have the keeping of her three with the moreen [stout wool] coming from them, where they have been usually kept. The corn already cut to be equally divided between wife and daughter, and the corn ready to be cut, after cutting and reaping likewise to be equally divided between wife and daughter. Hemp on the hempland also to be equally divided, and wife to have yearly a stone of hemp. To wife MARYAN, two beds as they stand upon the hall chamber, one brass pot, and one framed table; two formed stools, one chair, one cushion, three beares [pillow cases], two milk pails, two bowls. To daughter JUDITH a cow called Fiske. To daughter MARY, a cow called Lugghorne. To daughter ANNE a cow called Jay. Son-in-law JOHN MORSE is bound with the testator in a bond of £60 to repay £32. 5s. at Lady Day; JOHN MORSE to receive because of this, the close called Colshill. To son-in-law WILLIAM BENDY his best cloak. To son-in-law JOHN MORSE second cloak, corslet with pike, sword a pair of wheel locks [rifles]. To brother ANDREW, riding cloak, and all other wearing apparel. To grandchild FRANCES MORSE 20s. to be paid her by daughter JUDITH within one year of testator's decease. To wife MARYAN, a mare and another cow, to be sold towards payment of £6 due by bond. Residue of goods to JUDITH towards payment of debts, funeral expenses, and probate. Wife MARYAN and daughter JUDITH to be executrixes. Witnesses: THOMAS MORSE, JOHN MORSE, WILLIAM NORMAN, THOMAS MORSE. Pr. at Southelmham 24 Feb. 1631/2.

R(W) JEREMY PIPE of Laxfield. 20 February 1630/1 (329)

To be buried in Laxfield church yard. To wife MARGARET PIPE, all lands called Crispes at the Rookes, and Osgates in Laxfield, with all appurtenances, with liberty to take sufficient timber and fire wood for own needs and for necessary repairs. To wife MARGARET, all movables and household goods, provided she pay all debts; if she refuse to pay debts, then MARGARET to receive only three milk cows, and the bull to be sold by executors. The close called Hastedill with the piece taken out at the nether end, being part of the said close as it appears by the division of the Whitethorne hay, and certain trees adjoining towards the meadow in the south, lying in Laxfield, the whole containing 12 acres, to be reserved for the payment of a £200 legacy. To son THOMAS PIPE, and his sons THOMAS or JEREMY, the land called Crispes at the Rookes, and Osgate, save the excepted close referred to above, on the death of MARGARET PIPE. With regard to the close called Hastedill appointed for the payment of £200 legacy, THOMAS PIPE, testator's son, to redeem it and pay £200 -- £100 to be paid within one year after the date of the marriage of his sister ANNE MARTYN, and the second £100 to be paid in two installments -- £50 at Lady Day within six months after the testator's death, and £50 one year after the testator's death. If THOMAS PIPE does not pay the first £100, then the said THOMAS to redeem the close and repay the £100 in two installments as specified by his mother MARGARET PIPE, which sums are to be paid at her discretion to ANNE MARTYN. The second £100 to be kept by her if her son-in-law and daughter prosper not in order to relieve ANNE; if all well with the couple to pay the £100. Proviso that if THOMAS PIPE refuse to carry out these instructions, then the said close called Hastedill to pass to EDWARD & ANNE MARTIN and their heirs. If EDWARD & ANNE do inherit this close, and subsequently THOMAS PIPE is willing to redeem it, then EDWARD & ANNE MARTYN to release it back to THOMAS PIPE. THOMAS PIPE is directed to pay £40 out of the profits from Crispes at the Rookes and Osgates, at the direction of MARGARET PIPE, during her life time, and also to pay the £40 as directed by her in her will. If THOMAS PIPE, or his sons THOMAS or JEREMY die without issue, then the rent and profits from Crispes and Osgates to go, on the death of MARGARET PIPE, to testator's daughter ANNE MARTYN, for two years. After the two years the rents and profits to be accumulated and to be used for a legacy for THOMAS's daughter, viz. -- £50 on her 18th birthday, and £50 on her 21st birthday. After this legacy has been fulfilled the land to pass to JEREMY PIPE 'whom I brought up as a child.' Proviso that THOMAS PIPE is not to alienate Crispes and Osgates in his will; also THOMAS to have the close called Andrews (freehold) and Plumbs alias Nicholls (copyhold) provided he promise not to sell these closes, and to maintain them with their current tenant occupiers. If THOMAS leaves these two closes -- Andrews and Plumbs to his wife in his will, then THOMAS's wife to promise to maintain them in good order. THOMAS PIPE, further, has to pay on the death of his mother MARGARET PIPE, an annuity of £11 to his brother WILLIAM PIPE, for life on Lady Day and Michaelmas by payments of £6 and £5. Proviso that if WILLIAM die before receiving the legacy, then the sum to be paid to WILLIAM's sons -- JEREMY to have £6 and WILLIAM £5 for three years. If THOMAS refuse the legacy then the amount of the legacy is increased by 20s. for every feast day missed. To JEREMY PIPE, apprentice, £15. 5s. towards the binding to his trade, and £10 to be paid him at the expiring of his years, by testator's executor. Wife MARGARET PIPE appointed executrix. Pr. at Yoxford 22 Feb. 1631. Memorandum added [words omitted] that if THOMAS PIPE refuse to perform the £200 legacy then the close called Hastedill to pass to EDWARD & ANNE MARTYN and their heirs; if THOMAS PIPE subsequently performs the £200 legacy then the close returns to him. [This memorandum appears in both the register and on the original will.]

R(W) WILLIAM POOLE of Ellough, husbandman. (330)
23 December 1631

To three of his brother FULCHER's children -- namely MARY, ELIZABETH & PHILIP 10s. each, payable within 1 3/4 years after testator's death. To his sister KATHERINE FULCHER, widow, 10s. To JOHN FULCHER, son of CHRISTOPHER FULCHER, cloak, best doublet, best hat, ruff band, best shirt, pair of his longest boots, a pair of white stockings, his best garters and his best girdle. To MARY FULCHER, wife of JOHN FULCHER, 10s. within 1 3/4 yr. of testator's death. To JOHN FULCHER, son of JOHN FULCHER and his wife MARY, £3 within 1 3/4 yrs. of testator's death. To testator's brother ROBERT FULCHER's children which are living on the day of testator's death, 10s. within 3/4 yr. of testator's death. To sister ELIZABETH FLOWER, widow, 5s.; she to keep the sum which she owes to the testator; the 5s. to be paid within 3/4 yr. of testator's death. To sister ALICE BRANDON's children 10s. each within 1 3/4 yr. of testator's death. To JOHN REEVE, son of ALICE BRANDON, testator's coat, shirt, best hose, white hat, pair of blue stockings. To RICHARD BRANDON, son of ALICE BRANDON, best jerkin, grey hose, cloth doublet, a pair of short boots, shirt, pair of russet coloured stockings. To sister ALICE POOLE, 10s. within 1/4 yr. of testator's death. To wife ANNE, £10, she to receive £5 on the next Lady Day after his death, and a further £5 on Michaelmas. ANNE also to receive residue of unbequeathed household goods and movables in order to pay funeral expenses. To THOMAS BROWNE of North Cove, appointed executor, the surplus of unbequeathed money. Proviso, that if ANNE POOLE refuse to hand over to the executor the goods specified in the various legacies, then she looses the £10 legacy, and the exec. to distribute the £10 amongst the testator's kin as he think fit. Witnesses: WILLIAM BROWN (X), JOHN LAUGHTER (X). Note added: the names of R. FULCHER's children are -- ROBERT, MARGARET, & ELIZABETH. The names of the Widow BRANDON's children are RICHARD BRANDEN, JOHN REEVE, MARGARET REEVE, and ELIZABETH REEVE. Pr. at Beccles 7 Jan. 1631/2. [The note on children's names appears in both original will and register.]

R(W) EDMUND THOMPSON of Chattisham, yeoman. (331)
7 September 1631

Sick. To wife ANNE THOMPSON, messuage where he lives in Chattisham, and lands belonging to it lying next to the said messuage, viz. one parcell of land called Two Acres, one close called Broome close, two other closes called Steadcroft and Mowlecroft, one other parcel of land adjoining to the yard belonging to the said messuage called Three Acres; two other pieces of land called Rauscroft and Turners; one piece of land called Shieldcroft, one parcel of land called Birch land containing 60 acres in Chattisham and Washbrook; these to wife for life, provided she does [not] strip or waste the lands and maintain them in good heart and repair. On her death lands to pass to son EDMUND THOMPSON and his heirs. To son EDMUND, one parcel land/ meadow called Caprons, lying in Chattisham, containing 20 acres to him and his male heirs; if default of heirs male then land to pass to testator's son SAMUEL THOMPSON. To son SAMUEL THOMPSON, tenement called Wilkins with house and pasture in Chattisham, lately occupied by THOMAS WOOLVETT; also a tenement called Bulls in Chattisham, occupied by testator. Wife ANNE to enjoy the lands devised to EDMUND & SAMUEL, until they reach 21, she to pay yearly from the profits of these lands a sum of £7 to each son, in two yearly equal payments, for their maintenance. Also ANNE to pay to testator's daughters THAMAR & ANN, 40s. yearly to each daughter, until EDMUND & SAMUEL reach 21 when they inherit the lands. Remainder of the profit from those lands not used up in several sums of £7 and 40s., to remain with the executor in trust for testator's daughters ANNE & THAMAR. Wife ANNE THOMPSON to sell the land called Dawes in Needham, adjoining the meere (2 acres), the profits from the sale to be used in payment of testator's debts and legacies. To daughter SUSAN THOMPSON £100 within one year of testator's decease. To daughters THAMAR & ANNE £100 each on 21st birthday. Benefit of survivorship to the three daughters. To son EDMUND THOMPSON, tenement newly built in Chattisham called Sleyfield, and lands belonging to same, to him and his heirs, if the rent and profits from this are used by testator's exec. till EDMUND reach 21, towards the performance of the will. To wife ANNE, half goods, household stuff within the messuage where testator lives for life; then to be equally divided between SAMUEL, SUSAN, THAMAR, & ANNE. The other half goods etc. to go to EDMUND when 21. Residue of goods, etc. to go to exec. towards payment of debts, funeral expenses, and probate costs. Wife ANNE to be executrix; DANIEL MEADOWS, gent., ROBERT HAMBY gent. to be supervisors. ANNE as executrix, to enter within 2 weeks of testator's death, into bond with supervisors in 1,000 marks, to prove and perform will; if she remarry then she, and future husband before they marry to enter into new bond with the supervisors in £500 to perform the conditions of this will. If ANNE refuse to enter bond, then to forfeit executorship, and must not meddle in the execution of the will nor to have any profit from the will. Supervisors then to become executors, share all legacies etc.; supervisors to have 40s. each for their pains. To ELIZABETH CHEVINGTON, a bushel of wheat, bushel of rye, and bushel of barley. To godchildren ROBERT GARRARD, EDMUND ROVE, THOMAS CHEVINGTON & JOHN LEWIS 6s. 8d. each, within 2 yrs. testator's death. To the poor of Chattisham 20s. to be paid by executrix. Witnesses: JEFFERY ROUS, WILLIAM MARCHANT (X). Pr. at Ipswich 16 Dec. 1631.

R(W) HENRY TANN of Bramford (N). 31 October 1631 (332)

To daughters MARY, SUSAN, & ROSE TANN £40 each. Witnesses: JOHN MAPES of Henley, JOHN TANN of Bramford. Probate granted to ROSE TANN, widow 18 Nov. 1631.

R(W) ROBERT TUKELEY of Dunwich, yeoman (N).[no date] (333)

Sick. All goods, movables to daughters ELIZABETH and to wife DOROTHY, in order to pay debts and legacies. To THOMAS, JOHN & JAMES GALLANT, wife's grandchildren 20s. each. To ELIZABETH GALLANT, wife's daughter, one feather bed, one pewter platter. ELIZABETH to have her mother's share of testator's goods, if mother die before her. Witness: JOHN MELLS. Probate granted to DOROTHY TUKELEY and ELIZABETH GALLANT at Yoxford 2 Nov. 1631.

R(W) PHILIP STILES of Wortham, yeoman. 23 December 1629 (334)

£40 had been promised by testator on the marriage of his daughter BRIDGET to her now husband, and £20 of this sum had been paid. £20 now to be paid within one year of testator's death by exec. to BRIDGET and husband. To son PHILIP STILES and his heirs, lands and tenements and all reversions to them the lands lying on the north side of the common highway leading from Wortham church to Redgrave church. To daughter MARY STILES £40 within one year of testator's death. All household goods to be divided into four parts; three of these four parts to go to daughter MARY; one part to daughter SUSAN. Residue of money and other goods to go to son PHILIP STILES, appointed executor, to pay debts, funeral charges and probate expenses. Cousin HENRY KIRKE appointed as supervisor. Witnesses: JOHN KEWE, WILLIAM PRENTICE. Note -- that names MARY & SUSAN were inserted before sealing of the will. Pr. at Wickham Market 24 Nov. 1631. [This note appears on both the original will and registered copy.]

R(W) GEORGE STANNARD of Witnesham, yeoman. (335)
6 November 1631

To be buried in Witnesham churchyard. To wife GRACE, little tenement at Little Bealings, with the hempland, and all things belonging, for her life time. Property then to be sold by exec., and money thus raised to be equally divided amongst testator's children then living, except MARY CUTHBERT -- she to have 20s. within 6 months from the sale of this land. The exec. to sell land within six months of GRACE STANNARD's death; testator's children to have first refusal. If MARY CUTHBERT be dead then the 20s. be equally divided between remainder of testator's children. To wife GRACE, the best bedstead and the best bed with all its furniture, 4 pair of sheets, best cupboard, the cupboard table, coffer, form, two chairs, a little brass pot, two kettles, one little skillet, two pewter salts, six pewter platters, two firkins, three tubs, a keeler, two bowls, and all linen and woollens belonging to her; two cushions, a morter, a pestle, two stools, fire pan and tongs, cobirons, a spit, dripping pan, roast iron, candlestick, pail, pair of bellows, two board cloths, four napkins, and 40s. To grandchild GEORGE CUTHBERT 10s. payable out of land devised to GRACE, and 2s. 6d. to each of daughter MARY's daughters. To his three sons THOMAS, JOHN, & GEORGE STANNARD, 12d. each on his death; to the children of son JOHN 5s. each, to children of son GEORGE 5s. each and to daughter ROSE's children -- ROSE and MARY 5s. each, payable out of sale of messuage. To daughter ANN STANNARD 40s.; to daughter ELIZABETH WEBB 12d.; to son WILLIAM STANNARD the elder 30s.; to son WILLIAM STANNARD the younger 50s.; to ROBERT STANNARD, his son, 30s. within 6 months of testator's death. Residue of property and goods to exec. to pay debts, funeral and probate charges. After these met the residue to be sold within 40 days after the nearest Michaelmas and to be equally divided between children, excepting THOMAS STANNARD the eldest son, and MARY CUTHBERT. Wife GRACE STANNARD, and son WILLIAM STANNARD the younger executors. Witnesses: JOHN NICHOLLS (X), and me JOHN STANNARD (X), EDWARD LEECH. Pr. at Ipswich 25 Nov. 1631.

R(W) ANN SCARLET of East Bergholt, widow. 30 May 1631 (336)

Sick. To son GEORGE SCARLET, all shop stuff, all tools and implements concerning the dressing of cloth; also a little drinking pot tipped with silver and gilt, 1 desk. Remainder of goods, chattels, and corn to be equally divided, after all debts paid between testator's daughters -- ANNE, MARY & ELIZABETH SCARLET; the two youngest daughters to receive their portions from the exec. when they reach 21. ANNE SCARLET to receive her portion by the next Christmas after testator's death. Benefit of survivorship between daughters. GEORGE SCARLET to pay out of his legacy, 40s. to testator's grandchild JOHN SMITH, and to each of JOHN SMITH's daughters 10s. when they reach 21. ANNE SCARLET to have the guiding and ordering of testator's house until Michaelmas next after testator's death. GEORGE & ANNE SCARLET to be joint executors; brother-in-law THOMAS COLEMAN of Hadleigh, and JOHN LAYMAN of East Bergholt to be supervisors. Executors to be bound in 100 marks to the supervisors, within ten days of testator's death, to perform legacies specified in will; if refuse the bond, then to forfeit their executorship, THOMAS COLEMAN to take the place of whoever refuses the bond. Witnesses: JOHN LAYMAN, JOHN STANNUS, ANNE SCARLET (X). Pr. at Ipswich 10 Oct. 1631.

R(W) THOMAS SAMSON of All Saints SouthElmham, husbandman. (337)
19 April 1631

To son JOHN, one long table with a frame, a joined form thereunto belonging, one cupboard and a great chair, one posted bedstead with best feather bed, two feather bolsters, a pillow, two blankets, one quilt and a covering; a great chest, a little joined stool, and a little chair; one cauldron, and a bolting house and a skillet, one pewter platter, two saucers, one pewter candlestick, a spit, warming pan, and eight bolts, and a pair of andirons. To son HENRY, one livery bedstead with a featherbed, one bolster, a blanket and a covering, a salting tray, a milk kettle, an iron pot, a tumbling churn, a cheese tub, a cheese press, three keels, a pair of querns, one cart with a pair of wheels, a bunching block, a long ladder, and a plough with the furniture belonging to it; a beam, a pair of scales with the weights and a cow comb. To son SIMON and his wife ANNE, £3 within 2 months, paid by HENRY SAMSON out of his legacy. To daughter MARY, wife of SAMUEL FISKE, 40s.; 20s. of which to be paid within one month of testator's decease, 20s. within 3 months, by HENRY out of his legacy. To JOHN SAMSON, the yearling heifer, if he pay to THOMAS SAMSON, son of HENRY SAMSON, the sum of 10s. within one year of testator's decease. To goddaughter and grandchild ELIZABETH FISKE, 10s. within one year of testator's death, payable by HENRY SAMSON out of his legacy. To sons JOHN & HENRY SAMSON, 6 pair of sheets, 2 tablecloths, 2 pillow beres, 4 table napkins, 5 cheese salts, three cheese brigs, three beer vessels, these all to be equally divided between the sons with the allowance and consent of RICHARD DAVY and BENJAMIN HOWLETT, assigned by testator to part these goods. To son JOHN 4 milk neat, and to son HENRY 2 milk neat -- the one bought from GEORGE COOPER, and the other the eldest black cow; HENRY to have the use of all six until the Michaelmas next after the testator's death when the 4 are to be delivered to JOHN by HENRY; HENRY to pay JOHN £3 at Lady Day for this use. To son SIMON, all my clothes mordon, and also to SIMON and his wife ANNE 40s. -- 20s. to be paid by son JOHN and 20s. to be paid by son HENRY within 6 months of testator's death. If HENRY refuse this, then his legacy be void. To ELIZABETH, wife of HENRY SAMSON, 20s. to be paid by executor. Residue of goods to executor; JOHN SAMSON, of Rumborough, son, appointed executor. Witnesses: RICHARD DAVY, BENJAMIN HOWLETT, ROBERT DAVY. Pr. at Bungay 16 Nov. 1631.

R(W) ROBERT SMITH of Wickham Market, draper. (338)
22 September 1631

Sick. To the repair of the great town house of Wickham and the south window of the steeple there, £5. To the poor of Wickham Market £5, the poor of Pettistree 13s. 4d., the poor of Ufford 20s., poor of Dallinghoo 10s., poor of Easton 10s., Hacheston poor 20s., poor of Marlesford 13s. 4d., poor of Campsea Ash 10s., poor of Blaxhall 10s., poor of Tunstall 10s., poor of Little Glemham 10s., poor of Eyke 10s., poor of Bromswell 10s., and the poor of Melton 10s. To son-in-law MEADOWS, and son-in-law HEYMER a spurroyall to buy a remembrance. To daughters ELIZABETH & MARGARET £30 each payable in 1 yr. after testator's death. To daughter ANNE £30 within six months after her husband shall assure to her & her heirs begotten by him WILLIAM, in lieu of all her thirds and dower due to her out of his lands, lands to the yearly value of £40. To every one of his daughters three pair of sheets. Testator promised to JOHN BARKER, late son-in-law now deceased, to give him or his wife MARGARET £100, and JOHN BARKER in his will bequeathed this £100 to his son ROBERT BARKER; testator now devises the £100 to ROBERT BARKER when ROBERT reaches 21; if ROBERT die before 21, then £100 to go to testator's daughter MARGARET. To JOHN BARKER, grandchild, 40d., to buy a ring. To ROBERT BARKER £18. To each grandchild, other than JOHN & ROBERT BARKER, £10 on their 21st birthday. If a grandchild die before 21st birthday, then legacy to be void. To brothers GEORGE & JOHN SMITH, and sister MORRIS, sister NEWSON, and sister BRUDBANKE 20s. each to buy rings. To godson EDWARD BRUDBANKE 10s. To DOROTHY BOBBETT, wife of PATRICK, of Ufford 40s. To STEPHEN GREENHILL, ELIZABETH KNIGHT, & ELIZABETH BRANCH 20s. each. Residue of goods to son ROBERT SMITH, appointed sole executor. Witnesses: RICHARD THURSTON, JOHN STILES. Pr. at Ipswich 20 Dec. 1631.

R(W) SIMON ROSER the elder of Needham Market. (339)
14 November 1620

Sick; to be buried in Barking churchyard. To the poor of Inhitting in Needham 20s. on the day of his burial. To son SIMON and his heirs, messuage and tenement where testator lives, and all appurtenances in Needham Market, except the room where WILLIAM HART lives, and one little buttery adjoining this room, with free ingress/egress from same to the pump; likewise the benefit and use of the bakehouse to brew and bake, and the benefit and use of the herbs in the garden, and a convenient place in the yard to set sufficient wood for domestic needs -- all these to testator's wife BRIDGETT for her lifetime, and on her death to revert to SIMON. Executors to sell the close called Rolfsclose with adjoining pightle in Needham, and the meadow called Hacknell meadow held of Wolney hall manor in Creeting St. Olave, for the best profit; also to sell all leather, timber, hay, corn and cattle to use the money thus raised to pay debts, and meet legacies. To wife BRIDGETT £100 from executors. To daughter GRACE, one feather bed and a feather bolster, one pair of blankets, one pair of the finest sheets, one birded coverlet. If wife BRIDGETT die before receiving the £100 legacy, then this legacy together with all undevised goods, and the surplus from the sale of land and corn etc., to be equally divided among testator's eight youngest children, save that son JOHN may not have so much as the others by £10, and EDWARD, son, to have £20 more than the others. If BRIDGETT live to inherit the £100 legacy, then all the undevised household goods owned by the testator before his marriage, to be equally divided among the seven youngest children; and the surplus from the sale of lands and corn etc., be equally divided between the eight youngest children, except that son JOHN may not have so much as the others by £6. 13s. 4d. Executors to hold all these legacies on behalf of the young children, towards the cost of bringing up the five youngest children. BRIDGETT to have control and to care for these children until they are old enough to go for service, & executors to pay BRIDGETT 20d. in every £ in their hands every year towards the cost of maintaining the children and providing for them. JOHN to have his share at 25, THOMAS at 27, GRACE at 22, BRIDGETT at 22, ANNE at 22, EDMUND at 24, ROGER at 24, and ELIZABETH at 22. Provided that if JOHN die before reaching 21 then benefit of survivorship to pass to remaining children, but if JOHN does not die but one of the others does, then JOHN excluded from benefit. Also provided that when each of the five youngest children come of an age to be able to be sent into service, then their share shall be retained by executors and the profits accruing from that shall be used to benefit THOMAS and GRACE, that is only until the child whose portion is being thus used be under the age specified by the testator. When he/she comes to the right age to inherit then executors to hand over relevant share. To wife BRIDGETT all wood in the yard. Executors to sell two tumbrills (carts), posts, pales, planks, saws, hooks, hatchets, chisels, shovells, mattocks, hammers, road saddle, girths and stirrups, the two biggest brewing vessels, and all money thus raised to be equally divided amongst the eight youngest children. Wife to have the use of half the linnen which she had made since her marriage; on her death this to be equally divided amongst the eight youngest children. Wife BRIDGETT also to have use of little table, 4 buffet stools, and a short form and the use of two little back chairs; on her death all to pass and to be equally divided amongst the eight youngest children. To son SIMON, all skipps belonging to testator's trade, shaves, knives bean, knives and cromb, a black bean tub, pack saddles, longest ladder, shortest ladder in the stable, the hay ladder, and the longest alder ladder; all other ladders, stakes, pitch forks to be sold, and profits to be equally divided among the eight youngest children. Son SIMON to be executor; SAMUEL SALMON to be supervisor, and to receive 10s. Witnesses: WILLIAM SPARROW, SIMON ROSER. Pr. at Ipswich 16 Dec. 1631.

R(W) EDMUND ROGERS of Dunwich, husbandman. (340)
22 November 1631

Sick. To wife ALICE, tenement in Dunwich where he lives, purchased from FRANCIS ASHKETTLE. To brother's daughter MARGARET ROGERS £5 within one year. To mother MARY ROGERS 20s. within one month of testator's death. Residue of goods to wife ALICE; she to be sole executrix, and pay all debts, funeral and probate charges. Witnesses: THOMAS KEMPSTER, THOMAS HERFORD. Pr. at Yoxford 14 Dec. 1631.

R(W) MARGERY ROSE of St. James South Elmham, widow (N). (341)
14 November 1631

To ELIZABETH GRUDGFIELD, daughter of Mrs GRUDGFIELD, the silver salt. To ELIZABETH THOMPSON, daughter of RICHARD THOMPSON, a caldron. To godson RICHARD BATLEY, 20s. To ROBERT CORBOULD, son of ROBERT CORBOULD of St. Lawrence [Ilketshall?] 20s. To the three children of JOHN GOOCH 20s. each. To EDWARD BRIMBLE a bed fully furnished and one other pair of sheets. To MARY COLLINS, MARY SWAINE, ELIZABETH SWAINE, MARY BRAME, one pair sheets each. To MARGARET WRIGHT 10s; to RICHARD MARSHALL, son of JOHN MARSHALL 20s. To all the children of her brothers and sisters 20s. each. To brother GEORGE BATLEY, remainder of goods in order to pay debts of late husband WILLIAM ROSE and also to pay her own debts; also money to cover legacies given by her late husband WILLIAM and her own legacies. If any money left after meeting these debts and legacies then remainder of money to be equally divided amongst her brothers and sisters. GEORGE BATLEY to be sole executor and to meet funeral and probate expenses. Witnesses: JOHN GOOCH, KATHERINE GOOCH. Pr. at Bungay 8 Dec. 1631.

R(W) WILLIAM ROSE of St. James South Elmham, yeoman. (342)
24 June 1627

To wife MARGERY, messuage and tenement in Horstead (Norfolk) where JOHN GOSLING lives, being copyhold land; also pasture, late common lying in three enclosures in Horstead (28 acres); also land called Oakeyards and Abbescaier (4 acres) with all the freehold lands lying within the copyhold land and being within the land called Homestalls; these to her for life provided she commit no waste, strip the timber, maintain the same in good order and repair, and pay all rents and services due on the copyhold. Also within one year of testator's death, MARGERY, on the request of the lord of the manor of Horstead, to surrender 1 acre and 3 roods lying in Foldgate furlong in Horstead, part of MARGERY's jointure, to the use of HENRY WARDE of Horstead and his heirs. If MARGERY refuse to surrender this then the land given her called Abbescarr (2 acres) to be void and given to HENRY WARDE in recompense for the 1 acre and 3 roods; he HENRY, to hold this for the term of MARGERY's life. All lands devised hereby to MARGERY to pass on her death to testator's grandchild WILLIAM GOOCH and his heirs. To wife MARGERY, messuage and tenement called Acres (4 acres) in Horstead bought from HENRY WARDE, and also seven enclosures of land and pasture (30 acres) in Horstead, on the west side of the king's highway leading from Norwich to North Walsham. These to her to hold for one year after the tesatator's death, and then to pass to testator's nephew, JOHN ROSE, son of STEPHEN ROSE, testator's brother, and his heirs. JOHN ROSE to pay to EDWARD BROMLEY, testator's grandchild, £80 -- £30 to be paid on 21st birthday, £30 when 22, and £20 when 23; these sums to be paid in the church porch at Horstead; power of entry to occupy these lands devised to JOHN, if default; to enjoy the lands until legacy and arrears made good. If EDWARD BROMLEY die without issue before receiving £80, the legacy to remain with JOHN ROSE. To grandchild EDWARD BROMLEY a further £80 to be paid him by WILLIAM GOOCH out of his legacy of lands on the death of MARGERY ROSE. £80 to be given in form following, viz. £30 when 21, £30 when 22 and £20 when 23, to be paid in Horstead church porch. Power to enter and occupy the said lands until legacy and arrears are paid, if default. If EDWARD BROMLEY die without issue, before reaching 21 then the £80 to remain with WILLIAM GOOCH. If wife MARGERY think that the messuages given in this will for her jointure be not worth £20 per annum, then MARGERY to surrender back all her title to the messuages assured for her jointure to WILLIAM GOOCH and his heir, and she to revoke, and not enter into any benefit from any of the lands devised to her -- all to pass to WILLIAM GOOCH. He to enter and assure to MARGERY in lieu of dower £20 a year for life -- WILLIAM GOOCH to pay £14 a year at Lady Day and Michaelmas by equal portions at Bungay church porch (power to MARGERY to enter and distrain for full satisfaction if default in payment) and JOHN ROSE to pay £6 a year for life to MARGERY by two equal portions, as above specified, in Bungay church porch, with similar power to MARGERY of entry and distraint if default. To wife MARGERY, all goods in the parlour chamber, all her clothes and things belonging to her body; all linen, half the brass and pewter, 5 milk cows, one horse, one cart and all things pertaining to it, and one draught horse. To nephew WILLIAM GRUDGFIELD, gent., £10 to buy him plate. To the daughters of sister ELIZABETH HACON, £10 equally divided. To the daughters of sister MARGARET DENNY, £10 equally divided. To the daughters of sister BRIDGETT PITLING, £4 equally divided. All these sums to grandchildren to be paid at Michaelmas next after testator's death, at Horstead church porch. To grandchildren PRISCILLA & ANNE GOOCH £10 each; to MARY GOOCH the daughter of JOHN GOOCH of Ilketshall St. Margaret's £5 at Michaelmas. To sister-in-law DOUGHTY 20s. To the children of brothers-in-law GEORGE BATLEY, RICHARD BATELY and JOHN LAURENCE 20s. each, within one year of testator's death. To servant JOHN WELTON, if he is still with him on testator's death, £4. To apprentice ELIZABETH SWAINE, if still with him at time of death, 40s. covenanted to pay her on the ending of her apprentice term; paid within one year of death. To every servant serving him on the time of his death 6s. 6d. in one month. To the poor of St. James's Southelmham 20s. Residue of goods and chattels to executors to pay for the binding of testator's grandson EDWARD BROMLEY as an apprentice to a good trade and to pay for his bringing up and maintenance. Executors also to use money to pay debts, legacies, funeral and probate expenses. Wife MARGERY ROSE and son-in-law JOHN GOOCH to be joint executors; brother-in-law GEORGE BATELY to be supervisor and to receive £5 for his pains. Witnesses: WILLIAM BATELY (X), NICHOLAS CABLING (X), LAURENCE BIDBANK, WILLIAM DOUGHTY. Probate granted to MARGARET ROSE at Beccles on 14 Nov. 1631, and to JOHN GOOCH at Bungay 16 Nov. 1631.

R(W) GEORGE PARKHURST of Ipswich, grocer. (343
12 September 1631

Aged and diseased in body. To the poor of St. Laurence's parish where he lives 20s. To Mr UFORD, Ipswich town preacher 30s. if he preach a funeral sermon; if not to the preacher who does preach at funeral 20s. To RICHARD KEEBLE, esq. councillor at law in Ipswich 20s. and to JOHN LANG the younger of Ipswich 30s.; executors to pay all other fees to KEEBLE & LANG for costs in drawing up the will and their legal advice. To wife THOMASIN, in full satisfaction and payment of bonds entered into at the time of their marriage, £160. All household goods, implements, debts, wares, to be divided into three equal parts, after deducting funeral expenses, probate charges, payment of debts; wife to have one third share, grandson GEORGE PARKHURST another, and grandson ROBERT PARKHURST another, within six months of testator's death; benefit of survivorship. To ex servant HESTER CUTTING 20s. To the Widow MICHELL of Ipswich 20s. To THOMAS ROBERT who lives in a tenement owned by the testator in St. Margaret's parish Ipswich, near Mr LANG's back gate, 20s. To wife THOMASIN tenement and appurtenances, now occupied in part by testator and in part by THOMAS ROBERT, for life; on her death reversion to ROBERT PARKHURST and heirs male -- if no issue then to pass to GEORGE PARKHURST and his heirs male. To apprentice THOMAS MICHELL £3 if he finish his seven year term; if testator die before the end of the seven years, and THOMAS continue and finish the said term with testator's widow, then the legacy to increase to £5. Wife THOMASIN, to call in two honest men to make an inventory in writing of all goods and chattels in the chamber where testator's daughter ROSE PARKHURST lives and of all the goods and chattels in the house in St. Laurence where testator lives. There to be two copies of the inventory -- one for use of wife THOMASIN and one for ROSE PARKHURST. ROSE to have the goods she can prove to be her own by indifferent witnesses. All other goods given to her on her arrival to pass to testator's wife within one month of testator's death; if ROSE PARKHURST attempts to obstruct this transference and obstructs the same, then grandchildren GEORGE and ROBERT forfeit their share of household goods and these revert to THOMASIN. If ROSE PARKHURST remarry, then wife to have the chamber, the long gallery at the south end of the yard belonging to the messuage where the testator lives, with free entry to bake in the back house, use of the copers, water from the pump, liberty of the washhouse, and able to hang her linen in the yard and garden, and liberty to take her recreation and pleasure in the garden. If ROSE attempt to hinder this then grandson GEORGE PARKHURST to loose his legacy. Proviso, that before GEORGE & ROBERT PARKHURST receive their legacies, they have to enter in to a bond of £50 each, not to hinder THOMASIN PARKHURST, or to enter into any suits against her concerning testator's personal estate; if refuse the bond then they forfeit their legacies. Wife THOMASIN appointed sole executrix. Proviso; that if THOMASIN sells the tenement in St. Margaret's parish Ipswich, then THOMASIN to pay £10 to ROBERT PARKHURST in compensation for not receiving the said tenement as his legacy. Witnesses: JOHN EARNY, JOHN BRENN, ROBERT BRISTON, THOMAS MICHELL, THOMAS PORTER. Pr. at Ipswich 18 Dec. 1631.

R(W) MARGERY PLAYTERS of Sotterley, widow. 8 August 1631 (344)

To Sir THOMAS PLAYTERS, knight and baronet, £5, and two milk cows, one kettle (being the biggest save one), a little brass pot, a posted bedstead standing in the parlour with a feather bed; a bolster, a pair of blankets, a coverlet and a pillow belonging; two pewter platters, a little table in the hall chamber; all the hemp growing about the house; a great coffer standing in my chamber to the use of testator's daughter ELIZABETH, the wife of JOSEPH TYE, to be disposed of for her wants by the discretion of Sir THOMAS and Sir WILLIAM PLAYTERS his son, in lieu and full discharge of two bonds whereby the testator and her son are bound to Sir THOMAS PLAYTERS for £10 to the use of ELIZABETH TYE and her children. To son SAMUEL, one posted bedstead in the parlour chamber with the feather bed, bolster and blanket and coverlet as it stands; one chest standing by the said bed, and another chest in the parlour. To granddaughter ELIZABETH HUMFREY a one year old calf. Residue of all goods and chattels to sons MATTHEW & SAMUEL PLAYTERS to be equally divided between them, they to be joint executors and to pay debts, funeral and probate expenses. Witnesses: RICHARD HASSLETT, GILBERT CORKER, RICHARD CARDY. Pr. at Ipswich 31 Dec. 1631.

R(W) JOHN POPE of Ilketshall St. Margaret, husbandman. 28 October 1631 (345)

Sick. To wife ANNE, all houses and lands, free and copyhold, for life, provided she remain a widow, and if she keep property in good repair, and does not waste/strip it. If she remarry then legacy void. To son WILLIAM all lands and tenements on death of ANNE, or on her remarriage. On her remarriage WILLIAM to enter lands immediately, and pay ANNE £40 a year for life by equal portions, in compensation for dower rights. To son and daughter JOHN and ANNE POPE £16 each; JOHN to receive £4 in one year after wife ANNE's death; daughter ANNE to receive £4 within 2 years of mother's death; son JOHN to receive £4 within 3 yrs. of mother's death; daughter ANNE to receive £4 within 4 years of mother's death, and so on until each received £16. If default in payment then power given to JOHN & ANNE to enter lands devised to WILLIAM and to hold same until legacy fulfilled. To wife ANNE all goods and chattels in order to pay debts, funeral charges and probate expenses. ANNE to be sole executrix. Witnesses: ROBERT GOOCH, ROBERT POPE & JOHN MARSHAL. Pr. at Bungay 17 Nov. 1631.

R(W) MARY PITT of Bungay, widow. 29 October 1631 (346)

Sick. To son JOHN SPATCHETT £5 within one year of testator's death. To son HENRY SPATCHETT £5 within one year of testator's death. To son WILLIAM SPATCHETT £3 within one year of testator's death. To daughter ELIZABETH, the wife of HENRY SAMSON, £6 within 1 yr. of testator death. To daughter CHRISTIAN KERSEY 20s. within one year of testator's death. To daughter KATHERINE BALLS 20s. within one year of testator's death. To son-in-law JOHN LOVE 40s. to be paid by executrix to supervisor SIMON SELLING, in order to discharge a bond whereby JOHN LOVE is bound to Bungay town together with HENRY & WILLIAM SPATCHETT. Residue of goods to daughter ROSE SPATCHETT; she to settle debts, funeral and probate expenses. ROSE to be sole executrix; SIMON SELLING to be supervisor. Witnesses: SAMUEL STILES, EDWARD DALBY, SIMON SELLING. Pr. at Beccles 22 Nov. 1631.

R(W) JOHN MAY of Bucklesham, yeoman. 18 August 1631 (347)

To the poor of Bucklesham, Kirton, and Walton 10s. each, adding 10s. more to Walton. To brother ROGER MAY, the marsh called the Little marsh, with close adjoining it, and all appurtenances in Walton to him and his heirs; provided he pay to testator's daughter-in-law ALICE BRIGG £140 when she reach 21; if unpaid within six days of birthday, then power to enter and distrain -- this bequest in fulfillment of a legacy to the said ALICE by her father. Brother also to pay to testator's wife ALICE £5 a year out of the profits of the land; this money to be used for the benefit of ALICE BRIGG until 21. To wife ALICE a little freehold land and tenement in Kirton, late purchased from JOHN CURTON, provided she pay ALICE BRIGG when 21, £46 and also 40s. a year until ALICE BRIGG reach 21. Power to ALICE BRIGG to enter and hold till legacy fulfilled -- this payment in fulfillment of a legacy to ALICE BRIGG by her father. Brother ROGER owes a bond of £30 to testator; this £30 to go to testator's eldest sister's children by husband RAYMOND KING, namely RAYMOND, ELIZABETH & MARY KING when they reach 21 (£5 each) and to testator's eldest brother's children namely JOHN, ALEXANDER & ROGER MAY when they reach 21 (£5 each). To brother ROGER MAY all timber and boards in the barn, stack of hay, all lumber and portable household stuff. ROGER to enter into a bond to pay legacies specified in will within 3 months of testator's death, else all his legacies void. To sister JOAN, the wife of RICHARD ROSE, 20s., and to her daughter ELIZABETH 20s. Residue of ready money, all debts owed, to wife ALICE; she to be sole executrix, to pay debts, funeral and probate expenses. Memorandum added; that if this residue is over £200, then all sums over the £200 to go to brother ROGER. Witnesses: ROGER MAY, NICHOLAS BIRD (X), KATHERIN WISSEN (X). Pr. at Ipswich 13 Jan. 1631/2.

R(W) JOHN MALSTER of Hoo, yeoman. 28 August 1631 (348)

Sick. To grandchild THOMAS MALSTER £20 when 21, paid in South porch of Monewden church. To JOHN, son of THOMAS MALSTER, £20 when 21, paid in South porch of Monewden church. To son JOHN MALSTER £5 within one month of testator's death; this to be paid by JOHN MALSTER to his son JOHN MALSTER when he reaches 21 at south porch Monewden church. To son THOMAS MALSTER £3, and all clothes, linen and woollen. To wife ALICE MALSTER and daughter KATHERINE MALSTER residue of all movables and goods after payment of funeral and probate expenses and payment of debts/legacies. Son THOMAS MALSTER to be executor. Witnesses: THOMAS REYNOLDS, PRUDENCE HARROLD (X), JOHN MALSTER (X). Pr. at Wickham Market 15 Dec. 1631.

R(W) JOHN MINTER of Brantham (N). 23 October 1631 (349)

To son WILLIAM MINTER 40s., and all clothes with the hutch (cupboard) wherein they lie. To son JOHN MINTER £3 to bind him as apprentice. To daughter MARY MINTER 40s., and an old hutch that was her mother's; a pillow case and four pewter dishes. To wife ANNE rest of movables, in order to bring up youngest child THOMAS. Witnesses: RICHARD BATEMAN, ROBERT WOOD (X). Probate granted to ANNE MINTER at Ipswich 16 Dec. 1631.

R(W) JOAN MAN of Stoke next Ipswich, widow. (350)
22 October 1631

Sick and weak. JAMES MAN, husband of testator and now deceased, in his will leave tenement in Stoke to her to hold until their three sons JAMES, JOSEPH & JOHN MAN reached 21; the rent and profits from this tenement now go to executrix to use to maintain and educate these children until they reach 21. To daughter ELIZABETH MAN £10 on 21st birthday. Residue of goods once debts and funeral/probate expenses met to be equally divided between JOHN, MARY, SARA and ELIZABETH MAN. Sister FRANCIS BUTTER, wife of BENJAMIN BUTTER, executrix; THOMAS DADE, brother of Cotton, supervisor. To JAMES & JOSEPH MAN 30s. that ROBERT PECKETT owes the testator. Witnesses: GEORGE CATCHPOLE, public notary, WILLIAM STILES, EDWARD POTSUM, JAMES MAN. Pr. at Ipswich 4 Nov. 1631.

R(W) JOHN LAWSON of Waldringfield, shoemaker (N). (351)
18 October 1631

Sick. To cousin ANNE HALL, one feather bed and bedstead, 1 pair sheets, 1 blanket, 1 coverlet, 1 cupboard, 1 coffer. To cousin DORCAS HALL, one feather bed, one bolster, one pillow. To sister ALICE DRIVER all hemp. With regard to debt of 40s. owed testator by ROBERT BRADSTREET of Kirton, ROBERT BRADSTREET to retain 20s., and the other 20s. to be divided between WILLIAM & NICHOLAS SHEPPERD. To JOHN GOODLADD, one table, one form, two chairs, two cushions, four wedges, two cobirons, one rake, one grid iron, one fire pan. To brother JOSEPH HALL, the £5 he owes by bond to the testator. To poor of Waldringfield 20s. within one month of testator's death. Residue to brother WILLIAM SHEPPERD to pay debts, funeral/probate expenses. Witnesses: RICHARD ROSE, JOHN GOODLAND. Probate granted to WILLIAM SHEPPERD 30 Dec. 1631.

R(W) PETER LEVELL the elder of Baylham. 31 June 1628 (352)

Sick. To son JOHN LEVELL, messuage, tenement and orchards in Needham Market, late EDWARD DEANES, held of Barking manor; the little meadow called Stuntneys copyhold of Barking manor, to him and his heirs. To son NATHANIEL LEVELL, messuage and tenement in Baylham called Seagraves, and land pertaining to same, both free and copyhold, lately occupied by ROBERT COSSON; also £20 on testator's death. To PETER LEVELL residue of goods, chattels, household stuff. PETER & NATHANIEL LEVELL appointed executors to pay debts, funeral & probate charges. To the poor of Baylham 20s. Witnesses: ADRIAN ALDRITCH, JOHN THURKETTLE. Pr. at Ipswich 3 Feb. 1631/2.

R(W) FRANCIS JOLLY of Hemley. 7 October 1631 (353)

Sick. All goods, chattels, to wife ELIZABETH to pay debts, funeral expenses and probate charges; and to maintain her. Wife

ELIZABETH to be sole executrix. Witnesses: GEORGE COULTON, JOHN HART (X). Pr. at Ipswich 4 Nov. 1631.

R(W) JOHN HALTWAY of Hopton, yeoman. 23 October 1631 (354)

Aged and sickly; to be buried in Hopton church. To wife ELIZABETH all freehold in Hopton belonging to his tenement called Bees, where testator lives, lately purchased from ROBERT KEMPE, for life; provided she pay WILLIAM SHERMAN £20 owed to him by the testator; property then to pass to son JOHN HALTWAY and his heirs; if he has no heirs, then to pass to THOMAS HALTWAY and his heirs. If ELIZABETH refuse the £20 legacy, then JOHN HALTWAY to enter land immediately, and he to pay the £20 legacy to WILLIAM SHERMAN. To daughter ELIZABETH tenement in Fritton called Hethersett, lately purchased from RICHARD ELLIS, and also one carrucate of land containing 1 acre, purchased from GABRIEL WOODNOUGH; also £60 to be paid by executors to testator's wife within one month of testator's death; wife to keep this £60 until daughter ELIZABETH reach 21. If wife remarry then to pay daughter ELIZABETH the £60 immediately, or else to enter into bond to pay the £60 to daughter within one yr. of wife's second marriage; further wife to enter into bond as soon as she receive the £60 to pay the same sum to daughter on 21st birthday. To THOMAS, son, two tenements in Hopton, freehold, with all pertaining to them, bought from WILLIAM WIGGETT and ROBERT HAVERS; if THOMAS die without issue, then the lands to pass to testator's son JOHN. To son THOMAS also tenement in Fritton called Sheperds bought from GABRIEL WOODNOUGH with all appurtenances, provided THOMAS pay £20 to HENRY WINSTON, which said sum is owed by testator to HENRY WINSTON. To the children of WILLIAM SHERMAN, now living, 20s. each on 21st birthdays. To the child of THOMAS HALTWAY now being carried 20s. [missing in register, but present in the original will.] To the poor of Hopton 3s. 4d. Residue of all goods to sons JOHN & THOMAS who are appointed executors -- they to pay debts, funeral and probate expenses. Proviso that if any disagreement arise between testator's children over the provisions of the will, then these are to be resolved by two honest and independent men. Memorandum -- that JOHN HALTWAY to have £100 out of testator's stock. Witnesses: JOHN UNDERWOOD, clerk; JOHN UTTING, clerk. Pr. at Beccles 7 Nov. 1631.

R(W) THOMAS HARRISON of Wickham Market, haberdasher. (355)
25 November 1631.

Sick; to be buried at Wickham church. To wife SARAH, freehold tenement with all land belonging, one piece copyhold land containing 1 1/2 acres, in Wickham Market; these to be sold by wife within 1 1/2 yrs. after testator's death in order to settle debts. Wife also to have all goods and chattels, within and without doors, to sell to settle debts; residue of money after payment of debts to be used by her for the upbringing of children. SARAH to be sole executor, with WILLIAM HOWSDEN of

Rendham as supervisor. Witnesses: RICHARD HOWSDEN, BRIDGETT SPALDING, ELIZABETH ALLEN. Pr. at Wickham Market 1 Feb. 1631.

R(W) WILLIAM HARVEY of Frostenden, yeoman. (356)
13 October 1631

Sick. To wife ANNE, in lieu of dower, and for the maintenance and bringing up of testator's children, all that messuage and tenement where he lives, and all freehold land belonging to it in Frostenden and Wangford; and copyhold land lately purchased from GILES LEECE in Frostenden; also to ANNE all lands, meadows and marshes free and copyhold in Frostenden lately purchased from THOMAS PRESTON of Wrentham, provided she does not waste or strip the same, and only take such wood as necessary for fuel, not to exceed 5 loads of bond wood a year, nor to sell or cut the wood and only take what is needed for repair; provided also that ANNE shall, when their daughter ANNE reaches 15, give security by bond to the executors, to pay to daughter £80 on 21st birthday, and if she refuse the bond then executors have power to enter the devised lands to raise the £80, and wife ANNE can only re enter the said lands when the total sum of £80 has been raised in fulfillmant of legacy. If wife ANNE die before daughter ANNE reach 15 then executors have full power to lease the lands to raise the said £80. On the death of wife ANNE, son THOMAS HARVEY to have all the messuage where the testator lives, and all the freehold land, meadows, and pastures in Frostenden, unto the west side of the highway leading from Wangford to Wrentham; and one piece of meadow/pasture (2 1/2 acres) lying on the east side of the said way between the copyhold lands of the testator lately purchased of GILES LEECE on the east part, and the aforesaid highway on the west, and abutts on the copyhold land now or late of the said GILES LEECE on the north, and the lands of the testator on the south. To son THOMAS, on the death of his wife ANNE, all the copyhold land, meadow and marsh lately purchased of THOMAS PRESTON gent. and of GILES LEECE. To son ROBERT HARVEY, on death of wife ANNE, freehold land, meadow, and pasture in Wangford, and two closes of land and pasture lying together in Frostenden enclosed (11 acres) lying between the lands of ROBERT FETCH, gent., on the east, and the king's highway from Wangford towards Wrentham on the west, and abutts on the copyhold land of the testator called Longment in part and upon the testator's freehold land in part on the north, and upon the land of ROBERT FETCH gent. on the south. If THOMAS or ROBERT die before 21 survivor to have benefit of legacies. Executors, within 2 yrs. of testator's death, sell towards payment of debts and fines arising from the copyhold lands, a close of copyhold land called Longment in Frostenden, and also all that tenement and copyhold land belonging to it purchased from HENRY LEECE also situated in Frostenden. To eldest son EDMUND HARVEY, when reaches 22, all messuages and tenements in Wenhaston; executors to have all profits from this land in Wenhaston until EDMUND HARVEY of age, towards payment of legacies specified in this will. To daughter MARY HARVEY, £60 when 21, and 4 pair tearing sheets, one long table cloth, one dozen napkins, one pair of pillow cases, one coffer, and all the silver spoons given her on her christening -- all these items testator's wife to deliver to executors. If MARY die before reaching 21 then £60 to be equally divided between EDMUND & ANNE HARVEY when they reach 21. If ANNE, daughter, die before 21 her lagacy of £80 to be equally divided between EDMUND & MARY HARVEY when 21. With regard to the money in the executors' hands from the rents and profits from the Wenhaston lands, after deduction of £60 legacy for MARY, whatever sum there is when EDMUND reaches 22, to be equally divided between testator's children then living. JOHN LOVE, testator's father-in-law had promised on testator's marriage to pay £30; of this £30 some £20 to be paid by testator's executor to daughter ANNE on 21st birthday, and £10 to daughter MARY when 21; if JOHN LOVE die before ANNE or MARY reach 21 then the executors to receive the sum and hold on behalf of ANNE and MARY; benefit of survivorship if either daughter die. Residue of movables, household goods and implements undevised to go to wife ANNE towards payment of debts, maintenance of children and funeral/probate costs. ANNE to enter into bond with executors to do this, and if refuse loses her legacy of goods and chattels. Brother EDMUND HARVEY appointed executor with brother-in-law WILLIAM LOVE also. Witnesses: THOMAS JONES, THOMAS FLAYER, JOHN LOVE. Pr. 10 Dec. 1631.

R(W) JOHN HARRISON the elder of Sibton, gentleman. (357)
5 October 1631

To poor of Sibton 20s., poor of Yoxford and Peasenhall 10s. each. To son JOHN HARRISON all lands and tenements; six pair sheets, six napkins, four pillow cases, four hand towels. Residue of goods unbequeathed to be equally divided between testator's daughters. To daughter ABREA one livery bedstead, one featherbed, one feather bolster, one pillow, pair of blankets and a bed covering. To daughter MARY one livery bedstead, one feather bed, one feather bolster, a pillow, a pair of blankets, and a bed covering. Daughters to have use of dwelling house for three months after testator's death. To grandchildren JOHN & THOMAS DOCKING, WALTER & GABRIEL DOCKING 40s. each when 21. To grandchildren FRANCIS, PHILIP, ANN, WILLIAM, ELIZABETH, & MARY BROWN 40s. when 21. To grandchildren JOHN, WILLIAM, MARGARET & JUDITH PAYNE, 40s. when 21. To grandchild JEREMY KEMP £3 when 21. To grandchildren ERASMUS, WILLIAM, & THOMAS KEMP 40s. when 21. To kinsman JOHN HURRION 20s. within 4 yrs. of testator's death. To kinsman WILLIAM HURRION 20s. on his release of tenement called Okeys. Residue of goods to son JOHN, he to be exec., and pay all funeral/probate/debts. Witnesses: THOMAS BURWOOD (X), THOMAS KEMP. Pr. at Yoxford 2 Nov. 1631.

R(W) LIDEA GOULDING of St. Andrews Ilketshall (N). (358)
8 October 1631

To her mother, the wife of WILLIAM GOULDING £10. To her two brothers BARTHOLOMEW & AMBROSE £5 each. To sister DEBORAH, wife of EDMUND BARBER, £5. To WILLIAM son of HENRY BARNABY and wife ANNE £5 when reaches 21. To brother WILLIAM GOULDING £10. To sisters ANNE & DEBORAH all wearing apparel, to be equally divided. To cousins THOMAS GOLDING, WILLIAM BARBER & WILLIAM BARNABY a silver spoon each. To mother two silver spoons. Residue to executor; WILLIAM GOULDING appointed executor to pay debts and funeral expenses. Witnesses: GRACE HUNTINTON (X), WILLIAM GOULDING. Pr. at Beccles 28 Jan. 1631/2.

R(W) MATTHEW GODSON of Sandcroft South Elmham, yeoman. (359)
16 March 1625

Weak; to be buried in Sandcroft churchyard. To the poor of Sandcroft 5s., poor of Homersfield 5s.; poor of Flixton 5s. To nephew WILLIAM GODSON £10 within 1 yr. of testator's death to be paid by executors, provided WILLIAM come to claim legacy from them; if he does not then legacy to go to testator's brother-in-law CHRISTOPHER PYME. To brother-in-law CHRISTOPHER PYME £10 within 6 months of testator's death. To MARY & FRANCES BUNING, daughters of ANTHONY BUNING of Easton, 10s. each within three months of testator's death. To his late servant WILLIAM HALL 5s. within 6 months of testator's death. To apprentice JOAN SHERWOOD on completion of apprenticeship term 10 1/2s. To servants DANIEL HILL & ELIZABETH COOK 12d. each. To wife MARY GODSON residue of all goods, in order to meet legacies, debts, and funeral expenses and probate charges. She to be sole executrix. Witnesses: DANIEL HILL; JOHN CORVIN, scrivener. Pr. at Beccles 3 Dec. 1631.

R(W) DANIEL GIRLING the elder of Easton, yeoman. (360)
12 October 1631

Aged and sick; to be buried in Easton church. To wife ELIZABETH messuage and lands for life; then to pass to son DANIEL. To son DANIEL, one chest in the lower chamber, one copper and one brass pot, the biggest brass kettle -- these to him on the death of wife ELIZABETH. To daughter ELIZABETH AMYSON £10 within one year of testator's death. Residue of all goods and chattels to wife ELIZABETH, then to pass on her death to son DANIEL. Wife ELIZABETH and son DANIEL appointed joint executors, to pay funeral and probate charges, debts and legacies. Witnesses: EDMUND GARNELL, THOMAS GLADWIN, senior. Pr. at Wickham Market 24 Nov. 1631.

R(W) ELIZABETH GARDINER of Ipswich, spinster. (361)
31 October 1631

To sister SUSAN, the wife of FRANCIS MANISTER of Ipswich, 10s. within one year of testator's decease. To WILLIAM MANISTER, the youngest son of FRANCIS MANISTER, 20s. within one year of testator's decease. Residue of all goods, chattels, household stuff and implements, to THOMAS HAILES of Ipswich, clothier, who is appointed sole executor, to recompense him for his services and the charges borne by him in the care of the testator; also to cover cost of funeral and probate expenses, payment of debts and legacies. Witnesses: WILLIAM CHAPLIN, JOHN SHIPWRIGHT, HUBERT THORNBACK. Pr. at Ipswich 29 Nov. 1631.

R(W) JOHN GRYNNE of Needham Market, clothier. (362)
25 October 1631

Sick. Uncle EDMUND PISSEY appointed exec. to sell testator's house, pightle, and orchard with all appurtenances thereunto belonging in Needham Market within one year of testator's death, in order to meet debts, funeral expenses and probate charges; the residue then remaining to be equally divided by exec. between testator's wife and any of his children then living. To uncle EDMUND PISSEY all movable goods, chattels, household stuff and implements, and debts due to testator, to be sold within six months after testator's death, the money thus ensuing to be equally divided between testator's wife and children then living. Witnesses: THOMAS LOVE, RICHARD LOVE, PETER WARDE. Pr. at Ipswich 25 Nov. 1631.

R(W) THOMAS GILLET the elder of Yoxford, tailor (N). (363)
[blank] October 1631

To son ROBERT GILLET, a gold ring, a copper kettle, a feather bed, feather bolster, and a pillow. To daughter MARY GILLET, a posnett, and a kerchef. Witnesses: ANNE GILLET, DOROTHY, the wife of THOMAS YOUNGS. Probate granted to ROBERT GILLET at Yoxford 2 Nov. 1631.

R(W) WILLIAM FULLER of Badingham, yeoman. (364)
St. Simon & Jude's day [28 October] 1631

Sick. To wife PHILIPPA £100 within 3 months after testator's death; executor to pay her also an annuity of £10 due by equal portions on Lady day and on Michaelmas, to be paid in the church porch at Bramfield within ten days of either feast day. Also to wife, one feather bed and posted bedstead as it stands ready furnished in the parlour chamber, with the best coverlet and blanketts, two feather pillows and a feather bolster, one livery cupboard in the parlour; one little joined table standing in the kitchen chamber; one brass pan, one skillet, six pieces of pewter, one great chest, one long coffer, one trunk, 10 pair of sheets, four pillow cases, two dozen table napkins, two ells of broad cloth, and one great wicker chair. To son THOMAS FULLER, £200 payable in two installments, namely £100 when he reaches 21, and a further £100 when 23; also one feather bed and a livery bedstead whereon he now lies, with all furniture to it belonging, one little brass pot, and one bay mare colt. Also executors to pay yearly to THOMAS £3. 6s. 8d. by equal portions at Lady Day and Michaelmas until he reaches 21; the first payment to fall due on the first feast day after testator's death. To son OWEN

FULLER, £200 payable in two installments, namely £100 when 21 and a further £100 when 23; also one feather bed and livery bedstead with all furniture belonging to it as it stands on the wash house chamber, and one yearling bay horse colt. To daughter PHILIPPA FULLER £150, £100 to be paid within one month of testator's death, and a further £50 to be paid within 2 years after first payment. To daughter FRANCES FULLER £150, £100 to be paid when reaches 21, and £50 more when 23; exec. to pay her yearly £3. 6s. 8d. by equal payments on Lady Day and Michaelmas until 21; first payment to fall due on the first feast day after testator's death. Exec. to maintain her with meat, clothing and lodging. Alsoto maintain in similar manner testator's son OWEN until he reach 17, and when OWEN reach 17 exec. to pay £5 a year to him until he reaches 21 payable in like manner to bequests made before to THOMAS & FRANCES FULLER. Benefit of survivorship if any of testator's children die before receiving their legacies. To son WILLIAM FULLER, all freehold land in Bramfield to him and his heirs, provided he pay yearly to his mother PHILIPPA the £10 annuity specified in this will, PHILIPPA to have power of entry into the lands and to hold the same if default in payment of annuity. Further proviso that if PHILIPPA claimed dower rights in the lands at Bramfield, or refused to release the land in Walpole lately sold to WILLIAM CAINE, then her annuity is to be void. To son WILLIAM also residue of all unbequeathed goods etc. to pay legacies, funeral expenses and probate charges; WILLIAM to enter within 20 days of testator's death, into a bond of £800 to NICHOLAS WHINERY of Middleton to pay legacies. WILLIAM to be sole executor. Witnesses: NICHOLAS WHINERY, NICHOLAS CANNAP. Pr. at Yoxford 11 Jan. 1631/2.

R(W) THOMAS FELSTEAD the elder of Framlingham, yeoman. (365)
1 August 1630.

To wife GRACE messuage and tenement in Framlingham lately purchased of JOHN DURRANT, together with the malt houses, mill house, and all appurtenances; also the lead cistern and all implements belonging to the malt house and the horse mill there, for life provided she maintain the same and commit no waste. Then to pass to testator's son FRANCIS FELSTEAD and his heirs for ever. To wife GRACE, all other lands, tenements and hereditaments, free and copyhold in Framlingham, for life, provided she commit no waste; then to pass to son THOMAS. To wife GRACE, the lease of a messuage and lands in Sweffling, which lease is for 21 years. On her death the remainder of the term of years on the lease to pass to testator's son EDMUND. To son THOMAS £10. To son FRANCIS £10 within 1 year of testator's death. To son EDMOND £10 within 2 years of testator's death. To daughter MARY £20, within 2 years of testator's death, or on her marriage. To daughter ALICE £20 within 3 years of testator's death or on her marriage. Benefit of survivorship to these two daughters. To daughters GRACE & ANNE £5 each within 1 year of testator's death. To grandchild JOAN BANHAM £5 on 21st birthday or on her marriage. Wife GRACE and son THOMAS appointed exec., to pay legacies, debts, funeral expenses and probate, and to that end to receive residue of unbequeathed goods. Witnesses: JOHN CALVER, EDWARD MOULTON. Pr. at Wickham 6 Nov. 1631. [Registered copy is damaged -- damp -- so in the damaged areas the original will was consulted.]

R(W) PETER FASSETT of Ilketshall St. Andrew, yeoman. 20 August 1631 (366)

To wife ELIZABETH, all household stuff owned by testator standing in the houses of sons-in-law RICHARD BATTELY & SAMUEL COOK, as specified in notes written by the said sons-in-law. To the poor of Bungay 20s.; of Beccles 20s.; poor of Ilketshall St. Andrews 10s. To WILLIAM GOULDING clerk, 10s. Residue of all unbequeathed goods to son-in-law and executor RICHARD BATTELY in order to pay debts, legacies, funeral and probate expenses. Witnesses: JOHN ASHER, MARY LILLIE. Pr. at Beccles 12 Nov. 1631.

R(W) JOHN ETHERIDGE alias REYNOLDS of Gosbeck, yeoman. 4 March 1631/2 (367)

To daughter MARTHA ETHERIDGE, within one month of her marriage, with her mother's consent, £30. To grandchild JOYCE SPARROW, the only child surviving of testator's daughter JOYCE who married NICHOLAS SPARROW, all copyhold land. To wife MARTHA ETHERIDGE residue of all unbequeathed goods, chattels etc., for her own use, and to meet funeral and probate expenses. MARTHA sole executrix. Nephew WILLIAM STUDD of Gosbeck appointed supervisor. Witnesses: EDMUND MAYHEW, MARY BACON (X). Pr. at Ipswich 4 Nov. 1631.

R(W) ROBERT DURRANT of Iken, husbandman. 21 October 1631 (368)

Sick. To daughter MARY DURRANT tenement called Dooles, with all lands pertaining. To grandchild FRANCIS GOOLES two yearling calves, and when 21 the best bed with all things belonging to it. Residue of all unbequeathed goods to son-in-law ROBERT GOOLES and daughter MARY GOOLES, appointed joint executors, to pay debts and funeral and probate expenses. Also exec. to pay testator's kinsman JOHN DURRANT of Sibton, 5s. within six weeks of testator's death. Witnesses: EDWARD CHUSSING, EDWARD CROSS. Pr. at Wickham 12 Jan. 1631/2.

R(W) HENRY DEEKES of Hintlesham (N). [blank] November 1631 (369)

In the time of his sickness; all goods to wife ELIZABETH and to son HENRY to be equally divided. Witnesses: JOHN CLARKE, ELIZABETH DEEKES, ANDREW TASSARD. Probate granted to ELIZABETH DEEKES 17 Dec. 1631.

R(W) MARGARET CAMPELL of Chelmondiston, widow. (370)
7 January 1631/2

Sick. First that THOMAS CAMPELL late of Shotley, yeoman, deceased husband of testator, had made, in his will, testator and testator's son JOHN WRIGHT of Erwarton joint executors of his will, and that his goods were to be equally divided between testator and her son JOHN in order for each executor to pay half the debts and legacies of the said THOMAS CAMPELL. Now an independent valuer is to be appointed after testator's death, appointed by her executor, to value all her goods, corn, household goods, in order to meet the charges and legacies due under the will of THOMAS CAMPELL. Residue of any remaining money to be divided thus. To servant GEORGE WHITLOCK £3 within 1 year of testator's decease, and also the bed he now lies on. To EDMUND MARKES 20s. within 1 year of testator's decease. To grandchildren SUSAN & THOMAS POD 20s. each within 1 year of testator's death. To grandchildren ROGER & EDWARD CHENALL 20s. each in 1 yr. of testator's death. To granddaughters SARAH & ANN CHENALL 50s. each when 18. To son-in-law EDWARD CHENALL 40s. To granddaughter MARGARET COCK 20s. within 1 yr. of testator's death. To JOHN BURWOOD 20s. within 1 yr. of testator's death. To granddaughters ANNE & MARTHA FREEMAN 20s. on their marriage. Residue of money then to be equally divided into four -- one-fourth to go to son-in-law JOHN POD in 1 yr. of testator's death; one part to son-in-law JOHN COCK in 1 yr. of testator's death; half to executor. Further that the testator had received £30 from her son-in-law EDWARD CHENALL towards the upbringing of his daughters SARAH & ANNE CHENALL, and that the testator was bound to him to pay £15 each to SARAH & ANNE CHENALL when they reached 21 or on the day of their marriage. Executor appointed in this will is now to maintain these two children until 21 or their marriage, and to enter into bond with EDWARD CHENALL in £40 for the true repayment of the £30 to the said SARAH & ANNE. Proviso that if JOHN POD or JOHN COCK die before receiving their legacies, then the legacy to be equally divided between the relevant children. JOHN WRIGHT appointed sole executor. Witnesses: WILLIAM STONE, THOMAS BRANDESTON. Pr. at Ipswich 21 Jan. 1631/2.

R(W) JOHN COWPER of Ramsholt, yeoman. 30 December 1631 (371)

Sick. To daughter ANNE HOWELL, tenement and messuage where GEORGE BOONES used to live, with all its appurtenances and barns, provided that testator's wife ROSE has the corn in the barns, together with liberty of access to the corn whenever convenient for her. On daughter's death the land to be equally divided between her children then living, and if she have no surviving heir, then land to pass to testator's other daughter JANE COWPER and her heirs; if she die without heir then land to pass to testator's daughter MARY and her heirs. To daughter ANNE HOWELL 20s. in full discharge of any demand for further legacy. To daughter MARY when 16 £60 to be paid by exec. in Ramsholt church porch; exec. to care for and maintain MARY, cloth her and see to her education 'what shall be meet and fitting for such a one for her good.' MARY also to receive the posted bed in the parlour with everything belonging to it; the table in the parlour. To wife ROSE the posted bed standing upon the parlour chamber with all things pertaining to it, for life, then to pass to testator's daughter JANE. To son-in-law THOMAS COWPER £60 as specified in a deed made between THOMAS COWPER senior, and THOMAS COWPER junior, and testator, on condition that THOMAS COWPER senior and junior, father and son, endow testator's daughter JANE, the wife of THOMAS COWPER the son, with a sufficient jointure, good in the law. To servant THOMAS PELLS 10s. To JOHN COWPER 15s., and to ELLEN COWPER, testator's nephew and niece, 5s.; to all testator's sister's children 2s. 6d. each. To daughter JANE her bible, and testator's little coffer which he most commonly did use himself; his trunk with his name set on it, and all things in the said coffer. To wife ROSE cupboard in the parlour for life, then to pass to daughter JANE. Residue to wife ROSE and daughter JANE to be equally divided, for payment of legacies, debts, funeral and probate expenses. ROSE & JANE to be joint executors. Witnesses: JOHN SMYTH (writer of the will); HUMPHREY PRINCE (X). Pr. at Wickham 12 Jan. 1631/2.

R(W) MARY CLEMENTS of Ipswich, widow. 27 November 1631 (372)

Sick. To sister JOAN MOSBY, a cloth gown, green petticoat, one apron, one cloth waistcoat, two querns, two bands or ruffs, two quarters and two pair of best sheets; best feather bed, and one feather bolster; three pieces of the best pewter dishes, and 40s. within 2 months of testator's death. To THOMAS MOSBY son of my sister, 40s. within 3 months of testator's death. To MARGARET TYLER, wife of WILLIAM TYLER of Ipswich, best green rug, the taffeta apron, testator's gold ring, and 20s. To son JOHN JENKENSON, £5 within 6 months of testator's death; if he be dead by then, then the legacy to be split in 1 year equally amongst his children; if he die without heirs, then JOAN MOSBY receives 40s. and THOMAS MOSBY 20s. part of the £5 legacy. To kinswoman SARA LINFIELD, wife to GILBERT LINFIELD, best cloth gown, and 20s. To JOAN STRINGER, wife of NICHOLAS STRINGER, one pair of sheets. To kinswoman FRANCES HAYWARD, wife of RICHARD HAYWARD, one livery bedstead, one flock bed, one pair of sheets, two petticoats, one waistcoat, 20s., and 2 pewter dishes. To sister MARGARET SIMONDS, best feather bed, an iron jack with all the weights and lines belonging to it, the best posted bedstead where the testator now lies, with all its curtains, the red rug, and blankets on the said bed, and pillows. To kinsman WILLIAM TYLER of Ipswich 20s. To kinswoman KATHERINE NOOKES 2 pewter dishes. To kinswoman SARA LINFIELD, a silver whistle. ROBERT HOWE, friend, appointed executor, and given 40s. Residue of estate, after payment of legacies, debts, funeral charges and probate expenses, to be equally divided between son JOHN JENKENSON, sister JOAN MOSBY, THOMAS MOSBY and FRANCES HAYWARD the wife of RICHARD HAYWARD. Witnesses: WILLIAM ELLIS, THOMAS HAWKINS. Pr. at Ipswich 16 Dec. 1631.

R(W) ROBERT CULLIORS of Fritton. 17 December 1631 (373)

Sick; to be buried in the churchyard of parish wherever he dies. To ROBERT CULLIOR of Funwell (Norfolk) £12 within 1 yr. of testator's death. To WILLIAM CULLIOR, son of ROBERT, £5 within 1 yr. of testator's death. To the four children of ROBERT HASTINGS of Aslington (Norfolk) 25s. each within 1 yr. of testator's death, with benefit of survivorship. To the 4 daughters of ROBERT CULLIOR of Funwell 20s. each within 1 yr. of testator's death, with benefit of survivorship. To JOHN CULLIOR of Wyndham (Norfolk) son of GEORGE CULLIOR 60s. within 1 yr. of testator's death. To the poor of Pulham St. Mary 10s.; the poor of Harlston 10s.; Wortwell 10s.; Fritton 10s. To KATHERINE the wife of ROBERT HASTINGS £5 in 1 yr. of testator's death. To WILLIAM BROWNE of BrokenAshe (Norfolk) £5 in 1 yr. of testator's death. To WILLIAM & MARGARET BROWNE son and daughter of CHRISTOPHER BROWNE of Aslington 20s. each within 1 yr. of testator's death, with benefit of survivorship. To ALICE COANE 10s. To ANNE PENNY 5s. To MARY JACKSON 5s. To WILLIAM DIE of Tackleston (Norfolk) son of WILLIAM DIE the younger, 20s. within 1 yr. of testator's death. To [blank in both register and will] the sister of WILLIAM DIE 20s. within 1 yr. of testator's death. To THOMAS BATCHELLS of Fritton, appointed sole executor, one mare, and £6; he to pay debts, legacies, funeral and probate expenses, and to divide the residue equally between the testator's kin mentioned in the will. Witnesses: JOHN UNDERWOOD (clerk), JOHN FRANCES (X), THOMAS PINCHER (X). Pr. at Beccles 15 Dec. 1631.

R(W) WOOLFRAM AUBRY of Peasenhall. 9 December 1631 (374)

To eldest son JOHN AUBRY all lands, tenements, free and copyhold in Sibton. To younger son THOMAS AUBRY, all lands and tenements, free and copyhold, in Heveningham; also the horse mill as it now stands in the house of WILLIAM BLOCKE in which house the said THOMAS lives. Son JOHN AUBRY to be sole executor, and to have residue of all unbequeathed goods to pay debts, legacies, funeral and probate expenses. Witnesses: JOHN CATCHPOLE, LIONEL KNIGHT. Pr. at Yoxford 12 Jan. 1631/2.

R(W) THOMAS BENNETT of Washbrook,yeoman. (375)
15 December 1631

To wife ELIZABETH, a moiety (1/2) of lands and tenements in Washbrook, Easton, and Chattisham, provided she commit no waste. To daughter JANE BENNETT one half part of the house where testator lives in Washbrook, with all lands pertaining to same; the other half to her on the death of testator's wife ELIZABETH. To daughter MARY BENNETT, house with lands, freehold, in Easton, to have half the house and lands immediately, the other half on the death of wife ELIZABETH. To daughter ANN BENNETT, house and barn and lands in Easton, copyhold, to have half the lands and house immediately, the other half on the death of testator's wife

ELIZABETH. To WILLIAM & ELIZABETH HOW 10s. each. Proviso; that if by law the freehold lands owned by him have to be equally divided between his three daughters, then the copyhold lands in Easton given to ANNE to be sold, and the money thus raised used to pay debts, funeral expenses, etc. Wife ELIZABETH and daughter JANE to be executors. Witnesses JOSEPH CLARKE, JOHN PYMAN. Pr. at Ipswich 2 Feb. 1631.

R(W) JOHN BOTWRIGHT of Fressingfield, yeoman. (376)
19 December 1631

To son THOMAS BOTWRIGHT, messuage and tenement with appurtenances in Laxfield, where JOHN FULCHER lives, and all other lands in Laxfield on a 60 year lease, provided he pay in the south porch of Fressingfield church £260, namely to ELIZABETH & MARGARET BOTWRIGHT, daughters of the testator, £60 each within 6 months of testator's death; also to son JOHN BOTWRIGHT £70 within 1 yr. of testator's death, and also to testator's other son FRANCIS BOTWRIGHT £70 within 1 1/2 yrs. of testator's death. If default in payment, legacy void, and to pass to ELIZABETH, MARGARET, JOHN & FRANCIS BOTWRIGHT. To son WILLIAM BOTWRIGHT £40 within 3 months of testator's death; also one posted bedstead with a testor of the hour [sic] [hour glass?] as it stands on the great chamber parlour of the house occupied by the testator, with feather bed, feather bolster, coverlet, pair of blankets, the mat, and bedlinen now on the bed, and two pair of sheets. To daughter MARY BOTWRIGHT £60 in 3/4 yr. of testator's death. To FRANCIS SANDCROFT the younger of Fressingfield, all messuage, lands and tenement in Grundisburgh where ROBERT TOVELL lives, and all lands, tenements in Grundisburgh, Great Bealings, Culpho, and Playford, adjoining the said messuage; provided he pays by the next Lady Day £107 10s. to HENRY MEENE of Cratfield, gent., at or in the house of ROBERT WARNER gent., in Cratfield; further he pay £104 to WILLIAM CARR of Woodbridge, yeoman, at or in the house of WILLIAM CARR in Woodbridge, and further he pays £44. 10s. to THOMAS GREENE of Laxfield yeoman, in his house at Laxfield, and also pays to testator's executor £28 in the house where the testator lives. To son THOMAS, a cart, plough, harrows, cart rope, harnesses, and all the tools of husbandry. To sons JOHN, THOMAS, FRANCIS, and to daughters ELIZABETH, MARGARET & MARY, all goods household stuff, linen, brass, pewter, dairy vessell, unbequeathed in the house where testator lives, to be equally divided amongst them within 2 months of testator's death. Executor to receive all debts and moneys due to testator, and use same to pay his debts, and to pay funeral and probate expenses. Executor also to have residue of unbequeathed goods to help pay debts etc. After payment of debts surplus of money, together with the £28 due from FRANCIS SANDCROFT, to be equally divided between testator's sons and daughters. THOMAS BOTWRIGHT appointed executor; FRANCIS SANDCROFT appointed supervisor and to receive 40s. Witnesses: DANIEL LOCK, ROBERT ALDOUS, JOHN GILBERT (X). Pr. at Yoxford 31 Jan. 1631/2.

R(W) DOROTHY BACKLER of Chediston. 19 October 1629 (377)

To poor of Chediston 10s.; poor of Halesworth 10s.; poor of Darsham 10s.; poor of Theberton 10s. To her brothers and sisters children as follows -- JOHN BACKLER 2s. 6d.; EDMUND BACKLER 10s.; ROBERT BACKLER 5s.; MARY BACKLER 5s.; ALICE BACKLER 5s.; EZECHIEL BACKLER £4; MARY BLOMFIELD 10s.; JANE POLY 10s.; SARAH BACKLER 10s.; ROBERT ANTELL 10s.; JOHN ANTELL 10s.; and unto SUSAN their sister 20s.; EZECHIEL KNIGHT 10s.; NATHANIEL KNIGHT £4; KATHERINE BADLEY £5; SUSAN LEGGATT 40s.; PRISCILLA WOOLNOUGH £5 and PRUDENCE CLAXTON £3. To HESTER DIRECKE, widow, and PRISCILLA CHILSTON her sister 10s. each; and to ELIZABETH BURWOOD widow 20s. To godchildren JAMES BACKLER 10s.; JOHN MANN 2s. 6d.; ALICE SHEPPHERD 5s.; MARGARET SEPENS 2s. 6d.; SUSANNA HOWLETT 2s. 6d.; ELIZABETH WATES 2s. To ELIZABETH BIRD 2s. Proviso that these legacies to the children be paid when they reach 21. Proviso also that the £3 due to PRUDENCE CLAXTON be paid her in several installments, for her personal relief as she needs it. Kinsman WILLIAM KNIGHT appointed executor; brother ROBERT BACKLER appointed supervisor. In order for the executor to pay burial and funeral charges and debts he to have all ready money, one cow, all household stuff, linen, clothing and utensils. In order to meet legacies, executor to have all debts due to testator; any residue of money to go to executor in recompense for the care testator has yearly received EZECHIEL KNIGHT, father of WILLIAM KNIGHT executor and brother-in-law now deceased to the testator. To ROBERT BACKLER, supervisor, 20s. Witnesses: WILLIAM SMYTH, SIMON SEPENS, JOHN SEPENS, JOHN PIN, MATTHEW BOONE. Pr. at Beccles 3 Dec. 1631.

R(W) THOMAS BOISE of Belton (N). 22 November 1631 (378)

To wife MARY all his estate and goods. Witnesses: BARTHOLOMEW GREEN, ELIZABETH JEX. Probate granted to MARY BOISE, widow, at Beccles 31 Nov. 1631.

R(W) ELIZABETH BURTON of Charsfield, widow. 1 July 1631 (379)

To daughter ELIZABETH MANN, messuage, houses and lands in Kettleburgh occupied by THOMAS STRETCHAM, for her life; and on her death to pass to testator's grandchildren ELIZABETH & GRACE MANN, daughters of JOHN MANN and testator's daughter. Also to daughter ELIZABETH 2 cows and mares; one bedstead in the little chamber, one feather bed, one flock bed, two blankets and the best green coverlett, and the best birded coverlet, two ale vessels, one wicker chair, two stools, the best coffer standing in the little chamber with all its contents; one great chest with its contents in the parlour, one table standing in the parlour, one pair cob irons, ten pair sheets, 10 pillow cases, 1 dozen table napkins, 3 board cloths, 4 pillows and the biggest brass kettle that can be hung; one new smaller kettle; the best brass pot, the warming pan, and one iron dripping pan; two of the best cushions, one bedstead in the parlour chamber, the biggest skillet, a dozen pewter dishes, 6 pewter porringers, 2 silver spoons and the glass keepe in the hall; one churn, 2 keelers, 2 bowls, 4 of the best cheese vats with the brigs belonging to them; the best great tub, 2 great chairs, pair of querns, and all wearing apparell, linen and woolen. To son THOMAS BURTON £50 within 1 yr. of testator's death, to be paid in Charsfield church porch; also one feather bed, and one posted bedstead standing on the parlour chamber, one flock bed, one bolster, 2 blankets, 1 rug, 6 pair of sheets, 2 chairs, one table cloth and the little table standing in the hall; 2 pillows, 2 silver spoons, 2 of the best cushions, 2 cows, muskett with all things belonging to it; all the old iron, one morter of bell metal; 2 ale vessels, one brass pot and one brass kettle. To servant ROBERT SMITH 20s., also one flock bed, a bolster and a trundle bedstead. To servant ELIZABETH SEMAN 20s. To JOHN SYMPSON 10s. To all the poor who attend her funeral 2d. each. To son JOHN BURTON & daughter ELIZABETH, all ready money, debts, bonds due and all corn, in order to pay her debts, legacies, funeral and probate expenses. Residue of goods, to son JOHN BURTON, JOHN MAN, testator's son-in-law, and ELIZABETH MAN, testator's daughter, who were appointed executors. Witnesses: JOHN FOX, JOHN MAULSTER. Pr. at Wickham 24 Nov. 1631.

R(W) THOMAS BURRY of Carlton Colville, yeoman. 4 July 1631 (380)

Weak of body. To son WILLIAM BURRY, tenement where testator lives, with all lands pertaining; one close called Grove close in Carlton Colville, provided that the executor of this will takes the next half year's rent due from this close for the six months following testator's death, but if testator die before the next Michaelmas, then testator's wife MARY (executor) is to continue in the tenement until Michaelmas and use the rents for herself and not for the upkeep of testator's son THOMAS. Further that LAURENCE WINCOP, late of Blythburgh, and the testator of this will were executors of the will of JOHN CLARK of Blythburgh, and were charged with the payment of certain legacies to JOHN CLARK's children; now WILLIAM BURRY is charged with the payment of these legacies, and if he fail then the executor of this will is charged with the legacies, and can enter lands bequeathed to WILLIAM and to have and hold these lands until fulfillment of legacies under the will of JOHN CLARK. Further that if WILLIAM BURRY die without male heir then messuage and tenements to pass to testator's son THOMAS, provided he pay to testator's daughter ELIZABETH BURRY £60 when she reaches 21. To wife MARY BURRY, tenement called Brewere, occupied by RICHARD WARD, with all free and copyhold lands pertaining to it, until THOMAS BURRY reaches 21, this in satisfaction of her dower; also all profits from the tenement called Fleets, occupied by testator, -- the profits to be used to provide for the maintenance of testator's children THOMAS & ANNE BURRY until 21. Then when THOMAS 21 he to inherit these lands, provided he pay to his mother MARY BURRY an annuity of £9 in two equal payments at the feasts of Lady day and Michaelmas in full satisfaction of dower. If THOMAS die without male heir, then land to pass to WILLIAM BURRY and his heirs, provided WILLIAM pay to his sister ANNE BURRY £120 -- namely £60 within 1 yr. of WILLIAM's inheriting the land, and £60 in two years of his inheritance. If THOMAS die leaving heirs female, then WILLIAM to pay the girls £80 on his inheriting the land -- the £80 to be equally divided amongst THOMAS's daughters. To son THOMAS, a posted bedstead standing in the parlour, feather bed and 2 bolsters, a birded coverlet, blanket, feather pillow, mat, two pair sheets, the long table in the said parlour with a form belonging to the said table; a cupboard in the parlour, a great joined chest, two small buffet stools, a great candlestick of brass and a warming pan. To son-in-law AMBROSE PALMER, married to testator's daughter ELIZABETH, in fulfillment of a promise made of his marriage, £20 -- £10 within 1 yr. of testator's death, and £10 in 2 yrs.; this to be paid by WILLIAM BURRY in consideration of the Grove pightle devised to WILLIAM. To daughter ANNE BURRY, £20 payable by WILLIAM out of the Grove pightle profits -- £10 when ANNE 21, and £10 a year later. To son THOMAS BURRY £40 when 21, if he die before 21, legacy to pass to ANNE BURRY. To daughter ANNE BURRY £30 when 21; if she die before 21, legacy to pass to THOMAS. Residue of all goods, household stuff, implements, to wife MARY, in order to pay debts, and funeral expenses and probate charges, and to bring up testator's children THOMAS & ANNE. MARY BURRY to be sole executrix, and to enter bond of £140 with RICHARD BURRY of Bungay, yeoman, testator's brother, to perform legacies; if she refuse bond, then RICHARD BURRY to be executor. THOMAS WARD, brother-in-law, appointed supervisor. Witnesses: ROBERT BURRY (X), JOHN MAPLEDEN, the writer of the will. Probate granted to MARY BURRY at Beccles 22 Nov. 1631.

R(W) FRANCIS BUGG of Barking, yeoman. 13 September 1631 (381)

Sick. Executor to sell all movable goods, and to give £40 each to testator's daughters ELIZABETH & ANNE BUGG when they reach 21, with benefit of survivorship to his two sons FRANCIS & THOMAS. To granddaughter SUSAN, daughter of testator's daughter SUSAN, £5 and one feather bed. Residue of money to be invested at best rates to be equally divided between testator's sons FRANCIS & THOMAS when they reach 21. Brother-in-law WILLIAM COLEMAN and EDWARD TAVENER senior of Needham Market, yeo., appointed executors to pay debts, legacies, funeral & probate expenses. Witnesses: THOMAS COLVILLE, JOHN ROSE, JOHN MATTHEWS. Pr. at Ipswich 12 Nov. 1631.

R(W) THOMAS BOTWRIGHT of Withersdale (Mendham). (382)
15 April 1631

To wife ELIZABETH, messuage, house, lands, and tenements in Withersdale, Mendham, and Metfield, for life; then on her death daughter ELIZABETH SCARLET to inherit the parlour, parlour chamber, yard at the east end of the parlour from the hall windows unto the shed, with free ingress/egress, use of oven to bake, use of pump. To son THOMAS BOTWRIGHT his abode and use of the parlour and parlour chamber with sister ELIZABETH SCARLET as long as he remain unmarried. To son JOHN BOTWRIGHT, messuage, lands and tenements on death of testator's wife, giving to ELIZABETH SCARLET & THOMAS BOTWRIGHT £105, namely £50 to ELIZABETH and £55 to THOMAS -- ELIZABETH to receive £10 in 1 yr. after death of testator's mother, £10 in 3 yrs., £10 in 5 yrs., £10 in 7 yrs., and £10 in 9 yrs.; THOMAS to have £10 in 2 yrs. after death of testator's wife, £10 in 4 yrs., £10 in 6 yrs., £10 in 8 yrs., and £15 in 10 yrs. Power of entry into lands if default in payment, and to hold the lands until full satisfaction is made of legacies. To son JOHN, longest table in the hall, with 2 framed stools belonging to it. To son THOMAS bed in the chamber as it stands -- one feather bed, feather bolster, 2 blankets, the covering together with the line and mat; also longest chest in the parlour, and a glass case or keepe in the hall. To daughter ELIZABETH, the ceiled [sic] bedstead in the parlour as it stands, namely one feather bed and feather bolster, 2 blankets and a birded covering; one table, a chest, 2 buffet stools, one framed stool. Provision that all the goods devised to testator's children remain with testator's wife ELIZABETH until her death. Residue of all goods, household stuff to wife ELIZABETH to pay debts, funeral and probate expenses, and also to give each grandchild 10s. ELIZABETH appointed executor together with son THOMAS BOTWRIGHT. Witnesses: ROBERT FULCHER, BRYANT FOX, jnr. (X). Pr. at Beccles 29 Oct. 1631.

R(W) HENRY ALLEN of Kirton, yeoman. 13 September 1631 (383)

Sick. To daughter ROSE ALLEN, £200 when she reach 21 or on her marriage -- the money to remain with Sir PHILIP PARKER until then. To the poor of Kirton 20s. within 3 months of testator's death. To ROBERT ALLEN, son of testator's brother ROBERT ALLEN, £10 when 21. Residue of goods to youngest daughter ELIZABETH ALLEN, when she reach 21 or on her marriage. JOHN COLE of Kirton to hold the same until then, with proviso that if any of the goods are subject to decay then JOHN COLE to sell the same and to keep the money from the sale until ELIZABETH 21 or married. If any legatee die then benefit of survivorship to surviving legatee(s). Further proviso, that if ELIZABETH's legacy does not amount to £200 then the short fall be deducted from ROSE's legacy so that the two daughters receive an equal amount. Sir PHILIP PARKER & JOHN COLE appointed executors; if Sir PHILIP PARKER die before testator's daughters reach 21 then ROBERT MORGAN of Brantham to replace him. Witnesses: FRANCIS PLANFIELD (X), JOHN ROBERTS. Memorandum: ROBERT MORGAN to be supervisor; witnessed THOMAS CARTER rector of Shotley. Pr. at Ipswich 20 Oct. 1631.

R(W) JOHN SHARMAN of Weston. 4 October 1631 (384)

To son JOHN £20 which he already has on bond. To son-in-law ROGER BERT £10 in 6 months after testator's death. To son-in-law JOHN BARBER £20 due on bond. To son-in-law WILLIAM BIDBANKE £20 due on bond. To daughter ANNE SHARMAN £5 in 6 months of testator's death. To nephew THOMAS SHARMAN 20s. in 6 months of testator's death. To niece ELINOR WHAYBERE 10s. in 6 months of testator's death. To STEPHEN COLEMAN 20s. in 6 months of testator's death. To RICHARD SHARMAN 10s. in 6 months of testator's death. To the poor of the parish 40s. Residue to be equally divided amongst testator's five children by the executor within one month of the executor paying all debts funeral & probate expenses. Sole executor to be son-in-law WILLIAM BIDBANKE. Witnesses: JOHN BARBER, MARY BENTLEY, JOHN ELLIS. Pr. at Ipswich 5 Nov. 1631.

R(W) FRANCIS CUTTING of Sotherton, husbandman. 1 May 1631 (385)

Sick. To eldest son JOHN CUTTING 20s. in 1 yr. after testator's death. To son CHRISTOPHER 50s. in 1 yr. after testator's death. To son ROBERT 20s. in 1 yr. after testator's death. To son FRANCIS £4 in 1 yr. after testator's death. To son WILLIAM £5 in 1 yr. after testator's death. To daughter ELIZABETH £10 -- £5 within 1 month, and £5 in 1 1/4 yrs. after testator's death, with benefit of survivorship to children from all the legacies. Also to daughter ELIZABETH 4 pair of sheets; and if there be more than 8 pair in all then the remaining 4 to be divided between ROBERT, FRANCIS, and WILLIAM. Also to daughter ELIZABETH 5 table napkins, one long towell. All linen to be equally distributed amongst testator's children, by his neighbour THOMAS ALDRED, at his own discretion. Residue to son REGINALD CUTTING, to pay debt, legacies, funeral & probate expenses; he to be sole executor. Witnesses: HUMFREY BOHUN, THOMAS ALDRED. Pr. at Beccles 18 June 1631.

R(W) JOHN BIRKINSHAW of Bungay, draper. 30 November 1630 (386)

Weak, by constitution of nature. To the minister of Bungay St. Mary 10s. for preaching the funeral sermon. To the poor of both Bungay parishes 40s. To son JOSEPH BIRKINSHAW £80 immediately on testator's death. To son SAMUEL BIRKINSHAW £40 when he reaches 25. To daughter SARAH BIRKINSHAW £40 within 1 yr. of testator's death. To daughter BRIDGET BIRKINSHAW £20 when 21. To youngest daughter MARTHA BIRKINSHAW £20 when 21. To grandchild ELIZABETH MARSHALL 20s. within 1 yr. To son JOHN BIRKINSHAW the £20 owed to the testator by Mr HEALSTONE presently in the Fleet in London, if he can get the money from him. To son ROBERT house where testator lives within 1 month after testator's death, provided he pay to testator's wife ANNE an annuity of £8, and keeps property in good repair. To wife ANNE all household stuff, utensils, stock, and all lands and appurtenances both free and copyhold in Hedenham and Ditchingham (Norfolk) provided she sell the lands within 2 yrs. of his death in order to meet legacies. ANNE to be executrix. Brother-in-law ROBERT POPE of St. Margaret's and son-in-law THOMAS MARSHALL to be supervisors. Witnesses: HENRY CUNNINGHAM, RICHARD BENSLEY, THOMAS FRANCKLYN (script the will). Pr. at Beccles 22 Oct. 1631.

R(W) JOHN KNIGHTS of Lowestoft, innholder. 16 July 1631 (387)

To the poor of Lowestoft 2s. 6d. -- this to go to the 20 poorest and oldest. To eldest son JOHN KNIGHTS £40, namely £10 within six months of testator's death, and £10 a year thereafter; if he die before fulfillment of legacy, then remainder of legacy to be equally divided between his children. To second son WILLIAM KNIGHTS £40, namely £20 within 1 yr. of testator's death, and £20 within 2 yrs.; if he die without heirs then legacy to be divided between JOHN & RICHARD KNIGHTS, testator's sons, or the survivor of them, or their children. To youngest son RICHARD KNIGHTS messuage and tenement in Southwold with yard, salt houses, fish houses, that testator's brother RICHARD KNIGHTS bought from Mr THOMAS WARREN of Southwold and which is now occupied by JOHN JACKSON of Southwold. Also to RICHARD £40 on 21st birthday. Should RICHARD die without issue the £40 legacy to be equally divided between testator's children JOHN & WILLIAM KNIGHTS & ALICE BURGESS, or their survivors. To daughter ALICE BURGESS £15 within six months of testator's death; if she remarry, then legacy to go to testator's grandchild ALICE HERRINGTON when reaches 18. To grandson JOHN KNIGHTS £5 when 18, granddaughter ANNE NORRIS £5 when 18 and granddaughter ALICE HERRINGTON £5 when 18, with benefit of survivorship. Residue of goods to wife ELIZABETH KNIGHTS, to pay debts, funeral and probate expenses, she to be executrix. LAURENCE DEANE to be supervisor. Wife ELIZABETH and her brother JOHN EVERARD to be bound to LAURNECE DEANE of Reydon, yeoman, in £300 to fulfill will, pay debts etc., and should she refuse the bond, then LAURENCE DEANE has the power to call all the legacies away from the executrix and give the same to the legatees. Witnesses: JOSHUA SPRATT, STEPHEN WALLER. Pr. at Lowestoft 28 Sept. 1631.

R(W) JOHN WEBSTER of Monewden. 8 December 1630 (388)

Weak. To son ROBERT WEBSTER, appointed sole executor, £10. To grandchildren ROBERT & JOHN WEBSTER, sons of ROBERT WEBSTER, £10 each. To granddaughters MARTHA & ELIZABETH & MARGARET WEBSTER daughters of ROBERT WEBSTER £6 13s. 4d. each. Benefit of survivorship to all of grandchildren's legacies; grandchildren also to have all goods household stuff etc. to be equally divided once funeral and probate and debts are met; benefit of survivorship also applies. Witnesses: HENRY GARDENER, WALTER PEIRSON. Pr. at Shelley 5 July 1631.

R(W) JOHN TOKELOVE of Ufford, carpenter. 20 November 1630 (389)

Sick. To son JAMES TOKELOVE tenement where JOHN EAGLE lives, with all appurtenances and lands, both free and copyhold in Petistree and Loudham; also 2 pieces of meadow in the North meadow lately bought from THOMAS STILES, provided he pay to testator's wife MARGARET TOKELOVE, an annuity of £4 10s. at the south porch of Ufford church at Lady Day and Michaelmas; if default then lands to go to testator's wife for life. To JOHN TOKELOVE, eldest son of JOHN TOKELOVE, testator's son, deceased, all the copyhold lands and tenements held by JOHN TOKELOVE his father at the time of his marriage. To son NICHOLAS TOKELOVE, all lands bought from THOMAS COSEN senior, and NICHOLAS WHINERY, in Ufford, to enter these same lands the Michaelmas following after the testator's death, provided he pay to testator's wife an annuity of 20s. at the south porch of Ufford church on the two feasts of Lady Day and Michaelmas; if default then lands to go to testator's wife for life. To son JAMES TOKELOVE posted bedstead with the bed theron as it stands now furnished; all carpenters tools, half the stock of timber, plank and board, and £4. To son NICHOLAS TOKELOVE £20 within 1 yr. of testator's death. To daughter MARGARET CUSHIN £5 within 1 yr. of testator's death. To MARGARET TOKELOVE, daughter of testator's son ROBERT TOKELOVE, deceased, £6 when she reaches 21. To the poor of Ufford 20s. To wife MARGARET all corn in the granery bought from THOMAS COSEN and NICHOLAS WHINERY; also the use of granery till Michaelmas next after testator's death; all goods, chattel, movable goods, and 2 loads of wood yearly from the Petistree tenements. MARGARET to be sole executrix. Supervisor HENRY GROOME. Witnesses: HENRY GROOME, WILLIAM LONGE, HENRY NORMAN. Pr. at Ufford 12 Oct. 1631.

R(W) JOAN STILES of Ashbocking, widow. 25 September 1626 (390)

Aged. To daughter ELIZABETH ROOE, appointed sole executrix, all goods, chattels in order to pay legacies laid down in the will of ROBERT STILES late husband of testator and also to pay all legacies laid down in the will of testator's son EDMUND STILES also deceased. To the poor of Ashbocking 5s. in one month of testator's death. Witnesses: WILLIAM STILES, GEORGE FINCH (X), JAMES CASTON. Pr. at Ipswich 4 Nov. 1631.

R(W) JOHN SMITH of Holton, yeoman. 7 June 1631 (391)

Sick. To wife MARY, daughter MARY, daughter FRANCES and youngest daughter ELIZABETH all household stuff, bedsteads, cupboards, chests, hutches, tables, wool, linen, brass and pewter to be equally divided between them. To daughters MARY, FRANCES, & ELIZABETH one cow each. To wife MARY 2 horses. To son HENRY 1 cart, 1 tumbrell, 1 plough, 1 pair of harrows; also residue of all goods; HENRY appointed sole executor, to pay debts, funeral & probate expenses. Neighbour RICHARD BROWNING supervisor. Witnesses: RICHARD BROWNING (X), JOHN BARRETT, GEORGE STEVENS. Pr. at Ipswich 22 Sept. 1631.

R(W) EDMUND SIDNOR of Lound, gentleman. 16 September 1631 (392)

Very sick; to be buried in Lound church. To the poor of Lound 10s., and the poor of Blundeston 10s. To sister ELIZABETH DOWNING, niece ELIZABETH ALLEN, nephew ALLEN 10s. each to buy a ring; 10s. each to be paid by executor within 10 days testator's death. To nephew ROBERT SIDNOR £20 within 1 month of testator's death. To nephew HENRY SIDNOR £7 within 1 month of testator's death. To cousin ROBERT UNDERWOOD £7 within 1 month of testator's death. To the five children of testator's niece ALLEN -- WILLIAM, BENJAMIN, ANN, SAMUEL, and ELIZABETH GOSLING 10s. each. To cousin JOHN UNDERWOOD to preach at testator's funeral 10s. For a dinner for testator's friends after his burial at Lound £5. To godson JAMES UNDERWOOD 10s. within 10 days of testator's death. Residue of goods to nephew ROBERT SIDNOR, appointed executor, to pay debts, legacies, funeral and probate expenses. Witnesses: MARGARET UNDERWOOD (X), ROBERT UNDERWOOD, the writer. Pr. at Beccles 24 Sept. 1631.

R(W) JOHN SMITH of Ipswich, baker. 28 July 1631 (393)

Sick. To eldest son JOHN SMITH messuage and tenement where testator lives in St. Lawrence parish Ipswich, with all things pertaining to the same; all copper, tubs, hoggsheads, steeping vats, kilnes, and all implements for brewing and baking; also all land bought from ANTHONY PENYNG, both free and copyhold in St. Margaret's Ipswich, provided he pay to testator's wife ANNE an annuity of £12, payable twice a year in equal installments -- this in lieu of dower. JOHN SMITH also to pay to testator daughter ELIZABETH, the wife of RICHARD PAYNE £10 within 4 yrs. of testator's death. To son WILLIAM SMITH, messuages and lands in St. Margaret's parish Ipswich, where BENJAMIN NEVE, RICHARD HARROLD, & WILLIAM TOMPSON live, when WILLIAM reaches 24. These premises to remain with testator's wife ANNE until then to provide for WILLIAM's upkeep, and the care and maintenance of testator's youngest children. WILLIAM to have these premises when 24, provided he pay ANNE an annuity of £6 in two installments -- this to be in lieu of dower. To daughter ANNE SMITH messuage where EDMUND WARD lives in St. Margaret's parish. If she has no heir then messuage to pass to testator's sons JOHN & WILLIAM. ANNE to enter on 21st birthday -- until then wife ANNE to hold tenement to provide for upkeep of children; daughter ANNE to pay wife ANNE annuity of £6 in lieu of dower as in previous legacies to sons JOHN & WILLIAM. To poor of St. Margaret's 30s.; poor of St. Lawrence 10s. To ABIGAIL BAKER, a poor child brought up by testator, £3 to bind her apprentice within 3 months after death of testator. Residue, once debts, funeral and probate expenses met, to wife ANNE and son JOHN; ANNE & JOHN to be joint executors. Witnesses: RICHARD GRYMSTON (script), HENRY GREEN, WILLIAM TOFTS. Pr. at Ipswich 22 Sept. 1631.

R(W) THOMAS SKUDGEN of Copdock, yeoman. 5 September 1630 (394)

Sick. To the poor of Copdock 6s. 8d. Residue of goods to wife ALICE, who was appointed executrix. Witnesses: THOMAS GARTHWAITE, THOMAS CORNERS (X). Pr. at Ipswich 30 July 1631.

R(W) ANNE SMITH of Ubbeston, spinster. 28 July 1631 (395)

To ROBERT SMITH of Laxfield, son of RICHARD SMITH, testator's kinsman, 2 pair sheets, one pillow, one pillow case, 2 of the lesser kettles, one iron pot, one bolster, for as long as his wife shall live; then to pass on to his son THOMAS. To the wife of ROBERT SMITH, one upper coat, one under petticoat, the best apron made of say, one white apron. To ROBERT SMITH all the wood and boards, two iron wedges, one pair of wool cardes, on condition that he make for the testator a good coffin at his own expense, and also on condition that he cause no trouble to testator's executor. To RICHARD, son of ROBERT SMITH, one feather bed, one bolster, one trundle bedstead as it stands with everything belonging -- ROBERT SMITH to use it until RICHARD 21. To ALICE SMITH the daughter of testator's cousin RICHARD SMITH £3 within 1 month of testator's death; also black petticoat, one russet coat, one old red petticoat, 2 waistcoats, one upper bodice, one white apron, one pillow, one pillow case, one cushion, and the second best hat. To ANN SMITH daughter of cousin JOHN SMITH, chest and 10s. in 1 month of death. To MARY CLARK, daughter of THOMAS CLARK of Ubbeston, one little coffer. To the wife of WILLIAM WELLS, the great speinning wheel for life; then to executor. Residue of goods to executor to pay debts, funeral and probate charges. SARAH SMITH appointed executrix; SIMON JACOB of Ubbeston appointed supervisor. Witnesses: THOMAS CORNISH, SIMON JACOB, ELIZABETH WELLS (X). Pr. at Yoxford 19 Sept. 1631.

R(W) WILLIAM STEELE of Hoxne, linen weaver. 28 July 1631 (396)

To wife SUSAN for life, piece of land called Little Cawdwell, containing 3 acres, in Hoxne bought recently from JOHN BARKER of Syleham; provided she pay testator's son JOHN STEELE 20s. a year at Michaelmas and Lady Day. To son JOHN STEELE on the death of his mother Little Cawdwell close in Hoxne, and the messuage with lands pertaining in Hoxne where testator lives, containing 2 acres. The close, part of the land called Does, containing 4 acres, in Hoxne, bought by the testator from JOHN YOUNG, deceased, and held by copy of court roll of Hoxne manor to be sold within 1 yr. of testator's death by RICHARD COWPER the elder of Hoxne, and JOHN WOODE of Hoxne, for the best possible price, and the money thus raised to be used in paying debts and legacies of the testator. To wife SUSAN for life, cupboard in the hall with the stained clothes and other things therein; the long table with the form; one long form, 2 buffet stools standing in the hall, malt querns, and a kiln and the heare belonging. On her death these to pass to son JOHN. Also to SUSAN the greatest brass skillet; warming pan, chafing dish, mortar and pestle. On her death these to go to daughter ELIZABETH STEELE. To wife SUSAN for life, best posted bed as it stands, best feather bed and bolster, 2 feather pillows, best covering, one pair of blankets, flock bed, coffer, great chest and the little table with the desk thereon standing in the parlour; 4 pair best sheets, 4 pillow cases, 6 table napkins, one long towell, one table cloth, 2 blue and white cushions, 2 cushions, 2 low joined stools, 2 beer sacks, milk tub, 10 pieces of pewter being plates and dishes, roast iron, fire pan, frying pan, one cheese vat and cheese brigs, 2 candlesticks, double salt seller, 2 corn sacks and half the hemp on the ground; bolting hutch; all her clothes, two keepes, 3 combs of wheat; black cow with the white tail; weaned calf, one dripping pan. To son THOMAS STEELE one comb of wheat; one comb mustard. To daughter ELIZABETH STEELE 2 year old heifer; the joined chest standing between the two bedsteads in the parlour; wicker chair, greatest cheese vat and brigs to the same. To son JOHN STEELE ploughs, plough harnesses, the bay horse colt, brown mare, the old grey mare, cart and tumbrell with appurtenances, cart harness; the piece of the old haystack and the least of the new haystacks standing in the pightle near to the house. To wife SUSAN all unbequeathed brass; one haystack in the pightle called the Dry pightle; residue save for timber plank and wood and larch in the house and yard, together with any farm rents from lands held by Mr VINSENT on lease, are to go, once debts funeral expenses and probate charges met, to ANNE, ELIZABETH, SUSAN & JOHN STEELE who are appointed executors. Witnesses: JOHN BURGESS, ISAAC PRESTON, GREGORY BURGERY (X). Pr. at Stradbroke 15 Sept. 1631.

R(W) GEORGE REYNALDS of Walberswick, husbandman. (397)
11 March 1630/1

Sick; to be buried in Walberswick church yard. To wife FYRETT [sic] son JAMES, daughters MARY & SUSANNA all movables to be equally divided. Wife to have all movables until children reach 21. Wife to enter into a bond of £100 with HUGH STACEY & WILLIAM CHARROLD, friends of the testator, to give one third of the movables to these friends if she remarry before children reach 21 in order to provide for the careful upbringing of the testator's children. Benefit of survivorship to children. Wife appointed executrix, but if she refuse the bond, then HUGH STACEY & WILLIAM CHARROLD to be executors. Witnesses: JOHN CHESTER (X), THOMAS DURRANT. Probate granted to FYRETT REYNALDS at Yoxford 28 July 1631.

R(W) BRADLEY RANDALL of North Glemham (N). (398)
[blank] September 1631

To father JOHN RANDALL £20 given testator by his grandfather, and all else owned by testator. Witness: URSULA RANDALL. Probate granted to JOHN RANDALL at Wickham Market 20 Sept. 1631.

R(W) ELIZABETH PRYME of Halesworth, widow. 13 August 1631 (399)

First states that she was the daughter of ROBERT MAN of Brockford, deceased. For the use of THOMASIN LINSTED of Wortwell widow, and EDENY PEARSON of Wetheringsett, widow, £30 -- these two being sisters for the testator. For the poor and impotent in Brockford, the churchwardens of the parish are instructed to buy with legacy from testator, a piece of ground, which is to be let out to farm, and feofees are to be appointed to run this and to rent the ground; the money thus accruing is to be initially distributed by the churchwardens and overseers of the parish to testator's two sisters, and after their death to be distributed amongst the poor. Parson and churchwardens and overseers of the parish are to appoint the feofees to run the charity. To sister THOMASIN LINSTED one pewter platter, one petticoat, one smock. To sister EDENY PEARSON one petticoat, one smock, one pewter platter. Residue of goods to kinsman GEORGE PRYME of Halesworth, appointed executor to pay debts and funeral, probate charges. Witnesses: WILLIAM CHILSTON, NATHANIEL CHILSTON, THOMAS FELLA. Pr. at Yoxford 19 Sept. 1631.

R(W) GERVAIS PAYNE of Saxtead, cordwainer. 20 September 1631 (400)

To wife PRISCILLA for life, posted bedstead in the parlour, with a feather bed, 2 feather bolsters, 2 pillows, 2 coverlets, 1 pair sheets, 2 pillow cases, a testor mat and line; 2 coffers; box in the parlour with its contents; little cupboard, table, 1 low buffet stool, a little turned chair with a wicker bottom; warming pan, hand flask; one skillet, and a comb. On wife's death, these to go to testator's daughter MARGARET, wife of JOHN EMMERSON. To son ROBERT PAYNE £6 within 1 yr., paid by JOHN EMMERSON. To daughter MARTHA PAYNE £3 in 1 yr., paid by executor. Residue of goods to be equally divided -- half to JOHN EMMERSON provided he pay legacy to ROBERT PAYNE, and half to wife PRISCILLA for her life, then to go to daughter MARGARET. JOHN EMMERSON & wife PRISCILLA joint executors to pay debts, and funeral expenses, and probate charges. JOHN EMMERSON further to be bound in £12 to ROBERT PAYNE to pay ROBERT £6 in the north porch of Dennington church, and testator's executors to be bound in £6 to MARTHA PAYNE to pay her £3 at the north porch of Dennington church. If JOHN EMMERSON refuse the bond then his legacy to revert to testator's wife PRISCILLA and she to enter bond to ROBERT -- if PRISCILLA refuse the bond, then she loses the bequest of the bedstead with all furniture pertaining to the same standing in the parlour -- this to go to MARTHA. Witness: EDWARD MOULTON. Pr. at Wickham Market 19 Oct. 1631.

R(W) HENRY NORMAN of Ufford, yeoman. 15 September 1631 (401)

Sick. To son-in-law EDWARD HAMMOND all lands, free and copyhold, in Ufford and Petistree for the term of the life of testator's wife ROSE, provided he pay to JOHN MARTIN, testator's brother-in-law, an annuity during the lifetime of ROSE of £18 due on Lady Day and Michaelmas; if default, power of entry to JOHN MARTIN and his wife ELIZABETH to hold until payment of default with arrears. To MARGARET HAMMOND, daughter of EDWARD HAMMOND, all lands and tenements free and copyhold in Ufford and Petistree on death of testator's wife ROSE. Should MARGARET die without heirs, then lands to pass to ELIZABETH, the wife of JOHN MARTIN -- namely the lands which used to belong to EDWARD LONG and GEORGE BRIGHTWELL; the lands lately THOMAS COOTE's to go to HENRY MARTIN, son of JOHN MARTIN. To sister FAITH BRICE an annuity of 20s. payable out of THOMAS COOTE's lands. To ELIZABETH MARTIN, wife of JOHN MARTIN, 50s. to be paid by MARGARET HAMMOND. To each of the children of JOHN & ELIZABETH MARTIN, viz. HENRY, JOHN, ELIZABETH & MARY, 40s. a year to be paid by MARGARET HAMMOND, within 2 years of her entering the lands devised to her. To wife ROSE 40s. EDWARD HAMMOND & JOHN MARTIN appointed executors, to pay debts, funeral expenses. Witnesses; RICHARD HARRISON, THOMAS COOKE (X). Pr. at Wickham Market 12 Oct. 1631.

R(W) JOHN NUTTALL of Ipswich, clothworker. 24 July 1631 (402)

Sick. To son-in-law WILLIAM TIDYMAN all shop stuff, if he pay his 2 children WILLIAM & ELIZABETH 20s. each when 21. To daughter ELIZABETH TYDYMAN best wrought pewter dish, livery bedstead with the flock bed now on it standing in the chamber on the hall. To wife, all goods and furniture in the house where testator lives, which were there on their marriage, also one trundle bedstead with bed thereon in the chamber over the shop; also best down coverlett, best brass pot. To daughter MARYAN residue of all goods, to pay debts; she to be sole executrix. Witnesses: JOHN THURSTON, THOMAS BLOMFIELD, ROBERT CLARKE. Pr. at Ipswich 6 Aug. 1631.

R(W) WILLIAM MURDOCK of Saxmundham, joiner. 20 July 1631 (403)

Weak. To son WILLIAM 20s. within 3 months of testator's death. Residue to wife THOMASIN, appointed sole executrix, to pay debts, funeral and probate. Witnesses: WILLIAM ALDOUS, OLIVER MURDOCK, ROBERT REEVE. Pr. at Saxmundham 28 July 1631.

R(W) REGINALD MAYHEW of Debenham, yeoman. 8 November 1630 (404)

To grandchild JOHN MAYHEW, all free and copyhold land in Worlingworth, late bought from HENRY HAYWARD alias SADD, NICHOLAS BROWNE, & THOMAS VINCENT, provided he pay all debts, and legacies. Also one tenement called Glovers, copyhold, and 3 roods in Worlingworth lately bought from JOHN MYLES & RICHARD FRESTON. To daughter ELIZABETH £100 -- namely £25 a year for the following four years after testator's death, to be paid in the house of JAMES ALEXANDER in Worlingworth. She also to have and quietly to enjoy the little new parlour in the testator's house for one year after testator's death, provided she remain unmarried, with right of entry, draw water. After the year she to have liberty to remove her goods from the said chamber. To son-in-law JOHN THROWER and his wife JOAN, all the lands held by the testator in virtue of the mortgage between JOHN THROWER and testator, provided JOHN THROWER pays the £140 due at Michaelmas

1631, and £20 on every Michaelmas thereafter until 1637 in the house of JAMES ALEXANDER in Worlingworth. To grandchildren, SUSAN MAYHEW, MARY THROWER, JOHN THROWER, EDWARD THROWER, ELIZABETH THROWER, THOMAS THROWER, & MARGARET THROWER, £20 each when 21. To grandchild JOHN MAYHEW, the horsemill, one long table standing in the hall, one long table standing in the little parlour, one cupboard, one keep, one bedstead furnished with feather bed, bolster, coverlet, and blankets, two other bedsteads as they stand with bed linen to them belonging; one brass pot, one joined chair, one long ladder, one joined chest, one coffer. To the poor of Debenham 40s. and the poor of Worlingworth 20s. and of Monk Soham 10s. payable within 3 months of testator's death. Proviso that if any legacies are unfulfilled within 10 days that they fall due, then power to legatee(s) to enter and hold testator's lands. JOHN MAYHEW, son, and JOHN MAYHEW grandson, to be joint executors, to prove the will within 3 months; if they fail then daughter of testator ELIZABETH MAYHEW to be sole executor, holding the lands until full satisfaction of legacies -- she to receive a further £60. Witnesses: PETER ALDRICH, WILLIAM RISING (X), GEORGE LORD, JOHN MAYHEW (script). Probate granted to JOHN & JOHN MAYHEW at Ipswich 30 July 1631.

R(W) ROBERT KNIGHTS of Oulton, yeoman. 7 September 1631 (405)

To sister JANE wife of WILLIAM PLATER £10, none of which to go to her husband. To kinsman MILES GARDINER £10. To poor of Walberswick 30s.; poor of Blythburgh 10s.; Oulton poor 10s.; Easton 10s. Residue to brother ROBERT KNIGHTS who is charged with payment of above legacies, debts, funeral, and probate expenses; appointed executor. Witnesses: RICHARD CODD and his wife; SUSAN PARKER (X). Pr. at Beccles 14 Sept. 1631.

R(W) ALICE INGELL alias SANDERS of Horham, widow. (406)
8 June 1631

To be buried Horham churchyard. To niece MARY BOTTRIGHT, tenement bought from JOHN SMITH. To niece MARY MOWER £10 -- £4 within 1 yr., £3 in 2 yrs., £3 in 3 yrs of testator's death. To MARY MOWER one flock bed with bedstead and all furnishings belonging to it; one small coverlet, one blanket, 2 cushions, one pillow, 2 pair sheets, one pillow case, one cloth gown, one shift of my best wearing linen, the middle sized kettle, one skillet, two pewter dishes within 2 months of testator's death. To goddaughter MARGARET INGELL alias SANDERS 20s. and 1 pair sheets. To JOHN CHAPPEL, son of GEORGE CHAPPEL 20s. in 4 yrs. of testator's death. To the children of JOHN COLBY, 5s. each; JOHN COLBY to acknowledge receipt of same. To old STEVEN SANDERS of Stradbroke 5s. within 1 month of testator's death. To ELIZABETH COLBY wife of JOHN COLBY 10s. in 5 yrs. of testator's death. To the two children of DENIS CLUBB 5s. each in 5 yrs. of testator's death -- their father to acknowledge receipt of same. Residue to

MARY BOTTRIGHT; she to be sole executrix, pay debts, funeral and probate expenses. To ALICE MEEKINS, presently on my decease, best red petticoat. Witnesses: ROBERT BUCK (X), RICHARD HAILE. Pr. at Ipswich 14 June 1631.

R(W) MARY HOLLAWAY of East Bergholt. 3 June 1631 (407)

Weak. To father JOHN GOODWIN of East Bergholt £5 in 1 yr. of testator's death. To brother JOHN GOODWIN of Emmanuel College Cambridge, £10 when 21. To brother WILLIAM HUBBERT of East Bergholt £10 in 1 yr. of testator's death. To sister SARAH CHAPLEIN 10s. in 1 yr. of testator's death. To sister MARY WOODGATE 40s. to buy her a ring. To STEPHEN SKINNER the elder of East Bergholt 40s. in 1 yr. of testator's death, and to every child of his 40s. each when 21. To STEPHEN SKINNER the younger of East Bergholt 40s. in 1 yr. of testator's death. To MARY SKINNER, daughter of STEPHEN SKINNER the elder, a bible, in 1 yr. To MARY TRANHAM daughter of ROBERT TRANHAM when she can read perfectly in the Bible, a Bible. To MARY ALDHAM, daughter of ROBERT SKINNER, late of East Bergholt, 40s. in 1 yr. To ROBERT SKINNER, son of ROBERT SKINNER late of East Bergholt, 40s. when 21. To ELIZABETH TASSELL of East Bergholt, 20s. within 1 month of testator's death; a further 20s. in 1 yr., and 20s. in 2 yrs. of testator's death. To WILLIAM CLARK, son of ELIZABETH TASSELL, 40s. when 21. To the poor of East Bergholt £5. Residue of goods to be equally divided between sisters SUSAN BACON, ELIZABETH QUARLES, & ANN HEYWARD, save for one silver salt and spoon which are to go to nephew THOMAS QUARLES. Brother FRANCIS QUARLES of Newton next Sudbury clerk, to be sole executor. Witnesses: WILLIAM PERRIMAN, ROUS HARMAN. Pr. at Reydon 5 July 1631.

R(W) THOMAS HAIL of Hoxne, yeoman. 8 June 1622 (408)

Sick. To daughters MARY & DOROTHY all lands, free and copyhold, in Suffolk and Norfolk, and their heirs; if die without heirs, then lands to pass to testator's wife DOROTHY, and on her death to the right heirs of the testator. To wife DOROTHY and daughters all movables and household goods and stuff to be equally divided between them; provided if wife remarry then she has to enter into a bond before her second marriage, with JOHN SHERWOOD of Hoxne, her father, to give a true account of their legacy when they reach 14. If wife refuse then she has to account to her father; wife to care for daughters. Wife DOROTHY and father-in-law JOHN SHERWOOD joint executors. Witnesses: ROBERT ADAMS (X), GABRIEL TASSELL, MARTHA BRICE (X), WILLIAM MOLLING, JOHN SHERWOOD, junior. Pr. at Ipswich 22 Sept. 1631.

R(W) ELIZABETH GARRARD of Thurlston, widow. 29 March 1631 (409)

Sick. To the poor of Whitton cum Thurlston 20s. To ROBERT SOUTHGATE 20s. in 4 months of testator's death. To SARAH ISHAM one pair sheets; 6 table napkins. To MARGARET HAWYS 6s. 8d. in 1 month of testator's death. To FRANCES EADE, wife of ROBERT EADE, one pair sheets. Residue to FRANCES WAKE of Thurlston, widow; she to be sole executrix. Witnesses: JOHN ELLIOTT, RICHARD CROWE, ROBERT LEWES. Pr. at Ipswich 22 Sept. 1631.

R(W) THOMASIN FOSTER of Helmingham. 4 October 1630 (410)

Testator the wife of ABRAHAM FOSTER of Helmingham, husbandman, and that she is sick and aged; wishes to be buried at Helmingham. To son-in-law THOMAS BLOCK of Witnesham, yeoman, tenement called Blubbers in Helmingham, copyhold of Otley hall manor. To JOHN SHININ of Charsfield, testator's son £9 in 6 months of her death. To THOMAS SHININ, son of testator's son JOHN by his first wife, 20s. when 21. To WILLIAM, GEORGE, ANNE, THOMASINE, & MARY DORE, children of SUSAN & THOMAS DORE of Witnesham, testator's daughter and son-in-law, 20s. each when 21; should any child die then his/her share to revert to testator's daughter SUSAN. THOMAS BLOCK appointed executor. ABRAHAM FOSTER, agreeing to these legacies, is to have his dwelling in the new end of the premises which he built for himself, for life; further that JOHN SHININ is to pay to THOMAS BLOCK 10s. towards the yearly rent of the said ABRAHAM FOSTER for life. Witnesses: WILLIAM ARMIGER, ABRAHAM FOSTER, THOMAS SEAMAN. Pr. at Ipswich 26 Aug. 1631.

R(W) EMMA FORD of St. Clement's Ipswich. (411)
26 September 1628

To the poor of St. Clement's 20s. To daughter CHARITY wife of JOHN PICKAS 5s. in 2 months of testator's death. To KATHERINE MORGAN, wife of EDMUND MORGAN, of Ipswich, mariner, two tenements in St. Nicholas Ipswich occupied by testator's daughter JOAN HAYWARD, and by ROBERT BORDEMAN, weaver, for life; then tenement occupied by ROBERT BORDEMAN to go to EDMOND MORGAN, son of EDMOND MORGAN: tenement occupied by JOAN HAYWARD to pass to NATHANIEL MORGAN, brother of EDMOND MORGAN. To MARY ALEFOUNDER of East Bergholt, widow, BENJAMIN ALEFOUNDER, of East Bergholt clothier, and DANIEL MORGAN, brother of EDMOND MORGAN, £3 each in 6 months of testator's death. To JOAN BOTTON, the best gown. To PHILIP KENNINGHALL, 20s. Residue of all goods to EDMOND MORGAN, senior, to pay debts, legacies, funeral and probate expenses; he to be sole executor. [No witnesses -- not in register or original will.] Pr. at Ipswich 5 Aug. 1631.

R(W) EDMOND FRIENDS of Beccles, woollen draper. (412)
1 June 1631

Sick. To eldest son RICHARD, messuage late ELIZABETH SMITH's in Aldeby (Norfolk) and the best posted bedstead with furniture standing in the East chamber; feather bed and bolster, a birded coverlet which belonged to his grandmother HILL; one great chest used by testator to store woollen cloth in; a joined desk which was his mother's, 4 buffet stools; a framed table; salt seller of silver and gilt; small silver wine cup; 4 silver spoons given to his brothers and sisters late deceased; the best cloth gown. The land given to RICHARD used to belong to ELIZABETH SMITH -- the testator's mother. To son EDWARD, tenement where testator lives called Lennyes bought from Sir WALTER DEVERAUX in Beccles, near to the new market place; EDWARD to enter this tenement on death of testator's wife ELIZABETH. Also EDWARD to have tenement and 6 acres copyhold land in Aldeby bought from WILLIAM SEAMAN, on death of wife ELIZABETH; if EDWARD have no heirs, lands to pass to brother RICHARD. To daughter FRANCES two tenements in Beccles bought from EDWARD MILEHAM, gent., and from FRANCIS ARMIGER, now occupied by THOMAS BARKER & COXAGE. To son EDWARD one silver ball, silver and gilt wine cup. 6 silver spoons. To daughter FRANCES a silver ball. To EDWARD & FRANCES a posted bedstead and one drawing table each. To the preacher at testator's burial 10s. To poor of Beccles 40s. Residue after payment of legacies, debts, funeral and probate expenses, to wife ELIZABETH for life, then to EDWARD & FRANCES FRIEND equally. Wife ELIZABETH to be executrix. Proviso, that if EDWARD dies before his mother ELIZABETH, then the land devised to him to pass to FRANCES, with the exception of the land in Aldeby; like proviso if FRANCES die before mother, then legacy to pass to EDWARD. To maid servant MARGARET BARKER 10s. Witnesses: ROBERT HORNE, ROBERT ANTELL, ROBERT COBB. Pr. at Beccles 30 June 1631.

R(W) JOHN DRAPER of Erwarton, yeoman. 4 October 1631 (413)

Sick. To wife MARTHA messuage bought from ROBERT JENNER in Ashfield Thorpe, until son JOHN reach 21; all timber reserved to son JOHN from these lands. To son JOHN DRAPER messuage in Ashfield Thorpe on death of mother. To DOROTHY DRAPER £20 owed her in order to make up the sum of £200 to be paid as follows -- £100 in 6 months of testator's death, and £100 in 1 yr.; she to give acquittance of the sum. To poor of Erwarton 20s. in 6 months; poor of Brantham 10s. in 6 months. To Mr WICKS, minister of Erwarton, 20s. in 6 months of testator's death. To JONATHAN DRAPER all unbequeathed goods, chattels, when 21; if he die before 21 then £100 out of this residue to go to MARTHA DRAPER, and the residue to go to JOHN DRAPER when 21. JONATHAN DRAPER also to have 3 acres copyhold land, to be surrendered to JOHN DRAPER when JONATHAN reaches 21; should JONATHAN refuse to surrender the land, then he to give JOHN £60 in lieu out of his own portion. To wife MARTHA use and benefit of stock and money to care for JONATHAN. Also appointed executrix, to pay debts, legacies, funeral and probate expenses. If she omits to prove the will within 5 months of testator's death, then daughter DOROTHY to be executrix. Wife MARTHA to be bound to Mr WICKS of Erwarton, should she remarry, to pay legacies to son JONATHAN when 21. Witnesses: WILLIAM PUT, MARY ANDREWS, BENJAMIN BURROUGHS. Pr. at Ipswich 4 Nov. 1631.

R(W) THOMAS DUKE of Benhall, esquire. 12 April 1630 (414)

To nephew EDWARD DUKE, esq., all lands in Orford, and Benhall. To niece JUDITH HASSETT £25, and nephew EDWARD HASSETT £10. To goddaughter ANNE GLOVER, daughter of WILLIAM GLOVER esq., £5 in 6 months of testator's death -- to be paid by executor after he has received a debt of £400 due to testator from testator's nephew SAMUEL HASSETT. Residue of goods to nephew EDWARD DUKE, appointed sole executor. Witnesses: JOHN BOTOLPH, WILLIAM DAMART. Pr. at Ipswich 8 Aug. 1631.

R(W) JANE CORBRIDGE of Ipswich St. Peter's (N). September 1631 (415)

To daughter LYDIA CORBRIDGE all goods, chattels. Care and education of testator's child vested in kinsman JOHN COLE. Witnesses: EMMANUEL SORREL, EDWARD GOTT, jnr. Probate granted to JOHN COLE at Ipswich 22 Sept. 1631.

R(W) ANN COCK of Ipswich, widow. 19 August 1631 (416)

Widow of RICHARD COCK of Ipswich, gent. To son JOHN, appointed executor, messuage where she lives, bought from Mr FROBISHER, with all household stuff, to pay debts, legacies, funeral, probate expenses. To Mr SAMUEL WARD, preacher of Ipswich, 20s.; and Mr REYNER, minister of St. Mary the Tower, Ipswich 20s. To Mr FENTON 10s.; Mr SMART 10s.; Mr HUBBERD 10s.; Mr BERD 10s.; and Mr FOSTER the minister of St. Matthew's parish Ipswich 10s. To the poor of Ipswich £5, namely 20s. to St. Peter, 20s. to St. Matthew, and the £3 remaining to be split between the remaining parishes. To JOHN COCK's three children, DOROTHY, ANNE & JOHN £3 each when 14. To granddaughter ELIZABETH, daughter of son GEORGE, a great silver salt, a little silver and gilt salt with a silver beaker, a great beer cup of silver, a wine cup of silver, all of which GEORGE borrowed from testator, and now must give to his daughter, if he wants God's blessing, and testator's blessing. To daughter PRISCILLA MOYSEY's three children -- WILLIAM £10, PRISCILLA £20 and JOHN £20 when 14, with benefit of survivorship. To daughters REBECCA & ALICE COCK £30 each, in 1 yr. of testator's death. To LYDIA PIGGE, wife of HENRY PIGGE, £50 in 1 yr. of testator's death. To brother SAMUEL KNAPP £5 for a mourning gown. To sisters SALLEY, CARTER, & GRIMSHAW £3 each for a mourning gown. To ABRAHAM BRECHEN, sister's son, 40s., and to his sister SARAH 40s. To daughters REBECCA & ALICE COCK all clothes, and wearing apparel. To daughter PRISCILLA coach and all furniture relating to it. To son GEORGE £3 to buy a cloak. To sons-in-law LIONEL SHERWOOD, GEORGE KING, & WILLIAM MOYSEY £3 each to buy cloaks. To daughter PRISCILLA MOYSEY, & REBECCA COCK £3, and to daughter LYDIA PIGG £3. To son-in-law HENRY PIGGE £3 to buy a cloak. To daughter-in-law DOROTHY COCK £3 to buy a cloak. To sister PRISCILLA JOHNSON £3 to buy a cloak. To son JOHN COCK's wife 20s. Witnesses: BENJAMIN SOLLEY, ROBERT HAMBY, GEORGE GARDINER. Pr. at Ipswich 22 Sept. 1631.

R(W) ROBERT CANDLER the elder of Alderton, yeoman. 22 May 1631 (417)

Sick. To brother ROBERT's son, £30 -- £20 within 1 yr. of testator's death, and a further £10 in 2 yrs.; also a further £10 to be paid him on the death of his father. To FRANCIS PARKER £20 in 1 yr. of testator's death, provided he pay RICHARD OSBORNE £5 when he reach 24. To RICHARD OSBORNE £10 when 24. To ELIZABETH CATTEN, daughter of THOMAS CATTEN £10 in 1 yr. of testator's death. To son-in-law ROGER FOX £5 in 1 yr. of testator's death. To nieces, MARY CANDLER £5 in one year, and £5 to be held for her by her father, ALICE CANDLER 50s. in one yr., and 50s. to be held for her by her father, and AGNES CANDLER 50s. in 1 yr., and 50s. to be held for her by her father. To WILLIAM CANDLER £20 to pay legacies. To ANNE BOWINGE, maid servant £10 in 1 yr. of testator's death. To servant AGNES REVET 40s. within one year of testator's death. To servant THOMAS BACON 40s. when 20. To ROBERT SAY 40s. for making the will. Residue to testator's brother's son THOMAS CANDLER, and to testator's wife ANNE, to be equally divided, for payment of debts, legacies, funeral and probate expenses, they to be joint executors, but if wife refuse executorship, then THOMAS to be sole executor, and to pay testator's wife £220 in consideration of an obligation of £400 between testator and his father-in-law CHARLES ALLEN. ROBERT SAY supervisor. Witnesses: CHARLES ALLEN, snr., ROBERT SAY, WILLIAM BETTS. Pr. at Ipswich 30 July 1631.

R(W) HENRY BLUDD of Orford, yeoman. 16 April 1631 (418)

To the children of THOMAS CLARKE of Westleton, yeoman, £5 to be equally divided between them. To wife MARGERY £40. To godson RICHARD CURTIS, of Darsham 20s.; to his godson ALEXANDER EASTHALL, 20s.; to godson ROBERT GLOVER 20s. To the child of the Widow COOKE of Orford, which is the testator's godchild, 20s. To each of his servants presently living with the testator 20s. To THOMAS BOND of Orford 10s. To the poor of Orford 20s. To his sister's children, JOHN PACEY & ANTHONY KING £40 each. To sister MARGARET HARVEY 20s.; and to sister ANNE living in Framlingham 20s. Residue of estate to go to ROBERT GRIGGS & wife ANNE, and their children. THOMAS CLARKE of Westleton appointed sole executor to pay debts, legacies, funeral charges. Witnesses: HENRY WRIGHT, JAMES CORDY. Pr. at Yoxford 2 Nov. 1631.

R(W) EDMUND BEAST of Badley, yeoman. 30 May 1631 (419)

Weak in body. To wife MARGARET, all lands, both freehold and copyhold in Badley. To brother JOHN BEAST 20s. To EDMUND BEAST, son of testator's brother THOMAS 20s. To the children of THOMAS BEAST, his brother, £12 to be equally divided between them, viz. THOMAS, ROBERT, JOHN, ELIZABETH, ALICE, & MARY BEAST 40s. each. To the children of MARY KEEBLE, sister of testator, £12 to be equally divided, viz. STEPHEN, EDMUND, MARY, ELIZABETH, MARTHA, & ANN, 40s. each. That all these nephews and nieces to receive their legacy when they reach 21; also benefit of survivorship. To kinswoman BILTHA BEAST 40s. To godchild MARTHA FELGATE 20s. Residue of estate to wife MARGARET; she to be sole executrix. Uncle of testator RICHARD BEAST to be supervisor. Witnesses: JOHN RIVERS, EDMUND PISSEY, JOHN ROE, JAMES ROE, junior. Pr. at Ipswich 10 Oct. 1631.

R(W) ANN BIRD, widow. 3 June 1631 (420)

Weak. To kinsman WILLIAM FOWLER, one bed as it stands with one feather bed and feather pillow, one pillow beere, one pair sheets, 2 blankets, 1 green rug, 4 curtains and rods; one settle; 2 Dansk chests; 1 keep; 1 great brass pot; 1 great kettle; 1 iron dripping pan with cleaver; 2 pewter platters; 2 fruit dishes; 2 porringers; 2 saucers; 1 green chair; 3 buffet stools; 1 form; 1 silver cup. To kinsman HENRY BODMAN, 1 feather bed, and 1 £6 bond due to the testator by the said HENRY BODMAN, of which testator has only received 24s. To sister MARY HART, 40s. to remain with Goodman STUDD, malster, for him to pay to the said MARY whenever need arise. To kinsman WILLIAM FOWLER, 1 livery bed, 1 feather bed, 1 feather bolster, 2 blanketts, 1 pair sheets, 1 coverlet, 2 stools, 1 chair, 1 best kettle, 1 brass candlestick, 2 pewter platters, 2 porringers, 2 saucers, 1 box; WILLIAM FOWLER to take these and to deliver the same to BRIDGET HART, kinswoman of testator -- she to have the use of them. To kinswoman ELIZABETH HART, 1 trundle bed, 1 of the best feather beds in the chamber, 1 feather bolster, 2 blankets, 1 coverlet, 1 pair sheets, 2 pewter platters, 2 saucers, 1 little form, and 1 buffet stool. To kinswoman MARGARET HART, 1 livery bed, a feather bed and a feather bolster, 1 pair of sheets, 2 blankets, 1 coverlet, 1 little brass pot, a little buffet stool, 2 pewter platters, 2 porringers, 2 saucers. To kinswoman ELIZABETH BODMAN, 1 green birded coverlet of the best of the two, 1 pair sheets, pair of blankets, 1 little table with leaves to turn up, 1 long table and form, 1 chair to turn up, 1 middle sized kettle, 2 pewter platters, 2 fruit dishes. Witnesses: THOMAS WHITING, WILLIAM GRYMWOOD (X), HENRY BODMAN. WILLIAM FOWLER appointed sole executor to pay debts and funeral expenses. Pr. at Ipswich 12 Oct. 1631.

R(W) ROBERT BROCK of Stradbroke, cordwainer. 29 July 1631 (421)

To wife BLANDINA and her heirs, tenement in Stradbroke, where testator's son-in-law FRANCIS SPARKE, lives, with all pertaining to the same. Also to wife all goods, implements etc., to pay debts and funeral expenses. She to be sole executrix. Witnesses: FRANCIS GODFREY, SIMON BROCK (X). Pr. at Stradbroke 9 Aug. 1631.

R(W) ANN BUGG of Barking, widow (N). 1628 (422)

Sick. To son FRANCIS BUGG all goods which were her husband's JOHN BUGG; also all other goods etc., he to pay debts and funeral expenses. Witnesses: EDWARD TURNER, FRANCIS DAVIE. Probate granted to FRANCIS BUGG 20 July 1631.

R(W) THOMAS BITTON of Saxmundham, joiner. 27 July 1631 (423)

Sick. To wife ANNE, all house, lands in Saxmundham, recently purchased from JOHN RACKHAM, now occupied by ROBERT CARTER & RICHARD GUNER. ANNE to hold for life, then to be equally divided between testator's sons THOMAS & JOHN BITTON, and their heirs, provided they pay to testator's two daughters ANNE & SARA BITTON, £10 within 2 years of the sons inheriting the land -- namely £5 to each daughter. To son THOMAS £10 -- viz. £5 when 24, and the further £5 when 26. To son JOHN £5 to be paid when he reach 24. To daughter ANN £5 when she reach 21. To daughter SARA £5 when she reach 21. With benefit of survivorship; further proviso, that if THOMAS or JOHN refuse to pay these legacies, then power to enter lands, and hold until full payment of legacy. To wife ANN residue of movables etc., in order to pay debts and funeral expenses etc. She to be sole executrix. Witnesses: DANIEL SHEPPERD, THOMAS ALDUS, ROBERT REEVE. Pr. at Saxmundham 19 Sept. 1631.

R(W) MARY BLOYS of Ipswich. 16 June 1631 (424)

Stating that the testator is daughter of WILLIAM BLOYSE, deceased, portman of Ipswich. Executor to pay testator's mother Mrs FRANCES BLOYSE, £20 a year in two equal payments on feast days of Lady Day and Michaelmas. To nephew WILLIAM BLOYSE £100 when 20. To nephew ANTHONY BLOYS £100 when 20. To nephew THOMAS BLOYS £100 when 20. To niece and goddaughter ABIGAIL BLOYS £150 when 20; 7 spoons, all apparel and linen, excepting the mohair petticoat and 6 handkerchiefs which are to go to the wife of NATHANIEL STUART who is also to receive 10s. To brothers JOHN HODGES, & GEORGE DOWNING a gold ring value 40s. each. To sister DORCAS DOWNING £10 payable within 1 yr. of testator's death. To sisters CICELY BLOYS & ABIGAIL HODGES, all things in the closet, and all ready money; sister HODGES to have the silver can. To the preacher for Ipswich, Mr SAMUEL WARD £3. To NATHANIEL STUART, minister for St. Nicholas parish, Ipswich £5. To the poor of St. Nicholas Ipswich, 40s.; poor of Grundisburgh 40s. To RALPH BLOYS, MARY DAVY widow, ABIGAIL SWITTMAN, JUDITH HAYWARD 20s. each, and to ROBERT CLIFFORD 10s. To ABIGAIL POTTER 40s.; and to MARY LEAKE 30s. on her 15th birthday. To SUSANNA BADDESON 20s. Residue of estate, once debts, legacies, funeral charges met, to brother WILLIAM BLOYS; he to be sole executor. Witnesses: [not given]. Pr. at Ipswich 24 Sept. 1631.

R. CHRISTOPHER ALDERMAN of St. Nicholas Ipswich. (425)
4 September 1624

Sick. To the poor of St. Nicholas, Ipswich 10s., paid at the discretion of the minister. To wife SARA, the house where testator lives, with its appurtenances, for life; if the child she carries is a boy, he to inherit this tenement on SARA's death. To wife SARA, house called the Wodhouse, with all its furniture, in St. Nicholas parish, for life, provided she keep it in good repair; then to pass to boy child. Proviso that if unborn child be female, then on death of mother, child and testator's other daughter SARA to have both the houses. If the child be a boy and thus inherits both houses, son to pay his sister £80 when she reach 21. To wife SARA, customary land where MATTHEW MARTIN lives in St. Nicholas parish Ipswich, for life; she to maintain same in good repair. On her death this tenement to go to testator's daughter SARA, provided she pay to the unborn child, if it be female, £20 within 3 years of testator's wife's decease. To daughter SARA £40 when 21. To the unborn child, if female, £40 when 21. To Mr STUART, preacher at St. Nicholas 20s. within 3 months of testator's death. To wife SARA, residue of goods, movables, household goods etc., she to be sole executrix, paying debts, legacies, funeral charges. Brother JOHN ALDERMAN, to have £5, and testator's best suit; he to be supervisor of will together with testator's uncle THOMAS HAILE. Witnesses: THOMAS HAILES, JOHN BRAND, JOHN GRYMWADE. Pr. at Ipswich 13 Aug. 1631.

R(W) ELIZABETH WHAITES of Bungay, widow. 19 June 1631 (426)

Weak. To daughter ELIZABETH EDMUNDS, £6 within 6 months of testator's decease. To grandchild THOMAS EDMUNDS £3 when reaches 21. To grandchild WILLIAM EDMUNDS £3 when 21; proviso that if either grandchild die before 21, then his legacy to revert to mother ELIZABETH EDMUNDS. To daughter JOAN HOW, £3. To grandchildren ELIZABETH, JOAN, & ADRY HOWE £3 each when 16, with benefit of survivorship. To JOHN HOW grandchild, 20s. To daughter SARA HOWE, £5 within 2 years of testator's death; also £5 worth of household stuff to be delivered to her within 6 months of testator's death. To grandchild ELIZABETH CURTIS, £6 when 21; also 1 bedstead with a feather bed 2 bolsters, 2 pillows, 2 pillow beers, 2 pair sheets, 2 blankets, coverlet, pair of curtains; kettle, pewter, best gown and petticoat, half wearing linen. To grandchild THOMAS CURTIS 40s. within 6 months. To son THOMAS WHAITES all household goods unbequeathed, all bills, bonds, money; he to be sole executor, and pay bills, funeral charges, and legacies. Witnesses: JEREMIAH AGER, ANN DEBIDGE (X) and me NICHOLAS SAYER. Pr. at Beccles 7 July 1631.

R(W) JOHN WILTON of Shotley (N). 21 April 1631 (427)

To his two children JOHN & MARY WILTON £5 each. Wife MARY appointed executrix. Witnesses: ROBERT FULLER (X), CHRISTOPHER WILTON (X). Pr. at Ipswich 9 May 1631.

R(W) WILLIAM WEBB of Ipswich, tailor. 10 May 1631 (428)

Sick, but with about £24 in money to dispose of. Friend ROBERT HAMBY of Ipswich gent., appointed executor, and he to have the £24 and to use it to provide for testator's sister RACHEL, wife of ARNALD SIMPSON of Ipswich, tailor, and also for testator's nephew EDWARD EADE of Ipswich, according to his discretion. To nephew EDWARD EADE, one third of money in order to bind him apprentice -- the executor to hold this third in trust for EDWARD until he reach 24 and to put the said sum of money out to obtain the best interest thereon, in order to benefit the said EDWARD. To sister remaining amount of money, she to receive the same whenever need arise. To executor, 42 chisels, all patterns, until such time as EDWARD EADE reach 24, then to pass them on to him. Executor to sell stock of linen, wool, and clothes, in order to pay funeral charges. Witnesses: JOHN ALDUS, ANN BREND, NICHOLAS SANDERS. Pr. at Ipswich 7 July 1631.

R(W) JOHN WRIGHT of Shotley, husbandman. 7 March 1631 (429)

Sick. To the poor of Shotley 10s. To wife RACHEL, all the things she brought, and £36 more. To kinswoman ELIZABETH STARLING, wife of RICHARD STARLING of Wherstead, £10 within one year of testator's death. To his brother's daughter ANN STAFF, wife of ROBERT STAFF of East Bergholt, £4 in one year of testator's death. To brother ISAAC WRIGHT, of Falkenham, £4 within 1 yr. of testator's death. To the children of his brother BENJAMIN WRIGHT, namely BENJAMIN, MARGARET, & ELIZABETH WRIGHT 30s. each within 1 yr. of testator's death. To servant THOMAS MYLES 20s. when he reach 24. Testator forgives to GEORGE SMITH, servant, all that SMITH owes him, and gives a further £4. To JOHN & THOMAS WRIGHT, sons of testator's brother THOMAS WRIGHT 40s. each in 1 year of testator's death. To EDWARD WRIGHT of Wherstead, his brother's son, 40s. within 1 yr. of testator's death. ISAAC WRIGHT of Falkenham (brother) and PHILIP WRIGHT of Wherstead (nephew) are appointed joint executors. Witnesses: THOMAS CARTER, GEORGE SMITH (X). Pr. at Ipswich 9 May 1631.

R(W) LAURENCE WINCOPP of Blythburgh, yeoman. [no date] (430)

Sick. To the poor of Blythburgh 40s.; poor of Walberswick 30s.; poor of Westleton 10s.; poor of Dunwich 10s.; poor of Wenhaston 10s.; poor of Thorington 3s. 4d. To wife ROSE £30 within 1 year of testator's death; also 2 milk cows or £10 to be delivered or paid to her at the Michaelmas next after testator's death. Executors also to board ROSE and allow her a convenient room or chamber in which to lodge; wife also to receive £7 p.a. payable out of the Gillingham All Saints and Gillingham St. Mary's lands, in lieu of dower. To son RICHARD WINCOPP all lands in Gillingham All Sts., and Gillingham St. Mary. To sons RICHARD & WILLIAM WINCOPP, two leases -- one made between testator and Sir ROBERT BROOKE, and one made between testator and Lady CLEERE. To son LAURENCE WINCOPP £260 when he reach 21. Proviso that if LAURENCE die before inheriting said sum, then executor to pay out of this £260 the sum of £60 to testator's daughter ALICE, and the remaining £200 to be equally distributed between children by executor. Proviso that executor also to bring up and maintain LAURENCE WINCOPP, keeping him at school until he is able to read and write sufficiently well and to keep him until he reaches 21. To son LAURENCE WINCOPP one feather bed or £3 when he reach 21. To daughter ALICE WINCOPP £110 when she reaches 21 or on her marriage, whichever occurs first. If she dies before inheriting, then executor to divide the legacy equally between testator's sons then living. To daughter ALICE, one feather bed or £3 when 21; also one desk that was sometimes her mother's on the death of the testator. To wife's daughter REBECCA CHAPMAN £10 when 21. To his three menservants 10s. each, provided they serve out their terms with the testator's executor. To his three woman servants 6s. 8d. each provided they serve out their terms with the testator's executor. To his shepherd JOHN MILLER the 20s. which MILLER owes the testator. To THOMAS MILLER, shepherd's son, 10s. due on St. James's day, next after testator's death. Residue of goods to sons RICHARD & WILLIAM WINCOPP to be equally divided between them, they to be joint executors, and to pay debts, funeral charges. Witnesses: BRUCE WARD, THOMAS NEALE. Probate granted to RICHARD WINCOPP at Yoxford on 3 June 1631, and to WILLIAM WINCOPP at Yoxford on 21 June 1631.

R(W) WILLIAM WRIGHT of Dennington, husbandman. (431)
[blank] October 1630

To be buried in Dennington. To son RICHARD, all goods, household stuff. To daughter-in-law ANNE BOOTEMAN, provided she take care of testator during the rest of his life, feather bed on the hall chamber, feather bolster, pillow, coverlet, pair of blankets, the old straw bed with a mat, line and settle belonging to it. If she fail in the care of testator, then legacy to go to RICHARD. Residue of goods to be divided into three parts -- one part to go to son RICHARD, one part to daughter-in-law ANNE, and one part to MARY BOOTEMAN. Benefit of survivorship. Witnesses: EDWARD MOLTON, FRANCIS BROWNING. ANNE BOOTEMAN appointed executrix. Pr. at Wickham 6 June 1631.

R(W) THOMAS WOLNOUGH junior, of Mendham. 1 May 1629 (432)

To be buried at Mendham. For the repair of Mendham church 12d. To father THOMAS WOLNOUGH, all goods and chattels; he to be sole executor, to pay debts, funeral expenses. Witnesses: THOMAS WOLNOUGH, SUSAN TRENDELL, ABIGAIL CLOPPATHE. Pr. at Beccles 2 July 1631.

R(W) ROBERT TALBOT of Whitton (N). [no date] (433)

To FRANCES WAKE, all goods, she to be executrix. Witnesses: JOHN ELLIOTT, & wife ANNE, RICHARD CROWE. Pr. at Ipswich 7 July

1631.

R(W) JANE SETTELL of Pakefield (N). [no date] (434)

To ROBERT STEDMAN all her goods. Witnesses: ELIZABETH CLARK, THOMAZINE REDE, widow. Probate granted to ROBERT STEDDMAN at Beccles 14 June 1631.

R(W) MATTHEW SWAN of Kessingland, yeoman. 10 May 1631 (435)

To his youngest daughters ELIZABETH & BRIDGETT £50 each when they reach 21 or on the day of their marriage, whichever happens first; benefit of survivorship. To wife's brother ROBERT EDWARDS £5. To wife's sister ELIZABETH EDWARDS 20s. To sister ALICE CULLINGFORD 20s. To MATTHEW SWAN and GEORGE BELWARD, kinsmen, 10s. The house and lands mortgaged to the testator by WILLIAM BRAME to be redeemed, and the money given to testator's wife BRIDGET: if the mortgage is not redeemed, then BRIDGET to have the use of the property for her lifetime, and then the property to pass to testator's daughters ELIZABETH & BRIDGET. To eldest daughter WATTSON, £15 payable within 2 years of testator's death, provided that she then rest content and does not make any claim to testator's estate. If she contest any part of the will then her legacy to be null and void. Residue of goods, household implements etc. to wife BRIDGET, appointed executor, together with testator's brother-in-law ROBERT EDWARDS. Witnesses: GILBERT CORKER, CIPRIAN HULLOCK, ALICE CORKER. Pr. at Beccles 29 June 1631.

R(W) THOMAS SCOTT of Bucklesham, yeoman. 12 May 1631 (436)

Sick and weak. To eldest son THOMAS SCOTT, 1 tenement in Kirton, 6 acres of which is wood, now occupied by WILLIAM MILNER. Also 1 tenement in Bucklesham, from which tenement testator's wife ELIZABETH has a jointure during her lifetime. To son WILLIAM SCOTT tenement in Waldringfield, Newbourne and Henly. To son ROBERT SCOTT, tenement in Swilland, late TURNER'S & JAQUES. To son CHRISTOPHER SCOTT tenement in Trimley St. Martin, lately purchased from THOMAS PITT: he to receive this tenement together with tenement in Ipswich St. Lawrenc, late purchased from SIMON & SAMUEL TUNELL now occupied by one CHIRCH, when he reaches 21. To his youngest son JOHN £100 when he reaches 21. To daughter ELIZABETH tenement in Bucklesham, late purchased from ANDREW COCK & ROBERT MAULSTER, when she reaches the age of 21. Benefit of survivorship to his children with regard to their legacies. To son THOMAS the biggest pot, one silver spoon. To son WILLIAM middle sized pot, one silver spoon. To son ROBERT the other pot, one silver spoon. To son CHRISTOPHER one silver spoon. To son JOHN one silver spoon. To daughter ELIZABETH one silver spoon. Residue of household utensils, other implements to be equally divided between the testator's wife and children; wife to retain childrens portions until they reach their majority. To the poor of Bucklesham 20s. Residue of goods to wife ELIZABETH and son THOMAS, they to be executors, and to pay debts and funeral expenses. Executors to enter bond of £200 with testator's brother-in-law ROBERT ARMOND, who is appointed supervisor and is given 10s. for his trouble. Executors to allow no waste or to strip lands, and also executors to pay admission fines when CHRISTOPHER & ELIZABETH take up their lands. Executors also to maintain and educate the younger children of the testator. Witnesses: SIMON PETTIWARD, THOMAS YONGES (X), MARGARET BENNETT (X). Pr. at Ipswich 22 June 1631.

R(W) KATHERINE RAWLING of Frostenden, widow. 21 April 1631 (437)

To son JOHN RAWLING, one tipped pot, and a ring given to testator by her husband, when he reaches 21. Executor to buy a new bible and to give it to her son JOHN RAWLING within three months of testator's death. To servant MARIE STEEDMAN, gown, and the best say apron within three months of testator's death, provided MARIE be then 21. Residue of goods, chattels, debts, implements, once testator's debts and funeral expenses have been met, are to go to executor in order to maintain and provide for LUCY RAWLING, testator's late husband's aunt. If LUCY RAWLING die before all is wasted upon her upkeep, then the surplus to be parted between executor and testator's son JOHN RAWLING. If the said LUCY RAWLING outlive the money raised and require more, then testator's son JOHN is to allow to testator's executor the necessary money. JOHN GEORGE of Wrentham, kinsman, appointed sole executor; FRANCIS MORSE of Uggshall supervisor, he to have the tuition and guardianship of JOHN RAWLING and to choose him a trade; JOHN is required to be ruled and guided by the said supervisor. Witnesses: FRANCIS MORSE, THOMAS JONES, JOHN GEORGE of Frostenden. Pr. at Wrentham 7 June 1631.

R(W) THOMAS ROE of Dallinghoo (N). [no date] (438)

To JOHN ROE, the son of JOHN ROE his brother £80; residue to his (testator's) brother JOHN. Brother JOHN ROE to be sole executor. Witnesses: WILLIAM RUSSELL, CHRISTIAN ROE, jnr., THOMAS BUCK, CHRISTIAN ROE, snr. Pr. at Wickham Market 23 June 1631.

R(W) BENJAMIN ROBLETT of Wantisden, yeoman. 6 June 1631 (439)

Sick. To wife MARGARET, for life, all lands and tenements in Wantisden; these to pass on her death to testator's son BENJAMIN and heirs for ever, provided that BENJAMIN, within 2 yrs. of MARGARET's death, pays to testator's daughter MARIAN £50 -- power for her to enter and hold the said property if arrears or default until the default satisfied. Under the will of JOHN TALBOT late of Wantisden, TALBOT's lands were to be sold and out of the money raised from the sale £300 was to be used to benefit MARY the wife of TALBOT's son JOHN and then to benefit her children by his son. Now BENJAMIN ROBLETT was executor for this will and so he now instructs his executor to pay to the said MARY the profits that arise from the said £300, and after her death to pay the same £300 to her children. Executor to become bond to WILLIAM BAKER of Tunstal and ROBERT SMITH the younger of Wickham Market within 3 months of testator's death in £500 to perform this will. Residue of goods, once debts and funeral expenses met, to go to executrix, who is to be MARGARET ROBLETT, testator's wife. If she refuse the bond or she die before this will is proved then testator's brother-in-law EDWARD TALBOT is to be executor. Witnesses: WILLIAM BAKER, ROBERT SMITH, JOHN KING, THOMAS ROBLETT. Pr. at Wantisden 7 June 1631.

R(W) THOMAS ROWE of Ipswich St. Peter (N). [no date] (440)

To son JOHN one of the feather beds whereon he lay, and all the furniture therof as it stands. To son WILLIAM a bed upon the chamber of his house as it stands, and his keep in the hall. To daughter ELIZABETH one featherbed. Witnesses: THOMAS GIBSON & BEATRICE his wife. Probate granted to HELEN ROWE, widow of testator, at Ipswich 23 June 1631.

R(W) MICHAEL QUINTYN of Ipswich, malster. 20 May 1631 (441)

Weak. To son SAMUEL £250 when he reach 21, also the tenement in Stoke with appurtenances, now occupied by JOHN WYNELL. Proviso that if SAMUEL die before inheriting then the tenement to pass to FERDINAND QUINTYN, son of FERDINAND QUINTYN, and his heirs; the money to be shared out between FERDINAND, ANN, FRANCES, & RICHARD QUINTYN -- but only £20 each, when they reach 21. To wife JOAN all household stuff. To brother FERDINAND QUINTYN £10 within 6 months of testator's death; he to be supervisor. Wife JOAN QUINTYN appointed executrix. Witnesses: WILLIAM LOCKWOOD, JOHN LASTER, FERDINAND QUINTYN. Pr. at Ipswich 7 June 1631.

R(W) GEORGE PHILLIPS of Debenham, yeoman. [no date] (442)

To youngest son ISAAC PHILIPS, copyhold messuage and tenement called Woodwards containing 3 1/2 acres, purchased of one WILLIAM MORPHELL and LUKE HAYLE in Framsden, now occupied by Widow GODBOLD and partly by ROBERT BLOMEFIELD. Also one piece of copyhold land held of Butly manor called Overdowe or Nights close in Debenham, now occupied by JAMES BORNE. To wife ANNE for life, and then to pass to sons JAMES & ROBERT, messuage and tenement in Debenham where JAMES BORNE, shoemaker, now lives, containing three lower rooms, three upper rooms with a little yard paled out at the east end therof with every their appurtenances now or late part of PHILIP TRUND's tenement late purchased of GEORGE TOVELL & SIMON JEFFRY. Also the copyhold close called Stevens, containing 7 acres in Debenham held of the manor of Wolston hall. To wife ANN one cow, the best she can choose out of all the cattle, within 1 month of testator's decease. There to be 2 penny doles to be distributed -- both at burial to the poor people that come. Executor to sell all outward goods, chattels not already given, in order to meet funeral expenses and debts. If not sufficient then executor to sell such inward movables to meet the shortfall, but no more than is necessary to be sold. Residue to be equally divided within 3 months by the executor amongst testator's children then living, including sons JAMES & NICHOLAS. These to be executors and to receive 40s. each. Witnesses: WILLIAM BUTTS, WILLIAM SCROTTON, JAMES SCROTTON. Pr. at Ipswich 7 June 1631.

R(W) WILLIAM PODD of Tattingstone (N). [no date] (443)

To wife JUDITH all his goods, but if she remarry, then she must give testator's son JOHN half of his estate, and JUDITH must enter into a bond with THOMAS SORRELL before her remarriage for the payment of the full value therof when JOHN reach 21. Should she refuse the bond then THOMAS SORRELL to take goods devised to wife, to hold them for the use of testator's son. Witnesses: THOMAS SORRELL, JAMES GRENE, MARIE TAYLOR. Probate granted to JUDITH PODD at Ipswich 9 May 1631.

R(W) THOMAS NOBLE of Theberton, husbandman. 30 April 1631 (444)

All goods and chattels, both unmovable and movable, to be valued by JOHN INGHAM, GODFREY IRELAND, ROBERT REEVE of Theberton, and then all to be sold by executor and the money thus arising to be divided equally -- 1/2 to GEORGE FERMLY of Kelshall, gent. he to hold this half until testator's son THOMAS NOBLE reach 21, the said sum then to be handed over by GEORGE FERMLY to THOMAS NOBLE. The other 1/2 to go to THOMAS LOUD of Theberton, yeoman, to hold until PHILLIPA NOBLE testator's daughter, reach 21 or is married; the said THOMAS LOUD to then hand over the money to testator's daughter. Payment of debts, and funeral expenses to be first deducted from the money. Also to be deducted the cost of educating testator's two children. Further that THOMAS NOBLE (testator's son) is to be put out as apprentice with some honest man to the occupation of some handy craft or trade. Proviso that if THOMAS NOBLE die then PHILLIPA NOBLE to receive when 21 or on the day of her marriage the full sums of money from both GEORGE FERMLY & THOMAS LOUD. If both children die before inheriting, then their legacies to go to ROBERT NOBLE, testator's brother within 4 months of the death of testator's surviving child. PHILLIPA NOBLE to be educated and brought up by THOMAS LOUD of Theberton until she be of age to provide for herself. GEORGE FERMLY & THOMAS LOUD appointed executors. Witnesses: SIBBELL BACKER (X), ANNE PERSE (X), ROBERT MOWER (X). Pr. at Yoxford 21 June 1631.

R(W) THOMAS MARSH of Coddenham, husbandman. 25 March 1631 (445)

Sick. Messuage in Ringshall with house and lands, now occupied by WILLIAM BALLDRY, to be sold by testator's friend JOHN BROWNING of Coddenham in order to pay testator debts. After these met then £40 to be put out for the best profit, on the advice of JOHN BROWNING, for the benefit of testator's daughter ALICE MARSH, the which £40 is to be given to the said ALICE when she reach 18. Until then the profit arising from the £40 is to go to testator's wife in order to maintain and bring up the said ALICE MARSH. Residue of money, after deducting the above £40, to go to testator's wife ALICE together with all household goods etc. Proviso that if the land in Ringshall does not reach £60, then the land is not to be sold, but it is to remain with testator wife ALICE until testator's daughter reach 21, in order to use the profits arising from the land in order to pay debts, and to maintain testator's daughter. When daughter ALICE MARSH becomes 21 she to inherit the land in Ringshall. Executors to be JOHN BROWNING & ALICE MARSH, wife of testator. Witnesses: BASSINGBOURNE COOPER (X), GEORGE GOSSE. Pr. at Ipswich 9 April 1631.

R(W) ROBERT LAMBERT of Tattingstone, husbandman. (446)
9 June 1630

Very sick. To eldest son ROBERT, tenement in Sutton with orchards and gardens, on the death of testator's wife ELIZABETH, she to hold it for her life. Provided that ROBERT on his inheriting the said tenement pays to testator's son WILLIAM, £5 -- power to WILLIAM to enter and hold the land if ROBERT unable to raise the £5, in which case WILLIAM to inherit the land and pay ROBERT £5. To eldest daughter MARY £3 within 1 year of testator's death; also to daughter JANE £3 in 3 years of testator's death; also to daughter ANNA £4 when she reaches 21, and to youngest daughter SARA £4 when 21. To wife's daughter ELLEN BEDALL 20s. within 6 years, and to wife's daughter ELIZABETH BEDALL 20s. within 7 years of testator's death. To sons WILLIAM & ROBERT 5s. each within 3 months. Residue of estate to wife ELIZABETH, appointed sole executor. Witnesses: GREGORY GOODWIN, AUGUSTINE STERNE, EDMUND WITHERS. Appointment of GREGORY GOODWIN of Tattingstone as supervisor. Pr. at Ipswich 9 May 1631.

R(W) MARY LAUNE of Wenhaston, widow. 23 May 1631 (447)

Sick. To kinswoman MARY WALES my little framed table and my buffet stool. To sister JULIE LAUN half the wood in the yard. To goddaughter MARY LAUN one pewter platter. To ANNE WALES one pewter platter. To kinsman LIONEL MURDOCK 5s. To kinsmen THOMAS LAUNE & REGINALD LAUNE 5s. To kinsman JOHN EADE of Baddingham the residue of the estate. to pay debts and funeral expenses; he to be executor. Witnesses: ALICE BUNDING (X), MARY LAUN (X), THOMAS LESLEY. Pr. at Yoxford 3 June 1631.

R(W) THOMAS KNAPP of Ipswich, merchant. 8 December 1630 (448)

To be buried in Ipswich St. Mary Quay. Executors to pay debts and funeral expenses, then to each grandchild ANNE KATTELIN THOMAS, JOHN, DANIEL, ELIZABETH, & MARY KNAPP £10, and to each great grandchild living on testator's death 5 marks each. To SAMUEL WARDE the town preacher of Ipswich £5, and he to preach a sermon on his funeral on the text of 2 Corinthians 5, 1. To JOHN ALLEN minister of St. Mary Quay 20s. To the poor of St. Mary Quay parish £10, to be distributed at the rate of 20s. a year on the feast day of St. Thomas the apostle in bread, as the executors think fit. Son ROBERT KNAPP, and grandchild JEREMY CATELIN appointed executors. Witness: EDMUND BARKER. Pr. at Ipswich 23 June 1631.

R(W) FRANCIS BALDWIN of Yoxford, plumber. 1 April 1631 (449)

To brother WILLIAM BALDWIN the great double gilt spoon. To sister BRIDGET CLERKE, wife of ROGER CLERKE, the best silver spoon. To sister ABIGAIL ALLEN, wife of JOHN ALLEN, the other silver spoon. To brother-in-law ROGER CLERKE, bellows, 2 vices, 2 hammers, grindstone and files, provided he pay to testator's mother AMY BALDWIN 10s. To mother AMY BALDWIN, residue of tools, lead, solder in order for her to pay his debts and funeral expenses; she to be executrix. Witnesses: THOMAS BLOCKE, THOMAS MILLER (X), AGNES FORDE (X). Pr. at Yoxford 3 June 1631.

R(W) HENRY KELLAM of Dennington (N). [no date] (450)

To eldest daughter MARY KELLAM a desk. To daughter ALICE CASBIE, the feather bed furnished as it stands, and chest with the linen in it. To son AUSTEN KELLAM all clothes. To grandchild DANIEL KELLAM 10s., or else the biggest kettle. To grandchild WILLIAM TOMSON my bible. To grandchild EZECHIEL TOMSON the new chest. To grandchild ALICE KELLAM a coffer, 2 pair sheets. To grandchild EZECHIEL TOMSON flock bed. To grandchild HENRY KELLAM cupboard table and testator's cooper's tools. To son ROBERT KELLAM, my lease; he to be sole executor. To son ROBERT KELLAM and daughter ALICE CASBIE, the residue of unbequeathed goods. Witnesses: ELIZABETH BOOTEMAN, wid., JOAN, wife of THOMAS KERRICH. Pr. at Yoxford 3 June 1631.

R. ROBERT KINGE of Martlesham, sailor. 14 July 1630 (451)

Well, but decided to make his will, a good thing 'especially for seafaring men which are always under the hand of God to undergo all chances by ill weather.' To wife MARGERY all goods, chattels; she to be sole executrix. Witnesses: ROBERT SCOTT, JOHN SMYTH. Pr. at Ipswich 9 May 1631.

R(W) ANN JOHNSON of Weybread, widow. 15 May 1631 (452)

All goods, and chattels to go to JOHN ADAMSON, GREGORY MEENE & SAMUEL BARBER of Weybread, for them to pay debts, and to bring up her children. Once these duties are discharged the surplus of the money from the goods which remain to be equally divided between the children who reach 21. If any of the executors named above, refuse the duties, then RICHARD JOHNSON of Huntingfield, shoemaker and JOHN MARKHAM of Fornsett of Norfolk, blacksmith, to be executors instead. Witnesses: JOHN THURLBY, clarke; JOHN BROWNE. Probate granted to GREGORY MEENE & SAMUAL BARBER 11 June 1631.

R(W) JOAN HAZELL of Bramford, widow. 13 May 1631 (453)

To eldest son THOMAS MAY 5s. within 1 month of testator's death. To son ROBERT MAY one bedstead, one featherbed, 2 bolsters, 1 coverlet, 2 blankets with appurtenances, save for 1 white linsey woollen blanket which is to go to goddaughter ANN WILLCOCKS of Bramford. To daughter MARY, wife of son ROBERT, 1 fustian pillow and one pillow case of the best sort; one holland apron the best of the four, and one laced handkerchief one holland kerchief marked with 2 M's, and a neckcloth. To grandchild GRACE BURROUGH one leather trunk. all the pewter, one kettle -- the biggest of the two; one skillet; a dutch wheel and a dutch reel; one little table 2 wine stools and a chair with a sagging bottom. To ELINOR WRIGHT, one cupboard, a bible, a warming pan, a wicker chair for her life, then to go to GRACE BURROUGH. To GRACE BURROUGH 2 pillows and 2 pillow cases. The rest of the linen to be equally divided amongst testator's daughters & sons MARY, ELIZABETH, EDMUND, ELINOR WRIGHT, & GRACE BURROUGHS -- MARY to have first choice of the best sheets. Residue of goods to go, with money, to testator's executor, to be used for the education of GRACE BURROUGH. ROBERT MAY of Claydon, testator's son, to be executor. Witnesses: JOHN SUCKERMAN, JOHN STILES, ROBERT MAY, SUSAN STILES (X). Probate granted to ROBERT MAY at Ipswich 7 June 1631.

R(W) ABRAHAM HELLOND of Melton, miller. 27 July 1630 (454)

Sick. To son ABRAHAM HELLOND, house and lands in Snape, copyhold held of the manor of Beckling in Snape, occupied by one GODDERD. Son to inherit these lands within 6 years after testator's death; rents and profits from these lands for the intervening 6 years to be used to provide for the education of testator's two daughters ELIZABETH & JUDITH. To son ABRAHAM 1 acre freehold in Farnham, with the same proviso. To daughters ELIZABETH & JUDITH £40 equally to be divided when they reach 18; until they reach 18 the said sum of £40 to be imployed and profits from it to be used to provide for their upbringing. Benefit of survivorship. All goods and movables to be sold by testator's executors in order to pay debts, also the money due to testator from THOMAS BURTON & PHILIP NEWMAN, also the money due next Lady Day (1631) from testator's tenant GOOD (£5 2s.) and from HENRY ASHLEY (£3 4s.)

due next Michaelmas. Executors to use all this money, after paying debts, to educate testator's two daughters. Memorandum: ABRAHAM HELLOND to have the copyhold land held from Mr BACON of Freston manor. THOMAS BURTON blacksmith, and wife KATHERINE to be executors. Witnesses: ROBERT HALLIFAX, JOHN SMYTH, script. Pr. at Wickham 21 April 1631.

R(W) EDWARD GOODING of Ipswich, gentleman. (455)
25 February 1630

Weak. To wife ABIGAIL, for life, houses in Ipswich, with all household stuff and all debts due to testator from wife's father HENRY GOULDINGHAM. To brother JOHN GOODING all houses in Ipswich, on death of testator's wife. To sister REBECCA HUMFREY £50 within 2 months of testator's death. To Mr TURNBULL, minister of St. Margaret's parish, 50s. To the poor of St. Margaret's 50s. To godson JONATHAN LONGWOOD son of JONATHAN LONGWOOD of Harwich, £5; this to be paid to JONATHAN LONGWOOD senior on testator's death, for him to hold for his said son when he reaches 21. To godson WILLIAM MAY, son of WILLIAM MAY of Harwich 40s.; this to be paid on testator's death to WILLIAM MAY the father, to hold for his son until he reach 21. To JOHN LAND the lieutenant of Landguard New Fort, my great sealed gold ring. Executors to pay legacies, debts, funeral expenses, and the residue to go to testator's wife ABIGAIL. Wife and brother-in-law HENRY HUMFRIE to be executors. Witnesses: WILLIAM THORNES, WILLIAM SEARLES. Pr. at Ipswich 29 March 1631.

R(W) JOHN FACEBROWNE of Earl Soham, yeoman. 9 June 1631 (456)

Weak. To brother WILLIAM FACEBROWNE, all copyhold land called Sparhawks in Earl Soham. If brother has no heir then land to go to kinsman JOHN FACEBROWNE. To wife ANN £5 annuity due to be paid in equal installments on Lady Day and Michaelmas, to be paid by either WILLIAM or JOHN out of the proceeds of the copyhold land. If they fail then wife to have the lands for life. To WILLIAM FACEBROWNE and his heirs, the yard called Tainterhooke yard in Framlingham. Also £20 payable within 1 year of testator's death. To sister ELIZABETH, wife of ROBERT HEMLEN £20 within 1 year of testator's death. To sister ANN FACEBROWNE £20 within 1 year of testator's death. To ROSE JEAMES, wife of WILLIAM JEAMES of Iken, 40s. in 1 year of testator's death. To ELIZABETH WIETH, daughter of GEORGE WIETH of Kenton, goddaughter of testator 20s. within 2 years of testator's death. To wife ANN £20 within 6 months of his death; one of his best cows at her own choice; one feather bed as it stands furnished; 3 pairs sheets; one board cloth -- the said bed sheets and board cloth at the choice of his wife. To the poor of Soham 13s. 4d. on his burial. To kinswoman ELIZABETH JOLLY 20s. within 18 months of his death. To ALICE WEBBER, daughter of JOHN WEBBER the younger, 10s. when 21. Residue to wife ANN, sister ELIZABETH, and sister ANN to be equally divided. Wife ANNE and ROBERT HEMLEN executors to pay debts, legacies, funeral expenses. Witnesses: THOMAS SALLOWS, jnr., and THOMAS SALLOWES senior. Pr. at Wickham 29 July 1631.

R(W) ISABELL DENNINGTON of Leiston, widow. (457)
25 January 1630

To eldest son THOMAS DENNINGTON 2 pewter dishes. To daughter MARY WEST, widow of WILLIAM WEST, residue of goods, movables etc., she to be sole executrix. ARNOLD DANFORD of Leiston, yeoman, supervisor, and to receive 5s. for his pains. Witnesses: REGINOLD WRIGHT, WILLIAM BELWARD, ENOCH GIRLING. Pr. at Yoxford 11 July 1631.

R(W) MARGERY FYNNIE of Ipswich. [no date] (458)

To cousin MARY WARNER, best petticoat and gown and hat, the bed linen, blankets, bolsters and coverlet, with the bedstead, and the chest at the bed's feet; one pewter platter and her uncle FYNNIE's chair; bellows, one pillow and pillow case; best coife and quarter with two napkins; one sheet. To MARGERY WARNER, red gown, hat, one red cloth petticoat, best waistcoat with the little smock; the finest of the two aprons; coife and quarter; one neckcloth; 1 pillow; 2 pillow cases; one box with a lock and key. To old THOMAS WARNER, testator's nephew, the bed above, the bolster, 1 blanket, coverlet with the bedstead; one pewter platter for my godson. To young THOMAS, the glass case, 2 pewter platters dishes, and the trammel. To HENRY WARNER of Orford, one dansk chest, one brass kettle, one ruff, one form, one white crock, one corset, one quarter. To brother EDGAR, cupboard and my cloak for his wife. To sister SMILES one new smock. To MARY HERETON a new red waistcoat. To ELIZABETH BUTLER my green stuff petticoat; one sheet. To JANE COLLIN the best smock. To ROBERT BROWNE the bed he lies on, 1 pillow; 1 sheet; 1 corset, and his mother's chair. To ANN WARNER the chest in the chamber. MARY WARNER to have residue of goods, and pay debts, whatever remains after the payment of debts and legacies to be equally divided between SUSAN EDGAR, BARBARA STILES & MARY HERRINGTON. Witnesses: RICHARD STUDD, THOMAS GIRLING, BARBARA STILES, MARY HERRINGTON, SUSAN EDGAR. Probate granted to MARY WARNER at Ipswich 7 June 1631. Memorandum: on the will are set down such debts as the testator did owe and money owing her viz. Owe Goodman BUCKELL 7s.; EDMUND DAVERON 6s.; CHRISTOPHER FRY 2s. 6d.; Mr BLUMFIELD, the draper 3s.; Goodman SHRUBS 1s.; Goodman BURTON 2s.; Mr ROUCE at Midsummer 15s.; Owed, Widow YOUNGS 10s.; Goodman GLEB 10s.; ADKINS 10s.; Goodman MESSE 17s.; Mr DAMERON 12s.; Widow WARD 1s. 4d.; Goodman MARHSALL 2s. 8d.; Goodman HALL, the butcher 8d.

R(W) THOMAS CORBOLD of Crowfield, yeoman. 27 April 1621 (459)

Sick. A true inventory of goods to be made in order to pay debts and funeral charges. Half residue to go to wife ALICE, and half to be equally divided between his children when they reach 21. Wife ALICE, and brother-in-law JOHN CLEMINGHAM appointed executors. Pr. at Ipswich 4 June 1631.

R(W) EDWARD CHANDLER of Reydon, husbandman. 26 May 1631 (460)

Weak. To daughter JOAN CHANDLER all household goods, chattels, etc. to pay debts and funeral charges, she to be executrix. Friend ROBERT TILLY of Sotherton to be supervisor and to receive 40s. for his pains. Witnesses: WILLIAM CHAPMAN (X), AUGUSTINE WARDE. Pr. at Yoxford 11 July 1631.

R(W) MARGARET COKE, widow. 7 April 1631 (461)

To son ROGER COKE, flock bed that is under my feather bed, and the flock bolster. To grandchild EDMUND COKE, my great bible. To cousin ESTHER DUNE best stuff gown. To Widow BROTHERTON, the grainy petticoat, best waistcoat, green apron. To son HENRY COKE residue of goods, he to be executor. To daughter-in-law ALICE, wife of HENRY COKE, stained petticoat. Witnesses: THOMAS FLAGGETT, FRANCIS MOORE, by me RICHARD BROMWELL. Pr. at Ipswich 7 June 1631.

R(W) RICHARD BUXTON of Denham, yeoman. 6 January 1630 (462)

To wife MARGARET, the lease of the house where they live, all household stuff therein, and all the cattle. To kinsman MOSES BUXTON 20s., and to kinsman RICHARD BUXTON 25s. To the five children of testator's brother JOHN £1 each. To the three children of WILLIAM BUXTON, son to my brother WILLIAM 20s. -- 6/8d. each. To three of the children of THOMAS BUXTON, son of my brother WILLIAM, called THOMAS, WILLIAM, & THOMASIN 6/8 each. To their sister ANN BUXTON, now my maidservant, 10s. To sister's son ABRAHAM CARTER, 20s; to her sister ESTHER 20s. To kinsman JOHN CLARKE, a debt of 20s. owed to the testator; also testator forgives him another old debt; also 10s. more. To kinsman WILLIAM CLARKE 20s. Testator is bound to THOMAS CLARKE, and the said THOMAS CLARKE owes £20 to the testator; now testator forgives £10 of the said £20, on condition that THOMAS CLARKE discharge the bond by which the testator is bound to him within one year of the testator's death; he is to pay to executrix of this will the outstanding £10 within one year; if he fail to do so then he must repay all £20. To kinswoman MARGERY CLARKE 30s.; to kinsman ROBERT HOLMES, testator's brother-in-law 20s., and to brother-in-law JOHN CRANE 20s. To kinsman PETER FEATE 20s.; to kinswoman JOSEPHENE BURGIS a debt of 50s. owed by her to the testator; to kinswoman MARY PURFROY, erstwhile my servant 20s.; and to kinswoman MARGARET FOWLSHAM 20s. To a servant who was employed by testator a long time ago FRANCIS EDWARDS 20s. To servant GILLIAN THURLOW 20s. To GEORGE SADD, JOHN IRELAND,

WILLIAM HOLLINGTON, 20s. -- 6/8d. each, being old servants whom I thought well of. To maidservant ELIZABETH PALMER 6s. 8d. All of these legacies to be paid within one year of testator's death, unless the recipient be under 21; he/she to wait till 21. 25s. to be laid out for the purchase of 5 bibles, to be bought for his five godchildren, they to have the bible as soon as they can read it -- to MOSES BUXTON, son of kinsman MOSES BUXTON; THOMAS CRANE, son of THOMAS CRANE my brother-in-law; JOHN CRANE, son of JOHN CRANE, my brother-in-law; ISAAC CARTER, son of ABRAHAM CARTER; MARY CLARKE, daughter of JOHN CLARKE. To the poor 30s. Wife to be executrix, and to have all his goods, pay debts, funeral charges. Witnesses: FRANCIS HOLMES, FRANCIS TILNEY. Note; the 6/8d. legacy to man RANDAL, has been erased, but executrix can give it to him, if he do and behave himself well as it becomes a servant as long as he shall remain to her service. Witnesses to this note: ROBERT HOLMES (X), FRANCIS TILNEY. Pr. at Yoxford 28 July 1631.

R(W) JOHN BROWNE alias PORTER of Sudbourne, yeoman. (463)
16 June 1631

Sick. To wife ELIZABETH, all lands in Sudbourne, with all goods, chattels, save for half the corn which WILLIAM HOLDING has sown to halve unto me -- this half to go to WILLIAM HOLDING. Wife ELIZABETH, appointed executrix, to pay debts, funeral expenses. Witnesses: ANTHONY CROSSE, JOHN MAY, THOMAS BOND. Pr. at Wickham 11 May 1631.

R(W) GEORGE BENNETT of Waldringfield. 10 May 1630 (464)

Sick; to be buried at Waldringfield. To wife ROSE, house and lands in Waldringfield for life; then she to appoint a friend to sell it for the good of their children. To son THOMAS £30 within 1 year of wife's death. To daughter ELIZABETH £30 in 1 yr. of wife's death. To daughter ROSE £40 in 1 yr. of wife's death. If not enough money is raised by the sale of the lands to meet these specific legacies, then the money to be equally divided between the three children. Benefit of survivorship. Movable goods to wife ROSE in order to meet debts, pay funeral expenses; she to be sole executrix. Witnesses: RICHARD ROSE, WILLIAM POOL (X). Pr. at Ipswich 9 May 1631.

R(W) MARTHA BRIGGS late of Ipswich (N). [blank] June 1631 (465)

To brother NATHANIEL BIRD of Ipswich her estate and part in messuage occupied by NATHANIEL BIRD & MARTHA BRIGGS in St. Peter's parish Ipswich. He to have movables. Witnesses: ABIGAIL CANSTON & SUSAN HUTCHENSON (X). Probate granted to NATHANIEL BIRD at Ipswich 7 July 1631.

R(W) JOHN BRINGLEY of Mendham, yeoman. 12 July 1631 (466)

Sick. Testator bound himself in a marriage settlement of 1 August 1627 to FRANCIS ALLDOUS, now testator's son-in-law, to confirm 8 acres land in Garboldisham or else its full value to the said FRANCIS ALLDOUS and his wife FRANCES -- the testator's daughter. Now testator's wife FRANCES to discharge this obligation by paying £40 to FRANCIS ALLDOUS at Mendlesham church porch within six months of testator's death. To son JAMES £10 on the next Christmas after testator's death. Wife to pay legacies, and to enjoy lands for her lifetime, then all to go to son JAMES. Proviso that if his wife FRANCES remarry then she to be bound to perform will. She to be executrix, and to receive £10 for her pains. Witnesses: THOMAS GOODBOLD, JOHN DEY, GRACE SIMPSON. Pr. at Beccles 20 July 1631.

R(W) NICHOLAS BARNES of Parham, taylor. 19 May 1631 (467)

To wife JOAN, for life, all lands and tenements, then on her death to go to daughter ELIZABETH. If she die without issue, then lands to be sold by executor to benefit the children of testator's brother-in-law JOHN & PETER SAWYER, to be equally divided between them. To wife JOAN all goods, chattels, but if she remarry before daughter ELIZABETH reach 21, then JOAN to pay daughter £30 on her 21st birthday. Wife JOAN, and brother-in-law WILLIAM SAWYER to be executors. Witnesses: ROBERT WARNER (X), WILLIAM SAWYER (X), EDMUND WHAYTES. Note: due from FRANCIS SCARLETT £4 2s.; HENRY BEART 28s.; JOHN SCARLETT 22/6; JOHN SCARLETT the elder 8s. Pr. at Wickham 6 June 1631.

R(W) WILLIAM BORRET the younger of Wilby, yeoman. (468)
2 July 1631

Infirm. To wife EM, new sealed bedstead on the parlour chamber furnished as it now stands; the other sealed bedstead there to be furnished with a feather bed, feather bolster, coverlet, pair of blankets, pair of pillows each a mat and line, 10 pair of sheets, 6 pillow cases, 2 long board cloths, 2 short ones, one dozen table napkins, 4 towels, 2 best chests, 2 desks, one long framed table in the parlour, one little framed table on the parlour chamber, 6 high buffet stools, 2 low ones; one great joined chair, 2 turned chairs, 4 of the best cushions; warming pan, fire pan, pair of tongues, pair of cob irons, 3 kettles; 3 skillets, 4 pewter dishes, 6 pewter porringers, 6 saucers, 2 pewter candlesticks, 2 pewter chamber pots, brass milk pan, little churn, one milk tub, 2 milk keelers, one busking tub, bolting hutch, 4 beer vessels; 1 frying pan, one roast iron, the best cart and one tumbrell with half the furniture belonging to them; one plough and its furniture, save for the collars, one pair of harrows; 3 milk cows and a horse called Buck, for ever. To have the use of a copper, the horsemill and cheese press and grindstone for life only -- these items then to go, with the house which wife also to enjoy for life, to testator's son

WILLIAM. To daughter DOROTHY £250 paid out of unbequeathed goods, to be paid by the executor within 2 years of testator's decease in the south porch of Wilby church. Wife EM to be executor, and to have all household stuff unbequeathed, all cattle, corn, hay, money, bonds, bills, towards payment of daughter DOROTHY's legacy, and to pay all debts, funeral and probate expenses. Wife to sell these goods to meet these charges, and if money raised is insufficient for payment of daughter's legacy, then EM to have the use and occupation of all freehold land and appurtenances not before given, provided she suffer/cause no waste, to use the rents and profits to meet costs and daughter's legacy. When these costs are met then the freehold land to go to son WILLIAM BORRETT. EM to be bound in £500 to will's supervisor to pay DOROTHY's legacy, within 20 days of testator's death. RICHARD REEVE to be supervisor and if wife fail in this bond, her legacies to be void, and to go to the said RICHARD REEVE of Wingfield, gent., testator's brother-in-law, who then becomes executor. Because of legacies given to EM she to maintain, keep and educate DOROTHY and WILLIAM till of age. Witness: EDWARD MOWLTON. Pr. at Yoxford 28 July 1631.

R(W) FRANCIS BALLARD of Dunwich, yeoman. 18 April 1627 (469)

Sick. To wife URSULA houses, buildings where testator lives in Dunwich on his death, she to keep the same in good repair; on her death to go to testator's son JOHN. To son JOHN best posted bedstead standing on the hall chamber at the testator's house, fully furnished as it stands, when JOHN 24; he to have the best cloak when he reaches 21. To daughter SUSAN £15 when 21 or marriage; one great chest standing in the parlour. To daughter URSULA £10 when 21 or marriage; 1 livery cupboard in my parlour. To daughter FRANCES, piece of ground lying in Dunwich by the sea side there, bought from ROBERT SOANE, comprising 1/2 acre, when she 21 or marriage. Also £4 when 21 or marriage. To daughter ELIZABETH £5 when 21 or marriage. Benefit of survivorship to all these children. Residue to wife to pay debts, legacies, funeral charge, she to be sole executrix. Brother EDWARD BALLARD clerk, supervisor. Witnesses: JOHN REEVE, JOHN BENET, THOMAS CRISPE, the JOHN REYNOLDS, script. Probate to son JOHN BALLARD at Bungay 4 July 1631.

R(W) WILLIAM BECKET of Trimley St. Mary. 7 March 1625 (470)

To FRANCIS SMITH of Larkwell 12d. To the two children of FRANCIS SMITH 20s. each when 21. To JOAN BECKETT 20s. within 1 month of testator's death. To REBECCA BECKETT, daughter of JOAN, 10s. within 3 months of testator's death. Residue to ROGER RAWLING of Lawshall, he to pay debts, funeral expenses. Witnesses: JOHN LOVE, ROBERT JAY. Probate granted to ROGER RAWLING at Ipswich 11 June 1631.

R(W) SAMUEL BYLES of Baylham (N).[blank] June 1631 (471)

To wife ELIZABETH, all goods; she to pay debts, and be executor. Witnesses: THOMAS MEDOWE, WILLIAM DOWZING. Pr. at Ipswich 23 June 1631.

R(W) JOHN BROWNE of Woodbridge, weaver. 28 April 1631 (472)

Sick. To son JOHN £10 when 24, and if he die before, then legacy to be equally divided between testator's other children. To wife JUDITH all goods, to educate and maintain children till 21, then to dispose of the same equally between the children. She to be executrix. Witnesses: THOMAS WEBB, [ANNCE?] (X). Pr. at Wickham 6 June 1631.

R(W) RICHARD BURRWOOD of Ramsey Essex, husbandman. 21 February 1622 (473)

To wife ANN a posted bedstead, furnished with bedding; 1 cupboard; 1 joined table with 6 buffet stools; 2 dansk chests; 3 chairs, 1 hamper, 1 little desk, warming pan. To son THOMAS £40 when 21; if he die before receiving legacy, then the £40 to go to testator's other son RICHARD. To servant ANN WOODS, 20s. at the end of her apprenticeship. All unbequeathed goods to be equally divided between sons THOMAS & RICHARD; debts and funeral expenses to be met; ROBERT MORGAN, testator's father-in-law appointed executor, and to be THOMAS's guardian until he reach the age of 21. Witnesses: WILLIAM SUCKLING, WILLIAM CARD. Pr. at Ipswich 7 June 1631.

R(W) JOAN ATTELBRIGG of Ipswich, widow (N). 19 May 1631 (474)

To MARY ATTLEBRIGG, my only child all goods, household, chattels; she to pay to testator's grandchild DOROTHY ATTELBRIGG 10s. within 1 year of testator's death. Witnesses: AGNES SEALON, RACHEL NORTH, widow. Probate granted to MARY ATTELBRIGG at Ipswich 13 July 1631.

R(W) WILLIAM GOODELL of Pakefield, sailor. 27 June 1631 (475)

To be buried in the churchyard of Pakefield. To wife ESTHER, all houses and yards in Pakefield for life, then to pass to his eldest son JOHN GOODELL; if he die without heir, then to pass to other son THOMAS and his heirs. To 3 youngest children THOMAS, ABIGAIL, & ALICE 40s. each to be paid by JOHN GOODELL within three years of ESTHER's death -- namely 40s. to THOMAS in 1 year, 40s. to ABIGAIL in 2 yrs., and 40s. to ALICE in 3 yrs. If default, power of entry into the said lands. Wife appointed sole executrix. Witnesses: CRAIG HORTON, THOMAS PIGEON. Pr. at Beccles 9 July 1631.

R(W) HUMPHRY GIBON of Frostende, shoemaker. 26 May 1631 (476)

To son JAMES £20 when 21, to be paid him in the south porch of Frostenden church. To LETTICE ROPEING, wife's mother-in-law, 10s. to be paid within 6 months of his death. Residue of all goods, plate, jewells, money, household stuff, to wife ELIZABETH, she to be sole executrix. Witnesses: THOMAS JONES, GEORGE HADLEY, AMIE ASSEY. Pr. at Blythburgh 3 June 1631.

R(W) ROBERT ROBSON of Wissett (N). [blank] 1631 (477)

To brother-in-law GEORGE SMITH all goods. Witnesses: EDMUND GOSLINGE & wife MARY. Probate granted to GEORGE SMITH at Beccles 19 May 1631.

R(W) THOMAS DUNET of Blythburgh. 25 April 1631 (478)

Sick. To ELIZABETH TUBBY 10s. within 12 weeks. To the poor of Blythburgh 5s. To brother ROGER DUNET, £10 at the rate of 40s. a year until the £10 fully paid -- the first payment to begin 12 weeks after testator's death. Residue to JOHN MOUSER, he to be executor, to pay debts, funeral expenses. Witnesses: ELIZABETH WELLS, STEPHEN PILBARROW. Pr. at Beccles 19 May 1631.

R(W) HENRY WAKE of Thurlston, yeoman. 23 March 1630 (479)

Sick. To the poor of Whitton and Thurlston 20s. within 14 days of his burial, to be paid by RICHARD CROWE and ROBERT LEWES, sons-in-law. To FRANCIS LEWES, son of ROBERT LEWES £5 when 21. To ROBERT LEWES, son of ROBERT LEWES £20, when 14; on 14th birthday he to choose a guardian to employ this sum to its best advantage, until ROBERT reach 21. If he die before inheriting, then £15 of the said £20 to go to WILLIAM WAKE, testator's brother, and to HENRY WAKE son of the said WILLIAM, and FRANCES WAKE daughter of WILLIAM WAKE, and to testator's sister JOAN ADAMS, to be equally divided between them, namely £3. 13s. 4d. each. To brother WILLIAM WAKE 40s. within 1 year of testator's death. To HENRY WAKE, son of WILLIAM, £4 when 21. To FRANCES WAKE, daughter of WILLIAM, £4 when 21. To sister JOAN ADAMS 20s. within 1 yr. of testator's death. To THOMAS PODD, son of ROBERT PODD, of Dedham, 6s. 8d. To SARA ISHAM, 6s. 8d. within 1 yr. of testator's death. To wife FRANCES WAKE, residue of estate, she to pay debts, funeral expenses, and to be sole executrix. Witnesses: JOHN ELLIOTT, ANN ELLIOTT, RICHARD CROWE. Pr. at Ipswich 22 April 1631.

R(W) WALTER WHITBY of Orford (N). [no date] (480)

To son JOHN WHITBY, 20s. due next Michaelmas. To son NATHANIEL 20s. when 21. Residue to wife BRIDGET. Witnesses: JOHN WHITBY,

JOHN CAXALL, RICHARD COPPINGE, gent. Probate granted to BRIDGET WHITBY at Wickham 31 March 1631.

R(W) ROBERT TOVELL of Cretingham, yeoman. 24 April 1631 (481)

To daughter ANNE all lands, tenements, free and copyhold in Cretingham, and Brandeston, until his grandson ROBERT TOVELL reach 22. MARGARET WHINERY, mother of testator's grandchild ROBERT TOVELL, to educate and maintain the said ROBERT, and testator's daughter ANNE to pay £5 a year towards the maintenance of the said ROBERT. To grandson ROBERT TOVELL all lands when he reaches 22. To granchildren FAITH & MARGARET TOVELL & ROBERT BEIDSHAM £40 each when they reach 21, with benefit of survivorship. To grandson ROBERT TOVELL, all furniture and household stuff that is in the hall and parlour in the house at Cretingham; also all shelves, glass in the windows and wainscotts about the house, a copper, cheese press, salting trough and all brewing vessels in and belonging to the messuage; also the horsemill. If ROBERT die then goods and the residue of goods, debts, plate, money to go to daughter ANNE, she to be sole executrix. NICHOLAS REVELL, esq., and brother-in-law WILLIAM GAME to be supervisors and to receive 20s. each for their pains. Witnesses: GEORGE RUSSELL, THOMAS ELLIOTT (X). Pr. at Wickham 11 May 1631.

R(W) JOAN TURVIE of Aldeburgh (N). [no date] (482)

To daughter MARGARET SAWYER, wife of ALEXANDER SAWYER, half household stuff. To BURTON, TIMOTHY & ROBERT GILDERSLEEVE, children of testator's daughter ANN, the wife of THOMAS WILLIS, the other half of the household stuff. To ALICE COBB £3 within 1 yr. of testator's death. To ADRIAN LINFORD, wife to WILLIAM LINFORD, £3 in 1 yr. of testator's death. Witnesses: ELIZABETH DANNIELL, ANN BRIGHTWELL. Probate granted to MARGARET SAWYER 21 June 1631.

R(W) JOHN REDBEARD of Leiston, yeoman. 6 February 1630 (483)

To son JOHN ROBERT, £100 to be paid him by JULIAN REDBEARD, my wife when 21; if he die before inheriting, then £100 to be divided between testator's two daughters when they reach 24, with benefit of survivorship. To son JOHN REDBEARD one feather bed, and all things pertaining to the same. To daughter ELIZABETH REDBEARD, £120 when 22, and one feather bed. To daughter MARY REDBEARD £120 when 22, and one feather bed, and one cupboard. With benefit of survivorship. To wife JULIAN her habitation in my house called Baxters in Leiston, for life; on her death the messuage to go to son JOHN REDBEARD, provided he pay to his sisters ELIZABETH & MARY £10 each within 1 year of their mother's death. If wife remarry, contrary to the will, she to have nothing, and to have no control over his legacies to his children. THOMAS FRANE of Halesworth appointed supervisor and he to control legacies instead. Wife JULIAN and son JOHN appointed joint executors; THOMAS FRANE to receive 20s. for his pains taken as supervisor. Witnesses: ROBERT MARC, RICHARD SPALLDING. Pr. at Wickham 31 March 1631.

R(W) ANN RIPPS of Nacton, widow. 26 March 1631 (484)

To be buried at Nacton. To ROBERT BRANSON of Nacton, and his wife ELIZABETH, the annuity due to the testator from Sir RICHARD BROOKE of £7 p.a.; also all movables to them, provided he provide for her until her death, and to see her buried in a coffin and to ensure the preaching of a sermon on her burial. ROBERT BRANSON to be executor. Witnesses: ELIZABETH JARRALLS, JOAN REEVE. Pr. at Ipswich 22 April 1631.

R(W) ELIZABETH ROLFE of Great Bealings, widow (N). 26 March 1631 (485)

To ELIZABETH WOODE, widow, all goods, to pay her debts, and funeral expenses; this to her for taking care of me when ill. Witnesses: GEORGE BACON & ANNE his wife; JOHN FOX. Probate granted to ELIZABETH WOODE at Ipswich 1 April 1631.

R(W) JEREMY PIPE of Laxfield (N). 5 November 1630 (486)

To wife MARGARET, all movables, she to pay some debts, but son THOMAS to pay other debts. To son WILLIAM PIPE an annuity of £10 to be paid by son THOMAS on the death of their mother. Witnesses: HENRY BORRETT, ANN FASSETT (X). Probate granted to MARGARET PIPE at Stradbroke 26 April 1631.

R(W) SAMUEL PAYNE of Brandeston (N). 9 March 1630 (487)

Sick. To each of the six children of ZACHARY PAYNE, testator's brother, deceased, 10s. apiece within 1 yr. of testator's death. To godchild SAMUEL SPURLING, son of THOMAS SPURLING of Cretingham, 5s. in 1 yr. To RICHARD PAYNE of Brandeston, best suit of apparell, save the best cloak; an axe, hatchet, hook, shovel, mattock, and a pair of boots. Residue to wife MARGARET, she to be executrix, pay debts, and funeral expenses; she to leave half her goods on her death to testator's kindred. Witnesses: JOHN LOWE, clerk; ROBERT LEE gent. Pr. at Wickham 31 March 1631.

R(W) GRACE PAYNE of Walton. 4 April 1623 (488)

The wife of ROGER PAYNE of Walton. To husband ROGER all that he already has and has promised to pay to WILLIAM LEMMING, clerk, and SIMON PETTIWARD, clerk, by the following Michaelmas. To WILLIAM BROOME of Shotley cum Kirton, £9 part of the £30 by which

ROGER PAYNE is bound to him. Also 40s. more, which I lent to him. To MARY, sister of WILLIAM BROOME, and wife of JAMES MOSES £10, part of the above £30. To MARGARET BROOME, sister of WILLIAM BROOME, £8, part of the above £30. To WILLIAM LEMMING, clerk, and SIMON PETTIWARD, clerk, 30s. each, they to be executors. Witnesses: WILLIAM PETTE (X), PHAROA SMITH (X), ALICE HARRIS (X). Pr. at Ipswich 22 April 1631.

R(W) PRISCILLA NORTEN, widow. 30 March 1631 (489)

Sick. To daughter GRACE, one bed and bedstead that she lie on, coverlet on the same bed; one dansk chest; one copper kettle; 6 pieces pewter; a bolster; a pillow; one little table in the chamber, and the cupboard in the parlour; one silver spoon, and 50s. to be paid in 2 years of testator's death. To daughter ELIZABETH, one bed and bedstead, bolster and a pillow in the chamber; one brass kettle; one dansk chest; coverlet; cupboard in the hall, 6 pieces of pewter; one silver spoon, and 50s. within 2 years of testator's death. To daughter PRISCILLA WARNER 20s. within 2 years of testator's death. To daughter REBECCA 10s. and to daughter BILES 10s. in 2 years of testator's death. To every grandchild when they reach 21 5s. each, save for granddaughter SUSAN ALLEN she to receive 5s. more. To daughter REBECCA, the bed she has and the bolster and the trunk and 5 pieces of pewter. Son JOSHUA to be executor, pay debts and funeral expenses. Witnesses: JOHN ALDERMAN, RICHARD WALLS. Probate granted to JOHN NORTEN at Ipswich 9 May 1631.

R(W) FRANCIS LOVE of Ufford (N). 24 February 1624 (490)

To be buried in Ufford. To eldest son JOHN all lands, both free and bond, in Ufford. To youngest son THOMAS all movables and other goods. Brother ANTHONY GIRLING of Stradbroke and SIMON SANDCROFT of Eaton to be executors. Witnesses: THOMAS STILE, HENRY NORMAN, GODFREY BURNETT. Pr. at Wickham 21 April 1631.

R(W) THOMAS KEEDE of Dallinghoo, yeoman. 7 August 1630 (491)

Sick. To eldest son ROBERT KEEDE, messuage where testator lives and all lands in Dallinghoo, provided he let ROSE KEEDE, testator's wife, live in the best parlour, with free access, freedom to bake bread, draw water; also to pay to her £10 in two installments -- one at Lady Day, the other on Michaelmas, payments to begin on the first feast day to fall after testator's death. Also to let ROSE have a cart load of firewood. ROBERT also has to pay FRANCES PELLS, wife of HENRY PELLS of Bromeswell £35 within 2 years of inheriting lands in order to free ROBERT from any outstanding bonds; also to pay THOMAS KEEDE, testator's son £20 within 3 years of inheriting, RICHARD KEEDE, his brother, £40 in 4 years, and GEORGE KEEDE £40, his brother £40 in 5 years; also to pay a further £40 to RICHARD KEEDE in 6 years time, and a further £40 to GEORGE KEEDE in 7 years time, and to THOMAS son of

THOMAS KEEDE £5 when he reaches 16, and to pay to another grandchild HENRY PELLS £5 when he reach 16. All payments to take place in Dallinghoo church. To kinsman RAINBOROW STARKE 10s. To wife ROSE, all linen and bedding and household stuff in the parlour; also a brass pot, kettle, skillet; 8 pieces pewter; and the use of 4 silver spoons for life, then these to go to son ROBERT. To son ROBERT one feather bed, also feather bed to son GEORGE. Residue to son ROBERT, he to be executor. Witnesses: WILLIAM THOMPSON, ANTHONY BURWOOD. Codicil - if ROBERT fail in payments, power to legatees to enter and enjoy lands till legacy, and arrears, met. Witnesses to codicil: ANTHONY BURWOOD, WILLIAM THOMPSON. Pr. at Wickham 30 March 1631.

R(W) THOMAS JOLLY of Carlton Colville, yeoman. (492)
3 February 1624

Sick. To wife CHRISTIAN, £20 in 6 months of testator's death; 2 bedsteads one posted and another trundle bed, now both standing in the old parlour, with the feather beds, bolsters, pillows and covering belongings; also 2 chests now standing on the new parlour; 2 boxes to lay linen in, all my sheets and pillow cases, 3 table cloths and 1 1/2 doz. napkins; little table standing in the hall; the great brass pot; the great cauldron; great trivett; 6 pieces best pewter, spit and pair of andirons. Also £5 annuity payable by equal payments on Lady Day & Michaelmas. To son ISAAC £20 within 1 year of testator's death. To two grandchildren RICHARD JOLLY & HENRY HAGAR £5 each when 21. To grandchild CHRISTIAN HUCKERTON 20s. when 21. To son GEORGE JOLLY all movables, corn, cattle, household goods and money; he to be executor. Witnesses: PHILIPA WARD, EDMUND GILBERT (X). Pr. at Beccles 25 April 1631.

R(W) JEREMY HALL of Needham Market, hopman. (493)
30 March 1630

To wife ANNE copyhold tenement where THOMAS CARR lives, the hall abutting and all the chamber and the yard so far as lieth against the hall, with a convenient going unto the well to fetch her water. Then to son WILLIAM HALL. The other part of the tenement called the parlour and the parlour chamber to FRANCES HALL and her heirs, and if none then this to revert to brother WILLIAM. To wife ANNE £10. To children ROBERT HALL, & WILLIAM HALL & daughters MARY, ALICE & FRANCES all unbequeathed goods. Also 20s. to son JOHN if he come before the movables be divided. HENRY SAVEADGE of Needham Market and wife ANNE HALL to be executors. Witnesses: HENRY SAVEDGE, jnr.; JOHN GRYNE; GEORGE BLOMFIELD. Pr. at Ipswich 1 April 1631.

R(W) WILLIAM GISLINGHAM of Dunwich (N). 20 March 1630 (494)

To wife all the goods she had on her marriage, to be valued by two independent men; if the value comes to less than £12 then it to be made up to that sum. Residue of estate to his two brothers JOHN & THOMAS GISLINGHAM, they to be joint executor. Witnesses: THOMAS TURNER & GEOFFREY DAYNES. Pr. at Yoxford 30 March 1631.

R(W) ISAAC GOODWIN of Holbrook, yeoman. 20 March 1630 (495)

Sick and weak. To poor of Holbrook, 10s. within 6 months of his death. To daughter MARY £40 when 21. To the child which his wife is now carrying, if a boy, all copyhold land in Holbrook when 21; if it be a daughter then £40 when 21,but if it be a boy them daughter MARY have an additional /40 when 21. If the child be female, then the lands to be sold when she is 21 for as much as possible, and the proceeds of the sale be equally divided between the two girls. Benefit of survivorship -- if both girls die, then land to wife MARY together with residue of all goods; she to be sole executrix. JOHN WICKES to be supervisor. If wife remarry, then she to be bound to supervisor in £200 to perform this will. Witnesses: NATHANIEL HODGES, JOHN BROTHERTON. Pr. at Ipswich 1 April 1631.

R(W) ELIZABETH FOX of St. Nicholas SouthElmham, widow (N). (496)
[no date]

To son SIMON one featherbed, and to daughter ALICE, wife of THOMAS DRAKE, the same. Witnesses: SIMON FOX & SUSAN his wife; THOMAS DRAKE & wife ALICE. Probate granted to SIMON FOX & THOMAS DRAKE 26 March 1631.

R(W) MARY FREEMAN of Walberswick, widow (N). (497)
19 February 1630

To youngest brother, feather bed she used to lie on and the best coverlet. To eldest brother one of the other feather beds, coverings and 2 bolsters. To sister one yearling calf, waistcoat, ruff and forehead cloth, 1 pair sheets. To daughter SARAH one cow, £3 to be used to bind her as an apprentice. To Goodwife BARRETT one skip of bees. To ELIZABETH BUMYS a featherbed as it stands, and one ruff. To the son and daughter of GEORGE REYNOLDS, one ewe sheep. To HUGH STANE 1/2 bushel rye, pair sheets, one piece of leather, 1 pewter dish, 1 pillow. To Widow CARTWRIGHT 1 great chair, warming pan, 4 lbs. hemp, 1/2 bushel rye. To WILLIAM CHARROLD 1 feather pillow; 1 pair sheets; 1 pewter dish; 1 rake; 1 pair spoons. To Goodwife BUMYS 1/2 bushel rye; 4lbs. hemp. To ANNE DEEX striped pillow; pair sheets; 1/2 bushel rye; 1 peck barley. To GEORGE REYNOLDS a shirt cloth. Residue to be equally divided among the 4 children of Widow BUMYS. GEORGE REYNOLDS & HUGH STACIE appointed executors. Witnesses: WILLIAM CHARROLD, ANN DEEREING. Pr. at Yoxford 20 April 1631. [last gathering of register]

R(W) GRACE DOWE of Rushmere Street, Friston. (498)
20 March 1629

To executor, all goods in trust to sell to pay debts, legacies, pay funeral expenses and to bring up testator's 4 youngest children. If anything left after meeting all these charges then to be equally divided amongst testator's children. ANDREW FELGATE of Earl Stonham, yeoman, and THOMAS SALLOWS, yeoman to be executors. Witnesses: THOMAS SEAMAN, NICHOLAS PAYNTER, MARGARET BROWNE. Pr. at Ipswich 1 April 1631.

R(W) ROBERT DRURY of Kirton, husbandman (N). [no date] (499)

To son TIMOTHY HAWKINGS, a cloak, and to daughter HAWKINGS one kettle. To grandchild TIMOTHY HAWKINGS 1 little chest as it stands; 1 old flock bed. Residue of apparell to nephew WALTER DRURY. Witnesses: EDWARD DRURIE & ROBERT BRADSTREET. Probate granted to TIMOTHY HAWKINGS at Wickham 21 April 1631.

R(W) JOHN COCKE of Foxhall, yeoman. 24 March 1630 (500)

Sick. Wife MERCIE COCK to be sole executrix, to have all lands, goods, to pay debts, and to educate his children; she also to pay to eldest son JOHN COCK when 21 40s. a year whilst she lives. JOHN to inherit the lands when MERCIE dies, and he then to pay to testator's other children 40s. each a year. MERCIE also to pay each child £8 when they reach 20, or if she die before they reach 20, they to receive legacy on her death. Wife also to pay to testator's kinswoman ALICE BEDDELL 20s. within 1 year of testator's death, and wife also to give testator's man servant MATTHEW POOLY the suit of clothes he usually wears. Wife to enter bond in £40 with cousin WILLIAM COCK of Bucklesham, supervisor, to perform this will. Witnesses: JOHN SKYNER, minister; WILLIAM COCK; THOMAS PORTER (X). Pr. at Ipswich 1 April 1631.

R(W) JOHN CRISPE of Marlesford. 22 March 1630 (501)

Sick. House/tenement called Goodcheap in Little Glemham, now mortgaged to WILLIAM SEAGER of Ipswich for £32. 8s., to be sold and said debt discharged. To youngest daughter AMY £10 when 21. Remainder of money to be equally divided between testator's son JOHN and testator's daughter MARTHA. Implements also to be sold. JOHN BRIDGES of Little Glemham testator's brother-in-law, and ANN HOSKER of Marlesford appointed executors; DANIELL POTTELL of Glemham, yeoman, supervisor. Witnesses: JAMES POTTELL, THOMAS STANNARD. Pr. at Wickham 31 March 1631.

R(W) JOHN COLMAN of Hoxne, yeoman. 16 March 1630 (502)

To the poor of Hoxne 20s., and the poor of Denham 5s. Daughter

MARY to have the messuage where she and her husband live and the yard adjoining for the residue of the lease; also to have the remainder of the lease from Sir THOMAS SOUTHWELL, save the lease from HELEN SHEREWOOD. Residue of property to be independently assessed and valued by brother-in-law WILLIAM BARKER, and friends HILLARY FERMER & THOMAS YOUNGS, so that testator's son JOHN to sell within 3 years of testator's death. To wife ANNE 1/2 the linen. To son ROBERT, lease from HELEN SHEREWOOD after death of testator's wife. To son NICHOLAS COLMAN £10 within 3 years of testator's death, and to grandchild NICHOLAS son of son NICHOLAS £5 in 8 years of testator's death. To grandchild THOMAS, son of son NICHOLAS 11s. within 8 years. To grandchildren THOMAS BAXTER -- £4 to bind him an apprentice; to JOAN BAXTER £3. 6s. 8d. in 3 years of testator's death and 3 pair sheets; and to GRACE BAXTER 22s. in 3 years and 2 pair sheets. To grandchildren ALICE & JOHN, children of son JOHN 22s. each. To grandchild MARY, daughter of son STEPHEN 22s. in 5 years and 1 pair sheets. To son ROBERT £20 within 2 yrs. of testator's death. To grandchild JOHN COLEMAN, son of son ROBERT, 2 pieces of 44s. in 4 yrs. of his death. To daughter MARY, 1/2 linen which was left to testator when his first wife, her mother, died. To rest of grandchildren not specified by name in the will, 1/2 a piece of 11s. in 6 years of testator's death. To servant ALICE 10s. a year for the term of the Hoxne lease. To servant WILLIAM SALLETT 10s. within 1 yr. of testator's death. To son STEPHEN COLEMAN 30s. a year for the term of the Hoxne lease. The overplus from the sale to be equally divided amongst children, legacies, debts having been met. JOHN COLMAN, son, appointed sole executor. Witnesses: WILLIAM BARKER, JOHN KENE, BRIDGET EASTHAUGH the wife of FRANCIS EASTAUGH (X). Pr. at Stradbroke 26 April 1631.

R(W) BEATRICE CAGE of Ipswich, widow. 30 March 1631 (503)

To MARY WOODS, daughter of son RICHARD WOODS, now living with testator, £20 in 3 months of testator's death. To THOMAS WOODS, son of son THOMAS £10 when 21. To SUSAN WOODS, daughter of son THOMAS £10 when 23 -- if die before inheriting, then legacy to go to her brother THOMAS. £200 to be left with executor, and 40s. a year, interest accruing from the said sum, to be used for the education and clothing of JOHN WOODS, son of son JOHN WOODS. Son JOHN WOODS to have interest on £10, but if he come to live such an orderly and civil and hopeful course as meets with approval of Mr SAMUEL WARD of Ipswich, preacher, Mr EDMUND DAY of Ipswich, and cousin THOMAS WOODS of Dedham, then son JOHN can have the yearly benefit of the £200 in the executor's hands. If he fail, then he to have the yearly interest of the £10 referred to above, kept in the executor's hands, and on his death, this £10 to be paid to his children, save for JOHN WOODS, towards the cost of their education until they reach 21; then when they reach 21 they to have the principal equally shared amongst them. If son JOHN has no further child, other than his son JOHN, then grandson JOHN to have 1/2 the benefit of the £200, and the other half to go to THOMAS WOODS, son of THOMAS, for life, and if grandson JOHN die then all to be held in trust for THOMAS WOODS children. To the poor of Burstall, 40s. -- 1/2 on the day of her burial, and 1/2 within 6 months; to the poor of St. Nicholas parish 20s. To grandchild MARY BLOSSE, a gold ring which was GEORGE WOODS. Son JOHN WOODS already has £80 belonging to testator, this sum to go to some friends hands, and he to have the interest on it towards his maintenance; but if he does not wish this to be so, then he can have the same £80. To daughter RABEDGE, wife of WILLIAM CAGE, gent., my great desk and its contents; green birded coverlet; round hooped ring; 1 pair of large flaxen sheets; 2 silk gowns 2 kirtells and my best petticoat. To grandchild, the wife of THOMAS BLOSSE, gold chain for remembrance. To son-in-law WILLIAM CAGE and wife RABEDGE the beer cup, 6 silver spoons which were her late husband's EDWARD CAGE. To daughter MARTHA, wife of SAMUEL HADLOCK, 20s., and the scarlet coloured petticoat which I made last. To widow BASETT who keeps JOHN WOODS, my grandchild, best bay gown and the bodice and kirtle of the same; petticoat lined with fur; cloak I usually wear fur lined. To MARY WOODS, daughter of son RICHARD gown of watered stuff; 1 of 2 other petticoat whichever she choose, the other petticoat to go to SUSAN, daughter of son THOMAS. To MARY, daughter of son RICHARD and to BEATRICE & SUSAN daughters of son THOMAS all wearing linen to be equally divided within 1 month of testator's death. To the servants of my son CAGE 3s. 4d. To son JOHN WOODS, silver pot; 12 silver spoons, late GEORGE WOOD's, in 1 yr. of my death. To bind THOMAS WOODS, son of son THOMAS, as apprentice £10. Son CAGE owes £30 for 6 months rent on Burstall land -- he to now deduct the money for her board from this sum, and to have a further £6 from the remainder. Any money then remaining from the £30 to be used to pay probate charges. To MARTHA WOODS, daughter of son THOMAS WOOD £5 when 20. To son JOHN, one of my feather beds, bolster, pillow, pair of blankets, curtains of linsey woolsey, pair of ordinary sheets. Son-in-law WILLIAM CAGE, to be executor. Witnesses: JOHN HORNIGOLD, JOHN CASTLYN, THOMAS FASTOLFE, EDWARD DIXON. Pr. at Ipswich 30 April 1631.

R(W) AVICE BRANCH of Melton, widow. 7 April 1631 (504)

Sick. To son-in-law THOMAS ROSEYER £15. To son-in-law STEVEN CHANDLER £6. To grandchild ROBERT, son of STEVEN CHANDLER £3 when 21. To grandchild AVICE, daughter of STEVEN CHANDLER £3 when 21 and 1 pair sheets. To THOMAS, AVICE, & STEVEN CHANDLER, grandchildren 20s. when 21. Benefit of survivorship. Residue of estate, goods, to be equally divided between THOMAS ROSEYER & STEVEN CHANDLER; they to be joint executors. Witnesses: THOMAS BURTENS (X), WILLIAM PATRICH, RICHARD HARRISON. Pr. at Ipswich 22 April 1631.

R(W) JAMES BETTES of Baylham, husbandman. (505)
14 December 1630

Sick. To sons JAMES & JOHN BETTES all clothing to be equally divided. To grandchildren JAMES & MARY BETTES, 2s. each, and to the two children of JOHN BETTES 2s. each, and to the two children of THOMAS PECKE of Bramford, namely THOMAS & JAMES PECKE, testator's grandchildren 2s. each. Residue to wife JOAN, she to be sole executrix. STEPHEN BETTS of Barking to be supervisor, and to have 6s. for his pains. Witnesses: JOHN MOWER (X), MARY WHITEING (X). Pr. at Ipswich 22 April 1631.

R(W) ROBERT BEELIE of Benacre. 20 January 1626 (506)

Sick. To daughter ANN £15. To brother WILLIAM £10 within 6 months of testator's death. Residue to wife BARBERA, she to be sole executrix; JOHN CAPPS of Oulton, my brother, to be supervisor and to have the best horse. Witnesses: ANN BEESE (X), ROBERT DERBY (X). Pr. at Beccles 9 April 1631.

R(W) ROBERT BOYSE of Chelmondiston, mariner. (507)
11 March 1630

Sick. To the poor of Chelmondiston 10s. To son JOHN, house where JOHN FOLSTACKER lives, if he pay to his aunt JUDITH STAPLETON 40s. p.a., as testator is bound to do; JOHN also to have £40. To daughter MARGARET £30 when 21 or marriage, and the same to daughter ELIZABETH and to daughter MARGERY. To son NICHOLAS BOYSE, tenement purchased from JOHN WOODWERD in Shotley; also £28 when he reach 21, and he to be maintained at school for the next two years. To son ROBERT, tenement now occupied by WILLIAM STAFFORD, provided he surrender to GEORGE FENN of Holbrooke, clothier, his interest in a tenement in Holbrook; if son ROBERT refuse, then GEORGE FENN to have tenement given to ROBERT; also £28. Benefit of survivorship. To servant SUSAN SMITH 49s., and to servant JAMES 5s. Residue of estate to be equally divided amongst testator's children. WILLIAM WHITEBREAD of Chelmondiston and JOHN BOICE, testator's son, appointed joint executors; CHRISTOPHER ANDREWS of Chelmondiston appointed supervisor, and given 10s. Note that son ROBERT BOYSE also to be maintained at school till he finish his education, and that further the executors to be bound in £200 to the supervisor to perform the will, and if they refuse then supervisor to become executor. Witnesses: WILLIAM LENINGS, JOHN BROTHERTON. Pr. at Ipswich April 1631.

CHAPTER III

[The register for 1632 is missing, so that the wills for 1632 are all original Wills and not registered copies.]

W. ROBERT AMYSON of Dallinghoo, yeoman. (508)
27 September 1632

Sick. To eldest son WILLIAM, messuage and tenement in Dallinghoo where testator lives, with all pertaining to the same, and a horse mill, provided he pay to his sister ELIZABETH a yearly annuity of £7 due in two equal installments at Dallinghoo church porch. If default, lands to go to the said ELIZABETH. To son WILLIAM, messuage in Dallinghoo where NICHOLAS COOKE lives, provided he pay to his brother JAMES an annuity of £5 p.a. at Dallinghoo church porch in two equal installments one every six months. ELIZABETH & JAMES to acknowledge receipt of these payments every year, and if they refuse such receipts, then WILLIAM to keep the annuities. WILLIAM to be executor, and if he refuse, then daughter ELIZABETH to be executrix. Witnesses: NICHOLAS ELLINGER, GREGORY NICHOLLES, THOMAS BUCK (X). Pr. at Wickham 20 Nov. 1632.

W. ELIZABETH ADREW of Halstead, widow. 13 February 1632 (509)

Visited with age and disquieted in body. To be buried at Halstead. To eldest son JOHN, 1 large table, 1 cupboard, 1 bench which stands in the parlour, and all things that are belonging to the dairy, and backhouse -- the quernes, lead, troughs, ladders, and all necessary things for outdoors work. Also the £10 he owes to the testator to be paid by him at the rate of her death. To daughter PAINTER the glass case that stands in the parlour, and to her daughters 6 pieces of pewter -- 2 each and 20s. each within 6 months of her death. To son CHRISTOPHER one green chair, 4 cushions, 1 great chest that stands in the chamber. To his son CHRISTOPHER the chest in the parlour by the bedside, and to the five children of son CHRISTOPHER 20s. each, and to son CHRSITOPHER's daughter ELIZABETH the salt seller with brass on top. To daughter SUSAN COPPER, the flocked keel, the new featherbed, 2 blankets, 1 coverlet, 1 pair sheets, 1 new boulster, 1 pillow and pillow case, 2 cobirons, 1 pair tongues, a fire pan, a grogan and peale, warmingpan, mortar, and the chest that stand now under the glass case in the parlour, £5 and a great brass pot, 1 silver spoon immediately on testator's death. To grandchild ELIZABETH COPPER, 1 trundle bed, 1 bed, 2 blankets, 1 coverlet, 1 bolster, 1 pair sheets, 1 pelow, as it stand in the parlour. £5 to my daughter COPER's children to be equally divided between them, and to her eldest daughter one brass caskett, immediately on testator's death. To daughter POODE the black cover and the wicker chair in the parlour, 1 silver spoon, and to her 4 children 20s. and to her daughter ELIZABETH 1 pewter salt seller with a knop on the cover. To daughter MARGARET the brindled cover, 1 chaffing dish, 1 silver spoon. To son JOHN's wife, silver tipped pole, and then it to go to her daughter ANNE. To daughter PAINTER the violet waistcoat; to daughter COPPER my gown and stained petticoat and the waistcoat that GOODWARD made, and all workaday apparell. To daughter POODE violet petticoat and my bedding sheet. To daughter MARGARET best cloak. To the three youngest daughters all the linen, pewter and brass to be equally divided. 10s. to the poor of Halstead. JOHN ANDREW appointed sole executor, and any spare money after payment of debts and legacies to be equally divided amongst the four daughters. Witnesses: ANTHONY BROOKE, STEVE LESESTON, THOMAS OLE (X). Pr. at Ipswich 29 Sept. 1631.

W. STEPHEN ANGIER (N). 24 October 1631 (510)

To wife all goods for life, then to be equally divided between the 4 children. His share of the shop goods also to be equally divided among children. Mother and brother to go half shares in the shop whilst testator's mother lives, and they to employ testator's children in the shop. Mother to be executor. Witness: Mr STEVENS. Probate granted to MARTHA ANGIER widow, at Ipswich 1 July 1632.

W. JOHN BERT of Henstead. 28 May 1623 (511)

Sick. To son ROGER one of my best chests, and 30s. within 1 yr. of my death. To daughter SUSAN 1 of my best chests, and 30s. in 6 months of my death. To daughter MARGERY, standing cupboard, and 40s. when 21. Wife MARGARET, to have the use of these chests and cupboard for her lifetime. If his children be not content and trouble their mother, and be in any things disobedient unto her, their legacies to be void. Residue of estate to wife, who is to be executor. Witnesses: THOMAS JONES, snr.; JAMES & MARGARET B'EBEM (X). Pr. at Beccles 29 June 1632.

W. WILLIAM BACON of Great Blakenham, gentleman. (512)
22 August 1620

To ROBERT BACON, my son, £100 in 1 year of testator's death, this to release his interest in testator's estate; if he refuse to release his interest, legacy void. To WILLIAM BACON, grandson, £100 when 21 -- until then he to be paid £5 a year out of the interest on the £100, by quarterrly payments. To the two daughters of JOSEPH BARKER of Ipswich, haberdasher, £15 each within 1 year, in full satisfaction of £10 legacy to each under the will of WILLIAM BACON, deceased, testator's son, if then they discharge the £10 legacy; if they refuse, then the £15 legacy to be void. To the poor of Little Blakenham and Bricett 40s. each in 1 month of my death. To son TOBIAS BACON, copyhold in Little Blakenham, held of that manor, and freehold in Bricett, Ringshall, and copyhold in Great Bricett and Ringshall held of the manor of Great Bricett; also copyhold land held of JOHN ACTON of Ipswich from the manor of Berlyes and Normans in Bramford, save for one piece occupied by ROBERT BOWLE lying between lands late FRANCIS COLTHORNE's called Murks on the east, the king's highway on the west. Residue of testator's lands in Little Blakenham and Bramford remain to the uses made in an indenture made between testator and GEORGE LINCOLNE & EDWARD BALDEYE. To wife ELIZABETH and all his children not named in the will, 40s. each within 3 months of his death -- the reason is why I give them no greater portion in this my will is for that I have otherwise provided for them by former acts and assurances. Residue to son TOBIAS, he to pay debts, legacies, funeral and probate charges within one month of testator's death. TOBIAS to enter bond of £500 with GEORGE LINCOLNE of Stutton and FRANCIS COXAGE of Drinkstone, to performe the will, if refuse then [PERCY ?] BACON to be executor and to inherit lands above devised to TOBIAS. TOBIAS appointed executor. Witnesses: THOMAS EASTER, cleric; ROBERT BRISTOW, GEORGE BREEME. Pr. at Ipswich 14 July 1632.

W. RICHARD BASSE of Dennington, tailor. 31 January 1632 (513)

All household stuff and implements to be sold by executors with as much convenient speed; the money arising from such sale, together with the money from weaving and debts due to be used to pay his own debts and funeral expenses, and residue of money to go to son ROBERT BASSE when 21. Uncle JOHN MAGGS, to be sole executor, and have care and upbringing of testator's son ROBERT, and to bring him up in a virtuous education. Uncle to use the interest on the sum remaining from the sale of goods, to help in the upbringing of ROBERT, and if the interest be insufficient he is empowered to take such as he needs from the capital provided 2 men supervise the withdrawal. If son die, then money to go to testator's nephew WILLIAM BASSE within 6 months of ROBERT's death. Witnesses: EDWARD MOULTON (X), GRACE WEBB. Pr. at Yoxford 20 Feb. 1632.

W. ELIZABETH BROWN of Oulton (N). [no date] (514)

To ELIZABETH wife of JOHN BROWNE, 3 pewter dishes, salt seller, brass candlestick, one pot. To the wife of WILLIAM KETTLE woollen clothes. To MARY daughter of WILLIAM KETTLE, green apron, stuff petticoat. To JOHN GROSE one box. Residue to MARGARET MILLENTON. Witnesses: RICHARD CROSWELL (X), JOHN CRICKE (X), JOHN GROSSE, FRANCIS DOWIN, ELIZABETH, the wife of JOHN BROWN. Probate granted to MARGARET MILLENTON 3 July 1632.

W. ALICE BRADLEY of Beccles. 12 September 1632 (515)

Sick. To father NICHOLAS BRADLEY of Beccles. 8 acres close in Beccles and Engate, occupied by WILLIAM BAKER & WILLIAM YEOMANS, and other piece occupied by THOMAS SMYTH, cordwainer, for life; then to go to brother-in-law JEREMY COLMAN and his wife REBECCA.

Out of the profits of the land they to give each of their children 40s., save to their daughter REBECCA, testator's goddaughter -- she to have £3 within one year of the death of NICHOLAS BRADLEY. Also to pay to the children of JOHN BRAGGS, testator's uncle, 40s. each. To wife of WILLIAM MATCHETT 40s. NICHOLAS BRADLEY appointed sole executor, he to have all movables. Witnesses: ROSE COBBE, ELIZABETH MUD (X), SUSAN CHEVERS (X), ROBERT HAWES, EDMUND SKELT. Pr. at Beccles 12 Oct. 1632.

W. THOMAS BRADLIE of Bungay, alehouse keeper. (516)
26 April 1632

To wife MARGARET alehouse stock and all estate to pay debts and funeral charges; she to be executor. Witnesses: JOHN GIRLINGE (X), WILLIAM BREMONDE, JOHN CHANDLER. Pr. at Bungay 1 May 1632.

W. JOHN BUSSE of Belton, husbandman. 25 December 1626 (517)

To THOMAS, son of JOHN SMYTH of Great Yarmouth, godson, 10s. to be paid into the hands of EDWARD WATSON for him to hold until THOMAS 21. To JOHN POPE, godson, son of JOHN POPE of Belton 2s., and to THOMAS FALK, son of EDWARD FALK, godson, 5s., both of which sums to be paid into the hands of EDWARD WATSON, for him to hold until they reach 21. To maid BILLIS HENNELL, 3s. 4d. To the poor of Belton for ever one bond obligatory which JOHN BOYCE owes to the testator; this sum to go to churchwardens and overseers to put out the money into some able sufficient manner, at 12d. the pound interest, with the consent of the majority of headboroughs of Belton; the interest to be bestowed on the poorest people on EDWARD WATSON's searchings and to be paid on the feast day of St. Thomas the apostle; after EDWARD WATSON's death, the overseers to decide the poore. Residue to wife ANNE, she to be executrix; EDWARD WATSON to be supervisor, and to receive 20s. for his pains. Witnesses: JOHN FALK, CICELY FALK. Pr. at Belton 30 May 1632.

W. BARBARA BRADLEY wife of NICHOLAS BRADLEY of Beccles. (518)
30 May 1632

To the preacher at her burial 10s. To her husband NICHOLAS BRADLEY £3, to buy him a cloak. To daughter ELIZABETH, wife of WILLIAM BRADSHAW, one fine fustian white cloak, one black grogram cloak furred; one pair of Holland sheets; one diaper table cloth, one dozen diaper table napkins; one silver sugar dish and the little spoon to it and a little tipped pot. To her daughter BARBARA BRADSHAW one diaper cupboard cloth with lace on it, one silver spoon. To her daughter MARTHA, wife of GEORGE WALLS, all of testator's goods which she left in WALL's house; also one fustian waistcoat. One long table diaper board cloth, one square table board cloth, one diaper cupboard cloth, one long towel, one damask napkin, one nut(cracker?) tipped with silver, to her daughter. To her daughter BARBARA WATTS, one silver spoon. To her son THOMAS FIDELL, one pair sheets; one plain board cloth; one diaper board cloth and towell; one pair pillow cases; one square canvas board cloth; six diaper napkins, one dozen plain napkins; one new towel; one silver taster. To MARY, the daughter of testator's son THOMAS, one silver spoon. To ANNE the daughter of testator's son-in-law NEAVE and to the husband of daughter BARBARA one silver salt; residue of all other goods, chattels to go to son-in-law THOMAS NEAVE in order to pay all debts, he to be sole executor. Witnesses: ROBERT COBB, JOHN ELLMYE, ALICE BRAD. Pr. at Beccles 6 July 1632.

W. ALICE BOISE of Ipswich St. Clement, being now of the parsonage house of Tattingstone. 8 March 1631 (519)

Sick in body. To MARK BRAND, son of MATTHEW BRAND, £10 within six months of testator's decease. To brother THOMAS BRADLEY, £10 within two months of testator's decease. To niece ALICE, wife of WILLIAM BARNARD, £5 within six months of testator's decease. To ELIZABETH, daughter of MATTHEW BRAND and wife MAY £5. To ALICE daughter of MATTHEW BRAND and wife MAY £5. To MARY, daughter of MATTHEW BRAND and wife MAY £5. Legacy to testator's niece to be paid when she reaches 20, or if she has already reached 20 when the will is proved then legacy to be paid her within six months. Same proviso to apply to her kinswoman ELIZABETH, ALICE and MARY. Also benefit of survivorship. All woolen, linen, cloth, money, jewels, plate, and household goods to be shared among the above mentioned kindred as it seem fit by EDWARD L EVERICK minister of St. Clements and by EDMOND MORGAN, mariner who are to be executors, and receive £5. To the poor in the parish of her burial 5s. Witnesses: JOHN COLE, ANNE COLE, JEREMY AUGUR, ANNE STUNE (X). Pr. at Ipswich 28 June 1632.

W. EDMOND BRANSTON of East Bergholt, clothier (N). 7 July 1632 (520)

Sick. To his wife JUDITH, all goods whatsoever, she to pay £5 or £4 to each of his children. Whatever left of his goods at the time of his wife's death to be equally divided amongst his children. Witnesses: CORNELIUS FISHER, WILLIAM MAXCEY (script). Probate granted to wife JUDITH BRANSTON 2 Aug. 1632.

W. JOHN BELSON of Oulton, yeoman. 29 August 1625 (521)

Sick. To wife MARY all my lands and tenements with appurtenances in Oulton to her and her heirs for ever; also all goods chattels, movables and immovables. Wife to be sole executrix, and pay all debts, and funeral expenses. Witnesses: THOMAS BUSSEY, JOHN CAPPS. Pr. at Lowestoft 23 Nov. 1632

W. FELIX BETTS of Shadingfield, yeoman. 22 October 1631 (522)

Weak. To my kinswoman DOROTHY BIDBANKE £4 within one month of my decease. To my kinsman GEORGE BIDBANKE of Shadingfield £4. To the poor of Shadingfield 20s. WILLIAM BIDBANKE of Shadingfield appointed executor, he to have residue of all goods. Witnesses: THOMAS ROBINSON, EDMOND BIDBANK. Pr. at Beccles 18 Aug. 1632.

W. WILLIAM BUCKENHAM of Yoxford, gentleman. 22 June 1632 (523)

To WILLIAM BUCKENHAM, eldest son, and his heirs, after my decease and the decease of my wife ABRA, all copyhold land and tenements in Alderton or near. By a deed of 13 August 1628 an annuity of 40 marks was given to my son WILLIAM payable out of freehold lands in Middleton and Fordley (excepting the water mill, house and lands late held by copy of court roll of Leiston manor) during the lifetime of testator and wife ABRA, with the proviso that if my son WILLIAM died before testator and his wife ABRA, then an annuity of £20 was to be paid to son WILLIAM's wife DOROTHY, she surviving him; this annuity of £20 was also to be charged on testator's lands in Middleton and Fordley. Now, my wife ABRA, within two days after my death, is to be bound to son BENJAMIN BUCKENHAM and to kinsman WILLIAM WINCOPP of Middleton, in £300, with the condition to pay every year to my son WILLIAM and his wife DOROTHY out of the estate given to ABRA in my lands in Alderton, the said 40 marks and the £20 during the lifetime of ABRA. In consideration of this undertaking ABRA to receive all household stuff, linen, woolen, bedding, corn, wood, carts, tumbrells, ploughs, harrows, implements of husbandry, neat beasts, horses, swine, fowles and skeps of bees. If my wife refuse the bond, then all gifts to her are void. To son BENJAMIN my water mill with the stones and furniture with the same, and all lands tenements and appurtenances in Middleton and Fordley, and Darsham; also my moity of the parsonage of Middleton and all tithes and obligations belonging. If BENJAMIN die without heirs to pass this on to then this legacy to pass to testator's son JOHN BUCKENHAM and his heirs, and if in turn JOHN die without heirs, then lands to go to testator's son ROBERT BUCKENHAM and his heirs, and if ROBERT has no issue then lands to go to testator's son WILLIAM BUCKENHAM. To son JOHN BUCKENHAM, an annuity of £12 payable out of the profits of the free hold lands in Melton and Fordley, until JOHN reach 24 years; annuity to be paid him by even payments on Lady Day or Michaelmas or within eleven days of them; the first payment to be due on the first feast day next after testator's death. When JOHN reaches 24 the annuity is to cease, and JOHN to receive an annuity instead of £20 out of the same lands for life, payable at the same feast days or within twenty days of same, by equal portions, the first payment to begin on the first feast day after JOHN reach 24. If the annuity be unpaid or fall into arrears, then JOHN has power to enter and distrain and take distress until annuity and arrears be paid together with costs, and also 40s. 9p. extra for every default suffered. If JOHN should die with issue then an annuity of £10 to pass to his heirs out of the same lands and on the same feast days. Son BENJAMIN to pay to testator's wife ABRA or her assigns provided she remain a widow, an annuity of £10 out of the same lands in Middleton on Lady Day and Michaelmas by equal portions; the first payment to be on the first Michaelmas one year after testator's death. If ABRA die or remarry then the £10 annuity to go to WILLIAM WINCOPP until son JOHN BUCKENHAM reach 24. To sons BENJAMIN & ROBERT and to the heirs of son ROBERT, a freehold cottage in Yoxford occupied by one STAFF; and the freehold pightle adjoining, with a little long orchard like a spong adjoining to the said pightle. To son ROBERT and his heirs, rest of messuages, cottages, land, tenements unbequeathed, lying in Yoxford. Wife ABRA or her assigns can take the profits from lands and tenements before devised to ROBERT from the time of the testator's death until ROBERT reach 21 (provided wife remains a widow) towards the cost of bringing ROBERT up and educating him in learning or a trade of which he shall be most capable. If ABRA die or remarry before ROBERT reaches 21 then WILLIAM WINCOPP or his assigns to have the profits to put to the same use until ROBERT is 21. BENJAMIN BUCKENHAM at the present time is copyhold tenant to a close called Scyers croft and to one piece of meadow in Yoxford, being one acre, held of the manor of Yoxford cum Membris. BENJAMIN is, on demand by ROBERT when ROBERT BUCKENHAM has reached 24, to surrender these lands to testator's son ROBERT, and in the meantime ROBERT is to have the profits from the meadow and close. If ROBERT die without issue then the croft and meadow and all lands devised to ROBERT to pass to testator's son BENJAMIN and his heirs, and if BENJAMIN die without heir, then these lands to pass to testator's son JOHN. To son JOHN, house or shop in Saxmundham, adjoining the market stead there, and all lands in Walberswick, held of the manor of the priory of Blythburgh. To daughter MARY £200 within one year next after her marriage, and until she marry, testator's executors to pay her or her assigns towards her maintenance an annuity of £10. To daughter FRANCES 200 marks within one year next after her marriage, and until she marry, testator's executors to pay her or her assigns towards her maintenance an annuity of £10. To my two daughters £100 more, to be equally divided and paid between them within 5 years next after my decease. If either die unmarried, then executors to keep the money due to the dead daughter and to divide the said sum among BENJAMIN, JOHN & ROBERT BUCKENHAM. To the poor of the parish £5 at my burial. Wife ABRA, son BENJAMIN, and WILLIAM WINCOPP appointed executors. Witnesses: THOMAS BARKER, ROBERT GILLET, JOHN BALM, THOMAS DADE. Probate granted to ABRA BUCKENHAM, widow, and BENJAMIN BUCKENHAM, son of testator at Yoxford on 26 July 1632, and to WILLIAM WINCOPP on 27 July 1632 at Yoxford.

W. JOHN BALLARD of Dunwich, taylor. 1 April 1632 (524)

House with its appurtenances to executor, so that he may at his discretion sell the same within four years of testator's decease. Money thus raised to be equally divided amongst testator's three sisters -- URSULA, FRANCES, & ELIZABETH, each to receive their legacy when they reach 21 or on the day of their marriage. To

THOMAS PEARCE, clerk, 13s. 4d., presently after my decease. To my cousin ROBERT HARY the elder, one of my sheep. Residue of goods to be equally divided amongst my three sisters by my executor. ANTHONY CARY of Dunwich to be sole executor, he to pay debts and charges of the will, and to receive 15s. to buy himself a ring for remembrance. Witnesses: WILLIAM BIRD, EDWARD HODIERNE. Pr. at Yoxford 27 April 1632.

W. SUSAN BALLARD of Dunwich, spinster (N). [blank] 1632 (525)

In the time of her sickness. To her brother JOHN BALLARD £3. To her sisters BALLARD £3 each. To sister ELIZABETH £4. To JOHN CARTE 20s. To ROBERT HARPER 5s. Clothes to be equally divided between her three sisters. ANTHONY CARY appointed to dispose of her estate. To Mr PORTE 40s. Witnesses: THOMAS PERSE, ROBERT ALDUS. Probate granted to ANTHONY CARY at Yoxford 26 April 1632.

W. THOMAS BERRIE, singleman. 3 June 1632 (526)

Sick. To JUDY PARSON, wife of JOHN PARSON, £37 presently on my decease. To my brother JOHN BERRIE all my working tools and shop things such as shoes and leather boots and all household stuff whatsoever. To my servant ANTHONY BRUNE alias PORTER £4. Brother-in-law JOHN PARSONS appointed executor to pay debts and legacies. He is also to deliver to ROBERT REYNOLDS an obligation of £8. Memorandum -- that JOHN BERRIE is to have all testator's apparell, and testator's sister to have all linen, one iron pot, one kettle, one skillet. Brother JOHN BERRIE to pay to WILLIAM KETSONNE the tanner for two hides which I owe him. Witnesses: ROBERT REYNOLDS, THOMAS BLOCKE, JOHN SMITH. Pr. at Wickham Market 14 June 1632.

W. ROBERT BEAST of Badley, cooper. 20 December 1631 (527)

Aged, but of perfect memory. To my wife MARY BEAST, for life, for her to live in or let, freehold cottage and tenement called Gantries with all houses barns, stables, yards, in Badley bought of THOMAS GOODALL of Ipswich, shipwright. However she must not dig or put in tilth any of the land, nor cut any wood or timber without the consent of youngest son FRANCIS BEAST and his heirs, in writing and under seal. On her death premises to go to the youngest son FRANCIS BEAST and his heirs, held of the chief lord of the fee, provided FRANCIS pays to testator's 4 grandchildren £9, namely £4 to ALICE BEAT who is lame of one hand; 20s. to ROBERT BEAST her brother, and 20s. to JOHN BEAST their brother, and 30s. to ELIZABETH BEAST their sister, and 30s. to MARY BEAST their sister, to be paid them after the death of testator's wife MARY, or when they reach 21, and provided they tender a receipt for their legacy. Benefit of survivorship. To my wife MARY, best bed and bedstead with all the furniture as it stands; all her linen woolen and apparell and so much of my brass and of all other mine other household stuff as thought fit and necessary by the advice of 2 or 3 of mine honest neighbors, with consent of exec. or supervisor. To son FRANCIS BEAST bed and bedstead on which he commonly lies, with sheets, blankets, coverlets and all other furniture as it stand; biggest brass pot, and all working tools belonging to my trade of coopering and chair making; also half the rough and unwrought timber on my death, FRANCIS helping to pay for it; also he to have half the boards and all the turned timber in the shop and house. To each one of the children of daughter MARY KEBLE 20s. paid out of all my other goods by the executor; those who reach or are 21 within 1 year next after wife's death to have their legacy immediately; rest to wait until they reach 21. Also all to provide a receipt for the legacy; benefit of survivorship. Wife MARY to have use and benefit of all household stuff not before given; use of all corn, grass, cattle, and white meat until the Michaelmas next after testator's decease; then all goods, cattle, not before absolutely given, to be inventoried by exec., and sold; the money thus arising to be put for wife's benefit. If exec. refuse to do this, then executor has to pay to MARY testator's wife for her life an annuity of 40s., payable by equal portions four times a year, the first payment to be made on the Christmas next following after the Michaelmas next after testator's death. To BITHA BEAST 20s. after testator's wife's death; also whatever can be spared or whatever is left after wife's death out of and from the payment of the said annuity of 40s., to go to paying legacy to BILTHA BEAST and a legacy to the children of MARY KEBLE. After these are paid the surplus of all goods, properties which are left, which I doubt not will be a good portion, to go to son JOHN BEAST and his heirs provided he act as executor and pays all debts, legacies, and funeral expenses. Also within 3 months of testator's wife's death, JOHN BEAST to enter into bond of £80 with brother FRANCIS and brother-in-law STEPHEN KEBLE to prove this will and pay debts; if son JOHN REFUSE the bond, then son FRANCIS to be executor and pay his brother JOHN £10 within one year of testator's wife's death. Also if FRANCIS refuse to pay annuity to his mother, and all her other legacies, then mother MARY BEAST to have to her and her heirs the cottage called Gantries. STEPHEN KEBLE to be supervisor and to receive 20s. for his pains. Residue of goods to executor. Witnesses: JOHN ROE, WILLIAM FLINT (X), RICHARD MANNING (X), THOMAS BEAST. Pr. at Ipswich 26 May 1632.

W. ALICE BONNER widow, Lowestoft (N). 11 May 1632 (528)

To her daughter ELIZABETH WILSON, wife of WALTER WILSON of Yarmouth, all goods whatsoever. Witnesses: EGERIE ARNOLD, ANN MUNNS. Probate granted to ELIZABETH WILSON at Lowestoft 16 May 1632.

W. EDWARD COOKE of Bungay, yeoman. 19 March 1631 (529)

To wife WINIFRED, lands called Synins field in Bungay consisting of 4 acres, and 1/2 acre situated in the little field of St.

John's which testator bought of THOMAS BACON of Bungay, gent. Within 10 days of WINIFRED's death lands devised now to go to WILLIAM COOK, brother of testator, and to his heirs for ever, provided he pay his brother THOMAS COOKE £10 within 2 months of WINIFRED's death. Stating that testator has received £10 from his father JOHN COOKE of Wickham Skeith,yeoman, which £10 is a legacy given to the testator from his grandfather and which should have been given to testator after the death of his father, but the testator pays his father 15s. a year and so received the legacy of £10. Now if testator dies before his father, the said JOHN COOKE, then testator's wife WINIFRED is to repay the £10 to testator's father on the Michaelmas one year after testator's death or within 10 days of the said Michaelmas. To brother THOMAS COOKE £10 to be paid by WINIFRED COOKE within 10 days of the Michaelmas one year after death of testator. To brother WILLIAM COOKE £10 to be paid by WINIFRED COOKE within 10 days of the Michaelmas one year after death of testator. To ANN COOKE, the daughter of my brother JOHN COOKE 40s. to be paid by WINIFRED COOKE within 10 days of the Michaelmas one year after testator's death. To daughter-in-law SUSAN KNIGHT 40s. to be paid by WINIFRED COOKE within 10 days of the Michaelmas one year after testator's death. To sons-in-law REGINALD BURWOOD and ROBERT BURWOOD £3 each to be paid by WINIFRED COOKE within 10 days of the Michaelmas one year after testator's death. To the poor of Bungay 40s. to be equally divided between the poor in both parishes within one week of testator's death. To brother EDWARD PEIRSON 20s. for him to buy himself a ring, within one year. Residue of all goods to wife WINIFRED, she to pay debts, legacies, and funeral expenses. To Mr CHAPMAN 10s. for a funeral sermon. Wife WINIFRED appointed executrix. To GEORGE WOOD, gent., 20s. and he to be supervisor. To THOMAS BACON, gent., 10s. to buy himself a ring. To brother RICHARD PRYM of Beccles, hatter, 20s. Witnesses: THOMAS BACON, THOMAS WHAITES, EDWARD PIERSON, DRUE WEBSTER. Pr. at Bungay 9 July 1632.

W. ROBERT COOKE of Alderton, yeoman. 1 July 1632 (530)

Sick; to be buried at Alderton churchyard. To wife SARAH one piece of land consisting of 3 acres called Salters close in lieu of her dowry, for life; then close to pass to testator's son JOHN and heirs. To son ROBERT COOKE 1/2 house in Alderton, namely the hall, butlery, shop, and the chamber thereunto belonging; 1/2 the backhouse and 1/2 the barn, with free liberty to yards and well, and to go into the barn. Also 1/2 the land in Millfield. To son FRANCIS other 1/2 of house and land, namely the parlour and parlour chamber, 1/2 the backhouse, 1/2 the barn with the house at the barn end; liberty to yards and to the well. Also rest of lands in Millfield. To daughter ELIZABETH COOKE a piece of land, one acre, copyhold of the manor of Fenhall in Sutton. Sons ROBERT & FRANCIS to join together and to pay to testator's wife SARA 20s. a year out of their shares in the house and lands in Alderton, this annuity to continue until £10 has been paid, and payments to start on the Michaelmas next after testator's death and payments to be made in the north porch of Alderton church.

If the annuity is not paid, then power to enter and distrain to SARAH. To ROBERT COOKE, my best coat. To FRANCIS COOKE my best suite of clothes. Wife SARAH to have all corn, cattle, movables to pay debt, and burial expenses; rest after these expenses met, to be equally divided between wife and children. Wife SARAH appointed executrix; JOHN HARRISON of Alderton, supervisor. Witnesses: CHARLES ALLEN, WILLIAM BETTS. Pr. at Wickham Market 27 July 1632.

W. WILLIAM CUTHBERT of Barking, yeoman. 12 May 1632 (531)

Sick; to be buried at Barking. To brother ROBERT £4 within 6 months of testator's death. To niece ANN CROSE £4 within one month after she reaches 21. To niece SUSAN CROSSE 20s. soon after testator's death. Benefit of survivorship for these three bequests. To servant ELIZABETH MANYNGE 40s. within 6 months of testator's death. Residue of goods to WILLIAM PITTES the younger of Barking, he to be sole exec., to pay debts and legacies and funeral expenses. Witnesses: SIMON COLCHESTER, JOHN PULFORD, WILLIAM PARKER (X). Pr. at Ipswich 16 June 1632.

W. WILLIAM CRANE of Chelmondiston, yeoman. 19 June 1628 (532)

Sick. To each child 2s. when they reach 21 or the day of their marriage whichever first. Residue of goods, corn, cattle, jewels, ready money, once debts and legacies met to go to wife JUDITH in order that she might bring up their children and for her own maintenance. She to be sole executrix. Witnesses: CHRISTOPHER ANDREWS, JOHN MASON (X), JOHN HAVELL, script. Pr. at Chelmondiston 31 May 1632.

W. EDMOND CLOD of Parham, twill weaver. 11 December 1627 (533)

Sick. To wife BEATRICE all goods whatsoever, and all things belonging to the testator so that she can pay debts. She to be sole executrix. Witnesses: ISAAC HARLOND, GEOFRY CORBOULD (X), JOHN HUNT. Pr. at Wickham Market 31 Jan. 1632.

W. ROWLAND CHAPMAN of Mutford, yeoman. 21 December 1632 (534)

Sick; to be buried at Mutford. Wife EME to be executrix, and have all goods, chattels, bonds, movable, and bills, whatsoever in order to provide for maintenance of their children, and to pay legacies. To son WILLIAM, land and tenement called Fayerwethers, both bond and free in Henstead and Batley, provided WILLIAM pay to EME £10 each year for the rest of her life, by equal portions at Michaelmas and Lady Day. Also EME to live in the parlour chamber of the house and to have the orchard on the north side of the house with free liberty of ingress and egress. Further WILLIAM to pay to his brother HUGH CHAPMAN £50 when he reaches 21. To son HUGH CHAPMAN £50 more when he reach 21 to be paid by executrix. To daughter RACHEL £100 to be paid when 21 by executrix. To daughter ELIZABETH £100 when 21 to be paid by executrix. Executrix to pay the fine when WILLIAM enters the copyhold part of his lands. [Benefit of survivorship for legacies crossed out. No witnesses given, unless they were on another sheet of the will now missing.] Pr. at Beccles 19 Jan. 1632.

W. JOHN CRANE of Lowestoft (N). [no date] (535)

In the time of his sickness. To wife MARY house and lands in order to educate children, and all goods. Witnesses: THOMAS JENTLEMAN, WILLIAM KETTLEBURGH, ALICE ALLEN, ELIZABETH the wife of THOMAS FULWOOD. Probate granted to MARY CRANE 7 Nov. 1632.

W. SUSAN CHURCH of Sudbourne, widow. 31 October 1632 (536)

Sick. To son JOSEPH SIDEY, freehold lands and tenements in Hitcham, provided he pay to MARY BARNARD, daughter of the testator, and wife of RICHARD BARNARD, £4 annuity payable at Christmas, Lady Day, St. John the Baptist and Michaelmas by equal portions the first payment to be made on the first feast day after death of the testator; if default then daughter MARY to inherit the lands. To son JOSEPH a silver and gilt pot. To SUSAN BARNARD & JOAN BARNARD, daughters of RICHARD & MARY BARNARD £5 each. To the poor of the parish where testator is buried 40s. To godchild SUSAN GARRARD 20s. Son-in-law FRANCIS BURWELL to be sole executor and to have residue of goods to pay debts and legacies and funeral expenses. Witness: WILLIAM SMYTH. Pr. at Ipswich 12 Jan. 1632.

W. THOMAS CLARKE of East Bergholt, clothworker. 14 May 1630 (537)

Sick. To brother EDWARD 15s. that he owed to testator, and a further 5s.; also 30s. due to testator by a bill of debt from JOHN STANTON of Tollesbury in Essex -- EDWARD to receive it when it fall due and payable. To cousin ELIZABETH DUKE of East Bergholt, singlewoman, 40s. within 3 months of testator's death. To THOMAS KENTE the youngest son of THOMAS KENTE of East Bergholt, 40s. in 3 months of testator's death, to be paid into the hands of cousin ABRAHAM NEWTON to be put out by him or kept in his own hands to the best advantage and use of THOMAS KENTE the younger, and to be paid him when he reaches 21; if he die before reaching 21 then money to be paid to his brother ROBERT KENTE. Residue of goods and chattels to go to wife ELIZABETH CLARKE, she to be sole executrix and pay debts and funeral expenses. Witnesses: JAMES MEATER, ROBERT FERROUR, JOHN STEVENSON. Pr. at Ipswich 26 May 1632.

W. RALPH CUBITT of Bulcamp, gentleman. 26 April 1632 (538)

To son SIMON messuage and tenement in Henham where WILLIAM GAYE lives, with houses and orchards and land belongings; he to inherit lands immediately on testator's death. To wife MARY messuage and tenement in Bulcamp where testator lives with all lands belonging thereunto in Bulcamp and Henham, for her lifetime with all household stuff, stock, corn, hay, plates and utensils, except the ready money and debts due to the testator; also one horse to be taken by SIMON at his own choice, and also one bed fully furnished with all things needful to be delivered to son SIMON by testator's wife. Wife to have the rest with these exceptions in lieu of dowry. To son HENRY messuage previously given to MARY for her life; HENRY to inherit these lands on the death of his mother provided he pay to testator's other children as follows -- to son RALPH £50; to daughter ELIZABETH £40; to daughter MARY £50, and daughter MARTHA £50; and to testator's grandchild REBECCA WILKENSON £10 -- all these legacies to be paid by HENRY within six months of the death of his mother. Benefit of survivorship. If however HENRY die before MARY, the testator's wife, or if he refuse to pay the legacies above specified, then HENRY's legacy to be void and land to pass to testator's son SIMON, and SIMON has to pay the several legacies -- to HENRY £60, RALPH £40, ELIZABETH £40, MARY £50, MARTHA £50, and REBECCA £10; benefit of survivorship. Proviso that if any of the children die before they inherit but are over 18 on their death then they can dispose of their legacy as they wish. Residue to son SIMON, he to pay debts, funeral and probate charges, and to be executor. Witnesses: HUMFREY BOHUN, REGINALD LESSEY. Pr. at Yoxford 24 May 1632.

W. MARY CRISPE of Fressingfield, widow. 22 March 1631 (539)

To JAMES BRAME, testator's father, a piece of gold of 10s. To the two daughters of brother JAMES BRAME, piece of gold of 20s. each, all of which three pieces of gold now in the hands of my sister-in-law the wife of JAMES BRAME. To MARY MEENE, servant of son GODFREY CRISPE, best waistcoat and a kerchief, presently after my death. To goddaughter MARY BORDWELL, pair sheets and best ruff. To the wife of JEREMY BOTWRIGHT, green waistcoat. To Widow LEBOLD old cloak and tawney petticoat. To GRACE LEBOLD, russet petticoat and a coarse white apron. To JOAN NOYSE, tawney waistcoat, all of which gifts of clothes are to be made presently on death of testator. To the wife of GODFREY CRISPE and to HENRY DOWNES, my son-in-law, a silver spoon each presently on testator's death. Executor to receive all debts due to testator, and pay her debts and see her buried. Residue of goods to GODFREY CRISPE, provided that within 20 days after her death, he enter into bond with brother JAMES BRAME in £10 to pay an annuity of 20s. a year to MARY, testator's daughter and wife of HENRY DOWNES -- payments of the annuity to be made by equal installments at Lady Day and Michaelmas at the south porch of Fressingfield church. Also HENRY DOWNES to let GODFREY CRISPE have access to remove all household stuff, linen, bedding, brass and pewter. To daughter MARY kersey gown, little red petticoat, denser kersey petticoat, best cloak and the little box with the linen therin. GODFREY CRISPE appointed executor. Witnesses; JAMES BRAME, FRANCIS SANDCROFT. Pr. at Stradbroke 17 April 1632.

W. MARY DRANE of Framlingham, spinster. 7 May 1632 (540)

Sick. To sister ROSE DRANE of Saxtead, 20s. yearly payable at Christmas, Lady Day, Michaelmas and Midsummer at Framlingham church. To kinswoman ANNE KERRIDGE, wife of MILES KERRIDGE 20s. in 1 yr. of testator's death. To kinswoman SUSAN BROWNE, wife of ROBERT BROWNE of Leiston, 20s. in 1 yr. To kinsman THOMAS LOUNYS of Framlingham and ALICE my kinswoman his now wife, and after their deaths to ALICE's son called JOHN CULLIE, rest of goods, chattels, household goods and implements. THOMAS LOUNYS to be sole executor, pay debts. Witnesses: THOMAS MORSE, JOHN BORRELL. Pr. at Wickham Market 25 May 1632.

W. WILLIAM DAVY of Wantisden, husbandman (N). (541)
18 February 1632

To FRANCIS & WILLIAM WOOD sons of JOHN WOOD of Wantisden, one sheep each. Rest of goods to EDMUND TILLETT of Pettistree, my late master, and to his son EDMUND TILLETT; EDMUND TILLETT the elder to bury me decently at Pettistree. Witnesses: FRANCIS CRANE, JOHN WOOD. Probate granted to EDMUND TILLETT 19 Feb. 1632.

W. THOMAS DURRANT of Marlesford (N). [no date] (542)

Sick. All goods to be sold in order to pay debts, and residue to go to the maintenance of JOHN his youngest son. Witnesses: JAMES POTTE, clerk, MARGARET SWAINE, GEORGE KNOWLES, the grandfather of JOHN the son of the said testator. Probate granted to GEORGE KNOWLES at Wickham Market 20 Jan. 1632.

W. HENRY DOWE of St. Margaret's Ilketshall, husbandman. (543)
17 November 1632

Sick. To ANNIS DOWE, his wife, appointed executrix, all goods and chattels to pay debts and discharge legacies. To HENRY DOWE, son £5, namely 20s. within 1 year, and 20s. yearly thereafter; if son die before the £5 is all paid, then residue to executrix. Witnesses: RICHARD BATTELYE, CIPRIAN BATTELYE, RICHARD BATTELIE, jnr. Pr. at Beccles 15 Dec. 1632.

W. ALICE ELLIS alias PILKINTON, widow (N). (544)
28 January 1632

Sick. To daughter ANN PILKINTON all goods that were hers before her marriage with EDWARD ELLIS her late husband. Witnesses: ANN, wife of THOMAS DEERINGE; FAITH TOMSON, widow. Probate granted to ANN PILKINTON at Beccles 4 Feb. 1632.

W. EDWARD ELLIS of Blundeston, yeoman. (545)
17 December 1632

Very sick; to be buried in Blundeston church on the south side against my seat where I sit in church. To son JOHN ELLIS all household lands and tenements both free and copyhold, provided he pay to his sisters ELIZABETH & MARY £10 each -- namely to ELIZABETH in one year of testator's death, and to MARY £10 within 2 years. If he fail or default in these payments then power to enter and distrain until full satisfaction obtained. Residue of all goods and chattels whatsoever to go to wife ALICE, appointed sole executrix to pay debts and funeral charges. Witnesses: JOHN SPORLE (X), ROBERT UNDERWOOD, ANNE PILKINTON (X). Pr. 4 Feb. 1632.

W. WILLIAM EDGAR of Ipswich St. Nicholas, shoemaker (N). (546)
30 March 1632

To wife MATTHEE all goods, desiring her not to see his son suffer want and on her death she to leave whatever remains of testator's goods to his son. Witnesses: JOHN GRAY, MARY MORGAN. Probate granted to MATTHEE EDGAR at Ipswich 7 April 1632.

W. JOHN EDRIDGE of Woodbridge (N). 7 May 1632 (547)

To wife PRUDENCE £10 annuity to be paid out of the house in Woodbridge. To son JOHN £50, but in case son JOHN dies before he receive his legacy, then it should be given to wife PRUDENCE she to dispose of it equally between her other children. Witnesses: SAMPSON FENN, JOHN BENNET. Probate granted to PRUDENCE EDRIDGE at Wickham Market 25 May 1632.

W. WILLIAM FYNCH of Melton, yeoman. 26 May 1632 (548)

Sick. To son-in-law FRANCIS LEBOLD one black colt in Iken, on testator's death, the said FRANCIS to pay the charge for the pasturing of it. To MARY the wife of FRANCIS LEBOLD 20s., which she oweth to me. To daughter-in-law ROSE SHEWELL, £5, presently on the death of testator's wife SUSAN. To AVIS SHEWELL daughter-in-law £5 presently on the death of testator's wife SUSAN, her mother. To ROGER GODBOLD, brother-in-law, one suite of stuff, apparell and one coat. To brother THOMAS FYNCH of Woodbridge, husbandman, 20s. within one year of testator's death. To the four children of brother THOMAS FYNCH £4, to be paid to them as 20s. each within one year after death of wife SUSAN. Residue of goods and chattels to wife SUSAN, she to be sole executrix, pay debts. Witnesses: RICHARD HARRISON, THOMAS PLAKEY, HUMFREY

HARRISON. Pr. at Wickham Market 14 June 1632.

W. ANDREW FELGATE of Earl Stonham. 4 May 1632 (549)

Very sick and weak. To wife ELIZABETH, all lands and tenements, goods and chattels, if she execute the will. Also she to give a dower to SAMUEL KEABLE & GRACE ALDRED, her kinswoman, on their marriage, and also if the jointure offered at the time of this marriage does not amount to £40, then ELIZABETH to add to the sum offered to make it up to £40. If the amount offered is more than £40 then the surplus is to go to the said SAMUEL & GRACE. To the town of Earl Stonham £5, to be paid to the churchwardens of the town when or if wife ELIZABETH remarries, or on her death. To the poor of Earl Stonham 20s., to be distributed on his burial. To WILLIAM WHITBIE clerk, 20s. for a sermon. Wife ELIZABETH appointed sole executrix, she to pay debts, legacies, funeral charges. Witnesses: WILLIAM WHITBIE, JOHN VINSENT. Pr. at Ipswich 26 May 1632.

W. THOMAS FATTER of Ipswich, grocer. 2 January 1632 (550)

Executor to distribute to poor of [left blank] parish on his burial, the sum [blank]. To JOHN MICKLEFIELD of Bucklesham in satisfaction of all debts owed by testator to him, and for and towards burial, and payment of such fines as will be due for testator's sister LIDEA on her admittance to copyhold, one piece of meadow ground called Brodemeadow, with appurtenances, consisting of 9 acres, also one piece of land or pasture called Britell field, being 6 acres, and one piece of pasture lying at Butrell's lane and next to Bucklesham heath, being 4 acres, the same all lying and being in Bucklesham. Rest of lands and tenements in Bucklesham and Levington, both free and copyhold, to JOHN MICKLEFIELD for 10 years after testator's death, provided he support and maintain the said lands, and commit no waste or strip timber, and pay to testator's sister LIDEA a yearly annuity or rent of £6 by equal payments due on Lady Day and Michaelmas, the first payment to be made on the first feast after testator's death. Payment to be made in Bucklesham church porch. JOHN MICKLEFIELD is also to pay £20 to ROSE KNOCKES of Nacton, £10 to JOAN HAYWARD of Tuddenham, £8 to REBECCA BLECHINGHAM wife of THOMAS BLECHINGHAM, £4 to Widow RIVETT of Witnesham, £4 to THOMAS SMYTH, 40s. to SUSAN INNOLDES, and also pay the interest on these sums which shall be due on them on testator's death. To sister LIDEA after the 10 year term to JOHN MICKLEFIELD, all copyhold land above leased to JOHN MICKLFIELD. Testator is bound in £40 to pay £20 to sister LIDEA, now she to deliver this bond and shall also discharge and acquit executors of this will of and from one legacy of £40 given to LIDEA under the will of WILLIAM FATTER, our father. If LIDEA refuse to do so then exec. to occupy and enjoy messuages devised to LIDEA until they have received £60 from these lands, and until then LIDEA to have nothing to do with the said lands devised to her. Also if LIDEA die without lawful issue then lands devised to her to pass to

JOHN MICKLEFIELD and his heirs, provided he pay to THOMAS & MARTHA BLECHINGHAM, the children of THOMAS BLECHINGHAM £5 each within six months after LIDEA's death, and to pay to THOMAS, WILLIAM, EDMOND, JOHN PEACH & ELIZABETH ELLIS, the children of ROSALAINE PEACH £6 each within 2 years of LIDEA's death, and to pay to RICHARD STUD of Ipswich malster and THOMAS GOSLING of Ipswich husbandman, £4 each within 3 months of LIDEA's death; also to pay to ANN SEPSENGE of Ipswich widow £4 in 1 month of LIDEA's death, and to ROSE KNOCKES of Nacton spinster £6 in 2 1/2 years of LIDEA's death, and to pay to THOMAS, EDWARD, & ANN MICKLEFIELD testator's cousins £20 each within 4 years of LIDEA's death. All of which sums are to be paid at the Corn hill cross in Ipswich. Residue of all goods and chattels to sister LIDEA in recompense for all the legacies given her by her parents WILLIAM & MARGERY FATTER. Uncle JOHN MICKLEFIELD, sole executor; RICHARD STUD of Ipswich and THOMAS GOSLING appointed supervisors, and to oversee the £6 rent paid to LIDEA, and also LIDEA to have their advice with regard to her marriage. They to have 40s. each for their pains. Witnesses: WILLIAM COCKE, THOMAS COCKE. Pr. at Ipswich 2 Feb. 1632.

W. JOHN FLINTE of Badley, yeoman. 6 February 1631 (551)

Sick, to be buried at Badley. To wife ANNA copyhold tenement in Badley where he lives, and all appurtenances, for her life, she to maintain and keep in good repair. Then on her death lands to go to testator's son WILLIAM and his heirs provided he pay to testator's son EDMOND £60 -- if EDMOND reaches 21 before the death of ANNA his mother, then WILLIAM to pay the £60 within the first three years ensuing next after ANNA's death at a rate of £20 p.a.; if ANNA has died before EDMOND reaches 21, then WILLIAM to pay £20 to EDMOND on his 21st birthday, and then £20 a year for the subsequent two years. Power to enter and hold, and EDMOND then to pay the £60 to WILLIAM in three years, if default made by WILLIAM. To wife ANNA messuage in Stowmarket for life, then to pass to son EDMOND. To daughter SUSAN ASHLYE 20s. within 1 year of testator's death. To daughter RUTH WELLAM 20s. in 2 years of testator's death. All movables and goods remaining to wife, appointed sole executrix, to pay debts legacies and funeral charges. Witnesses: FRANCIS WITHERBEE, PHIL BARNES. Pr. at Ipswich 23 April 1632.

W. NICHOLAS FORD of Bramford, yeoman. 13 November 1632 (552)

Diseased in body. To daughter SUSANNA £40 when she reach 21. To second daughter ANN £40 when she reach 21. To youngest daughter MAY £40 when she reach 21. To that child which my wife is now with £40 when 21. Benefit of survivorship. Wife ANN to be sole executrix, and she to enter into bond of £300 with HENRY YORKE my father-in-law and kinsman JOHN FORD of Needham Market, within 4 months of death, being bound to pay legacies. If she refuse then HENRY YORKE & JOHN FORDE to be executors. Residue of goods whatsoever to wife ANN, hoping she will be a kind mother.

Witnesses: SAMUEL ASHTON, RICHARD HAYWARD. Pr. at Ipswich 15 Dec. 1632.

W. THOMAS FYNCH of Trimley St. Mary, yeoman. 8 December 1631 (553)

Sick. To wife FRANCES £20 which is in ALLEN COVES hands. To wife £30 more within 3 months of testator's death; also all household stuff of his and all which was hers before their marriage, except six silver spoons which were the testator's before he married her. To brother JOHN FYNCH £10 in 1 year of testator's death. To sister BUTTALL of Campsey Ash £5 in 1 year of testator's death. To sister BUN of Hasketon, £5 in 1 year of testator's death. To JOHN FYNCH of Gifford's hall, and to his wife £5 each in 1 year of testator's death. To son-in-law ALLEN COVE £10 in 3 months of testator's death. To CHARLES SMYTH of Ipswich £5 in 1 year of testator's death. To JOHN FARRAR, clerk, 40s. in 1 month of testator's death. To ROBERT ARCHDALE, clerk, 20s. in 1 month of testator's death. To his late partner DANIEL SMYTH of Walton 20s. To the poor of Walton 20s., and the poor of Trimley St. Mary 20s. in 1 week of death. To MARY LANGHAM, widow, 40s. in 3 months of testator's death. To JEFFERY BLINES & JOHN SPINKE of Trimley 20s. a year, being 10s. each, for life. Residue of all goods and chattels to son-in-law JOHN CRANE, and all the land being in two several closes lately had in mortgage of JOHN SCRUTTON in Trimley St. Martin. JOHN CRANE to perform all legacies, pay debts and burial expenses, he being sole executor. Witnesses: NICHOLAS BETTS, WILLIAM CUMFEILD (X), CHARLES SMYTH. Pr. at Ipswich 20 Dec. 1632.

W. JOHN GIRLING of Wherstead, carpenter. 25 August 1632 (554)

Sick. To JAMES GARNHAM, of Barking, carpenter, all household stuff and household implements, and all things else, and the reversion to a tenement in Great Bricett bought from JOHN WHELER of Bricett. Also JAMES GARNHAM is jointly bound with testator to NICHOLAS SORRELL in £20 to pat £10 -- JAMES GARNHAM now to satisfy the bond out of the estate. Surplus of estate once this bond is met, to be equally divided out amongst testator's children. JAMES GARNHAM to be executor, pay funeral expenses. Witnesses: NICHOLAS SORRELL, ELIZABETH LAYE. Pr. at Ipswich 20 Sept. 1632.

W. ANDREW GOYMER of Tuddenham, yeoman. [blank] July 1632 (555)

To wife SARAH all goods, chattels, household implements both indoors and out, in order for SARAH to pay debts and legacies to his daughters and for their maintenance, all lands and tenements in Tuddenham to wife until his son ANDREW reach 24, he to inherit lands on the Michaelmas next after his 24 birthday. To son ANDREW, houses and tenements, both free and copyhold, in Tuddenham when 24, provided SARAH has the sole use of the parlour and parlour chamber for life, with free egress, and use of the garden at the end of the said parlour. ANDREW also to pay mother for life an annuity of £8 due in equal installments on Lady Day and Michaelmas. Power for SARAH to enter and distrain in the lands, if default. To son JOHN GOYMER, land in Fen field, and a little meadow lying above Tuddenham Bridge, he to inherit these lands when ANDREW inherits his land. Also ANDREW to pay to him £10 when he reaches 24, and a further £10 within one year next after provided he surrender all copyhold land to ANDREW if need require. To daughters SARAH, ANN, & MARILYN £20 each, when 21, with benefit of survivorship. Also ANDREW to pay to his sisters the said SARAH, ANN & MARILYN 20 nobles each when they reach 21. When ANDREW reaches 21 he is to receive 40s. a year until his 24th birthday, to be paid him by testator's wife SARAH. Wife SARAH appointed executrix to pay debts, legacies; brother THOMAS GOYMER to be supervisor. Witnesses: JOHN BALLARD, ROBERT STEFFE, WILLIAM SEELY, HENRY PYNSON (X). Pr. at Ipswich 28 July 1632.

W. ALEXANDER GARNON alias STAYNER of Sutton, yeoman. (556)
1 January 1630

Sick. To JOHN GARNON alias STAYNER, my son, all lands and tenements, both free and copy hold, he to pay all debts, legacies and funeral expenses. To son WILLIAM £10 within 2 years next after testator's death -- namely £5 a year. To wife ELIZABETH £40, to be raised out of his stock, valued by two independent men one of whom to be appointed by wife and one appointed by son; also to wife all the goods and chattels she brought with her on marriage, and all those which were her mother's. Residue of goods, chattels, to son JOHN appointed sole executor. Witnesses: JOHN BRILL (X), WILLIAM TYE (X), RICHARD HARRISON. Pr. at Wickham Market 5 July 1632.

W. ANTHONY GRENLING of Stradbroke, yeoman. (557)
11 September 1632

To wife MARGARET an annuity of £35 payable out of lands at Stradbroke called Shelton's which were ROGER GRENLING's, now deceased, testator's father; this in full satisfaction of dower claims; payments to be made at Lady Day and Michaelmas by equal portions, and to begin on the first feast day which falls due after testator's death. If default, then power granted to enter and distrain into lands. To son ANTHONY, messuage called Sheltons, now inhabited by testator, and all lands, tenements whatsoever belonging to it in Stradbroke; also tenement in Stradbroke where JOHN GRENLING lives late purchased called Pulhams, and all copyhold lands in Stradbroke; ANTHONY to enter lands when 21. Also to receive bedstead with all the furniture thereunto belonging as it stands on my parlour chamber at the messuage where he lives; 6 pair sheets; copper and a livery table standing on the said parlour chamber -- all when ANTHONY reach 21. To daughter ELIZABETH £200 when 17; also posted bedstead with the feather bed and furniture belonging to it as it stands on the kitchen chamber; 6 pair sheets; great chest and the desk in the closet -- all when she reaches 17. To son ANTHONY all freehold land and tenements with appurtenances in Stradbroke late Pulham's, with all belonging to it, when he reaches 21, provided he pay to sister ELIZABETH £100 when she reaches 21 or within 6 months after the death of testator's wife MARGARET, whichever happens first. Payment to be made in the south porch of Stradbroke church, and if ANTHONY refuse or fail in this payment then power to ELIZABETH to enter Pulhams tenement and hold until received 200 marks. To wife MARGARET, two best bedsteads and featherbeds, unbequeathed, with all furniture belonging to them; also all unbequeathed linen. Rest of goods, chattles, brass and pewter to be divided into two -- half to go to wife MARGARET and half to be shared equally between ANTHONY & ELIZABETH. Executors to maintain and educate ANTHONY & ELIZABETH in learning and in good and virtuous education until ANTHONY 21 and ELIZABETH 17. Exec. to have use of all lands until ANTHONY reach 21 to use for the education and maintenance of testator's two children. Also to pay debts and legacies, maintain buildings in good repair, pay such rents as are due, commit no waste using timber only for essential repair and using only wood from hedges for fuel. To niece ANNE CURTEIS one white weaning cow calf. Rest of goods and chattels, and the lease of his parsonage, all cattle, to be sold by executors for uses already detailed; executors to call in all debts owed to him to pay his debts and funeral expenses. Executors, within 40 days of ANTHONY reaching 21 to give a true account of all their financial dealings to testator's daughter ELIZABETH, giving all receipts for sale of lands and goods to her, and within 4 days of rendering this account to give her any surplus of money remaining in their hands. Wife MARGARET, JOHN GOULDSMITH, gent., and THOMAS GORBOLD, gent., executors. To sister ANNE CURTEIS, widow, £3 in 1 year of testator's death. To FRANCIS LUFFE, widow, 40s. in 1 year of testator's death. FRANCIS SANDCROFT the younger, testator's friend, appointed supervisor and has £5. Witnesses: RICHARD ANDREWS (X), JOHN GRENLING (X), SAMUEL WRIGHT (X). Pr. at Stradbroke 25 Sept. 1632.

W. MARGARET GOBSEN of Stratford. 17 October 1632 (558)

All goods, small and great, to daughter GRACE CHAMBERLAIN. Witnesses: JOHN GILLY, WILLIAM SHARP. Probate granted to GRACE CHAMBERLAIN at Ipswich 19 Nov. 1632.

W. JOHN GOODWIN of Walberswick, singleman. 28 July 1631 (559)

Sickly and weak of body. To mother KATHERINE GOODWIN, all messuages and lands, she to pay out of these lands to WILLIAM BARTON, the son of RICHARD BARTON of Southwold £3 within 1 year. To mother all goods and chattels whatsoever, she to be sole executrix. Witnesses: THOMAS BURFORD, WILLIAM MUNNES, AUGUSTINE WARDE. Pr. at Yoxford 20 Feb. 1632.

W. FRANCES GOODWYNE of Shadingfield, spinster. (560)
23 May 1632

Sick. All goods, money, chattels, save charge of funeral, to go to the bringing up of her son THOMAS, to be expended at the discretion of the overseers of Shadingfield parish. If he die before money expended, surplus to be divided between those that were her helpers in the time of her sickness, to ELIZABETH BOSTON of Shadingfield is appointed executrix. Witnesses: FRANCIS CADDEW, MARY CADDEW, MARY ROSYER. [No note of probate.]

W. RICHARD GOOCH of Wissett, yeoman. 27 February 1631 (561)

Sick. To wife MARTHA, messuage and lands where he now lives, and all other lands and houses belonging in Wissett, for her lifetime, provided she maintain them and keep them in good repair, commit no waste, cut no timber, save for whatever necessary for repair, and fencing, she to pay such rents as are due for copyhold. Also she to pay out of the rents and profits of the lands, within the next 5 years after testator's death, to his two daughters MARY & MARTHA £5 each on Michaelmas and Lady Day by equal portions, the first payment to be made on the first feast day after testator's death. After 5 years has finished, wife to pay to her two daughters MARY & MARTHA £8 each a year as previously out of profits of the said lands, in the porch of Wissett church. Benefit of survivorship; also power to enter and distrain if default. MARY & MARTHA to inherit these lands on death of their mother. Wife MARTHA and brother-in-law RICHARD LOPHAM, to organise sale of all outward stock, cows, heifers, horses, sheep, and all other movables belonging to husbandry; this sale to be made as soon as possible after testator's death to raise money in order to meet debts. To daughter MARY, bedstead and bed fully furnished in the parlour, and the cupboard there; long table with the frame; one joined form standing in the hall -- all these to her within 3 months next after her marriage. To daughter MARTHA best bedstead and best bed fully furnished, next unto the bed given unto MARY; long table with the frame and one joined form standing in the parlour within three months of her marriage. Benefit of survivorship to apply to these gifts of furniture to MARY & MARTHA. Rest of goods, after debts, legacies, funeral expenses, and probate charges met, to go to wife MARTHA, she to be sole executrix, and to be a careful mother and to provide for his two daughters and give them good counsel. RICHARD LOPHAM of Wangford brother-in-law, appointed supervisor, and has 20s. Witnesses: JOHN HARVYE, NICHOLAS HARVY, ROBERT MIGHELLS. Pr. 12 May 1632.

W. JUDITH GODDARD of St. Margaret Southelmham. (562)
28 February 1631

Executor to sell all movable goods, corn, cattle, implements of household and household stuff at the best possible price in order to raise money to pay debts, probate and funeral expenses. Rest of the money remaining after this done, to be put out according to exec. discretion and the profits from that to be used in the education and maintenance of testator's children. Exec. also to sell 9 of the best oaks and 4 of the elms standing in her lands for the binding of testator's son WILLIAM to some trade. Executor instructed to lease the messuage and all such houses and lands where testator now lives together with all meadows, lands and pastures, excepting the land and all other benefits given to MARION PIGEON late wife of RICHARD PIGEON to provide her with an annuity of £5 a year as laid down in RICHARD PIGEON's will, late father to testator, rest of lands to go to executor in order for him to educate and maintain testator's children. Within one year of MARION PIGEON's death executor to sell those lands for the best price and money thus raised to be equally divided between testator's three children, or the survivors of them, provided also that her sons do not inherit such money until they have reached 24 and her daughters 21. If the lands are sold before children have reached these ages then the money to be employed by executor to the best profit and advantage of her children. Executor also to render an annual account of all moneys to supervisor of the will, and exec. to enter into bond with supervisor to perform the duties laid down in the will and to deliver accounts, and money as specified. Should the exec. die or refuse to enter bond then JOHN MORSE appointed executor in his place. Brother-in-law WILLIAM BENDY alias BACON, appointed exec; EDWARD HAM of St. Margaret's and JOHN PIGEON of Stowmarket, gent., appointed supervisors. Witnesses: EDWARD HAME, MARY MORSE (X), ANN BEDFORTH (X), JOHN SAGAR, script. Pr. 29 March 1632.

W. THOMAS GIRLING of Wherstead. 1 April 1632 (563)

Sick. To daughter SARAH, best brass pot, 4 best pewter dishes, 1 pair best sheets to be given to JOHN GOODING when he shall require them for her use. To daughter SARAH £40 to be given to JOHN GOODING for her use when she is 21, or on the day of her marriage. To wife MARY the use of all household stuff whilst she remain a widow, then this to go on her death to daughter SARAH: should wife remarry then 1/2 household stuff unbequeathed, or else its equivalent in money the amount having been apprised in an inventory to be made soon after testator's death by men of JOHN GOODING's choice to go to SARAH. The remaining half of goods to go to wife, MARY. Wife MARY appointed sole executrix; JOHN GOODING appointed supervisor. Witnesses: SAMUEL SUMMARES, RICHARD GOODING. Pr. at Ipswich 30 April 1632.

W. WILLIAM HERRINGTON of Hintlesham (N). 24 June 1632 (564)

Sick. To brother SAMUEL HERRINGTON best suit of clothes. To JAMES son of said brother SAMUEL 20s. To MARY, daughter of said brother 20s. To MYLES CRAMFILD, nephew, 20s. Residue of goods to sister BARBARA HERRINGTON, to pay debts, legacies, funeral. Witnesses: MARGARET, wife of JOHN STEWARD of Hintlesham; JEREMY MARCHANT of Hintlesham. Probate granted to BARBARA HERRINGTON 30

June 1632.

W. MARGARET HOWELL of Stradbroke (N). 2 January 1632 (565)

To daughter FRANCES, wife of HENRY KING, all her goods. Witness: ANN FOSTER. Probate granted to FRANCES KING at Yoxford 30 Jan. 1632.

W. JOAN HERING of Stradbroke, widow. 25 January 1632 (566)

Sick; to be buried in Stradbroke churchyard. To son WILLIAM, all shop tools, a cupboard, and an ale stool in the little buttery; 2 pair sheets; 2 plain pillow beers; 6 table napkins -- three of the best, three of the worst. To son JAMES, coffer on the hall chamber, 2 pair sheets, 2 pillow beers of the middle sort, 6 table napkins. To daughter ANNE, posted bedstead on the parlour chamber with the worst feather bed, a rug, a pair of blankets, a silver cup; all wearing linen and all woollen. To son JOHN livery bedstead, and a trundle bedstead with one feather bed and one flock bed, one bird covering, and one other covering on the trundle bed, 2 pair blankets in the parlour. To son THOMAS one livery bedstead, one trundle bed on the hall chamber; one feather bed, one flock bed and the best covering with one other covering; one of the best silver spoons, two pair blankets. To sons WILLIAM, JAMES, JOHN, & THOMAS all silver buttons, equally divided. To sons WILLIAM, JAMES, JOHN & daughter ANN, all books, trenchers, wooden platters and cups, equally divided. To sons JOHN, THOMAS & daughter ANN, all movable goods, chattels, household implements whatsoever, half going to sons and half to her daughter. To RICHARD ALLDUS of Wingfield and JAMES ALLDUS of Stradbroke, brothers-in-law, all right title, term of years possessed by testator, under her husband's will, but before they enter these lands, they to give security that they will pay legacies, and bring up her two youngest sons and apprentice them; also pay her debts and funeral expenses. At the end of the term of years fixed by testator's late husband in his will RICHARD & JAMES ALLDUS to yield up to son WILLIAM HERING an account of all monies received from these lands, which money is then to be divided between sons JOHN & THOMAS, & daughter ANN. To Mr BUCK, the preacher 20s. To the poor of Stradbroke, 20s. RICHARD & JAMES ALLDUS appointed joint executors. Witnesses: WILLIAM THROWER, JAMES HUBBARD. Pr. at Beccles 9 Feb. 1632.

W. EDWARD HOULTON of Sproughton (N). 27 May 1632 (567)

Sick. That Master FRANCIS FOWKES, clerk, has £4 belonging to testator, of which £3 to go to testator's fellow servant ALICE JEEVE, and 20s. to fellow servant ANN FOWKES, both of which sums to be paid them by their master FRANCIS FOWKES. Rest of profit from his estate to go to mother JANE HOULTON for her maintenance, and on her death to pass to his sisters children, to be equally divided between them. To brother RICHARD, all wearing apparel, if he accept. FRANCIS FOWKES & RICHARD HOULTON appointed to see to his estate. Witnesses: CHRISTIAN PRENTYS, JANE PRENTYS. Probate granted to FRANCIS FOWKES, RICHARD HOULTON at Ipswich 9 June 1632.

W. STEVEN HOWELL of Stradbroke (N). [no date] (568)

To wife MARGERY all goods for her maintenance, save to each grandchild an Alchimie spoon. Witnesses: JAMES HUBBARD, WILLIAM GROWER. Probate granted to FRANCIS & HENRY KING, sons of the Widow HOWELL. 30 Jan. 1632.

W. EDWARD HARDYE of Darsham, yeoman. 25 July 1631 (569)

To the poor of Darsham 6s. 8d. on his burial. To wife ANNE, house and lands in Carbrooke, Norfolk, for her lifetime, then to pass to son THOMAS HARDYE, provided he pay to his sisters ANNE, ROSE & SUSAN £10, to be paid in Darsham church porch in the following manner -- £5 to ANNE in one year, £5 to ROSE in two years, £5 to SUSAN in three years, £5 to ANNE in four years, £5 to ROSE in five years and £5 to SUSAN in six years following testator's death. Power given to his daughters to enter and hold lands if default until fully paid. To son THOMAS HARDYE £10 within 1 yr. of testator's death. To his three daughters ANNE, ROSE, & SUSAN, £10 each to be paid in 1 year of testator's death by his executrix. Residue of goods, chattels, to go to wife ANNE, appointed sole executrix, she to pay all debts, legacies, and funeral expenses. Witnesses: THOMAS TRUMPES, WILLIAM HARDYE, WILLIAM SKOTT. Pr. at Yoxford 20 Feb. 1632.

W. BEATRICE HOLLAND of Baddingham, widow. (570)
19 November 1629

Weak. To grandchild WILLIAM DAVYE £5. To grandchild BEATRICE DAVYE £20 when she reach 20, and if she die before this, then £20 to go to JOHN DAVYE. To grandchild HOLLAND DAVYE £10 when 20, and if he die before this, then it to go to JOHN DAVYE. To grandchild JOHN DAVYE £50, when 20, and if he die before 20 then legacy to go to FRANCIS DAVYE. To grandchild FRANCIS DAVYE £16 which is now remaining in the hands of testator's son-in-law WILLIAM DAVYE. To each child of LAWRENCE PELLS of Sweffling 40s. Rest of goods, chattels, once legacies, debts and funeral expenses paid, to go to FRANCIS DAVYE, and executor to hold the money until FRANCIS comes of age. Executor to pay to testator's daughter ANNE, the wife of WILLIAM DAVYE, for the use of testator's grandchildren, half the interest arising from the various sums, until grandchildren come of age to receive their legacies. Executors to be WILLIAM DAVYE, grandchild; and LAWRENCE PELLS of Sweffling. Witnesses: THOMAS WEST, ANN LANG, ANN PELLS. Probate granted to LAWRENCE PELLS at Wickham Market 1631; and granted to ANNE, wife of WILLIAM DAVYE at Yoxford 27 April 1632.

W. KATHERINE JESSOP of Weybread, spinster. (571)
6 November 1630

To kinswoman ANNE ALGAR, feather bed as it stands with all things therunto. To brother-in-law WILLIAM ALGAR and wife ROSE, 2 chests, 2 coffers, a bolting hutch, three kettles, 1 pewter dish, 3 pair sheets; 2 pillow beers. Also £12. To kinswoman SARAH BEECROFT 10s., also best petticoat, one of the best smocks; one of the best aprons. To Mr THUBEE 5s. for a sermon based on the epistle to Timothy, 4th chapter -- 'I have fought a good fight...' To those who accompany testator to her burial 5s. in beer and bread. FRANCIS GODFREY and ANNE ALGAR, kinswoman, appointed executors, they to pay debts, funeral and probate expenses. Witnesses: JOHN BROWNE, NATHANIEL NICCOLLES (X). Probate granted to JOHN BROWN & NATHANIEL NICOLS at Stradbroke 25 Sept. 1632.

W. HENRY JORDEN of Bentley, husbandman. 2 October 1632 (572)

Sick. All freehold land, house and messuages called Kirtens in Bentley, to wife ELIZABETH for life, provided she pay to HENRY JORDEN, testator's son, 20s. until 10 years be expired from the first payment -- first payment to be made when HENRY 21. On her death son HENRY to inherit lands, and if he has no heir then lands to go to second son THOMAS JORDEN. To son THOMAS JORDEN £12 when 21. To daughter ELIZABETH JORDEN £12 when 21. Rest to wife ELIZABETH to pay all debts, legacies, and funeral charges; she to be sole executrix. Witnesses: JOHN REWSE, clerk; THOMAS JORDEN (X). Pr. at Ipswich 31 Oct. 1632.

W. JOHN JUBY of Oulton, husbandman. 22 April 1632 (573)

Weak. To wife MARGARET, tenement and dwelling house with all things therunto belonging for life; then to be equally divided between testator's daughters -- JOAN, MARY, ELIZABETH, ALICE and their heirs. If they decide to sell the premises, then the profits to be equally divided between them, and daughter MARY's husband to be given the first refusal to the premises. To wife MARGARET, all goods, and household implements and stuff, corn, and cattle, for life; then to be equally divided between his daughters. Wife appointed executrix. Witnesses: JOHN BELSON (X), JOHN DAVYE. Pr. at Oulton 30 May 1632.

W. ALICE IBROOKE of Southwold (N). 26 January 1632 (574)

To grandchild JOHN IBROOK a silver spoon, and a net. To grandchildren MARTHA & ELIZABETH HALL, silver spoon and a net each. To daughters MARGARET & MARIAN, all wearing apparel, linen, and woolen, a pot and a kettle each. Rest of goods to be equally divided between her three children HENRY, MARGARET & MARIAN, save to son HENRY she gave the best bed with a little bedstead with all its furniture, it being the bed wheron she lay.

Rest sold and money raised to be used to educate son HENRY. Sister JUDITH BARRETT appointed executrix. Witnesses: RICHARD STANNARD, EDWARD HALL. Pr. at Southwold 14 Feb. 1632.

W. ROBERT KYSSE of Culpho. 30 June 1632 (575)

Sick; to be buried at Culpho. To son THOMAS KYSSE 10s. within 1 year after testator's death. To daughter AGNES SCOULDYNG, best brass pot, and to ANNIE her daughter, best posnet. To grandchild ELIZABETH KYSSE, the bedstead and bed where testator lies, with all the furniture belonging. Bequests to grandchildren, and to his daughter to be delivered presently on his death. Rest of all goods, chattels, household stuff and implements to be sold by his executors to pay all his just debts, and the surplus of money once debts be paid, to be paid by executors equally between testator's children, RICHARD KYSSE, DOROTHY CLYFFE & AGNES SCOULDING. To daughter DOROTHY CLYFFE, messuage and tenements with cottage in Playford for life, she to use the rents arising there from to pay the debts owed to her by the testator. On her death lands to revert to his son RICHARD. DOROTHY also to pay to sister AGNES SCOULDYNG 40s. a year for as long as DOROTHY shall live, the first payment to begin within one year after DOROTHY has received all the money due to her in debt by her father, the testator. If DOROTHY default in these payments to her sister, then son RICHARD to enter and have premises and pay annuity, but only until £6 has been paid. To granddaughter ELIZABETH KYSSE 13s. 4d. a year to be paid by DOROTHY out of the lands aforesaid, and if she default, then RICHARD to enter the lands, and pay the legacy. If daughter AGNES pays to testator's executors 20s., then she to have the cow he had of her husband, to be delivered presently on testator's death. To granddaughter ANNE SCOWLDYNGE £4. GABRIEL SCOULDYNG & RICHARD KYSSE appointed executors to pay debts, legacies and funeral expenses. [No witnesses] Pr. at Ipswich 28 July 1632.

W. JOHN KEMPE of Easton (N). 19 May 1632 (576)

All goods and chattels whatsoever to wife BRIDGET, who is to be executrix. Witnesses: ROBERT & JOHN LANE. Pr. at Wickham Market 28 July 1632.

W. EDWARD KENES of Stratford, husbandman (N). 2 December 1632 (577)

To grandmother ANN GOFFE £20. To aunt WILES, widow £5. To GEORGE WILES, her son, £5. To DANIEL WILES, her son, £5. To NATHANIEL & ABIGAIL DEATH £5 equally divided. Witnesses: ERASMUS TILLETT, senior; ERASMUS TILLETT, junior. Admon. to ANN GOFFE at Ipswich 11 Jan. 1632.

W. JUDITH KERRINGTON of Ipswich (N). [blank] June 1631 (578)

All goods, chattels and things whatsoever to DOROTHY, wife of GEORGE DEATH, her sister, and to GEORGE DEATH and their heirs; and that not one of the testator's brothers or sisters should have one penny worth of them. Witnesses: JOHN WEBB, SUSAN SNELL, REBECCA BRUGG, DOROTHY NEWPORT of Ipswich. Admon. to DOROTHY DEATH Ipswich 26 May 1632.

W. ROBERT KERESONNE of Southwold, sailor. (579)
21 February 1632

To wife ELLE all goods whatsoever for life, then to go to children ROBERT & JUDITH KERESONNE, only with this proviso, that JUDITH shall have the better part. Witnesses: HENRY HARRISON, JEFFREY KING (X). Admon. to ELLE KERESONNE, Southwold, 14 Feb. 1632.

W. GEORGE KERRICH of Bramford, yeoman. (580)
10 February 1632

Diseased in body. To son GEORGE KERRICH tenement in Claydon called Butlers, and houses belonging; all land, free and copyhold in Claydon, save one pightle of hempland which abuts on Akenham rectory, and other premises also excepted lying in Gowtye field. GEORGE to enter these lands when 21. To son JOHN KERRICH the great field lying before testator's tenement abutting on the highway towards the west, and the east head abutts on a close called Bushie close; also one pightle adjoining to the same field containing by estimation 2 acres, and one piece of 5 roods in Jennye meadow, lying between the lands of SAMUEL ELLMER; JOHN to enter when 21. To son SAMUEL KERRICH the orchard before the house lying in Akenham, and one little piece called the hempland adjoining in part the rectory land of Akenham, and one other piece adjoining the hempland towards the south west and upon the rectory land aforesaid being 1 1/2 acres; SAMUEL to enter when 21. To son AYLMER KERRICH field called Last lodge field, being 11 acres in Akenham, and one other close called Gowtye field being 7 acres, and one pightle lying at the east end of the said close, being 2 1/2 acres; enter when he reaches 21. Benefit of survivorship with all these bequests of lands to his sons. Son GEORGE to pay to his brother JOHN £10 when JOHN reaches 24, and GEORGE also to pay to his brother AYLMER £10 when 23. To son SAMUEL £100 when 21; this sum to be employed within 2 years of testator's death, and the profit arising from the amount be used for and remain with SAMUEL. Wife BARBARA to have use and profits from all lands until sons reach 21, she to commit no waste, strip no timber. Also she to have residue of all goods and to be executor, pay debts and funeral expenses. Witnesses: ANTHONY KERRICHE, ROBERT MAY, GEORGE CUPBARD, THOMAS HAYWARD. Pr. at Ipswich 22 Feb. 1632.

W. FRANCIS KINGE of Dennington, yeoman. 31 December 1631 (581)

To the poor of Bruisyard 20s.; the poor of Framlingham 40s.; poor of Badingham 13s. 4d.; poor of Dennington 20s.; poor of Brundish 13s. 4d.; poor of Tannington 13s. 4d.; poor of Worlingworth 20s.; poor of Peasenhall 6s.; poor of Sweffling 6s.; poor of Rendham 6s.; poor of Cransford 6s.; poor of Great Glemham 5s.; poor of Laxfield 13s. 4d.; poor of Saxtead 10s.; poor of Bedfield 5s.; poor of Parham 5s.; all of which sums to be paid to the overseers or churchwardens to be distributed by them before testator's burial so that then the poor of the said towns be not troublesome to themselves or to executors. To servant RICHARD BROWNE £5, if he be dwelling with testator on the day of his death, to be paid within 5 years next after testator's death. To each of the children of WILLIAM KINGE, son of HENRY KING, testator's brother now dead, save HENRY KING son of the said WILLIAM, 40s. in 5 years of testator's death. To servant MARY GARRARD, dwelling with testator on his death, £5 in 5 years. To apprentice MARGARET GOODALE £5 when she reach 21. To each child of ELIZABETH NORTON, the wife of RICHARD NORTON 40s., excepting FRANCIS, testator's godson, to be paid in 4 years of testator's death. To poor of Dennington £5; poor of Framlingham £10, poor of Bruisyard £3, poor of Badingham 40s., poor of Worlingworth £5, poor of Clopton 40s., to be paid by his executor within 4 years of his death, to the churchwardens or overseers of these parishes to be improved by them and their successors every year in the nature of a stock for the benefit of the poor forever, and the interest from it to be distributed on St. Thomas' day (21 December). To each of THOMAS GOSLING's children 40s. in 6 years of testator's death. To each tenant that lives in testator's houses at Bruisyard on the day of testator's death so inhabiting, 20s.; tenants of houses at Framlingham likewise 10s.; tenants of houses at Clopton likewise 10s.; tenants of houses at Dennington likewise 10s.; and to the two tenants of his house in Tannington 10s.; all of which sums to be paid them within 3 years after testator's death. To each godchild, namely FRANCIS ANTLEBY, son of JOHN ANTLEBY; FRANCIS KEEBLE son of ANTHONY KEEBLE; THOMAS ALDRED son of HUGH ALDRED; THOMAS KERITCH son of THOMAS KERITCH; FRANCIS SPARHAM, son of MATTHEW SPARHAM; ANNE PAGE, daughter of BENJAMIN PAGE; 10s. each within 6 years of testator's death. To brother-in-law ROBERT COBB of Beccles £5 in 3 years of testator's death. To nephews HENRY & FRANCIS KING, houses in Framlingham where JOHN MORRYS & JANE HAYWARD live, together with appurtenances, during the lifetime of ELIZABETH SHEMYNGE, wife of EDWARD SHEMYNGE, they to enter premises Michaelmas next after testator's death, and receive and hold the profits from the premises to the use of the said ELIZABETH, they first deducting whatever money necessary to maintain properties in good repair. On ELIZABETH's death, premises to go to her eldest son JOHN FRISTON. Nephews HENRY & FRANCIS also to give to ELIZABETH SHEMYNGE £5 within 3 years of entering premises, as they think fit. To each child of ELIZABETH SHEMYNGE 40s. within 6 years of testator's death. To godson FRANCIS NORTON £5 in 5 yrs. of testator's death. To godson FRANCIS AUSTEN £5 in 5 yrs. of testator's death. To sister ALICE WINCOLL, wife of GEORGE

WINCOLL £10 in 3 years of testator's death. To ALICE WINCOLL, daughter of ALICE WINCOLL 40s. in 5 years of testator's death. To ANNE WINCOLL, daughter of FRANCIS WINCOLL my nephew and godson, 40s. when 21. To goddaughter ELIZABETH NORTON, wife of RICHARD NORTON, £5. To MARGARET FISKE, wife of AMOS FISKE 40s. To ALICE LORD, wife of LIONEL LORD, 40s. To ANNE KEBLE, wife of ANTHONY KEBLE, 40s. To ANNE PAGE, wife of BENJAMIN PAGE, 40s. To DORCAS BATEMAN 40s. All of which sums of 40s. and £5 above devised to be within 3 years of testator's death. To each child of ANNE AUSTEN, wife of FRANCIS AUSTEN late deceased, excepting godson FRANCIS, 40s. within 6 years of testator's death. To each child of BARBARA BRISLIE, wife of MILES BRISLIE, late deceased, 40s. in 5 years of testator's death. To godson ROBERT URVIS, son of WILLIAM URVIS £5, and to RACHEL URVIS daughter of WILLIAM URVIS 40s., both bequests to be paid in 6 years of testator's death. To FRANCES FISKE, daughter of AMOS FISKE, 40s. in 5 years of testator's death. To [missing] BARKER, daughter of MARY BARKER, niece now deceased sometime wife of EDWARD BARKER, gent. 40s. in 6 years of testator's death. To the daughter of ELIZABETH TYLER, niece, wife of JOHN TYLER, 40s. in 5 yrs. of my death. To SUSAN LONGE, wife of NICHOLAS LONGE, 40s. in 3 years of testator's death. To JOHN WARDE, minister of Dennington £5, and to Mistress RAYMOND his wife's sister 40s. to be paid in 3 years of testator's death. To WILLIAM & THOMAS BATEMAN, sons of CHRISTOPHER BATEMAN, 20s. each in 3 yrs. of testator's death. To JOHN KINGE of Clopton, son of THOMAS KINGE, 40s. in 3 years of testator's death. To tenant EDWARD BACON 20s. in 3 years of testator's death. If anyone who is due to receive a legacy be under 21 at the time that the gift be due, then whoever be under 21 has to wait until they reach 21; every one receiving legacy to give a lawful receipt for the same, and if they refuse then the legacy to be withheld until such receipt be forthcoming. To nephew FRANCIS KINGE and his heirs, messuage, lands and tenements with appurtenances, both free and copyhold, in Bruisyard and Baddingham where JOHN MAN now lives, provided the said FRANCIS pay to testator's executors an annuity for 6 years of £20 from these lands, the first payment to be made in 1 year of testator's death, or within 10 days of it, and if he default, then exec. to have power to enter and distrain until £20 and arrears and £5 for every default be made good. Also FRANCIS to have close, messuages both free and copyhold in Bruisyard and Baddingham where GEORGE BALDRYE lives, provided he pay to his brother HENRY KINGE an annuity of £20 for 6 years, payable in the North porch of Dennington church, the first payment to be made in 1 year of testator's death or in 10 days of same, and if default then power to enter and distrain until default and arrears and an extra £5 per default made good. Also FRANCIS to have all land, free and copyhold in Bruisyard and Baddingham where RALPH LUNNYS lives, but if HENRY KINGE, the testator's heir by common law on the 20th day after testator's death, make a release in Dennington church porch to FRANCIS of all his rights in the above lands, then HENRY to have lands occupied by RALPH LUNNYS. To ALEXANDER KINGE, son of testator's brother HENRY KINGE deceased, lands in Clopton occupied by THOMAS TYE, provided he pay testator's exec. an annuity for 6 years of 40s., the first payment to be made in 1 year of testator's death or within 10 days of it, and if ALEXANDER default then power to exec. to enter and distrain for 40s. and arrears and for 10s. for each time arrear made. To HENRY KINGE, son of WILLIAM KINGE testator's nephew deceased, messuage and appurtenances in Framlingham adjoining to a way leading from the market place to the castle, against the churchyard on the part of the west, with the well thereunto belonging (save such liberties to the well as is hereafter bequeathed) which lands are now occupied by EDWARD BACON, ROBERT SEAMAN, ROBERT WARNER, THOMAS SKYNNER & ROBERT KINGE. Also to HENRY one pightle of 3 roods in Framlingham, occupied by EDMUND CROSSE, all of which premises in Framlingham were purchased by testator from ROBERT SPALDINGE. HENRY KINGE to pay to testator's executors an annuity of £5 for 6 years, the first payment to be made in 1 year of testator's death, or within 10 days of it, and if HENRY default then power to exec. to enter and distrain for arrears and 10s. for every default. All annuities to be paid to executors in the north porch of Dennington church, and to be used by them towards payment of legacies specified in will. Nephew THOMAS GOSLINGE & nephew and godson FRANCIS WINCOLL to be executors; each to have £40 and the surplus of goods, chattels left after payment of debts, legacies, funeral expenses. JOHN SCRIVENER of Sibton to be supervisor and have £5. To THOMAS GOSLING & FRANCIS WINCOLL the messuage where testator lives in Dennington, to enter it immediately on his death and use the profits arising from it towards the performance of this will; they to hold the same for 6 years and to keep it in good repair; then after 6 years all lands in Dennington to go to nephew HENRY KINGE. To THOMAS GOSLING & FRANCIS WINCOLL, in order to help in the performance of this will, messuage late purchased by testator of HENRY KINGE, his nephew, being in Worlingworth and Tannington. If nephew HENRY KINGE releases and discharges all actions & suits whatsoever he may have, as heir to testator by the common law, to THOMAS GOSLING & FRANCIS WINCOLL, of all rights in these premises, after the said THOMAS & FRANCIS have enjoyed these lands for 4 years after death of testator, and further that if HENRY on the 20th day after the Michaelmas next after testator's death makes a release in Dennington church porch to all legatees of estates of his rights in the lands (excepting the land given to FRANCIS KINGE for which HENRY is already bound to release); then if both these releases have been given, then HENRY KINGE to inherit lands in Worlingworth and Tannington after the 4 years. To NICHOLAS KINGE of Ubbeston, all that part of the house where GODFREY WOODE lives in Framlingham, together with the orchard, and free liberty of egress to the well, and to take water therefrom as is the custom. He to enter premises on the Michaelmas next after testator's death. To ROBERT KINGE, who was testator's servant and who is the son of NICHOLAS KINGE the other part of the house in Framlingham inhabited by ERASMUS GREEN, together with the orchard, and free liberty of egress to the well and to take water therefrom; he to enter premises on the Michaelmas next after testator's death. To servant MARY SKOWE, if she be dwelling with testator at the time of his death, and to her husband as she shall happen to have, messuage and tenement in Dennington late purchased of ROGER STONE and now occupied by

LAWRENCE GOODLAD, for her lifetime, or the longer liver of the two, and then to her child; if she have no heir, then premises to revert to the right heirs of FRANCIS KINGE, the testator. To executors THOMAS GOSLING & FRANCIS WINCOLL, cottage in Dennington with the yard belonging purchased of one ROBERT MOULTON, now occupied jointly by the testator and HUMFRY SMYTH; exec. to enter immediately on testator's death and to have its profits until RICHARD FRISTON, son of RICHARD FRISTON, late of Tannington cordwainer now deceased, reaches 24 or ends his apprenticeship. Executors to perform no waste, and when RICHARD FRISTON is 24 to hand over lands to him. HENRY KINGE, testator's nephew shall, within 10 days of testator's death on request made by testator's executors, enter into bond with executors in £30 to allow executors to enjoy these lands in Dennington, and to allow RICHARD FRISTON to have lands thereafter, without challenge from HENRY KINGE, and if the said HENRY refuse the bond, executors to hold premises. To EDWARD MOULTON of Saxtead, and THOMAS ARLIP of Tannington 20s. each in 3 years of testator's death. To REGINALD KINGE, son of NICHOLAS KINGE of Ubbeston, 10s. within 3 years of testator's death. To godson FRANCIS KINGE, second best feather bed, second best boulster and feather pillow, second best blanket and coverlet; 2 pair sheets, one of two bord cloths, 6 table napkins, 2 bedspreads as they stand in the parlour chamber in the house where JOHN MAN lives in Bruisyard. To godson FRANCIS WINCOLL, son of GEORGE WINCOLL, testator's brother-in-law, third best featherbed, boulster, feather pillow and blanket and coverlet, 2 pair of third best sheets; 6 table napkins. To HENRY KINGE, son of WILLIAM KINGE testator's nephew deceased, one feather bed, boulster, and 1 pair sheets. To ELIZABETH SHEMYNGE, wife of EDWARD SHEMYNGE of Framlingham, one feather bed, two pair sheets, for her lifetime, then to go to her son JOHN FRISTON. To nephew THOMAS GOSLINGE, fourth best featherbed and boulster and feather pillow, and blanket and coverlet; 2 pair of fourth best sheets; 6 table napkins. Executors to have to expend at my burial or within ten days of it, at the house where testator lives, in reasonable manner, all the provisions of food, and corn. Residue of goods to HENRY KINGE, testator's nephew, son of HENRY KINGE, testator's brother, except all bonds, bills, debts, rents due to testator on the Michaelmas after testator's death to go to executors, to pay testator's debts and funeral expenses. Witnesses: ROBERT DOWNING, RICHARD SAYER, EDWARD MOULTON, JOHN BAYLIE (X). Probate granted to FRANCIS WINCOLL at Dennington on 17 Aug. 1632, and to THOMAS GOSLING at Dennington on 19 Aug. 1632.

W. EDMUND KINGE. 17 July 1629 (582)

Two sons JOHN & ROBERT KINGE to be executors. To wife GRACE, lands and houses in Snape and Farnham for her lifetime; also 14s. annuity to be paid her by executors. To eldest daughter MARY, BOUTE's wife, 20s. To wife GRACE one feather bed and all things belonging to same, a chest, coffer, a chair, cupboard and as much pewter as is worth 5s.; 2 pair sheets, 2 pillow beers, a table and a form. Executors to sell all lands, and goods chattels, money thus raised to be parted equally between testator's children JOHN, ROBERT, WILLIAM, JEREMY, ELIZABETH, ANNE, GRACE, SARAH, & MARTHA KINGE within six months of sale, provided they be of age; if they be under age, then they have to wait until 21 or the day of their marriage. Executors to retain £9, in order to pay 14s. annuity to wife. On her death, this is to be equally divided amongst testator's children all receiving 20s. each. Benefit of survivorship. Witnesses: GEORGE PARKER. Pr. at Ipswich 15 Oct. 1632.

W. EZECHIEL KNIGHTS of Chediston, yeoman. [blank] 1630 (583)

To the poor of Chediston 20s.; poor of Halesworth 20s.; poor of Wissett 5s.; poor of Cookley 5s.; to be paid by churchwardens immediately on testator's death. To HESTER DERICKE of Halesworth 10s. immediately on testator's death. To wife MARGERY, all messuages, house, gardens and appurtenances in Chediston for life, provided she claim no dower and keep lands in good repair; she to bring up and maintain and educate three daughters until they reach 21. If wife should die before daughters reach 21, then testator's son EZECHIEL to pay to whoever brings them up £4 each a year until 21, to be paid twice a year by equal portions towards the cost of their maintainance. If son EZECHIEL refuse to do so, then exec. to take houses and lands in Chediston and use profits from same towards the maintainance of the daughters. To executor, all houses and lands in Laxfield and Stradbroke to hold until son EZECHIEL reach 30; the profits from these lands to be used by executor to pay funeral and probate expenses, debts and legacies; exec. to keep property in good repair. To daughter FRANCES KNIGHTS £80 when 21, paid in south porch of Chediston by exec. To youngest daughter MARY £80 when 21, paid in S. porch of Chediston by executor. If default made in these payments by exec., then power to daughters to enter and occupy lands in Laxfield and Stradbroke until legacy paid. To wife MARGERY, all household stuff, cattle, chattels, corn, provided she claim no dower, for life; then equally to be divided between testator's three daughters. If wife claim dower, then she to loose all legacies of household goods and the lands in Chediston which she has for life, and legacies to then go to executor. To daughter ELIZABETH surplus of profits from all his lands and personal estate when she reaches 21. Wife to supervise daughter's education until they reach 21 or marry. If wife remarry during her daughters minorities, then executor to have control of daughters and to receive the £12 a year toward their maintainance. Executor to be WILLIAM SMYTH of All Saints Southelmham and to receive 12 nobles. He to pay all debts, legacies, and funeral expenses. Witnesses: BENJAMIN FAYER FAXE, WILLIAM KNIGHTS. Pr. at Beccles 9 Feb. 1632.

W. JOHN KIDDALL of Reydon, husbandman. 12 September 1632 (584)

Sick; to be buried at Reydon. To wife ALICE, all movable goods of whatever kind, provided she pay WILLIAM SYEARS £12 within 6 months after testator's death, he then to put this sum out to its best advantage in order to provide an annuity for wife ALICE, until the child that she now is with reaches 21. WILLIAM SYEARS then to pay the £12 to that child. If that child die before 21, then WILLIAM to pay £12 to testator's wife. Wife ALICE appointed executor, she to pay debts, funeral expenses. Witnesses: THOMASINE GREANWARD, widow (X), WILLIAM SYARS (X), THOMAS DURRANT, JOHN PIGHING (X). Pr. at Beccles 15 Sept. 1632.

W. WILLIAM LANCASTER of Walberswick, chapman (N). (585)
14 November 1632

Sick. To wife SUSAN, house and appurtenances in Walberswick for ever. Witnesses: BRIAN WARDE, clerk; ROBERT EDMUNDS & ALICE the wife of RICHARD WRIGHT. Admon. to SUSAN LANCASTER 24 Nov. 1632.

W. JOHN LINDOE. 27 November 1632 (586)

To wife MARY, all lands and tenements until his son JOHN LINDOE reaches 21, he then to inherit, provided JOHN LINDOE pay to his brothers and sisters £4 each a year, beginning at the eldest £4 at the year ending after he shall accomplish 21, and so to all the rest of his brothers and sisters every year £4 until they be all paid, to so many as then shall be living. Wife MARY to be executrix to pay debts and funeral expenses. Witnesses: ROBERT SAINE, SIMON BOTSWYNE, WILLIAM GORBALL. Pr. at Beccles 31 Dec. 1632.

W. ROBERT MOYSE of Witnesham. 18 November 1631 (587)

Weak of body. To be buried at Witnesham. To wife ANNE, all goods, cattle, chattels, household stuff, implements, and utensils, and the lease which testator has in tenement where he lives in Witnesham. To kinsman ROBERT MOYSE £10 in one year of testator's death, and £30 owed by the said ROBERT to the testator. To each child of kinsman JAMES MOYSE, lately deceased, £5 to be paid as they come to the age of 21; benefit of survivorship. To ROBERT MOYSE, feather bed, to be delivered when the lease of testator's farm where he lives be ended. To kinsfolk JOHN GARNHAM & wife ANN, £10 in one year of testator's death, and the £10 owed by them to testator. To sister MARGERY 20s., to be paid by WILLIAM RIVERS of Burgh yearly for her life, in two installments of 10s. a year; also WILLIAM to lay out for the needful necessaries of the said MARGERY from time to time as need shall require. To THOMAS GOSNELL the younger, testator's landlord, £10 in 1 yr. of testator's death. To WALTER GOSNELL, ANTHONY GOSNELL, ROBERT, HENRY, URSULA, DOROTHY, & ANN GOSNELL, brothers and sisters to THOMAS £5 each in 1 yr. of testator's death, with benefit of survivorship. To ROBERT MOYSE, kinsman, messuage and tenements occupied by the Widow SMITH in Ashbocking on the death of testator's wife ANNE. To the poor on his burial 2d. each. To the inhabitants of Witnesham 40s., to be put out and employed with the town stock there to the best use and the benefit therof to be distributed from time to time amongst the neediest poor. To THOMAS GOSNOLD of Bentley, £10 in 1 yr. of testator's death. Wife ANNE to be executrix, pay all debts, legacies, prove will, and funeral expenses. Friend WILLIAM DRANE of Otley supervisor. Witnesses: WILLIAM DRANE, THOMAS SEMAN. Pr. at Ipswich 1 Feb. 1632.

W. JOHN MASON of Beccles, linen weaver (N). 23 May 1632 (588)

To wife ANNE all movable goods, credits and chattels, she to pay debts. Witnesses: JOHN VAUGHAN, ELIZABETH KNIGHTS. Admon. to ANNE MASON 30 May 1632.

W. THOMAS MAYHEW of Oulton, husbandman (N). 1 March 1631 (589)

SAMUEL MAYHEW, brother, to be executor, and he to give out of testator's goods unto GEORGE JOLLY, man servant to testator, 20s.; also to ELEANOR JOLLY, dame servant 10s.; to THOMAS LEECE, servant 5s. and to MARGARET JESOPP 5s., and ROBERT BULL 5s. Rest of goods and chattels to executor. Witnesses: GEORGE JOLLY & wife ELEANOR, THOMAS LEECE & MARGARET JESOPP. Pr. at Beccles 29 June 1632.

W. JOHN MARCAN of Wenhaston, husbandman. (590)
22 November 1631

Sick; to be buried in Wenhaston by the side of wife JANE. Wife JANE, executrix; she to have all movables for life; then to go to daughter ELIZABETH BUCKNAM one flock bed with the bedstead as it stands, one great kettle, one hutch, one little table, two chairs. Rest of goods on death of wife, to go to daughter ANN MARCAN. Witnesses: JOHN PEASE, JOHN FISHE, ROBERT GOWINGE. Pr. at Wenhaston 7 June 1632.

W. PHILIP MOLLE of Laxfield, husbandman. 20 March 1631 (591)

To daughter SUSAN MOLLE £20 to be paid her in the church porch of Laxfield when she reach 21; also one featherbed and feather bolster belonging to it when 21. To brother JOHN MOLL, best cloak and hat. Residue of goods whatsoever to wife SUSAN, she to be executrix, and pay debts, and legacies. THOMAS CORNICH of Ubbeston to be supervisor. Witnesses: THOMAS CORNICH, SIMON JACOB. Pr. at Stradbroke 17 April 1632.

W. ROBERT MURREL of Mutford, singleman. 1 February 1632 (592)

To the poor of Mutford 10s. in one month of testator's death. To WILLIAM MURRELL, son of THOMAS MURRELL, testator's brother now deceased, and to ANNIS MURRELL, daughter to the said THOMAS, all lands and tenements, provided they pay to JOSEPH MURRELL, son to WILLIAM MURRELL testator's brother, £13. 6s. 8d. in 4 months after he reach 24 -- JOSEPH to give notice of his age in writing within one month of his 24th birthday. Also they to pay to SUSAN MURRELL, daughter of WILLIAM MURRELL, £13. 6s. 8d. within 4 months after she reach 24 -- SUSAN to give notice in writing of her having attained that age of 24. Legacies to be paid in the south porch of Mutford church. Also to WILLIAM & ANNIS MURRELL all goods and chattels. MARGARET, wife of testator's late brother THOMAS, and her brother JAMES ALDRED, to be executors and to receive for their trouble 20s.; also to give 40s. for burial, and to pay the preacher 10s. Witnesses: RICHARD CODDE, WILLIAM HEKAME, FRANCIS CODDE. Pr. at Beccles 16 Feb. 1632.

W. HENRY MARCHANT alias TYLER of Monk Soham, yeoman. (593)
1 October 1632

Sick; to be buried at Monk Soham. To son EDWARD MARCHANT alias TYLER, tenement in Monk Soham where testator lives, and 20 acres and 1 rood of copyhold land belonging thereunto in Monk Soham when 21. To son HENRY MARCHANT alias TYLER, freehold land in Worlingworth on the death of testator's wife ELIZABETH; until then wife to hold same, and to render no account to the said HENRY. Rest of lands to son JOHN MARCHANT alias TYLER when 21. Wife ELIZABETH to hold all copyhold lands until his sons reach 21, and to use the profits from same towards cost of maintaining his children, and also to make up a portion for each of his two daughters. Wife to be sole executrix. Witnesses: NATHANIEL ALLARD, JOHN BICKAR (X), HENRY EWEN. Pr. at Yoxford 3 Jan. 1632.

W. JOHN MURDOCK of Framlingham (N). [blank] June 1632 (594)

All goods devised to wife ANN. Witnesses: RICHARD GOLTIE, THOMASINE SICKEMORE, wife of JOHN SICKEMORE. Probate granted to ANN MURDOCK at Wickham Market 21 Feb. 1632.

W. EDITH MOYSE of Holbrook, widow. 18 May 1631 (595)

Sick. To the poor of Holbrook 20s. within 3 months of testator's death. To MARGARET MOYSE, her daughter, 3 or 4 sheep that are with JOHN CHASE, with the benefit and profit of them, and also all the money due to the testator from her son-in-law NATHANIEL HODGE. To daughter ELLEN HODGE, brass copper which now hangs in her house, and 10s. to buy a ring in remembrance. To daughter MARY GOODING, brass kettle, feather bed and a flock bed now in her house and the £3 due to testator from the down is to go to testator's two grandchildren, MARY & MARGARET GOODING, to be received by their mother, and put out to their best advantage, and when they reach 16 to be equally divided between them; benefit of survivorship. To daughter MARY, one table more. To daughter ELLEN one brass kettle bought from the miller. Residue of goods to daughter MARGARET, she to be sole executrix, pay debts. Witnesses: WILLIAM MAPLETOFT, NATHANIEL HEDGE. Pr. at Ipswich 16 June 1632.

W. EATH MILSE of Little Glemham. 22 March 1631 (596)

To daughter ELIZABETH, JOHN FLATMAN's wife, 5s. and one pair of sheets. To grandchild ELIZABETH FLATMAN, a livery bedstead, one pair of sheets. To servant JOHN BUSH all lasts and seats. To daughter JOAN MILSE all movables, to pay debts, and she to be sole executrix. Witnesses: DANIEL POTTLE, JOHN SCARLETT (X), WILLIAM BARNES (X). Pr. at Wickham Market 8 April 1632.

W. MARY MAN of Woodbridge, widow (N). [no date] (597)

Sick. To son THOMAS £10 when 23 or 24 depending on executor's discretion. To son JOHN £5 when 23 or 24 depending on executor's discretion. Residue of goods, chattels to daughters ANN & KATHERINE, with benefit of survivorship to sons. Executor to be GEORGE WARREN. Witnesses: SIMPSON FEN, JULIAN ALDUS. Pr. at Wickham Market 10 Jan. 1632.

W. THOMAS NEAVE of Helmingham, yeoman. 9 January 1631 (598)

Sick and weak. To eldest son THOMAS messuage and tenement in Wattisham, and all other messuages, houses, buildings in Wattisham, Ringshall, Bricett, immediately on testator's death. To son LIONEL, an annuity of 40s. payable by THOMAS out of lands bequeathed to THOMAS during the lifetime of testator's wife JOAN, the first payment to be made at the end of the first year after testator's death. Also to LIONEL messuage and tenement in Brandeston on the death of testator's wife JOAN. To wife JOAN tenement in Brandeston, provided she pay to son LIONEL an annuity of 40s. during her lifetime, the first payment to be made at the end of the first year after death of testator. JOAN, before will is probated, to enter into bond of £20 with LIONEL to pay him the annuity. JOAN also to have one feather bed, feather bolster with the bedstead as it stands furnished in the lower chamber; she also to be executrix, pay debts, legacies, funeral expenses, and probate charges. Rest of personal estate to be divided -- 1/2 to son THOMAS, and 1/2 to wife JOAN, and of JOAN's half, half to be given to son LIONEL, and wife to have the rest for her lifetime. LIONEL to have his half in 10 days after his marriage, and to have JOAN's half on her death. All gifts given to wife JOAN are in full recompense of all dower claims on lands devised to son THOMAS. Witnesses: JAMES WYTHE, ROBERT NEWTON. Pr. at Ipswich 13 April 1632.

W. JOHN NEWMAN of Sutton (N). 20 June 1632 (599)

To wife MARY, house and lands in Sutton for life, then to go to son JOHN and his heirs, provided he pays ROBERT NEWMAN & LAWRENCE

NEWMAN, his brothers £15 each on the death of testator's wife MARY, and when they reach 21; benefit of survivorship. To wife all goods and chattels. Witnesses: THOMAS MILES, JOHN HALES, WILLIAM MARSH. Admon. to MARY NEWMAN 5 July 1632.

W. ADAM NEAVE of Shotley, taylor. 27 August 1632 (600)

Sick. All land in Shotley to DANIEL POD of Bramford on death of testator's wife, he to pay to testator's sister JOAN FOSET £1. 6s. 8d. a year for her lifetime, and then on her death to pay the same annuity to her son WILLIAM FOSET. To wife FRANCES all lands for her lifetime, and all goods and chattels, she to pay £1. 6s. 8d. to testator's sister JOAN and then to her son WILLIAM as above. She to be executrix and pay debts. Witnesses: THOMAS FRELLOW, THOMAS BOWSETT (X), MARGARET SKOT (X). Pr. at Ipswich 8 Oct. 1632.

W. JOHN NUN of Aldeburgh (N). Middle November 1632 (601)

To mother ROSE NUN, one chalder. To Mr TOPCLIFFE's daughter a noble or an angel. Rest of estate to brother FRANCIS NUN. Witnesses: JOHN GRASE, MARY wife of EDMOND PARSONS. Admon. to FRANCIS NUN at Yoxford 20 Feb. 1632. [Mr Topcliffe was rector of Aldeburgh at this time.]

W. THOMAS PALMER of Monewden, yeoman. 20 December 1631 (602)

Aged. To son JOHN PALMER, messuage and tenements in Kettleburgh with all appurtenances. To grandson THOMAS, son of JOHN, 1 silver spoon when 21. To daughter DOROTHY MAULSTER, wife of THOMAS MAULSTER, copyhold tenement called Coockoes, and all copyhold held of Cotton Hempnalls and Skeith manor in Cotton. To grandchildren THOMAS, JOHN, SAMUEL, & DOROTHY MAULSTER, 1 silver spoon each when 21. To daughter MARY AMYSON, wife of GEORGE AMYSON £60 to be paid by testator's executor -- £30 on the day in 1 years time after testator's death, and £30 in 2 years time, payable in Monewden church porch. Also one featherbed and bedspread where testator lies, 1 of the best coverletts, 2 blankets, 2 pair sheets, 1 table cloth in one month of testator's death. To each grandchild GEORGE, MARY & MARIAN AMYSON, 1 silver spoon when 21. Rest to executor to perform will, pay legacies, probate and funeral expenses; JOHN PALMER, son, and THOMAS MAULSTER, son-in-law appointed executors. Witnesses: ROBERT MORSE, MARY BOORE, THOMAS TURNER. Pr. at Wickham Market 25 May 1632.

W. JOHN POFFORD of Ipswich St. Margaret, innholder (N). (603)
8 March 1631

All goods to wife ANN for life, with remainder of the goods to son JOHN and daughter ELIZABETH NORMAN to be divided equally.

Witnesses: EDWARD MAWSTON, ELIZABETH JOHNSON (X). Admon. to ANN POFFORD 6 April 1632.

W. MARY PENDLETON of Pettaugh (N). 25 June 1632 (604)

Daughter of ROBERT PENDLETON. Sick. To mother 40s., best petticoat and best ruff. To sister FRANCES £10 towards her bringing up; 1 chest and its contents. To rest of brothers and sisters £10, to be equally divided. Residue of estate to father to pay burial costs. Witnesses: JANE SALLOWES, MARGARET MILNER. Admon. to ROBERT PENDLETON 25 July 1632.

W. JEAN PRATT of Hoxne, widow. 25 January 1631 (605)

Sick; to be buried at Hoxne. To daughter MARY, bed as it stands, and bedstead; flock bed, feather bolster, feather pillow, flock bolster, 2 coverlets, best red petticoat, best ruff and a joined chair. MARY to sell the cupboard and use the money from the sale to bury testator; MARY also to have 2 pair sheets, 2 smocks the best gown and 3 waistcoats. To daughter ANN 2 pillows, flock bolster, worsted red petticoat, 2 kettles, and a towe comb; one pewter dish, and a saucer; 2 coffers, 2 stools, 1 pair sheets, and a green say apron, and a coarse white apron; one smock and 2 pillow beers. To daughter MARY, baste and skillet. A pewter dish, a rack, pair of tongs a roast iron and all household implements, she to be executor. Witnesses: ROBERT EARNESON, JOHN ROPER, FRANCES BAXTER. Pr. 17 April 1632.

W. ROGER POPE of Hasketon, yeoman. 19 June 1632 (606)

Sick; to be buried at Hasketon. To grandchild JOHN FINCH, son of WILLIAM FINCH of Hasketon the elder, yeoman, the reversion to all lands and tenements in Dallinghoo due to come to testator ROGER POPE on the death of ELIZABETH the wife of GEORGE GARNER of Dallinghoo. To grandchild WILLIAM FINCH, son of WILLIAM FINCH, lands and tenements, both free and copyhold in Sutton, together with all predial, personal and all tithes whatsoever kind in Sutton. To grandchild MARY FINCH, daughter of WILLIAM £50 when 21. To grandchild ELIZABETH FINCH, daughter of WILLIAM, £50 when 21. To daughter SUSAN, wife of JEFFRY CLARKE of Sutton, glover, £20 if she outlive her husband. To son-in-law WILLIAM FINCH the elder £10, and to daughter MARY the wife of WILLIAM FINCH £5; also to the said WILLIAM & MARY rest of goods, corn, chattels, household goods whatsoever, they to pay debts, legacies, funeral expenses as executors. Witnesses: ANTHONY BURWARD, JOHN BURWARD, RICHARD SEWETT. Pr. at Ipswich 7 July 1632.

W. WILLIAM PEACOCKE of Saxmundham, husbandman. (607)
27 February 1632

All goods and chattels whatsoever to wife MARGERY for life; then to go to cousin WILLIAM GENTRY who is appointed executor. Witnesses: JOHN BASE, RICHARD GUNNER, WILLIAM ADUS. Pr. at Saxmundham 11 [missing date?].

W. SIMON PEEKE of Bungay, linen weaver. 25 July 1632 (608)

Weak of body by constitution of body. To be buried in Holy Trinity churchyard. To son ROBERT PEEK, messuage and tenements, houses and buildings and meadow late purchased of JAMES BATEMAN & BARNARBY BATEMAN in Bungay Trinity; also tenement called Darlett, where testator now lives. To daughter MARGERY for life tenement and yards in Bungay purchased from one SKYNNER and the use of the well standing in testator's own yard; on her death they to go to son ROBERT PEEKE. To son ROBERT PEEKE 2 houses used for a barn and a stable purchased from JOHN RUSHEMER in Bungay on the backside near to the castle yard there; also close of pasture ground lying at the Ollance in Bungay enclosed with pales, copyhold of Bardolph's manor; also one little piece of ground enclosed, being 1 rood, lying at the backside of the castle yard purchased of MATTHEW BARDWELL, copyhold of the manor of Borrough of Bungay. Also whole stock of linen cloth and yarn, all looms, stays and all implements for linen weaving in testator's house and also in any other man's possession but owned by testator. To daughter MARGERY an annuity of 40s. to be paid quarterly by son ROBERT -- first payment in 1/4 of year next after testator's death; if default then she to enter lands devised to ROBERT as often as need shall require, and hold lands until paid. She also to have livery bedstead with a mat and coverlet, one featherbed, feather bolster, a covering, pair of sheets as now stands or lately stood furnished in the chamber over testator's hall. To THOMAS FRANCKLYN of Bungay, scrivener 5s. shortly after testator's death. Debts and legacies to be paid, and expenses of funeral and probate, and whatever remains to be divided by two impartial men of discretion to be chosen by testators children ROBERT & MARGERY after testator's death, and ROBERT to have first half and MARGERY the second. To the poor of Bungay Holy Trinity 20s. and Bungay St. Mary 20s. in 1 month of death. ROBERT PEEKE and grandchild SIMON PEEKE to be executors and to prove will in 1 month. Witnesses: THOMAS FRANCKLYN, snr.; EDMUND ROSE; SIMON FOSTER. Pr. at Bungay 1 Dec. 1632.

W. JOHN PAINE of Petistree, yeoman. 11 November 1632 (609)

Sick; to be buried at Petistree. To wife ANN all movable goods, chattels, implements, in order that she may bring up his children till they reach 20. When they reach 20 wife to pay to sons JOHN, WILLIAM & THOMAS £20 each. Wife also to pay all debts, and to pay to testator's mother an annuity of £4. If one of his sons dies or more, then benefit of survivorship. Wife ANN to be sole executrix; brother-in-law THOMAS ALDRED, and friend FRANCIS HILL supervisors. Witnesses: SAMUEL WARD, cleric, THOMAS BALDING (X). Pr. at Wickham Market 13 Dec. 1632.

W. STEPHEN PRATT of Wickham Market, gentleman. (610)
27 March 1632

All lands, both free and copyhold, and all goods and chattels to be sold by his executors for the best price and from the money thus arising to pay debts, and from the remainder executors to pay legacies. To eldest son SAMUEL PRATT £100; to eldest daughter PHILIPA PRATT £80, and the rest of the money to be equally divided between the rest of his children being 5 in number -- sons to receive their legacies when 24, daughters when 20, with benefit of survivorship. Executor to take a charitable care of children, and place them in an honest trade and maintain them. Executors - WILLIAM GLOVER, EDWARD BLENHARSETT gent., and THOMAS CUTTING, gent. Witnesses: HENRY STERLING, THOMAS BROWNE, THOMAS PENSE (X), THOMAS HOLMES (X). Pr. at Wickham Market 20 Nov. 1632.

W. ROBERT PETTYTT of Framlingham, husbandman. (611)
19 June 1628

Sick. To wife ELIZABETH, her dwelling in testator's house in Framlingham, for lifetime, with half thereunto belonging. Also best feather bed and feather bolster for life and all such household stuff and chattels which were her own on marriage. To son ROBERT messuage and lands in Framlingham with all things pertaining to same provided he pay to his brother THOMAS 20s. before he enter these lands devised to him presently on the death of testator's wife. ROBERT to live in the messuage with testator's wife ELIZABETH for her lifetime. Also to ROBERT the covering which testator bought from RICHARD BALDEO, and a feather pillow. Sons ROBERT & THOMAS to equally divide testator's wearing apparel, both linen and woolen. Rest of goods, excepting legacies to wife and to son ROBERT, to go to son THOMAS for him to pay debts and legacies, and to provide him with a legacy. He to be executor and to have all corn and cheese and butter which is in the house at the time of the death of ELIZABETH testator's wife. If THOMAS fails in the performance of the will then ROBERT to be executor and receive residue of goods. Witnesses: THOMAS WADE, CHARLES WRITHOKE. Pr. at Wickham Market 30 Oct. 1632.

W. LAURENCE PELLES of Cransford, gentleman. 2 May 1631 (612)

To each of the grandchildren of WILLIAM NAUNTON esq., £5 in 2 months of testator's death. To ROBERT NAUNTON, son of WILLIAM NAUNTON, the great iron chain to draw timber, and the desk at Cransford to be delivered within 2 months of testator's death. To KATHERINE & ELIZABETH HORSEMAN, daughters of JOHN HORSEMAN, gent., testator's son-in-law, £12 each when they reach 21; also to ELIZABETH HORSEMAN a featherbed and to KATHERINE HORSEMAN a down feather bed. To FRANCES MARIOTT, daughter of ROBERT MARIOTT, son-in-law to testator, £12 when 21; also one joined table and joined stools in Kettleburgh and Cransford. To each child of CHRISTIAN WADE, testator's sister, 40s. each, and to sister CHRISTIAN WADE 40s. in three months of testator's death. To the wife of testator's cousin WALTER WADE 30s. and also 30s. each to her two daughters, and 40s. to her son, all within 2 months of testator's death. To testator's godson, son of THOMAS WADE, 40s. in 2 months of testator's death. To sister LITLER, widow, 40s. in 2 months of testator's death. To JOHN HORSEMAN and wife ELLEN, testator's daughter, all movable goods and chattels of testator's now in their custody and mansion house. To ROBERT MARIOTT and wife FRANCES, testator's daughter, all movable goods and chattels of testator's now in their custody and mansion house. To son-in-law ROBERT PELLES, horsemill and all timber in the old barn at Kettleburgh. To NATHANIEL HORSEMAN, bedstead in the parlour at Kettleburgh in 2 months of testator's death. To grandchild JOHN PELLES, bedstead, blankets, ruggs and coverlets (save the red one) wheron testator now lodges at Cransford, and one livery table in the chamber, and firepan, tongs and cobirons and wicker chair and the other chair in the chamber where testator now lodges in Cransford, and his gold ring, in 2 months of death. To executor £30 in order to pay burial and funeral expenses; also 30s. each to executors. Rest of goods to be divided between JOHN HORSEMAN, ROBERT MARIOTT, and ROBERT PELLES. WILLIAM NAUNTON & ROBERT HEIGATE appointed executors. FRANCIS MARIOTT & KATHERINE HORSEMAN to have a trunck each -- one in Kettleburgh, one in Cransford. Witnesses: RICHARD EDWARDS, JOHN NUTHILL (X). Pr. at Wickham Market 30 Oct. 1632.

W. WILLIAM PARISH of Snape. 3 April 1632 (613)

To be buried at Blaxhall. To wife ELIZABETH, in lieu of her dower claims, freehold messuage and tenement in Blaxhall occupied by HENRY LODGE, for her lifetime; then lands to go to daughters KATHERINE & MARIAN PARISH. Wife to maintain same lands in good repair, suffer no waste, and to pay to daughters KATHERINE & MARIAN PARISH 10s. a year in half yearly installments, the first payment to be made on the first feast day, either Michaelmas or Lady Day, after testator's death, or within 20 days of that feast, and if default made, then power to daughters to enter and distrain till paid. If wife refuse to release her dower rights then legacy to her is void. To daughters KATHERINE & MARIAN PARISH all land called Shortland, both free and copy; also 3 acres of fen, copyhold of Dunningworth manor, now mortgaged to HENRY BULLINGE -- this to be sold within two years of testator's death, and the money thus raised used to pay testator's debts. To wife ELIZABETH one bed ready furnished which she had on their marriage; also 2 coffers, one small brass pot, one brass kettle, 1 pair sheets, 1 brass skillet. To JOHN PEACHELL of Saxmundham 30s. in 6 months of testator's death, he to be supervisor. Residue of all goods to daughters KATHERINE & MARIAN PARISH, they to be executors and pay all debts, funeral expenses. Witnesses: RICHARD GROWE, WILLIAM MYLES, JOHN PEACHELL. Pr. at Saxmundham 27 April 1632.

W. JOHN ROBERTSON of Horham, husbandman. 4 March 163[?] (614)

To FRANCES ELMER of Horham, kinswoman, tenement in Horham, with all lands, both free and copyhold, all houses, stables, appurtenances, provided she enter into bond with DENNY CLUBBE of Allington [Athelington?] yeoman, supervisor of will, in £30 in two months of testator's death, to pay legacies specified in will. To the five children of JOHN STANTON of Stradbroke £6. 13s. 4d. equally when 21. To kinswoman MARY CEBLE 40s. in 2 years of testator's death. To the four children of MARY CEBLE 40s. each. To JOHN SADD, testator's sister GRACE SADD her son, 50s. to be paid 20s. in 5 years, 20s. in 6 years, 10s. in 7 years of testator's death. To EDMOND ROBERTSON of Eye 20s. in 1 year of testator's death. To MARTHA RICHARDSON, kinswoman, 40s. -- 20s. in 3 years, 20s. in 4 years of testator's death. To BATHOLOMEW JESSOPP of Horham 3s. immediately on testator's death. To the poor of Horham 10s. on his burial. To FRANCES ELMER rest of movables, chattels, she to be executor and pay debts, and funeral expenses. DENNY CLUBBE to be supervisor. Witnesses: GUY HAYLE, DENNY CLUBBE. Pr. at Horham 16 Aug. 1632.

W. GEORGE RAYMOND of Ipswich St. Clement's, clothier. (615)
14 August 1632

Weak. To son JOHN RAYMOND £40, and to son GEORGE RAYMOND £10, provided they make no claim or demand on testator's executor. To son JAMES RAYMOND £10 when 21. To daughters ANNE & MARY £10 when 21. To wife MARY all goods, chattels, debts, linen, wool, iron and silver, in order to pay legacies to his children, and to pay his share of the legacies to the grandchildren of his father to which he is bound as joint executor of his father's will with brother JEREMIAH RAYMOND. Wife executrix. Witnesses: RICHARD RAYMOND, PEDINE ALLEN. Pr. at Ipswich 8 Oct. 1632.

W. ALICE RICHARDSON of Blakenham on the water, widow(N). (616)
1 February 1632

Son WILLIAM RICHARDSON to be executor, and pay debts. To son ANTHONY RICHARDSON 5s. immediately on testator's death. To daughter DYANA, wife of ABRAHAM SUTTON 5s. immediately on testator's death. To daughter ALICE, wife of JOHN GIPPS 5s. immediately on testator's death. Residue, once debts paid, to be equally divided between WILLIAM, SOLOMON, EDWARD, ANN RICHARDSON, JOAN, wife of ROBERT ASHLYE, MARY & PHILIP RICHARDSON, children of testator. Witnesses: WILLIAM SMYTH, RICHARD PATTERICHE. Pr. at Ipswich 22 Feb. 1632.

W. JOHN RISINGE of Ilketshall St. Margaret's, yeoman. (617)
24 April 1632

To wife SUSAN, messuage where ROBERT WOLLNOUGH of Barham lives, and all lands, and meadows, pastures in Barham and Ringsfield;

also all goods, chattels, plate, linen, household stuff, corn, debts and ready money (save 2 pair of sheets, one pair to go to ALICE DOWE, one pair to FRANCES DOWE, kinswomen). Also £60 presently on testator's death. To WILLIAM GOOCH of Mettingham £20 in 1 year of testator's death. To JOHN MARSHALL of Ilketshall St. Margaret £5 in 2 years of testator's death. To the two children of JOHN RIXE, late of Westhall deceased £10 each when 21. To LIONEL EDWARDS of Blyford £15 in 2 years of testator's death. To JOHN BENNETT of Westhall, brother-in-law, £10 in 1 yr. of testator's death. To ANN, wife of JOHN SYTE of Westhall £5 in 2 years of testator's death. To MARY CROWLAND of Reddenhall (Norfolk) £5 in 3 years of testator's death. To MARY CROWLAND of Hopton £5 in 4 years of testator's death. To ELIZABETH DOWE of Ilketshall St. Margaret £5 in 5 yrs. of testator's death. To THOMAS CROWLAND of Aldborough (Norfolk) linen weaver 40s. in 5 yrs. of testator's death. To ELIZABETH CROWLAND of Alborough (Norfolk) 40s. in 5 yrs. of testator's death. To MICHAEL EDWARDS of Earsham (Norfolk), linen weaver, £5 in 6 yrs. of testator's death. To servant ANN WOOLLNOUGH 40s. in 4 years of testator's death. To servant ROBERT SEAMAN 10s. in 4 years of testator's death. To SUSAN, the wife of JOHN PIXTON of Harleston 40s. in 2 years of testator's death. To godson JOHN SWAYNE and ANN, goddaughter, daughter of LIONEL EDWARDS, 5s. each. To the poor of Ilketshall St. Lawrence 20s., and 2d. to each poor person from other towns present at testator's funeral. Rest of money and debts due to testator to go to ROBERT RIXE of Wangford, he to pay funeral expenses, legacies, and debts and be executor. To WILLIAM RIXE of Ilketshall St. Margaret's messuage where THOMAS MALLETT lives in Ilketshall St. Lawrence and all lands pertaining to it in Ilketshall St. Lawrence and Ilketshall St. Margaret, provided he pay £20 to ANN SHANKE of Pulham (Norfolk) widow in 1 year of testator's death; £20 to MARGARET, wife of TOBIAS DOWNING of Ilketshall St. Margaret in 2 years of testator's death; £20 to MARY, wife of JOHN GEORGE of Wrentham in 3 years of testator's death; £40 to FRANCES DOWE, spinster of Wissett in 5 years of testator's death; £50 to ALICE DOWE of Ilketshall St. Margaret's in 6 years of testator's death; all legacies to be paid in the south porch of Ilketshall St. Lawrence church, with power to enter and distrain if default in payment of any legacy. Brother-in-law JOHN BENNETT appointed supervisor. Witnesses: SYMON MAN, jnr.; DANYELL PRYOR. Pr. at Beccles 19 Jan. 1632.

W. THOMAS RANSOME of Blyford, husbandman. (618)
13 February 1632

Sick. To wife SUSAN £10 within 6 months of testator's death; also feather bed in the parlour, 2 pillows, 2 blankets, boulster, best coverlet with the bedstead and all other things belonging to it; best cupboard in the parlour, warming pan, pair of tongs, firepan, great buffet stools and a little one; a needlework cushion; pair of cobirons; chaffing dish; pestle and mortar. Wife to enter into bond of £7 with exec., within 1 month of testator's death, to return all these household items devised to her, to executor on her death. Also to wife annuity of 30s. -- 15s. to be paid every six months, first payment to be made on the first Lady Day or Michaelmas next after testator's death. Executor to enter into bond of £10 to pay this annuity. Wife is also to have half the total amount of provisions in his house on testator's death. Son-in-law JOHN THURSTON to have rest of goods, movables, and chattels, to pay debts and burial expenses, he to be executor. Witnesses: THOMAS LEFFY, PRUDENCE CARMAN (X). Pr. at Beccles 23 Feb. 1632.

W. NICHOLAS ROSSE of Falkenham, yeoman. 25 March 1632 (619)

Sick. To wife JOAN, the best bed and bedstead as it stands in the parlour with all things belonging to it; 2 pair sheets. To JEFERY MEDOWE of Buckelsham 20s. in 1 year of testator's death, provided he be a good friend to testator's youngest son JOHN ROSSE. Residue of goods to be equally divided into four parts -- 1/4 to wife JOAN, 1/4 to eldest son NICHOLAS ROSSE, 1/4 to son THOMAS ROSSE, 1/4 to son JOHN, but if JOHN dies before he reach 21 then his share to be equally divided amongst the others. JEFERY MEDOWE of Bucklesham appointed executor. Witnesses: ROGER DRACKFORD, ROBERT JAY. Letters of administration granted at Ipswich 30 April 1632.

W. THOMAS RUSSELLS of Ipswich, clothier. 1 March 1631 (620)

To son MYLES £5 in one year of testator's death, he to give a receipt to executor. To daughter SUSAN, wife of GEORGE DAMRON of Woodbridge £15 in 1 yr. of testator's death. To daughter KATHERIN, wife of RICHARD PILBROW of Ipswich £5 in 1 yr. testator's death. To granddaughter ABIGAIL BOWLE, or her guardian, £10 in 1 yr. of testator's death. Residue to wife ALICE, she paying all debts, legacies, probate and funeral expenses; she to be executrix. Witnesses: ROBERT BURRAGE (X), ROBERT LORD. Pr. at Ipswich 22 Feb. 1632.

W. WILLIAM RIX of Ilketshall St. Margaret, husbandman. (621)
24 January 1631

To maid ELIZABETH REVE, 10s. in 1 year of testator's death. To godchild JOHN WRIGHT of Rumburgh 8s. to buy a bible, and give it him when 10. To son WILLIAM RIX, all goods, chattels whatsoever, he to pay debts, legacies, and to be executor. ROBERT GOOCHE of Ilketshall St. Margaret, landlord, supervisor. Witnesses: ROBERT HUNT (X), JOHN MARSHALL. Pr. at Beccles 27 Oct. 1632.

W. JOHN SMITH of Lowestoft, miller. 20 August 1632 (622)

Sick; to be buried at Lowestoft. All debts, duties to be paid by executor. To servant RICHARD COLMAN 20s. within 6 months of testator's death, and all best apparell -- coat, doublet and breeches immediately on testator's death. Rest of goods to wife DOROTHY, she to be sole executrix, and she to enter into bond within 6 days of testator's death, in £100 with his brother THOMAS SMITH of Hingham (Norfolk) not to claim dower in lands. If she refuse then all lands and estate to go to brother THOMAS. Witnesses: HENRY WODSHED (X), ROBERT MENDHAM (X), WILLIAM UNDERWOOD. Probate granted at Beccles 19 Oct. 1632.

W. JOHN SPICER of Ipswich, mariner. 8 February 1629 (623)

To wife PRUDENCE, messuage and tenement where testator lives in St. Margaret's parish in Ipswich, with all yards belonging; also messuage where GEORGE COBYE instrument maker lives, in the same parish; she to hold these for life, maintaining them in good repair. Also all movable goods and chattels for life; on her death goods and chattels to be equally divided between his children JOHN, ROBERT & ELIZABETH. To son JOHN, messuage where testator lives in St. Margaret's parish on death of mother, and if he pay 20s. a year to his sister ELIZABETH on the feast of St. Thomas the apostle (21 December); power to enter and distrain if default. If JOHN die without issue then daughter ELIZABETH to inherit. To son ROBERT, messuage where GEORGE COBYE lives in St. Margaret's parish on death of mother, if he pay 20s. a year to his sister ELIZABETH on the feast of St. Thomas; power to enter and distrain if default and if ROBERT die without issue then ELIZABETH to inherit. Should ELIZABETH inherit lands then annuity ceases. Proviso that the water courses between the houses shall run as they do now. Witnesses: RICHARD RAYNSFORD, EDWARD HONK, JOSEPH BURROUGH. Admon. to PRUDENCE SPICER 20 Aug. 1632.

W. AMEA SWATWAY of SouthElmham St. Michael (N). (624)
6 August 1632

To son THOMAS SWATWAY, a spit, latchpan, an iron. To son THOMAS's daughter a pair of sheets. To son ROBERT pair of sheets, pillow beer, 2 napkins and £5. Rest of goods to daughters JOAN & SARAH to be equally divided. Brother ROBERT BALLS to be executor. Witnesses: WILLIAM & ELIZABETH TAILOR. Pr. at Beccles 1 Sept. 1632.

W. ALICE SAWER of Bungay, widow. 14 March 1632 (625)

To her four children £10 each, given to the testator by RICHARD IVES late of Mendham. Testator's executor to receive this money from ROBERT ROPE of Mendham, the executor for RICHARD IVES. To son RICHARD SAWER 1 old cow or neat beast; one posted bedstead, mat, cord, one feather bed, one bolster, one pillow and pillow case; 2 blankets 1 coverlet, 1 pair of sheets and a coffer. To son THOMAS one posted bedstead, mat, cord, on which testator now lies, bed of feather and flock; bolster, pillow, pillow case, 2 blankets, coverlet, pair of sheets, and one coffer. To son JOHN, one trundle bedstead, one flock bed, bolster, coverlet, blankets, one pair sheets and a coffer. All of these bequests of goods to sons to be delivered immediately on testator's death. To son THOMAS £4 to bind him out as an apprentice. Residue of goods to daughter ELIZABETH SAWER, to pay debts, legacies, and bind out son THOMAS, and pay funeral expenses. Executor EDWARD PEARFORD of Bungay, beerbrewer; he to assist testator's children, and to receive 5s. for probate expenses. Witnesses: JOHN ELLMER, ROBERT HOLBRUCK (X), THOMAS FRANCKLYN. Admon. to EDWARD PEARFORD at Bungay 18 April 1632.

W. THOMAS SMITH of Cratfield, taylor. 9 April 1632 (626)

To ROBERT SMITH, son 100 marks when 23; one posted bedstead with featherbed and things necessary for bed when 23; if he die before inheriting then to testator's brother and sister £20 in one year after son's death, equally divided between them, and to wife's brother and sister £10 equally divided between them. To wife ELIZABETH residue of goods, chattels in order to bring up and maintain son and to bind him out as an apprentice. Exec. to enter into bond in 15 days of testator's death, of 200 marks together with ROBERT BROODBANCKE & JOHN WILLIAMS, to SAMUEL SMITH, testator's brother to perform this will. Witnesses: GREGORY SMITH (X), GREGORY SMITH, snr., GREGORY ROUSE. Probate granted to ELIZABETH SMITH at Yoxford 24 May 1632.

W. JOAN SMITH of Holbrook. 26 May 1632 (627)

To daughter FRANCES NORMAN, bed in the chamber, the shorter of the two; bolster, blanket, the least kettle, one pair sheets, pillow beer. To son THOMAS, larger of the two beds in the chamber with furniture belonging to the same; bolster, pillows; one piece of large pewter; one dipper. Three sheets, one pillow beer, middle sized kettle, brass pot. To the poor of Holbrook a bushel of rye at the funeral. Rest of estate, all corn, cattle, household stuff to son WILLIAM he paying debts, and funeral charges -- he letting testator's sister POOLE of Chelmondiston have black waistecoat and gray petticoat, and MARGARET SAKERS 2 old petticoats, and sister COOPER an old petticoat. To daughter FRANCES one red petticoat, an old cloak, and handkerchief. Son WILLIAM SMITH to be executor. Witnesses: EDMUND MAPLETOFT, WILLIAM JORDAN (X), EDITH GOSLING. Pr. at Ipswich 6 July 1632.

W. FRANCIS SAWER of Shotley, singleman (N). (628)
13 October 1632

Sick. Master HENRY CHETTLEBURGH to be executor, and he to pay to testator's grandfather SAWER of Boulge the profits from £10 for his lifetime; then pay the profits on the £10 to mother for life, and on her death the £10 to go to brother ROBERT SAWER. Also to pay profits on £5 to grandfather for life, then to pay profits on £5 to mother, and then on her death the £5 to go to the three children of testator uncle JOHN LAUNCE. Witnesses: ELIZABETH KENDALL (X), SUSAN LAUGHTER (X). Pr. at Ipswich 3 [blank] 1632.

W. KATHERINE SCOTT of Martlesham, spinster. (629)
1 November 1632

To her master JOHN ROSE of Martlesham and his wife BRIDGET and his son JOHN, all her goods and movables, they to pay to her brother RICHARD, now an apprentice in Bradfield, 20s. when he ends his apprenticeship. Witnesses: WILLIAM RICHER, apothecary, and MARY BOTTRITT. Admon. to JOHN ROSE at Ipswich 1 Feb. 1632.

W. SARAH SHIRLANDS of Bungay, widow. 13 October 1632 (630)

All goods whatsoever to daughter ELIZABETH SHIRLAND, she to be executrix and pay funeral expenses. Witnesses: ROBERT BIRKINGSHAW, RICHARD BENTLEY, THOMAS FRANCKLYN, script. Pr. at Bungay 5 Nov. 1632.

W. JOHN SHEPHEARD of Creeting St. Mary, weaver. (631)
[no date]

Sick. To son JOHN 20s. when 21, also best cupboard which standeth in the hall, with the little round table and hooped chair -- on death of testator's wife. To son WILLIAM 20s. when 21; also best bedstead in the hall, great chest in the hall chamber after death of testator's wife. Rest of goods, chattels to wife SUSAN, she to pay debts, legacies, and funeral expenses; she appointed sole executrix. Witnesses: JOHN BALDRY snr., JOHN BALDRY, jnr., JOHN FREBURNE, SUSAN BUGG. Pr. at Ipswich 11 Jan. 1632.

W. RICHARD SKEET of Ilketshall St. Andrew, yeoman. (632)
24 May 1630

Sick. To wife MARGARET tenement where testator's daughter lives, and all lands thereunto belonging, for life; then to be equally divided between three daughters SUSAN, KATHERINE & ELIZABETH, with benefit of survivorship. To daughters £4 in equal portions to be paid them when they reach 18 by his wife MARGARET, she being his executrix. To daughter SUSAN posted bed new furnished in the hall chamber; cob iron in the butlery, and a great chest in the chamber. To daughter KATHERINE a bedstead and bedding in the chief house chamber; one desk with the letters R and S on it. To daughter ELIZABETH trundle bedstead and bedding; cupboard table in the hall, one desk with the letters R and F on it; 2 joined stools under the desk. Residue of goods to wife MARGARET, she being sole executrix, to pay debts, legacies and funeral expenses. Witnesses: WILLIAM GOLDING, BARTHOLOMEW SKUT. Pr. at Beccles 5 May 1632.

W. RICHARD TALLEMACH the elder of Coddenham, yeoman. (633)
31 August 1632

Sick. To the poor of Coddenham 20s. in one month of testator's death. To wife JOAN all tenements and lands in the three Creetings, occupied by one ROSE, both free and copyhold, for life; then to go to grandchild ELIZABETH TALLEMACH, daughter of testator's son RICHARD. Keep in good repair, allow no waste. To wife JOAN freehold land called Kendalls, lying to the south side of testator's house, and also all land in Shampford meadow. Also bed and bedstead where testator usually lies, and all furniture upon the chamber; also all linen, brass and pewter; the best chest, and all the hemp in the house; 2 chairs 2 cushions, 2 little stools, 2 firkins, 1 trammel. 1 firepan, 1 pair tongs, best gardiron, and all brewing utensils; 8 bushels of barley, 6 bushels of malt, and free use of house where testator lives, and the lands that belong to it, and firewood and profits from cattle until Michaelmas next after testator's death. If JOAN, his wife die before grandchild ELIZABETH reaches 24, then executor to hold lands until ELIZABETH inherit, and once ELIZABETH has inherited, she to pay to her brother RICHARD TALLEMACH £5 within 1 year, and to her sister ALICE TALLEMACH £5 within 1 year next after having paid her brother. To grandson WILLIAM TELLEMACH, son to son RICHARD, the reversion to Scotchmere's tenement in Coddenham occupied by WILLIAM CLERKE on the death of the said WILLIAM CLERKE. To granddaughter ANN TALLEMACH, daughter of son RICHARD, one posted bedstead, one bed as it stands on the chamber with all things belonging to it, except the sheets. To WILLIAM STUD of Gosbeck, son to testator's first wife, 40s. -- 20s. that testator owes him and 20s. more. To REBECCA & ANNE WOODWARD 30s., which should have been paid to their sister ELIZABETH, testator's servant had she lived. To ANN COOKE, daughter to HENRY COOKE, 3s. 4d. To son RICHARD TALLEMACH, all goods and chattels whatsoever, and residue of estate, he being executor, and RICHARD COBBOLD the elder, supervisor, he to receive 6s. 8d. Witnesses: ANNE TALLEMACH (X), WILLIAM STUD, MATTHIAS GILLET alias CANDLER. Pr. at Ipswich 20 Sept. 1632.

W. WILLIAM THOMPSON, yeoman. 13 August 1632 (634)

To son JOHN £20 when 22. To daughter ANNE £60 when 21 and to daughter MARGARET £60 when 21. To son JOHN, livery bedstead, feather bed, feather bolster, coverlet, 2 blankets, mat and bedline. To daughter ANNE, posted bedstead with a feather bed, bolster, curtains and all other furniture, in the little chamber. To daughter MARGARET, posted bedstead with a feather bed, bolster and furniture belonging to same in the little chamber. To ANNE POSTERS widow, 2 bushels of rye. Residue to wife MARGARET, to pay legacies, and maintain his daughters until they reach 21, and pay funeral expenses; she to be executrix, and within 14 days of his burial to be bound to brother-in-law JOHN CULLHAM in £200 to pay legacies. If she refuse, then gifts to wife to be void, and gifts then to be equally divided between his children, and JOHN CULLHAM to be executor. Witnesses: REGINALD LEFFY, MICHAEL REACE, JOHN BEAR. Pr. at Yoxford 18 Sept. 1632.

W. ROBERT THROCKMORTON of Bungay, gentleman (N). 3 April 1632 (635)

Sick. All goods within the house to go to son JOHN. Witnesses: JOHN DOWSING, jnr., JOHN WALBYE. Probate granted to JOHN THROCKMORTON 18 April 1632.

W. THOMAS TROANTE of Ufford, weaver. 6 February 1631 (636)

To son THOMAS, house where testator lives, with all land belonging thereunto; also two joined chests, desk and all testator's books. To brother ROBERT of Capel, all clothes. Residue of estate to executor to be sold and money thus raised to be put to use of son THOMAS. Also £30 is owed to testator by his brother-in-law JOHN HALES of Sutton, and this sum is also to be laid out for use of son THOMAS. If he die before reaching 21 however, then lands to go to ROBERT of Capel, provided he pay to sister KATHERINE HAMOND £10 within 1 year of death of THOMAS; also ROBERT to pay to sister CICELY FRANCIS £10 likewise, and to sister FRANCES BROOK £4 within 2 years of son THOMAS' death. Brother ROBERT also to be sole executor, paying all debts, and bringing up testator's son THOMAS, and rendering him an account of all profits from house and lands when THOMAS reaches 21. Witnesses: WILLIAM PRATT, THOMAS BOLDEN. Pr. at Wickham Market 28 April 1632.

W. UNDERWOOD VESEY of Belton, husbandman. [no date] (637)

Sick. To eldest son FELIX, house and lands where testator lives. To other son ROBERT, tenement and lands belonging in Belton, near the parsonage; also £10 within 1 year of testator's death, and 1 bedstead now standing on the chamber with feather bed, bolster, one pair blankets and one coverlet lying on it, one brass pot, 1 little table, 1 form, 2 pewter dishes, one chest of furring deal, all in 6 months of testator's death; also 1 yearling colt in 1 month. To daughter KATHERINE £10 in two years of testator's death; lessest brass pot; one framed table of furring deal, in one month of testator's death. To brother ROBERT VESEY 20s. within 6 months of testator's death. Residue of estate to son FELIX, he to be executor and pay legacies, debts. Witnesses: TEMPERANCE PULLEN, JOAN POPE, GABRIEL WOODRUFF. Pr. at Beccles 23 June 1632.

W. ROGER WOOD the elder of Halesworth, tanner. 8 June 1632 (638)

To son-in-law THOMAS TAILER of Rumburgh, yeoman, all movables and chattels. To grandchild MARY WOODE one chest in the chamber, which her grandmother gave her. To ELIZABETH & ANNE WOOD, grandchildren 10s. each when 21. To wife ANNE 20s. in 1 year next after testator's death. To son ROGER WOOD salting trough. To poor of Halesworth 10s. THOMAS TAILER sole executor, pay legacies and debts. Witnesses: NICHOLAS DAWKIN (X), MARTIN FOUNTAINE the elder (X), HENRY KEBLE. Pr. at Beccles 16 July 1632.

W. THOMAS WADE of Bradwell. 3 April 1632 (639)

Sick; to be buried at Bradwell. To mother MARGERY £10. To brother JOHN WADE £10 in 2 years of testator's death. To brother ROBERT WADE £10 in 2 years and a day of testator's death. To sister BRIDGET PEASECOD £10 in 2 years and 2 days of testator's death. To ANNE SAYE, wife of JOHN SAYE, brother-in-law, £10 in 2 yrs. and 3 days of testator's death. To THOMAS, son of JOHN SAYE £3 in 2 years and 4 days of testator's death. Rest of estate to JOHN SAYE, he to be executor and pay debts, legacies, and funeral expenses. Witnesses: BENJAMIN CAROWE, WILLIAM BASTARD, WILLIAM RYSINGE (X). Pr. at Beccles April 1632.

W. FRANCIS WOOLNOUGH of St. NicholasSouthElmham (N). (640)
20 January 1631

To brother JOHN £10, and to brother EPHRAIM £10 in 2 years of testator's death. To SARAH WOOLNOUGH, daughter of BENJAMIN WOOLNOUGH £5. To PRISCILLA, daughter of THOMAS SOUTHE, brother-in-law of testator £5, in 6 years of testator's death. Rest of estate and clothes to mother and brother JOHN; brother to be executor. Witnesses: HENRY WOOLNOUGH, CICELY WELTON, widow. Pr. 28 April 1632.

W. THOMAS WOOLNOUGH of Bramfield, yeoman. (641)
23 February 1631

To eldest son WILLIAM WOOLNOUGH tenement in Westhall, and Sotherton, he to pay legacies, and if he fail then wood and pasture called Goddards meadow, late purchased of JOHN LENNY, and all movables and money owed by son WILLIAM to the testator to go to testator's son-in-law JOHN MILTON, and he to pay legacies. To THOMAS WOOLNOUGH lands in Bramfield both free and copyhold; the horsemill and all furniture belonging. To son-in-law JOHN MILTON £16 lent by testator to him. To daughter ANNA, wife of JOHN MILTON, and her children £20, to be equally divided between them in 6 months of testator's death. To THOMAS REVE of Westhall, son-in-law £16 lent by testator to him. To daughter MARY, wife of THOMAS REVE and her children £10 to be equally divided between them in 6 months of testator's death. To son THOMAS £20 in 6 months of testator's death. To son THOMAS's children, all the money owed by THOMAS to the testator. Linen to be equally divided between testator's children on his death. To son THOMAS 1 feather bed, 1 bolster, 2 pillows, 2 blankets and coverlet. To and 1 coverlet. To daughter MARY 1 feather bed, bolster, 2 blankets and 1 coverlet. To poor £10. To son-in-law JOHN MILTON 2 loads of timber. To son WILLIAM £30 out of profits of wood, and £20 he owes testator for the farm of testator's tenements. Rest of estate and goods to son WILLIAM and to his five children £5 each; WILLIAM to pay debts, legacies, probate expenses. Witnesses: THOMAS FULLER, RICHARD WELTON, ELIZABETH COLMAN, widow. Probate granted to WILLIAM WOOLNOUGH at Beccles 7 Jan. 1632. [this will has parts missing; damaged]

W. JOAN WYSEMAN of Ipswich, widow. 20 April 1632 (642)

Sick. To daughter ELIZABETH WYSEMAN, the little box with linen in it, save 2 pair pillow beers one of the finest and the other of the ordinary sort -- these to go to son THOMAS WYSEMAN. To son THOMAS, testator's part of the lighter, a hoy called the Welcome Home John of Ipswich, with all things belonging; also 1 flockbed, 1 feather bolster, feather pillow, 1 livery bedstead. To daughter silver beaker, and all clothes, save old gown and best red petticoat. To son, pair of bed blankets, 1 rug. To daughter 10s. of gold. Rest to be equally divided between her son and daughter at the discretion of testator's brother JOHN ALDERMAN, and ROBERT CLARKE, gent. To sister STAPLETON, best red petticoat, and a ruff. To son old gown. To poor of Ipswich St. Clements 20s. To the minister Mr SCOTT, for a sermon 10s. Benefit of survivorship to children. Brother JOHN ALDERMAN to be sole executor. Witnesses: PETER TALBOT, ROBERT CLARKE. Pr. at Ipswich 26 May 1632.

W. ROBERT WHAYMAN of Framlingham. 12 January 1632 (643)

To son ROBERT, lands and tenements in Monk Soham and Kenton, provided he pay to testator's wife ALICE an annuity of £15 on Lady Day and Michaelmas by equal installments; first payment to be made at the first feast day next after the testator's death, and if default made, power to ALICE to enter and distrain for payment, arrears and an additional 40s. for every default made. To son DANIEL, lands, both free and copyhold, in Framlingham, provided he pay to testator's wife ALICE an annuity of £5 due by equal installments on Lady Day and Michaelmas, first payment due on the first feast day next after testator's death with power to enter and distrain if default. To wife ALICE, second best bedstead, best bedding, little joined chest in the parlour, with all the linen. To brother JEFFERY WHAYMAN, annuity of 20s. out of the lands in Monk Soham, to be paid by son ROBERT in two equal installments at Lady Day and Michaelmas, first payment to be made at the first feast next after testator's death. Executor empowered to use £200 to buy more lands and tenements, and the rent from these lands to be paid by executor to testator's son-in-law JOHN CULHAM and his wife SUSAN, for life by equal portions at the two usual feast, and the first payment to be made within 1 1/2 years after testator's death. If the executor fails to buy more lands, then instead executor to pay to JOHN CULHAM and wife SUSAN the yearly interest on the £200 for their lifetime. To grandchild SAMUEL CULHAM £60 when 21. Executor to have £140 and divide this sum equally between testator's grandchildren, the children of JOHN & SUSAN CULHAM -- excepting SAMUEL; they to receive their legacies when 21, with benefit of survivorship. Sons ROBERT & DANIEL to be executors, pay debts, funeral expenses, and legacies and to have residue of all goods and chattels. Witnesses: EDWARD MOULTON, THOMAS CALVER (X), MARY MOYES (X). Pr. at Ipswich 5 Feb. 1632.

W. HENRY WINSTON of Blundeston, yeoman. 20 December 1631 (644)

To the poor of Blundeston 20s. To son WILLIAM WINSTON £160 -- in six months of testator's death to receive £50, a further £50 in the next six months, then £40 in the next six months, and the remaining £20 in 1 year thereafter. To grandchild HENRY, son of WILLIAM WINSTON, £10 when 16. To daughter ANN WINSTON £80 at Michaelmas 1636. To son ANTHONY WINSTON, messuage and lands occupied by EDMOND WHETACRE; and 4 acres more of land of which 3 acres abut on a certain meadow called Speare meadow towards the east, and upon the said messuage towards the west; the other acres lies in the east field called Croftwent, and abuts on town lands of Blundeston on the west, both of which pieces are occupied by the testator. Also one piece of land in East field abutting on the lands of the rectory of Blundeston on the north and containing 2 acres late purchased of JOHN WOOD. All these said lands lying in Blundeston, and ANTHONY to hold these lands, provided he pay to testator's daughter ANN £120, namely £60 on Lady Day 1637 and £60 on the Michaelmas next following. If default, power to ANN to enter and enjoy lands, but if she die before legacy paid her and she have no heir, then whatsoever is due to her, to be divided between testator's sons JOHN, WILLIAM, & ANTHONY. To ANN, for her maintenance from the day of testator's death until the first payments of her legacies £5, every half year. To grandchild HENRY, son of son ANTHONY, £15 when 14. To grandchild ANTHONY, son of son ANTHONY £10 when 14. To grandchild HENRY, £5 within 2 years of testator's death. To grandchildren HENRY & ANNE WINSTON, children of son HENRY, £5 each when 21, no benefit of survivorship. To grandchildren JOHN, MARY & ELIZABETH ELLIS £5 each when 21, benefit of survivorship. To daughter ANN bedstead testator used to lie on, 1 of the beds, pair of blankets, a covering of rugs, 3 pair sheets, and to his sons, save HENRY 4 pair of sheets. Reciting that testator's wife BRIDGET, had before her marriage, when she was known as BRIDGET GUNTON of Belton, widow, become bound to testator's son HENRY in £240 to pay £100 to testator, which sum had not been paid; also that testator had lent her for her own use £21. Now within one month of testator's death, wife to release her dower claims in the lands devised to ANTHONY to which HENRY could claim, and further she to enter bond to discharge testator's executor of all legacies due to her from PETER GUNTON, her late husband; if she do these then the £240 bond to be delivered to her to be cancelled, and the £21 gift not to be called in from her.

Reciting that by deed of 16 September 1618 testator was to hold lands and tenements in Blundeston from HENRY WINSTON, for term of his life and for four months after the Michaelmas following his death; now testator wills that son ANTHONY to hold these lands until term be expired. To son JOHN £10 in 3 years of testator's death. To grandchildren THOMAS & HENRY, sons of son JOHN, £10 each when 21, with no benefit of survivorship. Residue of estate to son ANTHONY he to be executor, pay debts, legacies, funeral. Witnesses: ROBERT MELLING, THOMAS FELTHAM, EDWARD HOWLETT. Pr. at Beccles 15 Oct. 1632.

W. SAMUEL WRIGHT of Grundisburgh, wheelwright. (645)
19 December 1632

Sick. To son SAMUEL all timber, both converted and unconverted; all working tools. To son JOHN 20s. in 1 year of testator's death. To daughter FRANCES, wife of HENRY STILES 20s. in 1 yr. of testator's death. To son-in-law ROBERT MOISE 5s. in 2 years of testator's death. To grandchildren ELIZABETH, ROBERT, JAMES, SAMUEL, JOHN, JOSEPH & WILLIAM MOISE 5s. each when 21. Rest of goods to wife JOAN, but if she remarry then she to loose bequest and the residue of his estate to be equally divided between his children. If any one of his children die, then their share in goods to descend to their heir(s). Wife JOAN to be executrix, pay debts, legacies, funeral expenses. Witnesses: ROBERT HOWE, jnr., THOMAS CULLINGTON, ANDREW FOSDICKE (X). Pr. at Ipswich 11 Jan. 1632.

W. HUMFRY WYARD of Saxtead. 1 December 1632 (646)

To son JOHN, all lands and appurtenances, provided he pay to testator's daughter ELIZABETH, the wife of WILLIAM WYETH, £20 -- £10 in six months, and £10 in 1 year after testator's death, in the south porch of Saxtead church; if default, then power to ELIZABETH to enter and hold, until paid, together with arrears and 40s. more for every default suffered. To daughter ELIZABETH, little joined chest. Rest of estate to son JOHN, he to pay debts, funeral expenses, and be executor, and prove the will within six months of testator's death; if he does not prove the will in the time limit, then testator's brother ANTHONY WYARD to be executor, and to hold lands above devised to son JOHN for 3 years. Witnesses: EDWARD MOULTON, PHILIP RUMSYE (X). Pr. at Yoxford 9 Jan. 1632.

W. THOMAS WILSON of Beccles, blacksmith (N). (647)
30 January 1632

To WILLIAM RUSSELLS senior of Ringsfield, all goods, chattels, he to pay debts and educate testator's children. Witnesses: FRANCIS WARNE (X), JOHN WARNE (X), HANNA WOODWARD (X). Probate granted to WILLIAM RUSSELLS at Beccles 4 Feb. 1632.

W. ROBERT WILLS of Bungay, cordwainer. 25 June 1632 (648)

To RICHARD WILLS, brother WILLIAM's eldest son, best bedstead and all bedding, save one feather bed given to ANN WILLS, testator's brother JOHN WILLS of Halesworth his daughter; RICHARD to pay 15s. to testator's cousin FRANCES CHAPMAN, the eldest daughter to testator's brother WILLIAM. To cousin RICHARD WILLS, a black chest standing at the bed's feet, and a brass kettle. To brother JOHN WILLS of Halesworth, chest being of a yellow colour. To cousin JOHN WILLS, brother JOHN's eldest son, joined table with a long stool thereunto belonging. To cousin GEORGE WILLS, a great chain, and a flock pillow. To cousin ROBERT WILLS, a little table with a little form. To cousin HENRY WILLS one little skillet. To son-in-law FRANCIS WILLS, 2 small coffers which testator wills be given to cousin JAMES WILLS on his mother's death. To cousin SUSANNA WILLS, one old livery cupboard, trundle bedstead, 1 little brass kettle. To cousin ELIZABETH WILLS 1 yellowish coffer standing at the one end of the table above in the chamber, and a brass pot. To cousin RICHARD CHAPMAN one small brass kettle. All these bequests to relatives, with peace and quietness to enjoy. Executors to be RICHARD WILLS & RICHARD CHAPMAN. Witnesses: JOHN HALLAM, RICHARD NOLLETH. Pr. 19 July 1632.

W. ELIZABETH WRIGHT of Falkenham, widow. 8 May 1632 (649)

Sick. To sister's son ROBERT PASCOLE £5 when 21 -- the interest on it before then to be used to his benefit. To sister's daughter MARY PASCOLE £5 when 21 -- the interest on it before then to be used to her benefit. To the wife of WILLIAM COSSE of Walton, 20s., and 1 pair of best sheets, best pillow and pillow beer; cloak and smock of the best. To the Widow BETH's child, testator's husband's godchild, the price of a sheep, namely 6s. 8d. To JOLLYES child of Newbourne, testator's husband's godchild, the price of a sheep, namely 6s. 8d. Rest of goods to sister's husband HENRY PASCOLE, he paying testator's apprentice MATTHEW RINGE £11 when 21; he also to pay all debts, legacies, funeral expenses. Witnesses: JOHN HART, JAMES SUSBUX, ROBERT LAY. Probate granted to HENRY PASCOLE at Ipswich 1 Aug. 1632.

W. BENJAMIN WILSON of Theberton. 14 January 1632 (650)

If wife MARGARET be now conceived with child, then to that child and its heirs, all testator's moiety of lands in Theberton late JEREMY WILSON, testator's father, when child is 21. Until then wife to have profits to maintain and educate. If there be no child, then wife to have no moiety, and all goods and chattels; she to be executor. Witnesses: WILLIAM FULLER (X), WILLIAM MILLES (X). Pr. at Yoxford 30 Jan. 1632.

W. JOAN YOUNGES of Felixstowe, widow. 13 December 1631 (651)

To JOHN & MARY YOUNGES, children of ELIZABETH YOUNGES of Walton, widow, 5s. each in one month of testator's death. To MILDRED PATEMAN, daughter of JOHN PATEMAN of Felixstowe, 5s. in 6 months of testator's death. To ROSE BATEMAN, singlewoman, of Felixstowe, 10s. in 1 month of testator's death. To SIMON PETTEWARD of Walton, clerk, 6s. 8d. in 1 month of testator's death. Rest of goods and chattels to sister's son WILLIAM COEL of Trimley St. Martin, husbandman, for the use of his children; he to be executor. Witnesses: SIMON PETTEWARD, GEORGE KING (X), JOHN SCRUTTON (X). Pr. at Ipswich 19 Nov. 1632.

W. DOROTHY YOUNGS of Ipswich St. Peter, singlewoman (N). (652)
6 January 1632

Sick. All goods to GEORGE HARVY of St. Peter's Ipswich, if he bury her. Witnesses: THOMAS MORFALL and wife REBECCA. All goods to GEORGE HARVY save for old petticoats and a waistecoat which she gave to her sister. This the following week -- witnesses MARGARET, wife of WILLIAM SMITH and SUSAN HILL. Admon. to GEORGE HARVY 14 Jan. 1632.

W. ANN LABORNE of Pakefield [Very faint will]. (653)
12 [blank] 1632

Sick. To son WILLIAM LABORNE, 2 doles of herring nets in readiness for the sea, but if testator lives till they be sent to sea, then WILLIAM to have the doles of herring and nets with all the venture thereunto belonging; also 2 dole of the best and choicest mackerel nets; a dole of flues; a dole of pearling nets with all the line she now has for the repair; spurling nets -- WILLIAM to choose the best ones. Also feather bed, 2 blankets, coverlet, pillow, 2 bolsters; pair of sheets all in the hall chamber, best brass pot, frying pan, kettle, long chest, little table, best bedstead in the parlour. To son BARNABY LABORNE, biggest pillow, pair of sheets. To SUSAN, daughter of BARNABY, 1/2 dole of mackerel nets, 1/2 dole herring nets. To daughter MARGARET 2 doles herring nets, 2 doles mackerel nets; dole of flues dole of spurling nets. To son WILLIAM and daughter MARGARET 8 pieces of pewter to be equally divided, and to each of them a pewter pot. Rest of goods to daughter MARGARET LABORNE, she to be executor, pay debts, funeral charges. Witnesses: WILLIAM GYRLING, clerk, MARGARET GIRLING (X), JOHN WOOD. Pr. at Beccles 8 Oct. 1632.

CHAPTER IV

Abstracts of Wills contained in Register No. 62 and/or files nos. 69 and 70 of Wills proved in the Court of the Archdeacon of Suffolk.

R(W) JOHN BARRETT of Stratford. 5 June 1633 (654)

ANN my loving wife to have and enjoy all my freehold and copyhold land and tenements lying in the valley during her life as assigned to her for her jointure. Also to have the letting and setting of the messuage or house wherein I now dwell with the woadhouse, lead vats and all the implements belonging to the woadhouse, and all the outhouses, barns, stables, yards, gardens, orchards, lands, meadows and pastures on the backside of the said house. My wife is to receive all the rents and profits of the above property until the Michaelmas after my son ROBERT attains the age of 24. My wife to carry out any repairs thought necessary by my trusty and loving friends, Mr JOHN BRAGG and DANYELL WALL. She is also to use rents and profits from this property to bind out as apprentices my sons WILLIAM and JOHN, and to pay my daughter SARAH an annuity of £4. Any surplus from the profits to be equally distributed amongst the three sons as they reach the age of 24. Until my son ROBERT is 24, ANN must also pay £8 a year to SARAH as a jointure. This payment is to be made in two equal portions at Michaelmas and Lady Day in the north porch of Stratford parish church. When ROBERT is 24 he is to inherit all the land and buildings left in trust to his mother until he attained his majority. When he is of age ROBERT is to pay the £4 annuity to SARAH, who has power to distrain. After ANN dies, the land in Stratford valleys left to her for life is inherited by sons WILLIAM and JOHN. If ROBERT dies before he is 24, then the property bequeathed goes to JOHN with benefit of survivorship to WILLIAM. The testator had mortgaged to his brother WILLIAM CHAPLIN [i.e. brother-in-law] a 12 acre wood held copyhold of the manor of Roydon Hall, and had forfeited this wood. Since then he had repaid all but £5 of the mortgage and CHAPLIN had promised to restore the wood to him or his heirs when the £5 was paid. The executors are asked to pay this £5 to CHAPLIN and to ask him to surrender the 12 acres of wood to ROBERT BARRETT. 10s. to my daughter ANN BARKER and 10s. each to any children she has at the time of my death. These legacies are to be paid when the children attain the age of 21 or on their marriage days, whichever shall happen first. To my daughter MARTHA WOLWARD 10s. besides the £40 promised in marriage with her. To my daughter ELIZABETH £40, one half to be paid within one year of her marriage or when she is 21, whichever first happen, and the other £20 within 12 months of the first payment. In the meantime my executor is to maintain ELIZABETH out of the interest from her portion. To my kinsman JOHN BRIDGES 20s. to be paid one year after my decease or within one month after he has served out his apprenticeship. 20s. to be distributed amongst the poor people of Stratford at my burial. All my unbequeathed goods and chattels, both within the house and without, after my debts and legacies have been discharged, are to be equally divided amongst my wife and children. Wife appointed sole exrx. and must enter into a bond for £500 to my friends JOHN BRAGG and DANIEL WALL to perform my will. If she refuses to do this, these two men are to be exors. Witnesses: JOHN BARRETT, EDWARD CARDYNALL and JOHN BARWICK. Pr. at Ipswich 20 July 1633.

R(W) ELIZABETH BROWNING of Stratford, widow. 18 May 1633 (655)

£18 to my grandson ARTHUR RAND. £18 to my grandson JOHN RAND. Both these legacies are to be paid within one year of my decease. To ARTHUR RAND one great copper kettle, one posted bedstead, a featherbed, a flock bed, a coverlet, two blankets, a feather bolster, a flock bolster, a great brass pot, a musket with all the furniture belonging to it and half the pewter. To JOHN RAND the posted bedstead that I lie in, a Birds coverlet, a pair of blankets, a feather bed, a flock bed, a feather bolster, a pillow, half the pewter, a brass kettle, a little brass posnett, and a danske chest. ARTHUR and JOHN are to receive these legacies after their mother's death. All the rest of my movable goods and chattels I leave to my daughter ELIZABETH RAND, who must pay my cash legacies and is sole exrx. Witnesses: JOHN BARWICK and THOMAS BACON. Pr. at Ipswich 7 Aug. 1633.

R(W) ROBERT BORNE of Sudborne, gentleman. (656)
12 December 1632

To my beloved kinsman, DANIEL DEANE the younger gent, all and singular my goods and chattels, cattle, corn, ready money, plate, household stuff, movables and implements of household. DANIEL DEANE appointed sole exor. Witnesses: GEORGE UPPERSTALL, THOMAS MORRIS, and KATHERINE wife of ROBERT YORKE. Pr. at Beccles 17 Aug. 1633.

R(W) ROBERT BUTTELL of Boyton, singleman (N). (657)
4 June 1633

His sisters, ELIZABETH LETHERMAN widow and MARY BUTTELL singlewoman, to see his body brought to the ground in Christian burial, and all his goods to be equally divided between them. Witnesses: MARGARET MILES and MARY FALE. Pr. at Wickham Market to his two sisters on 7 Aug. 1633.

R(W) AUDREY BREDGHAM of East Bergholt, widow (N). (658)
2 June 1633

I give to my kinswoman JUDITH the wife of JOHN SMITH 1 hutch, my flannel petticoat, 1 pair sheets, 5 pieces of pewter, 1 shift of head linen, 1 handkerchief and £5 in money. I give to my sister-in-law HELEN NORMAN wid. the sum of 20s. I give to my kinsman

NICHOLAS COLLEN the younger my livery bedstead, a flock bed and the bedding to it as it stands in the chamber, 1 hutch, 1 handkerchief and 20s. in money. I give to my kinsman THOMAS COLLIN 1 hutch, 1 handkerchief and 6s. 8d. I give to my kinsman THOMAS HAVELL my middle kettle, 3 pieces pewter, 1 pillow, 1 sheet, 1 handkerchief and 6s. 8d. in money. I give to ELIZABETH HAVELL 1 brazen candlestick. I give to my kinsman DANIEL NORMAN 6s. 8d. I give to my kinswoman MARY BUNNER my stuff gown, my old flannel petticoat, 3 quarters and 1 handkerchief. Declared in the presence of ELIZABETH wife of NICHOLAS COFFEN and SUSAN GOATE (X). Probate granted at Ipswich to SAMUEL NORMAN alias TURNER of East Bergholt, brother of the testator, 22 July 1633.

R(W) HENRY CHETTLEBURGH of Shotley (N). 13 June 1633 (659)

I give to the inhabitants of Shotley £10 to be employed for ever towards the provision of bread and wine for the administration of the sacrament. To my daughter ELIZABETH the land and tenements mortgaged to me if they are forfeited, but if the mortgages are redeemed she is to have the money. To my wife ELIZABETH for her own use so much of my goods and chattels as are equal in value to the sum owed me on mortgage. The rest of my goods, together with the debts due to me, to be equally divided between my wife and daughter, but my wife to have £60 more than my daughter. Wife sole exrx. Declared in the presence of THOMAS CHURCH of Dallington, WILLIAM BROOME and THOMAS FULLER. Pr. at Ipswich 22 June 1633.

R(W) ANTHONY CROSE of Orford, yeoman. 9 June 1633 (660)

I give to the poor people of Iken 10s. to be distributed to them on the day of my burial or within one week of it. To my eldest son EDWARD CROSE all the land in Iken which I bought from my brother JOHN CROSE and his son SAMUEL, on condition that he pays £10 p.a. for 4 years to my daughter ANN MARTHA. £5 to my grandchild ALICE MAYE to be paid to her at the age of 21. I give £5 to DOROTHY MAYE to be paid when she is 21. All my movable goods and chattels to my son EDWARD, who is sole exor. Witnesses: THOMAS MARTEN (X), THOMAS FOULSER. Pr. at Wickham Market 7 Aug. 1633.

R(W) CIPRIAN COLCHESTER of Needham Market, clothier. 13 July 1633 (661)

Sick in body. To be buried in Barking churchyard. The tenement I live in to my wife JANE for her natural life. Part of this house is occupied by STEPHEN CIMBALL. After my wife's death I bequeath the said messuage or tenement to my son WILLIAM, on condition he pays £5 each to his sisters SARAH and ELIZABETH. If WILLIAM defaults on these payments the messuage is left to SARAH and ELIZABETH, who must then pay £10 to WILLIAM within 3 years of their mother's death. I give to my wife JANE all my movable goods and household implements towards paying my debts and funeral expenses. Wife sole exrx. Witnesses: JAMES HARLIRIN, EDWARD MILES, JOHN SERDIN, GEORGE BLOMEFEILD. Pr. at Ipswich 7 Aug. 1633.

R(W) WILLIAM COTTWYN of Woodbridge, yeoman. (662)
27 January 1632/33

Sick in body. I give to the poor people of Woodbridge 40s. to be distributed at my burial by the churchwardens and overseers of the poor. I give 10s. to the preacher at my burial. 50s. each to ELIZABETH and ALICE, daughters of ROBERT BLOCKE, to be paid within 6 months of my decease. To ALICE EWEN my kinswoman and wife of THOMAS EWEN my best posted bedstead with the feather bed upon it and 1 birded coverlet, a white rug, 2 blankets, and 1 pair of green curtains belonging to the bed, 2 pairs sheets, 2 pillows and 2 pillow beeres, my glass keep, a joined chair, 6 table napkins, 1 board cloth of diaper, 2 holland towels, 1 silk cushion, my best trunk and also 3 other of my best cushions. To ALICE EWEN, my god-daughter and daughter of THOMAS and ALICE EWEN, £10 to be paid to her father within 1 year of my decease. Also to her a silver cup, a silver and gilt salt cellar and 5 silver spoons. To my kinsman WILLIAM COTWYN £10, and to his wife ELIZABETH 40s. I further bequeath to ALICE wife of THOMAS EWEN one of Mr Perkins books and also my prayer books. 20s. to my godson WILLIAM RUDDOCKE. 20s. to my kinsman GILES KEBLE. 20s. to my god-daughter ANN, daughter of THOMAS WEBB of Woodbridge gent. 20 s. to THOMAS BAKER of Woodbridge apothecary. To my kinsman WILLIAM COTWYN my great bible and my clothes. To my kinsman THOMAS EWYN 40s., and to his wife ALICE my long table standing in the hall of my dwelling house. I bequeath to JAMES KEBLE, gent. of Halesworth, the freehold yards and gardens belonging to the messuage where I now dwell. He must pay all the above legacies. I leave my unbequeathed goods and chattels to JAMES KEBLE, whom I appoint sole exor. Witnesses: THOMAS WEBB, JOHN TOFTES. Pr. at Halesworth 13 Aug. 1633.

R(W) GEORGE COLE (X) of Kelsale. 21 March 1632/33 (663)

£15 to my daughter ELIZABETH wife of ROBERT DENINGTON. £20 to my daughter MARGARET wife of WILLIAM DENINGTON. £15 to my daughter ANNA wife of PHILEMON DOCKING. I forgive PHILEMON DOCKING the sum of £5 he owes me. All the rest of my goods and chattels I give to my three daughters and MICHAEL COLE, sole exor. of my will. Witnesses: THOMAS SEILTOME, THOMAS EADE. Pr. at Sternfield 27 July 1633.

R(W) NICHOLAS DOWNES (X) of Somersham, carpenter. (664)
25 July 1630

Whole in body. To MARGARET DOWNES, widow of Somersham, and my sister-in-law, all my goods and chattels. She is to pay my debts and funeral expenses and divide my goods amongst her children. Exrx(s). MARGARET DOWNES and her daughter MARGARET. Witnesses: EDWARD WARNER, FRANCIS PENNING and RICHARD GRIMSTON snr. Pr. at Ipswich 7 Aug. 1633.

R(W) ROSE DRANE of Saxtead, spinster (N). 13 June 1633 (665)

She gave all her ready money to her cousin ROBERT DRANE of Earl Soham, and all her movable goods to MARGARET WROTTS, whom she made her exrx. Witnesses: NICHOLAS DAVYE and ELIZABETH his wife, and FRANCIS WROOTS. Pr. at Saxtead 20 Aug. 1633.

R(W) HENRY GOSLING of Barking, yeoman. 20 May 1633 (666)

Being somewhat weak in body. To ELLEN my beloved wife all my lease lands and tenements in Ringshall for the term of 60 years or for her life, whichever expires first. However, if she remarries she is instead to be paid £3 p.a. by my exor. If she remains single she can take 3 loads of firewood yearly from the land in Ringshall. Until the Michaelmas after my decease she is to continue to live with my exor. at my farm of Mr BLOMFEILD's. After this time is up she is to choose 2 of my best milk cows and depart. I give more to her my bedstead, feather bed, feather bolster, flockbed and pillows whereon I lie, and all my linen. I give to her more my cupboard standing in the hall, £10 to be paid within 6 months of my decease, my least brass pot and my warming pan, 4 combs of my best wheat, 2 combs of malt, half a way of my best cheeses, half a firkin of rawing butter and 1 hog. £40 to my son-in-law GEORGE CHITTOCK and daughter MIRABEL CHITTOCK. To GEORGE CHITTOCK the black cow I bought of him and one calf weaned this year. £40 to my son-in-law JOHN CAGE and my daughter ELIZABETH CAGE. To JOHN CAGE a one-year old bullock now in his possession, a calf weaned this year, my 2-year old colt, my tumbril coop and wheels, 1 pair of harrows, my livery bedstead in the entry chamber, a flockbed, a bolster, a pair sheets and blankets, a coverlet, my middle brass pot and £8 to divide between his 2 children. £16 more to GEORGE CHITTOCK to be divided between his children. 20s. to my sister ELIZABETH GOSLING. 10s. to my servant ELIZABETH ALLIN. 10s. to the poor people of the parish of Barking. To my eldest son HENRY all my freehold and copyhold lands and tenements, and all my lease lands after my wife's death or remarriage. Also all my corn, grass, cattle and goods without doors, a posted bedstead standing upon the chamber with a feather bed and bolster belonging to it. Half my unbequeathed goods to HENRY and half to my wife. Exor. my son HENRY. Witnesses: JOHN BADWICKE (X), GEORGE BRANTON and DANIEL PULFORD. Pr. at Ipswich 20 July 1633.

R(W) CECILY HOLLAND of Lowestoft, widow. (667)

10 March 1628/9

I give to my daughters MARY, wife of THOMAS WIGG, and HESTER HOLLAND singlewoman the copyhold tenement I now dwell in with the yards and garden and half a well. My daughters are to sell the house as soon as they can conveniently find a buyer, and meanwhile HESTER is to live there and pay her sister 26s. 8d. p.a. £4 to my daughter MARY WIGG, also my second feather bed, my best truckle bedstead, a flock transom, my second bird covering, a danske chest, 1 pair sheets, 1 smock, 1 pewter platter, 3 saucers and a joined box. 20s. apiece to my sons THOMAS and MATTHEW HOLLAND. Residue of goods to my daughter HESTER, who is sole exrx. Witnesses: NICHOLAS PARYE, JOSEPH WILD and Mr JOHN WILDE snr. Pr. at Beccles 28 July 1633.

R(W) NABOTH HUETT of Ipswich. 25 May 1628 (668)

Being very aged and expecting the time which I have here to live in this world to be very short. To be buried in parish churchyard of St. Tellans (St. Helen's) in Ipswich. To my daughter ELIZABETH, wife of JAMES NORTON of Ipswich sailor, my house and yards on condition she pays my legacies. My wife MARGARET is to have her dwelling in my house so long as she lives. To my grandson THOMAS BACON, son of THOMAS BACON of Westerfield, a bedstead and feather bed, a coverlet and blankets, a bolster and a pair sheets, and 20s. These gifts to be given to him by my exor. at his age of 21. To my grandchild MARY BACON a trundle bed, flock bed, blanket, coverlet and bolster, a pair sheets and 10s. She is to receive these legacies when she is 18. Exrx. ELIZABETH NORTON, my daughter. Witnesses: NICHOLAS HUETT (X), JOHN ALDUS, THOMAS MANING. Pr. at Ipswich [no date given].

R(W) WILLIAM HUBBERD of Bedingfield, yeoman. (669)
20 December 1630

To my son ROBERT when he is 24 my house wherein I now dwell with all the land, meadows and pastures belonging to it, and my mill which is also in Bedingfield and is called by the name of Linkons Alleins or Linckons. When ROBERT inherits this property he must pay the following legacies: £50 to my daughter MARTHA when she is 24, £50 to my daughter MARY when she is 24. These are to be paid in the south porch of Bedingfield church. To my wife JOAN the house I dwell in with its land until ROBERT is 24. She is to keep the house and buildings in good repair with thatch and daubing. When ROBERT inherits the house and land he must pay his mother £10 p.a. in two equal portions at Lady Day and Michaelmas. As long as JOAN remains unmarried she is to have her dwelling in my parlour and parlour chamber, and ROBERT is to put 3 loads of wood at the parlour's end for her every year. She is also to have free access to the bakehouse to bake in the oven and to the pond to fetch water. If JOAN remarries, ROBERT immediately inherits the property and all legacies to JOAN become void. But ROBERT is to pay her £5 p.a. ROBERT must pay legacies to my grandchildren when they reach age of 21: £5 to JOHN THURSTON, 20s. to GRACE THURSTON and 20s. to THOMAS THURSTON. My daughter GRACE THURSTON must release to ROBERT her right in a piece of land or the legacies to her children will be void. To my wife JOAN my musket furnished. To my son JOHN all my copyhold land lying in Occold and called Wasses and held of the manor of Bennyngham Hall. JOHN is also left a posted bedstead with a feather bed and feather bolster, my best coverlet, 1 pair sheets, 2 blankets, 1 pillow, one of my best shifts, 1 of my best chairs and a silver spoon. I give to my son WILLIAM a silver ring. To my grandson WILLIAM HUBBERD my great cauldron. To my daughter MARTHA HUBBARD a posted bedstead standing in the parlour chamber, 1 feather bed and all that belong to it, 1 great hutch in the parlour chamber, 2 silver spoons, 1 brass posnet, a lesser cauldron and 1 buffet stool. To my daughter MARY HUBBERD 1 square table in the parlour, 1 great chair, 1 buffet stool, my middle brass pot, 1 great kettle, my best joined chest, 1 little chair, 1 silver spoon, 1 posted bedstead, 1 feather bed and all that belong to it. To my son ROBERT 1 long table and form in the parlour, my biggest brass posnet, 1 buffet stool, 1 silver spoon, my best bedstead in the parlour, my down bed and all that belong to it, and 1 great brass pot. JOAN my wife shall have the use for her lifetime of all these goods bequeathed to my children and grand children. She is also to have to bequeath as she thinks good my warming pan, 1 kettle, 1 skillet and all such movable goods as were hers before I married her, and all her linen and woollen. She may also take half the fruit growing in the orchard during her widowhood. All the rest of my brass and pewter to be divided amongst my 4 children. Residue of my goods to my wife whom I ordain sole exrx. She is to pay my debts and funeral charges. Witnesses: JOHN and ROBERT FENN. Pr. at Kenton 20 Aug. 1633.

R(W) FRANCIS INGAM (X) of Theberton. 18 July 1633 (670)

All my lands and tenements in Theberton to my daughter ELIZABETH INGHAM, who must pay 30s. a year to my son THOMAS. These payments are to be made in equal portions at Lady Day and Michaelmas in my now dwelling house in Theberton. If ELIZABETH fails to make these payments or leases the property for more than 1 year, the land and tenements go to THOMAS. To JEREME my wife my milk cow. All goods and chattels to my daughter ELIZABETH, who is sole exrx. Witnesses: ROBERT BACKLER, JOHN INGAM and THOMAS EADE. Pr. at Yoxford 5 Aug. 1633.

R(W) DOROTHY PLAYTERS [no place given but probably of Sotterly as the Playters family lived there] 1 January 1632/3 (671)

£40 to my daughter ELIZABETH to be kept in my exor.'s hands until the day of her marriage. 40s. to LIONEL PLAYTERS and 10s. to his wife. To the wife of my son AMBROSE 10s. To my daughter DOROTHY 10s. £40 to my daughter BEATRICE. To my daughter CURDY all my implements of household which are in her house at Sotterly, except 1 cloak; these are to be equally divided between her and her children. 10s. to RICHARD GILDER, my son-in-law, and to his wife, my daughter, 10s. 20s. to my grandchild FRANCES GILDER. To my grandchild ELIZABETH CURDY 1 little feather bed, a bolster, a blanket and a covering. To ELIZABETH CUDDON, wife of WILLIAM CUDDON gent., my little square table with a cupboard in it standing in my chamber. To Mr DAYNES preacher at Beccles 10s. To Mr VAUGHAN the minister 10s. To the poorest people of Beccles 13s. 4d. to be divided amongst the poorest. The rest of my movable goods to be divided amongst my 5 daughters: ELIZABETH PLAYTERS, ANN TOMPSON, FRANCES GILDER, BEATRICE PLAYTERS and ANN MANNING. ELIZABETH PLAYTERS to have half and the other 4 to share the second half equally. Exor(s). my kinsman JOHN HARBEN/HARBORNE and my loving friend GILBERT CORKER. 30s. to each of them for their pains. Witnesses: LIONEL SEAMAN, THOMAS KERĪDG, ABRAHAM TODD. Pr. 19 July 1633.

R(W) EDMUND POPE (X) of Belton, yeoman. 27 March 1629 (672)

To my brother JOHN POPE of Ashby 1 black milk cow, which I bought of him, and to his 3 children, NICHOLAS, ELIZABETH and MARY 5s. apiece. 5s. to MARY POPE daughter of HENRY POPE late of Aldeburgh. These legacies to be paid by my wife GRACE within 1 year of my death. 5s. each to EDWARD, MARY and ANN SMITER and ELIZABETH CURRIER, the children of ELLEN CURRIER. These sums to be paid by my wife within 2 years of my decease. Within 3 years of my death my wife is to pay 5s. each to ELIZABETH, MARY and GRACE BURRAGE, the children of my sister MARTHA and her husband JOHN BURRAGE of Belton; and 5s. to [missing] POPE son of my brother RICHARD POPE of Lammas in Norfolk. To JOHN son of JOHN POPE of Ashby my tenement abutting upon the east end of Shanckes heath in Belton and the land belonging to it, after my wife's death. To the same JOHN when he is 21 40s. to be paid by GRACE my wife. All my goods and chattels, except the cow bequeathed above, to my wife, whom I appoint sole exrx. Witnesses: JOHN MARTIN, JOHN POPE (X), EDWARD WATSON. Pr. at Belton 15 Aug. 1633.

R(W) ELIZABETH POINTER (X) of Kessingland, singlewoman. (673)
8 July 1633

I give and bequeath to my sisters PRUDENCE PETERS and PHILIPPA POINTER all my lands and tenements lying in Kessingland and held of the manor of Kinstons. I also give all my movable and unmovable goods to my sisters, whom I appoint exrx(s). of my will. Witnesses: JOHN CAPPS, EDWARD PACKARD, THOMAZINE FRAUNCIS. Pr. at Gisleham 16 Aug. 1633.

R(W) JOHN TOVELL of Wickham Market (N). 13 June 1633 (674)

Sick in body. I do give unto JOHN and ELIZABETH TOVELL my children the sum of 40s. apiece. Witnesses: WILLIAM TOVELL of Parham, THOMAS DUCKETT of Little Glemham and EDWARD NELSON. Pr. 14 June 1633. Admon. to his widow MARGERY.

R(W) JOHN FREED (X) of Somerleyton, husbandman. (675)
15 May 1633

To be buried in Somerleyton churchyard. To my daughter ELIZABETH a tenement with 1 acre of land, now in the occupation of JOHN EDEWELL, and lying on the east side of my mansion house where I now dwell. Also to her £20 to be paid by my exrx. at the rate of 20s. p.a. Also my best feather bed, 1 posted bedstead now standing in the hall, 1 livery bedstead, 1 leaf table and the form belonging to it, 1 long frame table in the hall, 1 coverlet which is now upon the bed wherein I lie, 1 pair blankets, 1 bolster, half my sheets, 1 great chest now standing upon the parlour chamber, 1 little chest now standing in the parlour, 4 pewter dishes, the second brass pot, 1 brass kettle, 1 copper kettle, 1 iron kettle, 1 little spit, half the brewing and half the dairy vessels. I give and bequeath to my 2 grandchildren MARY and SUSAN BOYSE, daughters of the late THOMAS BOYSE of Belton, £10 when they come to their age of 21. To my daughter ANN wife of EDMUND PENN of Corton the featherbed whereon I now lie. To my daughter ROSE wife of BARTHOLOMEW GREENE all my houses and land in Somerleyton not already bequeathed. ROSE GREENE sole exrx. Witnesses: HENRY ALLEN (X), WILLIAM SEGSTED (X). Pr. at Somerleyton 15 Aug. 1633.

R(W) NICHOLAS AUSTEN (X) of Earl Stoneham, clothier. (676)
1 June 1633

Sick in body. To WILLIAM AUSTEN my son £10. To ANN my daughter the wife of THOMAS HARDAYE £10. To ELIZABETH my daughter £10. To SUSAN my daughter £10. All these legacies to be paid by my exrx. within 1 year of my decease. All the rest of my goods, money and chattels I give to JOAN my loving wife, whom I make sole exrx. of my will. Witnesses: JOHN WAGE (X), JOHN GODDARD. Pr. at Ipswich 21 Oct. 1633.

R(W) DANIEL BACON (X) of East Bergholt, yeoman. (677)
2 May 1633

Weak in body. To my son ANTHONY my piece of meadow ground in East Bergholt which I bought of JOHN COOCKOE and which contains by estimation 5 rods. Also to ANTHONY £60, which is to be paid into the hands of my brother THOMAS BACON of Winston, who is to put it out for the best advantage of my son who is to receive the money at his age of 24. The rent of the meadow left to ANTHONY is also to be paid to THOMAS BACON. If my wife SUSAN or THOMAS

BACON decides to apprentice ANTHONY to a trade, the rent of the meadow is to be used to pay the expenses. 20s. to my brother THOMAS BACON. The remainder of all my goods and chattels I give to my wife SUSAN, who is to pay my debts and funeral charges. Exors. SUSAN and THOMAS BACON. Witnesses: ABRAHAM PAYTE, JOHN BURKITT (X), JOHN STEVENSON. Pr. at Ipswich 7 Aug. 1633.

R(W) JOHN BAMBRICK (X) of Martlesham, singleman. (678)
9 August 1633

Sick of body. I give and bequeath to my loving mother ELIZABETH, the wife of NICHOLAS ELLENGER, £10 to be paid within 1 year of my decease. To my nephew JOHN STILES, son of JOHN STILES, £40 within 1 year of my death. To my 2 sisters SUSAN wife of EDMUND YOUNGES and MARY wife of JOHN STILES £60 to be divided equally between them within 1 year of my death. To my nephew EDMUND YOUNGES my meadow in Raydon. Whereas my sister MARY is now great with child, if it shall please God the child be born and live in the world for 1 year, I do recall from my sisters SUSAN and MARY £10 each of their portions and give this sum unto the child my sister MARY is now withall. To my half sisters AVIS and ELIZABETH ELLINGER £10 each within 1 year of my decease. £20 to SUSAN daughter of EDMUND YOUNGES. I bequeath all the rest of my goods to my brother-in-law EDMUND YOUNGES, whom I appoint sole exor. Witnesses: NICHOLAS ELLINGER, THOMAS ELLENGER (X), THOMAS TYE. Pr. at Ipswich 20 Sept. 1633.

R(W) ELIZABETH BARKER alias HAMOND (X) of Helmingham, (679)
widow. 6 August 1633.

Sick in body. To my kinsman JOHN HARWYNE, son of my brother JOHN HARWYNE deceased, £60 to be paid out of the debts he owes to me. To my other kinsman JOHN HARWYNE, son of my brother THOMAS HARWYNE deceased, £60 to be paid within half a year of my decease out of my ready money and debts. To my kinsman ROBERT HARWYNE, son of my brother JOHN HARWYNE deceased, £30 out of my debts owing to me within 1 year of my decease. £5 each to kinsmen THOMAS, RICHARD and ROBERT HARWYNE, sons of my brother THOMAS HARWYNE deceased, to be paid out of my debts within 1 year of my death. £20 to my brother EDMUND HARWYN and £20 to my sister BARBARA HUNT widow to be paid within 1 year of my death. The moneys and debts owed to me by bonds and bills amount to £210. My exor. has £30 in his hands and owes me £80, and I have bonds in my hands for £20 owed by LIONEL WYTHE, £20 owed by Mr JAMES CASTON, £15 owed by WILLIAM BROWNE, £15 owed by WILLIAM FOLKARD, £20 owed by CHARLES ALLIN and £10 owed by RALPH CURTIS. My exor. is to have the use of these bonds and debts to pay the legacies before given, and the surplus to be used for the expenses of my burial and proving my will. Anything left over I give to my exor. I give to JOHN HARWYNE, son of my deceased brother THOMAS HARWYNE, and who now dwells with me all my movable and immoveable goods of household except such goods as I shall by word of mouth or with my own hands give to any person before my decease. I make sole exor. my right trusty and dearly beloved kinsman JOHN HARWYNE, son of my deceased brother JOHN HARWYNE, and supervisor of my will JOHN HARWYNE son of THOMAS HARWYNE deceased. They are to deal well with those that take pains with me in my sickness. Witnesses: ANN BAIGITT (X), BARTHOLOMEW RUSSELLS. Pr. at Ipswich 14 Sept. 1633.

R(W) SARAH ALDERMAN (X) of Ipswich, widow. 10 July 1633 (680

Sick in body. Whereas my husband CHRISTOPHER ALDERMAN deceased did bequeath the tuition of his and my children to me until their age of 21, I now bequeath their tuition to my brother-in-law JOHN ALDERMAN of Ipswich, clothier. Until the children are 21 he is to receive the rents and profits of all the houses and lands in St. Nicholas parish in Ipswich which were left to them by their father. He is to use the money for their education, bringing up and maintenance. I will that my exrx. sell all my goods and household stuff towards the payment of my debts. I make and appoint my loving mother JUDITH SENDALL sole exrx. Witnesses: ROBERT HOWE, G. CATCHPOLL, public notary, and RICHARD CUTBERT (X). Pr. at Ipswich 17 Aug. 1633.

R(W) AMOS FISKE of Dennington, turner. 4 June 1633 (681

To my son AMOS immediately after the decease of my wife MARGARET all my copyhold land and tenements held of the manor of Dennington, on condition that he pays the following legacies totalling £80. The payments are to be made in my mansion house where I now dwell in Dennington. £20 to my daughter FRANCES within 2 years of my beloved wife's death. £20 to my son WILLIAM within 3 years of my wife's death. £20 to my son JOHN within 4 years of my wife's death and £20 to my daughter MARGARET within 5 years of my wife's death. These 4 children have power to distrain. If AMOS dies WILLIAM inherits the land and the other 3 children receive £6 13s. 4d. extra each. To my wife MARGARET towards the bringing up of all my children in good nurture and virtuous education and towards the binding forth as apprentices as such of them as shall be fitting, all my ready money, clothes corn, hay, timber and ware ready turned, and my fat cow. I give to my son AMOS all my tools belonging to my trade, my birding piece and my sword and my horse mill with all the implements belonging to it. These items to be delivered to him within 1 month after my decease. All the rest of my goods and chattels I leave to my wife for her life. If she remarries she must bind herself in the sum of 200 marks to my exors. to maintain all my buildings in good repair and not to commit any strip or waste on my land. She must also pay my children £10 each if she remarries. After my wife's death my goods and chattels are to be equally divided amongst my children FRANCES, WILLIAM, JOHN and MARGARET. I make exors. of my will my kind and loving kinsman

ROBERT GIRLING and my right trusty friend EDWARD MOULTON, for both of whom I have great affection and trust. Witnesses: EDWARD HARSNUTT, JOHN GODBALD. Pr. at Stradbroke 24 Sept. 1633.

R(W) THOMAS GOSLING of Stonham Parva (N). (682)
[blank] August 1633

He gave £10 to his son ROBERT to be paid into the hands of ROBERT DENNY to the use of ROBERT. To his 3 daughters ANN, PRISCILLA and MARTHA 20 nobles apiece to be paid to them on Lady Day next. To his youngest daughter MARGARET 20 nobles to be paid to her when she comes to age of 21, and in the meantime his exor. to provide for her. These legacies to his children, all with benefit of survivorship, are in discharge of the sums of money left to them by their uncle MEWSE. To his daughter MARY EADE his smallest brass kettle. Rest of his goods and chattels to his wife MARY for her use during her lifetime, and after her death to be equally divided amongst his 5 youngest children: ROBERT, ANN, PRISCILLA, MARTHA and MARY. Wife sole exrx. ROBERT DENNY supervisor. Witnesses: BARNABY GIBSON, ROBERT DENNY. Pr. at Ipswich 16 Sept. 1633.

R. ROBERT HARDING (X) of Bruisyard, wheelwright. (683)
19 March 1632/3

Sick in body. I give to my son JOHN my tenement called Morrells and all my customary and lease lands held of the manor of Bruisyard. To my son GEORGE £20. To my daughter MARGARET wife of THOMAS STOFER £6. To my daughter ALICE wife of ROBERT TURNER £6. To ALICE my daughter my best great chest, and to my 2 daughters MARGARET and ALICE 2 keeps, 5 pewter dishes, 2 kettles, 1 posnet, 3 chairs, 1 stool, 1 livery table, 1 roast iron, 1 pair bellows, 2 spits, 1 dripping pan, 2 brass candlesticks, 1 mortar and pestle, 1 great bowl, 1 brewing tub, 2 beer vessels, 1 old cauldron, 1 pair mustard querns, 2 mud scuppets, 1 mattock, 1 pick, 1 hatchet, 1 hook, 2 pitchforks, 1 small pair scales and 5 lead weights, 1 great iron beam and a cutting shovel. All these items to be equally divided between them immediately after my decease. To my son GEORGE 1 little feather bed, 1 feather bolster, 1 blanket, 1 trundle bedstead, 1 hook, 1 hatchet, 1 shovel, 1 scuppet and 1 old chest. The unbequeathed residue of my goods I give to my son JOHN whom I make sole exor. of my will. Witnesses: HENRY CANNAP, JOHN HELLWIS. Pr. at Yoxford 5 Aug. 1633.

R. WILLIAM HAREN junior of Theberton (N). [no date] (684)

Made in the time of his sickness about 2 days before his death in the presence of WILLIAM MILLS and his wife. £10 to his uncle JONAS KING. £10 to WILLIAM HAREN the elder, his uncle. To ANN BLOBOLD a desk, to Goodwife FULLER a chest and to WILLIAM MILLS a sheep. All the rest of his goods he willed to be bestowed about his burial. Pr. at Yoxford 10 Oct. 1633. Admon. to JONAS KING and WILLIAM HAREN, the principal legatees.

R(W) MARION HECKFORD (X) of Saxmundham, widow. (685)
10 April 1633

Sick in body. I bequeath to REBECCA HECKFORD, my grandchild, one of the daughters of my son RICHARD, 1 bedstead, 1 feather bed, 3 pillows with the blankets and coverlets thereunto belonging, 1 pair white curtains belonging to the bed and 1 great chest. To ELIZABETH HECKFORD daughter of my son RICHARD, 1 table and form, 1 pewter platter and 1 pair of my best sheets. To ABIGAIL, my grandchild and daughter of my son RICHARD, 1 brass pot, 1 silver spoon and 1 pewter platter. To ANN, daughter of my son RICHARD, 1 long chest, 1 silver spoon and 1 pewter platter. I give MARY, the daughter of my son RICHARD, 1 old coffer, 1 small box, 1 large pewter platter and 6 pieces of small pewter, and 1 dripping pan and a spit. To ELIZABETH HECKFORD, my grandchild and one of the daughters of my son THOMAS HECKFORD of Fornham, 5s. to be paid to her by my exor. when she is 21. To my grandchild THOMAS, son of THOMAS HECKFORD, 5s. when he is 21. All the rest of my goods, chattels and household implements I bequeath to my son RICHARD, whom I make my sole exor. Witnesses: THOMAS ALDUS, RALPH SNELLING. Pr. at Saxmundham 18 Sept. 1633.

R(W) ROBERT READE of Brandeston, husbandman (N). (686)
11 August 1633

To WILLIAM PAULE of Framlingham £5 to be paid to him when 21. He bequeathed all his goods and chattels to his wife MARY by delivering to her one salt cellar of pewter in the name of all his possessions. Witnesses: JOHN LOWES clerk, BRIDGET FAYREWEATHER, RICHARD WILSON, WILLIAM WILSON and JAMES CRACKNELL. Pr. at Wickham Market 19 Sept. 1633. Admon. to the widow, MARY READE.

R(W) THOMAS SHUCKFORD of Ipswich, maltster. 8 May 1633 (687)

Sick in body. First all such debts as I owe to be well and truly paid by my exrx. as soon as convenient after my decease. To my mother ELIZABETH SHUCKFORD £3 and to my sister GRACE SHUCKFORD £3, both sums to be paid within 3 months of my decease by my exrx. To my son THOMAS £50 to be paid my my exrx. when he is 21. Until then the interest on this sum is to be used towards his bringing up. If my wife remarries before THOMAS is 21, she must give security to THOMAS CLEERE gent. of Ipswich for payment of this £50 to my son. After payment of my debts, legacies and funeral expenses I give all the residue of my goods to my loving wife ANN, whom I make my sole exrx. Witnesses: JOHN BOATWRIGHT, ROBERT LORD. Pr. at Ipswich 3 July 1633.

R(W) WILLIAM TYLER (X), husbandman. 6 February 1628/9 (688)

Sick in body. I make ELIZABETH my wife my whole exrx. She is to make sale of such things as are mine to pay my debts, and the remainder of my goods I bequeath to her for ever. I give to JOHN WADE son of ROBERT WADE one halberd to be delivered to him within 10 days after my decease. Witnesses: THOMAS HUMFERIE mariner and ELIZABETH SEARLE the younger. Pr. at Ipswich 11 Sept. 1633.

R(W) WILLIAM WATLING of Tannington. 13 August 1633 (689)

To be buried in Worlingworth churchyard. To MARY my well beloved wife all my white wheat growing in Powlens and in King's ground. Also all my corn I have in my chambers, both wheat and malt. I give unto MARY my wife 5 cows, of which 4 are at the house where I now dwell in Tannington and the other is at WILSON's in Worlingworth. Also all the hay in my barn at Tannington, all my cheese and butter that I shall have when it shall please God to call me, my hogs and shots, all my sheep and fowls. I give unto MARY my great bedstead wherein I now lie as it stands in the hall chamber with the feather bed, bolsters, pillows and curtains. My will is that all my movables, except those already bequeathed, in my house at Tannington shall be inventoried within 1 month of my death. MARY my wife shall have as many of them as she desires during her life, and after her death I give them all to my daughter CLAYDON. To my grandchild ANN CLAYDON £100 to be paid when she is 21. To my daughter CLAYDON all my bedsteads and bedding that are in my house at Worlingworth, also all my tables, forms and other household stuff in the same house. To ANN CLAYDON my grandchild my gilt cup. To ROBERT CLAYDON, my son-in-law, my cart, tumbril, ploughs, harrows and all my harness belonging to them; my ladders, grindstone, scuppets and shovel. Also all my corn on the ground and my hay, except the corn and hay already bequeathed. Also all money due to me by bond or in any other way. To my servants JOHN WATLING and ANN WRIGHT 20s. apiece. To ELIZABETH WESTROPP £20 to be paid to her at the age of 23. To HENRY WATLING of Worlingworth 40s. every year to be paid to him quarterly so long as he shall live. To FRANCIS WELTON's wife 20s. All my land, except 1 piece of copyhold, to my son-in-law ROBERT CLAYDON and his wife AUDREY, my daughter. The excepted piece of land I have already given to my grandson ROBERT CLAYDON. My son-in-law ROBERT CLAYDON to be exor., but if he refuses all the legacies made to him are to go to my brother-in-law STEPHEN BLOMFEILD of Stonham, if he consents to act as exor. Witnesses: WILLIAM and ELIZABETH DADE. Pr. at Tannington 23 Sept. 1633. Admon. to ROBERT CLAYDON.

R(W) HENRY SMITH (X) of Trimley St. Martin, husbandman. (690)
12 May 1633

To [a blank in both register and original will] my wife £5. To my brother JOHN SMITH £10. To RICHARD LEECH the elder 20s. To MARJORY BARKER 10s. To MARGARET KEENT 10s. All the rest of my goods I give to WILLIAM SMITH my brother, who is to be my exor. and to pay my debts and legacies. Witnesses: THOMAS SMITH (X), RICHARD LEECH (X). Pr. at Ipswich 7 Oct. 1633.

R(W) WILLIAM ESTO of Bramfield. 10 September 1633 (691)

To ELEANOR my wife during her life all my houses and land in Wetheringsett on condition that she keeps them in good repair and pays my son JOHN ESTO 30s. on every Michaelmas day at Wetheringsett church. JOHN has power to distrain. After my wife's death I give to my son JOHN the above houses and lands. I give to my wife 4 of my best cows and so much of my household goods as shall be worth £5, at her own choice. I will that she shall have the use for her life of my best posted bedstead and all things belonging to it, and after her death I give it to my son JOHN. To my son ABRAHAM £100 to be paid within a year of my death. To my daughter ELEANOR £100 to be paid within a year of my death. £40 to my son JOHN. To ABRAHAM my best brass pot, a bedstead, a feather bed upon it and all other things belonging. To ELEANOR a bedstead, a feather bed on it and all other things belonging. All my unbequeathed linen to be equally divided between my wife and 3 children. To my wife's sons ROBERT and JOHN SCOTT £6 13s. 4d. each, and to her son WILLIAM SCOTT 20s. All my movable goods to my wife and son JOHN to pay my debts and legacies. If this is not sufficient, JOHN must use the first 2 years' profit of the land bequeathed to him for this purpose. Exors. wife and son JOHN. Witnesses: MATTHEW ELMY, JAMES CLOUGH (X) and THOMAS EADE. Pr. at Yoxford 10 Oct. 1633.

R(W) MARGARET LATER (X) of Bramford, widow. 9 September 1633 (692)

To be buried in Bramford churchyard. To ROBERT and JOHN, the sons of JOHN BETES of Ipswich, 40s. each when they come to the age of 21. To JOHN BETES their father a piece of pewter. To BRIDGET HOLMES my smallest brass pot. To my kinswoman ALICE COOKE my gown and a ruff, and to her daughter MARY COOKE a ruff and my best petticoat. All the rest of my goods I give to my exor., my neighbour ROGER RASE. Witnesses: GEORGE REEME and THOMAS NOONE. Pr. at Ipswich 7 Oct. 1633.

R(W) WILLIAM MAYHUE of Gosbeck, singleman. 9 May 1633 (693)

To be buried in Gosbeck churchyard. To KATHERINE my mother-in-law [i.e. stepmother] 40s. To EDMUND MAYEHUE, my elder brother, 20 marks. To my eldest sister SUSAN, wife of JOHN FEVERYEARE of Kenton, 20 marks. £10 each to JOHN, SUSAN and MARY, the children of JOHN and SUSAN FEVERYEARE to be paid by my exor. when they are 21; with survivorship. £5 to my sister MARJORY MAYHUE. To my youngest brother RICHARD MAYEHUE £5 when he is 21. 30s. to THOMAS son of WILLIAM STUD of Gosbeck, and 30s. to SUSAN STUDD the sister of THOMAS. To ALICE DOVE my servant 30s. 20s. to

BRIDGET PIGOTT of Gosbeck. £5 to GEORGE BURROUGH parson of Gosbeck. I appoint JOHN FEVERYEARE of Kenton, my loving brother-in-law, my sole exor., and I give him all my lands, ready money, debts owing to me and to my movable goods towards the payment of my debts legacies and funeral charges. I make WILLIAM STUDD of Gosbeck, my loving neighbour, supervisor of my will desiring him to advise and assist my exor. And for his Christian kindness to me in my life and the hope of his care according to this my last request to him, I give him 40s. Witnesses: JAMES SARNHAM, THOMAS STUDD, WILLIAM POTTER. Pr. at Ipswich 8 Oct. 1633.

R(W) THOMAS WRIGHT (X) of Clopton, yeoman. 16 July 1633 (694)

Sick in body. 10s. to the poor people of Clopton to be distributed at the discretion of the overseers of the poor of the parish. I give £40 to my son THOMAS within 1 year of my decease, and 1 posted bedstead, with a feather bed and bolster, 1 coverlet, 2 blankets and 4 pairs of sheets. I bequeath £25 to my son JOHN to be paid within 1 year of my decease. Also to him 1 bedstead, 1 bolster, 1 feather bed, 1 coverlet, 2 blankets and 4 pairs of sheets. £5 to MATTHEW my son within 1 year of my decease, and £5 to be paid to MATTHEW's daughter MARGERY at her age of 21. £2 to THOMAS, son of my son MATTHEW, when he is 21. Within 1 year of my death £25 to my daughter KATHERINE, and 1 livery bedstead, 1 feather bed, 1 bolster, 1 coverlet, 2 blankets and 4 pairs sheets. The residue of my goods and chattels I leave to my wife MARJORY, whom I make sole exrx. provided that within 10 days of my death she binds herself to my cousin SAMUEL FULLER in the sum of £200 truly to perform my will. If she fails to do this, I make THOMAS WRIGHT my eldest son sole exor. of my will. He must then pay my wife £100 and bind himself to SAMUEL FULLER to perform my will. If my wife marries again she must pay each of my 4 children £15 over and above the legacies already given to them. I leave 10s. to my cousin SAMUEL FULLER, whom I make supervisor of my will. Witnesses: ELIZABETH BOOTMAN (X), BRIDGET STARE. Pr. at Ipswich 8 Oct. 1633. Admon. to widow.

R(W) KATHERINE BACKLER of Wickham Market, widow (N). (695)
23 July 1633

Being asked what she would bestow on her kindred, she answered I will bestow that little which I have on God's people who are my brethren and sisters. I will that my scholars ROBERT, ELIZABETH and ANN, children of Mr GHNESTON of Wickham Market, have 5s. apiece. To Mr SIMON DAWSON the elder I give 20s. and to his 2 sons, ROBERT and JOHN, a brass pot each. To JOAN GIRLING and the Widow ALDRED a pair of sheets each. 10s. each to Mr WILLIAM WINGFEILD and WILLIAM PORTER. All the rest of my goods and chattels I give to Mr WALTER BRIDGES minister whom alone I entreat to see me decently buried and my will performed. Witnesses: WILLIAM WINGFELD, WILLIAM PORTER (X). Pr. at Wickham Market 9 Oct. 1633. Admon. to WALTER BRIDGES.

R(W) JOHN COOK of Hintlesham, husbandman. (696)
21 September 1633

Sick in body. To be buried in Hintlesham churchyard. 6s. 8d. to the poor of Hintlesham to be distributed at my burial. I give to my 2 elder sons, JOHN and THOMAS COOK, to be equally divided all my freehold messuages, tenements, houses and land, both arable, pasture and meadows lying in Combs and Battisford and which I lately bought from NICHOLAS REVETT esquire, ROBERT ARMIGER gent. and ROSE SICKLEMORE, exrx. of her late father an Ipswich fishmonger. To my son JOSEPH all my copyhold land in Combs, Buxhall or Finborough, which I lately bought from JOHN SOWEGATE of Combs, husbandman. £60 to JOSEPH, and £55 each to my 3 daughters SUSAN, MARY and REBECCA. Until these legacies are paid within 3 months of my death, my 3 daughters are to be maintained at my exors.' expense. The residue of my goods and chattels are to be equally divided amongst my children. Exors. my son JOHN and my daughter SUSAN, who are to take my stock and monies into their hands to fulfill my will. Supervisor of my will, my loving friend EDMUND DENNY, yeoman of Combs. Witnesses: HENRY SMITH, JOAN PIPER (X). Pr. at Ipswich 16 Nov. 1633.

R(W) MARGARET FATHER (X) of Yoxford, widow. (697)
15 July 1633

Infirm of body. I bequeath to EDWARD HAMOND of Westleton my nephew and to SARAH his wife all my messuages and land in Ufford, Melton and Bromeswell. They must pay their eldest son WILLIAM £5 p.a. Also to EDWARD HAMOND all my goods, chattels, cattle, corn, ready money, plate, bonds, bills, debts due unto me, brass and pewter. By an agreement made on 16 April 1612 between my late husband, JOHN FATHER, and HENRY GROOME, then of Petistree and now of Ufford, HENRY GROOME and his wife MARGARET came into possession of the manor house in Ufford called Otlyes, where they now live, on condition that they pay £300 to the persons named in my will as follows. £150 to my nephew EDWARD HAMOND within 6 months of my decease, and the other £150 to him within 6 months more. Both these payments are to be made within Ufford church porch. I leave £30 to ROBERT GAITON of Sutton yeoman to be paid within 3 years of my death at £10 p.a. To JOHN MAN £10 and the bedstead, bolster, blankets and coverlet now used with the bed whereon the said JOHN usually lies. More to him 1 pillow, 1 pillow beer and 2 pairs of sheets. £5 to MARY CULHAM. 40s. to JOAN TILL, widow. These legacies are to be paid by EDWARD HAMOND within 7 months of my decease, provided that he has received the first payment of £150. I make EDWARD HAMOND sole exor. of my will. Witnesses: JOHN WOODCOCK senior, JOHN WOODCOCK junior, GEORGE DENNY. Pr. at Yoxford 29 Oct. 1633.

R(W) HENRY LOVEDAYE of Chediston, gentleman. (698)
16 October 1632

To the poor people of Chediston 20s. and to the poor people of Halesworth 10s. To the poor people of Wissett 10s. and 10s. to the poor people of Linstead Parva. I give £150 apiece to my 3 daughters ELLEN, ALICE and KATHERINE to be paid to them at their several ages of 16 or at their day of marriage, whichever shall first happen. To my son MAPES LOVEDAYE £150 when he is 16 or on his marriage day. To pay these legacies I empower my exors. to sell my house at Yarmouth in Norfolk, my copyhold land and tenements in Linstead Parva which are let to GEORGE SMITH, and my 10 acres of fen in Mendham. As exor. of the will of my late father ANTHONY LOVEDAYE I am charged with the payment of legacies to my brothers and sisters, and I ask my exors. to see these legacies paid according to his will. If necessary to pay all these legacies my exors. are to sell my land and tenements in Metfield, let to JOHN PEARE and my copyhold meadow in Linstead let to Widow WELTON. If my son ANTHONY is made a ward of his Majesty, all the expenses of obtaining his wardship shall be paid by my exors. out of the remainder of the money raised by the sale of my land. My exors. are to sell all my household stuff, plate and corn within 1 month of my decease, to pay my debts, legacies and funeral charges. My exors. must give an account of any money left over to my loving brother-in-law ROBERT SKARTH and my loving friend FRANCIS JERMY of Metfield, gent. These 2 men are to divide any surplus money between my 5 children: ANTHONY, ELLEN, ALICE, KATHERINE and MAPES, with benefit of survivorship. Until my 3 daughters and my son MAPES reach the age of 16 my exors. are to pay each of them £12 p.a. for their maintenance. All my other messuages and lands I leave to my son ANTHONY. To my loving wife ALICE my little bay mare, 2 of my best feather beds and bolsters, 2 pillows, 1 coverlet, 1 rug, 2 pairs blankets, 2 pairs holland sheets, 4 pairs coarse sheets and the bedstead, curtains and valance that I now lie in, and a trundle bedstead. I also give her £100 or £100 value in goods at her own choice. To my son ANTHONY my down bed and bolster with a rug and a livery bedstead. I give to my loving mother 40s. to make her a ring and to each of my brothers and sisters 10s. apiece, except my sister ANN LOVEDAYE to whom I give a feather bed and bolsters. I leave 5s. each to all my servants. To JEREMY CLARKE 20s. To my loving friend Mr PRICK of Halesworth 20s. to make him a ring. £10 each to my exors., and 40s. each to my supervisors to make a ring. My brother PEREGRINE died before receiving the £50 left to him in my father's will, and I ask that this sum be equally divided amongst my brothers and sisters. Exors. my loving cousin FRANCIS CLAXTON gent. of Pulham St. Mary in Norfolk, and my singular good and loving friend THOMAS GODBOLD, gent. I commit the tuition and education of my son ANTHONY to their care, desiring them to see he is brought up in the fear of God and humane learning. Supervisors: my trusty and truly loving uncle WILLIAM LOVEDAYE and my most loving friend FRANCIS JERMY. I desire my exors. and supervisors to assist my loving wife in my children's education. Witnesses: JOHN GREY, THOMAS TYRELL, ANTHONY FRESTON, JEREMY CLARKE (X). Pr. at Beccles 25 Oct. 1633.

R(W) ELIZABETH LAREME of Falkenham, widow. (699)
20 April 1633

Sick in body. To my son THOMAS GRIMSON all the apparel that was my husband's, 1 chest and 1 stool and 1 pot. Also all the crop on the ground to see me buried like a woman at his charge, and to pay the rent and my debts. I give him a debt due to me from Mr MALLETT of Woodbridge. I give to my daughter ANN GRIMSON 1 red petticoat, a linsey wolsey petticoat, my best waistcoat, and a livery bedstead as it stands with a pair of sheets, 1 great kettle, 1 powdering tub, 1 chest and 1 form. I give to JANE GRIMSON my other daughter, my gown, 1 petticoat, 1 cloak, my best hat and a green apron, 1 trundle bedstead, 1 flock bed, a bolster, 2 pillows, 2 blankets, 1 sheet, 1 chest, 1 table, 1 form, 1 old cupboard, 1 tub, 2 kettles, 2 skillets, and a hale. All the rest of my goods I give to be equally divided between my daughters. To my daughter JANE GRIMSON a bowl, 40s. in the hands of ROBERT COLL and 20s. in the hands of Mr MILLNER. Exor. my son THOMAS GRIMSON. Witnesses: JOHN BROWNE, JEREMY GODWARD and ROBERT JAY. Pr. at Ipswich 20 Sept. 1633.

R(W) MARGERY PAGE of Ipswich, widow. 2 September 1633 (700)

Weak in body. To be buried in churchyard of Blakenham on the hill where my father and mother were buried. 20s. to the poor of parish of St. Matthew in Ipswich. To my loving cousin, Mrs MARY FROBUSHER, 20s. to buy her a ring. To my loving Mrs LAMBE, the wife of JOHN LAMBE, 20s. to buy her a ring. To my servant ANN CORBOLD all my wearing linen. To ANN BUCK, servant with my cousin LAMBE, 10s. To my niece Mrs ELIZABETH PAGE her grandfather's and grandmother's pictures. To goodwife LOFTES my jack which I used to turn a spit and the weights belonging to it. All the rest of my goods, chattels, money, plate and jewels I give to my loving cousin Mr JOHN WENTWORTH of Ipswich towards the payment of my debts and the performance of my will. I make him sole exor. Witnesses: JOHN LAMBE, ROBERT AMBY. Pr. at Ipswich 1 Nov. 1633.

R(W) JOHN ROASE (X) the elder of Martlesham,yeoman. (701)
[blank] October 1633

To my wife BRIDGET £5 towards the bringing up of an apprentice. 10s. to the poor of Martelsham. To my wife and to my son JOHN all my movables and chattels to be equally divided between them. Exors: wife and son. Witnesses: FRANCIS NOONE, WILLIAM REDGRAVE. Pr. at Ipswich 8 Oct. 1633.

R(W) EDWARD FAYERWEATHER (X) of Kessingland, husbandman. (702)
8 December 1633

Sick in body. To THOMAS PACKORD my master £10 to be paid within 1 year, and £10 to ELIZABETH FRANCKES within 18 months of my decease. Both these legatees have power to distrain. To WILLIAM and ALICE HAMILL my kinsfolk 20s. apiece. I give all my lands and tenements lying in Flixton to my brother JOHN FAYREWEATHER for his lifetime and after his death to my kinsman JOHN HUNT and his heirs. JOHN FAYREWEATHER to pay my legacies. To my kinsman JOHN PEAPES 20s. and to one PETERS, a poor lame boy dwelling with him 10s. To JOHN GILLAM the younger 20s. To THOMAS PACKARD the younger 10s. To MARGARET MERIMAN 10s. and to MARY HAMER 10s. To the poor people of Kessingland 20s. and to the poor of Hopton 20s. To RALPH WATCHET a cloak or suit of apparel. To ROGER GREGGS a pair of shoes and hose and a linen slop. To JAMES BURGIS a pair of shoes. To my brother JOHN FAYERWEATHER all my land and tenements in Hopton for his lifetime and after his death to GEORGE HUNT and his heirs. Residue of my goods to JOHN FAYREWEATHER, whom I make sole exor. hoping that he will carefully perform my will. Witnesses: FRANCIS GREGGS (X), EDWARD PACKARD. Pr. at Beccles 16 Dec. 1633.

R(W) ANN PETINGELL (X). 29 July 1633 (703)

To my daughter CHRISTIAN my best feather bed, a bolster and 2 pillows, a blanket and a coverlet with a bedstead. I give to her all my wearing apparel and a coffer that stands at my bed's feet, a chair and 2 stools. I give my other bed with a bolster, 1 pillow and 1 blanket to JAMES BERRY my son. Also I give him my long table and a form. The rest of my goods I give to be sold towards my burial and the probate of my will. I name JAMES BERRY to be my exor. I desire VALENTINE DEY, our minister, to be supervisor to see that my will be truly performed. Witnesses: VALENTINE DEY and MARY BERRY (X). Pr. at Beccles 4 Jan. 1633/4.

R(W) JOHN WARRECK senior (X) of Pakefield, fisherman. 26 December 1633 (704)

To MARGARET my loving wife the house wherein she now dwelleth during her natural life, and after her decease to my son JOHN. I nominate my wife sole exrx., she to take my debts to pay my debts. To WILLIAM my son 2 herring nets. Witnesses: ROBERT BRANSBY, SARAH PORTE (X), WILLIAM WROTH. Pr. at Beccles 11 Jan. 1633/4.

R(W) ANN ANDREW (X) of Holbrook, widow. 12 December 1633 (705)

Sick in body. To my eldest son OLIVER ANDREW 1 brass pot and 1 pillow beer. To ANN TOWNEHILL my daughter 1 pair of my best sheets, a holland sheet and the rest of my childbed linen. Her sister SUSAN to have the use of the childbed linen when she needs it. To SUSAN £10 and a seventh part of my pewter, all my unbequeathed linen and all my wearing apparel except 1 blue petticoat, which I give to my daughter TOWNEHILL. To my son SAMUEL a seventh part of my pewter. To ANNA TOWNEHILL, my grandchild, 1 of my best sheep. I will that my son SAMUEL be educated by my daughter TOWNEHILL. To the poor of Holbrook 5s. The rest of my goods to my other 3 children: WILLIAM, JAMES and DANIEL. Exors: son ANDREW and my brother JOHN PODD. Witnesses: EDMUND MAPLETOFT, JOHN COLMAN (X), JUDITH BUNDISE (X). Pr. at Chelmondiston 23 Dec. 1633.

R(W) JOSHUA BROCK of Yoxford. 27 November 1633 (706)

To ALICE my wife and ROBERT COWARD my son-in-law all my goods and chattels and implements of household, and I make them exors. Witnesses: SIMON HAYLE, THOMAS EADE. Pr. at Yoxford 29 Jan. 1633/4.

R(W) JOHN DAWSON (X) of Ipswich, blacksmith. (707)
1 October 1633

Sick in body. My wife ELLEN shall have and enjoy my messuage wherein I now dwell with the yards and garden for her life. After her death it is to be sold and the money divided equally among my 4 sons: JOHN, THOMAS, LAWRENCE and EDWARD, and my daughters MARY and ELIZABETH. If any of my children is able to purchase my messuage he shall have it for 40s. cheaper than anyone else. The sale of my house to be undertaken by my beloved friends Mr THOMAS CLEERE and EDWARD WETHERDALL, or if they are both dead by the bailiffs of Ipswich. To my wife all my household stuff and implements, hoping she will hereafter remember my children as God shall enable her. But my bellows, hammers and all the rest of my working tools I give to my son THOMAS, hoping he will be a help to his mother in bringing up his younger brethren. Wife sole exrx. Supervisor my friend in Christ GEORGE NOYE the younger. Witnesses: JOHN WITTOM, NICHOLAS SAUNDERS. Pr. at Ipswich 16 Nov. 1633.

R(W) THOMAS EWEN of Woodbridge, yeoman. (708)
13 December 1633

Sick in body. To ALICE my daughter my house in Pound Street in Woodbridge and £60 when she is 21 or on her marriage day, and £40 more on my wife's death. To ELIZABETH my daughter my house in New Street in Woodbridge after the death of my wife, and £40 when she is 21 or married. To my mother ALICE EWEN £10 and to my sister AMY 20s. To my uncle HENRY EWIN 30s. to buy him a ring to wear for my sake. The overplus of my goods and personal estate I give to my dear wife ALICE on condition that she gives security to my uncle EWEN for the payment of my legacies. Wife sole exrx. Supervisor HENRY EWIN of Marlesford gent. Witnesses: ANDREW RUDDOCK, ROBERT ALDHOUSE. Pr. at Woodbridge 30 Jan. 1633/34.

R(W) RICHARD FOX of Badingham, yeoman. 19 August 1633 (709)

To my loving wife SARAH for her life the messuage wherein I now dwell in Badingham and known by the name of Ploughwrights, and my land in Badingham. After her decease I give the messuage and land to RICHARD FOX my nephew, son of my brother THOMAS, but if he dies without heirs before he is 31 the property then passes to RICHARD FOX, son of BRYANT FOX of Withersdale. If my wife dies before my nephew reaches the age of 21, I desire TOBIAS FRERE, gent. of Harleston in Norfolk, to hold the house and land until RICHARD is 21. Within one year of my death £100 is to be paid into the hands of TOBIAS FRERE for the benefit of my nephew, RICHARD FOX, and any of it remaining when he reaches 21 is to be then paid to him. If RICHARD FOX dies before he is 21, the money is to be paid to KATHERINE and ELIZABETH SKEETE, daughters of my sister MARGARET SKEETE. Within 6 months of my nephew RICHARD FOX reaching the age of 13, my exrx. is to pay £10 to TOBIAS FRERE, which he is to use to bind forth RICHARD as an apprentice. Until he is 14 my exrx. is to maintain and keep my nephew or pay TOBIAS FRERE £8 p.a. for his maintenance. To my loving friend TOBIAS FRERE, whom I make supervisor of my will, £10. Wife sole exrx., and I give her all the residue of my money and goods. Witnesses: TOBIAS FRERE, WILLIAM COOKE, RICHARD ROGER, THOMAS LOWE(X). Pr. at Beccles 18 Jan. 1633/34.

R(W) JOHN KING (X) of Benhall, yeoman. 19 November 1633 (710)

To EDITH my wife for her lifetime all my land and tenements in Hacheston towards bringing up my children, and after her death to my son JOHN. Two years after inheriting he must pay FRANCES my eldest daughter £5, £5 to my daughter MARY 4 years after and £5 to my daughter ANNE 6 years after. These payments are to be made in the porch of Hacheston church. The 3 daughters have power of distraint. £10 to my wife and a £5 legacy left by my father to be divided among my 4 children. After my debts are paid the residue of my goods to be divided amongst my 4 children at the age of 21, with right of survivorship. Wife sole exrx. Witnesses: THOMAS CURTIS, LAWRENCE PELLS. Pr. at Wickham Market 12 Dec. 1633.

R(W) WILLIAM LOFTE of Ipswich, mariner. 25 May 1628 (711)

In good health. To my mother BRIDGET wife of JOHN JACOB, mariner of Ipswich, a messuage in the parish of St. Clement's in Ipswich now inhabited my HENRY ROWNEKETLE. After her death I leave this messuage to her son JOHN JACOB. All my goods and chattels I do bequeath to my well beloved mother, whom I make my sole exrx. praying unto God now in my lifetime to direct her the right way to Salvation. Witnesses: JOHN CARNABYE, RICHARD DAWTREY. Pr. at Ipswich 10 Jan. 1633/4.

R(W) ROBERT LOPPAM of Beccles, glover. 6 December 1633 (712)

Sick in body. To HENRY LOPPAM my son the messuage wherein I dwell in Beccles when he reaches age of 21. After my daughter MARY attains the age of 21, HENRY must pay her £5 p.a. until she has received £30. When MARY is 21 my exor. is to give her a certain quantity of linen. To my son JAMES £20 when he is 24. To my son THOMAS £5 when he is 21. To my sister MARY £3. To ANN WASE my maidservant £10 in full satisfaction of such money as I owe her. All these legacies are to be paid within the great south porch of Beccles parish church. The residue of my movables to remain in the hands of my exor. towards paying my debts and well educating my children. Anything left over when they are of age to be divided amongst them. My exor. to hold the messuage left to HENRY until he is 21. Exor. JAMES BUNGAY of Ilketshall St. Andrew and I give him £5 for his pains. Witnesses: ROBERT COBBE, ROBERT DEMSKEL (X), HEREMY DAVY. Pr. at Beccles 7 Jan. 1633/4.

R(W) SUSAN MALSTER of Ramsholt, widow (N). (713)
[blank] October 1633

About three weeks before her death. £5 to JOHN MALSTER, son of my late husband, when he is 21. £20 to my son THOMAS WAYLAND, half within 1 month of my decease and half when he attains the age of 21. Also to him a 2-year old mare colt and a brass pot. To my daughter ELIZABETH MARSH the sum of £30, 1 brass pot and 1 bed as it stands when she is 21. ROBERT FULLER my son-in-law to maintain ELIZABETH until she is 21. The rest of my goods I give to ROBERT FILLER to pay my legacies and debts. Witnesses: JOHN MOORE (X), ISAAC CLEVELAND. Pr. at Ipswich 18 Dec. 1633. Admon. to ROBERT FILLER.

R(W) THOMAS MOWLSON of Ipswich, drawer. (714)
14 November 1633

Sick in body. To SYBIL my wife for life all those 3 rooms wherein ROBERT MOULSON my son now dwells with 1 little shop next the street, and liberty to go to the well in the yard belonging to my house and take water. Also to her for life the fruit of my pear tree growing on the ground belonging to my house. Immediately after my wife's death I give the 3 rooms and shop to my son ROBERT, who within 1 year must pay £10 to my son JACOB, who has power to distrain. To my son ROBERT all my houses, yards, gardens and orchards in St. Nicholas parish in Ipswich. He must pay £10 to my grandson THOMAS, son of my son THOMAS, when he is 21. To my daughter ALICE my cloak, a new horseman's coat, 1 horse cloth, 1 danske chest on the chamber and 1 posted bedstead in the chamber over the hall. 2s. 6d. each unto THOMAS, ABRAHAM, ISAAC and NATHANIEL MOWLSON. £3 each to my 3 daughters MARY, DORCAS and ALICE to be paid by my son ROBERT at yearly intervals starting 2 years after my decease. They have power to distrain. To my wife all my coal and unbequeathed household stuff and implements. All sums of money due to me to my son ROBERT, whom I appoint sole exor. and who is to pay 40s. to my wife within 3 months of my death, and also my debts and funeral charges. Witnesses: G. CATCHPOLE, notary public. Pr. at Ipswich 15 Dec. 1633.

R(W) SYBIL MOULSON of Ipswich, widow (N). (715)
[blank] November 1633

To her son THOMAS such goods, household stuff and legacies as were willed to her by her late husband THOMAS MOULSON. To MARY MOULSON her flannel petticoat and a murry waistcoat. To her sister PEARSYE 1 stuff petticoat. To DORCAS MOULSON 1 old petticoat and 1 old waistcoat. She asked that Mr ROBERT HOWE of Ipswich, clothier, should educate and bring up her son JACOB and manage his legacies. Witnesses: ROBERT, JOAN and MARY MOWLSON. Pr. 19 Dec. 1633. Admon. to ROBERT HOWE.

R(W) ROSE MYNTER (X) of Tuddenham, widow. 30 July 1628 (716)

Aged yet hale of body. To be buried in church or churchyard of Tuddenham. To WILLIAM MEADOWE, my son-in-law, my posted bedstead standing in the parlour in Witnesham Hall. To his wife, my daughter GRISELL MEADOWE £10. To MARY wife of ROBERT HALLIFAX of Melton £10. To JULIAN MINTER my son £3. To GEORGE, son of MARY HILL my daughter, £10. £8 each to MARGARET and MARY daughters of MARY HILL within 1 year of my decease. £8 each as they reach age of 21 to MARY HILL's children: JOHN, THOMAS, MARGERY, ROSE and ELIZABETH with benefit of survivorship. 40s. each when 21 to RICHARD son of my son RICHARD MINTER, and to my godson [blank in original will] son of my son EDMUND MINTER and to MARY daughter of my son ROBERT MINTER. To RICHARD WARNER, son of JOHN WARNER my godson, 10s. when 21. JOHN PYSSEY of Clopton tailor and WILLIAM PYSSEY of Helmingham tailor have mortgaged to me for £100 land and tenements in Witnesham. If they fail to repay the money on the due date, I bequeath the land to my grandson GEORGE HILL. To WILLIAM son of THOMAS SEAMAN, my son-in-law, my red rug and to his brother EDMUND my best featherbed. To GEORGE son of THOMAS SEAMAN my best covering. To MARGARET HILL my sewing desk. All the rest of my goods, clothes, linen and household stuff I bequeath to my daughter ROSE, wife of THOMAS SEAMAN. To the poor people at my burial 40s. I make GEORGE HILL my sole exor. and I give him all money due to me by bonds or bills. Witnesses: CHRISTOPHER CUTBERT (X), THOMAS SEAMAN, CHRISTOPHER COTTLER (X). Pr. at Wickham Market 12 Dec. 1633.

R(W) HENRY NUSSIE the elder of Beccles. 9 September 1633 (717)

In reasonable health of body. To my wife MARGARET a 5 1/2 year lease of houses and rooms in Great Yarmouth rented from JOAN and JOHN GROSSE of Great Yarmouth. Also I give to her for ever my house situated in the City of Norwich, which I lately purchased from NATHANIEL CULLIE, but if he redeems the covenant made between us, then I give the sum of money due to me to my wife towards the payment of my debts and legacies. £30 each to my sons WILLIAM and ROGER if my wife can spare so much out of my estate after paying my debts and allowing a sufficient sum for her own maintenance. Wife sole exrx. Witnesses: MATTHEW TROTT, RICHARD WAKEFEILD (X), HENRY NUSSYE. Pr. at Beccles 21 Nov. 1633.

R(W) WILLIAM PAYNE the younger of Charsfield, yeoman. (718)
30 November 1633

I give to my son WILLIAM PAYNE 3 closes of land that lie together in Charsfield. The first lies between the late GEORGE STERLING's land, which formerly belonged to ARTHUR DOWE gent., on the east and the messuage of my father WILLIAM PAYNE on the west and contains 2 acres. The second enclosure is to the west of the first, and the third lies between the lands of the late Sir JOHN LEMAN knight, commonly called Mill hill, on the west and the second piece to the east and contains 2 1/2 acres. This land was bought from ARTHUR DOWE gent. My son WILLIAM is to have this land on condition that he pays my son THOMAS £40 on 28 December 1645 in Charsfield church porch. THOMAS has power to distrain. I give to WILLIAM PAYNE my father all my freehold land and tenements now in his occupation for his lifetime, and after his death to my son WILLIAM. I give to my daughter ELIZABETH one 4 acre close of land and pasture commonly called Heringland or Mensers and lying in Charsfield. She is to enter into this land immediately after my wife's death. I give to my son WILLIAM all the residue of my copyhold lands now in the occupation of my father. I give to WILLIAM PAYNE my son my posted bedstead, which I bought from my brother-in-law NICHOLAS SYMED, with the curtains belonging to it and a feather bed which I had of my brother-in-law WILLIAM PAYNE deceased. Also a feather bolster, my coverlet, 2 pairs sheets, 1 pillow, 1 blanket and all other necessaries belonging to the bed. I give more to WILLIAM my son my silver cup and half a dozen of my best table napkins, my best saddle and bridle, all my apparel and my best cow. I give to my son THOMAS my other posted bedstead, which I bought of EDWARD SMITH, with the curtains and curtain rods belonging to it together with a featherbed, a feather bolster, a coverlet, 1 pillow, 2 pairs sheets and 1 blanket, and half a dozen of my best napkins. I give more to him my biggest brass pot. All these goods are to be delivered after my decease to my brother JOHN PAYNE, who is to give them to my son THOMAS at his full age of 22 years. I give to THOMAS my son £60, which my exrx. is to pay to my brother JOHN and my brother-in-law HENRY PAYNE on Michaelmas day 1638 in Charsfield church porch. Ten days after my death my exrx. is to enter a bond for £60 with JOHN PAYNE for the payment of this sum at the date and place named above. Until the money is paid my exrx. is to keep THOMAS in sufficient meat and drink and apparel and also to use the money to bind him apprentice to a trade thought fit by THOMAS PAYNE my brother-in-law and by JOHN and HENRY PAYNE. When THOMAS reaches the age of 22 the sum of £60, with any profits, must be paid to him. I make my wife ELIZABETH sole exrx., and bequeath all the rest of my money, goods and chattels to her towards paying my debts and legacies. If she refuses to prove my will within one month of my decease or to enter into the above bond, then I make my brother JOHN PAYNE and my brother-in-law HENRY PAYNE exors. and my brother-in-law THOMAS PAYNE supervisor of my will. In this case my exors. are to receive all my movable goods, except those which were my wife's before marriage, and are to sell them and use the money to maintain my son THOMAS until he is 16 when he should be bound apprentice. Witnesses: JOHN PAYNE, JOHN LYNG, THOMAS HOLMES (X), WILLIAM COOPER (X), WILLIAM PAYNE. Pr. at Wickham Market 9 Jan. 1633/4. Pr. to JOHN and HENRY PAYNE.

R(W) WILLIAM PARKINS of Great Bricett (N). (719)
30 January 1632/3

He gave all his goods whatsoever to his wife AGNES and named her exrx. Witnesses: EDWARD WATKINS, MATTHEW EVOLD. Pr. at Ipswich 10 Jan. 1633/4.

R(W) ROBERT ROGERS of Iken, husbandman (N). (720)
30 October 1633

He gave to MARY his daughter £10 to be paid by his exrx. 1 year after his decease. Also to her 1 bed with all that belongs to it standing at the entering into his parlour, a table, a form and a great hutch in the same room. To his son ANTHONY £10 and 1 bed as it stands in the hall chamber and a table in the same room. To his other son JOHN £10 and 1 bed with all that belongs to it. ANTHONY and JOHN are not to have their money and household stuff until after his wife's death or remarriage. The rest of his goods he left to his wife, whom he appointed sole exrx., towards the payment of his debts and funeral expenses. Witnesses: WILLIAM ALDUS, WILLIAM SHIPMAN, ROBERT BIRDE (X). Pr. at Wickham Market 15 Nov. 1633.

R(W) JOHN SMITH of Northwood in Cratfield, yeoman. (721)
18 April 1632.

In perfect health and memory. I give to EDMUND SMITH my son all the free and copyhold land and tenements in Cratfield which I inherited from my late father EDMUND SMITH, that is to say the messuage where I now dwell with the land adjoining it, one close called Wynters, a meadow called Wynters brook, 2 pightles called the Sumpe and all my land lying in the Park and now divided into 3 separate closes. My son ROBERT stands bound to several men in several sums of money for the debts of my son EDMUND, and if the latter does not release ROBERT from all his engagements and debts, then I leave all the aforesaid messuage and land to ROBERT to sell to pay EDMUND's debts. If any money remains, ROBERT is to pay it to EDMUND's children. My son EDMUND must pay yearly to my son JOHN £5 in equal portions at Michaelmas and Lady Day in the porch of Cratfield parish church. JOHN has power to distrain. Any dispute between JOHN and EDMUND must be referred to the arbitration of my nephew ROBERT SMITH of Wickham. I give to ROBERT SMITH my son one close known by the name of Semps close as it is now divided, and all the copyhold lands in Cratfield which I purchased from ROBERT WARNER gent. Also all the freehold land and tenements in Cratfield I bought from ROBERT WARNER and which is called Barfeild, and also a close called Bernes with a little meadow adjoining. I will that my son ROBERT shall pay out of the land I have given to him the following sums: to my nephew ROBERT SMITH of Wickham £100 which I owe him; to my son EDMUND £40 in 2 equal payments to be made one and two years after my decease; an annuity of 50s. to my son JOHN; and to my grandchild MARGERY POYNTE £10 to be paid to her when she reaches her age of 24. All these legatees have power to distrain. I give and bequeath to HENRY SMITH my son all the land and tenements which I purchased from JOHN FILBY and all those I lately bought from JOHN and RICHARD CALVER lying in Ubbeston, Cratfield and Laxfield. Out of these lands HENRY must pay the following sums: to ANN BIRTCH my daughter £15 in payments of £5 to be made over 3 years; to MARGERY POYNTE my grandchild £15 in 3 annual installments beginning 4 years after my death; and an annuity of 50s. to my son JOHN to be paid in Cratfield church porch at Michaelmas and Lady Day. These legatees have power to distrain. If JOHN assigns or sells his annuities they shall cease to be paid. If either EDMUND or HENRY try to interfere with the land left to their brothers, they will lose the land left to them. To my good friend Mr ELAND, minister of Cratfield, 20s. To my son EDMUND my silver salt and 1 of my silver cups, my brewing copper, the hakes in the hall and the back iron and cobirons belonging to it. I give to my son ROBERT my horse mill as it now stands fully furnished, my other silver cup, 1 diaper board cloth and 6 diaper napkins. I give to everyone of my servants 10s. All my unbequeathed goods, chattels, ready money, plate, debts owing to me, household stuff and implements of husbandry (my debts being paid and my funeral charges being deducted) I give to be equally divided among my 5 children: EDMUND, JOHN, ROBERT, HENRY and ANN the wife of WILLIAM BIRTCH, by my nephew ROBERT SMITH. I make my sole exor. my son ROBERT, who is to bind himself in the sum of £500 to my nephew ROBERT SMITH to truly perform my will. If he refuses to do this, the gifts made to him shall be void and I appoint my brother-in-law ROBERT BRODBANCKE exor. I appoint my nephew ROBERT SMITH supervisor and give him 20s. to buy a ring to wear for my sake. I charge my children in the fear of God and as they owe duty unto me to refer all matters of difference that may arise between them out of my will to my supervisor. Witnesses: AUDRY BARNETT (X), WILLIAM BURWARD (X), JOHN HYNDE, WILLIAM BURWARD. Pr. at Beccles 18 Dec. 1633. Probate to ROBERT SMITH, son of the deceased.

R(W) JOHN SUSHAM (X) of Sandcroft (South Elmham St. Cross), butcher. 4 December 1633 (722)

I give to ANN my well beloved wife for her lifetime towards the bringing up of my children until they reach age of 21 my tenement in St. Cross called Orenges with the orchards and yards belonging to it. This is in the occupation of myself and JAMES CORNELL. After my wife's death I bequeath this property to my son JOHN and his heirs. JOHN must pay 20s. each to my other 6 children as follows: to my sons EDWARD and WILLIAM and my daughter ELIZABETH 20s. each on the Michaelmas day next after my wife's death, and 20s. each to my sons GEORGE, HENRY and JAMES on the next following Michaelmas day. All these payments are to be made in the porch of St. Cross parish church. Further I give to my son JOHN my 3 butcher's stalls in Harleston and Beccles and £5 to be paid to him by my exrx. at his age of 20 and another £5 at his age of 21. To my son EDWARD £30 to be paid by my exrx. when he is 21. To my daughter ELIZABETH £50 to be paid by my exrx. when she is 21. Also to her my posted bedstead with its bedding standing in the parlour chamber where I now dwell immediately after my wife's decease. To my sons WILLIAM, GEORGE, HENRY and JAMES £25 each to be paid by my exrx. as they reach age of 21. All these legacies are to be paid in St. Cross parish church porch, and are with benefit of survivorship. I give to my father HENRY SUSHAM 4s. per annum during his natural life to be paid by my exrx. on the 4 quarter days. To ANN SKEETE 5s. to be paid immediately after my death. To the poor of St. Cross 5s. to be distributed by the churchwardens and overseers of the poor. All my unbequeathed movable goods, debts and money I give to my wife, whom I make sole exrx. and who is to bring up my children in the fear of God, good nurture and learning. Witnesses: THOMAS SEAMAN, JAMES GODBOLD, RICHARD BUNNING. Pr. at Beccles 4 Jan. 1633/4.

R(W) ROBERT SKOULDING of Walpole, yeoman. 16 June 1633 (723)

Whole of body. I give unto ALICE my much respected and loving wife all my movable goods and chattels, and the lease I hold from THOMAS GRAYE of Wenhaston yeoman of the land and tenement wherein I now dwell. She must pay my debts and burial expenses and prove my will. I make her sole exrx. and my loving friend SAMUEL NOLLOTH of Halesworth yeoman supervisor. Witnesses: ROBERT HUGGART clerk and THOMAS SKOULDING with others. Pr. at Halesworth 24 Dec. 1633.

R(W) THOMAS WRIGHT (X) of Great Glemham, husbandman. 2 November 1633 (724)

Sick in body. I will that ELIZABETH my wife shall have my tenement and lands in Benhall until my daughter ALICE shall reach the age of 21, towards the bringing up of my children. When ALICE reaches 21 I give the land and tenement to her and she must pay my wife 40s. p.a. in two equal payments on Lady Day and

Michaelmas. I bequeath to my daughter ANN £30 to be paid to her when she is 21. Exors. my brother-in-law ROBERT NEWSON and my wife. Witnesses: JOHN BULLEN, SIMON BROME, LAURENCE PELLS. Pr. at Wickham Market 15 Nov. 1633.

R(W) ALICE WRIGHT (X) of Kelsale, widow. (725)
16 October 1633

To my daughter ANN BENNS £40 when she is 21 if she be then living, but if she is dead I bequeath this sum to my exor. I give to my daughter ANN all my brass, pewter, linen and bedding when she reaches age of 21; until then these goods are to remain in hands of my exor., who inherits them if ANN dies. I bequeath the residue of my goods to my beloved friend LAURENCE SHANCK of Kelsale to pay my debts and funeral charges, and I make him sole exor. Witnesses: THOMAS REVE, GEORGE JERMY. Pr. at Yoxford 14 Nov. 1633.

R(W) HENRY WRIGHT of Beccles, yeoman. 20 July 1633 (726)

To be buried in churchyard of Beccles parish church. I will and bequeath to ELIZABETH my wife all my lands and tenements in Beccles for ever, and all my land and tenements in the parish of Redenhall in Norfolk for ever. Also all my movable goods and chattels, bills, bonds and debts. I make her my sole exrx. and she is to pay my debts. Witnesses: WILLIAM MATCHETT, JOHN GREENE (X). Pr. at Beccles 26 Nov. 1633.

R(W) THOMAS KENT of Monewden. 16 March 1632/3 (727)

Sick in body. To ANN my wife during her life all my houses standing in Crowfield with the land belonging to them, and after her death I bequeath them to to my eldest son THOMAS. If THOMAS dies without heirs, this property then goes to my son JOHN and if he has no heirs to my son JAMES. To my son THOMAS £20 and to my sons JOHN and JAMES £40 each, and to my 3 daughters ANN, SUSAN and SARAH £20 each to be paid as follows with benefit of survivorship. The residue of my goods and chattels I bequeath to ANN my wife, who must pay my debts, my funeral expenses and the charges of proving my will. She must also within a year of my decease pay £47 to my exors., who are to pay her the income from this sum towards the bringing up of my children. The legacies I have given to my children are to be paid by my exors. as they reach their ages of 21. I nominate as exors. my well-beloved in Christ our true and dearest friend JOHN HASELL of Gosbeck, my father-in-law, and my cousin JOHN HASELL his grandchild, also of Gosbeck. I do humbly and earnestly entreat them to undertake this business for my wife and little children. I do also earnestly desire my loving uncle Mr ROBERT MANKNOLD to be supervisor of my will and a friend to my wife and children. Witnesses: ROBERT MANKNOLS, FRANCIS KENT. Pr. [no place given] 9 Jan. 1633/4.

R(W) ROBERT NUDDS (X) the elder of Pakefield, fisherman. (728)
26 January 1633/4

Weak in body. To MARGARET my wife for her life that house wherein I now dwell and all the land belonging to it, and the tenement next adjoining in which ROBERT STROUD now dwells, and after her death to my son ROBERT. If he has no heirs the houses and land are to be sold after his death for the best price and the money divided between my 5 grandchildren: THOMAS and JOHN SWALT, ALICE SWALT now the wife of RICHARD MANNING, ROBERT and RICHARD WOLSIE. I give to these 5 grandchildren 5 doles of herring nets and 5 doles of mackerel nets to be equally divided between them after my decease. I give to ROBERT my son my third share of the great North Sea boat called the Hesse, my two thirds parts of my 2 mackerel boats, my 2 ferry boats and my line boat with all the appurtenances that belong to me concerning the aforesaid 6 boats. I also give to my son ROBERT my set net and all that belongs thereunto. I give to my brother WILLIAM NUDDS 20s. All my unbequeathed goods and chattels I give to my wife for her life. She may dispose of one-third of them as she wishes at her death, and the other two-thirds are to be divided after her decease between my son ROBERT and my daughter RUTH WOLSYE. Exors. wife and son ROBERT. Witnesses: WILLIAM GIRLING clerk and ROBERT STROUD. Pr. at Beccles 4 Feb. 1633/4.

R(W) JOHN MUNDS (X) of Lowestoft, cordwainer. (729)
12 December 1633

Very sick of body. I will and bequeath to ISRAEL and JAMES MUNDS my sons all my tenement wherein I now dwell with its yards and situated in Lowestoft, immediately after the decease of ANN my wife. After her death my will is that my sons shall sell the house and yards and divide the money equally between them. Whereas my late son WILLIAM MUNDS bequeathed 20s. each to my grandchildren ANN, JOHN and MARY UGGS and this money has been paid into my hands by his widow and exrx. MARGERY MUNDS, I will that my exrx. should pay these legacies as my grandchildren reach the age of 21. All the residue of my goods and chattels I bequeath to ANN my loving wife, whom I ordain and make my sole exrx. I make ISRAEL MUNDS supervisor. Witnesses: JOHN ARNOLD, WILLIAM UNDERWOOD. Pr. at Lowestoft 22 Jan. 1633/4.

R(W) HENRY WOODSHED (X) of Lowestoft, yeoman. (730)
23 November 1633.

Weak in body. I give to RICHARD FISHER my son-in-law and to MARY his wife all my houses and tenements in Lowestoft after my wife's decease. Also my bed as it now stands whereon I now lie, 5 pieces of pewter, 1 silver spoon, 1 candlestick, 1 chair and 1 cushion to be delivered to him after the decease of my wife. Also 40s. to be paid to him as soon as it is received on a bond owing to me. I give to my daughter JANE 40s. to be paid in the same manner, and 5 pieces of pewter, 1 silver spoon, 1 candlestick, 1 chair, 1 cushion, my cupboard and 1 of my beds as it now stands in my chamber over the parlour, being the best bed there. I give to my son-in-law ROBERT BALLS my little bed as it lies on the trundle bedstead standing in the parlour chamber, to be delivered to him by my wife at her discretion. To my grandson HENRY BALLS 40s. I give to my wife ANN the rest of the money due to me on bond as it can be recovered. I give to my daughter JANE my long table and form. I give to ROBERT BALLS 5 pieces of pewter. I give to ANN my loving wife all my fireing which now lies in my yards. My wife is to keep the goods I have bequeathed until she remarries or dies. My unbequeathed goods I give to my wife and son-in-law RICHARD FISHER, whom I make exors. of my will. Witnesses: JOHN SMITH (X), JOHN FISHER, OLIVER ASHLY (X), and RICHARD LINSEY. Pr. at Beccles 11 Jan. 1633/4.

R(W) HENRY RICHARDSON (X) of Westleton, yeoman. (731)
16 July 1633.

To my grandchild PHILIP RICHARDSON all my houses, lands and tenements in Westleton, but my son HENRY may hold and occupy my tenement called Burmans, with its yards and grounds, during his lifetime, or receive an annuity of £3 from the hands of PHILIP RICHARDSON as he chooses. I give £5 each to my 4 daughters to be paid by PHILIP RICHARDSON at the rate of 20s. each a year starting at the Michaelmas which falls a year after my decease. My intent is that my wife AGNES shall have and quietly enjoy her dower or thirds of my lands and tenements without any molestation by my grandson PHILIP. I give to AGNES my wife all the household stuff and implements that were hers before we married, and 1 good featherbed, 1 bed coverlet, 1 feather bolster and 1 bed blanket. All the rest of my goods and chattels shall be equally divided by my exor. between my 4 daughters immediately after my decease. Exor. PHILIP RICHARDSON. Witnesses: THOMAS EARNE and me THOMAS FELLA. Pr. at Beccles 11 Feb. 1633/4.

R(W) ROBERT RYSING of Beccles, shoemaker (N). (732)
13 January 1633/4

He gave all his goods and chattels to AUDRY his wife towards the payment of his debts and the charges of his burial, and revoked all gifts and legacies formerly given to JOSEPH RYSING his kinsman. Witnesses: SAMUEL MUNFORD, JOHN DADE junior. Pr. at Beccles 1 Feb. 1633/4.

R(W) JONAS BRETTON (X) of East Bergholt, shearman. (733)
30 December 1633

Sick and weak in body. I give 12d. apiece to my 4 kinsfolk the children of THOMAS BRETTON, that is to say JOHN, THOMAS, FRANCIS and MARGARET BRETTON to be paid by my exor. within 3 months of my decease. I give to DOROTHY my beloved wife all that my cottage or tenement wherein I now dwell with its garden and yards for ever. My debts being paid, I give the remainder of my goods and household stuff to my wife, whom I make sole exrx. I make my trusty and well beloved friend JOHN BUCKLE supervisor. Witnesses: JOHN PHILLIPPS, CHRISTOPHER DOWE. Pr. at Ipswich 18 Jan. 1633/4.

R(W) ROBERT COLE senior of East Bergholt, yeoman. (734)
26 December 1633

Sick and weak in body. To my son MARTIN COLE my messuage and lands now in the occupation of WILLIAM STROWD. I bequeath to my two daughters GRACE and ELIZABETH COLE my freehold messuage with garden and yards lying in East Bergholt and now in my own occupation. I give £10 to each of my daughters to be paid by my exor. 3 months after my decease. I give all my firewood and £5 to my son-in-law EDWARD LEWIS to convey me decently to the ground. The rest of goods and household stuff I give to be equally parted between my 3 children, MARTIN, GRACE and ELIZABETH. Son MARTIN sole exor. Witnesses: JOHN PHILLIPPS, ABRAHAM NEWTON and THOMAS KENT (X). Pr. at Ipswich 31 Jan. 1633/4.

R(W) KATHERINE FOSDICK (X) of Framlingham at the Castle, (735)
widow. 10 December 1630

I give to my son JOHN FOSDICK the coffer which was his father's and all such linen as is therein, fastened up in a shirt. Also a great pewter platter given to him by his grandmother, and his father's great Bible. I give unto GRACE FOSDICK my daughter my great chest and all the things fastened up in a apron in the same, and 1 great kettle being the best I have. I give to my daughter MARY FOSDICK my feather bed and bolster, the whitest fustian pillow, 2 of my best blankets, my best covering, my best bedstead and my biggest coffer with such things as are fastened up in an apron inside it. As MARY has no share in the house left to the rest of my children by my late husband JOHN FOSDICK, because she was not born, I give her £12. If I do not leave so much in money or bonds then this sum is to be made up by household goods. All my wearing apparel, both woollen and linen, to be equally divided between my two daughters, GRACE and MARY. My children are to have all such linen as is marked with their names, and the rest is to be divided between them. If my daughter MARY dies unmarried, then my son WILLIAM is to have the bed bequeathed to her and all things belonging to it; and the money due to her should be divided equally between my son JOHN and my daughter GRACE. If any other of my children die without heirs, then their legacies are to be divided amongst their surviving brothers and sisters. The residue of my goods I give to my exors. to pay my funeral expenses and the probate of my will. Exors. sons WILLIAM and JOHN. I appoint my trusty friends

ROBERT MOLLYNG and NICHOLAS DANFORD as supervisors. Wit. JOHN ASHBURNE, SUSAN HABERGHAM (X). Memorandum that the names of the supervisors were added on 10 Aug. 1631. Witnesses: ANNE MILLING (X), JOHN BEART. Pr. at Wickham Market 20 Feb. 1633/4.

R(W) WILLIAM KEBLE (N) of Iken. [No date] (736)

In the time of his sickness he gave to ROBERT and KATHERINE his children £10 apiece. He gave to ANN his wife all the rest of his goods and named her exrx. Witnesses: ROBERT SKUTTON, ALICE CLARKE. Pr. at Wickham Market 30 Jan. 1633/4.

R(W) KATHERINE PEARSE (N) of Leiston, widow. [No date] (737)

About a fortnight before her death being asked by THOMAS CRESNER alias HOXEN how she would dispose of her goods, she answered that the said THOMAS should have all her goods and pay out of them the following legacies: to her grandson HUMPHREY PEARSE, a lame boy, £5; to ROBERT AWCOCK, her daughter's son, £5; to the servants of THOMAS CRESNER alias HOXEN and to such as attended her 55s. Witnesses: RICHARD GIRLING, ENOCH GIRLING, ROBERT FULLER and others. Pr. 19 Feb. 1633/4. [No place given.]

R(W) MIRABEL POTTER (N) of Brandeston, widow. (738)
[blank] May 1632

She bequeathed to MIRABEL POTTER, daughter of GEORGE POTTER, 1 chest with certain linen in it and standing in a chamber at the house of GEORGE POTTER in Stonham Aspal. All the rest of her goods, chattels, money and debts she willed should be delivered into the hands of her loving friend ROBERT BLOMEFEILD of Stonham Aspal, yeoman. After he has paid her funeral charges and the expenses of proving her will, he is to divide the remainder equally between her children. Exor. ROBERT BLOMEFEILD. Witnesses: SAMUEL DAMONT, MARY BETTS, GEORGE POTTER and MARGARET BUTTON. Pr. at Ipswich 21 Feb. 1633/4.

R(W) JAMES DAWSON (X) of Wrentham, bricklayer. (739)
8 January 1632/3

I bequeath to ELIZABETH DAWSON, my brother's daughter, the sum of £5 to be paid to her by my exor. when she reaches the age of 20. Until then MATTHEW ARMESTRONG, whom I name my exor., is to use this money to her best advantage. If ELIZABETH dies before she is 20, the £5 is to be divided equally between all the children of my brother PHAMUELL. £3 to the children of MATTHEW ARMESTRONG, to whom as my exor. I give all the residue of my goods. Witnesses: THOMAS FELLA and ELIZABETH FELLA. Pr. at Beccles 15 Feb. 1633/4.

R(W) JOHN PLOWMAN (X) of Bungay, locksmith. (740)
21 February 1633/4

Sick in body. I give to my wife ELIZABETH, until my son WILLIAM comes to age of 21, my messuage in Bungay wherein I dwell, that is to say the house and the shop together with a little yard in the occupation of JEREMY MENTLE. When WILLIAM reaches the age of 21 I give him the messuage, shop and yard for ever. I give all the rest of my houses and yards in Bungay wherein ROBERT YOUNGMAN, JOHN DUNCKHORNE & JEREMY MENTLE dwell to my wife for her life towards bringing up of my children and the payment of my debts and legacies. After my wife's decease I give all these houses and yards to my son WILLIAM on condition that he pays £10 to my other son JOHN within 2 years of my wife's death. JOHN has the power to distrain. I give £20 to my son JOHN to be paid by my exrx. when he reaches the age of 21. This sum is to be put out for him immediately after my decease and the profits to be used to his best advantage. £10 to my daughter MARY when she is 21, and until then the money is to be invested and used in the same way as JOHN's. I give to PETER PLOWMAN my apprentice £3 to be paid to him at his age of 24. And also I give to him 1 pair of great smith's bellows, 1 smith's vice, 1 borwte hammer, 1 uphand hammer, 1 beake iron and 1 stythe. All these are to be delivered to him by my exrx. when he is 24. I give to ELIZABETH my wife all the residue of my goods, implements of household, utensils, goods, bonds, and ready money towards the bringing up of my children and the payment of debts and legacies. I make ELIZABETH my wife sole exrx. Witnesses: RICHARD BAISPOOLE, RICHARD BENSLYE (X). Pr. at Bungay 3 March 1633/4.

R(W) ANNE SAUNDERS (X) of Monk Soham, widow. (741)
2 August 1633

I give and bequeath unto ANN SAUNDERS my daughter all my movable goods and money, except 1 trundle bedstead with a flock bed and feather bolster as they now stand in the hall and 1 red chest with 2 locks and the keys belonging to them standing in the chamber. All these I bequeath to JOHN SAUNDERS my son and they are to be delivered to him by my exrx. within 6 days of my burial. £6 is to be paid to my son JOHN at Michaelmas after my decease in the south porch of Monk Soham church. I also give to him 1 pair of sheets. Daughter ANN sole exrx. Witnesses: JAMES MAYEHEW, JOHN MAYEHEWE, JOHN MAYEHEWE, snr. Pr. at Yoxford 19 Feb. 1633/4.

R(W) LYDIA ALAND (X) of Covehithe, widow. (742)
4 October 1633

I bequeath to JOHN & LYDIA ALAND, my son and daughter, all my tenement wherein I dwell together with the hempland belonging to it, to be equally divided between them. I also give to them all my goods and household stuff, and make them exors. of my will. Witnesses: JOHN YOUNGES, ROBERT BLYTHE (X), EDWARD WIGGATT (X). Pr. at Beccles 6 Oct. 1633.

R(W) WILLIAM ASHKETLE (X) of Dunwich, weaver. (743)
30 January 1633/4

I give to my daughter ELIZABETH ASHKETLE a posted bedstead, a featherbed, a feather bolster, a pillow, a blanket of linsey wolsey, a black and white woollen coverlet, 1 pair of sheets, a cupboard table, a joined form, a brass pot, 2 pewter platters, a chair, my little bible and a little coffer to be delivered to her by my exrx. when she reaches the age of 20. I give to my daughter MARY ASHKETLE a livery bedstead, a feather bed, a feather bolster, a pillow, a blanket of linsey wolsey, a black and white wool coverlet, 1 pair of sheets, 1 iron pot, 2 pewter platters, a little table and a chair to be given to her by my exrx. when she is 20. I give to WILLIAM my son a livery bedstead, a featherbed, a feather bolster, a blanket, a black and white wool coverlet, a brass pot, 4 pewter platters, a great chair, a long table with a form, a pair of sheets and a pillow to be delivered to him by my exrx. when he is 21. I give to my son FRANCIS £10 to be paid by my exrx. when he comes to age of 21. I name ELIZABETH my wife my sole exrx., and give her all the rest of my goods, money, plate, corn, cattle and implements of household and trading, on condition that she pay my debts and bring up my children with wholesome food and rayment for their bodies, and places them in service at suitable times as she sees good according to her motherly affection. Witnesses: THOMAS PEARSE, WILLIAM SYKES. Pr. at Yoxford 19 Feb. 1633/4.

R(W) JOAN ELLIS of Thorington, singlewoman. (744)
7 January 1633/4

She gave to MARY, one of the daughters of WILLIAM SCOTT of Thorington, her gown, her best petticoat and all her best wearing linen, 2 boxes, her best coverlet, a pewter platter, her best purse and as much wool as will make her a hat. To ELIZABETH, another daughter of WILLIAM SCOTT, she gave her cupboard, a coffer, and 1 of her best sheets. To MARGARET PRIMROSE, her godchild, she gave her best chest and 1 sheet. She gave to the 2 daughters of EDWARD ELLIS 2 of her best sheets, 2 yard kerchiefs and 2 pillowberes. To HENRY SCOTT her dark coloured petticoat, and as much wool and yarn as will make him a doublet and a pair of stockings. She gave to KATHERINE, the wife of THOMAS SCOTT, her cloak, a yard kerchief and three-quarters of a pound of wool yarn. She asked her brother WILLIAM SCOTT to sell her featherbed, bolster, pillow and brass pot for the best price. This money and any unbequeathed goods to be divided among WILLIAM SCOTT's children, except OLIVE the wife of ROBERT HAYWARD who was not to have a share. Half the £5 owed to her by WILLIAM SCOTT was to be divided among his children, except OLIVE HAYWARD, and the other half she gave to WILLIAM SCOTT, whom she made her exor. Witnesses: HARBONE FELTHAM, FRANCIS SEPEMES. Pr. at Yoxford 19 Feb. 1633/4.

R(W) GRACE FORMAN (X) of Bramfield, (745)
widow of THOMAS FORMAN of Bramfield. 11 June 1630

In bodily health, but thinks it best to settle her worldly affairs before she is unfitted to do so by sickness or in case she is called suddenly to her long home. I bequeath to AGNES, wife of NICHOLAS VESEY of Bramfield, 20s., 1 pair of my best sheets, my tow comb and my warming pan. I give to EDITH, wife of JOHN PULHAM the younger of Bramfield, 25s. To MARGARET, wife of JOHN ROWSE of Cratfield, 40s. and to JOHN ROUSE her son 6s. I give to MARY, daughter of NICHOLAS VESEY, 45s. To MARGARET, wife of WILLIAM FELLA of Bramfield, 20s. and to her daughters HANNAH & JANE FELLA & ELIZABETH COPPING 6s. 8d. each. I also give to MARGARET FELLA 1 pair of sheets marked with blue, 1 pillow and 1 pillow bere. I give to ROBERT, son of WILLIAM FELLA, 3s. and my roast iron. I give 5s. to MARY, daughter of JOHN PERISON of Bramfield. Also 20s. each to ANN, wife of EDMUND WATLING of Bramfield and to their son JOHN. I give to JOHN, son of JOHN COLLETT of Bramfield, 5s. to be paid to him when he is 21. I give to PARNELL TOKELOWE, late of Bramfield widow, 30s. I forgive her son JOHN the debt of 40s. he owes me on condition he pays 10s. each to his brother and sisters, THOMAS, PARNELL & HANNAH TOKELOWE, within 6 months of my death. I give to SUSAN, wife of ROBERT DURRANT of Cookley, 5s. and 5s. each to their children SUSAN, JOHN, FRANCES & ANN as they reach the age of 21. I give to DOROTHY WHYTE, daughter of my late husband THOMAS FORMAN, 30s. and to ALICE WITTINGHAM, another daughter of my late husband 45s. I also give to ALICE WITTINGHAM my best bedstead and bolster and all other things belonging to it. I give 35s. to each of her children to be paid when they are 21. I give 6s. to the poor people of Bramfield. Also 20s. to REGINALD VESEY of Bramfield, 6s. to WILLIAM HURRION of Bramfield, and 3s. each to WILLIAM, MARY, CLEMENCE and MARGARET, the son and daughters of WILLIAM CHERRY of Darsham. NICHOLAS VESEY sole exor., to whom I give all my unbequeathed household goods, ready money and debts owing to me to pay my debts and legacies. Wit. GEORGE VESEY, THOMAS FELLA (X), JOHN PULHAM jnr. Pr. at Yoxford 19 Feb. 1633/4.

R(W) JOHN TANN of Bramford, yeoman. 1 November 1633 (746)

To be buried in Bramford churchyard. I give to JOHN son of HENRY TANN my son all my freehold and copyhold land and tenements immediately after my decease. To MARY, daughter of my son HENRY, £13 6s. 8d. when she is 21 or on her marriage day. Similar bequests of £13 6s. 8d. each to grandchildren SUSAN and ROSE TANN, with benefit of survivorship. To ELIZABETH my wife all my household provision and firewood and all my apparel. She is to have the use of all my household stuff during her lifetime. I give 15s. to the poor of the parish of Bramford to be distributed at my burial by my exors. I give to the 4 men who shall bear me to church 4s. I give to the ringers that shall take pains to ring at my burial 5s. Exors. my trusty friends THOMAS BACON gent. and HENRY HERME yeoman, both of Bramford. On 15 Oct. 1633 I JOHN TANN attended the court of the lord of Bramford manor and surrendered my copyhold land to the use of my will. Witnesses: DOROTHY HAYEWARD (X), JOHN FRANCIS (X), and NICHOLAS HAYEWARD. Pr. at Ipswich 21 Feb. 1633/4.

R(W) WILLIAM LACY of Yoxford, tanner. 8 November 1631 (747)

I give to my wife JANE during her life my close in Yoxford called Churchfield and abutting on my land called Pyesage, on condition that she pays 40s. p.a. in 2 equal payments at Michaelmas and Lady Day in the north porch of Yoxford church, to the churchwardens for the use fo the poor of Yoxford. The churchwardens have power to distrain. I also give to JANE my wife all my other land and houses in Yoxford for her life, all the household stuff she brought to me, my little silver cup worth 30s., and all my cows. If I have no cows at the time of my death, then I give her £30 instead, and if I have fewer than 10 cows, I give her £3 for each cow less than 10. These bequests to JANE are void if she refuses to release to my grandchildren, ANNE & WILLIAM DUNSTON, all her right of dower in my lands and tenements in Bramfield, Mells hamlet and Earl Soham, and if she refuses to confirm the lease I have made to JOHN COPLAND of my tan office and buildings in Yoxford, or if she does not keep my houses, fences, tan vats, pump and other buildings in good repair during her life. If JANE forfeits her legacies, then they go to my grandson WILLIAM DUNSTON. I give to my grandson WILLIAM DUNSTON for ever all my houses and land in Bramfield and Mells hamlet after the death of my wife. I give more to him my land and tenements in Yoxford. I give to ANNE DUNSTON my grandchild for ever all my land and tenements in Earl Soham. I give to WILLIAM DUNSTON my bedstead standing in my parlour at Yoxford and the featherbed, bolster, pillows, blankets, coverlet, curtains and curtain rods belonging to this bed. Also to him my double silver salt, 5 silver spoons, my best brass pot, my furniture for my light horse and horseman, my great chest which was my first wife's, my brewing copper as it hangs, and my spit jack. But my will is that my wife shall have the use of the copper and jack during her lifetime. I give to ANN DUNSTON another posted bed-stead and all the bedding belonging to it, my silver beaker, my silver lipped pot, 5 silver spoons, my second brass pot. All money due to me, after payment of my debts, legacies and funeral charges, is to be divided between these two grandchildren. To WILLIAM LACYE of Earl Soham, my brother's son, £20. 40s. to the poor of Yoxford, 30s. to the poor of Sibton, 10s. to the poor of Peasenhall, 13s. 4d. to the poor of Bramfield, 10s. each to the poor of Darsham, Kelsale and Westleton. To each of my servants 10s. To WILLIAM BUCKENHAM the elder of Yoxford 40s. To MARY BRENDALL, my sister's daughter £5. Until my grandchildren

WILLIAM and ANNE DUNSTON reach their ages of 21, their father WILLIAM DUNSTON is to receive the yearly income from the land bequeathed to them and is to use it for their benefit. When these grandchildren come of age their father must account to them for this money, and can deduct from it the cost of their education and any legal expenses connected with their land. My son-in-law WILLIAM DUNSTON is to covenant with Mr JOHN SCRIVENOR esquire of Sibton to make the above accounts. I make Mr JOHN SCRIVENOR supervisor, and my son-in-law WILLIAM DUNSTON exor. of my will. I give to the latter all my unbequeathed money, plate and household stuff to pay my debts and legacies. Any surplus is for his own use. If my exor. dies before his children are 21, or refuses to covenant with Mr JOHN SCRIVENOR, then my kinsmen RANDOLPH WYARD the elder of Earl Soham and his son JOHN WYARD are to manage the property left to my grandchildren. Witnesses: JOHN COPLAND, JAMES JULIANS (X), HENRY JULYAN & RICHARD CRISPE. Pr. at Yoxford 12 March 1633/4.

R(W) ROBERT MERRELL (X) of Shotley, sailor. (748)
28 January 1631/2

In perfect health. I give to my kinsman THOMAS FULLER of Shotley, mariner, all my messuage and land in Shotley and now in his occupation. Within 2 years of my decease he must pay £5 to each of his 4 children. I bequeath all my goods and chattels to THOMAS FULLER, whom I appoint sole exor. Witnesses: ROBERT CLARK, WILLIAM COPIN. Pr. at Ipswich 1 March 1633/4.

R(W) WILLIAM BLANCHFLOWER (X) of Rendham, singleman. (749)
26 February 1633/4

To my brother ROBERT BLANCHFLOWER all my copyhold land, held of manor of Staverton with Bromeswell, in Eyke, on condition he pays my mother MARGARET BLANCHFLOWER £3 15s. 0d. in 2 equal sums at Michaelmas and Lady Day. My mother must pay my brother ROBERT £5 within 6 weeks of my decease. I give £5 to my niece and nephew ELIZABETH and JOHN KING to be paid by ROBERT BLANCHFLOWER as follows: 20s. within 3 weeks of my death and the remainder 7 years after my decease. To my brother ROBERT BLANCHFLOWER 4 ewes and lambs on condition he gives JOHN & ELIZABETH KING an ewe and lamb each 1 week after my decease. To my sister PENELOPE BLANCHFLOWER all my sheep which Mr BLUNDRETH of Sweffling has of me to halves. I give my mother 4 sheep and 3 lambs on condition she pays JOHN PECK her man 6s. 8d. and the same sum to ISABEL CORDILL within 8 weeks of my death. I give to ROBERT BLANCHFLOWER my cloak. All my unbequeathed goods I give to my mother towards the cost of my burial. Mother his sole exrx. Before making my will I surrendered all my copyhold land to the use of my will. Witnesses: DANIEL DRYVER, WILLIAM HURRION (X), JOHN PECK. Pr. at Wickham Market 13 March 1633/4.

R(W) JOHN WALPOOLE (X) of Beccles, yeoman. (750)
6 March 1633/4

Sick in Body. I give to MARCIA [MARKE in manuscript] BARNWELL, wife of HENRY BARNWELL of Hardley in Norfolk, my daughter £30. To JOHN, GRACE, MATTHIAS & LAWRENCE YNCKLE, the children of MARCIA BARNWELL, £40 to be equally divided amongst them as they reach the age of 21, with benefit of survivorship. I give £100 to my son THOMAS on condition he releases my son-in-law JOSEPH GARRARD from a bond by which he stands surety in the sum of £100 for the payment by my son THOMAS of £50 to Mr SMITH of Bungay. If THOMAS refuses to do this, the £100 is to be paid to JOSEPH GARRARD to redeem the bond, and any money then left over to be paid to my son THOMAS. I give £60 to my daughter GRACE ESTON within two years of my decease, or if she has died to her son JOHN at the age of 21. £30 when she is 21 to MARY, the daughter of SIMON KING, my son-in-law, or if she dies to be divided between the rest of his children. Until MARY KING is 21 my exors. are to pay her 40s. p.a. from the profits of her legacy towards her education and maintenance. The 40s. is to be paid in 4 installments at Michaelmas, Christmas, Lady Day and the feast of St. John the Baptist. £10 each when 21 to SIMON KING's children TIMOTHY, SAMUEL, ANN and ALICE, with benefit of survivorship. I give £20 to my son-in-law JOSEPH GARRARD, and my best bedstead and the furniture belonging to it. £10 when 21 to JOHN WALPOOLE my grandchild and to my grandson JOHN, son of JOSEPH GARRARD, £5 at his age of 21. All the rest of my goods, cattle, bills, bonds, mortgages, plate and household stuff I give to my son THOMAS and my son-in-law JOSEPH GARRARD, whom I nominate my exors. I give to MARY KING, my grandchild, a trundle bedstead with its bedding, and a joined box to be delivered to her immediately after my decease. Witnesses: THOMAS MARSHALL, THOMAS HALLES, THOMAS COLMAN (X). Pr. at Beccles 17 March 1633/4.

R. JOHN HOPWOOD (X) of Bungay, husbandman. (751)
18 September 1633

Sick in body. I bequeath to ELIZABETH my wife for ever my shop in Harleston in Norfolk. To HESTER HOPWOOD my daughter one little desk after my wife's decease. To ALICE HOPWOOD my daughter a bible which she is to have after my wife's death. I bequeath all the residue of my goods, chattels, household stuff and implements and working tools to my wife towards paying my debts and performing my will. I make her sole exrx. Witnesses: RICHARD BAYSPOOLE, WILLIAM HUNTMAN (X). Pr. at Bungay 13 March 1633/4.

R(W) JAMES BRAME (X) the elder of Fressingfield, yeoman. (752)
20 December 1632

To my daughter AVIS BRAME my best bedstead standing in the parlour of the messuage where my son JAMES now dwells. Also 2 of the featherbeds, 2 bolsters -- one of the best and the other of the meaner sort -- half the pillows, 2 coverlets -- one of the best and the other of the meaner sort -- 2 blankets -- one of the best and the other of the meaner sort -- all my pewter that I had before I was married to my last wife, the great cupboard in the pantry, 2 brass pots -- one of the best and one of the worser sort -- half my linen, my little cauldron, the brasen mortar with an iron pestle, a chair, a buffet stool, my great and my little candlesticks, 2 little coffers, a little table and a silver spoon. All these items are to be delivered to AVIS on reasonable demand after my deceaase. The rest of my goods, chattels, debts, pewter and linen I give to my son JAMES towards the payment of my debts and legacies. My exor. is to receive and pay my debts and bring me honestly to the ground in Christian burial. Exor. son JAMES, in whom I repose my trust and confidence. Witnesses: ROBERT CRISPE, FRANCIS SANDCROFTE. Pr. at Yoxford 12 March 1633/4.

R(W) THOMAS SHEMMING (X) of Earl Soham, cooper. (753)
6 April 1633

I give to SUSAN my well-beloved wife my messuage in Framilingham for her life and after her decease to JOHN SHEMMING my son. To my son THOMAS £25 to be paid 1 year after my decease. Also my best bedstead and all my timber, planks, hoops, clapboard and all my tools for my trade. This gift to THOMAS is in satisfaction of £10 which I owe to him. In satisfaction of 50s. that my son THOMAS has laid out for me in buying timber I give him my part of the profit from the land which he and I jointly rent from ROBERT RENANS, yeoman of Kettleburgh. I give to my son ROBERT the sum of £25 to be paid to him within 1 year of my decease, and to my son MICHAEL £25 to be paid a year after my death. I give to my son JOHN £5 to be paid within a year of my death. I give to JOHN SHEMMYNG my nephew [i.e. grandson], son of my son JOHN £5 towards binding him apprentice to a trade. I give £5 to my son-in-law NATHANIEL ROE of Framlingham, tailor, to be paid within 1 year of my decease. I give £5 to the rest of the children of my son JOHN to be equally divided between them, and £5 to THOMAS ROE my nephew [grandson] the son of NATHANIEL ROE, to be paid within 1 year of my death. All the residue of my goods I give to my wife SUSAN to pay the debts which I owe and my legacies. Upon the real trust and confidence which I repose in my wife I make her sole exrx. desiring her in the fear of God to see my will performed in every point according to my true intent. Witnesses: EDWARD CRICK (X), MICHAEL SHEMMYNG (X), THOMAS ALEXANDER junior. Pr. at Wickham Market 14 March 1633/4.

R(W) CHRISTOPHER STACKHOUSE of Bungay, yeoman. (754)
17 December 1633

Sick of body. My desire is that ANN my loving wife should peacably enjoy the estate settled on her, comprised of a copyhold messuage and land in Wrentham and 2 freehold messuages in Bungay.

I also give her for her lifetime all the rest of my messuages and land, both free and copyhold, in Bungay and elsewhere, towards the payment of my debts and legacies. She must keep the buildings in good repair, and pay an annuity of £10 to my only daughter ELIZABETH, the wife of Mr JOHN WHEELER, in 2 equal payments at Lady Day and Michaelmas within the church porch of St. Mary Bungay. My son-in-law and daughter must give a lawful receipt in writing for each payment. After my wife's death I leave all my messuages and land to my only daughter ELIZABETH WHEELER, and ask her to settle them on her children. I give to the poor people of the town of Bungay £3 to be equally divided between the two parishes. I give to ELIZABETH WHEELER my grandchild 1 of my silver tankards, and to my grandson [blank] WHEELER my other silver tankard. Both these gifts are to be given to the children when they are 21. I give to my son-in-law Mr JOHN WHEELER my seal ring in token of the love I bear to him. I give unto my good friend Mr ROBERT CHAPMAN, clerk, a piece of gold worth 20s., and to my very loving good friend Mr GEORGE GOOCH of Bungay another piece of gold of 20s. value. I make ANN my loving wife sole exrx. and I give her all my goods and chattels towards payment of my debts and legacies. Witnesses: THOMAS SEAMAN, JOHN NEWCOMEN, ROBERT CHAPMAN, GEORGE GOOCHE. Pr. at Bungay 20 Dec. 1633.

R(W) JOHN COCKE (X) of Trimley St. Martin, yeoman. (755
20 May 1630

Sick in body. I give to my loving wife during her lifetime 1 featherbed, 1 bolster, 2 pillows, half the sheets, half the pillowberes, 1 cupboard standing in the hall, 1 brass pot, half a dozen of pewter, 1 table, 1 buffet stool, 6 bowls, 3 cheese vats and 1 chair. I give to her more 1 black northern cow, 1 red cow, 4 ewes, 1 sow, 4 great shotts and 2 small ones and half the poultry. I also give to her 2 combs of rye, 1 comb of wheat, 2 combs of barley, 1 comb of peas and half the hempland called Hempshackells, to be given to her 1 month after the Michaelmas after my decease. I give to my wife for her life my messuage in Trimley St. Mary, now in the occupation of RICHARD MARCHANT, and after her death I give it to my son THOMAS. I give to my son THOMAS a cottage with a hempland and orchard in Walton and now in the occupation of WILLIAM POOPE, and another cottage in Walton which I purchased from ROBERT & ALICE NOBBS and which is now occupied by JOHN LOWNES. Also a messuage with an orchard and a piece of land in Walton, which I lately bought from THOMAS COURTUP and which is now in the occupation of WILLIAM MASE, and also a 4 acre enclosure of land in Walton and a cottage in Shotley, which I purchased from JOHN NELLY. THOMAS is to have this last cottage after the death of the Widow NELLY who now lives in it. Also I give to THOMAS a piece of land in Trimley St. Martin which I lately bought from HENRY EVEN. I give to JOHN COCK, my youngest son, a panelled chest, 1 silver spoon and my black cloak which I bought of CRICKMORE. I also bequeath to JOHN all the messuages I bought from ROBERT SIGER of Walton with 2 hemplands and an orchard belonging to them. I also give to my son JOHN a house at Shotley standing by the ten acres. I will that my exor. sell my marsh in Walton, sometime THOMAS CRICKMER's, towards the payment of my debts. I give the residue of all my goods to my son THOMAS towards the payment of my debts and the rent I owe my landlord THOMAS TYE. I make THOMAS my sole exor. Witnesses: THOMAS TYE, THOMAS CARLOE, NICHOLAS BETTS. Pr. at Ipswich 14 March 1633/4.

R(W) BARBARA GODSALVE. 8 August 1633 (756)

To be buried in the church of Stpleb in instead [sic] by my good husband. I give £3 to the poor of Gorleston to be distributed at Christmas next as the minister shall think best. I give to my 2 daughters £100 to be equally divided between them. I give to ANN BOSTOCKE my servant as much more as her wages shall come to at Michaelmas next. As for my son ROGER, there is about £500 of my husband's in the hands of Sir WILLIAM CAMPION, which he owes for the land which was my jointure. I desire ROGER to pay himself what is due to him from me out of this £500, and I also leave him the residue hoping he will remember the rest of my children. I appoint my son RICHARD GODSALVE my exor. I desire that my son THOMAS shall have all my plate that is in the house as an heirloom, except 1 silver ewer. I give to my god-daughter BARBARA GODSALVE 40s. to be paid by my exor. when she marries. [No witnesses] Pr. at Beccles 3 Jan. 1633/4.

R(W) MARY EDWARDS of Bungay, widow (N). 11 May 1634 (757)

Sick of Body. She willed that her daughter MARGARET should have all her goods and household stuff. Witnesses: THOMAS SMITH, THOMAS SEAMAN. Pr. at Bungay to MARGARET, daughter of testator, 16 May 1634.

R(W) THOMAS BALLARD. 23 April 1633 (758)

I give my land and tenements to my brother JOHN BALLARD, who is to pay my legacies that follow. I give £100 to my brother CHRISTOPHER within 1 1/2 years of my decease. My brother JOHN is to have the use of all the rooms that COVEL BANCTON now occupies, and my mother is to have the rest of the house during her life. After her death JOHN is to have the whole house. Five years after my decease 40s. each is to be paid to MARY CLARKE, to her brother ROBERT CLARKE, to ANN HARROL & MARY BALLARD. Ten years after my death £10 is to be paid to THOMAS BALLARD if he be living. I leave 2s. a week to my mother during her life. My brother JOHN is to pay this and my funeral charges. Exor. JOHN BALLARD. Witnesses: THOMAS BACON, JAMES SMITH & COVILL BANCTON. Pr. at Ipswich 7 Aug. 1633.

R(W) JOHN LANY the elder of Ipswich. 24 January 1631/2 (759)

Being above the age of four score and four years and knowing I have not long to live in this world. I give to my most loving and kind wife MARY over and above her jointure for her lifetime all my freehold land and tenements in Cratfield. At the earnest request of my son JOHN and his wife ELIZABETH I conveyed to him, amongst other things, my messuage in Basinghall Street in London, which was settled on my wife by my father as part of her jointure. I now ask my son JOHN to allow my wife to take the rents and profits of my copyhold land and tenements in Cratfield for her better maintenance. I doubt not that he will perform this request for his mother's comfort, and I bequeath to him all my copyhold lands after my wife's decease. I give to my son BENJAMIN a rent charge of £10 p.a. from my lands in Chediston. To my poor daughter MARY CLARKE I give a rent charge of £5 p.a. from my lands in Chediston, which I give to my son JOHN. I also give to JOHN my basin and ewer of silver, my best coverlet of verdners which was my father's, my long green carpet embroidered about the verges and all my law books. I give to my son BENJAMIN my standing cup of silver and gilt with its cover. To MARY my daughter my gilt tankard, which she already has, and to her and to the rest of my daughters and to my daughter-in-law 2 spurre ryalls apiece for a remembrance. I give to my brother JAMES LAMY 40s. and a ring of that value. Also I give to the poor of Cratfield 40s. and to the poor of the parish of St. Margaret in Ipswich 40s. To every one of my servants I leave 10s. each. I give to my grandchild ANNE BREAD £10. All the rest of my goods, money, plate and jewels (except hangings and window curtains which I will shall remain with my house) I give to my loving wife wishing they were more because she deserves more. I make her exrx. together with my 2 sons JOHN & BENJAMIN, beseeching Almighty God to bless them all. I have written this my last will with my own hands. If it shall please God to take my wife out of this world before me or before she has proved this will, then all my goods given to her shall be equally divided among my 6 daughters and my daughter-in-law. No witnesses. Pr. at Ipswich 4 Nov. 1633. Pr. granted to JOHN LANYE, esquire and BENJAMIN LANY, professor of theology.

R(W) GEORGE BUTTON (X) of Saxtead, yeoman. (760)
23 November 1629

I give to ROBERT my son my 7 acre close of land, meadow or pasture in Saxtead called Whinny Alland and which adjoins HENRY SINGLE's tenement, and my bottom meadows containing 5 acres. ROBERT must pay an annuity of £10 to ALICE my beloved wife in 2 equal portions on Lady Day and Michaelmas day in the south porch of Saxtead church. She has power to distrain. ROBERT must also pay the various sums he and I stand bound to pay to WILLIAM SENDALL my son-in-law and to HENRY SMITH of Saxtead. If ROBERT refuses to pay these debts, then my exor., EDWARD MOULTON of Dennington, shall have the land left to ROBERT until the money due to my son-in-law is paid. All my other land and messuages in

Saxtead I bequeath to my son ROBERT. I give to my wife ALICE my posted bed in the parlour chamber, my best featherbed and bolster, my best coverlet, a pair of my best blankets with the tester, hangings, mat and line belonging to the bedstead. I give to her more 4 pairs of my best sheets, a pillow bere, a broad cloth, my little brass pot, my best brass pan, my best kettle, 1 skillet, a little spit, my warming pan, 6 pewter platters, my square table in the hall, a turned chair, a great joined hutch that was her brother's, her coffer, 2 milk cows and £5. Also all the corn, both wheat and malt, in my chamber. Further my will is that she shall have the use during her life of my meat keep and table chair, which after her death I give to my son ROBERT. I give to my daughter ALICE, the wife of WILLIAM SENDALL 2 silver spoons, my double table and my lesser spit. I give to my daughter ELIZABETH 1 silver spoon and 2 pewter dishes. All my other goods, chattels and implements I give to my son ROBERT on condition he proves my will within 1 month of my death. If he refuses to do this, I give these goods to EDWARD MOULTON, who is joint exor. with my son ROBERT. Witnesses: WILLIAM RAVENS, HUMPHREY WARD. Pr. at Stradbroke 22 April 1634.

R(W) RICHARD BOWLTON (X)of Homersfieldin South Elmham, husbandman. 2 January 1633/4 (761)

Sick in body. To MARY my wife all her woollen and linen that was hers before marriage. The rest of my goods to be equally divided between her, my son HENRY and my daughter MARGARET. My wife is to choose her share first and then sell my children's shares. My son's share is to remain in my wife's hands towards his maintenance until he is provided for and part is to be used to bind him apprentice to a trade. Wife sole exrx. Witnesses: THOMAS MORSE, NATHANIEL HARRISON, WILLIAM BENDY, JOHN BOWLTON (X). Pr. at Homersfield 24 April 1634.

R(W) ROBERT BROADBANCKE of Linstead Magna, yeoman. 10 February 1633/4 (762)

Being visited with sickness. I give to MARY my loving wife for life my messuage with its copyhold land held of the manor of Cratfield, and also all my freehold land except one piece called Sallow pightle, which I bought from my nephew EDMUND BROADBANCKE. I also give her for life all the free and copyhold land I purchased from my brother CHRISTOPHER BROADBANCKE, and the copyhold land in Cratfield which I bought from ROBERT CARSEY. I give the Sallow pightle to my son EDMUND on condition he pays a legacy of £50 which my brother CHRISTOPHER left to his son RICHARD BROADBANCKE. I also bequeath to my son EDMUND a parcel of ground called Birds, which came to me by mortgage from my nephew EDMUND BROADBANCKE, on condition that he my son shall discharge a bond for the payment of £43 to ROBERT SMYTH of Kelsale on behalf of my nephew EDMUND. RICHARD BROADBANCKE and ROBERT SMYTH both have power to distrain. After my wife's death I give the land bequeathed to her for life to my son EDMUND on condition that he pays my daughter ELIZABETH BALDRY £30. To my daughter MARY WARD £10 to be paid within 2 years of my wife's death. £10 each to my grandson RICHARD BROADBANCKE and granddaughter MARGARET HULL within 4 and 5 years of my wife's death. All these 3 legatees have power to distrain. To MARY my loving wife all my movable goods and implements of husbandry, ready money and debts on condition that she pays my debts and the following legacies: £50 to my daughter ANN BROADBANCKE and £50 to my daughter PRISCILLA LEAGGAT. I make my wife sole exrx. and she must be bound in the sum of £100 to my nephew ROBERT SMITH of Cratfield to perform my will. If she refuses to do this, I appoint ROBERT SMITH my exor. Witnesses: ROBERT SMYTHE, SAMUEL NEWSON, GREGORY ROUSE and THOMAS LEGATT. Pr. at Yoxford 26 March 1634.

R(W) GEOFFREY CLARKE (X) of Sutton, glover. 2 April 1634 (763)

I give to my sister MARY CLARKE £10 on condition she discharges all bonds made between me and my uncles JOHN BUTTON and THOMAS POWIS. To SUSAN my wife all the rest of my goods. I make her sole exrx. Witnesses: SIMON BURWELL gent. and HENRY YORKE singleman, both of Sutton. Pr. at Wickham Market 7 April 1634.

R(W) ALICE CHRISTMAS of Woodbridge Hasketon, widow (N). [blank] April 1634 (764)

She gave all her goods to ANNE CHRISTMAS her grandchild, but they were to remain in the custody of THOMAS GOODDALL until ANNE came of age. Also she gave her £10 to remain in the hands of THOMAS GODBALDE until she is of age. Witnesses: GEORGE MANN. Pr. at Wickham Market to THOMAS GODDALL 16 April 1634.

R(W) WILLIAM CURDIE of St. Margaret Ilketshall, singleman. 4 January 1633/4 (765)

Sick of body. To be buried in Ilketshall St. Margaret churchyard. To my brother ROBERT CURDIE my tenement called Martins and all the land belonging to it in Ilketshall St. Margaret and now let to NICHOLAS ROMSEY, on condition that he pays my debts and legacies. If he refuses to do this my brother THOMAS WARREN shall have my tenement Martins. If my brother ROBERT dies before he is 21, then THOMAS WARREN inherits Martins and must pay £20 to my brother JOHN WARREN, £20 to my brother-in-law RICHARD RATCLIFFE and £20 to my brother GEORGE when he attains the age of 21. To my brother ROBERT CURDY my tenement and land in the parish of South Elmham St. Margaret, which is now in the occupation of JOHN NORMAN, but if he dies before he is 21 this property is left to my brothers THOMAS & JOHN WARREN, RICHARD RATCLIFFE & ROBERT GOOCH. I give £25 to THOMAS WARREN and £20 to JOHN WARREN two years after my decease. I give £20 to RICHARD RATCLIFFE 3 years after my death and £20 to ROBERT GOOCH 5 years after. I leave £4 to RICHARD RATCLIFFE, son of RICHARD

RATCLIFFE, when he is 21, and to THOMAS RATCLIFFE, my godson, £5 when he is 21. I bequeath £3 each to my nephews JOHN & ROBERT RATCLIFFE when they are 21. I give 40s. to my kinswoman MABEL AYCKRIN within 2 years of my decease. I give 10s. to the poor of the parish of Ilketshall St. Margaret, and 10s. to ROBERT SAMPSON now servant to my father. All the rest of my goods and chattels I give to my brother ROBERT CURDY, whom I make sole exor. Witnesses: GEORGE GOOCH, WILLIAM GIRLINGE (X). Pr. at Beccles 15 April 1634.

R(W) SARAH EDWARD (X) of Beccles, spinster. (766)
22 April 1631

I bequeath to SARAH EDWARD my mother all my fine hose yarn. I give 40s. each to my sisters MARY GIRLING, ABIGAIL NOBBS & SUSAN, the wife of WILLIAM COLLYNS. I bequeath 20s. each to REBECCA & SARAH, the daughters of my sister MARY GIRLING, when they are 21. I give 20s. each when they are 21 to ELIZABETH daughter of my sister ABIGAIL NEWSON and to MARY daughter of my deceased sister ELIZABETH FITLING. Also 40s. to THOMAS son of WILLIAM & SUSAN COLLYNS when he is 21. All the residue of my personal estate I bequeath to my father WILLIAM EDWARD, whom I make sole exor. Witnesses: THOMAS DAYNES, EDWARD DENNINGTON (X). Pr. at Beccles 24 April 1634.

R(W) EDWARD GOFF (X) the elder of Ipswich, clothworker. (767)
17 February 1633/4

In reasonable good health. I give to EDWARD GOFF my son £100 to be paid to him on Christmas day next after the date of this will. To my son TOBIAS £80 and £20 to my daughter ELIZABETH wife of THOMAS LAYTER and £50 to my daughter ALICE wife of EDWARD ELLETT, all to be paid on Christmas day after the date of my will. I give to my 14 grandchildren 6s. 8d. each to be paid them at Christmas next. All my unbequeathed goods and chattels I give to my sons EDWARD & TOBIAS, who must pay my legacies and funeral expenses and prove this will. I appoint them to be exors. Witnesses: JOHN GOFF and ROBERT LORD senior. Pr. at Ipswich 28 March 1634.

R(W) JOHN GARNHAM the elder of Gosbeck, yeoman. (768)
25 November 1633

Sick of body. To JOHN my son, after the death of ANNE my wife, all my messuages and land both free and copyhold. My wife is to have the occupation of my land during her life. She must commit no strip or waste. I will to ANNE my daughter for life one little chamber and in the chamber 1 posted bed with its bedding as it stands, 1 cupboard, 1 square table, 1 buffet form and an old chair. I will that she shall have free access to the fire in the hall to do such business as she shall have to do and doing as little harm as she can. ANNE my daughter is not to object if my wife wants to make use of the little chamber bequeathed to her for 1 or 2 nights. I bequeath all my movable goods to my wife, who must maintain my children until they can support themselves. My wife is to pay £25 each to my daughters ELIZABETH and EALES [sic] at the rate of £5 p.a. starting when they reach age of 21. They have power to distrain. If my wife remarries all the legacies made to her are void, and my son JOHN shall take possession of my house and land and pay my wife £3 p.a. in satisfaction of her dowry. My wife is to pay my daughter ANNE 40s. p.a. in 2 equal sums at Lady Day and Michaelmas, and £3 p.a. to my son JOHN in 2 equal payments on the feast of St. John the Baptist and Christmas day. After my wife's death, JOHN is to continue the payment of 40s. p.a. to my daughter ANNE, who has power to distrain. I bequeath to my son JOHN a long table, a cupboard and a buffet form in the hall, a cheese press, a long stool and all the shelves in the dairy and one cart. I give all the rest of my moveable goods to my 3 daughters, and if my son JOHN dies my land is to be equally divided among my 3 daughters. Wife sole exrx. Witnesses: THOMAS GARNHAM & MARGARET HALL (X). Pr. at Ipswich 28 March 1634.

R(W) JOHN GENTRY of Little Wenham, husbandman. (769)
2 April 1630

I give 20s. apiece to my sons WILLIAM, THOMAS, ROBERT & JOHN, to be paid to one son a year starting 1 year after my decease. I give £3 to my daughter ELIZABETH wife of THOMAS HARVEY of Ramsey in Essex to be paid to her husband within 6 months of my death. The remainder of my goods, as horses, cows, sheep, pigs, household stuff and implements of husbandry I give to TAMSIN my wife to pay my debts and funeral expenses. I make her sole exrx. of my will. Witnesses: SAMUEL TAYLOR clerk and JAMES IFORDOM. Pr. at Ipswich 7 April 1634.

R(W) WILLIAM GOSLEN (X) of Stonham Aspal, (770)
blacksmith. 17 April 1634

Sick of body. I give to JOAN my wife and her heirs for ever that tenement at the Street which I purchased from DENECIOUS DRYE and is now let to GREGORY BLOMFILD & JOHN LORD, except the shop and travis. I give the shop, travis and the yard between them and all my shop tools to JOAN my wife for her life, and after her death to my eldest son WILLIAM, who must pay 40s. each to my sons JOHN & THOMAS and to my daughters ANNE & JOAN at yearly intervals on St. John the Baptist's day. These payments are to be made in the south porch of Stonham Aspal church and the recipients have benefit of suvivorship. If WILLIAM dies, the shop, travis and yard pass to JOHN. All the rest of my movable goods, cattle corn and money I give to my wife whom I make sole exrx. and who is to pay my debts and bring up my children. Witnesses: STEPHEN BLOMFIELD, ROBERT CATCHPOLE junior, JOHN BLOMFILD (X) & THOMAS SALLOWES. Pr. at Ipswich 5 May 1634.

R(W) ROSE LACIE (X) of Wickham Market, widow. (771)
13 January 1633/4

To my daughter ROSE LACEI the 2 rooms wherein I now dwell for her life and after her death I give them to my son WILLIAM. I bequeath to my son WILLIAM all my lands and tenements in Wickham Market in which REUBEN GODFERYE late did dwell. I give 40s. a year to my daughter ROSE to be paid by WILLIAM. ROSE has power to distrain, and is sole exrx. Witnesses: HENRY ASHLY, SAMUEL FORDE (X) & WILLIAM WINFIELD. Pr. at Wickham Market 27 March 1634.

R(W) ELIZABETH LEEDS (X) of Ipswich, widow. (772)
26 November 1633

Sick in body. I give to my 4 children JOHN, STEPHEN, ELIZABETH & SARAH my messuage in the parish of St. Margaret in Ipswich now in the occupation of JOHN COLBY. I give to my son JOHN my silver beaker and my late husband's cloak and sword. I give to my daughter ELIZABETH my silver cup and my marrying ring. I give to my son STEPHEN 4 silver spoons, a piece of gold worth half a crown and my late husband's dagger. I give to SARAH my daughter 2 silver spoons, a blue pot tipped with silver. These gifts are to be given to my children by my exors. as they reach the age of 21. All the rest of my goods and chattels, my debts and legacies being paid, I give to be equally divided amongst my children by my exors. I appoint JOHN WITTAM and LUKE TOWER of Ipswich exors. of my will. Witnesses: RICHARD GRIMESTON snr. and SUSAN CORIE (X). Pr. at Ipswich 28 March 1634.

R(W) ANN RECCARDE of Ilketshall St. Andrew, singlewoman. (773)
10 November 1630

To be buried in churchyard of Ilketshall St. Andrew parish church. My grandfather, PETER LANGLY, left me £5 in his will and I ask my exrx. to pay this sum to my loving sister ELIZABETH RICCURD when she attains the age of 21, and also to give her 1 silver spoon now in the custody of my exrx. My father, SAMUEL RICURD, in his will left £40 to be paid to me at my age of 21, but he left so many debts it is doubtful whether I shall ever receive so much money. Nevertheless, I ask my exrx., my loving mother ANN wife of WILLIAM URTIES and exrx. of my father's will, if the money ever comes into her hands to pay £20 to my sister ELIZABETH and the remainder to be equally divided between my 5 brothers: SAMUEL, WILLIAM, PETER, JOHN & TIMOTHY when they are 21. I give £5 to my mother towards my burial and funeral charges. I give to ROBERT & RACHEL URTIES, my brother and sister-in-law, 2 silver spoons. Mother ANN URTIES, sole exrx. Witnesses: WILLIAM URTIES, GRACE HUNTINGTON (X). Pr. at Beccles 26 April 1634.

R(W) LIONEL RAYDON of Cretingham, yeoman. 14 April 1634 (774)

First I give to my wife MARY all the goods and household stuff that were hers before my marriage with her. I give to my cousin JAMES WITH my messuage and all my land until my son LIONEL shall reach the age of 21. JAMES WITH is to use the profits from the land to educate my son, once my debts have been paid. I give to my exor. all my bonds, bills, debts, cattle and household goods towards the payment of my debts. If there is any money left over after my debts, funeral charges and the expenses of proving my will have been paid, the surplus is to be paid to my son when reaches the age of 21. I make my loving son-in-law JOHN DAYNES sole exor., and my cousin JAMES WITH supervisor. Witnesses: JEFFREY CURTIS, HENRY CROWFOOTE. Pr. at Ipswich 1 May 1634.

R(W) ROBERT SPENSER of Rendlesham, esquire. (775)
14 February 1633/4

Sick in body. To be buried in the chancel of Rendlesham church. I bequeath to EDWARD my eldest son my capital messuage, commonly called Naunton Hall, and all its land lying in Rendlesham and Wantisden. This house and land is now in my own occupation. EDWARD must pay £200 to my second son HENRY SPENCER in the space of 1 year after my decease. If my sons HENRY, WILLIAM & LEONARD and my daughter MARY JERMINE have no lawful heirs, I give to my son EDWARD my messuage in Reigate, Surrey. I give to my wife ELIZABETH for her life my messuage and land in Campsea Ash, Tunstall and Blaxhall and now in the occupation of PHILIP CRAPNELL. She must within 1 month of my death release all her right of dower in my other property. After her death I give the land and house left to my wife to my son WILLIAM, who must then pay £100 each to my son LEONARD and to my daughter JOAN SPENCER. Within 6 months of my death £600 is to be paid into the hands of my wife, who is to use the interest on this money to educate and maintain my sons WILLIAM & LEONARD and my daughter JOAN. She must enter into a bond of £1000 with my exor. to pay £200 each to these 3 children when they reach the age of 21. I give all my goods and chattels to my son EDWARD to pay my debts and legacies. Immediately after my decease he must enter into a bond for £2000 with WILLIAM DADE esquire of Tannington and GERVASE HUBBALD of Rendlesham clerk, truly to perform my will. I nominate my son EDWARD sole exor. Witnesses: WILLIAM DADE, WILLIAM GOODWYN, GERVASE HUBBALD, THOMAS AMMOND. Pr. at Wickham Market 7 April 1634.

R(W) ELIZABETH TRAFFORTH (X) of Aldeburgh, widow. (776)
9 April 1634

I give to ELIZABETH BUCKE my daughter 1 old cupboard standing in the hall next to the chamber, 1 turned chair in the chamber and 1 board cloth. I give to SARAH GODBALL, my grandchild, 1 feather bed in the chamber with a truckle bedstead, 2 feather bolsters, 1 feather pillow, 1 pair sheets and a coverlet. These gifts are to be left in the hands of EDMUND BIXBEY, beer brewer of Aldeburgh, until SARAH is 16. If SARAH dies before then, these goods are to go to my daughter CATHERINE COOKE. I give to THOMAS GODBALL, my grandchild, a table standing in the hall chamber with a form belonging to it; these are to remain in the hands of JOHN LYNASH until THOMAS reaches his age of 24. If THOMAS dies before he is 24, these gifts are to go to JOHN GODBALL, my other grandson. I give all my wearing apparel, both linen and woollen, (except for 1 old under petticoat which I give to MARY WARD my maid servant) to be equally divided between my 2 daughters ELIZABETH & CATHERINE. All the rest of my movable goods I give to EDMUND BIXSBEY to pay my debts and see my body brought to the ground. Any surplus to be given to my daughter CATHERINE COOKE. Immediately after my decease EDMUND BIXSBY shall cause an inventory to be made of all my goods not bequeathed in this will by 2 honest men of Aldeburgh in order that there may be no fraud by him. Exor. EDMUND BIXSBY. Witnesses: THOMAS TIRNALLE, THOMAS COOKE, ROBERT GARERD. Pr. at Yoxford 16 April 1634.

R(W) RICHARD WYTH (X) of Sibton, yeoman. 11 April 1632 (777)

I give to ELIZABETH my daughter £5 to be paid within 1 year of my decease. I give to ANTHONY BAKER my grandchild all my movable goods (unless otherwise bequeathed), which are either in the possession of ANTHONY BAKER my son-in-law or at my house in Pettaugh, or their inventory value, when he reaches the age of 21. I give my best bedstead furnished, all my linen, 1 pair of needlework valences, 4 embroidered chairs and 2 stools to my wife. I give to ELIZABETH BAKER my grandchild £120 to be paid to her when she is 21 or on her marriage day, whichever shall happen first. If my wife remarries before my 2 grandchildren are 21, their legacies are to be given immediately to their parents, ANTHONY & ELIZABETH BAKER. I give all my bonds, bills and money to my exrx. to pay my legacies and debts. I make my wife sole exrx. Witnesses: JOHN BOTTERED (X) JOHN HILL, ANNE BARBER. Pr. at Yoxford 16 April 1634.

R(W) JOHN WAYLAND (X) of Farnham, singleman. 6 April 1633 (778)

I give to WILLIAM PITT jnr. of Farnham £20 when he is 21, and to his sister ELIZABETH PITT the younger £10 when she is 21, and to their brother THOMAS PITT £10 when he is 21. These legacies are with benefit of survivorship. I give £10 each to ANNE & LAWRENCE, daughter and son of LAWRENCE PELLS the elder of Bromeswell, to be paid when they are 21; with benefit of survivorship. I give to WILLIAM PITT the elder 1 bed and bedstead furnished as it now stands in the house of LAWRENCE PELLS of Bromeswell, and I give a box and a chest now in the same house to WILLIAM PITT jnr. I make WILLIAM PITT the elder my exor. Witnesses: JOHN TOMPSON, RICHARD BOUTMAN (X). Pr. at Wickham Market 26 March 1634.

R(W) HENRY GROOME of Ufford. 3 April 1634 (779

Sick of body. I make EDMUND GROOME my brother sole exor. of my will, and give him all my corn growing at Pettistree towards the payment of my legacies. He is to take the money from the sale of the timber I lately sold to SOPHFORD of Ipswich and use it to pay my legacies. I give to MARGARET my loving wife for her life all my land in Ufford lately purchased from JEFFREY BURWELL esquire, THOMAS STYLE, ANTHONY BURWOOD, NICHOLAS TOOKLY and others. After her death I give these lands to EDWARD GROOME my nephew. I bequeath all my household stuff and plate to my wife. After her death I will that my nephew EDWARD GROOME shall have my cypress chest, my brazen andirons and my gold seal ring. I give to my wife all my cattle and all my corn growing in Ufford. After my wife's death I give to my nephew EDMUND GROOME my manor of Utleys in Ufford. I give £100 to RICHARD ERRINGTON, my brother-in-law, to be paid by my brother EDMUND GROOME within 2 years of my decease. If RICHARD ERRINGTON has died before this time, then the £100 is to be divided between his 3 children. I give to my brother EDMUND my silver buttons which I usually wear on my doublet. I give to my sister MARGARET SANSBY 20 nobles to be paid to her every year in 2 equal portions at Lady Day and Michaelmas. I also give to her all my clothes. I give £10 to each of her children to be paid as they reach the age of 21. I give to the poor of Ufford £10 to be paid in 5 annual installments of £2, and £5 to the poor of Pettistree to be paid in 5 installments of £1. I give £5 to the poor of Wickham Market to be paid within 1 month of my decease. I give 4 sheep to my servant GEORGE GOLDBALD, and to JOHN SARNON my servant 2 sheep. My will is that my exor. shall pay to EDWARD HAMMOND of Westleton the £150 left to him in the will of MARGARET FATHERS. Witnesses: EDMUND BURWELL, JOHN BURWELL, EDWARD STYLE. Pr. at Wickham Market 7 April 1634.

R(W) RICHARD SMITH of Spexhall. [no date] (780)

His will is not extant, but the following notes, made 19 Oct. 1633, are. To finish the last will and testament of RICHARD SMITH of Spexhall. My wife ALICE, my sole exrx., is to hold for her life my messuage and land in South Elmham St. Margaret and St. Nicholas. She must pay my daughter MARY £5 p.a. towards her maintenance. After my wife's death the messuage and land left to her are to go to my daughter MARY, or, if she dies without heirs, to ROBERT son of ESDRAS SMITH. I give £120 to be paid by my exrx. to my daughter MARY when she is 21, but if she dies before then my exrx. is to keep this money, and after her death it is to be divided amongst the daughters of my brother and sisters. I give to my daughter MARY immediately after my decease my best bed fully furnished, 8 pairs of sheets, my best brass pot, my 2 brass kettles, 6 pewter dishes and my cupboard in the hall where I now dwell. I give all my goods to my exrx. I give 10s. to my god-daughter PHINITE [sic] HOWELL, and 10s. to the poor of Halesworth. Supervisors of my will: my cousin WILLIAM SMITH & JOHN ROPE; I give 10s. to each of them. Pr. 15 May 1634 [no place given].

R(W) JOHN BRABONE (X) of Syleham, potter. 8 April 1634 (781)

He decided to make his will by the holy counsel and discretion of his wife and most merciful God. I give to my brother ROBERT BRABON all my close called Dentons in Weybread and my close called New Close in Syleham for his life, and after his death to RICHARD BRABON, son of my brother SAMUEL. I also give to my brother ROBERT my half share of the land in Weybread which he and I lately purchased from ANTHONY BARRY the younger of Syleham. I give to SAMUEL BRABON, my brother, all my movable goods and £5. I give £5 each to the following: my sister AGNES wife of JOHN TIBENHAM; my sister CHRISTIAN wife of ROBERT COOKE; my sister CATHERINE BARROW widow; my sister LYDIA wife of WILLIAM BADCOCK; and to AGNES & ESTHER, the daughters of JOHN TIBENHAM. All these legacies are to be paid within 2 years of my death in the south porch of Weybread church. I give £5 each when they are 21 to RICHARD, AGNES & ANN the children of my brother SAMUEL BRABON. I give £5 each when they are 21 to MAGDALEN, daughter of my sister CATHERINE BARROW and to FRANCES daughter of JOHN TIBENHAM. I give £10 to CHRISTIAN wife of JOHN SANDERS. I give 20s. to the poor of Weybread and 20s. to the poor of Syleham to be distributed within 1 month of my decease. My brother ROBERT is to be my sole exor. Supervisor JAMES MEENE of Weybread. Witnesses: JAMES MEENE, JOHN BROWNE. Pr. at Beccles 3 May 1634.

R(W) THOMAS FENN of Monk Soham, yeoman. (782)
1 December 1633

I give to FRANCES my wife all my free and copyhold land and tenements in Tuddenham for her life and after her decease to my son LIONEL. I give to LIONEL my church bible. I give to my son THOMAS my book called Luther, and to my son BARTHOLOMEW my book called Perdicall [possibly Pardicall]. I give to NATHANIEL my son my book called Cooper on Romans, and to RICHARD my son my book called Dade on the Commandments. I give to my son WILLIAM my great bible. I give to my daughter SUSAN, wife of HENRY GLADES, the book called the Treatise of the Church, and to my daughter ANNE the book called The Way of Life. I give all my other books to be equally divided between my daughter FRANCES, and THOMAS & LYDIA FENN, children of my son THOMAS. To all my other grandchildren I give 2s. 6d. each. I give £3 to my grandson THOMAS, and £2 to his sister LYDIA when they reach age of 21. I give to FRANCES my wife my best bedstead with featherbed, bolster and all that belongs to it. Also all my linen and her own clothes. My movable goods are to be sold and, after my debts and funeral charges have been paid, the money is to be divided as follows. £10 each to my sons BARTHOLOMEW and NATHANIEL, and the residue to be divided among my other children: SUSAN wife of HENRY GLADES, ANN, RICHARD, FRANCES & WILLIAM, but RICHARD's and WILLIAM's shares are to be £5 larger than those of their sisters. However, my wife is to have the use of all my stock and movables during her lifetime, and must be bound to my supervisor to leave these goods at the time of her death as directed in my will. She must also be bound to keep my house and buildings in Tuddenham in good repair. If she refuses, all legacies made to her become void, and my son LIONEL shall be my exor. I appoint my wife sole exrx. I give 10s. to the poor of Monk Soham. I make my brother ROBERT FENN supervisor and give him 10s. for his pains. Witnesses: JOHN CULLAINE, HENRY CUTTENNE (X). Pr. at Yoxford 8 May 1634.

R(W) WILLIAM WOLSEY (X) of Pakefield, yeoman. (783)
26 April 1634

Weak in body. I give to ROBERT WOLSIE my son all the messuages and buildings in Pakefield Street which I lately purchased from JOHN COLBY the elder, after the death of my wife RUTH. I also give to ROBERT when he is 21 all my lands, houses and woods, both free and copyhold, in Carlton Colville. ROBERT must pay £5 to my grandson WILLIAM THIRKITTLE when he is 21, and 40s. p.a. to my son WILLIAM. I give to my son RICHARD when he is 21 all my messuages and land in Pakefield, now in my own occupation, and which I bought from Sir OWEN SMITH, on condition he pays £4 to my grandchild SARAH THIRKITTLE when she is 21 and 20s. p.a. to my son WILLIAM. If ROBERT & RICHARD die without heirs, the property left to them is to go to my daughter CHRISTIAN THIRKITLE, to whom I give £40 to be paid within 1 year of my death. I bequeath £120 to my son ROBERT to be paid to him when he is 16, and £20 to be paid to my son RICHARD when he is 18. The residue of my goods, chattels and credits I give to my wife RUTH whom I make sole exrx. Witnesses: WILLIAM GIRLING clerk, JOHN COBB, THOMAS BRANSBYE & JOHN EVERARD. Pr. at Pakefield 3 May 1634.

R(W) THOMAS POTTER of Chediston, yeoman. 27 May 1633 (784)

Weak in body. I give 20s. to the poor of Chediston to be distributed immediately after my decease, and 40s. for a stock for the poor of the same parish. I give 40s. to the poor of Halesworth, 10s. to the poor of Wissett, 10s. to the poor of Linstead, 5s. to the poor of Cookley; all these sums to be paid immediately after my death by my exrx. to the churchwardens of each parish. I give to BRIDGET POTTER my loving wife the use and occupation of all my lands and houses until the Michaelmas day after my decease. After this date I give to my son THOMAS all my land and tenements in Wissett and Chediston, which I bought from ROBERT STANTON gent. and his son JOHN which are now in THOMAS's occupation. Also to THOMAS all my free and copyhold land in Halesworth and Cookley. I give to my wife for her life all the houses and land I purchased from WILLIAM GOODWYNE, my deceased father-in-law, and after her decease to my son RICHARD. I give to my wife the use and occupation for life of all those my houses and land which were in the possession of one SMYTHE and are now in the occupation of RICHARD SPATCHETT & ROBERT GOODWYNE. After my wife's death I give this property to RICHARD the son of my son

THOMAS. I bequeath to my daughters MARY, ALICE & ELIZABETH £120 each to be paid to them by my wife within 1 year of my decease. I give £40 to my daughter MARY KNIGHTS, £20 to my daughter SUSAN FELLA and £20 to my daughter FRANCES SAMPSON to be paid by my wife within a year of my death. I give 10s yearly for 4 years to my sister ALICE SONE, if she live so long, to be paid by my wife, and 20s. to my sister SUSAN BURWARD to be paid by my wife. I give to my son RICHARD all the land I lately purchased from SAMUEL GARROLD, from NATHANIEL, EZEKIEL & WILLIAM KNIGHTS and from EDMUND KEMPE. If my wife remarries she is to release all her right of dower in my lands to my sons. All my bonds, bills, ready money, goods and chattels, except my mill which is to remain in the mill house, I leave to my wife after my debts, legacies and funeral charges have been paid. I make her sole exrx. I appoint my loving son RICHARD supervisor, desiring that peace, unity and concord may continue between my wife and children. I give RICHARD £5 for his pains and care. If my wife dies before she has proved my will, then my son THOMAS shall be exor. Witnesses: BENJAMIN BULLER, HENRY FISKE. Pr. at Beccles 19 May 1634.

R(W) ELIZABETH CARVER (X) of Shotley, widow. (785)
20 October 1632

In perfect health. 20s. to be distributed amongst poor of Shotley on day of my burial. All my lands and tenements I give to my grandchild ADAM FULLER, son of my deceased son ADAM FULLER. Also my best posted bedstead with my best featherbed, feather bolster and all other things belonging to the same as it stands. I also give to him a flock bed with a bolster, 2 pairs of sheets, 4 sheep and a lamb to be chosen by him, a milk cow, a copper kettle, my best cupboard, my best chest, a form in the chamber, a hutch at the bed's foot, my best framed table, 6 of my best pieces of pewter, my largest brass pot and my biggest brass pan. I give to ADAM FULLER £30 when he reaches his age of 21. I give to my grandson THOMAS, son of ADAM FULLER, an ewe and a lamb and 40s. when he is 21. I give to my grandchild GRACE, daughter of ADAM FULLER, a posted bedstead, a featherbed and a flock bed on it and everything else belonging to this bed. Also a little box with a lock and key, a little cupboard, a frame table and £5 when she is 21 or on her marriage day, whichever comes first. I give to ELIZABETH, daughter of ADAM FULLER, £5 when she is 21 or on her marriage day. I give to my grandchildren ELIZABETH and ANNA, daughters of my son THOMAS FULLER, 20s. each when they are 20 or on their marriage days. To ELIZABETH CLAY alias WENTFORD, my grandchild, my new featherbed, bedstead and bolster as it stands, a brass pot, a little box with a lock and key, a great chair and £5 when she reaches age of 21 or marries. I give also to her a danske chest and half of my clothes, except my silk apron and scarf which I give to MARGARET wife of my son ROBERT. The other half of my clothes I give to my grandchild GRACE FULLER. I give 20s. when he is 21 to my grandson PHILIP FULLER. I bequeath 10s. to my son THOMAS and 40s. to my son ROBERT, both sums to be paid within 3 months of my death. If my son THOMAS makes any attempt to interfere with my bequests to my grandson ADAM FULLER, then all my legacies to him and his children shall be void. ADAM is to have the profits of the land left to him immediately after my decease, and my exor. is to pay 1s. in the pound interest on the legacies to my other grandchildren until they are paid. My funeral charges, debts and legacies being paid, I leave the residue of my goods to be equally divided among the sons and daughters of THOMAS FULLER, who is not to benefit from this clause in my will. I make my son ROBERT and my grandson ADAM exors. Supervisors: CHRISTOPHER ANDREWS mariner and THOMAS BRANDESTON gentleman, both of Chelmondiston. I give them 10s. each. My son ROBERT is to enter into a bond with CHRISTOPHER ANDREWS and my grandson ADAM to pay all my legacies, and if he refuses to do this then I make CHRISTOPHER ANDREWS my exor. in his place. Witnesses: THOMAS BRANDESTON, SAMUEL BENNET (X). Codicil made 3 April 1634. Growing weak in body. I do give to my grandson ADAM FULLER the messuage in which I dwell with all the land belonging to it and held of the manor of Erwarton Hall. Witnesses: THOMAS CARTER, ROSE FULLER (X), SUSAN COOKE (X). Pr. at Ipswich 5 May 1634.

W(R) MARGARET LUDMAN (X) of Kettleburgh, widow. (786)
1 March 1633/4

Sick of body. I give £20 to my nephew JOHN MAWLINGE of Kettleburgh and £25 to my nephew THOMAS MAWLINGE of Stonham Aspal; both legacies to be paid 2 years after my death. I give £60 to JANE MAWLYNGE, my niece and servant, to be paid within 1 year of my decease. I bequeath to JANE MAWLYNGE and to EDENY [sic] BERY, daughter of JOHN BERY and my servant, all my chests and coffers and all the linen in them on the day of my death, except any chests or linen otherwise bequeathed, to be equally divided between them. Also to JANE MAWLYNGE my best posted bedstead, 2 feather beds, 2 feather bolsters, 2 coverlets, 2 blankets, 6 pillows, my best petticoat, my 2 best waistcoats, 1 cupboard standing in the hall, 1 warming pan and a wicker chair. All these gifts are to be delivered to her at Michaelmas next after my decease. I give to THOMAS BERY of Terling in Essex £10 to be paid within 1 1/2 years of my death, and to him at Michaelmas after my decease my best bedstead now standing in the chamber over the buttery and the hangings round it, 1 featherbed, 2 feather bolsters, 2 down pillows, 2 blankets, 1 coverlet, 1 pair of sheets and 2 pillow beeres. I give to ROBERT BERY, my servant and son of JOHN BERY late of Easton, £13 to be paid within 8 years after the date of this will. I give to EDENY BERY £25 to be paid to her when she is 22. These legacies to ROBERT & EDENY are with benefit of survivorship. I give to EDENY BERY at Michaelmas next a coffer standing at the foot of my trundle bed, a little framed table, a little joined form, 2 buffet stools, 1 pair of sheets, 2 pillow beeres, one trundle bedstead, 1 flock bed, 2 feather bolsters, 1 coverlet and 1 blanket. I give 40s. each, with benefit of survivorship, to the children of my late sister-in-law MARGARET PALMER: ROGER PALMER, SUSAN wife of RICHARD HEYWARD and MARGARET wife of JOHN STEVENSON. I give 1 pair of sheets to my nephew WILLIAM son of JAMES MAWLING, and to his sister REBECCA £3 when she is 21 and a pair of sheets. I leave 5s. to MARGARET DENNY, widow of Saxtead, to be paid within 1 month of my decease. My nephew JAMES MAWLINGE owes me £36. My late husband left him £10 and I now discharge this legacy by forgiving him £10 of this debt, and I do further forgive him £20 as my own free gift on condition that he acts as my exor. I give 20s. to MARY daughter of JOHN MAWLINGE, late of Butley, within 2 years. I give 10s. each to JOHN BACON the elder and his son JOHN, both thatchers, to be paid within 1 year of my death. I give £10 to ROSE daughter of my deceased brother HENRY MAWLINGE late of Charsfield and now wife of WILLIAM WARNE to be paid within 1 year of my death. To her sister EDENYE, now wife of JOHN SAVAGE, I give £6 13s. 4d. to be paid within 1 1/2 years of my decease. I give £6 13s. 4d. each, with benefit of survivorship, to my nieces MARGARET & WINEFRED, daughters of the late HENRY MAWLING, when they are 22. My nephew JAMES MAWLINGE sole exor., to whom I give all the unbequeathed residue of my goods and chattels to pay my legacies and see me decently buried. I make my good friend GEORGE RUSSELL of Cretingham supervisor and give him 40s. for his pains. Witnesses: FRANCIS RUMSEY (X), JOHN BACON (X), GEORGE RUSSELL. Pr. at Wickham Market 7 May 1634.

R(W) RICHARD GLOZIER/GLAZIER of Burgh castle, husbandman. 10 May 1634 (787)

Sick of body. I give to ELIZABETH my wife all my house and lands in Burgh Castle for ever. I give to my daughter ELIZABETH KING £5 and to my son WILLIAM £4 to be paid 1 year after my decease. I give to ELIZABETH TURNER, daughter of my daughter ELIZABETH KING, 40s. when she reaches age of 21; and 20s. to JAMES, son of ELIZABETH KING, when he is 24 (with benefit of survivorship). If my son WILLIAM dies before his legacy is paid, half is to be given to his wife and half to my daughter ELIZABETH KING. If she dies before receiving her legacy, it is to be divided between her children. I make my wife sole exrx. Supervisor RICHARD TAYLOR of Burgh Castle. Witnesses: THOMAS FALKE, WILLIAM NEWSON (X), EDMUND REEVE (X), ERASMUS REALL (X). Pr. at Burgh Castle 22 May 1634.

R(W) JOHN BENNET of Washbrook, yeoman. 9 November 1633 (788)

I bequeath unto 6 of the poorest people of Washbrook 10s. p.a. for 5 years after my death to be equally divided among them by my exors. on the 9th day of October each year. I give to my brother EDWARD BENNET and his heirs male all my copyhold land, called Millers, in Aldham. He must pay £5 apiece to each of the children of PHILIP GALLANT, glazier of Ipswich, at the age of 20; £5 each to the children of THOMAS WEST, back stiller of Hadleigh, at the age of 21; and £5 each when 21 to the children that my deceased sister CLIFFORD had by RICHARD CLIFFORD. All these payments are to be made in the south porch of Aldham church, and the legatees have power to distrain. I give to my exors. for 6 years my messuage called Wynnowes and its land in Thurleston, Akenham and Westerfield which is let to JOHN ELLET. Exors. are to use the profits of this property to pay £20 p.a. to my daughter KATHERINE for her maintenance in food, drink and apparel. My exors. are also to pay £60 each when 21 to THOMAS, JOHN and MARGARET, children of my brother-in-law WASPE and £5 to his son SAMUEL, and to pay the expenses of putting out SAMUEL as an apprentice. The residue of the profits are to be used to pay my debts, and any surplus is to go to my daughter ANNE. When the 6 years are up, the house and land called Wynnowes are bequeathed to my daughter KATHERINE or if she dies to my daughter ANNE. I give to my daughter ANNE BENNET all my copyhold land in Washbrook called Clies, which is let to JOHN PERMAN; also my barn and 2 fields called Haerewords Downs in Chattisham; also the lease of the farm where I dwell in Washbrook. Within 6 months of my decease my exors. are to sell to the best advantage my stock of corn, cattle, household stuff and implements. The money is to be used to pay my debts, and I give the overplus to my daughter ANNE. However, if my loving master Sir THOMAS TURPLE otherwise provides, then my will is that my daughter ANNE should have my corn, cattle and household goods immediately after my decease. All my other goods and chattels I give to my daughter MARY. Exors. BESLEINE BARKER esq., and my daughter ANNE BENNET. As a small remembrance of my great respect for him I give BESLEINE BARKER 40s. to buy a ring. Witnesses: JOHN BENNETT, JOSEPH CLARK, JOHN SMART, SAMUEL WARD (X). Pr. at Ipswich 20 Jan. 1633/4.

R(W) WILLIAM LAXHAM of Charsfield, yeoman. [blank] 1629 (789)

Sick in body. I bequeath to my wife ELIZABETH for life all my houses and lands in Charsfield. She must pay to MARGERY, wife of JOHN FOX, £4 p.a. towards the bringing up and better education of my 3 grandchildren. After my wife's death, I give my houses and land to my said three grandchildren MARGERY, MARGARET and ELIZABETH LAYHAM. They must pay their mother MARGERY FOX £3 p.a. All these payments are to be made in the porch of Charsfield church, and the legatees have power to distrain. I give to my grandchild MARGERY LAYHAM my posted bedstead, now standing in the parlour where I dwell, with a featherbed and bolster, 1 pillow, 1 coverlet, a pair of sheets and a pair of blankets. I also give to her my greatest table now standing in the hall where I dwell with a form belonging to it and 1 buffet stool. Also I bequeath to her my great cauldron and 2 great platters. All these gifts are to be delivered to her at her age of 21. I give to my grandchild MARGARET LAYHAM my table now standing in the hall, which I bought from JOHN WOULTON then dwelling in Otley, and 1 buffet stool. I also leave her my greatest kettle and 2 pewter platters. My wife is to have the use of these goods during her life. I give to my grandchild ELIZABETH LAYHAM 1 trundle bedstead with a flockbed and bolster, and a coverlet. Also my livery table now standing in the hall, my cupboard standing in the parlour, my brass pot which I had from my first wife and 2 pewter platters. My wife is to have the use of these gifts to

ELIZABETH during her lifetime. Wife sole exrx. and I give her the residue of my goods. Witnesses: GEORGE BRULL, THOMAS HOLMES (X), WILLIAM PAYNE. Pr. at Wickham Market 30 May 1634.

R(W) JAMES LEECH of Shottisham (N). 21 April 1634 (790)

He gave all his goods to his wife THOMASINE towards the payment of his debts and the education of his children. Witnesses: THOMAS CORBOLE and ROBERT MORE. Pr. at Wickham Market 30 May 1634.

R(W) REGINALD SKINNER (X) of Peasenhall, cooper. (791)
30 March 1631

I bequeath all my goods and lands to my son JAMES, provided he pays my legacies. I give 20s. to EMY SMITH my apprentice when she reaches age of 24; 10s. to the poor of Peasenhall. My son JAMES is to be sole exor. Witnesses: EDWARD BOUTH senior, THOMAS SMYTH. Pr. at Yoxford 29 May 1634.

R(W) JOHN THOMPSON of Aldeburgh. 9 December 1633 (792)

I give to MARGARET my loving and faithfull wife for ever my cottage wherein I now dwell. I give 40s. each when 21 to the children of my sister SUSAN ROBSON. Also 40s. each when 21 to the children of my sister ANN FUMIALL and to those of my sister MARGARET PULHAM. All payments to be made in the south porch of Aldeburgh church. I will that MARGARET my wife shall within 1 year of my decease enter into a bond of £50 with Mr THOMAS JOHNSON of Aldbridge to pay the above legacies. I give all my goods to my wife and make her sole exrx. Supervisor WILLIAM THOMPSON, whom I entreat to aid and assist my wife. I give him 20s. for his pains. Witnesses: EDWARD NOTTINGHAM, JOHN THOMPSON & WILLIAM THOMPSON. Pr. at Yoxford 29 May 1634.

R(W) ROSE WADE (X) of Capel, widow. 9 May 1634 (793)

I give to ANTHONY WADE my son £10, now in the hands of my well-beloved friend ROBERT KEED of Sutton, and also all my goods, chattels and household implements. If ANTHONY dies before he is 21, then I give £5 to be divided between the children of ELIZABETH RUSSELL, my well-beloved sister. Sole exor. ROBERT KEEDE of Sutton. Witnesses: THOMAS DAUSON, ROBERT MOSSE, THOMAS JOHNSON. Pr. at Wickham Market 30 May 1634.

R(W) ROBERT GRIMMER (X) of Bradwell, yeoman. (794)
11 April 1634

I give to my wife ALICE, after the death of my father ROBERT GRIMMER of Ditchingham, several pieces of land conveyed to me by a deed dated 7 June 1626. She is to keep this land until my son WILLIAM is 21 and is not to fell any trees growing on it. If WILLIAM has no heirs, the land goes to my youngest son ROBERT. I make my wife sole exrx. and give her all my goods and chattels to pay my debts and legacies. I give £20 to my son ROBERT. This money is to be paid 9 months after my decease into the hands of JOHN ANTELL, gent. and attorney dwelling in Ilketshall St. Andrews, who is to put the money out until ROBERT is 21. I leave £10 to my son WILLIAM to be employed as ROBERT's legacy. I give 20s. to Mr JOHN ANTELL whom I entreat to be supervisor of my will. Witnesses: HENRY REEVE, RICHARD CLARKE (X), THOMAS CLARKE. Pr. at Bradwell 22 May 1634.

R(W) SUSAN SWATMAN (X) of South Elmham St. James, widow. (795)
28 June 1627

Sick in body. To be buried in churchyard of South Elmham St. Cross. I give 3s. 4d. to the poor of St. Cross and 3s. 4d. to the poor of St. James to be distributed at the discretion of the churchwardens of each parish. I give £20 to my nephew RICHARD LONGE of Halesworth towards buying a house for him and his wife. After they are both dead I wish my exors. to sell this house and divide the money between RICHARD LONGE's children. I give to his 5 children 20s. apiece when they are 21. I give £5 each to my nephews NICHOLAS, JOHN & JAMES BOWLER; and 20s. each to RICHARD, JAMES & MARY RUSHMER, the children of RICHARD RUSHMER and MARY RUSHMER, my niece. I give unto RICHARD LYNG my best cupboard, my best feather bed & bolster with the bedstead. I give my sister SPIKE my best taffeta hat. I give the children of my cousin JOHN BOWLER 20s. apiece. I give to JOHN BOWLER my other feather bed and bolster. I give £5 to my niece PRUDENCE BOWLER. I give £6 to the children of LANCELOT ALGAR to be put out by their mother until they are 21. I give to WILLIAM ALGAR of South Elmham St. James £4 to be put out for his children until they are 21. I give £6 to LANCELOT BIDBANCK of St. James in the same way. I give to my nephew LANCELOT BIDBANCK a feather bed and a bolster belonging to it and my other cupboard. I give my niece LONG my best stuff gown, my best red petticoat and my best cloak. I give my niece BIDBANCKE my other gown and my lace guard. I give all my wearing linen to LANCELOT BIDBANCK's 4 daughters. I give all my goods in the custody and possession of LANCELOT BIDBANCK to be equally parted between JOHN BOWLER, RICHARD LONG and LANCELOT BIDBANCK after the expenses of my funeral and of proving my will have been paid. If LANCELOT BIDBANCK refuses to hand over any of my goods all legacies to him and his children become void. Exors. JOHN and RICHARD LONG. Witnesses: HENRY MOYSE, JOAN MILLS (X). Pr. at Beccles 5 July 1634.

R(W) WILLIAM BATTELLY of South Elmham St. James, yeoman. (796)
10 February 1625/6

Languishing of body. I give to my nephew RICHARD, son of my brother RICHARD BATTELLY, all my messuage called Parkers in

Rumburgh and all my freehold land, meadows and pasture called Nicholas and belong to the said house. All this land and messuage is now occupied by WILLIAM BAKER. I also give to this nephew all my movable goods, except ready money and bonds. He must pay the following legacies in the porch of Rumburgh church: £5 to MARY, daughter of my brother RICHARD BATTELLY when she is 21; and £3 each to MARGERY, ELIZABETH and HENRY, the daughters and son of my brother GEORGE BATTELLY within 2 years of my decease. I give £3 to my sister KATHERINE, now the wife of JOHN LAWRANCE of Rumburgh to be paid within 1 year of my decease. I give 40s. to JOHN and £5 to KATHERINE, son and daughter of JOHN and KATHERINE LAWRANCE within 2 years of my death. I give 20s. to my nephew WILLIAM GRUDGFILD gent. 1 year after my decease. I give to my brother GEORGE BATTELLY all my copyhold land in Wissett. I bequeath £5 each to my nephews ROBERT and GEORGE, sons of GEORGE BATTELLY, 1 year after my death; 10s. to my kinsman WILLIAM SMYTH of South Elmham All Saints and £10 to my sister ANNE DOUGHTY 1 year after my decease, and 20s. to her son WILLIAM DOUGHTY within 5 years of my death. I bequeath to my brother RICHARD BATTELLY all my land in the parish of South Elmham St. Michael; 20s. to my niece ELIZABETH THOMPSON, wife of WYARD THOMPSON within 1 year of my death, and 20s. each to her daughters ELIZABETH & SUSAN within 3 years. I give 20s. to ELIZABETH, wife of THOMAS MENDHAM, within 2 months of my death, and 12d. apiece to each of my godchildren when they shall come to be men. I leave 8s. to ELIZABETH SWAINE, servant of WILLIAM ROSE my brother-in-law, and 10s. to MARGARET, wife of my kinsman JOHN WIGHILLS within 1 year of my decease. I give £20 to my nephew RICHARD BATTELLY to help him pay the above legacies. 3s. 4d. is to be paid to the Widow MUFFORD of Rumburgh by my exors. All my ready money and bonds I leave to my brother GEORGE BATTELLY and to my brother-in-law WILLIAM ROSE to pay my debts, and they are to be my exors. Witnesses: JOHN WELTON, ROBERT MIGHELL. Pr. at Bungay 1 June 1634.

R(W) JOHN BYLES (X) of Great Glemham, yeoman. 24 May 1634 (797)

Sick in body. I give to ELIZABETH my wife for her lifetime all such goods and chattels as I shall leave behind, and after her death they are to be equally divided between my 2 children JOHN and ELIZABETH. If my wife remarries she is to bind herself to pay to my children the value of my goods. Wife sole exrx. Witnesses: HENRY WAYTHE, THOMAS BROWNE. Pr. at Wickham Market 10 July 1634.

R(W) GEORGE CANHAM of Chattisham (N). 18 June 1634 (798)

He gave to ANNE his wife all his movable goods whatsoever. Witnesses: JOSEPH LOCKWOOD, JOHN FLECOSTE. Pr. at Ipswich 20 June 1634.

R(W) RICHARD COOKE (X) of Hinton hamlet in Blythburgh, yeoman. 26 May 1634 (799)

Sick in body. I give to my son WILLIAM for his life all my tenements and land, both free and copyhold, in Westleton for his honest provisioning and maintenance, and after his decease I give these tenements and land to my son THOMAS and his heirs. I give to ANNE my wife, and after her death to ELIZABETH my daughter, my tenement with outhouses and garden in Blythburgh. I give to ANNE my wife my great cupboard during her life and after her death to my daughter ELIZABETH. I give to my wife 8 skeps of bees and 5 combs of wheat to be reserved for her out of the old corn. I give to my son WILLIAM a flock bed and bolster, a bedstead and other things necessary to the furnishing of a bed, together with an old featherbed. Also a pillow, 2 pairs of sheets, a little brass pot and a little skillet. I also bequeath to him the coffer that was mine before I married, a 4-footed chair and a cushion, 6 skeps of bees, my best suit of doublet and hose, a white doublet that was my father's, my best coat but one and 2 shirts. I give to THOMAS my son £40 to be paid to him within 5 months of my decease, and £20 to be paid to him within 1 month of my wife's death. I also give him from my old corn 4 combs of barley, 10 combs oats, 12 combs rye and 2 combs wheat. More I give him a bed and bedstead fully furnished, 3 pairs sheets, a pillow beere, the long table, the cupboard table, the best chest, 2 joined stools (a high one and a low one), 2 cushions (one of the best and another of the worst sort) and 1 chair. I give to THOMAS all my horses and colts, 1 brindled cow with her calf, 2 heifers, 2 bulls and all my sheep except for 6 ewes. I give him 2 boarded carts, the ploughs and all the traces and implements of husbandry. I leave to him my biggest brass pot save one, a great kettle and a skillet, all my unbequeathed bees and all the corn now growing on my land. He is to have the benefit of all my land until the Michaelmas after my decease, provided that he pays the rent and other charges, keeps the cattle on the premises and provides for that family I now have if they are content to remain quietly here until Michaelmas. I give £30 to my daughter ELIZABETH to be paid 5 months after my decease, a cow called her cow and 2 heifers that belonged to ARTHUR STYLES and another that was PARYS, a bull calf and 6 of my best ewes chosen out of all my sheep. I also give her a bed and bedstead well furnished, 3 pairs sheets and a pillow beere, the best brass pot except one, a kettle and a skillet, the least chest, 1 coffer, 2 stools, one of the best cushions and 6 skeps of bees. I give 20s. to the poor of the parish of Blythburgh and the hamlets belonging to it to be distributed according to need at the discretion of the churchwardens and overseers of the poor. All the rest of my goods, within doors and without, and my cattle I bequeath to my wife ANNE, whom I appoint to be sole exrx. I require my son THOMAS to be ready to help her in any reasonable matter. Witnesses: MARY MURDOCKE & BARTHOLOMEW GOLDING, who wrote this will. Pr. at Blythburgh 11 June 1634.

A particular as what is due from other men to RICHARD COOKE made 29 March 1634.

ROGER CHESNOLD 4 combs & 3 bushels of barley 57s.

Mr CORNWALLIS	40s.
THURSTON	28s. 10d.
ED RIVERS 2 bushels of malt	6s.
WELHAM	3s. 8d.
BUCK 2 bushels of malt	6s.
Item from BYRD for a bushel of malt	3s.

WILLIAM PARKER 12 combs of barley and more the 7th 11 combs and 2 bushels and 11 combs 3 bushels of malt. Item from running 2 combs of barley due to him £21 3s.
I give my brother JOHN COOKE 20s. I give £10 amongst WILLIAM PARKER's children, and I give £20 to THOMAS COOKE and £15 to ROBERT COOKE. This note was written in the presence of FRANCIS COOKE & WILLIAM PARKER, whom the testator desired to be exors. of his will. Witness: LAWRENCE WHITEING. Pr. at Ipswich 20 June 1634.

R(W) THOMAS GOLDSMITH/GOULESMITH (X) of Holbrook, locksmith. 25 August 1627 (800)

Very sick in body. I give to SARAH my wife for life my copyhold tenement with the shop and yard in Thorpe le Soken, Essex, held of the manor of Thorpe and called the town house. After SARAH's death, I give it to my son JOHN, or, if he dies without heirs, to my niece ELIZABETH GOLDSMITH. I give to my son JOHN my best bed standing in the chamber with its bedding. The rest of my household stuff, shop goods and tools, bills and bonds I bequeath to my wife, who is joint exrx. with my son JOHN. They are to sell my shop stuff and tools for the best price to pay my debts. Witnesses: ROBERT WILKER & JOHN BROTHERTON. Pr. at Ipswich 5 July 1634.

R(W) THOMAS GOODALL (X) of Ipswich, ship's carpenter. 1 October 1631 (801)

Sick of body. I give to ALICE my loving wife for ever the house I now live in. I give £3 to my daughter REBECCA, wife of GEORGE STANFORD, to be paid 1 year after my wife's death. I give £3 each to my daughters ELIZABETH and JOANNA GOODALL at the same time, and £3 to my grandson THOMAS HARRISON 2 years after my wife's decease. All my other goods I give to my wife, whom I make sole exrx. Witnesses: THOMAS EADE & RICHARD CROWE. Pr. at Ipswich 1 June 1634.

R(W) ISAAC JERMY of Stutton, knight. 18 June 1634 (802)

The £400 made over to the feoffees of a trust set up by me for the maintenance of my youngest daughter JUDITH RIDDLESTON is to remain as the settlement provides. I give to my dear, beloved wife ELIZABETH JERMY £50, my clothes, my coach horses and another £20 to buy mourning. I give to my poor sister GOLDINGHAM 4s. a week for life for her livelihood. I bequeath £5 each to Mr WARD, Mr SCOTT and Mr HEARDSON the elder. I give £5 to the poor, 40s.

to my man PATISON and 40s. to MARY BAKER, and 40s. more to be divided among the rest of my household servants by my wife. I will and bequeath to my eldest daughter MARY THORNEHILL for mourning clothes for herself and her husband £10, and £8 to my youngest daughter JUDITH RIDDLESTON for the same. I give £4 to my son EDWARD for mourning. I will and command my exor. to bury me privately. My wife has in her custody £100 besides other money lying in my desk in the closet. She is to collect the rents due to me. I give all the residue of my goods to my exor. who is to permit and suffer my wife to have the use for one year of the household stuff now in my house at Ipswich. I make my eldest son JOHN sole exor. I wish to be buried in the chancel of Stutton church next to my wife JANE. Witnesses: THEO PATTESON, WILLIAM SEWELL and MARY BAKER. Pr. at Ipswich 4 July 1634.

R(W) JOHN NORMAN of South Elmham St. Margaret (N). (803)
13 June 1634

He gave to SUSAN his wife all his goods and nominated her exrx. He asked her to pay £4 to WILLIAM NORMAN, son of his brother REYNOLD, on 20 May next. This sum being part of £6 due to him from ROBERT PORTER of South Elmham St. Michael on 20 May or thereabouts. This £4 is to be employed for the benefit of WILLIAM NORMAN until he is 21, with remainder to his brother. Witnesses: WILLIAM NORMAN and HENRY WOLNOUGH. Pr. at South Elmham St. Margaret 25 June 1634.

R(W) THOMAS SALTHORNE of Saxmundham, oatmeal maker. (804)
14 June 1634

I bequeath all my houses and yards lying in Saxmundham to my wife ALICE for her life, and she is to bring up my youngest son JOHN. After her death I give to FRANCIS my eldest son the part of the house wherein I now dwell and half the yard for access to the same. FRANCIS must pay my daughter MARY 40s. 6 months after my wife's decease. The other part of the same house, now occupied by JOHN KING, I give to my son ROBERT together with the other half of the yard, the mill house and the oatmeal house, after my wife's death. ROBERT must pay my daughter KATHERINE 40s. within 6 months of my wife's death. After the decease of my wife I give to JOHN my youngest son the house where JOHN KEEBLE now lives. I give all my movable goods and debts to my wife, asking her to pay my debts and give each of my daughters £3 within 2 years of my decease. Wife sole exrx. Witnesses: THOMAS BROWNE, ARTHUR DRYVER, THOMAS ALDUS. Pr. at Saxmundham 18 June 1634.

R(W) WILLIAM WHITING of South Elmham All Saints (N). (805)
12 June 1634

He gave to his brother NICHOLAS WHITING £5, and to WILLIAM CAULER £5 and his best jerkin. He gave to SYETH ENOULDS his sister £4 and to SARAH DAVIE 10s. He left to his sister CAULER 40s. and

40s. apiece to her 4 children, MICHAEL, EDWARD, JOHN and MARGARET. He gave 6s. 8d. each to 2 of his god-children, MARY SMYTH & WILLIAM COOKE. He bequeathed 30s. to his sister HALL and 20s. each to her 4 children. He gave £5 to Mr JOHN GOOCH. All these legacies to be paid within 1 year of his decease by his kinsmen ARTHUR and ROGER WHYTING, whom he made exors. He gave them all his movable goods towards the performance of his will. Witnesses: WILLIAM SMYTH, DOROTHEY TELLING and BENJAMIN HOWLET. Pr. at South Elmham St. Margaret 25 June 1634.

R(W) NICHOLAS WHYTING (X) of South Elmham St. Margaret, husbandman. 8 June 1634 (806)

I give to my wife MARY for life my tenement wherein I and my son ROGER dwell, and after her death I bequeath it to my son ARTHUR on condition he pays my son ROGER £20 within 1 year of inheriting the house. He must also pay £5 to my grandson JOHN, son of ROGER, when he reaches age of 21. If ARTHUR refuses to pay £20 to ROGER, then the house goes to ROGER on condition he pays ARTHUR £30 within 18 months of my wife's death. I give all my household goods and cattle to my wife for life, and after her death to be equally divided between my sons ARTHUR and ROGER by my exor. I make my exor. RICHARD KEEBLE of South Elmham St. Margaret, my only friend and neighbour, to whom I give 5s. for his pains. Supervisor: Mr SAGAR, parson of South Elmham All Saints. Witnesses: THOMAS KEEBLE (X), JOHN SAGAR. Pr. at South Elmham St. Margaret 20 June 1634.

R(W) RICHARD TAYLOR of Shadingfield, yeoman. 12 June 1634 (807)

Weak in body. I give to my wife KATHERINE for life my tenement in Mettingham with all the land belonging to it, and after her death my will and pleasure is that nephew ROBERT TENNY shall have them. I give all my household goods, cattle, and money to my wife, except for my weaving looms and all things belonging to them, which I give to my nephew ROBERT TENNY. After my wife's death, half of my movables are to be divided among my sister's children, with the exception of ROBERT TENNY to whom I have already given my land and looms, and the other half is to be disposed of by my wife as she wishes. Wife sole exrx. Witnesses: THOMAS ROBINSON, rector of Shadingfield, WILLIAM BIDBANCK (X), ELIZABETH ROBINSON (X). Pr. at Beccles 19 July 1634.

R(W) MARGERY CHAMBERS (X) of Sibton, widow. 28 March 1634 (808)

I give to WILLIAM CHAMBERS, my late husband's son, 40s. to be paid within 1 year of my death. The residue of all my goods I bequeath to my most kind and loving god-daughter ANNE, the wife of EDWARD WATLYNG yeoman of Bramford, to pay my debts, legacies and burial expenses and I make her sole exrx., desiring her to see my body brought to the earth in decent manner. Witnesses: JOHN PULHAM, JOHN FLUZZIAN. Pr. at Beccles 9 Aug. 1634.

R(W) JOHN CRANE (X) of Chelmondiston, (809)
[spelt Shenton in manuscript], son of CHRISTOPHER CRANE of Ipswich deceased. 6 December 1634

Lying very weak in body. First I give and bequeath to my son JOHN my house in Chelmondiston, where the pot kiln stands and which is now occupied by ROBERT PAMER of Chelmondiston, together with the yards and backhouses and all my land in Chelmondiston. JOHN must pay £40 to my son WILLIAM CRANE the younger in 4 equal annual payments of £10 starting 4 years after my decease. If JOHN dies without heirs, the above property is to descend to WILLIAM. I bequeath to my son WILLIAM my house in Woolverstone which I bought from HENRY HORNDE, and a barn and a yard in Woolverstone which I purchased from MATHEW STAPLETON. If WILLIAM dies without heirs, this property goes to JOHN. All my movable goods and debts due to me are to be equally divided between my 2 sons, who must pay my debts and £5 to ANNE TOWLESON or to her husband THOMAS TOWLESON. Exors.: my 2 sons. Supervisor: THOMAS TOWLSON. Witnesses: WILLIAM RUSSELL, ELIZABETH WOODGITT, LUCY CORISH (X), SUSAN LIFE (X), JOHN CORNISH. Pr. at Ipswich 14 July 1634.

R(W) ANNE FROGGETT (X) of Hoo, widow. (810)
24 January 1633/4

I give to my son ANTHONY all my stock of cattle save 1 heifer which I give to my daughter ANNE, to whom ANTHONY must pay £10 within a year and a day of my decease. I give also to ANNE a livery bed with a featherbed and all that belongs to it, 6 pairs of sheets, 3 holland pillow beeres, a casting kercher and 1 keep. I give to ANTHONY 1 keep, the posted bed with the best featherbed and all that belongs to it, the best flockbed with the bedstead with the half head and all that belongs to it. I give to my daughter the other flockbed with all that belongs to it. I give 4 great platters to my son and 3 to my daughter. The rest of the pewter is to be equally divided between ANTHONY and ANNE, and I give to ANNE all my wearing clothes both linen and woollen. The rest of my household goods are to be divided between ANTHONY and ANNE. I give to ANTHONY the long table with the cloth, 2 joined forms and 3 joined stools. I give to ANNE the best cupboard, 3 joined stools and the three quarter table with the long form. I give to both my children 3 pillows each, and to ANTHONY the great chest. To ANNE I give 1 silver spoon and the little coffer. I give the best box to ANNE and the other to my son; the best rug to ANTHONY and the other to ANNE. I give to ANTHONY the cupboard and long hutch, another hutch and the wicker chair. To ANNE I give the pilleon and its cloth. I give to my son the great brass pot, and the other two to ANNE. I give to ANTHONY the best and worst posnets and the other 2 to ANNE. To ANTHONY I give the great kettle, and the other 2 to ANNE. To ANTHONY the 2 new towels and to ANNE the 2 flaxen towels. I give 2 dozen napkins to be parted between them. I give to ANTHONY the great chair and to ANNE the child's chair. The other stools and chairs are to be parted between them. I give to ANTHONY a livery table and to ANNE my 2 wheels. To my son I give all such tools as belong to a husbandman, both within the house and without. I give a pair of pillow beeres each to my sons WILLIAM and THOMAS. I give to ANTHONY the malt querns and to ANNE the mustard querns. To ANNE I give the small cheese press and to ANTHONY the other. The dairy vessels are to be divided between them, but ANTHONY is to have the better part. Witnesses: THOMAS YELLOP, THOMAS FREGGETT, ANTHONY FROGGETT, ANNE FROGGETT (X). Pr. at Wickham Market 30 May 1634.

R(W) HENRY FACON (X) of Campsea Ash, yeoman. (811)
15 July 1634

I bequeath to JOHN my son £6 to be paid by my exors. into the hands of Mr JOHN LANE of Rendlesham until JOHN reaches age of 21 or marries, Mr LANE is to pay JOHN interest at the rate of 18 pence in the pound. Also I give to JOHN immediately after my decease my weaving loom with all things belonging to it and all my clothes. To MARY FACON, my eldest daughter, I leave £7 to be paid to Mr LANE to keep for her use as occasion shall require. To the rest of my children by my present wife, including that which my wife is expecting, I leave £5 each to be paid by my wife when they reach 16 (with benefit of survivorship). My wife is to bring up my children in nurture and fear of God. I bequeath to MARY my loving wife all my goods and cattle towards the payment of my debts and legacies, and the education and upbringing of my children. She is sole exrx. Supervisor: Mr JOHN LANE. Witnesses: EDMUND CAPON (X), and his wife MARY CAPON (X). Pr. at Wickham Market 31 July 1634.

R(W) WILLIAM GLADDEN (X) of East Bergholt. (812)
19 February 1633/4

Sick and weak in body. I bequeath to MARY my beloved wife for life my cottage and land, and after her death to my heirs. I also give her all my movable goods to pay my debts. The residue is to be divided between my 2 children, MARGARET and MARY, when they are 21 and until my wife is to have the use of these goods. My brother NICHOLAS GLADDEN and my brother-in-law JAMES MARLER are to see that these goods are kept for my daughters. My will is that my wife should build on to my cottage a room or little buttery to cost £3 or £4. Witnesses: JOHN PHILLIPS, THOMAS HAMDALL, JOSEPH CLERK, JAMES MARLER. No exor. named. Pr. at Ipswich to widow 14 March 1633/4.

R(W) ROBERT RICHARDSON of Butley (N). (813)
31 December 1633

He gave all his goods and estate to ROSE his wife. No exor. named. Witnesses: WILLIAM DRIVER, RICHARD HUDD. Pr. to widow at Wickham Market 31 July 1634.

R(W) LIONEL STANNARD of Debenham. 21 May 1634 (814)

To be buried in Debenham churchyard. I give 40s. each when they are 24 to all the children of my sister KATHERINE, wife of JOHN ISACKON. I give to the children of ELIZABETH and ROBERT LOCKWOOD, my sister and brother-in-law, 40s. each when 24, except that their son JOHN is to receive £3. I give to ANNE, daughter of ROBERT MORE, when 24 £5 and to his daughters MARY, ELIZABETH and JUDITH and to his son ROBERT 40s. each when 24. (All these legacies are with benefit of survivorship.) To JOHN, son of JOHN GOSELING of Mickfield, I give 20s. when he is 21 to buy himself a book. I leave 40s. to the poor of Debenham to be distributed by the overseers of the poor within 1 week of my death. The rest of my goods, my debts and legacies being paid, I give to my wife REBECCA provided she enters into a bond of £100 with JOHN GOSELING of Mickfield to truly perform my will. I make my loving wife sole exrx. and JOHN GOSELING supervisor of my will. Witnesses: JOHN GOSLING, NICHOLAS DOOLE, JOHN SHERMAN (X). Pr. at Debenham 21 July 1634.

R(W) JOHN WRITHOCKE of Wingfield, yeoman. (815)
24 November 1627

I give to my daughter ISABEL, widow of ROBERT WARREN , for ever my best house standing in my tenement Bulines, my stable and half my barn standing to north of the above house. She is to have right of access with horse and cart to the barn through the yard on its west side, and also the right to drive cattle through the yard, and to have access from the yard to repair her house and buildings. I also give her that part of the yard lying between the barn and stable as it is now dooled out. I also give her the newly planted orchard on the east side of the best house and stable, and a 1 1/2 acre pightle adjoining the end of the barn and stable. I also bequeath to her two more pightles. One has GEORGE BORRET's land called Coldhams on its north side and the King's highway at its east end; the other is next to the first. These 2 pightles are part of the Brines tenement and contain 4 1/2 acres. I leave more to ISABEL a 6 acre close, being part of the New Park, with SIMON FOXE's land on its east and south sides, JOHN FOXE's on the west side and the King's highway on the north side. The rest of my land called New Park and containing 26 acres I give to my grandson JOHN BARKER. I bequeath to my grandson JOHN PRENTICE my half-headed bedstead, my best featherbed but one, my best coverlet but two, my table frame and 1 long boarded stool standing in my hall and my tumbril. I give to my daughter ISABEL my best featherbed, my best bolster, my best coverlet, the best blanket, the best pillow, the best table, the best chair, one little framed stool, the shod cart, the iron harrows, the best spit, the frying pan, my cheese press, a salting trough, one boarding coate standing in the yard, the malt querns, the best ladder and a hand flasket. I give all these goods to my daughter ISABEL on condition that she enters into surety to my exors. that they shall be left to her daughter ELIZABETH WARREN immediately after her (ISABEL's) decease. I give to my daughter BRIDGET my second bedstead, a featherbed, a coverlet, a blanket, a feather bolster, a pillow, my second best cupboard, and two ladders. If BRIDGET dies childless, I wish the goods left to her to pass to my grandson JOHN BARKER. I give to the said JOHN BARKER my boarding coate standing in New Park, a trundle bedstead, a flockbed, a bolster, a coverlet and a pair of sheets. I give to ELIZABETH BARKER, my grandchild, a cupboard table and a pair of sheets. I bequeath to JANE BARKER, my grandchild, a little cupboard table, my best table and a pair of sheets. I give MARY BARKER, my grandchild, my mortar and pestle and a pair of sheets. To FRANCES BARKER, my grandchild, I give the chafing dish and a pair of sheets. I give ELIZABETH PRENTICE, my grandchild, a chest in the hall chamber. I give JOHN BARKER, my grandson, 2 coffers, 1 in my closet chamber and the other in my bed chamber, my smallest spit, my smallest skillet, my musket and a pair of mustard querns. I leave to ANNE my daughter my best Bible. All my unbequeathed books are to be equally divided between JOHN BARKER and JOHN PRENTICE, my grandsons. I give to WILLIAM PRENTICE my hagsaw. To my grandson JOHN BARKER I give my little brass pot, my grindstone, all my tools and iron things, and all my boards and planks. I give to ELIZABETH WARREN my great brass pot, a milk tub, one churn, 3 keelers, 2 beer vessells, 1 little tub, 1 cheese vat, 12 pieces of pewter, a bell metal mortar and pestle, a glass keep, 2 buffet stools, a chest, a flockbed and a little cupboard. WILLIAM PRENTICE owes me £10 from which 20s. each is to be given to JOHN, ELIZABETH, JOAN, MARY and FRANCES BARKER, to ELIZABETH WARREN and to FRANCIS GODFREY; the remainder is to be divided among WILLIAM PRENTICE's children. All my unbequeathed goods are to be equally divided between my grandsons JOHN & ROBERT BARKER. Exors.: JOHN BARKER, my grandson, and WILLIAM PRENTICE. Witnesses: THOMAS WRITHOCKE, THOMAS POTTELL, FRANCIS KENT (X). Pr. at Yoxford 9 July 1634.

R(W) WILLIAM MULLENNER/MULLEMER of Horham, yeoman. (816)
20 October 1630

To be buried in Horham churchyard. I bequeath to my beloved wife JOAN for life my piece of land in Horham called Crokshelmwent and containing 12 acres. After her death, I give these 12 acres to my son WILLIAM in order that he may pay the portions due after my wife's death to my sons JOHN of £60 and RICHARD of £50; these payments are to be spread over 10 years, and made in the south porch of Horham church. If WILLIAM refuses to make these payments, the land is to go to JOHN and if he refuses to make them, to RICHARD. Supervisor of will: my son JOHN, to whom I give 20s. for his pains. To my daughter MARY I leave my down bed which I usually lie on. To my daughter JOAN I give my livery bedstead fully furnished as it now stands in the parlour chamber. I give to my grandchild JOAN UBBESTON my trundle bedstead fully furnished in the hall chamber. I leave all my other goods to my wife for life, and after her decease to be equally divided between my daughters ANNE, ELIZABETH, MARY, JOAN and ALICE. My wife is sole exrx. Witnesses: ROBERT DOWNNING, EDWARD MOULTON. No probate.

R(W) ANNE LYLLY (X) of Halesworth, (817)
spinster and one of the daughters of HENRY LYLLY deceased.
1 May 1634

I bequeath 26s. 8d. to the poor people of Halesworth to be distributed at my burial. I give to my aunt SEPENCE 40s. and to her daughter ANNE, wife of JOHN NEWSON, 40s. I give to my godson HENRY, son of ANNE and JOHN NEWTON, 40s. and 20s. each to the rest of their children. I leave 20s. each to the children of my uncle LYLLY three years after my death. I give 40s. to my kinsfolk JOHN, ROBERT, MARY and ANNE ANTELL 2 years after my decease, and 30s. each to THOMAS and SUSAN, son and daughter of my uncle HENRY BALLS, 2 years after my decease. I give to my cousins JOAN, MARY and ELIZABETH KEBLE 40s. each to be paid 3 years after my death; they are the children of my uncle and aunt JAMES and JOAN KEBLE. I bequeath 30s. each to my Aunt BUGG, my aunt MILLS and to my aunt KEBLE to be paid within 2 years of my decease, and 20s. to be paid to my kinswoman ANNE SEMAN within 2 years of my death. I give 6s. 8d. to GEORGE GOODWYN and 5s. to MARTHA BROWNE, both servants to JAMES KEBLE. All these legacies are to be paid in the south porch of Halesworth church. Exor. my uncle JAMES KEBLE. Witnesses: GEORGE GOODWYN and JOHN MILLS. Pr. at Halesworth 11 June 1634.

R(W) ROBERT GILBERT (X) of Bungay, tailor. (818)
25 August 1634

Being sick. I give all my houses and land in Bungay to CHRISTIAN my wife for her life on condition that she brings up my 2 lame children, THOMAS and ALICE. After her death I give the house and land to these 2 children. I give all my goods to my wife towards the bringing up of my children, and make her my sole exrx. Witnesses: RICHARD BASPOOLE, RICHARD NUN, WILLIAM YOUNGES, and RICHARD BENSLEY. Pr. at Bungay 15 Sept. 1634.

R(W) RICHARD AMYSON of Easton, blacksmith. (819)
11 November 1620

Hale in body, but calling to mind that all flesh is frail and subject to death. I leave to my wife ELIZABETH my messuage and land in Easton for her life and after her death to my heirs. I give all my goods and chattels to my wife to pay my debts, and she is to be sole exrx. Witnesses: WILLIAM MORGAN, ROBERT CRISPE (X), ROBER GILL. Pr. at Wickham Market 18 Sept. 1634 to widow, ELIZABETH AMYSON.

R(W) GRACE BRAME (X) of Ipswich, widow. 7 July 1634 (820)

I leave to my son HENRY 1s., and to my son JOHN £6 when he reaches age of 18. To my son EDWARD I give my little bedstead with all the bedding on it in the fire room where I keep [i.e. live]; the bedding on this bed is a flock bed, a feather bolster, 1 blanket, 1 coverlet and a pair of sheets. These goods bequeathed to EDWARD are to be given to whoever he serves as an apprentice until he is 18. I give £6 to my son ROBERT when he is 18; also 1 posted bedstead in the parlour, a feather bed, a feather bolster, a coverlet and a pair sheets. I give £6 to my daughter GRACE BRAME when she is 18, and a close posted bedstead, a feather bed, a feather bolster, a blanket, a feather pillow and 1 pair of sheets and all my clothes both linen and woollen and 1 silver spoon. My exors. are to sell all my unbequeathed goods and household stuff and collect all the money due to me to pay my debts, funeral charges and the probate of my will. The overplus is to be equally divided amongst my children JOHN, EDWARD, ROBERT and GRACE. Exors. WILLIAM SOUNDE and PETER PETTERSON. Witnesses: ROBERT LORD and JOHN CHURCH. Pr. at Ipswich 8 Oct. 1634.

R(W) JOAN BUGGE, widow (N). 31 March 1634 (821)

She left to ANNE her daughter 1 kettle, 1 skillet, 1 petticoat, her best waistcoat and 1 pair sheets. All the rest of her household stuff she asked to be equally divided into 4 parts by STEPHEN REDLAND and HENRY COURTNALL for her other 4 daughters, MARY, WINIFRED, BRIDGET and SARAH. Exor. ROBERT MARKS. Witnesses: HENRY CURTNALL, HENRY SNELLING. Pr. at Ipswich 19 Sept. 1634.

R(W) EDWARD BARBAR senior (X) of Stradbroke, yeoman. 14 July 1634 (822)

Sick in body. I choose EDWARD BARBAR, my eldest son, my sole exor. and give to him all my land. He is to pay all my debts. I give to my sons WILLIAM and GILES, to be equally divided between them, all my looms and slayes with all the engines and other things belonging to them. I give to my son JOHN such things as he has most need of to the value of 20s. I give to my son WILLIAM the black heifer in the pasture which gives milk. I give to my daughter MARY my black heifer on the common which was bought of JOHN HERING of Dennington. The rest of my goods are to be equally divided between my children WILLIAM, GILES, MARY and ELIZABETH after the death of ELIZABETH my wife. Witnesses: WILLIAM CALVER and JOHN ALLEYEN. Pr. at Stradbroke 23 Sept. 1634.

R(W) THOMAS BOND (X) of Beddingfield, yeoman. (823)
28 August 1634

I give and bequeath to BRIDGET my right well deserving wife for ever a pightle of land in Beddingfield called Longwent which I lately purchased from ROBERT CLERKE. I give to MARGARET CURDIE my sister £10: £5 to be paid a year after my decease and the other £5 a year later. I give to my nephew JOHN BOND of Debenham, son of the late JAMES BOND of Debenham, £20 to be paid as the legacy to my sister. I give all my movable goods and debts due to me to my wife on condition she pays my debts and legacies. Wife sole exrx. Witnesses: ROBERT FENN, JOHN FENN. Pr. at Stradbroke 23 Sept. 1634.

R(W) WILLIAM ELLINGHAM of Flixton (N). [blank] August 1634 (824)

He gave to WILLIAM his son all his clothes and to MARGARET his wife all the rest of his goods and made her sole exrx. Witnesses: JONAS LAKERS clerk and JOHN REEVE. Pr. at Homersfield 24 Sept. 1634.

R(W) JOHN GISLAM the elder of Worlingham, yeoman. (825)
1 August 1634

Sick of body. I will and bequeath unto DIANA my loving wife the vance roof, the old stable and the garden plot at the parlour end with liberty of ingress and egress so long as she remains unmarried and keeps the premises in repair. She shall also have 4 loads of firewood p.a. while she dwells in these premises. I give to my son THOMAS all messuages, land, woods and rights of common in the parish of Worlingham on condition he pays my wife £18 p.a. while she remains a widow. The payments are to be made in my mansion house at Michaelmas and Lady Day. If DIANA remarries her annuity is then reduced to £16. (She has power to distrain.) If she makes any claim on my property all legacies to her are forfeit. I bequeath to THOMAS all my interest in the goods he had with his wife on their marriage, and all my outdoor goods, that is corn, horses, cows, sheep, hay and husbandry tools. I give to my wife for ever one silver salt and half a dozen silver spoons, and she is to have the use of all the bedding, linen, brass, pewter, and household stuff now in the parlour, parlour chamber and vance roof of the house where I now dwell. After her remarriage or death all these goods are left to my son THOMAS. I also give to him the tables, cupboards and other furniture now in the hall, one featherbed, and all the unbequeathed residue of my goods, money and plate. THOMAS sole exor. Witnesses: JAMES KING clerk, ELIZABETH TURNER (X), THOMAS FIDELL. Pr. at Beccles 13 Oct. 1634.

R(W) JOHN HAWKES of Ipswich, grocer. 24 July 1634 (826)

Sick and weak in body. I give to my two daughters THOMASIN and

MARY £100 each when 21 or on their marriage days whichever happens first. Until such time MARY my well-beloved wife is to have the use of this £200 towards the girls' education and upbringing. If one daughter dies, the other is to have her share, but if both die then my wife can dispose of the money as she wishes. I give £5 to my kinsman ISRAEL EXTON. My wife is to enter into a bond of £400 with WILLIAM INGLETHORPE, my father-in-law, and THOMAS CLEERE of Ipswich gent., to pay my children's portions at the time specified above. All my goods, chattels, plate, money and stock in the sugar house in Ipswich I give to my wife whom I make sole exrx. and who is to pay my debts and legacies. Witnesses: EDWARD SOLLERY, EDMUND MYLES, notary public. Pr. at Ipswich 7 Aug. 1634.

R(W) ELIZABETH JENOR (X) of Laxfield, widow. (827)
26 June 1629

I wish to be buried in Laxfield parish church. I give to my son JOHN SOONE all my land and tenements in Peasenhall and Heveningham, but if HENRY NORTH of Laxfield pays him £800 in Laxfield church porch in 2 equal payments, one a year and the other 2 years after my decease, then HENRY NORTH shall have all this property. If HENRY NORTH refuses to pay £800, then my son is to pay him £100 one year after my death and another £100 a year later. I give to my daughter SARAH, now wife of HENRY NORTH, 2 chairs and 2 stools covered with needlework. I give to my 3 grandchildren, MARY, SARAH and ELIZABETH NORTH £20 each to be paid by my exor. 2 years after my decease to HENRY NORTH in trust for these children until they are 21 or marry. I also give them each 1 pair of sheets, 2 pillow beeres and 1 dozen napkins. I give 10s. each to HENRY NORTH's household servants. I bequeath 20s. each to JOHN COLLISON and ELIZABETH PAINE, and 40s. to Mr SKYNNER, the minister of Laxfield. The rest of my goods I give to my son JOHN SOONE whom I make sole exor. Witnesses: WILLIAM GODBALD, JOHN NEWTON, JOHN COLLISON. Pr. at Yoxford 9 Oct. 1634.

R(W) SARAH LYNDSEY of Kessingland (N). 24 June 1634 (828)

She gave 40s. to ANNE DALE and all the rest of her goods to NATHANIEL REDHED to pay her debts and made him sole exor. Witnesses: THOMAS MANSERET, MARY COBY. Pr. at Beccles 30 June 1634.

R(W) NATHANIEL LEVELL (X) of Baylham, yeoman. (829)
17 August 1634

Sick in body. I give to PETER LEVELL, my eldest brother, my house and copyhold tenement called Segroms and now occupied by JOHN LUCAS. I also give him all my corn, rye, barley, horses, cows, sheep, hay, household stuff, bedding and all other movables. He must pay my debts, funeral charges and probate expenses. If £20 remains over, then I give that to my brother

JOHN LEVELL. I make my brother PETER sole exor. Witnesses: JOHN BIRD, JOHN JACKSON (X), THOMAS BOYCE (X). Pr. at Ipswich 19 Sept. 1634.

R(W) THOMAS MANNING (X) of Burstall, cooper. (830)
11 June 1634

Sick in body. I give to JOHN my eldest son £5 and 5s. each to his daughters ELIZABETH, SARAH and ANN to be paid within 1 year of my decease. I give to my daughter MARY GARWOOD 10s. and to her daughter MARY 5s. to be paid within 1 year of my death. I give to ANNE my beloved wife my best bed with all things belonging to it to dispose of as she thinks best, and all the rest of my household goods for life or until she remarries. She is to pay my debts. After her death or remarriage I give my goods to my son THOMAS and daughters ANNE, ROSE and ELIZABETH, but THOMAS is to have £5 more and ANNE 40s. more than the others. Wife sole exrx. I give my son JOHN for his trouble 10s. in addition to his portion given above. Witnesses: THOMAS ROWNING, THOMAS SHEREWOOD. Pr. at Ipswich 16 Aug. 1634.

R(W) SUSAN PALMER of Hasketon, widow (N). 8 August 1634 (831)

She gave THOMAS PALMER her son 1 livery bedstead, a flockbed, a pair of sheets, a feather pillow and a beere belonging to it, a covering, a blanket that is on the bed where he lies, a flock bolster, a skillet, a stool, and a great chest. All the rest of her goods and the profits for a year and day of the house and land she occupied she gave to her daughters ELIZABETH and HANNAH PALMER, whom she named exrxs. Witnesses: WILLIAM FARRER clerk and GEORGE MANN. Pr. at Wickham Market 18 Sept. 1634.

R(W) MICHAEL SAFFERY (X) of Wingfield, yeoman. (832)
15 July 1634

I give to ALICE my wife all my cattle, except for one old cow which I give to ALICE my daughter. I also give my wife all the husbandry utensils, except one ladder and 1 crouding barrow, on condition she pays £5 5s. 0d. due by bond to JOHN VALENT of Tibenham in Norfolk at Michaelmas next. My mind is that ALICE my wife shall have the use of all my household goods until the Michaelmas 12 months after my decease, and after that time SAMUEL VALENT my son-in-law shall have them. I bequeath my tenement and land in Gissing, Norfolk to my daughter ANNE, wife of SAMUEL VALIENT. Wife sole exrx. Witnesses: WILLIAM ELLIS, ROGER WARD, ROBERT HAYWARD. Pr. at Stradbroke 20 Sept., 1634.

R(W) The devise of JOHN WRITHOCK [of Stradbroke?], innkeeper. 9 September 1634 (833)

I give to my wife KATHERINE for life my little tenement now occupied by THOMAS SANDER and the Widow SANDER, and after her death to my son JOHN, who must pay 20s. p.a. to my son ANTHONY (he has power to distrain). I give also to my wife for life a 1 acre pightle called Pyes meere, which I lately bought from ROBERT JAMES and his wife, and after her death I leave it to my son ANTHONY. After my wife's decease I give to my son JOHN my copper and brewing vessels together with my mill, and all the tools belonging to my shop. All the rest of my goods I give to my wife to pay my debts and perform my will. Witnesses: ROGER CAVER, ISABEL BORRETT, ELIZABETH RASON. Pr. at Stradbroke 20 Sept. 1634.

R(W) EDMUND GROSSE burgess and alderman of Great Yarmouth. 20 August 1634 (834)

Sick in body. As SAMUEL DOUBLEDAY, merchant of Great Yarmouth, stands bound for me to various persons to whom I owe money, I give to him, so that he may be discharged of all obligations on my behalf, all my movable goods, cattle and plate, and make him my sole exor. Supervisor WILLIAM NUTTHALL, my son-in-law, to whom I give 13s. 4d. Witnesses: BENJAMIN COOPER, senior, JOHN ALLEN, RICHARD COBBE. Pr. at Beccles 17 Oct. 1634.

R(W) WILLIAM DAVIE of Walberswick, grocer. 4 June 1634 (835)

Sick in body. I give and bequeath to ANN my beloved wife all my houses and lands in Walberswick and Blythburgh for life, and after her death to my daughter HANNAH. If HANNAH dies without heirs before my wife, then the houses and land are left to the latter absolutely. I give to HANNAH £400 to be paid to her by my exrx. in the south porch of Walberswick church when she reaches 21 or marries, so long as she does not marry without first obtaining the consent of my wife, the right worthy Mr HENRY COKE esq. and HUMPHREY PYM my brother-in-law or the majority of them. If she marries without their consent, she must wait until she is 21 for her portion. Until she inherits the interest on the £400 is to be used for her meat, drink and apparell and education, and other necessary expenses. I will that she shall be grounded in the principles of the Christian religion and in the faith of Jesus Christ and to this end she shall be employed to school and learning until she is 15 years old for the learning of such things as are fit for one of her degree to learn. If HANNAH wishes to live apart from my wife after she is 15, she is to have £5 p.a. If she dies unmarried before she is 21, my exrx. is to pay £100 each when they are 21 to HENRY, ANN and BETHIA, the children of my brother-in-law HUMPHREY PYM. I give £5 each to JOHN, ELIZABETH, KATHERINE and MARTHA, children of my brother JOHN DAVY, to be paid within 4 years after my decease. I give to the poor of Walberswick 20s. p.a. for 5 years to be paid by my exrx. where she thinks most fitting. All the rest of my goods, money, plate, bonds, debts, ware, household implements and stuff, and cattle I give to my wife towards the payment of my debts, legacies, funeral charges and the probate of my will. Wife sole exrx. Within 1 month after my decease she must enter into a bond of £700 with Mr HENRY COKE of Thorington truly to perform my will. Supervisors: Mr HENRY COKE and Mr HUMPHREY PIM, whom I ask to aid and assist my wife with advice and counsel. Witnesses: FRANCIS MORSE, JOHN BOWMAN, NICHOLAS GIRLING. Pr. at Yoxford 9 Oct. 1634.

R(W) JOHN KNOWLES of Easton, weaver. 7 August 1634 (836

I give to MARY my wife for life my messuage and land in Marlesford after the death of GEORGE and ISABEL KNOWLES, my father and mother, towards the education and upbringing of my children. She must pay £2 p.a. to my son GEORGE in 2 instalments at Michaelmas and Lady Day in the church porch at Easton, starting when he reaches 24. After my wife's death the messuage and land are to go to my son GEORGE. If he has no heirs, this property passes after his death to my daughters MARY, ELIZABETH, ANNE, KATHERINE and SUSANNA. I give to my wife for life the messuage in Easton in which I live with its land, and after her death to my son JOHN, who must pay £5 each to his 5 sisters at the rate of one p.a. If my wife dies before JOHN reaches age of 21, THOMAS PELLS, my loving kinsman, is to have this house and land until JOHN is of age and is to let the property and divide the profits between JOHN and my 5 daughters. If JOHN dies without heirs, the house and land in Easton go to GEORGE, who must then pay £10 each to his sisters at the rate of one p.a. (The daughters have benefit of survivorship and power of distraint.) I give my 5 daughters £10 each to be paid by my exrx. when they reach 24. All my household goods and cattle I give to my wife towards bringing up my children and performing my will. She is sole exrx. Witnesses: FRANCIS COLEMAN, MARGARET ASKOWE and ROBERT FLINT. Pr. at Wickham Market 8 Oct. 1634.

R(W) KATHERINE SMYTH (X) of Parham, widow. 9 April 1630 (837

In health of body. I give to my daughter MARY, wife of ROBERT MENTLE, all my household goods now in the possession of her husband and half my linen. I give to my grandchild SUSAN COBB all my clothes, both linen and woollen, and 1 red coffer now standing in the parlour of JOHN SAWER, my son-in-law. I bequeath 20s. each to my grandchildren FRANCIS and PRISCILLA BRADWELL when they are 21, and to GEORGE SAWER my grandson my brass pot when he is 21. My household goods now in my hands and in those of JOHN SAWER I bequeath to my daughter KATHERINE SAWER. The residue of my goods, chattels and money, after payment of my debts and legacies, are to be equally divided between my 2 daughters, MARY and KATHERINE. Sole exor. JOHN SAWER. Witnesses: HUGH BARRY, EDMUND JORDAN, ROBERT MENTLE (X). Pr. at Wickham Market 8 Oct. 1634.

R(W) JOHN BROWNE (X) of Covehithe alias Northales, husbandman. 2 October 1634 (838)

I give and bequeath my house and tenement wherein I now dwell with the yard and all my household stuff to my loving wife ELIZABETH for ever, and make her sole exrx. Witnesses: JOHN YONGE, BENJAMIN STAFFORD, ELIZABETH JERNAS and others. Pr. at Beccles 7 Oct. 1634.

R(W) LIONEL CORNISH (X) of Ipswich, yeoman. 2 August 1634 (839)

Sick in body. I give 20s. to my father ROBERT CORNISH in token of a remembrance of my duty to him. I also give to him my small stock of cattle that is in his hands to be distributed amongst my brothers and sisters after his death. I leave £5 to MARGERY ABBS my elder sister, and to her son ROBERT ABBS a testament, which is in my chest, to learn to read in. To my younger sister KATHERINE CORNISH I give £8 and my bible which I commonly use. I make my brother STEPHEN sole exor. I do forgive my elder sister what I lent her and she shall never be called to pay a penny thereof. I give the residue of my goods, debts, bonds and wearing apparel to my exor. to pay my funeral charges, the apothecary and doctor for their physick in this time of my sickness, and my debts. I give to WILLIAM STYLES for his pains and the care he has taken with me a pair of gloves. Witnesses: THOMAS TOMLYN, WILLIAM STYLES. Pr. at Ipswich 5 Aug. 1634.

R(W) ROBERT MARSHE of Bromeswell, yeoman. 1 August 1634 (840)

I give and bequeath all my lands and tenements, free and copyhold, in Bromeswell to my daughter ELIZABETH PALMER for life, and then to her daughter ALICE and her heirs for ever one close of pasture called Meldam; to her daughter ELIZABETH and her heirs one close of arable called Nobs close which I bought from WILLIAM GARRARD; and to her son GEORGE and his heirs 2 pieces of arable or pasture which I purchased from JOHN GOSLING. To my grand-daughter ELIZABETH STILES I leave £10 to be paid to her when she is 20 by the then owner of Meldam close. (She has power to distrain.) Supervisor: GERVASE HUBBARD of Rendlesham, clerk. All the rest of my goods and chattels I give to GEORGE and ELIZABETH PALMER, my son-in-law and daughter, and I make them exors. and ask them to pay my debts. I give ELIZABETH STILES a featherbed and a feather bolster which I bought of her father and a half headed bedstead to be delivered to her when she is 21. To WILLIAM MARSHE, son of my brother WILLIAM MARSHE, I give my birding piece. Witnesses: GERVASE HUBBARD, WILLIAM MARSH (X). Pr. at Wickham Market 30 Oct. 1634.

R(W) ROBERT PETTIT of Tunstall.[blank] 1634 (841)

Sick of body. I give a 3 acre piece of land in Oulton to my wife AGNES for ever, and I give her for life, in satisfaction of her dower, a little tenement re-edified and built in a place called the Grove with the little house adjoining it, a hempland and a yard amounting to 1/2 acre, and all the fruit on both sides of the house. I also give her 1 posted bedstead now standing in the parlour chamber with the tester belonging to it, a featherbed and a transom, 2 pillows, 1 blanket and my bed covering, 2 pairs sheets, 2 pillow beeres, 1 table in the hall with the frame and form belonging to it, 1 great kettle, 1 little stand, 2 little kettles, 1 cobiron, 1 pair tongs and firepan, 1 little pair of malt querns, 1 great spring coffer, 1 great hutch standing on feet, 1 round stool and 1 livery stool. Also 10 cheeses and 6 pints of butter, 1 frying pan, 2 bushels wheat, 3 bushels malt, 1 great keep, 1 warming pan, 1 great and 1 little firkin, 1 feather pillow, 1 flitch of bacon, 1 hake, 1 great pewter platter, 1 brinded calf, 6 sheaves of femble hemp. After her decease all these goods are to go to my grand-daughter ELIZABETH PETTIT, except those things which were my wife's before her marriage with me. I leave £5 to my grandchild ANNA HARTWELL when she is 21. To my son HENRY I give all my tenement called Scuter or Scoter with its land, except the little tenement already given to my wife for her life. I also give him 2 milk neats, 1 roan nag, a featherbed, a posted bedstead, all my shop tools and all the rest of my goods. I make him sole exor. Supervisor: ROBERT CHANTRIE of Kelsale. Witnesses: WILLIAM BAKER, FRANCIS WILLET. Pr. at Wickham Market 18 Sept. 1634.

R(W) FRANCIS REEVE of Westleton (N). 1 October 1634 (842)

He left £5 to the poor of Westleton to be invested by the churchwardens and overseers of the poor with the intention that the income should be distributed to the poor on the anniversary of his funeral every year. All his own goods and those he inherited from his sister he gave to his cousins, the children of his uncle HUGGINS and his aunt DRANE. Witnesses: JOHN SWAYNE and ELIZABETH HACON. Pr. at Yoxford 9 Oct. 1634 to THOMAS HUGGINS.

R(W) FRANCES RAYNOLD (X) of Stonham Aspal, widow. 11 October 1634 (843)

I give 40s. to my eldest son JOHN and 20s. to my son RICHARD and 20s. to my daughter ELIZABETH, wife of WILLIAM COLEMAN and 20s. to my daughter FRANCES RAYNOLD. These payments are to be made at the rate of 1 p.a. at Michaelmas. I give the rest of my goods to my daughter PRISCILLA, whom I make sole exrx. and who is to pay my debts and legacies, and to see me decently buried. Witnesses: ANTHONY LIFT and THOMAS GALLOWES. Pr. at Ipswich 31 Oct. 1634.

R(W) JOHN SHALE (X) of Ipswich. 14 May 1634 (844)

Weak in body. I give to Mr SAMUEL WARD, preacher of God's word in Ipswich, £10. I bequeath to my sister's 2 sons and 2 daughters £10 each to be paid by my exrx. within 6 months of my decease. I will that £5 be bestowed on my burial and I give to the preacher that shall preach at my burial 10s. All the rest of my movable goods I give and bequeath to ANNE PETTEWARD, wife of WILLIAM PETTEWARD of Ipswich, for her great pains and care of me for many years, and I make her sole exrx. of my will. I give to my sister ROSE PINSON £10 and to Goodman WILSON, sexton of the Tower, 5s. I give to the poor of the Tower parish (St. Mary at Tower) 20s. Witnesses: SIMON PETTEWARD senior, MARY PETTEWARD, DOROTHY HORELY (X). Pr. at Ipswich 20 May 1634.

R(W) JOHN SHARKE the elder of Kelsale (N). (845)
17 October 1634

He gave all his goods to his wife BRIDGET. Witnesses: RALPH EADE, GEORGE EADE. Pr. at Yoxford 29 Oct. 1634.

R(W) JOHN SMYTH (X) of Holbrook, fisherman. (846)
20 October 1634

Sick and weak in body. I leave 10s. to the poor people of Holbrook to be distributed by my exrx. within 3 months of my decease. I give to JOHN SMYTH my son £5 to be paid within 1 year of my death, and 1 bed ready furnished in the chamber and on which he usually lies. To my son WILLIAM £7 within 2 years and to my son THOMAS £7 within 3 years of my death. These legacies are with benefit of survivorship. The residue of my goods and chattels I give to ELIZABETH my wife whom I make sole exrx., hoping that she will have a care to perform my will. Witnesses: JOHN CRANE (X), JOHN BROTHERTON, who wrote the will. Pr. at Ipswich 2 Nov. 1634.

R(W) JOHN SAWER of Campsea Ash. 15 July 1634 (847)

Sick of body. I give and bequeath to RICHARD WYNTER my uncle, the exor. of the will of my late father JOHN SAWER, £10. I give to JOHN SMYTH my master, with whom I dwell, and to ANNE his wife £10 each to be paid next Lady Day. I give £4 to ELIZABETH, wife of HENRY PAGE and daughter of ANTHONY TOWNRAWE; 40s. each to RICHARD, MARGARET & HENRY WINTER, the children of my cousin RICHARD WINTER; 20s. each to my cousin RICHARD WINTER and to ELIZABETH his wife; 10s. to KATHERINE, wife of THOMAS TOWNRAWE; & £10 to my cousin WILLIAM BLYTH. All these legacies are to be paid by 1st March next ensuing. I give £10 to be used by my exor. to bring my body to the ground in decent order, for a repast for my friends who accompany my body to the earth, to pay the bearers, ringers and other helpers, and to the poor. I make RICHARD WYNTER, my uncle, sole exor. Witnesses: THOMAS HOLMES

(X), JOHN GREENE. Pr. at Wickham Market 30 Oct. 1634.

R(W) JOHN SAGAR of South Elmham St. Michael, yeoman. (848)
18 November 1634

Weak in body. I wish to be buried in the parish of All Saints. I give and bequeath to JOAN my wife for life all my freehold land and tenements in Chediston. She must keep the house in good repair and bring up my children. After her death this land is to go to my daughters ELIZABETH & JOAN and to the child my wife is carrying. I give to my wife all the movable goods she brought with her when we married. She must give security to my father JOHN SAGAR to pay an annuity of £10 during his life and that of ELIZABETH SAGAR my mother; this is to be paid quarterly. The rest of my movable goods are to be sold and the money used by my exor. to pay my debts, funeral and probate expenses. I make my father, JOHN SAGAR clerk, sole exor. I give him 20s. for his pains. Witnesses: BENJAMIN FAIRFAX, ROBERT GOOCHE. Pr. at Bungay 20 Nov. 1634.

R(W) MARGARET LANGLEY of Mutford, (849)
widow of ROBERT LANGLEY. 9 June 1634

I leave 10s. to the poor of Mutford. I give to WILLIAM HERNE, my son-in-law, and to MARGARET his wife for their lives the tenement wherein I dwell with its land both free and copyhold. They must pay 20s. p.a. in quarterly payments to ELIZABETH, wife of JOHN HANCE of Easton. After the deaths of WILLIAM & MARGARET HERNE, I bequeath my tenement and land to my grandchild ROBERT PEEKE, son of JAMES PEEKE and of my late daughter PHILIPPA. ROBERT must pay his elder brother THOMAS £5 within 3 years of entering into possession of the tenement and land. If WILLIAM HERNE survives his wife he is to pay ROBERT PEEKE 20s. p.a. for his better maintenance. My posted bedstead, my table and my joined chair now in the parlour are to remain in my house for the use of its occupants for ever. The rest of my goods and chattels I give to WILLIAM & MARGARET HERNE, whom I make exors. Witnesses: WILLIAM LONE, RALPH MYLLES (X), MARY LINGLY. Pr. at Beccles 5 Dec. 1634.

R(W) WILLIAM CODON of Shadingfield, esquire. (850)
27 July 1633

I wish to be buried in the chancel of Shadingfield church. I give 20s. to the minister of this parish and 20s. to the minister that shall preach at my burial. I give 40s. to the poor of Shadingfield, and as for other deeds of charity I leave them to the discretion of my exrx. I have already given away some of my movables and real estate. First I give to FRANCIS my eldest son my plank table as it stands in the hall with the trestles and forms belonging to it. I give and bequeath to my daughter ELIZABETH SMITH for her life my tenement in Beccles, and after her death to her daughter ELIZABETH SMITH and her heirs for ever.

I give £3 each to my other 5 daughters: ANNE WADE, URSULA HAMOND, MARY BURWARD, DOROTHY TITHE and AUDREY LEE. The legacy to my daughter DOROTHY shall be void if her husband WILLIAM TITHE makes any claim to it. I give to ELIZABETH, my well-beloved wife, my plate, jewels, ready money, bedding, brass, pewter, linen, woollen, my geldings and all my unbequeathed movable goods in the parlour, parlour chamber, dining chamber and all the other rooms in my new building and also in Beadles hall, in the men's chamber, the stable, the brewhouse, the bakehouse or elsewhere. I make my wife sole exrx. and I doubt not but that she will lovingly and faithfully fulfill it. Witnesses: AMBROSE PLAYTERS, JOHN COLBUCK clerk. Pr. at Beccles 24 Dec. 1634.

R(W) ANNE GREENE (X) of Ipswich, widow. 30 October 1630 (851)

I give to my daughter ANNE AKELEY 12d., and to my daughter ELIZABETH 3 pairs of new sheets and half my apparel. My daughter CICELY is to have the other half, and I make her sole exrx. and give her the rest of my goods. Witnesses: RICHARD & MARY RAINFORD, WILLIAM COALE. Pr. at Ipswich 18 Oct. 1634.

R(W) THOMAS ROE of Walton, gentleman. 4 November 1634 (852)

Sick in body. I leave £5 to the poor of Walton. I give to FRANCIS HUMFREY of Walton 40s. and to his daughter ANNE 6 sheep, that is to say 4 wethers and 2 ewes. To my godchild ROBERT BROOKE I give 1 ewe. I give to JOHN LAND, gent. and Lieutenant of Landguard new fort, the ring I wear daily. I bequeath to JOHN SCRUTTON, gent., the bay nag I ususally ride in token of the old affection which was always between us. I give to my loving sister ANNE, wife of JOHN STILES draper of Woodbridge, all my freehold and copyhold land and tenements in Clopton for her life and after her death to her eldest son THOMAS STYLES. ANNE is to use the income from this property to bring up THOMAS until he is 21, to bestow on him some learning and to provide him with meat and drink, and clothing, both linen and woollen, and all things necessary for a manchild to have and wear. If ANNE refuses to do this my exor. is to have the tuition of THOMAS and £10 p.a. from the property left to ANNE. If ANNE is still alive when THOMAS reaches 21, she is to pay him £10 p.a. I give and bequeath to THOMAS STILES 1 silver bowl which his mother is to keep carefully for him until he is 21. If the sale of my movable goods does not raise enough to pay my debts and legacies, my exors. are empowered to sell some of the land left to my sister ANNE. I give £5 each to my exors. to buy a ring to wear for my sake. I bequeath 40s. to my aunt, MARION TALBOT, widow of Walton. I give to MARGARET, wife of FRANCIS HUMPHERIE of Walton, 10s. to buy a ring and ask her to wear it for my sake. I make exors. my sister ANNE STYLES and my kinsman DANIEL SMITH of Walton gent. Witnesses: JOHN SCRUTTON, JOHN COCK (X), JOAN MASON (X). Memorandum: I do further give to JOHN COCK, singleman of Landguard New Fort, a suit of clothes, doublet and hose which I daily wear, my new cloak and the friese coat I wear daily.

Lastly I give and bequeath 20s. to my brother-in-law JOHN STYLES, requiring him to buy a ring and wear it for my sake. Pr. at Woodbridge 9 Dec. 1634.

R(W) THOMAS TUNMER (X) of Helmingham, husbandman. (853)
10 August 1634

I give to ANNE my beloved wife all my movable goods for her life. After her death my daughter ELIZABETH CARVER shall have 3 of the best cows, a posted bedstead, a featherbed, a bolster and all that belongs to it as it now stands, and 1 pair of sheets which were her own mother's, 1 cupboard in the hall with the pewter standing on it, a table in the hall and a chest in the chamber. I give to AMY CORBULL 1 chest in the hall. The rest of my goods are to be equally divided between my son THOMAS and my daughter ELIZABETH CARVER. Wife sole exrx. Witnesses: REGINALD ABLE, RICHARD ALLING (X). Pr. at Ipswich 3 Jan. 1634/5.

R(W) ELIZABETH GARDNER (X) of Ufford, widow. (854)
10 February 1633/4

I give and bequeath to my daughter CICELY, wife of JOHN MOORE, all my land and tenements in Sproughton for her life and then to her son THOMAS for ever. I give to my grandchild ELIZABETH MOORE my bed and bedstead in the parlour where I now dwell with 2 bolsters, 2 pillows, 1 coverlet, 2 blankets, the curtains and curtain rods and all other things belonging immediately after the decease of CICELY MOORE. ELIZABETH must pay half the value of this bedstead to my daughter MARGARET BROOKE. I give to ELIZABETH MOORE 3 pairs sheets, 2 pillow beeres, 8 pieces of pewter, my biggest brass pot, 1 kettle, my cupboard, my biggest chair and my joined chair in the parlour. I give and bequeath to my grandson JOHN MOORE my bed and bedstead in the parlour chamber where I now dwell with the bolster, 2 pillows, 2 blankets, 1 coverlet and all other things belonging. Also I give to him 6 pieces of pewter, 1 brass pot, my table and form in the hall, 1 chair, 3 pairs of sheets, 1 table cloth, and 1 kettle. To my grandson THOMAS MOORE I bequeath my bedstead now in the possession of Widow BRYTH of Ufford, a featherbed, a bolster, 1 blanket, 1 coverlet, 1 brass pot, 6 pieces of pewter, 1 chair and 1 kettle. All these gifts to my grandchildren are to be delivered to them immediately after the decease of my daughter CICELY. I give to my daughter MARGARET BROOKE my best gown and my best petticoat. I give 20s. each to my grandchildren HENRY, MARGARET & THOMAS BROOKE. I give to my daughter CICELY MOORE all the money I have at the time of my decease and all that due to me by bond or otherwise, my debts, legacies and funeral charges having first been paid. She must divide this money between her 3 children when she dies, and she and her husband, JOHN MOORE, must enter into a bond of £100 with GERVASE HUBBALD, parson of Rendlesham, to do this. If they refuse, their children's legacies are to be kept by GERVASE HUBBALD until the children are 18. All the rest of my goods I give to my daughter CICELY and I make her and my daughter MARGARET exrxs. of my will. Witnesses: GERVASE HUBBALD, EDWARD GOULDING (X). Pr. at Wickham Market 8 Jan. 1634/5.

R(W) JOHN PROWDE of Halesworth, currier. 8 November 1634 (855)

Sick and weak in body. I give to my son WALTER that part of my house standing next the street with part of the yard. He must pay my daughter MARY £3 within 2 years of my wife's decease. I give to my daughter ELLEN the house wherein I dwell, and she must pay MARY 20s. within 2 years of my wife's death. I give to my daughter ELIZABETH my new house and the other part of the yard, which is to be divided from the end of the sill to the pale. These 2 daughters are to share this yard and live together as sisters ought. I make my wife MARY sole exrx. Witnesses: FRANCIS TAYLOR, SIMON CRISPE, RICHARD LONG. Pr. at Yoxford 10 Dec. 1634.

R(W) ANDREW SMITH (X) of Friston. 15 December 1634 (856)

Sick in body. I give £20 to JOHN DALINGER, my son-in-law within 2 years of my death; £15 to ARTHUR DALINGER my son-in-law within 3 years of my death; and £15 to SUSAN DALINGER my daughter-in-law within 4 years of my decease. [These 3 are probably step children.] These legatees have benefit of survivorship. I give to WILLIAM APE my apprentice 20s. when he is 24. Whereas I have taken ALICE PEARCY a poor child of Friston, I wish my exrx. to keep her with sufficient meat, drink and apparel until she 21 and then to give her double apparel at the end of her time. All the rest of my movable goods I give to MARY my wife who is to pay my debts and legacies and whom I make sole exrx. Witnesses: THOMAS FRENCH, THOMAS HARDING. Pr. at Wickham Market 18 Jan. 1634/5.

R. WILLIAM SMITER (X) of Kirkley, yeoman. (857)
20 December 1634

The unprofitable servant of God. Weak in body. I give and bequeath to my son ROBERT £5 when he is 21. All the rest of my goods I bequeath to my loving brother THOMAS SMYTER the elder of Lowestoft, whom I make sole exor., earnestly desiring him to discharge my debts and be helpful to my wife and with the bringing up of my son. Witnesses: RICHARD CHURCH and J. MAPLIZDEN, who wrote the will. Pr. at Beccles 2 Jan. 1634/5.

R(W) ROGER BEARE of Westhall, yeoman. 26 July 1634 (858)

Sick of body. I give to ROGER BEARE my eldest son for ever the messuage wherein I dwell with all its lands, which I purchased from ROBERT BENNET late of Westhall, on condition he pays the following legacies: £15 p.a. to ELIZABETH his mother in 2 equal portions at Lady Day and Michaelmas; to his sister KATHERINE £100 when she is 22; to his brother THOMAS £100 when he is 22; to his brother ROBERT £100 when he is 21; to his brother HENRY £100 when he is 21; and to ELIZABETH his youngest sister £100 when she is 22. All these payments are to be made in the south porch of Westhall church. The legatees have power to distrain and benefit of survivorship. I give to JOHN BEARE my second son the messuage wherein JOHN COZEN now dwells with its lands which I bought from EDWARD REEVE, late of Westhall. He must allow his mother to live in this house and occupy the lands during her widowhood, and she must pay him £10 p.a. in 2 equal payments at Lady Day and Michaelmas. The payments are to be made in this house. My son JOHN is to pay his brother HENRY £10 when he is 21. ROGER my eldest son is to pay £10 p.a. towards the upbringing and keeping at school of my children THOMAS, ROBERT, HENRY & ELIZABETH until they reach age of 17. If my wife dies before all these children are 17, then ROGER is to bring them up. I give to ELIZABETH my well-beloved wife £20 worth of cattle, bedding and household stuff to be delivered to her within 1 month of my decease. I will that she shall have the use of the little parlour, the buttery beyond it and the parlour chamber in the messuage where I now dwell for one whole year after my decease. All the rest of my debts, ready money, cattle, household implements, corn and timber I give to my eldest son ROGER to pay my debts and funeral charges, and I make him sole exor. Witnesses: SIMON SYMOND, JOHN BENNET. Pr. at Beccles 14 Feb. 1634/5.

R(W) ELIAZER FISKE of Withersdale, yeoman. (859)
10 November 1634

In good health. I wish to be buried in the church of the parish in which I die. I give to my son ELIAZER my messuage called Norris in Metfield, in which my brother-in-law JOHN SAWER lives, together with the buildings and land belonging to it. He must pay to SARAH FISKE, my loving mother, all the legacies left to her in the will made on 20 Oct. 1628 by my late father JEFFERY FISKE. He must also pay to ANNE my youngest daughter £50 as follows: £10 on 29 Sept. 1636 and £10 on that date every year until £50 is paid. As soon as my son ELIAZER reaches age of 21 he must dishcarge my exors. from payment to him of all sums of money given to him by the last will of MARY LANTER, widow of South Elmham St. James, dated 20 Sept. 1619. If he refuses to do this he must pay £10 each to my daughters MARY, SARAH & ANNE to increase their portions. I give to ANNE my daughter £100 to be paid by my exors. on 25 June next after she reaches age of 21, and £50 when she is 20. These payments are to be made in the porch of Metfield church. I give to my son JOHN, when he is 24, the messuage in which I now dwell in Withersdale with its land, which I lately purchased from ROBERT HARPER of Mendham. He must pay £20 each to his 3 sisters, starting the Michaelmas after he is 24 and paying one a year in Metfield church porch. If JOHN dies without heirs before he reaches age of 24, my son ELIAZER is to pay £40 each to his 3 sisters as above. My daughters have power to distrain. I give to my daughter MARY £50 owed to me by JOHN & EDWARD WATSON. To my daughter SARAH I give £140 when she is 24 on condition she does not demand from my exors. any money from the will of MARY LANTER. I give to my son ELIAZER one bedstead as it stands fully furnished with its bedding in the parlour of the house I dwell in, a table in the parlour of my house in Metfield and my best cart. I give to my son JOHN a bedstead fully furnished in the parlour chamber of the house wherein I dwell. All my unbequeathed cattle, corn, linen, brass and household stuff is to be equally divided amongst my 3 daughters within 1 month after my decease, but I leave my ready money to my exors. Daughters have benefit of survivorship. Exors. to hold my house and land in Withersdale until my son JOHN is 24, and are to use its profits to pay my legacies and keep my buildings in repair. I will that my son JOHN be bound apprentice to some honest man to the trade of a tailor as he desires, and I give my exors. £10 to pay to his master. I give 40s. to be distributed amongst the poor people who have most need, and 10s. to a faithful minister to preach a sermon at my burial for the good of the people present. I give my exors. £5 each and 40s. to my supervisor. My exors. are to put out my children's portions to the best profit. Exors.: RICHARD NEWSON of Westhall, yeoman and my brother-in-law, and my kinsman NATHANIEL FISKE of Weybread, yeoman. Supervisor, my kinsman FRANCIS VERDON, singleman of Linstead Parva. Witnesses: FRANCIS VERDON, JOHN SAWER, MILLICENT SAWER (X). Pr. at Beccles 14 Feb. 1634/5.

R(W) WILLIAM STEEDMAN (X) of Beccles, yeoman. (860)
27 January 1634/5

I give to my son THOMAS my messuage called Skinners and the yard belonging to it, which is now occupied by WILLIAM SMITH, JOHN CRISPE & [blank in manuscript]. I give to my daughter MARY all my goods in the parlour, viz. 1 featherbed, bolster and pillows, a coverlet and blankets with the bedstead, 1 long table, a little table, a chest, 3 buffet stools, a coffer, and a box. Also I give to MARY my biggest brass pot and a little one, a cupboard, a great chafing dish with the foot to it, the ewer, a brass kettle, a copper kettle, and a skillet. Also to her all my linen and woollen which was my wife's, except for 2 pairs of sheets which I give to my son THOMAS. I give to THOMAS my nether tenement called Skinners with the yard, now occupied by JOHN TUCKE my son [presumably son-in-law]. THOMAS is to have possession of this house immediately after my decease. I give to my daughter MARY my white cow and a 12-month old calf. All the rest of my goods, cattle, household stuff and implements of husbandry I give to my son THOMAS on condition he pays my gifts and legacies. I give 20s. each to ANDREW, MARGARET, EMMA, MARTHA & KATHERINE, the children of CLEMENT STEEDMAN deceased, to be paid within 1 year of my death. I give 40s. each to my sons ROBERT, PHILIP & WILLIAM to be paid within 2 years of my decease. My son THOMAS is to pay my debts and funeral charges, and he shall have all my clothes. Exors.: my loving friends FRANCIS LENGLEY, gent. of Toft in Norfolk, and MILES KEBLE gent. of Ditchingham in Norfolk. I give them 20s. each. Witnesses: HENRY COPPING, RICHARD MAPLIZDEN. Pr. at Beccles 9 Feb. 1634/5. MILES KEBLE renounced his executorship.

R(W) JOHN HUNT the elder of Needham Market, clothier. (861)
24 October 1631

I give to my wife MARY the house I live in and that occupied by JOHN KNAPP with the yard belonging to these houses. After her death I leave them to my son EDMUND, who must pay £20 each to his brother EDWARD and his sister SUSAN at the rate of £10 p.a. I give and bequeath to my son JOHN the house and yard where he now dwells for his life and afterwards to my son EDMUND. I give to THOMAS GLADEN and his wife ELIZABETH my houses and lands in Trimley and Walton. They must pay £10 to my son JAMES within 1 month of my death; £10 to WILLIAM DEBBICHE, my son-in-law, 2 years after my decease; and £10 to STEPHEN FLOWER, my son-in-law, 4 years after my death. If they refuse to pay these legacies, then I give this house and land to my wife MARY for ever. All my movable goods I give to my wife, whom I make sole exrx. Witnesses: THOMAS LONE, EDWARD CARVER. Pr. at Ipswich 9 Jan. 1634/5.

R(W) WILLIAM FULLER of Syleham, gentleman. (862)
20 January 1629

I give to the poor people of Ilketshall 20s. to be distributed by the minister of the parish the Lord's day after my decease. I give 10s. to the poor of Syleham, 10s. to the poor of Brockdish, 6s. 8d. to the poor of Hopton, 5s. to the poor of Needham, 10s. to the poor of Halesworth, 10s. to the poor of Mendham, 5s. to the poor of Weybread and 5s. to the poor of Wingfield. All these sums are to be distributed by the churchwardens of these parishes on the day of my burial. I give to Mr THOMAS DAINES preacher 40s. and to Mr BRIANT WHERELL of Syleham 20s. I give and bequeath to CLAIRE my wife £20 in lieu of her claim to a third of my estate. My exors. are to pay her £10 within 1 month of my death and the other £10 a year later. She is to have all such goods as were hers before our marriage, and any rents due to me. I give to my wife's daughter REBECCA STOWERS 40s., and to MARY, my late wife's daughter and now the wife of JOHN ALLEN, 40s. to buy a ring for remembrance. I give RICHARD PUCKEL the gilt salt that was his mother's, and to SAMUEL PUCKELL the broad silver gilt cup that was his mother's. I give 40s. each to GABRIEL, JOAN & ANN PUCKELL. I give to EDMUND GILES my wife's son and to EDMUND ELLES that married my wife's daughter the sum of £10 to be used for the benefit of ANN, the wife of [blank in manuscript] GODBOLD and daughter of my former wife GILES. This money is to be used for her good and that of the youngest children she had by her former husband GOSLING. I give and bequeath to ANNE BISHOP, now the wife of one PEIRSE of Pulham, 40s. I give 10s. each to ANTHONY GOODWYN, PETER, SARAH, GRACE & FRANCIS GOODING. I bequeath 10s. to my nephew WILLIAM BARBER. I give my apprentice GEORGE BERTE £5 when he is 24, and to every servant dwelling with me at the time of my decease 10s. I give all my linen to my daughters LYDIA & JUDITH; LYDIA is to have two-thirds and JUDITH one third. My plate, ready money and debts owing to me are to be equally shared amongst my children BENJAMIN, LYDIA and JUDITH. I will that the table in the hall, the 2 tables and the bench in the parlour and all the pictures in any of the rooms shall remain where they are for my son. I give my daughters LYDIA and JUDITH, wife of WILLIAM WOODS, annuities of £10 to be paid out of my land in Wingfield called Trollopes in 2 equal payments at Lady Day and Michaelmas. They have power to distrain. I give to my grandson WILLIAM WOODS £100 when 22, to my grandson THOMAS WOODS £60 when 24 and to my grandchild SUSAN WOODS £40 when she is 21. I bought from Mr THOMAS LAWRENCE 4 acres of land lying near my house for the benefit of my daughter LYDIA. If my son BENJAMIN pays her £50 she must surrender to him all her right to this land, but if she refuses to do so her annuity shall be forfeit. If LYDIA marries and bears a child which lives to the age of 20, my exor.is then to pay to him or her £100. When my grandson WILLIAM FULLER reaches the age of 21 my exor. is to pay him an annuity of £10 out of Trollopes as long as he lives with his parents and behaves himself dutifully towards them. I appoint my son BENJAMIN my sole exor., and give him towards the performance of my will all my hay and corn, all my implements of husbandry, my horses, cows and cattle and all my leases and chattels. Since I made my will I have received £300 for land sold in Ingate and Weston; this money is in the hands of my son's landlord, Mr SPALDING, who is to repay it after 3 years. My son is to have this £300 for his own use. My exor. shall see me buried near my late wife in the chancel of Syleham church, and shall lay a decent stone or stones over our graves within 1 year of the day of my burial. Supervisors: RICHARD GREENE of Wilby and LAWRENCE MAYHEW gent. of Norfolk, to whom I give 20s. each. My exor. must bind himself to them in the sum of £400 truly to perform my will. The will was signed and sealed on 2 Feb. 1633/4. Witnesses: ANTHONY & RICHARD BASPOOLE, JOHN BROWNE. Pr. at Beccles 31 Jan. 1634/5.

R(W) EDMUND PALMER of Rendham. 14 April 1634 (863)

I give and bequeath to my son EDMUND all my copyhold land and tenements in Rendham and Sweffling. He must pay my wife ELLEN an annuity of 5 marks in full discharge of her dower in 2 equal payments at Lady Day and Michaelmas. If he refuses to pay this, the above land is bequeathed to my wife for life. I give to EDMUND my best silver cup with a cover, my gown, the long table in the parlour, the bedstead with its valence and bed line in the parlour chamber, and all my armour both old and new with the pike and jackequett belonging to the same. After my son dies his son EDMUND PALMER is to have these gifts, except for the armour. I give to my grandson EDMUND PALMER the great brass pot now in the use of his father, the court cupboard in the parlour chamber, all my books and manuscripts and the keep in the parlour that the books usually stand or lie in; also the painted board, the earthen bason with a foot, the painted ewer standing on the court cupboard in the parlour chamber and the long drawing table standing in the parlour at his father's house in Carlton. I give to PRISCILLA, MARY & ELIZABETH, my eldest son's daughters, 2 silver spoons each, and to MARY and ELIZABETH 1 pair of sheets. I give to MARTHA, daughter of my son EDMUND, one double ducat [duckett in manuscript]. I give to ELLEN my wife my little new featherbed and a small bolster and all the household stuff that was hers before we married, and 3 loads of firewood. I give to THOMAS PALMER my brother my violet coloured cloak and my new cloth breeches, and to his son THOMAS a hat and 30s. I give to my kinsman THOMAS HIRRIN 1 pair of sheets and 30s. I give to my cousin RICHARD MORRIS 30s. I give 10s. each to THOMAS & EDMUND, sons of my deceased brother RICHARD PALMER; 20s. to my godson EDMUND PALMER; 20s. each to my sister SHENNING and to her children ELIZABETH & EDMUND, who is my godson. I give 20s. when 21 to the eldest son of my cousin CLAY. I give 20s. to the poor of Rendham, 10s. to the poor of the parishes of Sweffling, Snape and Saxmundham, and 5s. to the poor of the parishes of Stratford, Farnham, Sternfield, Friston and Bruisyard. These sums are to be distributed amongst the neediest poor at the discretion of the ministers of these parishes within 1 week of my decease. I give to my grandson EDMUND, son of my son JOHN, the house in Framlingham which I lately purchased from ANTHONY SHENNING and his sister MARGERY TOWELL. Until he is of age, the rent of this house is to be used towards his upbringing and that of his sister ALICE, to whom I give £20 when she is 21. I also give to ALICE the chest in the closet next to the parlour chamber, 6 pairs of my best sheets, a long board cloth of holland, 2 pairs of the best and 1 pair of the coarse pillow beeres, 2 dozen table napkins of the finest I have, a small holland broad cloth, 2 long towels and the spice box that was her grandmother's and which is inlaid on all sides and 1 dozen pewter dishes. All these gifts are to be kept locked up in the chest given to ALICE until she is 18. If she dies, they are to be given to her brother EDMUND when he is 20. All my unbequeathed goods and chattels I give to my son JOHN towards his further preferment, and I make him sole exor. Supervisors: my cousin WILLIAM BROWNE of Rendham, my son EDMUND and my brother THOMAS. JOHN must bind himself to my supervisors in the sum of £300 truly to perfrom my will. He must also bring up his children, EDMUND & ALICE, with meat, drink and apparel until they are able to get their own living. If JOHN refuses to be bound, then I will that Mr THOMAS PAINE of Charsfield, lately chief constable, and my beloved friend JOHN HUNT of Parham should be my exors. If they are my exors, they are to sell my house in Framlingham and all my goods and chattels, and use the money to bring up my grandchildren EDMUND and ALICE until they are 16 and then to bind them out as apprentices. Any money left over is to be given to EDMUND & ALICE when 21. If both these children die my son EDMUND is to have this money. Witnesses: THOMAS FRENCH, THOMAS BROWNE. Codicil dated 14 Oct. 1634. Testator discharged his son EDMUND from a bond obliging him to pay legacies given in his will. Pr. at Saxmundham 18 Feb. 1634/5.

R(W) GEORGE RIPINGE of Carlton Colville, yeoman. (864)
13 July 1634

Sick and weak in body. First I will that a dole of 3d. shall be given to each poor person who comes to my burial by my exors., whom I appoint my loving cousin Mr SEAMAN, parson of Carlton Coville, my good friend Mr ROBERDS, parson of Gisleham and my kinsman JOHN HULLOCKE, yeoman of Carlton Coville. I give 30s. to the poor of Carlton Colville to be distributed by the overseers of the poor during the 3 months after my decease, and 20s. to the poor of Lowestoft. I give £10 to my kinswoman MARY HULLOCKE, widow, and 2 gold rings already in her possession. Also to her and to JOHN HULLOCKE the younger all the household goods I have in the house of JOHN HULLOCKE the elder. I give £3 to Mr PHILIP HAWARD, 20s. to his son PHILIP and 20s. to his daughter FRANCES. I give 20s. to Mr HUMPHREY HAWARD as soon as he pays the money he owes me. I bequeath 30s. to Mr ROBERT MILDEN of Somerleyton to buy a ring, and another £5. I give 20s. to his wife and 10s. each to his children FRANCIS & SUSAN. I bequeath £6 to my kinsman Mr SEAMAN, 20s. to his wife and 20s. each to all his children. I give 20s. to my godson GEORGE LOWND and 10s. each to his 2 children. I give £5 to the son and £3 to the daughter of WILLIAM SEGSLYE and to his wife 40s., my best hat and a pair of murry stockings. Also to them all my goods in their possession at my house in Somerleyton, except a black mourning cloak. I give my kinsman JOHN LYNCOLNE and his wife 20s. each to be paid when he pays the money he owes me. I give Mr SELLING and his wife and Mistress ELIZABETH CHAPMAN 5s. each to buy a pair of gloves. I bequeath 10s. each to my kinsman ROBERT LYNCOLNE, to his wife and to their child which is my god-daughter. I give my kinsman SAMUEL LINCOLNE a long table with a long form standing in BLANCHFLOWER's house in Gisleham; also to him a musket fully furnished, a dozen silver spoons and 40s. on condition he renounces all claims to my estate. I give 25s. to ROGER HOLLOCK of Gisleham; 20s. to KATHERINE GRIGGS widow and 6s. 8d. each to her children JOHN, THOMAS & AMBROSE. I also give THOMAS GRIGGS one pair of murry-colored breeches and a white cut doublet, but without the silver buttons on it. A pair of sheets are to be shared by ROGER HOLLOCKE and KATHERINE GRIGGS. I bequeath to NATHANIEL COLBY of Pakefield the musket he already has in his possession and 10s. to his wife and to his daughter who is my godchild. I give to JOHN COLLYN 1 set of silver buttons. I give to ROBERT RIX the elder 1 set of silver buttons of the biggest sort and to his children JOHN, ROBERT & ELIZABETH the money he owes me. I bequeath to THOMAS, son of AMBROSE HOLLOCKE 6s. 8d. and a little coffer standing by my bed. To my kinsman WILLIAM LOWND I give 1 suit of clothes and 40s. I bequeath 3s. 4d. each to my godchildren ROBERT CAPE and GEORGE BENETT and the son of THOMAS BROOKE of Somerleyton. I give to Mr LIONEL SEMAN, attorney, 20s. and the debt owed to me by BIRTCHAM of Beccles. I give to Mr HODGEKINS of Rushmere 13s. 4d. if he preaches at my funeral. I give JOHN PAMPLING, ROBERT WIGGE, JOHN BANY, THOMAS GREENE & JOHN PLAYFORD, all of Carlton Colville, 5s. each to buy woollen cloth. I give GEORGE ANNIS and his wife, the daughter of my cousin BEALE, 5s. each. I give 10s. each to my cousin JOHN

HALLOCK of Thorpe and to his wife; 20s. to ROBERT MURRELL of Carlton Colville; 10s. each to my cousin RANDALL of Barney and to his wife. I bequeath to GEORGE & ANNE, the children of my cousin WILLIAM KEMPE of Gisleham, the £6 which he and his father owe me. I give 6s. 8d. each to WILLIAM GOODWYN of Carleton Colville and to his wife. To my cousin JOHN HALLOCKE the elder of Carlton Colville I give £10, 1 set of silver buttons and my best suit of clothes. I give 3s. 4d. each to all the servants living with my cousin JOHN HALLOCK at the time of my death. To Mr BRAMPTON of Oulton I give 4s. to buy a pair of gloves, and to GEORGE JOLLY and his wife 3s. 4d. each to buy gloves. I give 3s 4d. to THOMAS STONE of Somerleyton. £18 is due to me by bond from JOHN HALLOCK the elder of Carlton Colville. I give £14 of it to his son JOHN, and my exors. are to make the remainder up to £10 and give it to JOHN HALLOCK the elder for the use of his son THOMAS. JOHN HALLOCK is to give this money to his 2 sons when they are 18 together with interest of 12d. per pound p.a. If JOHN HALLOCKE the elder buys my land, he may use the above £24 for that purpose. I give to JOHN HALLOCKE the younger the feather bed on which I usually lie, the bolster and pillow belonging to it, my best coverlet, a pair of blankets, a field bedstead with mat and cord, a little box and a coffer. His father is to keep these goods until he needs them. Any man owing money to me is to have remitted half a year's interest when he pays his debt to my exors. I bequeath the rest of my movable goods, cattle, money, bonds and bills to my exors. to pay my debts and legacies. My loving friend PHILIP HAWARD is to see to the ordering of my burial, the entertaining of my friends, the interment of my body in the place appointed and the placing over it of a decent gravestone. Witnesses: RICHARD CHILDERS, WILLIAM BURRY. Pr. at Beccles 21 Feb. 1634/5.

R(W) JOAN HALES alias HAWES (X) of Sutton, widow. (865)
17 August 1632

To be buried in the church or churchyard of Sutton. I give £10 to CICELY TURNER, the daughter of JOHN TURNER of Sutton when she is 21, or, if she dies, £5 to RICHARD son of RICHARD GREENE of Sutton. I bequeath 10s. to the poor of Sutton. All the rest of my movable goods I give and bequeath to my kinsman ROBERT MAULBY, joiner of Woodbridge, and make him my sole exor. Witnesses: JOHN KEBLE, GEORGE LAMRYN & THOMAS RICHER. Pr. at Wickham Market 19 Feb. 1634/5.

R(W) ROBERT SCAPIE (X) of Barnby, husbandman. (866)
16 November 1634

I give 3s. 4d. to the poor of Barnby. I bequeath 20s. to my nephew JOHN SCAPIE. All the rest of my goods and chattels I bequeath to MARY my wife, whom I make sole exrx. She is to pay my debts and legacies, and see my body decently buried. I make my brother-in-law WILLIAM GISLAM supervisor to aid and assist my wife, and I give him for his pains 6s. 8d. Witnesses: ABRAHAM

JOHNSON, GREGORY STERAKER, WILLIAM GISLAM and WILLIAM LONE. Pr. at Beccles 14 Feb. 1634/5.

R(W) WILLIAM CARRE of Woodbridge, yeoman. 27 July 1634 (867)

Sick of body. I give to EDENY [sic] my wife in full satisfaction of her dower an annuity of £30 to be paid in equal portions on the 4 quarter days. I give her for her life the little chamber below and the little chamber above in the messuage where I live with free ingress and egress from these rooms and the yard belonging to the house. She is to have 2 loads of wood billets p.a. placed in a convenient outhouse. If she makes any claim to my land for dower, these legacies to her will become null and void. I give her 2 of my best featherbeds and the bolsters and pillows, coverings, blankets, sheets and all other things belonging to them. Also a gilt salt with a cover and 6 silver spoons. I give to my son JOHN CARR all my manors, messuages and lands in Woodbridge, Hasketon, Burgh, Boulge, Saxmundham, Kelsale, Middleton and Fordley. I give an annuity of £8 to my daughter JUDITH, wife of MICHAEL BULL the younger, yeoman of Walton. I also give her £100 to be paid 1 month after my decease, 2 silver salts, 6 silver spoons, a pot tipped with silver, a featherbed, a bolster, the coverings and blankets belonging to it. I bequeath £200 to ALICE CARR my daughter to be paid within 1 year of my decease. Also to her 1 silver salt, 1 featherbed and bolster. I give £5 each when they are 18 to all the children of my daughter MARY, wife of WILLIAM WARNE. I give to Mr JOHN WENTWORTH 20s. to buy a gold ring. I bequeath 40s. to the poor of Woodbridge, and 20s. each to the poor of Hasketon and Saxmundham. I make JOHN CARR my son sole exor., and give him all my unbequeathed goods and chattels. I nominate my kinsman THOMAS ATHEROLD to be supervisor and give him £5 for his assistance to my exor. Witnesses: ROBERT MARRIOTT, who wrote the will, and GEORGE FERRIMAN. Pr. at Ipswich 20 Sept. 1634.

R(W) JOHN WELTON of South Elmham St. James, husbandman. (868)
22 October 1633

Sick of body. I wish to be buried in the churchyard of St. James. I give £20 each to my sons THOMAS & JOHN when they are 21 (with benefit of survivorship). If both sons die then this money is to be divided between my mother, my brother THOMAS and my sisters. I make WILLIAM GIRLING, yeoman of Stradbroke, and EDMUND BAKER, yeoman of Bungay, my exors. and I give them all my movables towards the upbringing and education of my 2 sons and the payment of £20 each to them. I ask my exors. to have a special tender care of my sons. Witnesses: SAMUEL KNAPP, JOHN FLATMAN. Pr. at Bungay 21 Feb. 1633/4.

R(W) THOMAS ARMOND of Rendlesham, yeoman. (869)
21 November 1634

Sick in body. I wish to be buried in the churchyard at Bucklesham where my father and mother already lie. I give 40s. to the poor people of Bucklesham to be distributed where most need is. I give all my land in Glemham Parva and Stratford to my son THOMAS. In satisfaction of her dower I give to my wife ANNE for life all the land in Bucklesham, Kembroke and Kirton, which I bought from GEOFFREY BURWELL and THOMAS RANT gent. and which is now let to JOHN GIBSON. She must pay £10 p.a. to my son THOMAS, who will inherit this land after her death. I give and bequeath to JAMES my second son my tenement Mares with all its land in Bucklesham and Foxall and now let to THOMAS FLATHER. I also give to JAMES my tenement Stones with its land in Bucklesham and Foxhall and now let to WILLIAM SWANTON, and my tenement called the Fen House, which is now occupied by the Widow HAWARD and is in Bucklesham and Foxhall. JAMES must pay my wife £4 p.a. I give to my daughter ELIZABETH ARMOND £250 to be paid to her by my exors. when she is 21, or when she marries. If she marries a man whose estate is not equal to her own or marries against the will of my wife, then her portion of £250 shall remain in the hands of my son THOMAS, who is to pay her £12 p.a. After her death my son THOMAS, or his exors., are to divide the £250 between her children. I give £20 to my daughter DORCAS HART when she is 21, and £20 to my son-in-law JOHN HART when he is 21. I give to my sister SCOTT 20s. and 10s. to each of her children when 21. I give 5s. to each of my servants living with me at the time of my death. To my son THOMAS and to my daughter ELIZABETH I bequeath a posted bedstead with bedding each; these beds are in the chambers of my mansion house at Rendlesham where I now dwell. I give my son JAMES another posted bedstead and bedding standing in the parlour of THOMAS FLATHER's house at Bucklesham. I give to GERVASE HUBBALD, parson of Rendlesham, 20s. and I ask him to preach at my funeral if the minister of Bucklesham will allow him to do so. I will that my sons THOMAS & JAMES be bound apprentices to such good trades as my wife thinks fitting. The premiums for this are to come from my goods and chattels if enough is left after paying my debts and legacies; if not they are to be raised from profits of my land. My wife is to be guardian of my sons until they are 21, and must keep the houses and land in good repair. I give the residue of my goods to my wife, who is sole exrx. Witnesses: GERVASE HUBBALD, ROBERT TAVELL, FRANCIS HUBBALD. Pr. at Wickham Market 12 March 1634/5.

R(W) NATHANIEL BURROUGH of East Bergholt, clothier. (870)
13 January 1634/5

Sick and weak in body. I bequeath £20 to my eldest son PETER when he is 24; £80 to my son NATHANIEL when he is 24; £80 to my son JOHN when 24; £40 to my daughter SUSAN when 21 and £40 to the child my wife is carrying at the age of 24 if a son and at 21 if a daughter. (Children to have benefit of survivorship.) My exors. are to use the profits of my children's legacies for their education and upbringing. The remainder of my goods and chattels, my debts and funeral charges being paid, I give to SUSAN my loving wife. I make her and JOHN BARKER, my brother-in-law exors. Witnesses: JOHN GOODWYN, THOMAS ALLEN, ROBERT RICHERSON & JOHN STEVENSON. Pr. at Ipswich 13 March 1634/5.

R(W) MARY COOKE (X) of Laxfield, singlewoman. (871)
2 September 1632

Sick of body. I give and bequeath to MARGARET, daughter of my brother-in-law PHILIP PRIME of Wissett £20 when she is 21. Until then my exors. are to pay her 30s. interest p.a. If she dies before she is 21 this money is to be divided between THOMAS, ELIZABETH, ANNE & BRIDGET, the children of my brother-in-law THOMAS TAILOR. I give MARGARET PRIME my smallest black trunk with the linen in it as it now stands in THOMAS TAILOR's house in Laxfield. I give 20s. to the poor of Laxfield, and 10s. each to the poor of Walpole, Halesworth, Yoxford and Darsham. The rest of my goods, bonds, bills and household stuff I give and bequeath to the 4 children of THOMAS TAILOR when they are 21. The expenses of my burial and of proving my will must first be paid out of these goods. I appoint my well-beloved brother-in-law THOMAS TAILOR sole exor., and my well-beloved brother-in-law PHILIP PRIME supervisor of my will. Witnesses: JOHN DOWSING, SIMON MAN, WILLIAM STANNARD. Pr. at Beccles 13 March 1634/5.

R(W) MARY GODAWRD widow of Metfield. 24 March 1633/4 (872)

I give to my brother JAMES GREENE a featherbed, 3 silver spoons, and to his wife my best petticoat and hat, 1 ruff and 2 pairs sheets. I give and bequeath to my brother SAMUEL GREENE a featherbed, 3 silver spoons and 2 gold rings, and to his wife my riding suit and 1 ruff. I give and bequeath to my brother WILLIAM GREENE and to his daughter ANNE my chest of linen and my boxes of linen. I give to my sister TAYLOR all my wearing linen in a drawer and a ruff. I give to RICHARD BARCARE a feather trundlebed. I name HENRY WILBY my exor. and leave him all my goods not disposed of in this my will, trusting him to see my will performed. Witnesses: CLEMENT GREENE, JOAN GOWERE & RICHARD WILBYE. Pr. at Beccles 24 March 1634/5.

R(W) ELIZABETH BALDREY of Bramfield. 8 April 1634 (773)

I give to my brother JOHN KNIGHTS 40s. to be paid within 6 weeks of my decease. I bequeath to my sister JOAN PARTRIDGE my furrendale chest and all my clothes. To my kinswoman ELIZABETH CLERKE I give my bedstead standing in my parlour chamber with a featherbed, 2 feather bolsters, 2 feather pillows, the coverlet and blankets, and 1 pair of my best sheets. Also to her my best cupboard and best copper cauldron with ringles, 1 brass posnet, my little joyned table standing in the hall, 2 pewter platters, 2 joined stools and 1 pair of andirons. I give my godchild

ELIZABETH FISHER my counter table with my virginals which stand in my hall. To my kinsman JOHN KNIGHTS of Carlton I give 10s., and to my kinswoman ELIZABETH GRAY 20s. I give 40s. to my kinswoman ANNE CLERKE, and 2 pewter platters and 2 joined stools. To ELIZABETH CLERKE I give my best chest. I give 40s. to the poor people of Bramfield to be paid to the churchwardens and distributed by them at their discretion. I give to my kinsman THOMAS CLERK of Bramfield all my other movable goods, chattels and debts due to me towards the probate of my will, funeral charges and legacies. I make him my sole exor. Witnesses: ITCHINGHAM LOFTS and ROBERT VESTEY (X). Pr. at Yoxford 11 March 1634/5.

W(R) THOMAS COOKE (X) of Blythburgh. [No date] (874)

I give to AGNES COOKE my mother and to ELIZABETH COOKE my sister all my corn to be equally divided between them. I also give them all my cows, except one, all my horses, plough shares, carts, harness and implements of husbandry. I give to my brother WILLIAM COOKE £20 to be paid in 4 equal payments during the year after my decease. I give to my aunt TUMAR's children £11 to be divided amongst them. I give to my brother WILLIAM my father's best breeches and best coat, 1 brown cow and 1 coffer. I give all my household stuff to my mother and sister and make them exrxs. Witnesses: THOMAS SEPINS (X), RICHARD MARCH (X), NATHANIEL BROWNE. Pr. at Yoxford 11 March 1634/5.

R(W) WILLIAM DOBS (X) of Thurleston, yeoman. (875)
13 February 1634/5

Sick in body. First I wish all my debts to be paid. After my wife's decease I give £5 apiece to my grandchildren, the children of WILLIAM KEMPE, of WILLIAM GILDERSLEEVE & MICHAEL MARSHLAND. Any other money left after my wife's death is to be equally divided among my 3 daughters, the wives of WILLIAM KEMMPE, WILLIAM GILDERSLEEVE & MICHAEL MARSHLAND. (They have benefit of survivorship.) I make my wife sole exrx. and give her all I have, after my debts have been paid. Witnesses: FRANCIS REYNOLDS, JOAN ELLIOT (X). Pr. at Ipswich 13 March 1634/5.

R(W) JOHN SMITH of Woodbridge, carver. (876)
20 January 1634/5

Weak in body. I wish my body to be buried in the churchyard of Woodbridge in decent manner. I bequeath to my 2 sisters ANNE & MARY my house in Woodbridge wherein I now dwell with its outhouses and yards; this was lately purchased from THOMAS BERMAN. I give to my brother WILLIAM SMITH of Yarmouth £20 and to his son JOHN £20. I bequeath to my brother ARNOLD SMITH of Aldeburgh the £5 10s. 0d. owed to me by JOHN BARBER of Aldeburgh, and the use of my hired house there, the rent of which is paid to Lady Day next. Also to him the bed, bedding, bedstead, chests and all the other household stuff and utensils in this house and all the wood and billets there. To my sister ELIZABETH SMITH I give 30s. p.a. to be paid in 2 equal portions by my exors. I give to MARY HOOKER of Aldeburgh my horse. I make my 2 sisters ANNE & MARY my exrxs. Witnesses: WILLIAM ALSTON, NATHANIEL FLEMING, ROBERT CADE, clerk. Pr. at Woodbridge 12 March 1634/5.

R(W) EDWARD BALDRY of Ipswich, yeoman. 15 July 1634 (877)

Of good and perfect health. I give and bequeath to my brother JOHN BALDRIE £100 to be paid by my exors. within 6 months of my death. Also £5 each to his children ROBERT, JANE & MARY, to be paid within 6 months. I give to THOMAS, ROBERT, FRANCIS, ANNE & MARY, the children of my brother-in-law THOMAS WALKER, £5 each to be paid to those who are 16 within 6 months of my decease and to the rest as they attain age of 16. I give 40s. each to my cousins Mrs JOAN BROWNRIG, Mrs ELIZABETH BREWSTER and Mrs MARY SNELLING to buy rings to wear as a remembrance of me. I give my cousin JOHN HAVELL £5 if he pays to my exors. the money he owes me. I give £10 to MARGARET wife of RICHARD HARDIE if he pays my exors. the money he owes me by bond. I give 40s. to ANNE EDE, one of the daughters of THOMAS HAVELL. I give £10 each to HELEN & SUSAN, the children of my cousin WILLIAM BALDRIE, when they are 16. I bequeath £5 each when they are 21 to JOHN, SAMUEL, MARY, ELIZABETH, MARTHA, ANNE, ALICE & BENJAMIN, the children of my cousin MARY SNELLING (with benefit of survivorship). I give 20s. each when they are 21 to ROBERT, FRANCIS, HUMPHREY, JOHN & SAMUEL BREWSTER (with benefit of survivorship). To Mr SAMUEL WARD I give 40s. and to Mr CARVER of Belstead 20s. I give to my cousin ELIZABETH PHILLIPES of Wrentham 40s.; to my cousin MATHEW BROWNERIGGE clerk 20s.; to my cousin KATHERINE CARVER of Wilby 20s.; to ANN COLE daughter of JOHN COLE 20s.; to MARY wife of ROBERT BATEMAN 40s.; to ROBERT TURNER my godson and to ELIZABETH TURNER 20s. each; to JONATHAN BUTTER my godson 20s.; to ALICE GOSTE my god-daughter 20s.; to MARY THURSTON servant with my cousin Mrs MARY SNELLING 10s.; to Mr CATLYN clerk 20s.; to ANNE BEDDALL my god-daughter 20s.; to ELIZABETH daughter of JOHN HAVELL 20s. and to WILLIAM MENDHAM 20s. I give 10s. to the poor of the parish of St. Peter (in Ipswich). I give to Mr BEARD clerk 20s.; to RICHARD & EDMUND HARDING 20s. apiece. I bequeath to my cousin JOHN BEDDALL junior my danske chest. I give 20s. apiece to ROBERT, RICHARD, THOMAS, JOHN & ELIZABETH BRACKETT. I give to EDWARD WALLIS my godson 20s. Exors.: my loving cousin JOHN HAWIS, gent. of Ipswich and WILLIAM BALDRIE. I leave £10 to the former for his pains. My debts, legacies, funeral and probate charges being paid, I give all my household goods and chattels to my cousin WILLIAM BALDRIE. Witnesses: JOHN HAWYS junior, JACOB CALEY, WILLIAM HAWYS. Pr. at Ipswich 31 Jan. 1634/5.

R(W) THOMAS CRESSNER alias HOXON (X) of Leiston. (878)
15 June 1634

I give and bequeath to ALICE my wife all my lands and tenements in Brundish. She must pay £30 within 5 years as follows: £20 to FRANCIS and £10 to ANNE, the children of my deceased brother JOHN CRESSNER alias HOXON. These payments are to be made in the south porch of Brundish church. I give and bequeath to my wife all my lands and tenements in Theberton, Thorpe and Sternfield. I give £5 to MARY, daughter of THOMAS BELWARD deceased, to be paid by my exrx. within 5 years of my death. I give to MARY's sister ALICE, the wife of WILLIAM WHITE, 20s. I give to the 2 children of JOHN THRELKIN, tailor of Dunwich, 20s. each within 4 years of my decease. I give all my goods and chattels to ALICE my wife whom I make sole exrx., desiring her faithfully to perform my will. Witnesses: JOHN CHAPMAN (X), JOHN THORNTON (X). Pr. at Yoxford 9 Oct. 1634.

R(W) JOHN BARRICK (X) of Sutton, husbandman. (879)
31 October 1634

Sick in body. I wish to be buried in the churchyard at Sutton. I give £3 to my brother THOMAS BARRICK to be paid on 25 March next. To my sister ELIZABETH BARRICKE I give 40s. to be paid on the same day, and to my other sister MARGARET BARRICKE 40s. also to be paid on 25 March next. I give and bequeath 20s. to LANCELOT SCOTSONE. I give to RICHARD MOSE of Hollesley yeoman 20s., and to KATHERINE OCX 20s. to be paid on 25 March next. I give to HENRY YARCK of Sutton £10 to be paid on same date. I give £10 to the poor of Sutton to be paid to the churchwardens on 26 May 1635 and to be put to the best use for the benefit of the poor. At the end of their year of office, the churchwardens must pay this £10 to the next churchwardens and so on, so long as it shall please God the world shall endure. I give and bequeath to ROBERT COOPER and his wife SUSANNA all the rest of my goods, bonds and bills, and make them exors. of my will. Witnesses: THOMAS BROWNE, KATHERINE OXE. Pr. at Wickham Market 20 Nov. 1634.

R(W) FRANCES ARLE of Hoxne (N). [No date] (880)

She gave to JOHN RUSHMER her kinsman all her goods. Witnesses: JOAN SALLOWES, JOAN REDE, ELIZABETH SMITH & ELIZABETH HASELL widow. Pr. at Beccles 30 June 1634.

R(W) JOHN CATCHER of Ipswich, vintner. 27 May 1633 (881)

I give and bequeath to MARION, my dear and well-beloved wife, all my messuages and lands in Ipswich, Stoke by Ipswich and Sproughton, and all my goods, household stuff, plate, ready money, bills, bonds and mortgages for her life. She must keep the messuages in good repair, and pay my debts and legacies. I give £500 to my son EDWARD when he is 21, £300 to my son JOHN when 21 and £200 to each of my daughters, MARY, ELIZABETH, MARGARET, SARAH, MARTHA and DEBORAH, when they are 21 or on their marriage days, whichever is earlier, provided that they do not marry without the consent of my wife. To the child my wife is carrying I bequeath £200 if it is a girl or £250 if a boy, when 21. (All children have benefit of survivorship.) My wife must bring up and educate my children in the fear of God and in decent manner. I make my wife sole exrx. If she cannot raise enough money from my personal estate to pay my debts and legacies, she may sell my messuages and land except for the house wherein I now dwell. Any money left over from such sales is to be equally divided between my children. After my wife's decease I give the messuage wherein I now live in Ipswich to the eldest of my sons then living. I bequeath to my mother MARY CATCHER widow £8 p.a. to be paid to her quarterly. I do further give to my daughter MARY £50 over and above the legacy given to her above and to be paid at the same time. Witnesses: JEREMY REYMOND, EDMUND MILES notary public. Pr. at Ipswich 6 Jan. 1634/5.

W. GEORGE CANHAM of Chattisham (N). 14 June 1634 (882)

He gave all his movable goods to his wife ANN. Witnesses: GEORGE LOCKWOODD, JOHN FROSTE (X). Pr. at Ipswich 20 June 1634.

W. THOMAS CROSMAN (X) of Alderton, singleman. (883)
19 February 1632/3

I give and bequeath to ROBERT CROSMAN my brother my house and land in Bawdsey, on condition he pays ANNE DRYVER my sister £10; half a year after my decease and half a year later. If he refuses to pay her, I revoke this bequest to him and give my house and land to ANNE for 3 years and then to ROBERT's heirs. I give to WILLIAM BOWINGE, my brother-in-law, my apparel. I give 20s. to my nephew WILLIAM BOWINGE to be paid by my brother ROBERT 1 year after my decease. I make my brother ROBERT CROSMAN my exor., but if he does not prove my will within 6 months of my death then I make my sister ANNE DRYVER exrx. Witnesses: CHRISTOPHER REVE, THOMAS CORBIN & HENRY ROLLEISON. Pr. at [no place given] 9 Oct. 1633.

W. HENRY SKELTON of Corton, yeoman. (884)
circa 9 October 1634

He gave £20 to WILLIAM BURRELL, £20 to THOMAS BURRELL, £20 to THOMAS son of LUKE THORNTON, £20 to WILLIAM son of PAUL ALEXANDER, £20 to ANNE daughter of PAUL ALEXANDER. These legacies to be paid one per year starting with that to WILLIAM BURRELL 1 year after testator's decease. He gave MARGARET his wife all his goods and estate to pay his legacies and prove his will. Witnesses: HUSTINGS WILKINSON, GREGORY JOHNSON (X) and

THOMAS WHEELER. [no probate]

W. JOHN EVERARD of Gisleham, yeoman. 10 November 1634 (885)

In good and perfect health. I wish to be buried in Gisleham churchyard. I give 20s. to the poor of Gisleham, 10s. to the poor of Rushmere, 20s. to the poor of Pakefield, 20s. to the poor of Kirkley, 20s. to the poor of Carlton Colville, 20s. to the poor of Kessingland, 10s. to the poor of Mutford and 10s. to the poor of Barnby. These sums are to be paid by my exors. within 1 month of my decease and are to be distributed by the overseers of the poor of these parishes. I give to my nephew JOHN EVERARD when he is 21 my messuage and lands which were my father's, all the land I purchased from EDWARD HUBBERD esq., and the meadow I bought from JOHN LABORN of Pakefield. I also give him the counter in the kitchen and all the timber wrought things as they stand in the kitchen and cellar, the cupboard in the hall, the great andirons in the hall and the great iron rack with the 2 great spits, the bed fully furnished in my chamber where I lie, and all the other goods standing in that chamber with the cabinet with all the writings, excepting those appertaining to the land I late purchased of CAPON and now given to THOMAS EVERARD my nephew and his brother as hereafter specified. More to JOHN EVERARD I give my mazer tipped with silver, 12 silver spoons, the biggest silver cup and the biggest brass pot. All the movable goods bequeathed to me in my father's will are to remain in the house, namely the horse mill, 2 lead cisterns, 1 copper to brew in, all the brewing vessels, the cheese press, 2 tables, the long table in the hall and the great table in the parlour. If my nephew JOHN dies without male heirs, then all the messuages, lands and goods bequeathed to him shall descend to his brother THOMAS and his heirs. I give and bequeath to THOMAS EVERARD my nephew the house and land I bought of WILLIAM CAPON and all the lands I last bought of EDWARD HUBBERD esq. in Gisleham, together with all the household movables therein, which are a seeled bedstead, a table, a brewing copper and a [hole in manuscript] pot in full satisfaction of the legacies made to him by his father THOMAS EVERARD and which remain in my hands. I also give him a black cup tipped with silver, a mazer tipped with silver and the rest of my silver spoons, the biggest brass pot but one, the trunk with T & E on it and all the linen in it that was his father's. I give and bequeath to SUSAN GODFREY widow, my sister, an annuity of £6 to be paid out of their lands by my 2 nephews JOHN & THOMAS at Lady Day and Michaelmas. (She has power to distrain.) I give £6 each to CHRISTIAN & MARGARET MEREMAN to be paid by my exors. within 3 months of my death. I give £10 to GEORGE WOODGATE to be paid within 6 months, and £5 each to his 2 children MARGARET & JOHN when they are 21. (These legacies are with benefit of survivorship.) I give 40s. to GEORGE, the youngest son of GEORGE WOODGATE, when he is 21 and £10 to GILBERT WOODGATE 2 years after my decease. I give 20s. to ROBERT GARDINER my servant within 1 month of my death. All the unbequeathed movable goods in the house where I dwell and all my cattle are to be equally divided between my 2 nephews JOHN & THOMAS EVERARD. I make them exors. and they are to pay my debts and legacies. I make Mr JAMES HUBBERD, son of EDWARD HUBBERD of Langley in Norfolk, supervisor of my will and my exors. are to give him £3 for his pains. Witnesses: RICHARD TURNER, JOHN HASE clerk, and ELIZABETH EDWARDS (X). [no probate]

CHAPTER V

Abstracts of Wills Contained in Register No. 63 and/or File No. 71 of Wills Proved in the Court of the Archdeacon of Suffolk.

R(W) ROSE STANNARD of Worlingworth, widow (N). (886)
25 February 1634/5

My son-in-law WILLIAM WILSON of Worlingworth is to take my goods and pay himself for my diet and burial charges. Anything left over is to be equally divided between him and HENRY STANNARD of Worlingworth and JOHN STANNARD of Cratfield. Witnesses: PHILIP TYNCKE, rector of Worlingworth, RALPH TURNER. Pr. at Yoxford 27 May 1635.

R(W) JANE RUSLES/RUSSELLS of Adleburgh, widow. (887)
29 March 1635

I give and bequeath all my goods and chattels to my daughter MARY RUSSELLS, who is to pay my debts and bring my body to the ground. Daughter sole exrx. Supervisor: Mr THOMAS JOHNSON. Witnesses: ANNE BRYTELL widow and BRIDGET CHAPMAN (X) and WILLIAM THOMSON. Pr. at Wickham Market 28 May 1635.

R(W) JOHN DRANE of Earl Soham, yeoman. 18 December 1632 (888)

Hail of body. I give and bequeath to SUSAN my well-beloved wife for 6 months after my decease the messuage in Earl Soham wherein I dwell with all the land belonging to it. She must keep buildings in good repair and not plough up any more land than is now in tillage. She is entitled to any corn growing on the arable land at the time of my death, and has the right of access to the barn where grain is stored to thresh and winnow it until Feb. 2nd after the above six months is up. After 6 months has passed, I give the above messuage and land to my son ROBERT, who must pay £60 each to my sons JOHN & THOMAS at the rate of £20 p.a.; they have power to distrain. To my 2 daughters, SUSAN and MARGARET, I give £50 apiece to be paid by my exrx. within 1 year of my decease. My wife shall pay all the legacies that I stand charged to pay as exor. of the wills of my deceased brothers ROBERT and THOMAS DRANE. She must also pay to my children the legacies left to them in the will of SUSAN HUGGIN, their grandmother. My wife is to have the use of my goods, corn and cattle for 6 months after my death to help her pay my gifts and bequests. After 6 months everything left is to be equally divided between my wife and children; my wife is to choose her part first. After my son ROBERT has inherited my house and land he is to pay my wife an annuity of £10 in consideration of her rights of dower; she has the power to distrain. This annuity and all other gifts to my wife will be void if she makes any claim on my property. As long as she remains a widow, my wife is to have the use of the parlour, parlour chamber and vaunce roof over them together with the garden next to the parlour and the use of the mill to grind her own corn and grain, the use of the oven to bake her bread and the right to take water from the ponds for brewing and washing. She is to have 3 good cart loads of wood every year, to be felled, cut and made into faggots and great wood and brought into the yard next to the parlour, at the expense of my son ROBERT. I give to every one of my children 1 pair of sheets, and all the rest of my linen is to be divided equally among my wife and 3 daughters: SUSAN, ROSE & MARGARET. I give to my wife all debts owing to me by bond and my ready money towards paying my debts, legacies and the legacies due from me as exor. of the wills of ROBERT & THOMAS DRANE. She is to pay £10 to my sister-in-law MARY, wife of DANIEL COTWINE and late wife of my deceased brother ROBERT DRANE. This sum is due to her in lieu of dowry and is to be paid to her as follows: £5 on 1st July and £5 on 6th Jan. after my decease. I will that all the following items shall remain in my house as heirlooms: the long table in the hall with the 2 forms and benches, my muskett, my copper, my horse mill, my ladders and ladder pieces, my boards, planks and shelves both nailed and un-nailed, my cupboard under the stairs in the parlour, the beam and scales with the lead and other weights, the boards in the cheese chamber, my steeping vat, my hayre, my cheese press, my cart, tumbril, plough and harrow with all the traces for them, all my carpenter's tools and tools of husbandry, and all hewn and unhewn, sawn and unsawn timber in my yards. All payments specified in my will are to be made in my house at Earl Soham. My wife SUSAN is sole exrx. and is to bind herself in the sum of £200 to my brother-in-law ANTHONY WYARD truly to perform my will. If she refuses to do this within 1 month of my decease, then my son ROBERT is to be sole exor. Supervisor: my loving friend GEORGE RUSSELL, yeoman of Cretingham, and I earnestly desire him to assist my exrx., and give him 20s. for his care and pains. Witnesses: GEORGE RUSSELL, WILLIAM RUSSELL, OLIVER NEALE. Pr. at Wickham Market 28 May 1635.

R(W) THOMAS GILDERSLEVE (X) of Falkenham, yeoman. (889)
20 April 1635

Sick in body. I give and bequeath to my brother DANIEL GILDERSLEEVE 40s. to be paid over 2 years at 10s. every 6 months. I give 2s. each to my servants JOHN COOKE, ALICE BAKER & JOHN CURSPE. I give 20s. to JOHN BROWEN of Falkenham. I bequeath to JOHN CURSPE £5 that was given to him by the will of his grandfather ROBERT CURSPE to be paid out of a tenement in Melton. All the rest of my goods are to be divided into 3 parts between PHOEBE my wife, THOMAS my son and the child my wife is carrying. If Thomas dies before he is 21, half his share is to be given to JOHN, RICHARD & DANIEL, sons of my brother PHILIP GILDERSLEVE. JOHN BROWNE of Falkenham is to have my son's part until he is 21 and is to pay £12 to my wife toward the upbringing of THOMAS. I nominate JOHN BROWNE supervisor of my will and my wife as sole exrx. Witnesses: PHILIP GILDERSLEVE & ROBERT JAYE senior. Pr. at Ipswich 30 May 1635.

R(W) ROBERT BIRDE (X) of Hintlesham, husbandman. 7 May 1635 (890)

Sick in body. I give and bequeath immediately my tenement called Osbornes to my eldest son ROBERT, who must pay his brother RICHARD £20 as follows: £10 12 months after my wife's decease and £10 12 months later, both payments to be made in Hintlesham church porch. My 2 pightles of land in Chattisham, which are to let JOHN SMITH, taylor, I give to my daughter MARY immediately after the decease of my wife RACHEL, who is to have this land for her life. ROBERT is to pay her £2 p.a. for her maintenance. After my wife's death I give the bedstead with featherbed, flock-bed and bolster whereon I lie in the chamber to my daughter MARY. I give my other featherbed in the chamber to my son ROBERT after my wife's death. I give my son RICHARD a flockbed when he is 21. The rest of my movables, brass and pewter I give, after my wife's death, to be equally divided amongst my 3 children: ROBERT, RICHARD & MARY, but I give absolutely to my wife RACHEL my cow, cattle and corn. If my wife remarries she must bind herself to pay the value of my goods to my children. Son ROBERT sole exor. I make THOMAS FLACKE of Chattisham supervisor and give him 20s. Witnesses: THOMAS DENTON & THOMAS FLACKE. Pr. at Ipswich 29 May 1635.

R(W) JOHN TYKE (X) of Gorleston. 24 May 1635 (891)

I give to OLIVE TYKE my sister £10 to be paid by my exor. within 1 year of my decease. I give to WILLIAM TYKE my brother £5 when he comes to 16 years of age. The rest of my goods I bequeath to CHRISTOPHER TYKE my brother whom I make sole exor., not doubting that he will truly perform my will. I ordain BENJAMIN STEGOULD, my master, as supervisor and give him 10s. for his pains. Witnesses: CHRISTOPHER STEYGOULD & WILLIAM SHINGLES (X). Pr. at Beccles 20 June 1635.

R(W) BRIDGET BULL (X) of Aldeburgh, widow. 11 May 1635 (892)

Sick in body. I wish to be buried in Aldeburgh churchyard. I give and bequeath £5 each to my grandchildren MARY, LAWRENCE & JOHN BALDRIE when they reach age of 16. I give to my daughter MARY, wife of ROBERT ANTELL, 40s., and to my daughter ELIZABETH BALDRIE £8. I give and bequeath to WILLIAM BALDRY, my grandson, £60 now in the hands of my son-in-law ROBERT ANTELL to be paid to WILLIAM when he is 21. I also give £12 to be used to bind forth WILLIAM BALDRY as an apprentice to some good trade or science. I also give to him when he is 21 all my movable goods, linen, brass and pewter. My clothes I give to my daughter ELIZABETH BALDRIE. Grandchildren have benefit of survivorship. Any residue of my goods I leave to my son-in-law LAWRENCE BALDRIE, whom I make sole exor. He is to receive the debts due to me and pay my own debts. Witnesses: THOMAS TRENDLE clerk, MARIAN SCRUTTON (X). Pr. at Wickham Market 18 June 1635.

R(W) ROBERT BROWNRIGG of Willisham. 3 February 1634/5 (893)

Weak in body. On 12 Jan. 1622 I and my eldest son, JOHN BROWNRIGG, made a 60 year lease of the manor of Willisham Hall to JOHN SCRIVENER esquire, JOHN GOBBETT, JOHN GRIGGS & RICHARD SYER as security for the payment of £600 as a trust for my wife ANNE. I now declare that this manor and its land are fully discharged from any liability for the payment of £600. I ask my son JOHN to allow my wife and her servants to live in certain rooms of the manor house and to have the use of the kitchen, backhouse and brewhouse, room in the apple chamber to lay her fruit and space in the yards to put 16 loads of wood to be felled on the land of the manor every year at my wife's expense. She is also to have the use of the garden, a quarter of the fruit growing in the orchard and access at all reasonable times to the parlour, kitchen and other rooms and yards as long as she remains unmarried. My son JOHN must pay my wife £40 p.a. in four quarterly payments. If within 3 months of my death my son JOHN gives sufficient security to JOHN SCRIVENER & HARBOTTLE WINGFEILD esquire, his brother-in-law, to allow my wife the use of the above rooms etc. and to pay her annuity, then JOHN SCRIVENER and the other three named above are to surrender to him all their interest in the 60 year lease made in 1622. A marriage, which I utterly dislike, is likely to take place between my daughter HELEN MUDD & WILLIAM TAMPON of Great Bricett. If she relinquishes this marriage then I give and bequeath unto HELEN £40, but if she persists with this marriage then this gift to her shall be utterly void. I give and bequeath £100 to be divided equally amongst those of my grandchildren who shall be living at the time of my decease. I give £10 to be distributed to the poor of Needham Market, Barking, Darmsden, Baylham, Nettlestead, Somersham, Ofton, and Willisham who come to my funeral. I give £5 towards a stock for the poor of Willisham parish; the income to be distributed annually. I give to my well-beloved wife for life my goods, chattels and money to pay my debts, legacies and funeral expenses. I make my wife ANNE sole exrx., and my 2 sons JOHN and ROBERT are to be her exors. and divide between them all my goods which my wife still has when she dies. Supervisors: my loving kinsman JOHN SCRIVENER and Mr HARBOTLE WINGFEILD. Witnesses: EDMUND STYLE, JAMES JACKAMAN (X). Pr. at Ipswich 4 June 1635.

R(W) RICHARD COPPING of Orford. 2 April 1635 (894)

I give and bequeath to TOBIAS COPPING my son my freehold land and tenements in Wickham Market and Pettistree. He must pay my son JAMES £500 within 6 months of my decease in Orford church porch. If TOBIAS defaults on this payment, the above property is left to

JAMES. I give and bequeath to TOBIAS my messuage called Lames in Orford with 1/2 acre now occupied by FRANCIS PEIRCE, and also my land in Orford and Sudbourne that I purchased from Sir MICHAEL STANOP knight and FRANCIS DEEREHAUGH gent. Also my pightle called the saffron pan, my land in Orford and Sudbourne bought from the late [blank] BUCKLIE, but not my tenement and land in Orford now occupied by THOMAS TOKELY and the adjoining tenement and land now occupied by LAWRENCE TYRES. I also except my 2 acre marsh called Crowes marsh. I give to my son JAMES all my land and tenement in Kelsale and my horse mill, the two tenements with land and the marsh excepted above from my bequest to TOBIAS, and all my other land and tenements in Orford except my messuage and 1/2 acre of land let to WILLIAM HOLLOWBREAD. This messuage and 1/2 acre I give to WILLIAM COPPING my brother for life and then to my daughter MARGARET LEWES widow. I give to my brother WILLIAM £10 and all my clothes except my best cloak and coat. I give to my daughter MARGARET LEWES all the wearing apparel of my 2 deceased wives. My exor. is to pay MARGARET LEWES £100 for her use until her daughter ELIZABETH LEWES is 21 and £50 until her son WILLIAM is 21. She must be bound to my son TOBIAS in sum of £300 to pay the above sums to her children at the age of 21. I give my best cloak to TOBIAS and my best coat to JAMES. I have invested £100 in a mortgage of land and a tenement at Walpole for my sister JOAN CARY widow; this money is for her son WILLIAM when he is 21. I now bequeath this mortgage to my sister JOAN CARY. I give all my plate and household stuff to be equally divided among my 3 children. I give £5 to my sister JOAN, 40s. to ELIZABETH, daughter of RICHARD COPPING of Ipswich, and 40s. to THOMAS OSBORNE, clerk of Orford, to preach a sermon at my funeral. I give 20s. to THOMAS REEVE of East Green in Kelsale. I bequeath £10 to the poor of Orford and £5 each to the poor of Wickham Market and Pettistree. I leave £5 to ROBERT BROWNE my tenant. The rest of my unbequeathed goods I give to my sole exor. my son TOBIAS. If he does not prove my will within 2 months of my decease, then all gifts to him shall be void and my son JAMES is to be sole exor. Witnesses: WILLIAM FRENCH, JOHN JACKSON (X), THOMAS EADE. Pr. at Ipswich 15 May 1635.

R(W) HENRY FOX (X) the elder of Rendham, yeoman. (895)
28 October 1630

I give and bequeath to my son HENRY all my lands and houses in Rendham and after his death to his son WILLIAM. I give 10s. to the most needful poor of Rendham, and 6s. 8d. to the most needful poor of Sweffling. If my son HENRY dies before his son WILLIAM reaches 21, then my daughter-in-law MARIAN is to hold the property and pay WILLIAM £3 p.a. during his minority. She must also bring up her other children, allowing them sufficient food, drink and clothing. If MARIAN is still living when WILLIAM reaches 21, he must pay her £4 p.a. She has power to distrain. I also give her £10. After my son HENRY dies his wife is to have her dwelling in the parlour of the house left to him, with liberty to brew, bake and wash in the backhouse, to fetch water from the pond and ditches, and to place her firewood in a convenient place in the yards and to bring my white horse and cart into the yard. I give £10 to my daughter DOROTHY wife of ROBERT NEWMAN and 40s. each when 21 to my grandchildren ROSE, SARAH & ELIZABETH SPENCE. To my grandson THOMAS FOX £40 when 21, also a featherbed, a bolster and other things belonging at his father's discretion. I give to my grandson WILLIAM FOX my best featherbed, 1 bolster, 1 coverlet, 1 blanket, 1 pillow and the featherbed in the parlour, and the cupboard in the parlour. I give to my grand-daughter MARIAN FOX £20 when she is 21 and 1 featherbed, 1 bolster, 1 blanket, 1 coverlet, 1 pillow. To WILLIAM, son of my deceased son ROBERT FOX, I give £6 and 1 pair of sheets when he is 21. The rest of my goods I give to HENRY FOX my son whom I make sole exor. Witnesses: EDMUND SENIOR & WILLIAM CLAMP. Pr. at Yoxford 17 June 1635.

R(W) LYDIA GOULDING of Worlingworth, singlewoman (N). (896)
[no date]

Made about a month before her death. She gave to ROBERT SPINKE her house and land in Debenham asking him to pay his brother and his sister SARAH £5 each. She gave to JOHN WOLNOWE a cupboard, and to her sister MARY, wife of FRANCIS MORE, a petticoat and waistcoat. She left to SARAH SPINKE a trunk, an apron and other small items of linen. She gave all her other goods to her father ROBERT GOULDING in satisfaction of money due to him from her and for the expenses of her sickness and funeral. Witnesses: Mrs ANN JARMY & JANE LOUDE. Pr. at Horham 9 June 1635.

R(W) WILLIAM GARRARD (X) of Walton, butcher. 2 June 1635 (897)

Sick of body. I wish to be buried in Walton churchyard. I give to ANNE my beloved wife £30 and the bed and bedstead on which I now lie. I give to my daughters BRIDGET & MARY a posted bedstead with featherbeds, blankets and sheets. To my son JOHN GLANFIELD [son-in-law] I bequeath my house I now dwell in with a hempland and all the rest of my goods and the debts due to me. I make him sole exor. and ask him to sell my house and hempland to pay my debts, and to divide the residue between my two daughters. Witnesses: JOHN SCOTT, JOHN TALBOTT. Pr. at Ipswich 10 July 1635.

R(W) RICHARD HAYLE the elder of Horham, yeoman. (898)
30 April 1635

I give and bequeath to THOMAS HAYLE my son one posted bedstead standing in the parlour, 1 featherbed, 1 feather bolster, 2 feather pillows, 2 pillowbeeres, 2 blankets, 2 pairs sheets, 1 covering and the curtains of the same bed. Also I give to him my horse mill, my copper and brewing vessels, 10 milk bowls, my cart and all its furniture, my gelding and 1 hogshead to put beer in. I also give and bequeath to THOMAS 1 milk cow called the shield cow. I give to RICHARD HAYLE my son another milk cow called the black cow. I give and bequeath to ANNE HAYLE my daughter my best bedstead standing in the parlour chamber and all the furniture belonging to it. All the unbequeathed residue of my goods I give to be equally divided between my sons RICHARD & JOHN and my daughter ANNE. These three children are to have full liberty to come and go into my house and buildings to fetch away the goods bequeathed to them for one month after my decease. Exors. sons RICHARD & JOHN and daughter ANNE. Witnesses: DENNY CLUBB, FAITH GRIMSBIE (X). Pr. at Wickham Market 18 June 1635.

R(W) ANNE KERRY (X) of Wingfield, widow. 10 April 1634 (899

I assign all my household goods and all my estate to my sons JOHN GODFREY and GEORGE and my daughter ANNE GREENE widow, except all annuities and other yearly rents due to me for my lifetime for my maintenance, as apportioned in an attached schedule. Witnesses: FRANCIS WARNER, ANNE DEYE (X). Schedule made 9 Dec. 1634 dividing the goods which are mine at the day of my decease between my 3 children. I will that my son JOHN GODFREY shall have my best green cloth rug, 2 of the best cushions, my best featherbed and a little bolster, the yellow blanket, the chest at Syleham House, the cupboard at Wingfield Hall, the little table and 2 stools in the hall chamber, 1 little and 1 great pewter dish in the coffer in the cellar chamber, the coffer itself, my best skillet, 1 pair cobirons, the little spit, the chest that my linen lies in, 2 pairs sheets, 1 pair pillowbeeres, 3 table napkins, 1 towel, and the plank bench and warming pan at Syleham House. I will that GEORGE GODFREY my son shall have my best stuff gown and worst bed, my best bolster, a white blanket, my best coverlet, 2 pairs sheets, 1 pillow, 2 pillowbeeres, 3 table napkins, 1 towel, the other 2 cushions, the firepan and tongs, the press at Syleham House, the new chest in the hall chamber, the box in the kitchen chamber, 1 great and 1 little pewter dish, 1 skillet, the long form stool in the hall chamber and 1 handbell. I will that my daughter ANNE GODFREY shall have my box in the hall chamber with the linen in it and all my other wearing linen, my kirtle, my best petticoat and russet scarf, the biggest pewter dish and kettle. Any money left after paying my funeral charges is to be divided equally between my 3 children. I will that JOHN my son shall have my bedstead as it stands with curtains, valence, cords and mattress, and the worst coverlet. I will 5s. to the poor of Syleham and 10s. to the poor of Wingfield. Witness: FRANCIS WARNER. Pr. at Fressingfield to her 3 children 9 June 1635.

R(W) WILLIAM KENNETT (X) of Halesworth, husbandman. (900
21 July 1634

Sick in body. I give and bequeath to ELIZABETH my most loving and respected wife all my movable household goods and chattels for ever. I make her sole exrx., and my loving friend SAMUEL NOLLOTH supervisor. Witnesses: JOHN SEAMAN, GEORGE DAWSON (X),

EDWARD BUXTON junior (X), WILLIAM PRYNT (X) and HENRY KEBLE, who wrote this will. Pr. at Beccles 29 June 1635.

R(W) ROBERT KEY (X) of Harkstead, seafaringman. (901)
12 January 1631/2

Weak in body. I give to JUDITH my wife all and singular my goods and apparel, all my household stuff and implements of husbandry, and £4. I give £10 to my son JOHN to be paid within 1 year of my death. I give to my daughter ELIZABETH MARSH £7 to be paid within 2 years, and £8 to my son ROGER within 3 years of my decease. I give 20s. to my grandchild ELIZABETH MARSH when she is 21. If my daughter dies before her legacy is due, then I wish it to be divided equally between her 4 children: ELIZABETH, JOHN, FRANCIS and JOHN [sic.] at their ages of 21. Any unbequeathed money left after paying my debts and funeral charges I bequeath to my son ROBERT, whom I appoint exor. Witnesses: EITHE BROTHERTEN & JOHN BROTHERTEN, who wrote this will. Pr. at Ipswich 9 June 1635.

R(W) REGINALD LENNY (X) of Bungay, husbandman. (902)
26 June 1635

I give and bequeath to my youngest daughters SARAH & ANN LENNY all my goods and household stuff on condition that they pay 20s. to my eldest son REGINALD within 2 months and 40s. each to my children ROBERT & KATHERINE within 2 months of my decease. I give to my man WILLIAM SALLOWES 10s. to be paid within 2 months by SARAH & ANN. I give to my son REGINALD all my wearing apparel. The goods given to my two youngest daughters are: a mare, a long table and a form belonging to it, a cheese press, 2 vats, 5 bowls, 2 beer vessels which remain at Kings, a livery bedstead, a featherbed, 1 bolster, 1 pillow, 2 flockbeds, 2 shredding coverlets, a dornix coverlet, a trundle bedstead, 2 kettles, 1 pair of blankets, 1 firepan and a pair tongs, 6 pieces of pewter, 5 pairs of sheets, 2 chairs, 1 plank, 1 warming pan, 2 skillets, 1 bowl and 1 keeler. I nominate SARAH & ANN as my exrxs. Witnesses: ROBERT CHAPMAN, RICHARD NUN. Pr. at Bungay 2 July 1635.

R(W) THOMAS MOWLING of Bungay, grocer. 25 July 1632 (903)

Sick in body. I give and bequeath to ANNE my loving wife for ever the house I now dwell in with all the land belonging to it, my chapel close and the land called Dukes lying by Dukes bridge and all my land in Bungay field. Also my house and land in South Elmham St. Peter called Britwells, and all my other land in Bungay, Bungay Boyscot, Ilketshall and St. Peter's. ANNE must pay my debts, legacies and funeral charges. I also give to her all my goods and chattels, cattle, plate and household implements. I give 30s. to my sister the wife of BENNETT GILBERT and 20s. to ANN LENNIE daughter of REGINALD LENNIE. I give 40s.

to my sister CRISPE, wife of PHILIP CRISPE of Chediston and to her son and my godson 20s. I give 30s. to my mother-in-law [stepmother], wife of my deceased father VINCENT MOWLING and to my sister and her daughter ANNE MOWLING 20s. I give to my mother-in-law ANNE BIRKINSHAWE widow 20s. to buy a ring, and to my brother-in-law JOHN BIRKINSHAWE clerk 30s. and to his brother ROBERT 10s. to buy them rings. I give 20s. to my brother-in-law SAMUEL BIRKINSHAWE. I give and bequeath 30s. apiece to my 3 sisters-in-law SARAH, BRIDGET and MARTHA BIRKINSHAWE when they are 21, with benefit of survivorship. I give and bequeath 40s. each to ROBERT, JOHN & MARY the children of my brother-in-law WILLIAM REVE when they are 21, with benefit of survivorship. I give 20s. to CHRISTIAN, wife of JOHN WARD, and to my 2 servants JOHN JAYE & ANNE FAWSETT 20s. each. I give 16s. to the poor of Bungay St. Mary and 24s. to the poor of Bungay Trinity, of which parish I am a parishioner. I make ANNE my loving wife sole exrx. Supervisor GEORGE GOOCH of Bungay gent. to whom I give 40s. for his pains. Witnesses: JOHN DOWSING, JOHN SMITH, EDWARD DALBY. Pr. at Bungay 5 June 1635.

R(W) JOHN NICKOLLS (X) the elder of Tattingstone, yeoman. 15 November 1632 (904)

I give and bequeath to my kind and loving friend WILLIAM LING of Tattingstone my posted bedstead in the parlour, my cheese boards in the dairy and my 2 hanging shelves in the hall. I give and bequeath to JOHN NICKOLLS my grandson my brass pot. I give and bequeath to 12 of the poorest families in Tattingstone 24s., that is to say 2s. apiece to each family. After paying my debts and funeral expenses, I give and bequeath all the rest of my goods and chattels to LIONEL NICKOLLS. WILLIAM LING, in whom I repose great trust, I make my sole exor. Witnesses: EDWARD MOULTON, ROBERT PINCKNEY (X). Pr. at Yoxford 17 June 1635.

R(W) THOMAS POTTER of Wissett, yeoman. 27 February 1634/5 (905)

I give and bequeath to ELIZABETH my well beloved wife until my son THOMAS is 21 all my free and copyhold lands and tenements in Wissett, Chediston, Halesworth and Cookley. I give to my son RICHARD when 21 all the land in Wissett and Chediston which I bought from ANTHONY LOVEDAIE esquire, and all the land in Cookley and Halesworth that I bought from JOHN FELTHAM yeoman. All the rest of my land and tenements I give to my son THOMAS when he is 21. If my wife remarries she is to have an annuity of £30 to be paid by my supervisors from the land left to my son THOMAS, and she has power to distrain. I give and bequeath to my wife all my goods, household stuff and ready money for as long as she remains unmarried. She is to pay my debts and legacies, and be bound in the sum of £200 to my supervisors to deliver all the above goods to them if she remarries. If she does so, then my supervisors are to be bound to her in the sum of £300 to lease the land left to my sons and to use the profits for my children's upbringing and to increase their portions. I give and bequeath £160 to my daughter ELIZABETH when she is 21. If she dies before then, her legacy is to be equally divided between my 2 sons. If my wife remarries my supervisors are to pay her £10 p.a. until my 2 sons are 12 and thereafter £14 p.a. for their upbringing and education. They are also to pay her £8 p.a. for the bringing up and education of my daughter until she is 21. If all my children die before reaching age of 21, then my wife is to have all the land left to them for her lifetime. My supervisors are to pay her £100 if either all my children die or if she remarries. If my children die, I bequeath all my movable goods to my sisters. Wife sole exrx. Supervisors: my brothers-in-law NICHOLAS CURTIS and EDWARD FELLOWE. Witnesses: JOHN BARBER, HENRY PASEE (X), ROBERT ARTIS. Pr. at Beccles 2 July 1635.

R(W) RICHARD RUMBALL (X) of Woodbridge. 2 June 1635 (906)

Sick in body. I give to my brother WILLIAM RUMBALL of Nubery 2s. 6d. and 2s. to each of his children. I give to my sister MARGARET 2s. 6d. and 2s. to each of her children. I give 6s. each to my brother CRESWELL and to his wife, and to each of their children 2s. 6d. All these payments are to be made 2 months after my burial. The rest of my goods I leave to my wife whom I make sole exrx. Witnesses: NICHOLAS BEARDE, ISAAC EXTON. Pr. at Ipswich 19 June 1635.

R(W) WILLIAM RICHER of Woodbridge. 23 May 1635 (907)

Sick in body. I give and bequeath to ALICE my wife towards the maintenance and bringing up of my 2 children my house at Ufford with its land, and my shop and chamber over it at the upper end of Woodbridge market place. I also give her all my movable goods and make her sole exrx. Witnesses: ROBERT REYNOLDS, THOMAS BOND (X) & THOMAS MYTER. Pr. at Woodbridge 18 June 1635.

R(W) ELIZABETH SMALEHEAD (X) of Eyke, widow. (908)
7 November 1631

Sick in body. I give to my son JOHN SMALEHEAD 1 silver spoon and 2s. All the rest of my goods, cattle, household stuff and implements I give and bequeath to my kinsman JONAS WAYTH and my son-in-law ROGER SMALEHEAD [stepson] and make them my exors. Witnesses: GERVASE HUBBALD, JOHN SEAMAN(X), CHARITY SEAMAN (X). Pr. at Wickham Market 18 June 1635.

R(W) ANDREW SORRELL (X) the elder of Ipswich, yeoman. (909)
18 September 1632

I give and bequeath to my eldest son ANDREW and his heirs my messuage wherein I now dwell in the parish of St. Peter's Ipswich, and the great orchard on the east side of the messuage and my 2 small tenements next to the orchard now occupied by JOHN CHURCH & Widow BLACKMAN. I also give to him my tenement in the parish of St. Mary Elms, Ipswich, which is now in the occupation of JOHN FIRSE, and my lease of the manor and parsonage of Henley. I give and bequeath to ANDREW my brewhouse in St. Peter's parish which he now occupies, together with the dwelling house, millhouse, brewing vessels, coppers, leads, vats, coolers, millstones and all other lead pipes and other implements belonging, and all the yards and gardens. ANDREW is to pay my debts and legacies. I give to ANDREW all the sums of money in my possession when I die or due to me. If ANDREW dies without heirs, then all the land and goods bequeathed to him are to descend to my son EMANUEL. I give and bequeath to my son EMANUEL my tenement in St. Peter's parish standing against my present dwelling house with its yards and garden. EMANUEL has recently repaired this house for his own occupation. I also give him the wash yards belonging to the same house and now occupied by EDWARD GOAFE, and my tenement in Claydon with 5 acres of land, now let to one CLARKE. I give £10 p.a. to my son JOHN to be paid quarterly by my son ANDREW out of the property bequeathed to him. This gift becomes void if JOHN sells his annuity. All the household stuff in the tenement where I now live is to be equally divided by the supervisor of my will between my sons, ANDREW & EMANUEL. I give 20s. to the poor of the parish of St. Peter's. The unbequeathed residue of my goods I give to my son ANDREW, whom I make sole exor. Supervisor: son EMANUEL. Witnesses: EDWARD GOFFE junior, WILLIAM BLOMFEILD & THOMAS MARTYN. Pr. at Ipswich 10 July 1635.

R(W) THOMAS WIGG of Kirkley, fisherman (N). 15 June 1635 (910

He gave all his goods to his wife ANNE, and being asked what he would give to his sisters, he answered he would leave all to his wife. Witnesses: MARTHA PORTER (X), ELIZABETH GOODWYN (X). Pr. at Beccles to the widow 25 June 1635.

R(W) EDMUND YORKE of Holbrook, husbandman. (911
5 November 1634

Sick in body. I give to my wife SUSAN for her lifetime my tenement called Reves in Freston, and after her death to my son RICHARD. I give my tenement in Holbrook I now dwell in to my wife during her widowhood and no longer, and also all my movable goods. After her death or remarriage my goods are to be equally divided amongst my 4 children: EDMUND, SUSAN, MARY & RICHARD. The tenement I now live in I leave to my son EDWARD. I give my daughter SUSAN my copyhold tenement by Holbrook mill, and to my daughter MARY £20 when 21 or on her marriage day. I give 5s. to the poor of Holbrook. Exors: wife and son EDMUND. Supervisor: CHRISTOPHER HAYWARD, to whom I give 10s. Witnesses: ELIZABETH WHITING (X), JOHN BROTHERTON. Pr. at Ipswich 19 June 1635.

R(W) SIMON MERRIMAN (X) of Beccles. 22 March 1633/4 (912)

I give 20s. to Mr JOHN VAUGHAN minister of Beccles and to his wife 1 silver spoon and to each of his 3 children, JUDITH, JANE & AMIAS, a silver spoon. I give 40s. each to my sisters MARY SALLOWES, MARGARET REESON & ANNE CLAXTON. I give 20s. to MARY BULLOCK, daughter of my sister SALLOWES. All these legacies are to be paid within 1 month of my decease. I give to SIMON CLAXTON, my sister's son, my featherbed with the bedstead, 2 feather bolsters, 2 feather pillows, 1 rug, 2 coverlets, 1 blanket and all the residue of my goods to pay my debts and legacies. I make him exor. Witnesses: NICHOLAS PECKE, THOMAS REDE. Pr. at Beccles - no date.

R(W) SARAH HERRING (X) of Beccles, widow. 13 July 1635 (913)

Sick of body. My exor. is to pay himself out of my estate all such sums as I owe him and all my other debts. I give to HENRY son of RICHARD SPENDLOWE the bed and bedstead I now lie on with the coverlets, blankets and all other things belonging to it. I also give him 2 pairs of sheets, 6 napkins, 1 pair pillowbeeres and 2 hand towels. I give to JOHN son of RICHARD SPENDLOWE another bed with a livery bedstead with the coverlet, blankets and other things belonging to it as it now stands in the gatehouse chamber, and 2 pairs sheets, 6 napkins, 2 hand towels and 1 pair pillowbeeres. I give to MARGARET, wife of STEPHEN FOULEZER of Beccles, a coloured say apron, 1 smock and 1 pair hose. I give to MARY, wife of HENRY MAKINS, 2 red petticoats which I wear daily, the waistcoat I wear daily, 2 aprons (1 blue and 1 white) and a smock. I give to ELIZABETH, wife of RICHARD FARRER, my best hat, a smock, the coif wrought with white which I have now on, a linsey wolsey apron, a pair of old shoes and a pair hose. I give to HENRY SPENDLOWE 2 silver spoons and the bible that was my husband's. I give 2 silver spoons to JOHN SPENDLOWE. I give a silver spoon each to SARAH & MARGARET, the daughters of HENRY MAKINS. The residue of my goods are to be equally parted amongst the 6 children of THOMAS SPENDLOWE of Halesworth and the 3 children of HENRY MAKINS of Beccles when they are 21. They all have benefit of survivorship. I make JOSEPH GARRARD of Beccles, beer brewer, sole exor. Witnesses: THOMAS FIDELL, STEPHEN FOULDSER & FRANCIS BELL (X). Pr. at Beccles 20 July 1635.

R(W) JOHN BENNETT (X) of Linstead Parva, husbandman. (914)
13 June 1635.

I give ELIZABETH my wife all my goods and chattels, and all debts owing to me upon bills or bonds. Witnesses: THOMAS PEERE (X), BRIAN DEWE & JOHN ALEXANDER. Pr. at Yoxford 8 July 1635.

R(W) WILLIAM CALVER of Bedfield, millwright. 10 June 1635 (915)

Sick in body. I give and bequeath to my daughter SUSAN the bed, bolster, bedstead, blankets, sheets and covering as it stands in the parlour where I lie. I also give her £5. I give to ANNA my well-beloved wife all my cattle and household stuff, except what I have left to SUSAN, so that she may pay my debts, legacies and funeral charges. I make her sole exrx. Witnesses: JOHN CASSON, ROBERT CLAYTON & PETER ALDRICH. Pr. at Wilby 11 July 1635.

R(W) GILBERT COOKE of Beccles, keelman. 28 March 1629 (916)

I ask my exors. to show my remembrance of the godly poor people in Beccles according to my poor estate. I give and bequeath to ALICE my loving wife my houses in Beccles, my lands and movable goods during her natural life. She must keep the houses in good repair and within 6 days of my decease must make an estate in law to my 2 daughters and their heirs of this property after her death. My daughters are ELIZABETH wife of THOMAS AYLEWARD and ANNA wife of JOSEPH HILL. If ALICE my wife refuses to make this assurance to my daughters, then they shall immediately enter into possession of my houses, land and moveable goods. All my property is to be equally divided between my daughters after my wife's death. I ask them to be peaceable and charitable and to do no wrong to each other. Exrxs.: wife and 2 daughters. Witnesses: on 19 May 1629 by EDWARD TROTT, HENRY NUSSIE, THOMAS HORTH. Pr. at Beccles 27 July 1635.

R(W) THOMAS COOPER of Dallinghoo, yeoman. 11 June 1635 (917)

Sick in body. I give and bequeath to my daughter JOAN £60 to be paid 6 years after death of both myself and my wife MARY. I give and bequeath to my son WILLIAM £40 to be paid 4 years after the death of myself and my wife. I also give to him my house and land at Great Bealings 2 years after my death, and my house and tenement in Woodbridge after my wife's decease. I make my son THOMAS sole exor. I give my son WILLIAM my looms and all things belonging to them, and my posted bedstead in the parlour after my wife's decease. I give my cupboard in the parlour and a featherbed with all that belongs to it to my daughter JOAN after my wife's decease. After my wife's death all my unbequeathed movable goods go to WILLIAM & JOAN. I give JOAN a table in the parlour chamber, 1 posnet and 1 brass pot after my wife's death. I give WILLIAM one load of wood at the stub. Witnesses: THOMAS & WILLIAM COOPER. Pr. at Wickham Market 9 July 1635.

R(W) JAMES CLOUGH of Ilketshall St Margaret, yeoman. 19 June 1635 (918)

Sick in body. I give and bequeath to my eldest son JAMES my free and copyhold messuage and lands in St. Margaret Ilketshall and in South Elmham St. Peter and St. Michael. I give my second son

JOHN my messuage in South Elmham All Saints, which I purchased from JAMES SEALER, with all its buildings and land. I grant to JOHN's wife, MARGARET, in case she should outlive him, an annuity of £10 from this messuage in lieu of dowry. She has power to distrain, but if she attempts to claim a larger dowry her annuity will be void. I have already assured to my youngest son WILLIAM the messuage in Ilketshall St. Margaret which I purchased from JOHN GUYLE. He must pay my younger daughter MARTHA £100 when she is 21. This payment is to be made in my dwelling house in Ilketshall St. Margaret. The residue of my goods and chattels and movable goods I give to my 2 sons JAMES & JOHN towards the payment of my debts and legacies and funeral expenses, and I make them exors. Witnesses: THOMAS PYE clerk, DRUE WEBSTER. Pr. at Beccles 7 July 1635.

R(W) WILLIAM JOHNSON (X) of Westhall, linen weaver. (919)
12 July 1635

I give and bequeath to ELIZABETH my loving wife for her lifetime all my messuage in Peasenhall wherein JOSEPH BULLOCK now dwells, and after her death to THOMAS my second son. I give and bequeath to THOMAS £10 to be paid to him when 22 by my exrx. I give to WILLIAM my eldest son £20 to be paid to him at age of 20. I also give him immediately 2 pairs of weaving looms with the slayes and other things belonging. I give to my son ROBERT £25 to be paid to him when 21, and £23 to be paid to my son JOHN when 21. I give to the child my wife is with, if born alive, £20 at age of 21. Children have benefit of survivorship. All the debts owing to me are to be called in and the money put out towards the payment of my legacies. All my stock of cows, horses, corn, grass, cheese, butter and yarn is to be sold for the best price before the Michaelmas after my decease. The money so raised is to be put out at interest towards the payment of my legacies. My wife ELIZABETH is to use the income from this money for the education and bringing up of my children until they are of age. The residue of my household stuff I give to my wife, whom I make sole exrx. Witnesses: JOHN BENNETT, ROGER LAURANCE, ROBERT SWAINE junior. Pr. at Beccles 25 July 1635.

R(W) KATHERINE LINGE (X) of Clopton, widow. 15 April 1635 (920)

I give and bequeath to my daughter MARGERY, wife of Mr JOHN SUCKERMAN, 10s. and to my daughter ELIZABETH, wife of WILLIAM PORTER, 10s. I give to my daughter JOAN, wife of THOMAS CUSEN, 40s., and to my grandchild MARY NEWMAN 5s. I give to DORCAS LING, who now dwells with me, 40s. to be employed for her benefit by my exors. I give to my son-in-law THOMAS WILKESON my best featherbed and bolster, my best coverlet, 2 blankets, 1 pair sheets and 1 pillow, and to his wife my best petticoat. I give to LETTICE CUSEN my grandchild one of my best pewter dishes. The rest of my goods are to be sold by my exors. and daughter MARGERY, and the money divided equally between my 5 daughters: AMY, wife of ISAAC [blank], MARY NEWMAN widow, JOAN wife of

THOMAS CUSEN, ELIZABETH, wife of WILLIAM PORTER and MARGARET, wife of THOMAS CAPPS. Exors.: Mr JOHN SUCKERMAN and my neighbor THOMAS TYE. Witnesses: JOHN GODBOULD (X), JOHN SIPMAN (X). Pr. at Ipswich 31 July 1635.

R(W) WILLIAM LYKE (X) of Letheringham, husbandman. 30 March 1635 (921)

I give and bequeath to ELLEN, daughter of my sister ELIZABETH who is wife of THOMAS WILSON, all my goods and chattels. She is to see my body buried and discharge my funeral expenses. I make her sole exrx. Witnesses: RICHARD HARRISON, LAURENCE PLANT (X), JOHN CAGE. Pr. at Wickham Market 29 July 1635.

R(W) ROBERT LYNE of Dallinghoo, yeoman. 11 June 1634 (922)

I give and bequeath £20 to ELIZABETH daughter of my brother THOMAS LYNE, but if he has another son or daughter the £20 shall be equally divided between them. I give £20 to MARY SMITH, my sister's daughter, £5 to HENRY SKOCHMOR, 40s. each to THOMAS & DOWSEN CAMP, 5s. each to my godchildren ROBERT JAYE, PATIENCE ALLIN & FRANCIS WITTUME. I give 40s. to the poor of Dallinghoo to be distributed by the churchwardens and overseers where most need is. I give all the rest of my goods to my well-beloved brother THOMAS LYNE whom I make exor. and ask to pay all my legacies within 1 year of my decease. He is to bestow 40s. on my funeral expenses. No witnesses. Pr. at Wickham Market 9 July 1635.

R(W) EDWARD RAWLIN (X) of Shelley, blacksmith. 13 June 1635 (923)

Sick in body. I give and bequeath to my son JAMES the posted bedstead standing in the parlour. I give to my son EDWARD the bellows in the shop and also the stith. I bequeath to my son THOMAS all my clothes, both linen and woollen. I give to my daughter MARY, wife of THOMAS BLOSSE, 20s. to be paid to her 3 months after my decease, and £5 to my daughter ANNE to be paid at the same time. I give my grandchild MARY BLOSSE 10s. to buy her a bible. All the residue of my goods, my debts, legacies and funeral charges being paid, I give to my loving wife MARY whom I make sole exrx. Witnesses: ROBERT GOODWIN, THOMAS GRAVENER. Pr. at Ipswich 10 July 1635.

R(W) HENRY THURLOE (X) of Brantham. 15 June 1635 (924)

Very sick in body. I give and bequeath to ISABEL my beloved wife for her life my house with its yards. She must keep it in repair with thatching, plastering and fencing. If she fails to do this, after 3 months my son WILLIAM shall give his mother-in-law [stepmother] notice to undertake such repairs to the house or fences as are necessary and if she still refuses to do this, then he is to take possession of the house. After the death of ISABEL I give the house and yards to my son WILLIAM. I give my wife the posted bed I lie on as it stands and all the chests in the house save 1 trunk, 3 kettles, a joined table and a joined form belonging to it, the round table in the hall, all my working tools and other household vessels and all my linen. I bequeath to my son THOMAS my half-headed bed with 1 feather bed, 1 feather bolster and 1 coverlet, the trunk hooped with iron that stands in my chamber, the long framed table in the hall, the livery cupboard, the brass pot, an iron pot head and pot hooks, a copper that hangs between the hall and the chamber, my cloak and all my other apparel on condition he gives his mother 40s. to pay my debts. I give my son WILLIAM 2 pewter dishes and 2 saucers. All the rest of my household goods I give to ISABEL my wife and make her sole exrx. Witnesses: ROBERT WYLIS and JOHN GLANFEILD. Pr. at Ipswich 10 July 1635.

R(W) AUGUSTINE EDWARDS (X) of Beccles, yeoman. (925)
11 July 1635*

Sick of body. I give to my sister FRANCES, wife of JAMES WESSON, £20 to be paid within 1 year, and £20 to my sister ELIZABETH to be paid within 1 year of my death. If my sisters die, their legacies are to be parted among their children. I give 4 pairs of sheets to each of my sisters. I give to my sister MARIAN EDWARDS 40s. p.a. to be paid to her quarterly by my exor. and I also give her 4 pairs of my ordinary sheets. I give £5 to RICHARD EDWARDS of Harleston, son of RICHARD EDWARDS late of Bungay, to be paid within 1 year. I give 20s. apiece to ELIZABETH, MARY & MICHAEL children of MICHAEL EDWARDS of Earsham; 40s. of this is already in his hands. I give to my cousin ABRAHAM TODD the elder £3 to be paid within 1 year, and 5s. to his wife ANNE. I give 5s. apiece to FRANCIS JOHNSON, KATHERINE AYERS & MARY TODD, my fellow servants and 10s. to some godly minister of the town where I die to preach a sermon at my burial. I give to the poor of the town where I die 10s. The residue of my goods and chattels and ready money I give to JAMES EDWARDS of Norton, my brother, whom I make sole exor. Witnesses: ABRAHAM TODD, THOMAS FIDDELL, KATHERINE AYERS (X). Pr. at Beccles 8 July 1635.
[*This date appears in original will and register, but must be incorrect.]

R(W) ROBERT BATEMAN (X) of Wrentham, yeoman. 13 June 1635 (926)

I give and bequeath to MARY my daughter £100 when she is 21, and £100 to my son FRANCIS when 21. If my wife dies before these children reach age of 21, within 1 month of her death her exors. are to pay £200 in trust for my children into the hands of FRANCIS BREWSTER junior of Wrentham and FRANCIS MORSE of Uggeshall. Children have benefit of survivorship. I give to my eldest son WILLIAM £10 p.a. during my wife's lifetime, but during the first 2 years after my decease he is to have only £5 p.a. Payments to him are to be made in my house situated in the West End in Wrentham by my wife or her assignees. He has power to distrain, and must give a receipt for each payment to my wife MARY. All legacies given in my will are to be paid in this house and all the legatees are to give a written receipt to my wife. I bequeath to my son WILLIAM one of my posted beds with the best but one featherbed, 1 bolster, 1 pillow, 1 coverlet, 2 blankets, 2 pairs sheets, my best brass pot, 1 square copper kettle, my dansk chest standing in the old parlour and 1 trunk. These items are to be given to him 1 month after my death. I also give him after the death of my wife a frame table with its leaf, a form and a joined chair as they stand in the new parlour. I give to my wife for her life all my free and copyhold land and tenements in Wrentham lying to the west of the church. She must keep the house in repair, pay my debts and legacies and bring up my children until they are 21. After her death I give my messuage and land to my 2 sons WILLIAM & ROBERT. They have benefit of survivorship. If one wishes to sell his share, the other is to have the right to purchase it for £10 less than anyone else. If my wife dies before my children MARY & FRANCIS are 21, my sons WILLIAM & ROBERT are to pay £16 p.a. for the use of each of them into the hands of FRANCIS BREWSTER junior and FRANCIS MORSE. This money is to be used for their education until they are 21. They have power to distrain. If either WILLIAM or ROBERT dies without heirs, the survivor is to pay £50 each to MARY & FRANCIS at £10 p.a. They have power to distrain. I give to my son ROBERT £20 to be paid by my wife a month after he reaches age of 22. I give 10s. to the poor of Wrentham and 10s. to the repair of Wrentham church. I bequeath all the rest of my goods and chattels, cattle, bonds, bills, plate and money to my wife MARY towards the execution of my will, and I make my beloved wife sole exrx. She is to enter into a bond of £300 to perform my will with FRANCIS BREWSTER & FRANCIS MORSE, and if she refuses they are to be my exors. Witnesses: THOMAS MORSE, RICHARD NEWSON & GABRIEL BATEMAN. Pr. at Beccles 18 July 1635.

R(W) REBECCA GILDERSLEEVE (X) of Beccles, widow. (927
11 July 1635

All my goods and household stuff, except my linen and woollen, are to be sold by my exor., who is also to receive debts due to me and is to pay my debts. Anything left over is to be equally divided between my 2 daughters MARY & FRANCES when they are 21. I give to them my pightle at Rigbone Hill in Beccles when they are 21; until then my exor. is to use its rent for their benefit. I give to my daughter MARY my biggest pot, and 2 silver spoons (the biggest and the smallest) when she is 21. I give to FRANCES my lesser tipped pot and my other silver spoon when she is 21. I appoint SIMON BOATSWAYNE the elder of Beccles sole exor. hoping he will see my body decently brought to earth and my will proved according to my faithful trust reposed in him. I give him 30s. Witnesses: THOMAS UTBER, ROBERT HARMAN (X), & RICHARD MAPLIZDEN, public notary. Pr. at Beccles 23 July 1635.

R(W) JOHN BETTES of Pettaugh, husbandman (N). (928)
3 July 1635

He gave all his goods to ANNE his wife for her life to pay his debts and bring up his children, and anything left after her death to be divided among his children. Wife sole exrx. Witnesses: EDMUND MOUSE of Wetheringsett and his wife SUSAN, ANDREW HAYLE of Pettaugh and his wife MARY. Pr. at Ipswich 20 July 1635.

R(W) THOMAS BUNNYTE (X) of Ipswich, glover. 1 June 1635 (929)

Sick in body. First my will is that my debts should be paid and my funeral expenses discharged. I give and bequeath to my son THOMAS £10 when he is 21, and £10 to my daughter ELIZABETH at 21. Benefit of survivorship. I give all my movables to my wife ELIZABETH whom I appoint sole exrx. Witnesses: RICHARD STUDD, PEDINGANUELL ALLEN. Pr. at Ipswich 4 Aug. 1635.

R(W) WILLIAM HAYWARD (X) of Worlingworth. 31 August 1631 (930)

I give and bequeath to my nephew JOHN HAYWARD, son of late JOHN HAYWARD of Elmswell, £10 to be paid 6 months after my death. I give to my 2 nieces, daughters of late JOHN HAYWARD, £5 between them to be paid within 6 months. I give 6s. 8d. to my godson ROBERT son of JAMES PRICK, and 3s. 4d. to my god-daughter FRANCES, daughter of JOHN WISKE. I give the rest of my goods and chattels to FRANCIS JERMY of Metfield gent and to GEORGE JERMY of Buxlow clerk to be equally divided between them. I make them exors. Witness: THOMAS MOORE (X). Pr. at Beccles 26 Sept. 1635.

R(W) THOMAS ARMITAGE of Raydon, yeoman (N). 9 July 1635 (931)

He gave to MARGARET his wife and to WILLIAM his only son all his estate to be equally divided between them. Wife to have all his money put out on bond and all her linen, and son to choose the best horse. Wife and son joint exors. Witnesses: ROBERT RIXE & EDWARD CAPP. Pr. at Beccles 22 Aug. 1635.

R(W) ROSE BROADE of Hollesley, widow (N). (932)
[blank] August 1635

She gave to BENJAMIN her son £20 to be paid to him when 15. She gave £15 to her son ROBERT and £5 to her son JOHN to be paid to them when BENJAMIN attains age of 15. These legacies are to remain in hands of her daughter MARY, and the interest on them is to be used towards the education of BENJAMIN until he is 15. All the rest of her goods she gave to her daughter MARY, whom she named exrx. Witnesses: RICHARD MOSE & ELIZABETH CURSPE. Pr. at Wickham Market 2 Oct. 1635.

R(W) BRIDGET BAKER (X) of Ringsfield, widow. (933)
17 September 1635

My body is to be buried in the churchyard of Ringsfield. After my debts are discharged I bequeath to my son FRANCIS a legacy of £100 to be paid out of my movable goods when he is 21. I also give him a featherbed with all its furniture to be delivered to him by my 2 daughters HESTER & REBECCA whom I make exrxs. The rest of my movable goods are to be divided between my 2 daughters. Witnesses: ROBERT SHELFORD parson, JAMES GODBOLD, REBECCA GOOCH (X). Pr. at Beccles 9 Oct. 1635.

R(W) WILLIAM COLEMAN of Ringsfield (N). [no date] (934)

He gave all his goods and estate to his 2 children, WILLIAM & AGNES, to be equally divided between them. Witnesses: WILLIAM CRAMPTON gent. and his wife MARGARET, ELIGEUS BOOTIE and his wife FRANCES. Will made in the time of his sickness. Pr. at Beccles 4 Aug. 1635.

R(W) EDWARD COOPER (X) of Ufford, weaver. (935)
1 September 1635

Sick of body. I give and bequeath all my messuages and lands in Ufford and Melton to my exor. until my son EDMUND is 24. Exor may sell as much of my land as is necessary to pay my debts and the charges of my burial and probate of my will, over and above the value of my goods and chattels. Any money in hand after paying my debts, etc. is to be retained by my exor. for the upbringing of my children. Exor. to keep my houses in good repair and to pay for this out of the annual income from my land. I give to my son EDMUND my houses and unsold land when he reaches age of 24. Within 2 years he must pay £10 to my daughter MARY who has power to distrain. Exor. to bring up my children and maintain them with meat, drink and apparel during their minority. All the remainder of my goods, cattle, butter and cheese, except one weaned calf, I give to my wife. I make EDWARD GOULDING my exor. and give him the calf. Witnesses: GERARD HUBBALD, WILLIAM LONG, THOMAS WALTER. Pr. at Wickham Market 2 Oct. 1635.

R(W) GEORGE FARRER of Flowton, (936)
minister of the word of God. 23 May 1632

Weak in body. I give to ROBERT SPROWE, portman of Ipswich, for ever all my lands and tenements in Bentley. I give to MARY my wife for ever all my land and tenements in Chatisham and Hintlesham. She must pay £30 to GEORGE FARRER within 1 year and

£30 to JOHN FARRER within 2 years of my decease. I give to JAMES FARRER £30 to be paid within 3 years. I give to ELIZABETH DAIE my kinswoman £20 within 4 years and to ELIAS FARRER £20 within 5 years of my death. I give to the 6 sisters of JOHN FARRER, clerk of Langham, £60 to be paid within 4 years. The wife of WATSON has already received £5 and one other, being a widow, £3. I give 50s. each to the 4 children of EDWARD FARRER when they are 21. I give £5 to ROBERT FARRER of Bury St. Edmunds within 2 years and £5 each to his 2 sons when they are 21. To JUDITH FARRER I give 20s. to be paid within 1 year and to her 2 sons 50s. each when they are 21. I give £5 each to be paid within 7 years to STEPHEN & JOSEPH BARKER. I give £5 within 1 year of my decease to my kinswoman late the wife of JOHN BARKER of East Bergholt and £5 each to her 2 children when 21. I give to WILLIAM BOGGAS my son-in-law and to his wife £5, and £5 each to buy rings to MARY, RICHARD, JOHN & ANTHONY BOGGAS. I give 5s. each to my 6 servants. I give 13s. 4d. to the poor people of Flowton and 13s. 4d. to the poor people of Somersham. I give to MARY my wife all my goods and chattels and make her sole exrx. Witnesses: ROBERT SPARROWE junior, HENRY COURTNALL. Codicil: Whereas I have given in my will £30 each to GEORGE, JOHN, JAMES & ELIAS FARRER and to ELIZABETH DAIE* widow, I have already given them £10 each with my own hands, so there remains to be paid to them by my exrx. £20 each. The legacies of two of the sisters of JOHN FARRER of Langham have also been partly paid. Witnesses: HENRY COURTNALL & JOAN GARNER (X). Pr. at Ipswich 30 May 1635.
[*This does not quite tally with earlier part of will, but the register copy and the original will agree in this error.]

R(W) MARY GARRWOOD of Chatisham, widow (N). [no date] (937)

In time of her sickness. She gave to ROBERT GARRWOOD her son 10s., to THOMAS GARRWOOD her son 5s., to EDMUND GARRWOOD her son 40s. and to her son RICHARD £12. She gave £40 to her son JOHN, £12 to her daughter MERCY, wife of GRAVENER and £5 to her daughter MARY, wife of THOMAS WOLNETT. She named her son ROBERT as exor. Witnesses: RICHARD FLACKE & ELIZABETH his wife. Pr. at Ipswich 3 Oct. 1635.

R(W) WILLIAM HUMFRIE (X) of Benacre, yeoman. (938)
15 September 1635

I give all my houses and land in Benacre to JANE my wife for her natural life. She is to keep them in repair. After her death I give them to my son GEORGE and to my 4 daughters ELIZABETH, MARTHA, MARY & AGNES. All my movable goods I give to my wife on condition she pays £20 to my son JOHN when he is 26; payment to be made in porch of Benacre church. He has power to distrain. If he dies without heirs before age of 26, then £20 is to be equally divided among those of my children then living. JANE my wife I make sole exrx. Witnesses: NATHANIEL ROE, ROBERT TRAPNELL (X). Pr. at Benacre 8 Oct. 1635.

R. JOHN HUNT of Parham, yeoman. 7 September 1635 (939)

I give and bequeath to my son JOHN the messuage wherein I now dwell with all its land, except one piece called Calfer which I assign to my daughter ANNE. I also give to JOHN all my manuscripts and all my books which concern the laws of this realm and also a book called Downeham's Christian Warfare. All my other books which do not in any way concern divinity are to be kept for JOHN and delivered to him by my exrx. at his age of 18. I give and bequeath to my son LUKE immediately all the land in Parham which my deceased father JOHN HUNT purchased from EDMUND BURWELL. I give to my daughter MARY all my land and tenements in Great Glemham at once, and £50 when she is 21. I give to my daughter ANNE at once the 2 1/2 acre piece of land called Calfer, which adjoins land of FRANCIS WARNER esq. and ROBERT COLVILL gent. I also give her a 2 acre piece of land called Carters, which once belonged to ADAM HUNT my grandfather, and the 1/2 acre piece of pasture or fen in Parham which I lately bought from ROBERT WARNER the elder and ROBERT WARNER the younger. I also give to ANNE £40 to be paid to her by my exrx. when she is 21. All children have benefit of survivorship. I give £10 to REBECCA, daughter of BARNABAS FRYER linen weaver of Ipswich, to be paid 5 years after my decease. I give to WATCH LEGATT, my god-daughter, a little book entitled Mr Perkins's Six Principles and another book called The Practice of Piety. If it can be conveniently done, they are to be bound up together and given to her by my exrx. when she is 16. I desire her to read them for her instruction and godliness. I bequeath to JANE my wife all my goods and chattels to pay my debts and legacies, and I do appoint my loving wife to be sole exrx. of my will, asking her to see it fulfilled as my trust and confidence is especially reposed in her. I also ask her to be careful of the godly and religious education of my children, and to augment the portion of my son JOHN according to her promise made to me. JOHN must behave himself dutifully and honestly to her as he ought to do. I also especially desire her to be directed by the advice and council of my supervisors according to her solemn promise to me. I make my very loving friends ROBERT ROBERTSON, yeoman of Monewden, and GREGORY NICHOLAS, yeoman of Dallinghoo, supervisors of my will. I ask them to assist my wife truly to perform my will, and to have a circumspect eye concerning the education of my children and counsel their mother about their godly and virtuous upbringing and the continuance of quiet and peace amongst them. I give ROBERT ROBERTSON for his pains one of my books called The Institution of Christian Religion by Mr John Calvin, and 20s. Unto GREGORY NICHOLAS I give 20s. and a book which is a disputation between Reynolds and Hart. Witnesses: THOMAS COLLAM, EDWARD PALLANT, WILLIAM WADE. Pr. at Wickham Market 2 Oct. 1635.

R(W) THEOPHILUS LAKELAND of St. Mary at Elms Ipswich, dyer. 7 July 1635 (940)

Sick in body. I give to THEOPHILUS LACKLAND my son £40 when he is 21, and to my son ROBERT £30 when he is 21. To my daughters

DEBORAH, ABIGAIL, SUSAN & MARY I give £20 each when they reach 21 or on their marriage days. As long as my wife ALICE has the charge and tuition of my children she is to have the use of their portions, but if they be bound out as apprentices or go away to live away from home in service, then their portions are to be put out. Children have benefit of survivorship. All my goods and money I give to ALICE my wife. If she remarries she is to give good security to supervisors of my will for my children's portions before her marriage takes place. If she dies unmarried, all my goods bequeathed to her are to be divided among my children. After my wife's decease I give £10 to each of my children out of my goods. I give to DORCAS, daughter of WILLIAM PRESTON, 20s. I appoint my well-beloved brothers WILLIAM PRESTON, vicar of Rushmere, and ZACHARIE FISKE, glover of Wetherden, to be my supervisors. Witnesses: ROBERT LAKELAND, MARY FISKE (X), ABIGAIL LAKELOND (X). Pr. at Ipswich 18 Aug. 1635.

R(W) WILLIAM MARTIN of Cookley, clerk. 11 March 1634/5 (941)

Visited with sickness. Within 6 months of my decease my exors. shall pay to my well-beloved wife ALICE £30 or goods and chattels to that value in satisfaction of an agreement made on 26 July 1613. I give and bequeath to WILLIAM my eldest son all that part of my house wherein he now dwells with its land in the parish of All Saints in the City of Norwich, and to my son THOMAS the other part of the same house in which he lives with its land. If THOMAS should die without heirs, the whole house and land are to descend to my grandson WILLIAM and if he in turn has no heirs, to my grandson LUKE and if he has no heirs to my grandson JOSEPH. If any of these heirs attempt to interfere with the arrangements made in this my will, then they shall be deprived of all bequests to them. I give to my daughter ROBERTS, wife of FULKE ROBERTS clerk, my book called <u>Babington his Works</u> and to her husband my 2 books called <u>Thesaurus Concionatorum</u>. All the residue of my goods and chattels, after paying my debts, funeral charges and the expenses of proving my will, I give to be equally divided between my sons WILLIAM & THOMAS whom I make joint exors. I entreat my loving son-in-law FULKE ROBARTS to be supervisor and to aid and assist my exors. I give him 10s. for his pains. Witnesses: ROBERT HUGGARD clerk and HENRY MORE. Pr. at Bungay 20 April 1635.

R(W) GEORGE ROPPE of Ipswich, yeoman. 8 April 1635 (942)

Sick of body. I give to GEORGE my son all my messuage in the parish of St. Mary at Quay wherein EDWARD FEILD mariner now inhabits. I give my daughter ABIGAIL my messuage, adjoining the first, in which [blank in original will] REVETT mariner lives. They both have benefit of survivorship. I give to ABIGAIL my great brass kettle, my little brass pot, my joined great cupboard, my best bedstead, featherbed, bolster and all other things belonging to it and my best flockbed. All these things were mine before my marriage with FRANCES my present wife. I give to GEORGE my son my great brass pot, my little kettle, my other bedstead, featherbed, bolster and all other things belonging to it, and my other flockbed. These goods were likewise mine before my present marriage. All my other household stuff, brass, pewter and linen which were mine and were brought to me in marriage with FRANCES, I give to be equally divided between GEORGE and ABIGAIL. I give to MATTHEW & HENRY SHERMAN, children of my present wife's daughter, ANNE SHERMAN widow, £3 each when 21. I give 40s. to ABIGAIL BLACKSALL, my late wife's grandchild, and 20s. to ROSE BLACKSALL, sister of ABIGAIL. I give 20s. to my godson MICHAEL COLCHESTER. These sums are to be paid by my exor within 1 year of my decease. All my unbequeathed goods and chattels I give to my exor. to pay my debts, legacies and funeral charges. I give him 20s. If any money is left over, I give it to my daughter ABIGAIL. I appoint JOSEPH PEMBERTON, maltster of Ipswich, sole exor. Witnesses: RICHARD GRIMSTON senior, JOHN BELTE & RACHEL GRIMSTON. Pr. at Ipswich 3 Oct. 1635.

R(W) NICHOLAS RUMSIE of Ilketshall St. Margaret. (943)
13 July 1635

He gave to ANNE his wife all his goods and estate to pay his debts and educate his son RICHARD. Anything left at death of his wife he willed to his son RICHARD. Witnesses: RICHARD RUMSEY & MARK BATEMAN. Pr. at Bungay 7 Aug. 1635.

R(W) EDWARD SHEMYNG (X) of Framlingham, yeoman. (944)
7 September 1635

Sick in body. Immediately after my decease my exor. is to take into his hands all my goods and chattels, cattle and debts to pay my debts, funeral charges and the probate of this will. After this the surplus is to be used to pay my legacies. I make FRANCIS IRELAND, apothecary of Framlingham, my exor. and I give him £15 for his pains. I give to JOHN son of my brother FRANCIS SHEMYNG £30: £5 to be paid within 3 years of my death, £5 3 years later and £20 6 years later. I give to JOHN son of my deceased brother WILLIAM £5 to be paid within 10 years of my decease. If he dies I give this £10 to ELIZABETH FISKE. I give £10 to my brother FRANCIS 5 years after my death or if he dies before then, to his son JOHN. I give to my brother NICHOLAS £10: £3 to be paid within 1 year and £7 within 7 years of my decease. I give £10 to MARY SHEMYNG to be paid within 1 year. I will that MARY my wife and MARY TOMPSON her daughter shall hold for 3 years the messuage wherein I dwell with its yards, and a 15 acre close in Framlingham called Sone close and now occupied by MARY TOMPSON, in satisfaction of the sum I owe to EZEKIEL TOMPSON my wife's son. EZEKIEL is also to be paid £5 within 7 years of my death. Witnesses: JOHN LANE & WILLIAM TOMPSON (X). I do further give to ELIZABETH SHEMYNG my sister £5 to be paid within 3 years of my decease. All my legacies are to be paid in

Framlingham church porch. I do further give immediately after my decease to my loving kinsman JOHN LANE of Rendlesham my best bedstead. My wife is to have all such goods as were hers before my marriage with her. I give to EDWARD TOMPSON, my wife's son, 40s. to be paid within 7 years, to MARY TOMPSON her daughter 20s. and to WILLIAM TOMPSON 20s. Witnesses: THOMAS SEAMAN (X) & GEORGE BUTE (X). I give to the poor of Framlingham £3 to be distributed by the churchwarden and overseers of the poor. Pr. at Wickham Market 2 Oct. 1635.

R(W) MARGARET SMYTH (X) of Cratfield, widow. (945)
25 October 1630

I give and bequeath to my grandchild JOHN, son of my son ROBERT SMYTH, a posted bed with a tester, a featherbed, a feather bolster and all the furniture belonging as it now stands in the parlour of the messuage in Cratfield in which my son ROBERT now lives. JOHN is to have this gift when he is 21, and in the meantime his father is to have the use of it. I give to my son ROBERT my best gold ring and to FINETT his wife my best stuff petticoat. I give to GRACE CORNISHE my daughter my best cloak and safeguard, and £5 to her children: MARTHA, MARGARET, ELIZABETH & JOHN when they are 21. They have benefit of survivorship. I give to FRANCIS ALDOWES my son-in-law my other gold ring, a pot lipped with silver and a silver spoon, and to KATHERINE, his wife and my daughter, my best cloth gown. I give to ANNE ALDOWES my grandchild my best stuff gown and my second featherbed in value, 2 pillows and my new coverlet. To her sister SARAH I give my third featherbed in value, a linsey wolsey bolster and my third coverlet in value. I also give to ANNE & SARAH my hutch of linen standing under the table in the parlour of the messuage in Cratfield wherein FRANCIS ALDOWES lives. I give to my grandson WILLIAM ALDOWES my musket furnished, a silver spoon and my sermon book when he is 21. I give to my daughter MARY, wife of EDMUND TALMACHE, my second stuff gown in value and my best cloth petticoat. I give £5 each when 21 to my grandchildren MARGARET & FINETT TALMACHE. I will my exor. shall receive and pay my debts, and bring me honestly to the ground in Christian burial. The residue of my goods and chattels, bedding, linen, brass and pewter and all household goods I give to MARGARET ALDOWS my grandchild. I make my son-in-law FRANCIS ALDOWES sole exor., hoping he will faithfully perform my will according to the trust I repose in him. If he refuses to prove my will within 15 days of my decease, I give all the goods bequeathed to him to my grandchild MARGARET ALDOWES and make her exrx. Witness: WILLIAM FISKE junior. Altered and confirmed on 31 Dec. 1634. Witnesses: WILLIAM ALDOWES, JOHN FISKE. Pr. at Walpole 21 May 1635.

R(W) JANE INGELAND (X) of Gorleston, widow. (946)
28 September 1635

Sick in body. I wish to be buried in Gorleston churchyard. I bequeath to FRANCIS my son my new built house together with all the rooms and yards from the new house to the north corner of the old house and so down to the cliffside, and the stable belonging to the house and half the well. I bequeath to my daughters REBECCA & ELIZABETH my old house with all the rooms and yards belonging to it on the north side and the other half of the well. This house is to be divided between my daughters by my exor. and my brother JOHN ABOROWGH as they shall think fitting. My daughter ELIZABETH is to have for her part the fore rooms at the street end of the house. If either daughter dies without issue then children of my daughter ANNE are to have her property, and if both daughters and my son FRANCIS die without heirs, then EDMUND TALLOR is to have their houses. REBECCA & ELIZABETH are to pay my son FRANCIS 10s. a year each, starting 2 years after my decease, until they have both paid him 30s. FRANCIS is to give £5 to my daughter ANNE TALLOR or to her children if she dies. I give and bequeath to FRANCIS 1 trundle bedstead, 1 flockbed and certain spare feathers with a covering, a blanket, a bolster and a pillow. I give all my linen to be equally divided between my 4 children. I make my well-beloved and trusty friend WILLIAM TOWNESEN of Gorleston my sole exor. to see my debts paid, my body decently buried and my children brought up in such good and decent fashion as the overplus of my goods will allow. If the debts due to me and my movables are not sufficient to pay my own debts, then my exor. and JOHN ALBROWTH shall let my houses until enough money has been raised. I give my exor. 20s. Witnesses: THOMAS CHAMBERLIN, SIDRACK SCOILE, MARY ODE (X), CICELY CLARK (X). Pr. at Beccles 17 Nov. 1635.

R(W) MARGARET BOISE (X) of Benacre, widow. (947)
17 January 1634/5

I will the house in which I dwell shall be sold by my exor. and the money divided equally between my sons PETER & WILLIAM when they are 21. Anything spent on their education is to be deducted. After payment of my debts, all my movables are to be divided between my 2 sons. I make NATHANIEL ROE of Benacre, clerk, sole exor. Witnesses: MARGARET HARRIS (X), HESTER DAVIE (X). Pr. at Beccles 17 Oct. 1635.

R(W) ROGER DRIVER of Saxmundham, grocer. 19 June 1635 (948)

Sick in body. I give and bequeath to MARGARET my most loving wife all my houses and lands in Wickham Market and Pettistree and Ufford for ever. I also give to her all my household stuff now in the house where I dwell. I make my father ARTHUR DRIVER exor. of my will and desire him to have all the rest of my goods, shop and chandle debts and ready money to pay my debts and legacies and discharge my funeral expenses, and to keep the overplus for himself. Witnesses: JOHN FYNE, ROBERT HARVYE. Pr. at Saxmundham 11 Nov. 1635.

R(W) JOHN CLARKE (X) of Halesworth, yeoman. 1 April 1633 (949)

Sick of body. I give and bequeath to ALICE my loving and most respected wife a posted bedstead standing in the parlour chamber, a featherbed with all the furniture belonging, a great chest next to the bed, a trundle bed with all its furniture in the parlour chamber. I give to ANNE BARROWE my loving daughter £30 and to my son JAMES £30. Both these legacies are to be paid after the decease of my wife at the rate of £10 p.a. I give to my son WILLIAM my messuage in Halesworth wherein he and I jointly live with its yard and garden. He is to pay legacies to ANNE & JAMES, who have power to distrain. If JAMES dies before his legacy is paid, WILLIAM is to pay £10 to his wife. The rest of my unbequeathed movable goods I give to be equally parted between my 3 children. I make WILLIAM my son sole exor. Witnesses: JOHN CUDDON (X) & HENRY KEBLE, who wrote this will. Pr. at Yoxford 11 Dec. 1635.

R(W) WILLIAM KETTLE (X) of Beccles, yeoman. (950)
1 November 1635

Sick in body. I give to JOHN, son of my brother ROBERT, £25 to be paid 2 years after my decease, and £10 to his brother ROBERT within 3 years. I give £5 each to the 4 daughters of ROBERT KETTLE senior: ANNE, MARY, MARGARET & ELIZABETH, to be paid within 4 years. I give £5 each to the 4 children of my late sister TURNER of Leiston to be paid within 5 years. All these legatees have benefit of survivorship. I give £30 to MARION, daughter of WILLIAM ROWE, within 2 years of my death. I give to DOROTHY, my wife's daughter, £100 when she is 21, one of my best silver spoons, one of my tipped jugs and my largest silver bowl. I give my brother ROBERT an annuity of 40s., and all my clothes. I give the rest of my cattle, movable goods, ready money, plate and bonds to BARBARA my loving wife whom I make sole exrx. I appoint my good friend Mr AUGUSTINE PLUMSTED as supervisor and give him £5. Witnesses: AUGUSTINE PLUMSTED, THOMAS DAYNES. Pr. at Beccles 5 Dec. 1635.

R(W) JUDITH HIGATE of Leiston, widow (N). (951)
26 October 1635

She gave to DANIEL HIGATE her son all her goods and chattels, except her wearing apparel, which she gave to her daughters. She made DANIEL sole exor. Witnesses: THOMAS EADE & MARY SAVEDGE. Pr. at Yoxford 11 Nov. 1635.

R(W) JOHN MEEKE of Cookley, tailor. 21 August 1635 (952)

Sick of body. He gave the following sums, to be distributed by the churchwardens or overseers to the poor of each parish: 5s. each to the parishes of Cookley, Huntingfield and Chediston, 10 groats (3s. 4d.) to Walpole, 8s. to Halesworth and 4s. to Nether

Linstead (Linstead Parva). I give to my brother GEORGE MEEKE £8 9s. 0d. due to me from him on a bond, which is to be cancelled immediately after my decease. To my brother WILLIAM MEEKE I bequeath my house and land in Rumburgh and my land in Upton called Southwalsome and all my movable goods and chattels, except those otherwise bequeathed. WILLIAM is to use my moveables to pay my debts and legacies: £15 to my brother FRANCIS MEEKE to be paid within one year of my death and a set of silver buttons and a holland shirt. I give and bequeath to FRANCIS TAYLOUR my bedstead, mat and bed line with my featherbed, 1 feather bolster, 1 feather pillow, 1 pillow beere, 2 pairs sheets, 1 blanket, 1 rug, 1 birded covering, 1 long towel and half a dozen coarse napkins, 1 shopboard, 1 pressing iron, my best pair of shears, my best doublet and hose (but without the buttons on the doublet), and 1 keep. I give to EDMUND TAYLOUR £5 to be paid within 1 1/2 years of my death. I give to MARY, wife of RICHARD PAGE of Laxfield and my aunt, 40s. to be paid within 6 months. I give to JOAN, daughter of ROBERT SHILDRAKE of Peasenhall, 40s. when she is 21. I give 20s. to the 4 children of JOHN SNELLING of Cookley within 6 months. I make WILLIAM MEEKE of Wenhaston, my brother, sole exor. Witnesses: JOHN SNELLING, ROBERT GOWINGE. Pr. at Yoxford 11 Nov. 1635.

R(W) MARGARET PEDGRAVE (X) of Dallinghoo, widow. (953)
16 June 1635

I give and bequeath to MARGERY BRUNDISH my daughter 40s. to be paid within 1 year of my decease. I give to my grandchild RICHARD FAKEN 1 brass pot and £6 when he is 21. I give to my grandson THOMAS FAKEN £6 when 21, and to ANN FAKEN my grandchild 1 featherbed, my best bedstead, 2 feather bolsters, 1 feather pillow, 1 rug, 1 coffer, 1 box with the linen therein and £6 on her marriage day or when she is 21. These 3 have benefit of survivorship. I give to FRANCES, daughter of JOHN PEDGRAVE, my grandchild, 20s. when 21. I give to ANNE PAYNE my daughter the remainder of my movable goods. I make WILLIAM PAYNE of Dallinghoo and ANNE his wife exors. Witnesses: JOHN STANHAWE, HENRY HOMES (X), WILLIAM MARRIOT (X). Pr. at Wickham Market 22 Oct. 1635.

R(W) EDWARD PARKER (X) of Crowfield, tailor. (954)
14 October 1635

Sick in body. I give to MARGERY my daughter and the wife of LIONEL DENIE my cupboard. I give to EDWARD DENNY, my grandson, a black bullock with a white dug. I give my daughter ELIZABETH, wife of RALPH CLARKE, my joined posted bedstead, my warming pan and my red heifer. I give to MARY CLARKE, my grandchild, a 2-year old red heifer. I give to my daughter MARGERY my featherbed and feather bolster I now lie on, with one darneck coverlet and a blanket. I give and bequeath to ELIZABETH & SUSAN DENNY, my grand-daughters, a pewter dish each. I give to GEORGE, my eldest son, a brown cow. I give EDWARD my youngest son my dun cow, my best featherbed, best bolster, 1 pillow, 1 list coverlet and 1 blanket, 4 pewter dishes, 1 pair sheets, 1 pillow beere and my wicker chair. These goods are to be delivered by my exor. to AGNES my wife for the use of EDWARD, to whom I also give £10. I give to AGNES my loving wife all my goods and chattels and household stuff not listed in an inventory made by me with her consent and bearing the same date as this will. All the goods and household stuff in the inventory I give to GEORGE my eldest son, whom I make sole exor., desiring him to pay my debts and legacies and to see my body buried decently. Witnesses: ROGER ALLDRED & THOMAS SALLOWES. Pr. at Ipswich 19 Oct. 1635.

R(W) EDWARD CLARKE of Tattingstone, yeoman. 8 May 1633 (955)

I give to EDWARD my son my best bible immediately after my decease, and when he is 21 a trundle bedstead with a feather bed as it stands, a plank in the parlour chamber and a little framed table. All the rest of my goods, my debts, legacies and funeral expenses being paid, I give to REBECCA my wife and EDWARD my son to be equally divided between them when EDWARD reaches age of 21. I make my well-beloved wife and her son ROBERT NORMAN exors. They are to enter into a bond of £100 with WILLIAM MARTYN of Bentley to prove my will within 1 month of my decease and to fulfill it. Witnesses: GEORGE LINCOLNE, WILLIAM MARVEN. pr. at Ipswich 1 Dec. 1635.

R(W) BRIDGET DAMREN (X) of Walton, widow. 7 July 1635 (956)

Sick and weak in body. I wish to be buried in Walton churchyard. I give my daughter ANNE, wife of THOMAS COLE, 40s. to be paid within six months of my death, and also all my clothes both woollen and linen. I give her son ROGER COLE my bed and bedstead as they stand in the hall chamber of THOMAS COLE'S house, a pair of sheets, a livery cupboard, a danske chest, a pair of cobirons, 4 joined stools, 2 chairs now standing in the same hall chamber, 6 napkins, 1 dozen trenchers and a brass chafing dish. I also give him 40s. to be paid within 3 years. I give to JOHN COLE my grandson my trundle bedstead with a featherbed, 1 bolster and pillow on which he now lies and a cupboard, all standing in the parlour of THOMAS COLE's house. I also give him a roast iron, 3 pewter dishes, 5 napkins and 40s. This sum is to be paid within 4 years of my death to THOMAS COLE, who is to put it out to the best advantage. ROGER & JOHN COLE have benefit of survivorship, but if they both die all gifts given to them are to go to their mother. I give my grandchild ROBERT MICKLEFEILD a brass pot and 40s. to be paid within 3 years. I give to MARGERY MICKLEFEILD my grandchild a little kettle, a little box and 40s. to be paid within 3 years. I give 10s. to SIMON PETTEWARD, minister of Walton to preach at my burial. I give my son ROGER PAYNE all my money in his hands, which is due to me, towards the payment of my debts and I make him sole exor. Witnesses: WILLIAM GLOVER & JOHN SCOTT. Pr. at Ipswich 27 Nov. 1635.

R(W) ROBERT MORE of Chattisham. 3 November 1635 (957)

I will and bequeath to SUSAN my wife for her life the tenement I now live in, which is called Belshams, and after her death to my son ROBERT. I also give him my tenement called Beacons in Wifeneld, Essex. This latter tenement is to be let for 3 years after my decease to pay my debts. I give to PETER MORE £18 to be paid 1 year after the death of my wife, and £15 to ANNE MORE wife of THOMAS BENSHER 2 years after my wife's death; this money is to be shared between her children, THOMAS & ELIZABETH. I give £14 to ELIZABETH MORE to be paid 2 years after wife's death, and a featherbed and bolster, a brass pot and pothook, a pestle and mortar and a spinning wheel to be given to her 1 month after my wife's death. I give SUSAN daughter of PETER MORE 20s. 2 years after wife's death, and a brass kettle to ROGER MORE 1 month after her decease. All my unbequeathed goods I give to my son ROBERT, whom I make sole exor. He must be careful to please his mother. Witnesses: JOHN FORIM, ROBERT BARKE. Pr. at Ipswich 14 Dec. 1635.

R(W) ISAAC SEAMAN (X) of Sutton, miller. 28 March 1635 (958)

I give to JOHN MARTYN labourer my worser cloak on condition he pays 10s. to SUSAN GOODWYN. My exor. is to sell the rest of my apparel and divide the money between WILLIAM & FRANCES SEAMAN, son and daughter of my brother WILLIAM, when they are 18. I also give them 20s. due to me from Mr FLICKE, parson of West Creeting. All the rest of my goods and chattels I give to my kind master Mr FERNLIE esquire, whom I make sole exor. Witnesses: SAMUEL MERN, WILLIAM MOWDON. Pr. at Ipswich 2 May 1635.

R(W) ROBERT TOVILL the elder of Grundisburgh, yeoman. (959)
14 October 1631

Hail in body. I wish my body to be buried in church or churchyard of Grundisburgh at the discretion of my exors. I give and bequeath for ever to AGNES my beloved wife all my goods and chattels, cattle and household stuff on condition she performs my will. I give 20s. each to my grand-children ANN & RICHARD GOWEN when they are 21. I give to JOHN & DORCAS HART my grand-children 20s. each when 21. I give my grandson ROBERT, son of my son RICHARD TOVILL, all my lands and tenements in Huntingfield on condition he pays £8 p.a., in 2 equal portions at Lady Day and Michaelmas, to my son ROBERT during the lifetime of my wife AGNES. He must also make over to JOHN CARY of Huntingfield a piece of copyhold land in Huntingfield in fulfillment of an agreement made between me and TEMPERENCE TOVILL widow and mother of ROBERT. If ROBERT fails to perform these conditions, the legacies to him are void. I give to ROBERT my son all my land and tenements in Grundisburgh after the death of my wife. After he inherits he must pay £3 6s. 8d. each to JOHN, RICHARD, THOMAS, RACHEL, & ANNE TOVILL, the brothers and sisters of my grandson ROBERT TOVILL. One is to be paid a year and they have power to distrain. I give 40s. to the poor of Grundisburgh. I give 20s. to my daughter DORCAS JENOR. I make my wife AGNES exrx. and, as my trust is wholly in her, I desire her to receive the debts due me and pay the debts I truly owe and to see my body laid in earth in seemly manner. If she refuses to do these things, I appoint ROBERT my son exor. Witnesses: JOHN CONSTABLE, ROBERT HOWE junior. Pr. at Ipswich 15 Dec. 1635.

R(W) ROBERT CODD (X) of Beccles. 10 November 1635 (960)

He gave to MARGERY his wife all his movable goods to dispose of as she liked. Witnesses: THOMAS BARNEBY senior (X), ROBERT HARVY. Pr. at Beccles to widow 13 Jan. 1635/6.

R(W) WILLIAM BROWNE (X) of Ashby, husbandman. (961)
2 December 1635

Pained in body. I wish to be buried in Ashby churchyard. I bequeath 40s. apiece to my daughters FRANCES, ELIZABETH & JOAN BROWNE, ANNE, wife of JOHN STANDLIE tailor of London, MARY & MARGARET BROWNE. One is to be paid each 6 months starting 1 year after my death. I give 40s. to my son JOHN. The residue of my goods and chattels I give to my son WILLIAM, whom I make sole exor. Witnesses: EDWARD BRYSE (X), ROBERT UNDERWOOD, who wrote this will. Pr. at Beccles 1 Jan. 1635/6.

R(W) WILLIAM COTWYN of Beccles, tailor. (962)
9 February 1626/7

Sick in body. I give and devise for her life to LUCRETIA my loving wife my copyhold messuage in Beccles held of the manor of Roos Hall with Ashmans. After her death my 3 sons, NICHOLAS, ROBERT & WILLIAM, are to sell this messuage and divide the money between them. If my eldest son JOHN, or any of my sons, is able to buy this house, he shall have it for 30s. less than any one else. I give my bible to my son ROBERT. The rest of my goods and cattle I give to my wife to pay my debts and funeral expenses and to educate my 3 youngest children. I make her sole exrx. Witnesses: ROBERT COBBE, RICHARD PRINGE, EVERARD & CHARLES CHAPMAN, JOHN BRYANT (X). Pr. at Beccles 17 Dec. 1635.

R(W) DANIEL DRYVER (X) of Eyke, yeoman. 17 December 1635 (963)

Sick of body. I give my wife SUSAN my lease held of Lord BERCKLEY. I give her for life my backhouse wherein I now dwell, my part of the barn now occupied by myself and ROBERT GIRLING and my hempland. After her death my son JOHN is to sell the backhouse, barn and hempland and the money is to be equally divided among my 4 sons: JOHN, DANIEL, NATHANIEL & THOMAS. All the rest of my goods and chattels I give to my wife to pay my debts and burial expenses, and I make her sole exrx. Witnesses:

GERVASE HUBBALD, WILLIAM BUGG, GREGORY BAKER (X), ROBERT GIRLING (X). Pr. at Wickham Market 8 Jan. 1635/6.

R(W) CHRISTOPHER PAGE (X) of St. Clements parish, Ipswich, mariner. 8 December 1635 (964)

Visited with sickness. I will and bequeath for ever to SUSAN my well-beloved wife the house wherein I now dwell in St. Clements parish in the town of Ipswich with its yard, garden and orchard. I also give her all my goods and chattels, jewels, cattle and corn whatsoever. I give her my share in certain sea-going vessels with their tackling. I appoint her sole exrx. Witnesses: ALICE BROCK (X), GEORGE KENT, RICHARD WARREN. Pr. at Ipswich 9 Jan. 1635/6.

R(W) EDWARD PATTESUNE of Stoke by Ipswich, baker. 4 January 1635/6 (965)

Sick in body. I bequeath to JOHN PATTESUNN my son the mansion house wherein I now dwell in Stoke by Ipswich, my orchard in St. Peter's parish in Ipswich, my posted bedstead in the parlour with all the bedding on it and 1 pillow. All the rest of my household stuff is to be equally divided between the rest of my children: MARY, ELIZABETH, JUDITH & EDWARD. I give to my son EDWARD when he is 21 my house and barn in Stoke which I lately purchased from ROBERT DRANE. Until EDWARD is 21 my son JOHN is to receive the rent of this house, keep it in repair and pay 40s. p.a. to ROBERT DRANE. When EDWARD reaches age of 21, he is to discharge JOHN from this last obligation. I give to my son EDWARD my copyhold land called the wharf which abuts on the south side of the barn left to him. All the rest of my goods and chattels I give to my son JOHN to pay my debts, funeral charges and the probate of my will. I make him sole exor. Witnesses: WILLIAM SEELI, THOMAS PINBARAW & ROBERT LORD, who wrote this will. Pr. at Ipswich 29 Jan. 1635/6.

R(W) RICHARD WYNTER (X) the elder of Blaxhall. 13 August 1635 (966)

I wish to be buried in Blaxhall churchyard. I give to my son RICHARD all my free and copyhold land and messuages in Waldringfield for life and then to his son RICHARD, or if he dies to his son HENRY. I give £30 to my son WILLIAM, half to be paid within 2 and half within 3 years of my decease. I give £10 to my son THOMAS to be paid within 3 years if he comes in person to demand it. I give 40s. to my son HUMPHREY to be paid within 1 year. I give £5 each to the 3 children of my son RICHARD: RICHARD, MARGARET & HENRY at their ages of 24. They have benefit of survivorship. I give £10 to RICHARD, son of my son WILLIAM, to be paid to his father for his use within 1 year of my death. I give an annuity of £5 to my son PHILIP to be paid quarterly by my son RICHARD. Payments are to be made in the house of EDWARD

HAWSTED at Waldringfield. I give all my copyhold land in Wickham Market and Campsea Ash to my son RICHARD and his wife ELIZABETH. I will to my son PHILIP my best bedstead and featherbed, the bolster, blankets and covering belonging to it, 2 pairs of good sheets, 1 pillow, 1 pillowbeere and my best copper kettle. All the rest of my movable goods I bequeath to my son RICHARD, who must pay all my debts and legacies and prove my will, bring my body to the earth and pay my funeral charges. He must enter into a bond of £100 with my supervisor to perform my will. If he refuses, all the legacies to him are void and I give them to my son WILLIAM and make him exor. on the same conditions. Supervisor: my son-in-law RICHARD ROSE of Waldringfield. As a small remembrance I give him £5. Witnesses: ALEXANDER REVELL, HENRY HAYWARD. Codicil made on 4 Jan. 1635/6: I give to PHILIP my son an annuity of £10 to be paid quarterly starting 12 months after my decease. My exor. is to lay out £10 on my funeral and burial. Witness: ALEXANDER REVELL. Pr. at Wickham Market 28 Jan. 1635/6.

R(W) ROBERT POPE of Weybread. 5 December 1635 (967)

I give to JOAN my wife all my goods and chattels, bills and bonds due to me on condition she pays my legacies. I give £200 to my son WILLIAM to be paid 4 months after my decease. I give £130 to my son JOHN and £140 to my son GEORGE; both to be paid 1 month after my death. If insufficient money has come into the hands of my exrx. to pay these legacies to my 3 sons at the appointed times, she is to pay them £5 in £100, but must not keep them waiting for the remainder of their legacies for more than 1 year after my decease. I give to my grandchild RICHARD POPE £20 when 22, but if he dies before then this sum is to go to my 3 sons. I give ANNE MEENE my grandchild £5 when she is 18, or if she dies to her brother RICHARD. If my wife dies before these legacies are due to be paid, my sons are to pay them. I give 10s. to be distributed at the discretion of my exrx. amongst the poor people of Weybread that have most need. I make JOAN my wife exrx. and JOHN HOBART of Weybread overseer of my will. I give the latter 20s. for his pains. Witnesses: RICHARD MEENE, FRANCIS BURLIE (X) & RICHARD SOTEN (X). Pr. at Yoxford 27 Jan. 1635/6.

R(W) CHRISTOPHER CUBITT of Henham. 20 January 1635/6 (968)

Weak in body. I give to the right worshipful Sir JOHN ROUS knight my well affected master 20s. and 2 silver spoons. I give to the right worshipful JOHN ROUS esquire, Mr THOMAS ROUS the elder, Mr MICHAEL ROUS, Mr THOMAS ROUS the younger, Mistress ELIZABETH ROUS & Mistress MARY ROUS to each of them 20s. in remembrance of their many noble favours and of my dutiful affection towards them. I give my mother MARGARET CUBITT an annuity of 30s. to be paid at Michaelmas and Lady Day. I give to PRISCILLA my daughter £20 to be paid to her on the Michaelmas day after my mother's death. I give my sister ELIZABETH £40, of which £20 is to be paid within 1 month and £20 within 1 year of my decease. I give £10 each to my brothers JAMES, JOHN & RICHARD to be paid within 2 months of my death. I give to JOHN CAWSTON 20s. p.a. to be paid each Michaelmas until he has received £4, and all my boxes, dice, cards and counters; also my livery cloak and he is to pay the tailor for making it up. I give to JOHN ALLEN 20s. and my worst suit of apparel with a cloak belonging to it. I give 10s. each to EDMUND & ROBERT HARGRAVE and to EDMUND GOODALE. I give 30s. to NICHOLAS GOOCH of Wangford, and 20s. to RICHARD EMANS. I give 5s. each to JOHN ASHBY and [blank in original will] PITELYNGE, and 20s. to THOMAS GOODING the younger. I give to JOHN BELL my black cloak, and to OLIVER DEANE 2 double ducats, one half French crown and one spur royal. I make ROBERT CUBITT my sole exor. and give him the overplus of my personal estate after my debts, legacies, funeral expenses, and charges of the probate of my will have been paid. I give 10s. each to CHRISTOPHER ARMITAGE & KATHERINE, wife of ROBERT HOULETT. Witnesses: EDMUND HEYLOCKE (X), DANIEL DEANE. Pr. at Beccles 1 March 1635/36.

R(W) ELIZABETH HALTWAIE the younger of Hopton, singlewoman. 22 January 1635/6 (969)

Very sick and weak of body. I give and bequeath to ELIZABETH HALTWAY my loving mother for ever my tenement in Fritton with all its free and copyhold land, which is now occupied by JOHN UNDERWOOD. All my movable goods, bonds and ready money I bequeath to my mother, whom I make sole exrx. Witnesses: JOHN CANDLER (X), ROBERT PEIRSE (X), RICHARD GILBERT (X), MATTHEW LOCKLES (X) & ROBERT UNDERWOOD, who wrote this will. Pr. at Beccles 1 Feb. 1635/6.

R(W) ROBERT BENNETT of Dunwich, gentleman. 26 December 1635 (970)

Sick in body. He had conveyed all his land and tenements in Dunwich to JAMES WARD of Sharington in Norfolk in trust for his wife and two of his daughters, ANNE & ELINOR, with reversion after his wife's death to his son JAMES. ANNE my wife is to receive from JAMES WARD £50 committed to him in trust for her, and she and my son JAMES are to reach an agreement over the sale of the land to which JAMES has the right of reversion. I bequeath all my movable goods to my wife, whom I make sole exrx., hoping she will have a motherly care both in the education of my children and in providing them with such portions as she can afford. Witnesses: PETER THURKETLE (X), JOHN THREKELD, who wrote this will. Pr. at Yoxford 29 Jan. 1635/6.

R(W) JOHN COOPER of Dennington, yeoman. 20 May 1628 (971)

Hail in body. I wish to be buried in the church or churchyard of Dennington. I give and bequeath to MARY COWPER my daughter £20. All the rest of my land, tenements, goods and chattels, cattle, ready money, plate, jewels and corn I give to be equally divided between my 3 daughters, ELIZABETH, URSULA & MARY when they are 21. They have benefit of survivorship. I make my 3 daughters exrxs. and give them power to receive and pay my debts. Witnesses: EDWARD MARRYOTT & THOMAS SEAMAN. Pr. at Wickham Market 18 Feb. 1635/6.

R(W) LEWIS CRESEN alias HOXEN (X) of Snape. (972)
2 January 1635/6

Sick in body. I give my house and all its land in Snape which I lately purchased from WILLIAM DEALE of Snape to ELLEN HOXEN my wife and I give her full power to keep or sell or bequeath it as she desires. I give to RICHARD HOXEN my son an axe with which I usually hew timber. I give to ROBERT HOXEN my second son a buffet stool. I give to ALICE my daughter a chair with a cushion. I give all my other movable goods to my wife for ever and make her sole exrx. Witnesses: JOHN SCOLESMAN (X) & NICHOLAS KING. Pr. at Saxmundham 29 Jan. 1635/6.

R(W) THOMAS COCKE of Ipswich, merchant. (973)
18 September 1635

I am making my will to prevent future strife over my worldly goods and estate. I give and bequeath to MARY my well-beloved wife for life the messuage now occupied by me in the parish of St. Mary at Quay in Ipswich, and all my other messuages in the parish of St. Clement in Ipswich with all their yards, gardens, orchards and outbuildings. After her death I give the messuage in St. Mary Quay to my son WILLIAM or, if he dies without heirs, to my daughter ABIGAIL. All the rest of my messuages in St. Clement's parish now let to ZECHARIAS BROMWELL & ROBERT DAWES, mariners, and the adjoining tenement let to [blank in original will] SHUCKFORTH widow I bequeath to my daughter ABIGAIL after the death of my wife and of my sister ALICE MOORE, who has a life interest in this property. I also give to ABIGAIL after the decease of my wife, the messuage occupied by JOHN PEACOCKE mariner, which is situated behind the tenement occupied by widow SHUCKFORTH. I also give her my 2 messuages in St. Clement's parish formerly occupied by my late son THOMAS and now by [blank in original will] MOUTTON widow and THOMAS NEVETT. If ABIGAIL dies without heirs, I give all the houses left to her to my son WILLIAM. I give to my wife 2 messuages on the north side of St. Clement's church with their outbuildings, yards and gardens, to give away or sell as she wishes. I give £5 to MARY BLYTHE to be paid within 6 months of my death. During her lifetime my wife must keep all my houses in good repair and pay an annuity of £8 to my sister ALICE, wife of THOMAS MOORE. I give all my movable goods, plate, ready money, bills and bonds to my wife to pay my debts, funeral charges and the expenses of proving my will, and I make her sole exrx. I will that my son WILLIAM and daughter ABIGAIL shall pay £20 to my grandchild SARAH COCKE at age of 16. Witnesses: EDWARD MANN, PETER COALE junior, ROBERT LORD, who wrote this will. Pr. at Ipswich 29 Jan. 1635/6.

R(W) RICHARD CHISNALL (X) of Belstead, husbandman. (974)

Weak of body. I wish to be buried in Little Belstead churchyard in such decent order as shall be thought meet by my exor. I give to my wife MIRABEL 2 cows of her own choice, all the firewood in the garden when I die, and all the hay and straw of this present year or of that in which I die. She is to live in my dwelling house. I give her 8 bushels of rye, all my cheese and butter, and all my household goods. I give £3 to my son HENRY and 55s. each to my daughters ZAPHARAHE & ELIZABETH to be paid within 1 year of my death. I give 20s. to my grandson RICHARD CHISNALL when 21, and 20s. each when 21 to RICHARD & ELIZABETH, children of my son THOMAS. I give ELIZABETH OSBORNE my kinswoman 30s. to be paid within 1 year. I make my son ROGER sole exor. After my wife's death my goods are to be equally divided among my children. If my son ROGER dislikes my will I give him the £4 10s. 0d. in his hands, and make my wife sole exrx. Witnesses: HUGH PALLMER, MARGARET SHARPE (X). Pr. at Ipswich to ROGER CHISNALL 29 Jan. 1635/6.

R(W) JOHN GODBOULD of Wissett, yeoman. 27 November 1631 (975)

Within 2 years of my death my exor. is to sell the messuage I now dwell in and all its land in Wissett and Spexhall, and is to use the money to perform my will. I give my loving wife SARAH £40 to be paid within 1 year of this sale. I also give her 2 of my best milk cows, 2 livery bedsteads with 2 featherbeds, 2 feather bolsters, 2 pillows, 2 blankets and 2 coverlets. One bed with its bedding is in the hall chamber and other in the parlour. I also give her a cupboard in the hall, 6 pairs of sheets, 6 table napkins, 1 board cloth, 2 pillow beeres, 2 towels, 6 pieces of pewter small and great, 1 brass pot, 1 warming pan, 2 candlesticks, 1 middle sized kettle, 1 livery table in the hall, 1 box, 1 desk in the parlour, 1 back chair, 2 buffet stools, 4 cushions, 3 bowls, 6 wooden dishes, 6 wooden spoons, 8 earthern drinking pots, 3 coffers in the hall chamber, 2 firkins, 1 stand, 1 tub, 1 pair of cobirons, 1 pair tongs, 1 firepan, 1 pair bellows, 1 hale, 1 roast iron, 1 frying pan, 1 spit, 1 dripping pan, 2 sacks, 1 keep hanging in the hall, 1 pewter chamber pot, 1 tow comb, 1 pashel, 1 spinning sheel, 1 pair of woolcards, 1 pitch fork, 1 meadow rake, 1 little stool, 1 tunner, 1 bottle and 1 dozen trenchers. These gifts are made on condition that within 1 month of my decease SARAH my wife shall be bound in the sum of £100 to my exors. not to make any claim on my lands for dowry or thirds. I give £10 to my brother RICHARD GODBOULD to be paid at 20s. p.a. starting 1 year after my death, or to his children if he has died. I give to JOHN & WILLIAM, sons of my brother RICHARD, £14 each to be paid 18 months after my land is sold, and to their sister FRANCES 14s. p.a. during her marriage with JOHN MILLS and £14 one year after the death of her husband. These 3 have benefit of survivorship. I give and bequeath £4 to STEPHEN

GOWIN, £7 to JOHN GOWIN, and £15 to be divided between MARGARET, BRIDGET & DANIEL the children of the late DANIEL GOWIN. I give £20 to be divided between CHRISTOPHER & MARY, children of my brother-in-law HENRY WELTON. I give 40s. each to THOMAS BERT & PETER CHAMBERLYN, and 10s. to MARGARET HORNE. I give 13s. 4d. to the 7 children of ALICE WYET, lat wife of FRANCIS TYE deceased. I give 40s. apiece to 7 of the children of my sister ALICE CONE: JOHN, WILLIAM, ROBERT, JAMES, MARY, CICELY & ALICE, and £4 to FRANCIS CONE. All these legacies are to be paid 2 years after the sale of my land. I give 10s. each to WILLIAM & KATHERINE GODBOULD, children of the late wife of GEORGE MOULSER. I give 10s. to the poor of Wissett, 20s. to the poor of Halesworth and 5s. to the poor of the parishes of Rumburgh, Holton and Ilketshall St. Andrew. These legacies are to be distributed on or before the day of my burial. Eighteen months after the sale of my land 20s. is to be paid to the churchwardens of Wissett to be employed for ever towards the repair of the church. I give 3s. 4d. to each person who witnesses this will within 1 month of my decease. I give 2s. each for their pains to the 4 appraisers of my goods when my inventory is made. I give my wife £4 worth of goods if she agrees not to take her legacy of £40 until 1 year after my land has been sold. Until my messuage is sold she is to live there and have sufficient firing and 2 loads to take with her when she leaves the house. The rest of my goods and chattels are to be sold and the money used to pay my debts and legacies. Any money left over is to be used to educate, bring up and apprentice DANIEL son of late DANIEL GOWIN, and any remaining after that has been done is to be divided between him and his sister MARGARET when they are 21. I will that JOHN SPALDING the elder of Wissett shall have my livery cupboard in the parlour for 17s. on the day my goods are priced. I give to FRANCES CONE, lately my servant, 20s. and 1 pair of sheets. My legacies are to be paid in the south porch of Wissett church. I make JOHN SPALDEN the elder of Wissett my exor. and give him £10. Within 1 week of my decease my wife must enter into a bond of £200 with him not to remarry. I make my nephew CHRISTOPHER WELTON supervisor and give him 20s. If any legatee complains about his gift or tries to alter my will, then he or she shall not receive the legacy. Witnesses: ROBERT MOORE, WILLIAM SAMPSON, JOHN SPALDING junior. Pr. at Yoxford 29 July 1635.

R(W) HENRY PEELE (X) of Henham. 16 January 1635/6 (976)

Weak and sick in body. I give all my goods and chattels, bonds and bills to DOROTHY my wife, who is to pay £3 each to my sons FRANCIS, JOHN & HENRY when they are 24, and £4 each to my 5 daughters MARY, MARGARET, DOROTHY, ELIZABETH & ANNE when 21. I make my loving wife sole exrx. Witnesses: EDWARD KEY, GEORGE SUGAR, WILLIAM LEVETT & PETER LILLY (X). Pr. at Yoxford 17 Feb. 1635/6.

R(W) JOHN PAYNE of Ipswich, yeoman. 13 June 1634 (977)

Weak in body. I give to MARY daughter of GEORGE PICKERING deceased and to MARY daughter of FRANCIS BALDERSTONE deceased a tenement and land in Kesgrave to be equally divided between them. I give to my brother's sons RICHARD & EDWARD PAYNE, mariners of London, £5 each. I give to ROBERT son of ROBERT BRANSON of Nacton 50s. I give to GEORGE PICKERING, clothier of Ipswich, a feather bed, a bolster, 1 pair blankets and a coverlet. I did formerly make a will giving my land in Kesgrave to my grandchild MARY BALDERSTONE, but I now revoke this will and leave the land as above. I give all my movable goods to MARY PICKERING & MARY BALDERSTONE and make them exrxs. They are to pay my debts and my funeral expenses. I make RICHARD HARRIS, yeoman of Walton, my supervisor and give him 20s. Witnesses: SIMON PETTEWARD, ROGER MAY, RICHARD HARRIS (X). Pr. at Ipswich 19 Feb. 1635/6.

R(W) HENRY BOURNE of Felixstowe, yeoman. 14 October 1635 (978)

Weak of body. I give to the poor of Felixstowe £5 to be paid to the overseers of the poor as follows: 50s. on the day of my burial and 50s. one year later. This money is to be distributed amongst the poor by the churchwardens and overseers. I give to JOHN, son of WILLIAM SEAMAN yeoman of Felixstowe, when he is 21 my messuage in Felixstowe called Boyses or Hurries and now let to JOHN RAYNOLDES. I also give him the land I lately purchased from WILLIAM BLOWE: a pightle called Northfields, a pightle next to my messuage and 2 pieces of land containing 1 acre which I bought from WILLIAM MARE. One of these pieces is in Millfield and the other in Fields pightle. I also give him my lease of a 2 1/2 acre marsh next to the gate in Felixstowe and lying between Wrens Park and a meadow called Howbone. Until JOHN SEAMAN is 21 his mother ANNE is to receive the rents and profits of the messuage and land bequeathed to him and is to use them for his education. If JOHN dies before he is 21, the land and messuage are left to his mother for ever. I give to ANTHONY, son of my brother-in-law JOHN STANNARD of Butley, my lease of a 9 1/2 acre marsh next to the one left to JOHN SEAMAN. I give to HENRY, son of JOHN STANNARD, my lease of a 20 acre marsh in Felixstowe which has a wall on its east side, and Sterlings and Michaels marsh lands to the west. I give to SIMON PETTYWARD clerk £6 13s. 4d. and ask him to give my funeral sermon. I give to HENRY son of ROBERT BOURNE of Sutton the house wherein I live and all my other land in Felixstowe which my late father HENRY BOURNE bequeathed to me. I give £20 to my sister MARY, wife of HENRY STANNARD; they must give an acquittance to my exors. of all demands on my estate. If they refuse to do this, the legacy of £20 and those to their 2 sons ANTHONY & HENRY shall be void. I give 20s. to my brother-in-law JOHN STANNARD to buy a ring. I give 20s. to MARIAN DIMSTON, widow of Felixstowe, to buy a ring. I give £3 to ANNE, wife of WILLIAM BATEMAN of Felixstowe, £10 to JOHN BOURNE the elder of Shottisham and £10 to MARIAN, wife of HUMDEN HART of Grundisburgh. I give her son and my godson, HUMDEN HART, £5. I give 40s. and 2 combs of wheat to JOAN, wife of JOHN REYNOLDS of

Felixstowe, and 10s. to my godson ALEXANDER son of ALEXANDER SCRUTTON. I give 5s. apiece to all my other god-children. I give 10s. to ANNE daughter of WILLIAM SEAMAN, and 10s. to my servant ALICE MORFULL. I give 6s. 8d. to my servant ELIZABETH TOAKELEY and I give EDMUND MAY of Felixstowe 6s. 8d. I make THOMAS ELLETT, yeoman of Foxhall, and WILLIAM SEAMAN my exors. I give all my unbequeathed goods and chattels and personal estate to my exors. towards the performance of my will according to my true intent and meaning. Witnesses: ROBERT MARIOTT & ALEXANDER SCRUTTON. Pr. at Ipswich 10 Nov. 1635.

R(W) WILLIAM COOKE (X) of Debenham, joiner. 24 May 1635 (979)

Sick in body. I give to my exors. all my goods, movable and unmoveable, and all debts due to me. They are to pay my funeral charges and the cost of proving my will, and then to apprentice my 3 children. If possible my sons THOMAS & JOHN are to be apprenticed to the trade of a joiner and my daughter MARY to some good place. My exors. are to pay my debts and are to be allowed the expenses of proving my will and any necessary journeys connected with this. I give the inhabitants of Creeting St. Olive 20s. for the use of my mother ANNE COOKE to be given to her by them when she most needs it. The rest of my goods are to be divided among my children when 21. I make RICHARD SHEPPERD of Mickfield and THOMAS BETTS of Wetheringsett exors. Witnesses: THOMAS NICKOLL, ANNE BETTS (X). Pr. at Mickfield 8 Oct. 1635.

R(W) RICHARD HARPER (X) of Barnby, husbandman. 3 April 1635 (980)

I give and bequeath to DOROTHY my wife my posted bed which I now lie in as it stands in the chamber, the cupboard in the firehouse, 2 cows and all my brass and pewter except 4 pewter platters, 2 of which I give to my son EDWARD. I give to my daughter ELIZABETH 2 pewter platters and 10s. I give my son WILLIAM 15s. to be paid into the hands of THOMAS HERMAN senior of Mutford. I make my wife sole exrx. and give her all my unbequeathed linen and household stuff to pay my debts and legacies, and bring my body to the ground in decent manner. I make THOMAS HERMAN gent. of Mutford supervisor. Witnesses: GREGORY STERCKER (X), THOMAS HERMAN junior. Pr. at Beccles 6 Feb. 1635/6.

R(W) SUSAN CROWLAND (X) of Ilketshall St. Margaret, widow. 14 July 1634 (981)

In good health and memory, yet being aged consider it best to set in order my estate. I bequeath to JANE CLARKE my sister, if she be living at day of my decease, £5 to be paid at 20s. p.a. I give to her son JOHN £5 to be paid within 1 year of my death. I give to my kinswoman JANE, wife of JOHN FARRER of Flixton, 20s. within 1 year. I give to the daughter of my sister CHRISTIAN

CURMAN 30s. and my best gown. I give 20s. within 1 year to the daughter of my brother EDMUND CLARKE, and 40s. to be divided among the children of my brother JOHN CLARKE. I give 10s. to be shared by SIMON & EDMUND, sons of my cousin SIMON BORRETT of Wilby. I give 5s. to MARY wife of [blank in original will] HACON of Wissett, and 20s. to WILLIAM son of JOHN GOOCH junior of Ilketshall St. Margaret. I give 20s. each to PRISCILLA & MARY, daughters of JOHN GOOCH junior and to him 40s. I give 40s. to my cousin ROBERT, son of JOAN CLARKE widow of Buckham, and £5 to her son JOHN who is my godson. I also give him my bed fully furnished as it stands in my cousin CLARKE's house in Buckham, my best covering and my largest pillow. I give my sister JANE CLARKE 1 covering, 1 blanket and 1 pair sheets. I give to PRISCILLA GOOCH my chest and to MARY GOOCH my cupboard and to my god-daughter KATHERINE WALPOOLE my desk. Any money left over is to be divided between the children of my cousin JOAN CLARKE of Buckham: SARAH, KATHERINE, JOAN, JEREMY & MICHAEL. I make JOHN GOOCH & ROBERT CLARKE exors. Witnesses: TIMOTHY SAYER, NATHANIEL WELHAM (X). Pr. at Beccles 20 Feb. 1635/6.

R(W) CHRISTOPHER CHAPMAN (X) of Kelsale. 21 October 1635 (982)

I give and bequeath to my daughter SUSAN all my messuage and free and copyhold land in Middleton, Fordley, Inham, Sotherton and Wangford for her life, and after her decease to THOMAS & CHRISTOPHER, sons of my brother THOMAS CHAPMAN. I give to my exors. during the life of my wife ANNE my lands and tenements in Dunwich. They must pay her 40s. p.a. in performance of a covenant I made before our marriage. I give £100 to my brother THOMAS and £20 to my brother PHILIP one year after my death; £100 to my sister MARGARET, wife of JOHN HARSANT within 2 years; £100 to my sister OLIVE, wife of THOMAS PREWE within 3 years; £100 to my sister SUSAN, wife of JOHN ROBSON within 4 years. They have benefit of survivorship. I give 20s. to the poor of Wangford. The residue of my ready money, household goods and chattels are to be equally divided amongst the children of my brother PHILIP when they are 21. After the death of my wife I give my land and tenement in Dunwich to my daughter SUSAN for ever. Exors: DANIEL DEANES of Inham gent. and THOMAS EADE of Fordley yeoman. Witnesses: THOMAS TRAPNELL, THOMAS GRENE. Pr. at Beccles 3 Oct. 1635.
[This will appears to have been proved 18 days before it was written. The dates are the same in the original will, so there must be a contemporary error.]

R(W) ROGER GRIMMER (X) of Ilketshall St. Andrew, yeoman. 2 August 1635 (983)

Sick of body. I give to my son RICHARD £30, of which £20 is to be paid within 3 months and £10 within 6 months of my decease; payments to be made in south porch of St. Andrew's church. I give my daughter SUSAN £35 in two payments of £20 and £15 as to my son above, and £30 to my daughter MARY in the same way. I give 20s. to MARY LATER widow to be paid within 6 months. I give to JOHN BOND my apprentice 10s. I give to the minister who preaches at my burial 20s. I give 10s. to the poor of St. Andrew Ilketshall. I give 10s. to buy a ring to Mr THEOPHILUS VAUGHAN my landlord. I give £10 to RICHARD BATTELY & JAMES BULLYN of St. Andrew, whom I make exors. The residue of my goods is to be divided amongst my children. Witnesses: JOHN SHARDELOWE vicar, JOHN SADLER, WILLIAM LEAME (X), JOHN PAGE (X), JOHN YOUNGMAN. Pr. at Beccles 22 Aug. 1635.

R(W) JOHN WILKINS of Lowestoft, weaver (N). [no date] (984)
About a month after midsummer.

He gave his son JOHN a bed and bedstead, a table and whatsoever his wife thought fit. He gave his daughter ELIZABETH a bed with all its furniture and whatever his wife thought fit. The rest of his goods and chattels he gave to his wife JANE to pay his debts and funeral expenses. Witnesses: ANNE SHERINGHAM (X), ELIZABETH BROWNE (X). Pr. at Lowestoft 8 Jan. 1635/6.

R(W) RICHARD FOX of Metfield, gentleman. 24 October 1634 (985)

Sick in body. I give my wife SARAH, to increase her jointure and in full satisfaction of her right of dower, my messuage in Metfield wherein I now dwell with the land belonging to it for her life. She must keep the buildings in repair. I also give her an annuity of £20 to be paid from my land in Fressingfield, Stradbroke and Weybread at Michaelmas and Lady Day; payments to be made in my messuage called Foxes in Fressingfield which is now let to ROBERT DAVY. She has power to distrain. I give her 6 loads of firewood p.a. to be taken from my land in Weybread called Semers and Suffords. I give my exor. all my free and copyhold land in Fressingfield, Stradbroke and Weybread until my son ANTHONY is 21 to pay my debts and legacies, educate my son and defray the charges which may arise if he is made a ward. When he is 21 he is to inherit all this land. If he dies without heirs, my messuage in Fressingfield called Foxes with its land is to go to my brother-in-law ANTHONY BARRY the younger, and my messuage called Wolnoughes with its land in Fressingfield and Stradbroke, now occupied by WILLIAM SMITH, is to be sold for the best price. I give £600 to be divided equally between AMY, ABIGAIL, REBECCA, MARY, JOHN & THOMAS, the children of my father-in-law ANTHONY BARRY the elder. If my son ANTHONY dies without heirs my exors. are to sell my house and land in Metfield as soon as convenient after the decease of my wife, and the money so raised I give as follows: £100 to LIONEL GIRLYNG, £50 to his brother SAMUEL and £50 to his sister MARY, £20 to my uncle RICHARD WARD of Aldeburgh, £20 to his daughter ANN, £20 to JOHN son of SIMON GORBOULD of Fressingfield, £20 each to MARY, HENRY & FRANCIS children of HENRY BURROUGH, £20 each to CHRISTIAN & FRANCES daughters of RICHARD MOWSER of Bungay. I give £30 to LIONEL GIRLING and £10 to MARY GIRLING 6 years after my decease. I bequeath 30s. each when 21 to MARY, HENRY & FRANCIS BURROUGH.

I give £4 to JOHN GORBOULD within 4 years, and 50s. to ANN WARD. I give £5 when he is 21 to RICHARD son of JOHN GILLETT, and 20s. to the son of JOHN BURGES of Aldeburgh when 21. I give 30s. to my servant MARY FARROWE. I give to the churchwardens and overseers of Fressingfield £25 for the use of the poor, to be paid within 5 years. I give my wife all my linen, her clothes and other furniture, and her own choice of as much of my bedding and other household stuff as shall be worth £20. I give 20s. to the poor of Metfield. The rest of my goods and chattels I give to my exors. towards the speedier paying of my debts and legacies. Anything left over is to be paid to my son ANTHONY when he is 21. If my son is made a ward to His Majesty, then I humbly desire the Master of the Court of Wards and Liveries to grant his wardship to my father-in-law Mr ANTHONY BARRY. I make my loving friends Mr THOMAS GODBOLD of Mendham and ANTHONY BARRY the younger exors. I ask them truly to perform my will and see my body decently buried according to the manner of a man of my estate. I give them £10 each for their pains. I desire my loving friend ROBERT HARPER the elder of Mendham to be supervisor and I give him £4. Witnesses: WILLIAM SMITH, THOMAS BURROUGH (X), TOBY ASHBY. Pr. at Beccles 5 Dec. 1635.

R(W) HENRY NEAVE (X) of Ringshall. 19 March 1634/5 (986

Sick in body. I wish to be buried in Ringshall churchyard. I give to my son ERASMUS all my lease lands called Semons with houses on them in Ringsfield after the death or remarriage of my wife AMY. The lease of these lands was granted to my grandfather by WILLIAM GRESHAM esquire. If my wife remarries ERASMUS is to pay her £3 p.a. in 2 equal half-yearly payments. She has the power to distrain. If she is widowed a second time, then she is to have the use of my parlour and parlour chamber as long as she remains a widow. She is to have right of access to the yard with a horse and cart and to place in it her wood. She is to choose 4 apple trees in my orchard and have the right to gather their fruit as long as she is a widow. After her decease ERASMUS is to pay £30 to my children EDMUND, ANNE & JOHN, paying 50s. to one of them each year until the £30 is paid. They have power to distrain, and benefit of survivorship. If my wife ANNE dies before my children ANNE and JOHN are 21, ERASMUS is to pay 20s. p.a. to ANNE and 30s. p.a. to JOHN until they are 21. I give all my movable goods to my wife to pay my debts, prove my will and bring my body decently to the ground, and I make her sole exrx. Witnesses: JOHN WELHAM & THOMAS SKUDGIN. Pr. at Ipswich 13 June 1635.

R(W) WILLIAM WARNER (X) of Henley, yeoman. (987
27 December 1634

I give and bequeath to ROSE my well-beloved wife the use of the parlour and parlour chamber in the house wherein I now dwell in Henley, together with 5 loads of wood p.a., the liberty to lay her wood in the yard, to take water and to brew and bake in the outhouses for her own use. I give her all my movable goods except my horse mill which I give to my son WILLIAM. After her decease the goods are to be divided among my 4 daughters: ALICE, MARGERY, ANNE & JOAN. I give my eldest son WILLIAM the house I live in, its freehold land and a piece of copyhold land called Harrisons piece, on condition he pays my wife £6 p.a. in equal half-yearly payments and gives her 5 loads of wood p.a. Also 3 years after my decease he must pay £15 to my daughter MARGERY wife of EDWARD GARRETT, and £30 to my daughter ANNE wife of JOHN MILLES. They have power to distrain. I give to my son EDMUND all my unbequeathed land in Henley on condition he pays my wife £6 p.a., and £10 to my daughter ALICE wife of ROBERT ROOKE and £30 to my daughter JOAN wife of JOHN HUGGENS 3 years after my death. They have power to distrain. Upon receipt of their legacies my daughters are to give acquittances to WILLIAM & EDMUND. I make my wife ROSE sole exrx. as I repose great trust in her and desire her in fear of God to see my will carefully performed. Witnesses: MARTIN CASTLETON, ROBERT JAY, HENRY WEBSTER (X). Pr. at Ipswich 29 Oct. 1635.

R(W) ANN GOOCH of Lowestoft, widow (N). (988)
In June last past.

She gave to ANNE and DOROTHY her daughters all her goods and chattels to be equally divided between them. Witnesses: RICHARD BRATHIT (X) & MARY BRATHIT (X). Pr. at Lowestoft 13 Jan. 1635/6.

R(W) HENRY LAWES (X) of Wingfield, tailor. (989)
5 February 1634/5

I give and bequeath to ANNE my loving wife all my goods and chattels for her life provided she keeps herself unmarried. If she remarries, she is to have one third of my goods and my 2 sons WILLIAM & THOMAS one third each. She is to be bound to my sons in sum of £15 to abide by this condition. My goods are to be valued. I make my wife sole exrx. desiring her to receive and pay my debts, to perform my will and bring me to the ground. Witnesses: ELIZABETH VYNIOR (X), WILLIAM BROWNINGE, MARGARET CUPPER (X). Pr. at Yoxford 8 Oct. 1635.

R(W) JOHN MIXTER (X) of Chelmondiston, weaver. (990)
10 March 1634/5

I wish to be buried in the churchyard at Chelmondiston. I give to my son ROBERT one loom as it stands in the inner side of my shop. I give to my son ADAM 10s. to be paid 1 year after my decease. I give to my son THOMAS the loom that stands next to the street in my shop. I give my slays and wheels to be equally divided between my 2 sons ROBERT & THOMAS. I give to my daughter ELIZABETH, wife of JOHN TURLE, 5s. 3 months after my death. I give to my daughter ABIGAIL 1 featherbed, 1 feather bolster, 1 covering, 1 blanket, 1 feather pillow, 1 pair sheets and the half-headed bedstead corded that stands in my lodging parlour. I give to JOHN GREENE, son of my son ROBERT's wife, 5s. when 21. My will is that my wife shall keep to her use my 2 looms with their slays and wheels during her lifetime. All the rest of my goods and chattels I give to my wife whom I make sole exrx. Witnesses: WILLIAM STONE clerk and JOHN CLARKE (X). Pr. at Ipswich 23 April 1635.

R(W) ANN PITT (X) of Aldeburgh, singlewoman. (991)
6 March 1634/5

Sick in body. I give to RICHARD, son of FRANCIS CHAPMAN pump maker of Aldeburgh, 40s. and £4 to his sister BRIDGET. I give £4 to MARY, daughter of MARY RUSSELLS widow of Aldeburgh, and 6s to ELIZABETH daughter of WILLIAM PITT yeoman of Farnham. I give all my movables to my 2 sisters BRIDGET CHAPMAN & MARY RUSSELLS, my funeral expenses being first paid. I make my brother-in-law FRANCIS CHAPMAN and my sister MARY RUSSELLS exors. Witnesses: GEORGE EADE, ROBERT BROWNE (X), THOMAS BOONE. Pr. at Yoxford 8 April 1635.

R(W) JOSEPH RAINOLDS (X). 19 November 1634 (992)

I bequeath to my son THOMAS £40 immediately and to my son FRANCIS £40, to son JAMES £40 and to daughters DOROTHY & ANNE £40 each, all when 21. I give 12d. to my wife JANE. I give all my goods and household stuff in the house of JOHN CARVER in Marlesford to my children, and I make JOHN CARVER senior and my son THOMAS exors. Witnesses: ELIZABETH GODFRI, PETER RAWLINS. Pr. at Wickham Market 5 May 1635.

W(R*) THOMAS BACON of Bramford, gentleman. (993)
4 January 1634/5

Sick of body. Firstly I ask my exrx. to sell my land in Bramford called Home meadow and the copyhold land which belonged to my brother DANIEL; all this land was lately in the occupation of GEORGE ROPES. The money so raised is to go towards paying my debts. I make my wife exrx. and THOMAS BROOKE gent. supervisor. I give to my well-beloved wife for life half of all the rest of my land and messuages in full satisfaction of her right of dower. I give the other half of my land and messuages to my son THOMAS, and my wife's half as well after her decease. A 9 acre close called Pettie acre is also to be sold to pay my debts. If THOMAS dies without heirs, I give all my landed property to my wife for life and after her death to the eldest sons of my 3 brothers: THOMAS son of MATHIAS BACON, JAMES son of JAMES BACON and NATHANIEL son of NATHANIEL BACON. I give £5 to JAMES son of JAMES BACON to be paid to him by my son THOMAS when JAMES is 21. The rest of my goods and personal estate is to be divided between my wife and my son. I give to DANIEL my brother 40s. to buy him

a suit of apparel. Witnesses: EDWARD COLBORNE, TOBIAS BACON, FRANCIS BROCK. Pr. at Ipswich 10 April 1635.
[*Wills marked thus are in the register but on damaged pages and so can only be read completely in the originals.]

W(R*) MARY BAKER (X) of Ufford, widow. 31 January 1633/4 (994)

In good health. I give to my son PHILIP DOWE my house and land in Blaxhall and Dunningworth, and he must pay his sister MARY an annuity of 40s. If he refuses to pay this, she is to have the house and land and pay him 40s. p.a. I give to my son ABRAHAM DOWE my house, barn and land in Ufford, and he must pay his sister ANNE BAKER 30s. p.a. as above. If my sons die without heirs, my daughters are to have the land left to them. My sons are to pay £10 to my daughter ANNE and any legacies left in the will of their father ABRAHAM DOWE, made 24 April 1617, and remaining unpaid when I die. I give to my daughter MARY a featherbed, a chest, a brass pan and half my linen and pewter. I give to daughter ANNE BAKER a brass pot, a cupboard, 1 chair, 1 table and half my linen and pewter. Witnesses: RICHARD LOVEKIN, MARGARET LOVEKIN, JANE PRENTICE. Pr. at Wickham Market 9 April 1635.

W(R*) EDMOND KNAP of Needham Market, singleman. (995)
23 October 1634

Sick and weak in body. I give to JOHN my eldest brother a 8 acre copyhold close commonly called Gravel Pit Close, lying by Green Street at Needham town end towards Darmsden. I give to Master FLETCHER, rector of the parish of Barking in which I now live, 20s. to preach at my burial. [Needham Market was a chapelry of Barking parish.] I give £10 each to my sisters MARY LOWE & SUSAN WIGHTMAN, and 20s. to my cousin THOMAS KNAP, clothworker. I give 20s. to ELIZABETH, daughter of my uncle RALPH SPARROW. These legacies are to be paid within 1 year of my decease. I give to my cousin EDWARD HUNT of Norwich 40s. to be paid within 3 months. The rest of my goods I give to be equally parted between my brothers JOHN & EDWARD, but the close given to JOHN is worth £40 and this is to be counted as part of his half share. Exors.: my brothers JOHN & EDWARD. Witnesses: JOHN ROE, CHARLES SEAMAN, WILLIAM ROE. Memorandum written 20 Nov. 1634: Having forgotten to dispose of my freehold lands, I now give them to my brothers JOHN & EDWARD KNAP. I bequeath 50s. to the poor of Needham to be distributed immediately after my burial. Witnesses: SIMON NELLSON, THOMAS WHITEOAKE (X), JOHN ROE. Pr. at Ipswich 23 April 1635.

W(R*) THOMAS HOWARD (X) of Earl Soham, yeoman. (996)
9 April 1635

Sick in body. I give and bequeath all my land and my tenement called Godwardes wherein I now dwell to be sold by my exors.

within 1 year of my death to pay my legacies. I give to JOHN son of my brother ROBERT HOWARD £5, and £5 to ROBERT'S daughter MARY CATCHPOLE. I give to my sister ANNE EVENNE £5 and to her daughter MARGERY, wife of ROBERT RUSSELL, £5. I give £5 to MARY WRIGHTE widow, my sister's daughter, and to my sister MARGARET, wife of HENRY YOUNGES, £5. All these legacies are to be paid within 1 year of my decease. I give to PHILIPPA, daughter of ROBERT RUSSELL, 40s. p.a. to be paid quarterly until she is 14 and £20 when she is 21. All my legacies are to be paid in church porch of St. Mary Tower, Ipswich. The residue of my movable goods I give to my nephews JOHN & THOMAS CANDELLER and I make them exors. I charge them as they will answer at the day of judgement to see my will duly performed. Witnesses: THOMAS CULLINGTON, RICHARD BARBER. Pr. at Ipswich 23 April 1635.

W(R*) THOMAS FULLER of Shotley, sailor. 5 March 1634/5 (997)

In health of body. I give to ALICE my wife for life my houses, yards, outhouses and land: a field called Fen field, another called Green Close, one called New Close, a field called Little Downe and one called Peasecroft. After her death I give all this property to my daughter MARY. I also give to my wife for life my lease of a house and land that belonged to ROBERT MERELL and after her death to my daughter HESTER. I give 20s. to my daughter ELIZABETH HEAGH to be paid within 1 year of my decease. I give £10 to be paid to my daughter SARAH at her age of 24, and £20 to my daughter HANNAH which is to be paid to her at once or security for it given to my cousin STEPHEN COPING the elder of Ipswich. He is to take HANNAH and the income from her £20 until she is 21 when the portion is to be paid to her. Daughters have benefit of survivorship. I give to my daughter MARY my best posted bedstead with a feather bed, a feather bolster, 2 pillows and all other things belonging to it. I also give her a livery table, a copper kettle, and a danske chest. I give to my daughter HESTER a livery bedstead with a feather bed, a feather bolster, 2 feather pillows and all other things belonging to it. Also a livery table, my best framed table, 6 buffet stools, 6 cushions, 6 pieces of pewter, my best cupboard, a kettle with a copper bottom and 1 chest. All my unbequeathed goods I give to my wife whom I make sole exrx. and ask her to pay my debts and legacies. My meaning is that my daughter MARY shall pay her sister HESTER £20 out of the land bequeathed to her within 2 years of her inheriting it. Witnesses: WILLIAM BRAME, SUSAN BRAME (X). Pr. at Ipswich 10 April 1635.

W(R*) WILLIAM COVELL of Buxlow. 28 March 1634/5 (998)

I give and bequeath to THOMASINE my wife for life all my goods and chattels, my debts being paid and the expenses of my funeral and probate of my will being discharged. After her death I give them to my 2 sons WILLIAM & FRANCIS, except that I wish my wife to remember my son JACOB with something out of my goods. I make my wife and son WILLIAM exors. Witnesses: ALICE NEWSON (X),

GEORGE JERMY. Pr. at Wickham Market 9 April 1635.

W. ROGER SCOTFER [no place given but possibly Blythburgh] 20 May 1635 (999)

I give £5 each to my sisters CECILY & MARGARET and to JOSEPH & MILES SCOTFER. I give 20s. to the poor of Blythburgh. I give all that is in my house to EDWARD CEWELL and his children when they are 21. Witnesses: HUGH SMITH, TOBIAS MURDOCKE. [no probate]

W. MARTHA GOOCH (X) of Wissett, singlewoman. 6 May 1635 (1000)

Sick in body. I give 10s. to the poor of Wissett to be distributed by the churchwardens and overseers where they think most need is. I give £10 to my step-father SAMUEL SHERMAN for his great pains that he has taken with me in the time of my sickness. I give to my mother MARTHA SHERMAN my scarf and my black wrought waistcoat. I give a good pair of gloves each price 1s. to Master THOMAS LEE, a minister of Wissett, ROBERT MIGHELLS, his wife MARY and his daughters DOROTHY & ANNE, and to MARY daughter of ROGER MIGHELLS. I give a petticoat each to ANNE STANNARD & FRANCES BURROWE, servants to ROBERT MIGHELLS. I bequeath to MARTHA daughter of JOHN MILLES of Walpole and to his wife MARY, my sister, my reversion to half a messuage with its land in Wissett, which is now occupied by my step-father. This property was left to me, after the death of my mother, by the will of my late father RICHARD GOOCH of Wissett made on 27 Feb. 1631/2. Within 1 month of my decease JOHN MILLES must bind himself in sum of £40 to my uncle ROBERT MIGHELLS to pay my legacies and perform my will. If he refuses, then I bequeath my half of the house and land to my mother. I make JOHN MILLES sole exor., and give him and his wife all the remainder of my goods, but if he refuses to act as exor. my mother is to be exrx. Witnesses: SUSAN SMITHE (X), ANNE STANNARD (X), ROBERT MIGHELLS. Pr. at Beccles 23 May 1635 to JOHN MILLS.

W. ANNE HARDYE (X) of Westleton, widow. 18 April 1635 (1001)

I give 20s. to the poor of Westleton to be paid to the churchwardens who are to use the annual profits for the benefit of the poor of the parish. I give 2s. p.a. to JOHN my grandson, son of THOMAS HARDYE, until he is 21 when he is to have 40s. I give to my grandson HENRY, son of RICHARD WADE of Westleton, a great brass pan measuring 1 bushel. The rest of my goods and chattels I give to my daughters ROSE & SUSAN and make them joint exrxs. Witnesses: JOHN SWAINE clerk and EDITH KYNG (X). Pr. at Yoxford 6 May 1635.

W. ROBERT BOLTON (X) of Hollesley, yeoman. 9 April 1635 (1002)

I give £60 to my daughter SUSAN when she is 18, or if she dies £20 to my daughter KATHERINE, £5 to my daughter MARY and 50s. each to the 3 children of AGNES VALENTINE of Hollesley, and the remainder to my kinsmen THOMAS BUTTEHAM & FRANCIS PULLHAM. I give £40 to my daughter KATHERINE when she is 18, or if she dies to my daughter MARY. I give £40 to my daughter MARY when 18 and £3 p.a. out of my lands until she is 18. If she dies her legacy of £40 is to go to my son BARTHOLOMEW, to whom I give all my land. I give to my wife KATHERINE the best bed in the parlour as it stands with a bolster, bedstead, blankets and coverlets, a trundle bedstead with a flockbed on it in the parlour, 4 pairs of sheets, 1 board cloth, the long table in the parlour, my smallest brass pot, a skillet, my smallest kettle, the form in the parlour, 2 stools, the chest in the little chamber, a pewter candlestick, a hake, the wicker chair, 2 bushels of rye and 1 bushel wheat. I give to my brother MARGET my best suit of clothes and best coat. I give 5s. each to my sister MARGET's 2 children, and 5s. each to my kinsmen THOMAS BUTTEHAM & FRANCIS PULLHAM. I give 20s. each to RICHARD MOSSE and his wife. I give 40s. to my apprentice WILLIAM RUNNALLS if he is willing to be bound apprentice by my exor., and if not 20s. only. I give 2s. to the Widow RUNNALLS of Hollesley, and 4s. to my maid ALICE BEETS. I bequeath 20s. to the poor of Hollesley. I leave £10 to my kinsman JOHN BOLTON towards bringing up my children and seeing my will executed, and £5 to his wife MARTHA. I give 20s. to RICHARD VALENTINE. After payment of my debts and legacies, my goods and chattels are to be divided between my children. I make my cousin JOHN BOLTON guardian of my son BARTHOLOMEW until he is 21, and he is to hold my land until that time. Sole exor. my well-beloved cousin JOHN BOLTON of Hollesley gent. Witnesses: JOHN REVE, THOMAS BLOWERS. Pr. at Wickham Market 5 May 1635.

W. EDWARD ALGER of Wingfield, yeoman. 16 November 1630 (1003)

In health of body. I do bequeath to CECILY my wife for life my tenement wherein I dwell with its land. She is to keep the buildings in repair and pay 20s. p.a., half yearly, in the south porch of Wingfield church, to my son EDWARD who is to have my house and land after my wife's death. He must pay £10 each to my daughter SARAH and to my sons ANTHONY, JOHN, HENRY, ROBERT & THOMAS. He is to pay one each year starting one year after inheriting my house and land, and is to make payments in the south porch of Wingfield church. Children have benefit of survivorship. If EDWARD fails to make these payments, then my property is to go to ANTHONY on the same conditions, and if he fails to fulfill them to JOHN and so on. I give to EDWARD & ANTHONY all my looms, slayes and other implements belonging to my art of weaving. All the rest of my goods and chattels and ready money I bequeath to my wife for her life towards paying my debts, discharging my funeral expenses and the better educating of my younger children if any be unable to provide for themselves at the time of my death. After my wife's decease the goods and chattels that she leaves are to be equally divided among my children then living. If she remarries, then within 1 year she is to pay £20 to be shared among my children. I make my well-beloved wife exrx. and my son EDWARD exor. of my will, and my supervisor is my brother-in-law WILLIAM BETTS to whom I give 5s. Witnesses: THOMAS WRITHOKE, ANNE WRITHOKE (X). Pr. at Yoxford 8 April 1635.

W. LIONEL WYTHE of Little Blakenham. 10 July 1634 (1004)

I wish to be buried at Helmingham near where my ancestors are buried. I give and bequeath to MARGARET my loving wife for her life, towards the bringing up of my children and payment of my legacies, my tenement calles Wythes, Bregges & Powles in Helmingham with all its buidlings and land. After her death I give all this to my eldest son LIONEL, who, if he has no heirs, must not sell this property but must leave it to his brothers or their heirs as if it were entailed. I give an annuity of £8 to LIONEL which is increased by 20 marks p.a. if he marries. He has power to distrain, and right to give his wife a jointure from the property bequeathed to him. Within 1 year of inheriting LIONEL is to pay £20 each to my 4 sons: JOHN, THOMAS, CHARLES & ROBERT. These 4 sons are to be paid £40 each by my exrx. when they are 24. My exrx. is also to pay £40 each to my daughters FRANCES, AMY, ELIZABETH, MARY & SUSAN when they are 21. Benefit of survivorship. I give to my wife towards the bringing up of my children and performing my will all my goods and chattels, bonds, bills and ready money, and make her sole exrx. I doubt not that she will see my children brought up in a godly manner and my will performed. I chose my very loving brother Mr FRANCIS BURWELL as supervisor and give him a piece of gold of 20s. value for his pains. My wife is to be bound to him in sum of £400 within 1 month of my death or forfeit all legacies made to her and the executorship. In this case FRANCIS BURWELL will be my exor. Witnesses: THOMAS CRAMPTON, BENJAMIN FREND (X). Pr. at Ipswich 10 April 1635.

W. WILLIAM DOWE of Badley, yeoman. 15 November 1635 (1005)

Sick in body. I give to my wife MARY an annuity of £20 to be paid half yearly. I give to my son DANIEL £100 to be paid within 1 year of my death, and to my son ROBERT £100 when he is 21. I give £50 to my daughter CICELY when 20, £40 to my daughter KATHERINE when 20 and £40 to my daughter JOYCE when 21. I give £5 to ELIZABETH, wife of WILLIAM COCKE, and 10s. to MARY wife of WILLIAM BOWLE. All my houses and land in Helmingstone I give to my son WILLIAM on condition he pays my wife her annuity of £20. Exors. my wife and my son WILLIAM to whom I give all my goods towards paying my legacies. I give to MARY BOWLE my grandchild 20s. Witnesses: JOHN FORDE, EDWARD COLMAN (X), JOHN STANNARD (X) & FRANCIS BEART (X). Pr. 2 Dec. 1635. [No place give]

W. GEORGE NEALE (X) of Wickham Market. (1006)
28 February 1634/5

Weak in body. I give and bequeath to JOAN my wife all my lands and tenements in Wickham Market for ever, and also all my goods and chattels to pay my debts and bring my body decently to the ground in Christian manner. I make her sole exrx. Witnesses: RICHARD THARSTON, JOHN STYLES, ANNE GLADWINE (X). Pr. at Wickham Market 5 May 1635.

W. RICHARD RUSHMER of South Elmham St. Cross, yeoman. (1007)
1 May 1634

Weak in body. I wish to be buried in St. Cross churchyard. I give to my eldest son RICHARD my tenement called Vances and Fryndes with its land in St. Cross which I inherited from my father ROBERT RUSHMER. My wife MARY is to occupy this house and land until the Michaelmas one year after my decease. RICHARD is to pay my wife £10 within 1 year of my death, and thereafter 50s. p.a. in 2 equal payments. My wife is to lodge in the parlour and have free access to the yard, garden and outhouses, and sufficient fuel from land left to my sons RICHARD & JAMES. If they do not give her this fuel she has right to take it. If she remarries she is no longer to have the use of the parlour or my gift of fuel, but £5 p.a. must be paid to her by my sons. I give to my son JAMES a 8 acre close called Harcocks and a 2 acre pightle called Lygate and 2 meadows named Hatfeilds, all of which are in St. Cross. JAMES must pay my wife 50s. p.a. in 2 equal portions. My wife has right to distrain if either son fails to pay her annuity. I give 20s. each when 21 to RICHARD & JAMES sons of my daughter MARY COGSWELL. I give all my goods and chattels to my wife, whom I make exrx. I make JOHN BOWLER my brother-in-law supervisor. Witnesses: JOHN BARKER (X), JOHN NEWSON. Pr. at Beccles 23 May 1635.

W. ROBERT MOORE of Wrentham, grocer. 30 January 1634/5 (1008)

Sick of body. I give and bequeath to my loving wife JOAN all the goods and household stuff she brought to me, and all my bedding, brass, pewter, bedsteads and household implements on condition she leaves these goods to such of my children as she shall think best of. I give to my son JOHN my shop goods. He is to pay my debts and legacies. I give £5 each to my daughters MARGARET, BRIDGET, MARY, ELIZABETH & JUDITH; one to be paid each year. After my wife's death I give to my daughters ELIZABETH & MARY her house in Lowestoft. I give my stable to my son JOHN as it goes with his house. Witnesses: BENJAMIN FOXE, THOMAS SWATMAN. Pr. at Beccles 28 March 1635.

W. WILLIAM OTBYE (X) of Bungay, yeoman. 19 April 1635 (1009)

I give to my son ROBERT my messuage and land in Bungay. He must pay £20 each to my sons JOHN & CLEMENT and to my daughter MARTHA; one each 6 months starting 6 months after my death. I give £5 to my other daughter ELIZABETH, wife of LAWRENCE BIRDE, to be paid at 20s. per month. I give 20s. each when 20 to my 6 grandchildren: SUSAN, ELIZABETH, ALICE, LAWRENCE, JOHN & DANIEL BIRDE. I give all my goods and chattels to my children JOHN, ROBERT & MARTHA. I make my sons CLEMENT & ROBERT exors. Witnesses: JOHN SMYTH, JOHN JAYE. Pr. at Bungay 1 May 1635.

W. MATHEW WAKRING (X) of Mendham, clothier. (1010)
11 December 1634

I give to my sister, Widow CETELL of Bracon Ash in Norfolk, and to her son MATHEW and his 3 sisters £100 to be paid within 1 year of my decease. I give to my brother ROBERT of Yealdon in Essex £100 and to his son DANIEL £100. I give to NICHOLAS DANSE of Mendham the money he owes me if he uses me kindly and lovingly during my life. Exors. THOMAS FRESTON of Mendham gent. and ROGER SPOWNER of Fritton yeoman. Witnesses: CHARLES LOVE, MATHEW GOODWYN. Pr. at Bungay 2 April 1635.

W. BENJAMIN SMITH of Beccles, woollen draper. (1011)
18 December 1634

I give to my wife PHOEBE an annuity of £4 in lieu of dowry. My exor. is to sell my land and tenements and use the money and my goods, after paying my debts, as follows: half to my godson BENJAMIN son of my brother JOHN SMITH and the other half to be divided into 4 portions for my brother FRANCIS and my sisters MARY, wife of RALPH BOULTER, ANNE wife of THOMAS PARKER, and PHOEBE SMITH. I make my brother JOHN sole exor. I give a silver spoon to my godson and half my clothes to my brother JOHN, and one of my rings to my father GISLAME. Witnesses: SIMON GISLAME (X), PHOEBE SMYTH (X). Pr. at Beccles 1 April 1635.

CHAPTER VI

All original Wills; no register extant. Will bundle, reference no. 1C/AA1/67.

W. THOMAS BORRETT of Bramfield, yeoman. 11 July 1636 (1012)

To the poor of Bramfield 10s.; to the poor of Walpole 5s.; the poor of Halesworth 6s. 8d.; to the poor of Sibton 5s. To wife CHRISTIAN, the best bedstead and best bed, 2 pillows, a pair of blankets, the best coverlet, a trundle bedstead, the worst featherbed and the worst coverlet, all linen of napery, best chest and coffer, all the silver plate that is to say, the silver tun and silver spoons, and not others. Also an annuity of £16 payable quarterly on the feast days of All Saints (1 November), purification of Mary (2 February), feast day of Philip and James (1 May), and Animas [sic: this refers to all souls day I believe which falls on 2 November, and does not fit the quarterly pattern which should give a day in August, but with no register to cross check it is impossible to deduce whether this is a mistake.] All payments to be made in Bramfield church porch, and the first payment to be made on the first feast day which falls due after testator's death. These bequests to wife made in lieu of her dower claims on lands conveyed to testator by ROBERT SMITH of Cratfield. If she claim dower, then gifts made to her and the annuity to be void. Wife also to release her jointure to testator's son SIMON BORRETT, and if she refuse this then gifts and annuity given above to be void. Son SIMON BORRETT to enter into a bond of £200 to pay the annuity to CHRISTIAN. To daughter ELIZABETH, the wife of EDMUND ALDEN, £20 within 1 year of testator's death. To grandchild EDWARD ALDEN 40s. when he reaches 21. To grandchild SIMON HAYLE £3 when he reaches 21. To grandchildren SAMUEL, NATHANIEL, THOMAS, SARAH & ELIZABETH HAYLE 40s. each when 21. To grandchildren WILLIAM & MARY CARYE £3 each. To grandchild ROBERT CARYE 40s. when 21. To daughter JANE two year old heifer. To daughter MARGARET TUBBY £10 within 1 year of testator's death, and £5 in 2 years of testator's death. To grandchild THOMAS TUBBY, [missing], and to FRANCIS & MARY TUBBY 40s. when they reach 21. To daughter FRANCES HAYLE [missing] within 3 years of testator's death. To the vicar of Bramfield 20s. To MARGARET, wife of SIMON BORRETT 40s. Residue of all goods and movables to son SIMON, appointed executor. Witnesses: HOLMINGHAM LOFT, vicar; WILLIAM CARY. Pr. at Yoxford 20 Sept. 1636.

W. JONAS BLOMEFIELD of Leiston, yeoman. (1013)
12 September 1634

To son WILLIAM, house and lands with all appurtenances in Leiston, provided he pay at testator's now dwelling place in Leiston, to testator's daughter JOAN £20 within 3 months of testator's death. Also to pay in testator's now dwelling place to testator's daughter CHRISTIAN an annuity of £4 payable in equal shares on Lady Day and Michaelmas or within 6 days of these feasts; also to pay to testator's daughter PHOEBE an annuity of £4 payable at such times as the first mentioned annuity; also to pay to testator's granddaughter MARY CUPPER an annuity of £4 until she reaches 18 on the same feast days as above mentioned. All payments to begin on the first feast day which falls first within six months of testator's death. If default made in payments of sums, then power to enter and enjoy lands until the default, together with arrears and costs suffered be made good. To son WILLIAM, all goods and chattels, he to be sole executor. Witnesses: TRAYNORE JENTRE, WILLIAM JENTRE, THOMAS DADE. Pr. 20 Sept. 1636.

W. STEPHEN BLOMFIELD of Stonham Aspall, yeoman. (1014)
23 September 1635

To the poor of Pettaugh 40s. within 1 month of testator's death, to be distributed by the minister or other chief inhabitant; also to the poor of Earl Stonham 40s. within 1 month of testator's death to be distributed by the minister or other chief inhabitant. To eldest son HENRY BLOMFIELD, capital messuage and tenement called Mownyes where testator lives, in Stonham Aspall, together with all houses, lands, meadows, late purchased by testator from ANNE HASELL, widow, and ROBERT HASELL, being 38 acres. HENRY to hold these lands immediately on testator's death, provided he pay to testator's youngest son STEPHEN BLOMFIELD out of these lands £100 when the said STEPHEN reaches 21 or within 10 days of his reaching 21, in Stonham Aspall church porch; if HENRY default, then power given to STEPHEN to enter these lands and enjoy them until the £100 be paid in full. To son STEPHEN all lands purchased by testator from his brother LIONEL BLOMFIELD immediately on testator's death. To daughters JOAN & ELIZABETH £350 each to be paid by his executor out of testator's goods -- JOAN to receive her £350 in six months of testator's death, and ELIZABETH to receive her £350 when she reaches 21. Benefit of survivorship to children, if any of testator's children die. To son HENRY, the table standing in the hall given to testator by his father; the long table, livery cupboard, 2 chairs and all the stools in testator's parlour; all his hogsheads and ale stools in the buttery; salting tray standing in the dairy; cheese press in the backhouse; 2 coppers, brewing tubs, 2 best spits, pair of iron racks for the spits to turn in, the two best dripping pans; the horse mill as it stands furnished; 1 fowling piece, a musket furnished; a corslett furnished, beam and scales and leading weight of 64 lbs.; all lath and board lying over the cart house, and all timber and board and lumber lying over the calves; all ladders. Executors to have an inventory made of all household goods and implements and debts, not previously devised, and to use money left in his estate to pay all debts, probate charges and legacies. Remainder to be equally divided between testator's wife ANNE and his son STEPHEN. Sons HENRY & STEPHEN appointed executors. Witnesses: THOMAS TURNER, JOHN BLOIS. Pr. at Ipswich 7 Oct. 1636.

W. MARGARET BRADSHAWE of Framsden. 1 May 1634 (1015)

Aged about 75 or thereabouts; to be buried at Framsden. To the poor of Framsden 20s. within one month of testator's death. To eldest son JAMES HANWORTH £5 within 6 months of testator's death. To THOMAS WYARD, son of son-in-law THOMAS WYARD, one feather bed and feather bolster within 1 month of testator's death. To MARY HANWORTH, daughter of testator's son ISAAC HANWORTH, the great chest in one month of testator's death. To DEBORAH HANWORTH, daughter of ISAAC HANWORTH, one feather bed, one feather bolster, one feather pillow, one pair of sheets, best coverlet within one month of testator's death. To ELIZABETH HANWORTH, daughter of ISAAC HANWORTH, one cupboard, one pair of sheets, within one month of testator's death. To ALICE HANWORTH, daughter of testator's son JOHN HANWORTH, the great posted bedstead within one month of testator's death. To CICILY, the wife of testator's brother JAMES STONE, the glass keep, within one month of testator's death. Proviso that if any of the legatees be under age and unable to give a receipt for their gift, then their father to provide a receipt; and if any one refuse to give such a receipt then their legacy to be void. Rest of estate to go to brother JAMES STONE, he to be executor, and pay all debts, legacies, funeral and probate expenses. THOMAS POOLE appointed supervisor. Witnesses: JAMES STONE, MARY HANWORTH (X). Pr. at Ipswich 18 Oct. 1636.

W. WILLIAM BARROW of Huntingfield, gentleman. 3 August 1636 (1016)

To son ROBERT, messuage and tenement where Mistress COPPING, widow lives, together with houses and appurtenances in Halesworth; also 8 butchers stalls in the market place of Halesworth in consideration of the debts owed by testator to his son ROBERT. Also two leases of messuages and lands in Walpole and Cookley lately had of Sir JOHN HEVENINGHAM for the duration of those leases. To son HENRY £6 annuity payable by equal installments of £3 on Lady Day and Michaelmas or within 10 days of the said feasts; first payment to be made on the first feast day which falls due after testator's death. Annuity to be paid in executor's house and son HENRY to give a receipt for the same. Testator releases son HENRY from all bonds and debts due from him to the testator. To son ROBERT lease of messuage where testator now lives in Huntingfield, lease being held of Sir EDWARD COKE. To son WILLIAM and his wife, or the longer liver of them, mortgage on the lands of EDWARD ODIERNE of Walpole. To grandson JOHN, son of son ROBERT, the horse which testator most commonly do ride immediately on testator's death, together with all goods whatsoever in the shop and shop chamber where testator commonly used to work, immediately on testator's death. To the children of EDMOND BARROW, testator's brother late deceased, 40s. each, being WILLIAM the elder, EDMOND, a joiner, ANDREW a joiner, and TIMOTHY. To the wife of THOMAS KEBLE 40s. in 1 year of testator's death. To FRANCES BARROW, daughter of EDMOND, 40s. in 1 year of testator's death. To kinswoman ANNE BURWORD £5 when

21. To each poor person who attends testator's burial 4d. To the minister Mr CROSBY 40s. for a sermon at testator's funeral. Rest of estate to son ROBERT, he to pay all debts and legacies. Son ROBERT and wife ANNE to be executors and pay burial and probate expenses. Witnesses: WILLIAM NEWSON, ROBERT HUMPSON, and me THOMAS FELLA. Pr. at Beccles 1 Nov. 1636.

W. ROBERT COBBE of Beccles, gentleman. 25 March 1635 (1017)

Aged. That under certain articles of agreement made between the testator, JOHN YONGES of Earsham, Norfolk, and JOHN JOSHE alias CANNAM late of Barnham yeoman, dated 19 July 1630, being the testator's marriage settlement by virtue of which all his debts were paid. Now under this settlement to wife THOMASINE, all goods, chattels, and implements, she being appointed executor. Witnesses: JAMES BALEY, ROBERT HERVIE. Pr. at Beccles 7 Oct. 1636.

W. JOHN COLMAN of Bredfield, yeoman. 30 October 1633 (1018)

Sick. To wife ANNE, posted bed in the parlor with all things belonging to it, for life; 2 little tables in the said parlour for life; the great chest and linen in the parlour, 2 small kettles; one hooped chair, 2 joined stools. To son JOHN rest of goods and chattels, provided he pay to testator's wife ANNE an annuity of £10 if she need it, payable quarterly. To ALICE WRITE, testator's sister's daughter, 40s. in 3 years of testator's death. To JOHN WRITE her brother 40s. when he reaches 24. To MARY CHRISTMAS, testator's sister's grandchild 40s. in 1 year of testator's death. To RICHARD LYBBIS, testator's sister's son, 20s. when he reaches 24. Son JOHN appointed executor. Witnesses: JOHN SMYTH, script., ADRY TAYLER the wife of RICHARD TAYLER. Pr. at Wickham Market 4 Aug. 1636.

W. ABRAHAM HUBBERD of Great Wenham, yeoman. (1019)
31 January 1633

To the churchwardens of Brandeston 20s. for distribution amongst the poor of the parish; and to Mr HOPKING 10s. for the poor of Great Wenham. To grandchild JOSEPH HUBBERD, messuage and tenement, both free and copyhold in Brandeston; the close called Melfield being 12 acres, and all leasehold land in Brandeston, provided he pay to testator's grandchild THOMAS HUBBERD £10 within 3 years of testator's death, and also to pay testator's grandchild AGNES HUBBERD £20 in 4 years, and to pay testator's grandchildren ELIZABETH & MARY HUBBERD £15 each in 4 years, and to pay testator's grandchild ABRAHAM HUBBERD £30 in 6 years of testator's death; all these bequests made with benefit of survivorship, and also proviso that if default made in payment of money, then grandchild JOSEPH HUBBERD to loose Melfield close, and this close to pass to testator's son-in-law JOHN LEWSON for him to pay those legacies which are unpaid. JOHN LEWSON appointed supervisor and receives 40s. for his pains. To testator's three daughters MARY SMYTH, AGNES BAILEY & MARTHA LEWSON 5s. each. Residue of estate to testator's grandson JOSEPH HUBBERD, provided he prove this will within 3 months of testator's death; if he fail to do so, then all gifts of goods to him in this will to be void, and the goods and chattels to go to JOHN LEWSON, who is appointed executor. Witnesses: WILLIAM CARLETON, JOHN STEVENSON. Pr. at Ipswich 8 July 1636.

W. JOSIAS HUNT of Woodbridge, vintner. 16 August 1636 (1020)

Sick. To mother 20s. To father-in-law JOHN SMYTH 20s.; both bequests of 20s. made in order that they may buy themselves a ring. To sister MARY PARTRIDGE, wife of JOHN PARTRIDGE, £25 -- she to receive £12 10s. in six months after testator's death, and the further £12 10s. in 1 year after the testator's death; proviso that if sister dies before receiving all her legacy, then the sum remaining from the £25 to go to testator's executor; but if his sister leaves a son or daughter living at the time of her death then the sum remaining to pass to him/her/them. Also to sister MARY all the household stuff and household implements lately had by the testator off WOOLFRAM MANN of Woodbridge, excepting the linen and pewter. To sisters MARY PARTRIDGE & MILLICENT SMYTH all the linen and pewter which testator had from WOOLFRAM MANN to be equally divided between the two sisters. To sister MILLICENT SMYTH a ring worth £1 and a trunck to be delivered to her within 1 month of testator's death. To JOHN PARTRIDGE, the husband of sister MARY, one cloth cloak edged with satin lace within 1 week of testator's death. To WILLIAM PULHAM one black stuff cloak in full recompense of debts owed, and black gown, late the goodwife ARCHER's, within 10 days of testator's death. To JOHN PURDWAY long frise coat within 1 week of testator's death. To godson THOMAS WALKER, son of DANIEL WALKER, 10s., and to goddaughter ELIZABETH BARKER, daughter of PETER BARKER, 10s. to buy each of them a silver spoon, within six weeks of testator's death. To SAMUEL GIRLING 10s. within 1 week of testator's death. To brother SAMUEL HUNT £5, he to be executor, and to have all plate, jewels, debts, credits, money, household goods whatsoever, and he to pay all debts, legacies, and funeral expenses. To WILLIAM CATWAY's wife 2s. 6d. To cousin ROBERT KENLE 10s. To maid ELIZABETH BONDLE 2s. 6d. To LIONEL EDGAR 10s. to buy him gloves. Witnesses: GEORGE BUTTON, JOHN BUTTON, GEORGE JURY. Pr. at Woodbridge 7 Sept. 1636.

W. JOHN DAMRON of Ipswich, coke porter. 28 March 1636 (1021)

Sick. To wife KATHERINE, all lands in St. Margaret's parish Ipswich, with all appurtenances, until testator's son ANTHONY DAMRON reaches 26 when he inherits lands, provided he let his mother KATHERINE have a convenient dwelling in some of the tenements for her life; if he refuse then KATHERINE to keep all the lands for life. Also ANTHONY to pay to brother HENRY £5 when he reaches 24, and to pay to his sister LIDIA £5 on her marriage, and if ANTHONY refuse to do these, then power to HENRY & LIDIA to enter and enjoy messuages and appurtenances until legacies fulfilled from the profits of the said lands. Also if ANTHONY die before reaching 26 without any heirs, then lands and appurtenances to pass to HENRY & LIDIA DAMRON, and they to allow to their mother KATHERINE a convenient dwelling in some of the tenements. To son ANTHONY the posted bedstead and featherbed in the kitchen, when 26. To son HENRY, livery bedstead & featherbed in the chamber when 24. To daughter LIDIA, bedstead & featherbed in the hall on her marriage. To ALICE BODDYE 20s. To THOMAS DAMRON 10s. within 1 year of testator's death. To EDWARD, DANIEL & ALICE ELLINDER 20s. each on their marriages. Residue of estate to wife KATHERINE, she to be executrix. Witnesses: JOHN UPSON, THOMAS PARKER, EDWARD DIXON. Pr. at Ipswich 15 July 1636.

W. THOMAS FROST of Barnby. 26 June 1636 (1022)

Sick. To son THOMAS FROST, all lands and tenements in Northales alias Covehithe, both freehold and copyhold, to him and his heirs, but if he have no heirs, then lands to pass on his death to testator's brother CHRISTOPHER FROST. To son THOMAS 40s. within 3 months of testator's death. To brother CHRISTOPHER 40s. within 3 months of testator's death. Residue of estate to wife BRIDGET, she appointed sole executrix. Witnesses: PHILIP HOWARD, ROBERT MUNNS. Pr. at Beccles 9 July 1636.

W. ROBERT GOSLYNGE of Newbourne, yeoman. (1023)
27 November 1635

Sick. To son JOSEPH, all lands and tenements with appurtenances; if JOSEPH die without heir then lands to go to testator's daughters MARY & ANNE. All corn, cattle, and possessions of the testator, including ready money, to be inventoried by four men, and all debts to be paid, and legacies, and the overplus to be paid to son JOSEPH by executor. If there be not enough money to satisfy all debts and legacies, then JOSEPH is required to make good the shortfall, but if he refuse to do so, then whoever has not received payment of debt or legacy is empowered to enter into lands devised to JOSEPH and to enjoy the same until he receives satisfaction. To daughter ANNE GOSLYNGE £100 when she reaches 21; if she die before reaching 21 without heir, then money to be equally divided between son JOSEPH and daughter MARY. To grandchild MARY BUCKLE £10 when 21. To the four children now living of JOHN WATLYNGE of Sudbourne 10s. each when 21. To DORCAS & ELIZABETH FLOWERDEW, children of CHARLES FLOWERDEW of Grundisburgh, 20s. each when 21. To each of his servants being with him at the time of his death, 20s. within 1 year of his death. JOHN LANE of Rendlesham appointed sole executor; RICHARD KEEBLE of Ipswich to be supervisor and to receive 10s. Witnesses: CHARLES FLOWERDEW, ROBERT HOWE, junior. Codicil to will, dated 30 November 1635. To daughter MARY BUCKLE £20 within 6 months of testator's death. To grandchild ROBERT BUCKLE £10 when 21. To poor of Newbourne 20s. within 1 month of testator's death. Witnesses: JOSEPH HALL, CHARLES FLOWERDEW. Admon. at Wickham Market to CHARLES FLOWERDEW.

W. ROBERT INDYE of Wrentham, yeoman. 29 December 1633 (1024)

To be buried in Wrentham churchyard. To brother NICHOLAS INDYE £50, namely £25 within 1 year and £25 in 2 years of testator's death. To brother WILLIAM INDYE £50, namely £25 within 1 year, and £25 in 2 years of testator's death. Both brothers to enter into bond with testator's executor to pay testator's sister MARY AMYS an annuity of 10s. a piece for life, and if they refuse this payment of annuity, then gifts to them to be void. Wife JANE to keep and maintain testator's kinswoman MARGARET WOODYE until she reaches 16, and to pay her £20 when she reaches 21; JANE to have the house and tenement where testator now lives free from rent until the Michaelmas next after testator's death, and if brother NICHOLAS INDYE refuse to allow this to her, then NICHOLAS to loose his legacy of £50. To SUSAN INDYE, daughter of NICHOLAS INDYE £10 when 21. To uncle ROBERT INDYE 40s.; and to his youngest son 40s. in 2 years of testator's death. To WILLIAM CRISPE one suit of clothes and 20s. in 1 year of testator's death. To the poor of Wrentham 40s., the poor of Henstead 20s., and the poor of Covehithe 13s. 4d. all within one month of testator's death. Residue of estate to wife JANE, she being sole executrix, to pay legacies. Witnesses: RALPH TURNER, THOMAS SWATMAN. Pr. at Beccles 7 Sept. 1636.

W. ANN GARDNER of Rumburgh. 25 July 1636 (1025)

To CATHARINE GARDNER, daughter of JOHN GARDNER of Wenhaston deceased, £5 within 1 year, and to ANN SIMONDS, younger daughter of JOHN GARDNER of Wenhaston, £10 within 2 years of testator's death. To brother ROBERT GARDNER of Lowestoft 20s., which he owes to testator. To THOMAS, eldest son of ROBERT GARDNER, £5 in 3 years, and to JOHN, youngest son of ROBERT GARDNER, £5 also in 3 years of testator's death. All clothes, linen, wool, to go to the two daughters of brother JOHN GARDNER of Wenhaston, to be equally divided by executor, excepting the best bolsters and pillows which are to go to testator's partner ALICE CLARKE. To partner ALICE CLARKE £8, and the trunk standing in testator's master LAURENCE his chamber. To CATHARINE GARDNER, daughter of JOHN, chest in the little chamber at master LAURENCE, and to ANN SIMONDS, daughters of JOHN, the box in the same chamber. To CICLIE CLARKE, sister to ALICE CLARKE, cloak and sack excepted from the bequest to the two daughters of JOHN GARDNER. To GREGORY CLARKE, servant of GEORGE LAURENCE, 40s. in 1 year of testator's death. To godson ROBERT CLARKE, son of WILLIAM CLARK of Barrow in Norfolk, 20s. to be paid to WILLIAM CLARKE for his son's use within 2 years of testator's death. To Widow MARGARET WASH, 30s. to be bestowed in clothes for her by executor. Residue of estate to partner ALICE CLARKE, she to be executrix and pay debts, legacies, and funeral charges. Witnesses: WILLIAM GALLARD, JOHN FOX. Pr. at Beccles 22 Oct.

1636.

W. JOHN GIRLING of Wickham Market, husbandman. (1026)
2 July 1636

That WILLIAM PEMBERTON of Bredfield, yeoman, is to have the profits from testator's house and lands in Marlesford, except for the parlour of the house which is to go to testator's wife for her dwelling for life, until the said WILLIAM PEMBERTON has received from the same house and lands the sum of £13 10s., as has been agreed already. When the said WILLIAM has received this said sum, he then to surrender all copyhold lands to testator's son WILLIAM GIRLING, and the house in Marlesford and all freehold lands adjoining it to go to testator's sons JOHN & THOMAS GIRLING and their heirs. All goods, save 5 iron wedges, to go to WILLIAM PEMBERTON and testator's wife ANNE, to do as they think best. Wedges to go to son THOMAS. WILLIAM PEMBERTON and testator's wife ANNE appointed joint executors. Witnesses: MAXIMILYAN SMYTH, WILLIAM SAER (X), ELIZABETH ASHELY (X). Pr. at Wickham Market 4 Aug. 1636.

W. GEORGE JARVIE the elder of Woodbridge, shoemaker. (1027)
3 September 1636

Sick. To wife ALICE £3, also featherbed with all things thereunto belonging, for life; bed to be sold on her death and then the money arising from the said sale to go to his two sons GEORGE & THOMAS JARVIE and to his two daughters ROSE JARVIE & JOAN SHARPE equally to be divided. To sons GEORGE & THOMAS a flock bed each. To daughters ROSE & JOAN a flockbed each. Rest of goods to be sold, and money thus arising to be used to pay debts, and the money left once debts paid, to be divided equally between wife and children. Son GEORGE JARVIE appointed executor. Witnesses: HENRY USHERWOOD, THOMAS RICHER. Pr. at Wickham Market 22 Sept. 1636.

W. THOMAS KENT of Debenham, innholder. 30 May 1636 (1028)

Sick. To wife MARY, messuage and tenements with all appurtenances thereunto appertaining lying in Wetheringsett occupied by JOHN SADD; wife to sell these lands within one year of testator's death, and use the money from the sale, to pay debts and legacies. To son THOMAS KENT £100 within 6 months of the sale of lands, and a further £20 in six months after death of testator's wife MARY. To son ROGER KENT £80 within six months of the sale of land, and a further £20 in six months after death of testator's wife MARY. To wife MARY, all household goods, utensils whatsoever, she to be executrix, and pay debts and legacies. Witnesses: THOMAS WYBOVE, JOHN CATCHPOLL. Note: that the testator's will and meaning is that his son THOMAS should have the first refusal of testator's lands, and to have them provided he make a reasonable offer. Pr. at Ipswich 4 Sept. 1636.

W. ROBERT MANISTYE of Ipswich, yeoman. 7 September 1636 (1029)

To THURSTON MANISTYE, the son of testator's executor, £10 within 3 months of testator's death; also a feather bed and feather bolster and pillow on which the testator does now lie, with the coverlet and blankets. Stating that SAMUEL HALDOCKE of Whitton is in debt to the testator; now WILLIAM MANISTYE to receive and have the said debt, and that if SAMUEL HALDOCKE refuse to pay the same to the said WILLIAM, then the said WILLIAM is to receive a letter of attorney from testator's executor legally appointing the said WILLIAM the legal heir to the testator and thereby entitled to the said debt. Also to WILLIAM a brass pot. To all all children of JOHN COOPER 5s. each. To WILLIAM GALL, son of WILLIAM GALL, 20s. and to the rest of his children 5s. each. To FRANCIS MANISTYE junior, £5 within six months of testator's death; also a great brass kettle, flock bed and flock bolster, joined chest, and 1/2 the brass & pewter. To MARY BRADFIELD, wife of WILLIAM BRADFIELD, carved joined chest, and to the child of WILLIAM BRADFIELD 5s. To ANN COOPER, wife of JOHN COOPER half the brass and pewter. To all his godchildren 2s. 6d. Rest of goods to FRANCIS MANISTYE senior, he to be executor and pay all debts, and funeral expenses. Witnesses: WILLIAM TOFLER. Pr. at Ipswich 7 Oct. 1636.

W. THOMAS PRESTON of Wrentham, gentleman. (1030)
5 September 1636

Sick. That his executor shall give and execute the state of all those lands which are already sold by agreement to LIONEL PLAYTERS of Uggeshall, clerk, and the money to be used in payment of testator's debts. Also that part of his land is mortgaged to THOMAS TYE of Southcove for £100, and executor to redeem this land and pass it to the said LIONEL PLAYTERS. To wife FRANCIS the principal tenement where CHRISTOPHER BERRY lives, with all free and copyhold land thereunto pertaining, provided she maintain the said property and keep it in good repair, and on her death the property to pass to testator's son JOHN and his heirs. Also wife FRANCIS to enjoy and have the benefit from the land and houses belonging to testator in Southcove until son JOHN reaches 21 -- she to pay debts and any other charges out of these properties. When son JOHN reach 21 he to have and enjoy profits and lands in Southcove. Rest of goods to wife FRANCIS, she to be executrix and pay all debts and charges. Witnesses: ELIZABETH MARKE, MIRRABEL CAPPE, THOMAS SLATHE. Pr. at Beccles 13 Sept. 1636.

W. WILLIAM MANNING of Ofton. 14 March 1635 (1031)

To be buried in Ofton churchyard. To wife SUSAN £10 within one month of testator's death; also 40s. annuity for life to be paid in installments of 10s. each quarterly, provided she make no controversy over her dower claims, and if she does then her gifts void. Also if default made to her in the payment of these gifts, then she to enter and hold for term of her life the tenement called Coppinges. To son WILLIAM MANNING, two bonds worth £20 and £10 respectively, immediately on testator's death; also £20 more within 1 year of testator's death, provided he pay to his mother SUSAN £5, if she be then living. Also to son best brass pot, and all the shop tools. To son JOHN MANNING, all lands and tenements in Ofton; also one neat cow towards the cost of testator's funeral; also bedstead in the chamber, and all ready money, bonds being excepted, in order to pay legacies specified in this will. If JOHN fail to pay these legacies, then son WILLIAM to inherit the lands instead of JOHN. Rest of household goods and estate to go to wife SUSAN. Son JOHN MANNING appointed executor. Witnesses: RICHARD MICHELL, ROBERT SPARROW. Pr. at Ipswich 7 July 1636.

W. WILLIAM ROGERS of Shottisham, husbandman. (1032)
11 October 1633

Sick and weak; to be buried in Shottisham. To JOAN SMYTH of Bromewell, testator's aunt, £20, to be paid at the rate of 40s. a year by equal payments on Lady Day and Michaelmas, the first payment to be made on the first feast day following testator's death. If aunt dies before the whole £20 be used up, then the residue of the money to go to aunt's daughter ELIZABETH SMYTH. To WILLIAM BOTLIE of Shottisham and his wife ANNE, messuage and tenement in Hacheston. Also the rest of his goods to WILLIAM BOTLIE alias CUTBERD and to ROBERT CHURCH of Tuddenham who are appointed joint executors, to pay all debts, and legacies, and funeral charges. Witnesses: HENRY CHURCH, THOMAS SEAMAN. Pr. at Wickham Market 12 Oct. 1636.

W. ELIZABETH NEWSON of Northales alias Covehithe, single. (1033)
22 April 1636

Weak; to be buried at Northales. To THOMAS HARMAN and his wife ELIZABETH £4 which is now in the hands of JOHN ELLIS of Weybridge, in consideration of the long trouble, and the great and continual charges they have been at with testator in her manifold afflictions. To DOROTHY HARMAN, a coffer. THOMAS HARMAN appointed executor. Witnesses: MARK WYALL (X), JOSEPH HEAD. Pr. at Beccles 27 Aug. 1636.

W. THOMAS ROCHESTER of Halesworth, taylor. 6 June 1625 (1034)

Sick. To wife REBECCA £10 within one year of death of STEPHIMA ROCHESTER mother of testator, which £10 was given to testator by his father JOHN. To son JOHN, £10 in 1 year of death of STEPHIMA ROCHESTER, and if son JOHN dies before he inherits, then the said sum to go to testator's wife REBECCA. Also to son JOHN bedstead, one feather bed and all furniture thereunto belonging as it stands in the parlour. To wife REBECCA, 1 great chest, 1 keep, a great chair the best of the two, 1 little table, 1 brass pot, 1 dripping pan, 1 little spit. All the rest of household stuff to go to mother for her lifetime, and if she be in need of money, she to sell the movables. Brother-in-law DANIEL PRYME and cousin CHARLES RICHES to be executors. Witnesses: PETER WOOD, HENRY KEEBLE (writer). Admon. to PETER WOOD & HENRY KEEBLE at Beccles 1 Aug. 1636.

W. WILLIAM SELF of Bramford, innkeeper. 21 April 1636 (1035)

Sick. To wife FRANCIS, messuage and tenement and buildings in Eye and Denham inherited by testator from his father THOMAS and now occupied by his uncle ROBERT SELF. She to hold for life, and then to pass to testator's brother-in-law JOHN LEVERIDGE and his heirs. To kinsman ROBERT LEVERIDGE £5, to be paid within six months of testator's death in the south porch of Bramford church. Rest of estate to wife FRANCIS, she to be sole executrix, paying all debts, legacies and funeral expenses. Witnesses: HENRY ROWING, JAMES BACON, THOMAS RINSTON. Pr. at Ipswich 15 July 1636.

W. ROBERT PALMER of Chelmondiston, yeoman. (1036)
2 September 1636

To be buried at Chelmondiston. To daughter ELIZABETH PALMER, when she reaches the age of 22, house and tenement being freehold, and all lands belonging thereunto in Shottisham, having the yearly value of £6, held of Sir ANTHONY FELTON, provided she pay to testator's other daughter FRANCIS £10 out of these lands within 3 years of her having inherited these same lands. To daughter FRANCIS PALMER, when she reaches the age of 22, house and tenement being freehold, in Shotley, having the yearly value of 30s., held of Sir ANTHONY FELTON. Executor to give out of testator's goods £20 to testator's daughter ELIZABETH £20 within 4 years of her reaching 22, and likewise to give to daughter FRANCIS £20 within 4 years of her reaching 22. To THOMAS PALMER of Essex 5s., and to THOMASINE PALMER of Shotley 5s., both sums to be paid within one year of testator's death. Wife SUSAN appointed executor together with friend STEPHEN PALMER of Langham, yeoman. Witnesses: WILLIAM SIMCOCKS, RALPH BRAGG (X). Pr. at Ipswich 8 Sept. 1636.

W. JOAN STARKE of Woodbridge, widow. 24 March 1635 (1037)

Weak, to be buried at Woodbridge. To grandchild JOHN STARKE, all goods, chattels, movables, pewter, linen, wool, brass, beds, debts, bills, bonds, once debts and funeral expenses and legacies met, in order to sell the same for the best advantage, and the money thus arising to be placed in JOHN WARREN's hands, and to be used in the bringing up of the said grandchild JOHN STARKE. To SUSAN, wife of RICHARD PENNINGTON of Woodbridge, best petticoat and waistcoat, all firewood ready in the orchard and a skip of bees and the housing for them, presently on testator's death. To Mrs WARREN of Woodbridge another skip of bees and their housing. To goddaughter MARY BOTRICKE of Martlesham, red flannel petticoat, 3 coiffes presently on testator's death. To Widows SEWELL, AUSTEN, COCKE & CRISPE present in the almshouse, one of my new smocks each. To goodwife CORBALL an old petticoat. JOHN WARREN of Woodbridge appointed executor of will and guardian of grandson JOHN STARKE; if grandson die before he reaches 21, then the money arising from the sale to be equally divided between the children of GEORGE COLE, when they reach 21. Witnesses: ROBERT CADE, clerk; SUSAN PENNINGTON (X). Pr. at Wickham Market 4 Aug. 1636.

W. MARY SMITH of Friston, widow. 15 June 1636 (1038)

To JOSEPH BUTERS, the youngest grey mare; also 2 marks to be paid on the Michaelmas following her death. Residue of estate to be equally divided between son ROBERT and daughter MARY they to receive their legacies within one year of testator's death, provided that all debts, and funeral expenses and legacies have been met. JOSEPH BUTERS appointed sole executor. Witnesses: RICHARD HAMLERE (X), MARGARET BROWNE (X), ROBERT FENT, THOMAS HARDING, script. Pr. at Wickham Market 22 Sept. 1636.

W. WILLIAM PAINE of Charsfield, yeoman. (1039)
20 September 1626

To son JOHN, messuage and tenement with all thereunto belonging being in Woodbridge, provided he let testator's wife have the profits from these lands for term of her life. To daughter ELIZABETH £30 to be given her out of the money raised from the sale of testator's movables; she also to have the linen, and the linen on two beds, and also the best bed as it now stands. To MARGARET PAINE, daughter of THOMAS PAINE, the second best bed with all things thereunto belonging; also 40s. within 1 year of testator's death. To godchild WILLIAM PAINE one silver spoon, presently on testator's death. To godchild WILLIAM SYRED one silver spoon, presently on testator's death. To JOHN SYRED, testator's daughter's son, one silver spoon. To the rest of the children 2s. apiece. Residue of unbequeathed goods to be divided between testator's son JOHN and daughter ELIZABETH. Daughter ELIZABETH appointed sole executrix. To JOHN PAINE the third best bed with all its belongings. Witnesses: ROGER CLARKE, JOHN SMITH, script, JOHN SMYTH the younger. [Probate missing.]

W. ROBERT PAYNE of Yoxford, yeoman. 23 November 1635 (1040)

To daughter MARY PAYNE the close late WALTER WALPOLE's with the house and the hempland to the north east of it, being 6 acres 3 roods lying in Yoxford, with the king's highway from Sibton to Middleton on the north east, the common way from Sibton to

Ilketshall on the south west, the churchyard of Yoxford on the north west, and lands of HENRY HILL on the south east; this close to her provided she pay to testator's daughter CATHERYNE HURRION, £20 within one year of the death of testator's wife MARGARET, and payment to be made in Yoxford church porch and if she default, then power to CATHERYNE to enter and to take profits from this said close until the legacy of £20 be fulfilled. Further to daughter MARY PAYNE a meadow called Stowemeadow, purchased from MARY HURRION, widow, being 1 acre and a half in Yoxford, lying on the north side of the common mere; also to her the close of land called Bysorg, being 4 acres in Yoxford, lying between lands of WILLIAM LACEY and lands of NICHOLAS WHINERY; also to her a pightle called Market mere, late WALTER WALPOLE's, lying in Yoxford against the vicarage of Yoxford, and being 2 acres; also to her the land called Foxboroughs, and Hobbes yard lying together and enclosed in Yoxford between the vicarage in part and lands of JOHN FOX, gent., on the north, and lands of ROBERT CASTER, deceased, in part and lands of THOMAS BAYNE deceased, in part of the south, and abutts on Wildwoodlane on the east, and the king's highway from Yoxford to Kelsale to the west. Provided daughter MARY pays out of these lands to testator's wife MARGARET in full satisfaction of any dower claims, £9 a year due on the feasts of Christmas, Lady Day, St. John the Baptist, and Michaelmas -- or within 5 days of each of these feasts, payments to be made in Yoxford church porch and first payment to be made on the first feast day which falls next after testator's death. If default made in payment then power to wife to enter these lands and hold them until default made good. Daughter MARY also to give, within one month of testator's death, to her mother MARGARET, 2 cart loads of wood, and to let her mother have two cart loads of wood each year for life; MARY also to put this wood in some convenient place for her mother, and if default made in the cartloads of wood, then power to testator's wife MARGARET to enter Market mere pightle and hold it for life. To wife MARGARET and daughter MARY all goods and chattels equally to be divided; they to be joint executors. Witnesses: NICHOLAS WHINERY, THOMAS PULHAM, junior. Pr. at Yoxford 20 Sept. 1636.

W. THOMAS TODD of Saxmundham (N). Christmas 1635 (1041)

To KATHERINE, the wife of PHILIP CRANE, and sister of testator, his house and shop in Saxmundham together with the rest of his estate. Witnesses: NATHANIEL DRIVER, ROBERT HARVIE, RICHARD GUNNER, GRACE the wife of WILLIAM LEWIS (X). Probate granted to KATHERINE CRANE at Yoxford 13 July 1636.

W. ROBERT TOOLEY of Yoxford, yeoman. 1 August 1636 (1042)

To wife ALICE, all lands and tenements whatsoever in Yoxford, for life; then on her death these lands to pass to testator's maid SARA BURROUGH for life, together with all the goods in the house kitchen, kitchen chamber, buttery, backhouse, and backhouse chamber and barn; then on the death of SARA these to pass to

WILLIAM THORNE son of WILLIAM THORNE of Sibton, joiner, and to his heirs, provided he pay to WILLIAM CANDLER son of Widow CANDLER of Saxmundham £40 within one year of his entering these lands, and provided also that he pay to WILLIAM WOODWARD, son of WILLIAM WOODWARD late of Sibton £40 within 2 years of his entering these lands; payment to be made in Sibton church porch, and also if default in payments, then power given to whomsoever is in arrears to enter and hold these lands until the default is made good. Should WILLIAM WOODWARD or WILLIAM CANDLER die without heirs before inheriting their legacies, then gift to be void. To maid SARA, one long table in the hall and the stool belonging to it; cupboard and three chairs and the cushions in the hall; the little table in the shop chamber; 2 beds with their furniture; one coverlet with the bed sheets; 2 pairs of coarse sheets and one pair of the finer sort of sheet; one linen table cloth for the table in the hall; one little cloth for the cupboard table in the kitchen; also 30s. All these gifts to maid SARA on the death of testator's wife. To RICHARD TOWLEY £20 within six months of death of testator's wife. To ANN RACHAM wife of THOMAS RACHAM £5. To ROBERT RACHAM, son of THOMAS, 20s. and a dozen of pewter. To THOMAS RACHAM, son of THOMAS, 20s. and a dozen of pewter. To ANN RACHAM, daughter of THOMAS, 20s. and a dozen of pewter. To Widow CANDLER 50s. To the two daughters of WILLIAM WOODWARD 20s. and a dozen of pewter each. To JOHN THORNE, son of WILLIAM THORNE, 20s. and a dozen of pewter. To the father of SARA BURROUGH 50s. To the daughter of Widow CANDLER the wife of one MILLS of Saxmundham, 20s. and a dozen of pewter. To BRIDGET BURROUGH 20s. and a dozen of pewter. To PHILIP THORNE, son of WILLIAM THORNE, 20s. and a dozen of pewter. To ALICE DURRANT that was my servant 20s. and a dozen of pewter. To WILLIAM COWNES that was my servant 20s. and a dozen of pewter. To MARGERY the wide of WILLIAL THORNE 20s. All the above bequests of pewter and 20s., to be delivered to legatees within six months of testator's death. To THOMAS NUTTAL of Saxmundham, to Mr JONES, Mr SWEYNE, Mr EACHER of Darsham and Mr EACHER of Yoxford, 40s. each within 10 days of death of testator's wife. To whoever preaches at testator's burial 5s. To WILLIAM THORNE the elder £5 and all the copper in the kitchen, wicker chair, the long table in the hall chamber, bed and bedstead with its furniture in the hall chamber, the woolen coverlet woven with bucks, pillow; the musket with all its furniture. To WILLIAM SMITH of Sibton £5, and the great brass pot, brass pan and the bed that testator lies on with all its furniture. All spits to be equally divided between WILLIAM THORNE & WILLIAM SMITH. To the town of Yoxford £10 for a town stock. To the poor of Yoxford 10s. To WILLIAM CANDLER a bible; all these bequests within six months of death of testator's wife. Residue of estate to wife ALICE for life, she to be executrix together with WILLIAM THORNE the elder. WILLIAM SMITH appointed supervisor. Witnesses: JOHN BAYLE, ROGER CLARKE. Pr. at Yoxford 13 Oct. 1636.

W. NICHOLAS BEOMANT the elder of Wilby, joiner. (1043)
4 July 1636

To wife MARGARET, house and lands and tenements, both free and copyhold in Wilby, for her lifetime if she remain a widow, and keep property in good repair. If she allows ploughing on these lands and pastures, then she must pay testator's son NICHOLAS BEOMANT 30s. for every acre of land ploughed. Also to wife, the smallest chest standing in the parlour and all the linen; the joined bedstead without a trundle furnished as it stands on the said chamber; the brass warming pan, and all movables, chattels and utensils for as long as she remain a widow. To son NICHOLAS the long table in the hall with two joined forms belonging to it; the keep in the hall; the horse mill standing in the mill house; cheese press in the backhouse; cart and tumbrel, and one brass copper in the backhouse immediately on the death of testator's wife. To son ROBERT BEOMANT one long table in the parlour and six joined stools belonging to it; biggest brass pot, 2 great cobirons in the hall, one feather bed and the feather bolster; two feather pillows, one coverlet, one blanket lying on the best bed in the parlour chamber, and all timber in the house and yards and all working tools belonging to the trade of a joiner; best oak standing on the south side of the meadow adjoining the lands of FRANCIS FOULSHER, which oak is to be cut and used within one year of testator's death; also horse colt; grindstone and cupboard in the buttery; danske chest in the parlour chamber; best cloak; benches in the shop and one tun standing in the shop chamber -- the working tools, timber, grindstone, and horse colt to go to son immediately on testator's death, and the rest of the goods bequeathed to him to come to him on the death of testator's wife, or on her remarriage. Also ROBERT to have use and occupation of chamber next to the buttery, use and occupation of shop and shop chamber with free egress and ingress for the horse and carts in the yards and for him and his servant to and from the shop and chamber for as long as he remain single. To son JOHN BEOMANT one bedstead in the parlour with the feather bed and feather bolster, 2 feather pillows, one coverlet, one blanket, one pair of sheets, 2 pillow cases one mat and line; iron pot, great joined chest in the parlour, one pair of small cobirons -- all immediately on death of testator's wife; also curtains hanging about the bed in the parlour, one small table in the hall and two joined stools belonging to it; one great turned chair in the hall; one fire pan; one pair tongs, one iron spit, one iron dripping pan. To daughter MARTHA TOOKE, best posted bedstead standing on the parlour chamber; one joined table chair in the parlour immediately on death of testator's wife. To MARY BEOMANT joined cupboard in the parlour, one joined table chair in the parlour; one livery bedstead, the best, in the little bed chamber next to the hall furnished with a feather bed and bolster, two feather pillows, one coverlet, one blanket, one pair sheets, one mat and line lying on the said bedstead; two joined stools, one joined back chair, immediately on death of testator's wife. To wife MARGARET all bonds and ready money. Residue of unbequeathed goods to be equally divided between ROBERT, JOHN, MARTHA & MARY, testator's children, on death of testator's wife. To son ROBERT

BEOMANT £30 within one year of testator's death. To son JOHN BEOMANT £30 within one year of testator's death. To daughter MARTHA, wife of JAMES TOOKE, £10 in 1 year of testator's death. To daughter MARY, £10 in one year of testator's death; all monetary legacies to be paid in south porch of Wilby church. Testator is bound in £40 to pay £20 to his daughters MARGARET, SUSAN, MARTHA & MARY within one year of the death of ROBERT GRIMBLE -- testator's wife's uncle. Now executor is charged to provide £20 for these children to be paid within one year of death of testator's wife. To son NICHOLAS BEOMANT all leases, lands and tenements both free and copyhold, he to prove this will within six months of testator's death, and pay all legacies and to be executor. WILLIAM CALVER of Wilby the elder, to be supervisor. Witnesses: WILLIAM CALVER, LAURENCE CALVER, GUY HAYLE, script. Pr. at Yoxford 26 Oct. 1636.

W. ELLEN WOOLNOUGH of Sweffling, widow. 3 March 1635 (1044)

To HENRY, MARY & GRACE CHAPLEN, the three children of testator's brother THOMAS CHAPLEN half testator's goods. To brother HENRY, 40s. and the spit lent to him by testator. To sister ANN BOOTMAN, wife of JONATHAN BOOTMAN £3 in 3 months of testator death. Rest of goods and estate to brother THOMAS CHAPLEN the elder, THOMAS CHAPLEN the younger, WILLIAM, ROBERT & EDMOND CHAPLEN being the sons of THOMAS CHAPLEN the elder. THOMAS CHAPLEN the younger and HENRY CHAPLEN, sons of THOMAS CHAPLEN the elder appointed joint executors. Witnesses: WILLIAM HARVIE, LAURENCE PELLS. Pr. at Wickham Market 11 Oct. 1636.

W. CHRISTOPHER DOWE of East Bergholt, clothier. (1045)
28 June 1636

To kinsman JOHN BARKER, all goods whatsoever, he being executor. Witnesses: ROBERT NUNE (X), RICHARD MUTLEY. Pr. at Ipswich 25 Oct. 1636.

W. ROBERT WYTH of Southolt, yeoman. 12 September 1636 (1046)

To wife ELIZABETH, all household stuff and goods and implements for life; then to be equally divided between sons JOHN & GEORGE WYTH and daughter ELIZABETH BOALES, widow. To grandchild GLAMFIELD BOALES, son of ELIZABETH BOALES, £10 when reaches 21. Brother EDWARD WYTH appointed executor. Witnesses: MARGARET BRADSHAW, JOHN TYLER. Pr. at Saxmundham 12 Oct. 1636.

W. GREGORY WOOD of Wenhaston, husbandman. 2 April 1636 (1047)

Infirm; to be buried at Wenhaston, with a sermon to be made from the said church for the instruction and edification of the people. To wife SIBEL, all goods, chattels, stock and cattle. Also there is due a £100 bond to the testator from his brother

JOHN WOOD of London, of which £80 is left; JOHN WOOD is to pay interest on this sum to SIBEL for her and her children's use. To son PETER £40 when 21. To the unborn child which testator's wife is now carrying £29 when 21. Proviso that if son PETER die before reaching 21, the younger child to inherit his part which legacies to be paid out of the capital sum of £80 by JOHN WOOD; if both children die, then their legacies to go to SIBEL. Stating that a legacy is due from PETER & MARGERY WOOD to their grandchild JOHN ROCHESTER of £11, and that the testator is under obligation to pay this sum; now testator instructs SIBEL to pay this £11 to the said JOHN when he reaches 22, which £11 is to come from JOHN WOOD being part of the said bond of £80. When the legacies of £40, £29 and £11 have been paid, then SIBEL is to give the bond back to JOHN WOOD. To son PETER, bible in quarto embossed with brass. To poor of Wenhaston on the day of his burial 10s. Wife SIBEL appointed executor; JOHN WOOD to be supervisor. Witnesses: NICHOLAS HUNT vicar of Wenhaston; ELLEN GOODDEN (X). Pr. at Yoxford 16 Nov. 1636.

W. BARTHOLOMEW WOODWARD of Offton (N). [blank] July 1636 (1048)

Sick. To wife MARY all estate so long as she remain a widow; if she remarry, then half the estate to his children to be equally divided between them, save that his son should have the better part. Witnesses: THOMAS WOODWARD, DORCAS STYGOLD. Admon. to MARY WOODWARD at Ipswich 23 Sept. 1636.

W. WILLIAM CLUMP of Snape. 20 September 1636 (1049)

To daughter ALICE the barn and the piece of ground on which it stands from the hithermost gate post unto an ash right over against the gate post, and abutting on lands of THOMAS SMYTH on the west. To wife ANNE, house where testator lives, and rest of his lands for life, then these to go to son THOMAS. To son RICHARD £5 when 21. To daughter MARGERY £5 when 21. Rest of movables to wife ANNE, she to pay debts and legacies; also all the tools from the shop, and the shop, and all goods there and all iron, she to be executor. Witnesses: THOMAS HARVIE, MICHAEL CANNON, CHRISTOPHER SMYTH (X). Pr. at Saxmundham 22 Oct. 1636. (Note of the surrender of all copyhold land held of the manor of Snape by WILLIAM CLUMPE through JOHN SMYTH and THOMAS HARVIE, they being witnesses to the surrender.)

W. GEORGE WHINKOPP of Spexhall, yeoman. 24 August 1636 (1050)

In order to pay his debts and legacies specified in will messuage and tenement with all lands thereunto belonging being in Theberton purchased from RICHARD FARROW to be sold by executor within 3 years of testator's death. Then to second son JOHN WHINKOPP £30 when 21. To third son WILLIAM WHINKOPP £30 when 21. To fourth son GEORGE £30 when 21. To fifth son ROBERT £30 when 21. To sixth son LAURENCE £30 when 21. To daughter ROSE £30 when 21. Residue of money to wife MARGARET and eldest son EDMUND, who are appointed executors; they to use the money to bring up his children and pay debts and funeral expenses. Witnesses: PHOEBE WISEMAN, JOHN PLUME, WILLIAM WHINKOP. Pr. at Beccles 16 Sept. 1636.

W. JOAN GESSE, wife of EDWARD GESSE of Sandcroft. 3 May 1632 (1051)

To kinsman JOHN WHALL £10. To kinswoman MARGARET WHALL, sister to the said JOHN, £7. To kinswoman MARGERY, wife of THOMAS FEEKE, £5. To kinsman ROBERT HAYLE £5. To kinsman JOHN FEEKE, son of THOMAS, 20s. To kinsman EDWARD FEEKE, son of THOMAS 20s. To the eldest son of kinsman ROGER HAYLE £3. To JOHN & HENRY FENNE, sons of JOHN FENNE of Weybread, 20s. each. To THOMAS & ELIZABETH LYLLYE, children of STEPHEN LYLLYE of Metfield 20s., equally divided. To SUSAN, the wife of GEORGE HOWLETT, 6s. 8d. To BRIDGET SWAYNE 6s. 8d. To maid servant MARY SAMPSON 6s. 8d. All of these legacies are to be paid within one year of testator's death in the chapel of St. John's in Harleston. JOHN FENNE of Weybread appointed sole executor and he receives 20s. Witnesses: JOHN FENNE, SAMUEL FENNE, JOHN BARBER. Pr. at Yoxford 16 Nov. 1636.

W. HENRY YOUNG of Henley, yeoman. 16 June 1636 (1052)

In order to avoid all suits and controversies between wife MARGARET and his three sons ROBERT, RICHARD & EDMUND, all gifts to wife are made provisionally -- wife MARGARET is not to claim or challenge any gifts of lands in this will, or claim dower on them, and she is to surrender to their sons her right to any dower, to the said sons. If she does this, then son EDMUND is to allow MARGARET to enjoy and occupy the hall and the chamber over the hall, part of the copyhold tenement or cottage in Barham where WILLIAM BROOKE now lives, with a little room standing at the north side of the chimney there, also the yard adjoining unto the same. MARGARET to enjoy the same for life, with free egress and regress for water at the pond in the close there adjoining called Lucens. Also to wife, if she disclaim dower rights, an annuity of £5, and two able cartloads of wood for fuel, to be provided for her by sons EDMUND & RICHARD and delivered to her in the cottage -- EDMUND to provide 50s. of the annuity and one cart load of wood and RICHARD to provide the other half of the annuity and the other cartload of wood; annuity and wood to be made in equal payments on the feast days of Lady [Day], St. John the Baptist, Michaelmas and Christmas, and the first payment to be made on the first feast day which falls first after the testator's death. To son EDMUND, in order to help him fulfill the gifts of annuity and wood, two closes of land in Barham called the Lucens and Crosse close, and also one other piece called the Peeke lying within the lands of Mistress VEER, and also testators barn in Barham. To son RICHARD in order to help him fulfill the gifts of wood and annuity to his mother, the tenement where ROBERT MUDD lives in Barham, with the orchard and gardens, and also the closes and copyhold lands and a little grove next adjoining the said tenement, called Pigtle home close and Bushie close. Also testator's three sons shall yearly deliver unto their mother MARGARET for her life, 3 pecks of good, sweet and clean dressed wheat, 1/2 bushel of malt and also 4 pints of sweet butter; the wheat and malt to be delivered unto her between Christmas and Lady Day, and the butter to be delivered to her between Midsummer and Michaelmas; also each son to pay to MARGARET 2s. each between Midsummer and the feast of St. James, and also to deliver one indifferent cartload of wood for her fuel within one month after Michaelmas. To wife MARGARET a bushel of wheat, bushel of malt, 6 cheeses and 1 ale press on death of testator. Wife MARGARET also to have some convenient room in the house where testator now lives until the Michaelmas next after testator's death, with free egress and regress to take water at the pond. Also wife to have one livery bedstead with a flockbed and a flock bolster lying on the same, 2 pair best sheets, coverlet, a blanket, the best kettle but one, 2 of the best pieces of pewter, the little table in the hall, one hutch, one box and 20s. in 3 months after testator's death; these to be delivered to the cottage in Barham. Son RICHARD also to deliver to MARGARET every year to the Barham cottage, 1 bushel of pears, 1 bushel of apples at the feasts of Michaelmas and St. Bartholomew. All these legacies to wife are however conditional upon her giving up her claims on estates through dower; if she does give up her right of dower, then sons EDMUND & RICHARD are to become bound to MARGARET, in whatever sum two independent men see fit, to pay these gifts. If she refuse to give up dower claims then all gifts to her, to be void. To son ROBERT the meadow purchased from JOHN CHEEKE, gent. To daughter MARY 40s. in 1 year of testator's death. To son ROBERT's children namely HENRY, ANN, ROBERT, MARY & ELLIS £3 each in 2 years of testator's death. To three grandchildren HENRY, ANN & MARY MUDD 40s. each in 3 years of testator's death. To the poor of Henley 10s., and the poor of Barham 10s. Rest of estate to son ROBERT he to be executor, and within 20 days of testator's death, he to enter into bond with WILLIAM BLOMFIELD the younger of Little Stonham gent., in 100 marks, to perform this will, and if he refuse, then he to loose all gifts under the will, and to cease being executor; if so then son RICHARD to have the residue of estate and become executor and enter into bond to perform will. WILLIAM BLOMFIELD appointed supervisor, and receives 20s. Witnesses: JOHN MAPES, ANTHONY BLOMFIELD, SARA ELLETT (X). Pr. at Ipswich 6 Aug. 1636.

W. ELLEN BEARMAN of Woodbridge, spinster. (1053)
10 October 1636

To brother THOMAS BEARMAN £20 in six months of testator's death. To sister-in-law ALICE, wife of THOMAS, a riding suit, that is a safeguard riding coat and hood, presently on testator's death. To nephews THOMAS & WILLIAM BEARMAN, sons of THOMAS, a gold ring each to be delivered to their father THOMAS for their use. To brother WILLIAM BEARMAN one piece of silver plate valued at £5 in six months of testator's death. To brother NICHOLAS BEARMAN £20 in six months of testator's death. To sister MARGARET, wife of ROBERT BEVERSHAM, £20 in 6 months of testator's death. To sister MARY BEARMAN £20 in 6 months of testator's death. To the children of brother-in-law CHARLES BURWELL, namely FRANCIS, CHARLES, WILLIAM, ELIZABETH & MARY £10 each, when they are old enough in years and discretion. To niece ELLEN BALLET, daughter of brother-in-law FRANCIS BALLET, £10, to be given to the said FRANCIS for the use of his daughter in 6 months of testator's death. To sister ELIZABETH, wife of brother-in-law CHARLES BURWELL, rest of goods, she to be executor and to execute these legacies. Witnesses: ROBERT MARRYOTT, ROBERT MANNINGE. Pr. at Woodbridge 28 Oct. 1636.

W. JOHN HYNDES of St.James Southelmham, yeoman. (1054)
19 November 1632

To wife CHRISTIAN, all movables, stock and chattels, she paying out of the same the sum of £90 to such as are named in this will. Also to her all lands, and tenements both free and copyhold, for life being in Metfield, she paying out of these lands to testator's brother THOMAS HYNDES £5 a year; she to commit no waste and to maintain in good repair, and can, if she live on these lands, take wood for her fire, and as much timber as she need for repair, but no more than is necessary. On her death lands in Metfield to go to testator's brother THOMAS HYNDES of Ditchingham, Norfolk, and then on his death, lands to pass to testator's nephew JOHN, son of the said THOMAS of Ditchingham. THOMAS HYNDES to pay out of these lands £140 to persons specified in this will, and should he die before all the £140 be spent, then his son JOHN to continue meeting the legacies herein specified. To brother JEREMY HYNDES £20 to be paid by THOMAS HYNDES one year after the death of testator's wife; should THOMAS also be dead, to be paid by JOHN HYNDES. To sister PRISCILLA ALLDISSE £20 to be paid by THOMAS HYNDES 2 years after death of testator's wife; if THOMAS dead, then to be paid by JOHN HYNDES. To PRICILLA HYNDES, daughter of brother JEREMY HYNDES, £20 to be paid by THOMAS HYNDES in 3 years of death of testator's wife; if THOMAS dead, then by JOHN. To THOMAS HYNDES, son of brother JEREMY, £20 to be paid by THOMAS HYNDES in 4 years of death of testator's wife; if THOMAS be dead, then by JOHN HYNDES. To ROBERT HYNDES, son of brother JEREMY, £20 to be paid by THOMAS HYNDES in 5 years of death of testator's wife; if THOMAS be dead, then by JOHN HYNDES. Benefit of survivorship for JEREMY, PRISCILLA, THOMAS & ROBERT HYNDES. To WILLIAM ALLDISSE, son of brother-in-law JOHN ALLDISSE, £10 to be paid by THOMAS HYNDES in 6 years of death of testator's wife; if THOMAS be dead, by JOHN. To JOHN ALLDISSE, son of brother-in-law JOHN ALLDISSE, £10 to be paid by THOMAS HYNDES in 6 years of death of testator's wife; if THOMAS be dead, then by JOHN. To the daughters of JOHN & PRISCILLA ALLDISSE, £20 equally to be divided between them, to be paid by THOMAS HYNDES, in 7 years of death of testator's wife; if THOMAS be dead, then by JOHN HYNDES. Benefit of survivorship to the ALLDISSE family. To brother JEREMY £20 to be paid by executrix, in 1 year of testator's death. To sister PRISCILLA ALLDISSE, £10 to be paid by executrix, 1 year of testator's death. To the three children of JEREMY HYNDES, namely PRISCILLA, THOMAS & ROBERT HYNDES, 40s. each to be paid by executrix, in 1 year of testator's death. To JOHN ALLDISSE, son of brother-in-law JOHN ALLDISSE, £10 to be paid by executrix in 1 year of testator's death. To the other five children of brother-in-law JOHN ALLDISSE and wife PRISCILLA, £10 -- namely 40s. each, to be paid by executrix, when they each reach 21. To ELIZABETH VEZA, testator's sister and wife of EDMUND VEZA of Bramfield 20s., and to her son RICHARD VEZA 20s., to be paid by executrix in 1 year of testator's death. To RICHARD TUBBYE, the son of testator's wife CHRISTIAN, £15, to be paid by executrix in 3 years of testator's death. To FRANCIS TUBBYE, the son of testator's wife CHRISTIAN, £15, to be paid by executrix in 3 years of testator's death. To BENJAMIN FAYERFAXE, preacher of the gospel at Rumburgh, 40s. to be paid by executrix in 1 year of testator's death. To the poor of St. James Southelmham, if testator be living there at the time of his death, 20s., within 1 month of testator's death. Residue of estate to wife CHRISTIAN, she being appointed executrix, and she to pay all debts, legacies, and funeral charges. Witnesses: WILLIAM SMYTH, SARAH FAYERFAX. Pr. at Bungay 24 Feb. 1636.

W. THOMAS FYNCH of Martlesham, yeoman. 20 January 1635 (1055)

To be buried in Martlesham church yard or church. That testator's supervisors, or three of them, or if they refuse then three other persons, should as soon as possible, make an inventory of testator's goods, and then to deliver the inventory to executors, and that then the executors should sell all the goods for the most money as is possible, and use the resultant sum to pay debts and funeral expenses. The surplus, once these expenses met, to go to wife MARGERY, and to daughters MARGERY, MARY, ELIZABETH & ROSE FYNCH in equal shares. Should ROSE or ELIZABETH be under age or unmarried at the time of testator's death, then exec. to pay their share of the money to supervisors, and that the supervisors should be bound to the said ROSE & ELIZABETH to repay their legacies within six months of their reaching 21 or marriage, and that the supervisors to use the yearly income arising from these legacies, for the maintenance of the said two daughters. Benefit of survivorship to apply to wife and all daughters. Daughters MARGERY & MARY FYNCH appointed executrix, they to perform legacies. Supervisors to be JOHN REDGRAVE of Woodbridge, the elder and a merchant; NICHOLAS REDGRAVE, son of JOHN; WILLIAM FYNCH of Hasketon, yeoman; HENRY LEAKE the elder of Hasketon, yeoman; THOMAS CARR; JOHN POWER; RICHARD TYE of Hasketon, yeoman. Witnesses: JOHN BOORHAM (X), HENRY STYLES (X), RICHARD PERVELL. Pr. at Ipswich 14 Nov. 1636.

W. MARGARET HARVY of Fordley, widow (N). (1056)
[blank] August 1636

Sick. To daughters MARGARET & JANE £20 each. Rest to son JOHN. Witnesses: HENRY PATTRICHE and wife ELIZABETH. Admon. to JOHN HARVIE 12 Jan. 1636.

W. THOMAS MORSE the elder of St. Margaret Southelmham, (1057)
bricklayer. 16 December 1636

Sick; to be buried in the churchyard of St. Margaret's. To daughter ELIZABETH MORSE, one five or six year old milk cow in one year of testator's death. To wife MARGARET, all unbequeathed goods and chattels, provided she maintain and keep daughter MARY, and if she die then wife's executor to provide for daughter. Witnesses: ROBERT DAVIE, JOHN MORSE. Probate granted to MARGARET MORSE at Bungay 19 Jan. 1636.

W. RICHARD CLARKE. 28 December 1636 (1058)

Very sick; to be buried in Shotley. Wife and Goodman KEENE appointed executors. All testator's goods to be divided into three parts -- one third to go to wife, and the remaining two thirds to go to testator's two children. Wife ELIZABETH to have and enjoy all the goods so long as she remain a widow, and to use them to help in the bringing up and maintenance of the children. If she remarry however, she to enter into a bond before her remarriage, with the executors of this will, to pay the legacies to testator's children. Children to receive legacies when 21; benefit of survivorship. Witnesses: JOHN TOMSON, ELIZABETH TOMSON. Pr. granted to ELIZABETH CLARKE at Ipswich 10 Jan. 1636.

W. HENRY BENNETT of Bredfield, yeoman. 2 January 1636 (1059)

Visited with sickness. To wife ELIZABETH, both tenements in Tunstall, and four pieces of land called Crabtree pightle with appurtenances, for life. [Crossed out -- to son JOHN BENNETT £40; to daughter ELIZABETH BENNETT £40.] Wife ELIZABETH to keep property in good repair and maintain the same, with no waste or stripping of timber. If she fail to do this, then exec. to enter lands and use the profits from the lands to maintain and keep testator's wife and children. On death of wife, lands to pass to testator's son JOHN and his heirs. To son JOHN BENNETT £40 when 21. To daughter ELIZABETH BENNETT £30 when 21 or on her marriage. Benefit of survivorship to the two children. All movables to wife ELIZABETH, she to pay debts and funeral expenses from the same; she is also to call in all debts due to him in order to help pay legacies in this will, and if the amount called in as due to him does not cover the legacies, then she is empowered to abate their legacies, so that they can be covered. Wife to use movables to help maintain and keep testator's children. Brother JOHN BENNETT appointed executor. Witnesses:

RICHARD KEMPE (X), ADDARD TAYLOR (X). Pr. at Ipswich 9 Feb. 1636.

W. JOHN HARVIE. 27 December 1636 (1060

Wife appointed executrix of all his goods; she to have goods so long as she remain a widow. If she remarry, then she is only to have a child's part of his estate, and she to pay the rest of the estate to whom she pleases. If she remain a widow she to have the house where NATHANIEL MILES lives, and have all goods at her own disposing. Should she remarry, then her next husband to have no more than a reversion to testator's goods. Three men appointed supervisors; THOMAS HORNE of Lincoln; WILLIAM FRANKES of Shotley; GEORGE MOOR of Ipswich. Witnesses: HENRY KEENE, EDMUND SMITH. Pr. granted to Mistress HARVIE at Ipswich 10 Jan. 1636.

W. PETER HILLS of Woolverstone, fisherman. 2 April 1634 (1061)

To son ROBERT £40, provided he pay his brother PETER £10 in 1 year of testator's death. To daughter MARY £40, provided she pay to brother-in-law WILLIAM MARKHAM £5 when he reaches 24. Rest of household stuff and implements of the household to be equally divided between ROBERT and MARY, but MARY to have the feather bed in the parlour where testator now lies. ROBERT HILLS & MARY HILLS appointed joint executors. Witnesses: THOMAS RICE, JOHN LASBER. Pr. at Ipswich 29 Dec. 1636.

W. ELIZABETH MANING of Ringshall, widow. (1062)
26 February [blank]

Visited under the hand of Almighty God. To eldest son JOHN MANING, all copyhold lands in Ringshall, held of the manor of Linges in Battisford, provided he pay out of these lands £20, namely £5 to testator's daughter ELIZABETH GYE within one year of testator's death, and £15 to RACHEL MANING, testator's daughter, within one year of testator's death. If default, or if he refuse to pay these sums, then power to daughters to enter and enjoy the lands until legacies paid. To youngest son RICHARD MANING, copyhold land in Ringshall held of Ringshall manor provided he pay to testator's daughters ALICE & SUSAN MANING £10 each within one year of testator's death. Power to enter and enjoy these lands if default in the payment of legacies. To three daughters ALICE, SUSAN & RACHEL, all household stuff, equally divided. Rest of goods and chattels, once debts, legacies, and funeral charges met, to go to JOHN & RICHARD MANING and testator's three youngest daughters ALICE, SUSAN & RACHEL, equally to be divided. Note of debts -- 26s. 8d. owed to ELIZABETH GYE; 40s. to daughter RACHEL. Should anyone challenge their legacy, then they loose it. Son RICHARD MANING appointed executor. Witnesses: WILLIAM TOMSON, RICHARD ARCHER. Pr. at Coddenham 16 Aug. 1636.

W. ANN DADE of Crowfield, spinster. 22 October 1635 (1063)

Sick. To brother-in-law WILLIAM DADE, esq. of Tannington £30 in 1 year of testator's death. To cousin ELIZABETH WINGFIELD the elder £30. To cousin ELIZABETH WINGFIELD, daughter of ELIZABETH WINGFIELD, £5. To cousins FRANCIS & MARY WINGFIELD, two of the children of cousin WINGFIELD of Crowfield, 40s. each in one year of death of testator. To FERN, wife of NICHOLAS HILL of Henley 40s. in 1 yr. of testator's death. To all the servants with testator's cousin WINGFIELD 5s. each in 1 month of testator's death. To cousin HERBOTTLE WINGFIELD esq. unto whom I have been very much beholden £30. To sister MARGERY DADE all linen and wearing apparell in 3 months of testator's death. Residue of estate to be equally divided between brother THOMAS DADE and sister MARGERY DADE. HERBOTTLE WINGFIELD appointed executor. Witnesses: THOMAS GOODWYNE, JOHN BLOMFIELD. [Probate cut off].

W. RICHARD GLANFILD of Harkstead, husbandman. 1 January 1636 (1064)

Weak in body. To wife ALICE, messuage and tenement called Bowers, with all copyhold, bought from ROBERT WITTELL, gent. now dead; also all copyhold land held of Erwarton manor, for life; then to go to son JOHN, provided he pay to testator's daughter MARY when she reaches 21 £20 -- if she die before inheriting then son JOHN to pay the sum of £10 to testator's daughter ANN within 3 months of MARY's death. To daughter ANN £10 in 2 years of testator's death. To daughter ALICE RIVERS £20 in 3 years of testator's death. To wife ALICE, 2 of the best cows -- she to choose them; also one bedstead with a feather bed and all things thereunto belonging. Rest of goods to two sons GEORGE & JOSEPH, they to be executors, to pay debts and legacies. Witnesses: JOHN FRELOVE, JOHN HEAD. Pr. at Ipswich 8 Feb. 1636.

W. MARY WATLING of Tannington. 22 August 1636 (1065)

To FRANCIS DADE son to testator's cousin DADE of Tannington £150 -- this sum to be used for his benefit until he reaches 22 when he to inherit; should he die before inheriting then £100 of the money to be divided between the 4 youngest of his brothers and sisters, and £50 to go to testator's cousin DADE. Also to cousin ANNE DADE £50, and to goddaughter HEN DADE £5, and to FRANCES DADE daughter of testator's cousin DADE £50 when she reaches 18 -- but if she die before inheriting then her sister ANN to receive £10 and her other sister ELIZABETH to receive £10 and the remaining sum to be at her own disposal. To cousin THOMAS DADE £3. To cousin WILLIAM DADE £3. To cousin SOONE a silver tankard. To the rest of cousin DADE's children 20s. each. To cousin WINGFIELD of Crowfield £3 to buy him a cup of silver, and to his wife 30s., and to godson a silver porringer. To cousin THOMAS WINGFIELD £20, and to his brother FRANCIS WINGFIELD 30s.; to cousin JEREMY a silver cup; to my sister £5, and to sister SUSAN £5. To cousin BONNAR 20s.; to Mr CLAYDON £10; to aunt

ROSENTON 40s.; to cousin DADE 40s. To GOODY FISHAR 30s. to buy her a silver porringer; to Mr ARTIS 20s.; to MARGARET PARKER 10s.; to Mr LONG's wife 10s.; to cousin ELIZABETH DADE two silver spoons; to PRESELLY WEALS £3 and a pair of sheets and some wearing things fit for her wearing, and to her husband 20s. and to their two sons 10s. each, and to their servants 30s. To the town 30s. Requests to be buried in the night. Executor to be testator's cousin DADE who is to receive £5 and has to perform the various legacies in the will within one year. Testator wrote this will. No witnesses. Pr. at Yoxford 3 Oct. 1636.

W. MATTHEW BOONE of Chediston, yeoman. 20 July 1636 (1066)

To the poor of Chediston 10s. within one month of testator's death, and to the poor of Halesworth 20s. also in one month of testator's death. To son MATTHEW £5 within one month of testator's death. To daughter DOROTHY GYLL an annuity of 20s. a year payable by executor, twice a year, first payment to be made in 12 months of testator's death. To daughter DOROTHY's children £10, to be equally divided; they to receive their legacies within six months of death of their mother if they are over 21. To son-in-law THOMAS SAMPSON 20s. in 1 year of testator's death. To the five children of THOMAS & MARGARET SAMPSON, 20s. to each one now living, to be paid within one year of testator's death; THOMAS SAMPSON to hold sums until each child reach 21. To the children of son RICHARD BOONE 20s. each -- son to have the use of these sums till each child reach 21. To the children of son RICHARD BOONE 20s. each -- son to have the use of these sums till each child reach 21. Son RICHARD appointed executor; brother ROBERT appointed supervisor. To son RICHARD all debts and estate remaining, he to pay legacies, funeral charges and debts; once these paid the surplus remaining to go to him too. Witnesses: THOMAS CRANYLL, SIMON MAN, WILLIAM KNIGHTS. Pr. at Beccles 20 Aug. 1636.

W. JOHN BETTS of Ipswich, musicioner. 25 June 1636 (1067)

To grandchild HENRY VARNISH all movables and money, he to pay to testator's other two grandchildren something in rememberance of testator; and for the assurance thereof this day the testator gave to the said HENRY VARNISH, the bible; testator also gives to HENRY VARNISH the money that is in Master SICKLEMOR's hand, if any remain after testator's death. Witnesses: MARK BRAWLERD, THOMAS COOPER. Admon. to HENRY VARNISH at Ipswich 6 Jan. 1636.

W. JOHN STROUD of Lowestoft, fisherman. 11 May 1636 (1068)

To wife ELLIN, house and tenement in Pakefield for life, she keeping it in good repair; on her death, lands to go to son SAMUEL, provided he pay to testator's other children £5 each, namely to son ROBERT £5 in 1 year of inheriting; to daughter ALICE £5 in 2 years; to son HENRY £5 in 3 years; to son JOHN £5 in 4 years, and to daughter ELIZABETH £5 in 5 years of his inheriting. Benefit of survivorship. The oldest nets to THOMAS LANDEFIELD, SAMUEL STROUD & HENRY STROUD equally. To son JOHN 6 herring nets, 1/2 a dole of mackerel nets ready for the sea. To daughter ELIZABETH 1/2 a dole of herring nets; 1/2 dole of flewes nets, ready for the sea. Rest of goods to wife ELLIN, she to be executrix. Witnesses: HENRY WARD senior; JOHN WILDE, writer. Pr. at Lowestoft 8 March 1636.

W. JOHN MEDDOWE of Newbourne, husbandman (N). (1069)
11 January 1636

To wife MARGERY, all houses and lands in Martlesham for life, and all movables in Newbourne -- she to pay to testator's daughter MARGERY £10 a year when she reaches 20. If wife remarries, she to pay to daughter £10 a year from date of remarriage. To sister ROSE WHITLOCK, wife of WILLIAM WHITLOCK of Waldringfield, £5 in two years of testator's death, and if she too is dead by that time, then £5 to go to her child; if that child is dead too, then £5 to cease. To brother-in-law WILLIAM WHITLOCK 40s. in 2 years of testator's death, provided he useth his wife well. MARGERY MEDDOWE to be executrix. Witnesses: WILLIAM REDGRAVE minister of Newbourne; THOMAS BUTTON of Hemley. Pr. at Ipswich 8 Feb. 1636.

W. THOMAS SHEDWEEKES of Levington (N). 3 December 1635 (1070)

To cousin ANN HUMFREY who lives with testator's uncle HUMFREY of Walton, all money and movables. Witnesses: THOMAS BLICHENDEN, THOMAS VALENTINE. Probate granted to THOMAS BLICHENDEN & THOMAS VALENTINE at Ipswich 6 March 1636. Admon. to ANN HUMFREY 11 March 1636.

W. THOMAS BISHOP of Coddenham, taylor (N). (1071)
25 December 1636

To sister SARAH SPARHAM half testator's estate. Out of this half estate to JOHN & RICHARD CHAMBERLAIN sons of kinsman JOHN £5 each. Rest of estate to MATTHIAS CANDLER, clerk; he to be executor. Witnesses: JOHN DEYNES; JOHN CHAMBERLAIN of Coddenham, gent. Pr. at Ipswich 14 Jan. 1636.

W. THOMAS PALMER of Woodbridge, weaver (N). (1072)
28 January 1636

To brother-in-law ROBERT TOFTS of Woodbridge, with whom the testator lives and where he then lay sick, all his movables and chattels. Witnesses: IDEANNE SEXTEN, GEORGE SPALDING. Probate granted to ROBERT TOFTS at Wickham Market 3 March 1636.

W. THOMAS BRUNDISH of Wickham Market, woollen weaver (N). 14 January 1636 (1073)

To daughter SUSANA CARLOE of Needham Market 20s., due to testator by bond from JOHN COATES of Needham Market. Witness: ELIZABETH BOULTON. Probate granted to SUSANA CARLOE at Ipswich 8 Feb. 1636.

W. JOHN TUTHILL of Framsden, taylor. 29 December 1636 (1074)

To wife MARY, house and tenements in Framsden, with all lands, meadows whatsoever both free and copyhold, for life, in order she might bring up and educate testator's children, and for their, and her, maintenance. On her death, lands to go to son JOHN, provided he pay his sisters MARY, ANN, ELIZABETH, DIONISE & MARGARET TUTHILL £10 each when they reach 21. If default, then the lands to pass to testator's eldest daughter then living, and she to pay £40 to JOHN within 6 months of her inheriting and £10 each to her sisters. JOHN to pay the £10 legacies to his sisters in the south porch of Framsden church; if the sisters be under 21 when JOHN inherits, and have not reached that age within 6 months of their mother's death when JOHN inherits land, then those under 21 have to wait until reach 21. To wife MARY, all movables, she to maintain and educate children; she also to be sole executrix, pay debts. Witnesses: ROBERT SAYER, RICHARD GIRLING, GEORGE STEBBINGE, ROBERT HAYLE. Pr. at Ipswich 11 March 1636.

W. THOMAS BATEMAN of Belton, husbandman. 25 January 1636 (1075)

To wife KATHERINE, house and lands in Bungay for life, provided she keep them in good repair, towards the bringing up and maintenance of testator's children. On her death, lands to go to sons WILLIAM & THOMAS BATEMAN, each son receiving one house each. To daughter KATHERINE £10 when 21, and if default, she to enter into a house and enjoy the same until the £10 be fully paid. Rest of estate to wife KATHERINE, she to be sole executrix. Witnesses: WILLIAM THORN, WILLIAM POPE. Pr. at Beccles 31 Jan. 1636.

W. RICHARD FRANCIS alias FARROW of Dallinghoo, carpenter. 10 November 1635 (1076)

To son-in-law RICHARD ALLDOUS and his wife ANN, houses and lands in Dallinghoo, and all else. Daughter ANN appointed sole executor. Witnesses: THOMAS CHURCH, THOMAS COOPER. Pr. at Wickham Market 2 March 1636.

W. THOMAS WHITTMAN of Harkstead, yeoman. (1077)
22 January 1636

Sick. To each of his three daughters ELIZABETH, SUSAN & KATHERINE £15 when they reach 21; benefit of survivorship. To father CHARLES WHITTMAN, best suit of clothes, immediately on testator's death. To sister ANNA NASE, widow 10s. To sister REBECCA BELT, wife of JOHN BELT, 10s. To sister SARAH WHITTMAN 5s. To kinsman and friend THOMAS THROGGETT 10s. To MARY, the wife of THOMAS BULL, 5s. Wife ELIZABETH appointed sole executrix, she to pay all debts, legacies and funeral charges. Witnesses: SUSAN CONNY, EDWARD DAMERON, THOMAS BULL, THOMAS THROGGET, JOHN BELT. Pr. at Ipswich 8 Feb. 1636.

W. ANNIS MASON of Cookley, widow (N). (1078)
[blank] December 1636

To EDWARD GOOCH & DOROTHY GOOCH all her goods, to see her buried. Witnesses: JOHN BREWSTER & his wife MARY. Probate granted to EDWARD GOOCH at Beccles 21 Jan. 1636.

W. ALICE FAYTHERWETHER of Winston, widow. (1079)
16 October 1635

To the poor of Winston 5s. To son THOMAS £5. To son WILLIAM £5. To son EDWARD £5. To SUSAN, wife of son EDWARD 40s. To PRISCILLA, daughter of son JOHN 40s. To ELLEN, daughter of son THOMAS 40s. To servant JOHN FOSDICKE 10s. To son ISAAC £5 and one flock bed. To the five children of son ISAAC 5s. each. To the two children of son JOSEPH £10 each. To MIRABLE wife of son JOSEPH £4. To son WILLIAM one flock bed with one feather bolster, one flock bolster, one coverlet, one blanket with the bedstead as it stands in the parlour chamber. To granddaughter MIRABEL, daughter of son JOSEPH, best birded coverlet, 4 cushions. Son JOSEPH to be executor, and he to have all goods and chattels in order to deliver these legacies within one year and ten days of testator's death; each recipient of a legacy to give a receipt for the gift or else gift is void. Witnesses: JOHN CRAKNELL, ROBERT TOVELL. Pr. at Ipswich 10 Jan. 1636.

W. RICHARD SHELDRAKE of Sweffling, yeoman. 25 June 1636 (1080)

To wife JUDITH one of my worst featherbeds, one bolster, one coverlet, one blanket, one pillow, one trundle bedstead, one little table in the hall, one feather bed and bolster which testator's man lies on, one coverlet and blanket which was hers, one posted bedstead in the backhouse, one table in the kitchen which is used to mould bread on, one warming pan which was hers, and all the brass which was hers, save one copper and one little brass pot. Also all hemp and hemp seed, 4 combs of wheat, 3 combs of rye, all the oats, 1/2 the barley, 1/4 of the cheese, 1/2 the firkins of butter, and 1/2 the dairy vessels, provided she remain unwed. To son RICHARD one bond of £60 which REYNOLD READ & ROBERT MAYHEW are bound in, each paying £30; also a bond of £20 where DANIEL POTTELL is bound to pay £10; also £10 within one year of testator's death. Also 2 year old brown heifer; 4 pewter platters; 2 pair of sheets, one great chest on the hall -- all of these gifts being given him in discharge of legacies left to him by testator's brother THOMAS SHELDRAKE. To son ROBERT £40 -- being £20 within six months of testator's death, and the further £20 within one year next following; also one comb of wheat, one comb rye, and 2 pair of sheets. To daughter ELIZABETH £40 bond made by JOHN KINGE, gent. whereby he is bound to pay £20; also one bond of £12 whereby LAURENCE PELLS is bound to pay £6 -- these in full satisfaction of legacies made to her by her grandparents SMYTH now deceased. Also one bible, one keep for meat, one down bed, one featherbed, one trundle bedstead that the feather bed lie on, 2 feather bolsters, 2 feather pillows, two coverlets whereof one of them is new, 2 blankets, 2 pair sheets, 4 pewter platters of the largest, 2 other pewter platters, one coffer which was her mothers with all that is in it, one livery table, 2 buffet stools, one desk in the hall chamber, one little spinning wheel, one great milk kettle, one glass keep that was her grandmother SMYTH's, one great chest that was her mother's standing in testator's chamber where he lies; one of the best chairs, all within one month of testator's death; also one calf. To son JOHN, messuage and tenement in Monk Soham, provided he pay brother ROBERT a £5 annuity, due by equal payments on Lady Day and Michaelmas, paid in Soham church porch. If JOHN default, then ROBERT able to enter and hold lands. To servant GRACE CUTTING, trundle bedstead, one of the worst feather beds, one bolster, one blanket, one pair sheets, one coverlet. To grandchild JUDITH SHELDRAKE one of the best weaning calves. To AMOS SPURLINGE one chair, which was his father's. To MARGERY SPURLINGE one posted bedstead remaining at Kettleburgh; also 5s. To THOMAS SPURLINGE, one trunk and 6s. Residue of estate to son JOHN, he to be executor. Witnesses: NICHOLAS BROWN, LAWRENCE PELLS. Pr. at Wickham Market 9 Feb. 1636.

W. NICHOLAS TEMPLER of Ipswich, taylor. 14 March 1635 (1081)

Sickly. To wife SIBELL, all wearing apparell, linen and woollen, and all household stuff which she brought with her on marriage, immediately on death of testator. Also £4 annuity to be paid out of the house in St. Helen's Ipswich, in lieu of dower -- this to be paid her quarterly by even payments by son NICHOLAS; if he default, wife to sue for payments. Also to have all wood, coal and broom which are in the house when testator dies. To daughter MARY, wife of JAMES RAYMOND, and also to daughter MARGARET, wife of ROBERT KETTELLE, all cloth, linen, wool, both new or old, made or unmade, to be equally divided between them. To daughter JOAN, wife of JAMES SMITH, silver carp. To daughter MARY RAYMOND, best bed coverlet. To JAMES RAYMOND, testator's Rennes testament, and all boards in the yard. To ALICE RUSHMER, a bible. Son NICHOLAS to be executor, and to have all things that were his brother CHRISTOPHER's; and also to have all else due to testator, and the rest of the unbequeathed goods. Testator's son-in-law JAMES RAYMOND is to take charge of the will if the said NICHOLAS is away at sea, and JAMES to give an account of all his doings to the said NICHOLAS on his return. Witnesses: GEORGE LYNCH, ALICE WOODE, JAMES RAYMOND. [Probate missing.]

W. MARGARET HUDSONE of Chillesford, widow. (1082)
25 September 1635

To son SAMUEL BALLY, and to daughter JUDY BALLY all the part of testator's house which she owns, and also part of the hempland and all appurtenances in Butley which she owns. SAMUEL is also to pay to testator's daughter MARGARET 40s. in 1 year of testator's death, and daughter JUDY to pay to testator's daughter FRANCIS 40s. in 1 year of testator's death. If any default, then power to those wronged to enter into house and lands. To daughter JUDY all goods and household stuff, she to be executor and to pay debts and burial expenses. Witnesses: DOROTHY FOULSER (X), ROBERT FOULSER. Pr. at Wickham Market 30 March 1636.

W. SUSAN SHEMYNGE of Earl Soham, widow. (1083)
9 November 1636

To son JOHN £9. To grandson JOHN best trundle bedstead with all bedding and furniture; 1 pair of sheets. To grandson THOMAS 20s., and the desk which was his grandfather's. To granddaughter MARY 10s., 1 pair sheets and another desk. To grandchildren SAMUEL, NATHANIEL, DANIEL SHEMYNGE 10s. each. To son THOMAS SHEMYNGE £10, feather bed with a bolster, 2 pillows, pair blankets, coverlet commonly used with the best bedstead of the said THOMAS standing on the buttery chamber; table chair, 2 low buffet stools, green chair and cushion used in the buttery chamber; meat keep; boulting hutch, copper. To daughter-in-law, wife of son THOMAS, one shift of the best wearing linen; 2 of the best pillow beres; best red petticoat. To the child that daughter-in-law is now carrying, little brass pot. To son ROBERT, £10 and all the bedding and movables of testator that are in his custody, also little table with the form belonging to it in the parlour where testator now dwells. To grandchild ROBERT 20s. and the joined chest in the kitchen chamber. To grandchild ANNE 10s. To son MICHAEL £10 and the posted bedstead on the parlour chamber, and all bedding and its furniture. To grandchild ELIZABETH 10s. and the joined chest in the parlour. To son-in-law NATHANIEL ROE 20s. and the great kettle. To grandchild SUSAN ROE £5 and the great coffer in the parlour chamber with all the linen in it. To grandchild THOMAS ROE 10s. To grandchildren NATHANIEL & EDMOND ROE £5; all legacies to ROE grandchildren of money to be paid them, with the yearly interest on same, when reach 21. If they die before reaching 21, then benefit of survivorship. Son-in-law to hold these gifts of money until his children come of age on their behalf, and he is to enter bond of £30 to pay these legacies when they fall due. To brother THOMAS SAVERNE all the debts he owes to testator. To sister-in-law SAVERNE, his wife, red kersey petticoat. All movables which have been bequeathed, to be given within 20 days of testator's death, except the coffer to grandchild SUSAN ROE -- she to receive this when 20. To sons ROBERT & MICHAEL £10 each, in 1 year of testator's death. Sons JOHN & THOMAS to be executors and to pay all debts, funeral and probate expenses. Whatever is then left of her estate to be equally divided between sons JOHN, THOMAS & MICHAEL. Witnesses: EDWARD MOULTON, ADAM SPENCER (X), MARY PEPPER(X). Pr. at Wickham Market 9 Feb. 1636.

W. ELIZABETH UPSON of Battisford, widow (N). (1084)
[blank] October 1636

To EDMUND WHITE of Marlesford, all her estate. Witnesses: JOHN WHITE, HUMFREY BLOSSE (X). Probate granted to EDMUND WHITE at Wickham Market 8 Dec. 1636.

W. FRANCIS HAYLE of Wickham Market, yeoman. (1085)
7 November 1636

To wife ANN, house and lands in Wickham Market, now occupied by the testator, if she commit no waste; she to hold the same for seven years following after testator's death beginning on the first Lady Day or Michaelmas which first falls; also she to hold these lands only if she remain a widow, and she also to pay to testator's son JOHN HAYLE £10 a year by even payments every six months, and the first payment to be made in six months next after testator's death. Wife also to have 2 loads of wood for her firing and can also have the use for the said seven years of all household stuff, which is then to go to son JOHN. Also to wife, 1 weigh of cheese; one firkin butter, 2 combs wheat in the chamber, 2 combs barley; 1 hog; all the hemp; also she to have all her own goods. To son JOHN all lands and household goods after seven years, provided he pay to testator's wife ANNE £5 annuity out of these lands, payable by even payments on Lady Day and Michaelmas, the first payment to be made on the first feast day which falls due after the said seven years. Wife can distrain for payment of this annuity if there be default. JOHN is also to give a fitting allowance for the suitable maintenance of testator's other children HENRY, RICHARD, MARGERY & TOMASINE until they receive their legacies. To daughter MARY, wife of WILLIAM GOODING, £5 within 7 days after the seven years following testator's death. To daughter MARGERY £30 in 2 years following the 7 years after testator's death; also one bed, boulster, coverlet, and 2 pair sheets immediately on testator's death. To daughter TOMASINE £30 in 3 years following the 7 years after testator's death; also one bed, boulster, coverlet, 2 pair sheets immediately on testator's death. To son HENRY £30 when 24. To son RICHARD £30 when 24. If JOHN default in payment of legacies, then he to loose land, and son HENRY to inherit, and to pay the legacies. Rest of estate to son JOHN, he to be executor. Witnesses: MAXIMILYAN SMYTH, THOMAS LAURENCE, WILLIAM HOWELL. Pr. at Wickham Market 8 Dec. 1636.

W. ROGER MEENE of Weybread, yeoman. 7 June 1634 (1086)

Aged and not altogether of perfect health. To wife ELIZABETH, messuage in Weybread, where testator and THOMAS LINCOLN live, called Tagges tenement, with all appurtenances; also part of the commonage called Bromthwayte or Weybread green, lying on the foreside of the said tenement called Tagges, and adjoining thereunto, which has been lately enclosed by agreement between DANIEL de LUIGNE knight and his wife Dame ELIZABETH, and the testator; also testator's meadow lying next to the highway from Fressingfield to Harleston market; wife to hold these lands for life, provided she pay to FRANCIS TAYLOR and his wife ELIZABETH, testator's daughter, £10 a year from the time of testator's death until the sum of £40 be paid. On wife's death, messuage and commonage depasturage and feed of the said piece, part of Weybread common, and all other lands, except Mundes meadow which lies next to the highway from Fressingfield to Harleston, to go to sons THOMAS & NICHOLAS MEENE, and they to pay £40 to the said FRANCIS & ELIZABETH TAYLOR. To wife ELIZABETH, all goods, chattels whatsoever. Mundes meadow had been mortgaged to JOHN BANCROFT of Wingfield for £54 in 1634 and testator wishes his brother SAMUEL MEENE to redeem the same. When it has been reclaimed then the same is to be sold, within one year of its redemption, and the money thus raised to be used to repay testator's brother SAMUEL, and whatever costs and charges it took to reclaim the said land. Further, wife to take £40 out of this money to pay FRANCIS & ELIZABETH TAYLOR, but if this has already been paid by the time of the sale of this said land, then wife to keep this sum; any remaining money from the sale to go to testator's son THOMAS. If however, son THOMAS refuses to allow the sale of the said meadow on reasonable request so to do by testator's brother SAMUEL, then SAMUEL to inherit testator's other lands together with testator's son NICHOLAS on the death of testator's wife ELIZABETH, and gift to THOMAS to be void. Wife ELIZABETH appointed executor; brother SAMUEL MEENE to be supervisor. Witnesses: SIMON TURPIN, THOMAS WALES. Pr. at Beccles 7 Jan. 1636.

W. MYLES RYSING of Beccles, cordwainer. (1087)
27 February 1636

Sick. To eldest son JOSIA, shop and the house adjoining it, and the chamber above them, and all appurtenances, abutting on the north side on GEORGE AUSTEN's lands, and on the west on Northgate street, and so far on until he comes at the next turning in the yard which parteth GEORGE AUSTEN and testator, and so turning on the east until he comes at the way as testator has parted it. To daughter ANN, the next room joining unto it which testator has given to son JOHN as before, with the chamber and all belonging, abutting on the north on that which testator has given to son JOSIA before, and on Northgate street on the west, and on EDWARD CHYTTELLBOROUGH on the south, and so butting on EDWARD CHYTTELLBOROUGH from Northgate street unto Ravenerway, quite through and so according as testator parted it to come down from the one to the other, from Ravenerway to the Northgate. To son JOHN the house abutting on the east on Ravernerway, and on the north on lands of GEORGE AUSTEN with all the other houses belonging as they stand, and so butting on the north on GEORGE AUSTEN and so far on until he comes at the parting of that which testator has given to son JOSIAS before, and likewise butting on that given to daughter ANNE before on the south, and so right on until he comes at Ravenerway. Tenement given to JOSIA to be to him and his male lawful heirs, and if he have none then to his lawful children, equally to be divided between them, provided they keep the premises in good repair; if they fail to keep the said premises in good repair then the said premises to be leased out until JOSIA or heirs repair same. Premises given to daughter ANN to be to her for life, then to her male heirs and their descendants; if daughter have no male heir then premises to go on her death to testator's son JOHN, provided he maintain the same in good repair, for 10 years, and then premises to go to testator's son JOSIA and his heirs. Premises left to son JOHN to be to him and his heirs male, and if he have none, then to his lawful children, provided he keep the same in good repair; if he have no heirs then premises to go to testator's son JOSIA and his heirs, provided they maintain the premises in good repair. All three of testator's children to have free egress from their premises to the well. Wife ANNE to have these three messuages for life, provided she keep the same in good repair. Executor to be JOSEPH HARBOUR, and he is to lock up testator's shop immediately on testator's death, and also to lock up the shop chamber at the same time; the contents whereof to be inventoried, and used to pay testator's debts; also whatsoever in the house which can be conveniently spared to be sold, and also two cows, and mare to be sold to pay debts, and also to provide money for the finishing of the house bequeathed to son JOHN and to make it tenantlike. Rest of goods to be equally divided on the death of testator's wife, between daughter ANNE and son JOHN. JOHN and ANNE to keep well in good repair and allow free use of well between testator's three children. To wife ANNE meadow in Oakestones for life, and two cows; then to go to son JOHN for the residue of the term of years specified in the lease; but if executor does not have enough money from the sale of testator's goods to finish the house before devised to son JOHN, then executor to have this meadow and use the profits therefrom to help finish building the house. To executor 40s. Son JOSIA to keep and maintain a fence to his brother JOHN's part, from his own part unto the end of the house, on condition that testator gives him free passage and entry for a horse through his brother JOHN's ground, and also a cartway so far as ANN's corner; if he refuse to maintain the fence, then he looses these rights. JOSIA is also to give his brother JAMES if he comes again £5 in two installments of 50s. each, within 2 years after his entry to his property; ANN is also to give her brother JAMES if he comes again £5 in two installments of 50s. each within 2 years after her entry to the property; JOHN also to give his brother JAMES £5 in two installments of 50s. each, within 2 years after his entry to the property if JAMES returns. Should JAMES not return, then neither JOSIA, JOHN or ANN is bound to pay this sum, but should

JAMES return and any default in payment is made then power to JAMES to enter the house of whoever has defaulted, and to remain in that house until he receives the full sum of £5. Witnesses: THOMAS EDWARDS (X), AMOS CARTER (X), MILES RYZING (X). Pr. at Beccles 18 March 1636.

W. FRANCIS BALLET of Melton, gentleman. (1088)
1 November 1636

Sick. To son FRANCIS lands called Brickell house where ROBERT HAUGH senior lives in Melton, but executor to have the rents and profits from the premises until son FRANCIS reaches 15, and to pay to the said FRANCIS £10 a year at Lady Day and Michaelmas and executor to use the rest of the money arising from the premises to educate and maintain testator's other children. To daughter MARGERY BALLET £50 when 18. To daughter ALICE, messuage and tenement where BARBARA MORFOLD widow lives in Ufford, when 18; also £40 when 18. To daughter ELLEN messuage where testator lives in Melton when 18, and £20 when 18. To daughter MARY £40 when 18. Benefit of survivorship for children's legacies. Rest of estate to mother MARGERY and to brother-in-law THOMAS BEREMAN, they to pay debts, legacies and funeral expenses and be executors. Witnesses: WILLIAM PRATT, THOMAS BURTON(X), HUMFRIE HARRISON. Pr. at Wickham Market, 8 Dec. 1636.

W. JEFFRY NEANE of Frostenden, miller. (1089)
16 November 1636

Sick; to be buried at Walpole. All debts to be paid by executor, and also funeral charges; then with remaining money executor to fulfill the following legacies. To son JEFFRY £40 when 21; also to pay him 40s. a year until 21 towards his maintainance--payment to be made by equal payments on Lady Day and Michaelmas; first payment on the first feast to fall due after testator's death. To son JOHN £20 when 21. To son WILLIAM £20 when 21. Benefit of survivorship to apply to these gifts to his children. To wife SUSAN, freehold messuage and tenement in Walpole, which testator inherited from his father JEFFRY late of Walpole, also a wind mill on the said land, provided she pay legacies and act as executor; if she refuse then son JEFFRY to enter into the land, and he to pay legacies; if he refuse, then land to go to sons WILLIAM and JOHN and they to pay legacies. To wife SUSAN, all goods and chattels, she to pay debts, and educate and maintain testator's children; she appointed executrix, and JOHN ELLIS, of Frostenden, friend of testator to be supervisor. Witnesses: JOHN ELLIS, EDWARD LOCKWOOD. Pr. at Beccles 21 Jan. 1636.

W. THOMAS BROWNE of Sudbourne, husbandman. 1 July 1636 (1090)

To ROSE MANINGE, wife of JOHN, 40s. in 6 months of testator's death. To MARY BALLY, wife of SAMUEL, 40s. in 6 months of testator's death. To MARGARET DUNN, 40s. in 6 months of testator's death. To ROBERT FOULSER of Orford 40s. in 6 months of testator's death. To the poor of Orford 40s. and the poor of Sudbourne 40s. both in 6 days of testator's death. To ELIZABETH DUNN 20s. in 6 months of testator's death. To SAMUEL BALLY all testator's wearing apparel, save the linen. To THOMAS LAYSTONE 20s. in 6 months of testator's death. To ROBERT MALLINGE 20s. in 6 months of testator's death. To FRANCIS BARNARD 20s. in 6 months of testator's death. To ROBERT WALSINGHAM 20s. in 6 months of testator's death. To the LANKESTER's child, testator's godchild, and to NICHOLAS LASTOR's child and to THOMAS PETTET's child and also the Widow GLOVER's child, all being godchildren of the testator, 10s. each within 6 months of testator's death. To ROBERT TOOKE of Orford, house and lands in Orford, with all movables; he to be executor and pay legacies; if he refuse then ROBERT FOULSER to have the lands & goods and be executor. To JOHN MANNINGE 5s. to buy him a pair of [Rest of will missing.]

W. RICHARD SPATCHETT of Rumburgh, yeoman. 6 July 1636 (1091)

To wife MARY, in virtue of her jointure, lands in Rumburgh for life, which on her death are to go to testator's son THOMAS, as specified in their marriage settlement. Executors to have lands where testator now lives, and the homestalls there belonging, being 4 acres; also one piece of copyhold land called Wyards in Rumburgh, being 12 acres, for seven years beginning the Michaelmas first after testator's death. After the said seven years, lands to go to son THOMAS, provided he let testator's wife MARY enjoy these lands for her lifetime, and if he refuse then testator's son RICHARD to inherit. To son THOMAS £4, the sealed bedstead and mat and coverlet had from testator's father HENRY SPATCHETT, also 4 silver spoons when he reaches 21; also trundle bedstead, feather bed, coverlet, blankets, bolster as it stands in the buttery chamber now used by testator's mother ANN WOODS -- the said ANN to live in the said chamber for term of her life. Executors to have copyhold land in Rumburgh called Brake pightle being 14 acre for seven years beginning the Michaelmas first after testator's death, and after this, lands to go to testator's son RICHARD. To son RICHARD £10 and 4 silver spoons when he reaches 21. To daughter ALICE £20 when 21, but if testator's wife is still alive then, then ALICE has to wait for 6 months after the death of her mother before receiving this legacy. Legacy to be paid by testator's son THOMAS, and if he neglect so to do, then power to ALICE to enter into the freehold land previously given to testator's wife MARY which THOMAS is to inherit; ALICE to occupy this land until she receives her legacy. Also to ALICE £10 to be paid by testator's son RICHARD and if he neglect to do so, then power to ALICE to enter into lands devised to the said RICHARD and hold till payment of legacy in full is made. Also to ALICE, best trunk, a box, and half the wearing linen that was her mother's; also 5 silver spoons when 14. Rest of goods and chattels to be sold, and money thus raised to be used to pay debts and meet legacies, and also used to bind son RICHARD as an apprentice; executors to pay these debts, and funeral charges, executors being testator's wife MARY and GEORGE

DOWNING, they to receive £10. Whatever is then left, to go to testator's son THOMAS. Witnesses: JOHN HUNNE, WILLIAM STANNARD, ALICE FARROW. Pr. at Beccles 19 Nov. 1636.

Glossary To Abstracts Of Some 17th Century Suffolk Archdeaconry Wills

Andirons:	iron bars supporting the ends of log in a fire.
Backhouse:	outhouse or lean-to used for a variety of domestic purposes, and often containing an oven.
Back iron:	fire-back.
Back stiller:	an unidentified occupation.
Ballies:	bellows.
Bandore:	musical instrument similar to a guitar.
Battledore:	i. hornbook for teaching children the alphabet. ii. wooden implement for beating clothes being washed.
Bay:	of a reddish brown colour.
Bayes:	coarse woollen cloth, napped on one side.
Beake iron:	i. the pointed end of an anvil. ii. one of a set of bits that can be slotted into the body of an anvil to provide a working surface suitable in size and shape for a particular task.
Bean knife:	knife shaped like a bean.
Beare/Beir/Bere:	case; e.g. pillowbere—pillow-case.
Bed:	mattress.
Bedstead:	bed.
Bedstedle:	bedstead.
Bereing kettle:	kettle used in brewing.
Billaments:	ornaments, jewellery.
Birded coverlet:	a coverlet, perhaps embroidered with birds; but see also burditt, of which birded may be a corruption.
Blocks:	wood fuel cut into short lengths.
Board-cloth:	table-cloth
Bolt:	bundle of straw weighing 12 or 24 pounds.
Bolting:	sifting.
Bolting-house:	room where flour is sifted.
Bolting-hutch:	box with a sieve base and able to be agitated to sift flour.

Borwte hammer:	Heavy, two-handed hammer.
Braid:	board for pressing curd, being somewhat less in circumference than the vat in which cheese is being made.
Branched stuff:	figured material or fabric.
Brank:	buckwheat, *Polygonum fagopyrum*.
Bread/Breede:	see braid.
Breeds:	bread crocks.
Brendel/Brinded/ Brynded:	coloured a streaky, tawny brown.
Bucking cooler:	wash-tub.
Buffet stool:	generally one of a set of low stools for use at a long table, but may also mean either a high stool or a foot-stool.
Burditt:	a kind of cotton fabric.
Buttery:	store-room for food and relevant utensils and equipment.
Calfer:	calfret—material such as tow or oakum used for caulking the seams of boats.
Cardes:	implements similar to a wire brush, for combing the fibres of wool or hemp.
Carpet cushions:	thin cushions for benches and other forms of seating.
Casting kercher:	meaning uncertain. A casting hood was part of a judge's formal apparel, and some types of kerchief resemble a hood. So perhaps this was a garment for use on special occasions.
Ceiled:	see sealed.
Chappen/Chaffer/ Chafing Dish:	vessel or small enclosed brazier containing hot coals for heating food or keeping it warm.
Chair of easement:	commode.
Chair table:	chair with a solid back which could be turned over to lie flat on the arms, thus forming a table.

Chalder: a measure of coal (36 bushels), or of fish.

Chamber: an upper room. e.g. The parlour chamber was the room *above* the parlour.

Cheese brig: crossed bars of wood resting across the cream pan to support the skimming bowl.

Chenille: soft silken material.

Ches: unidentified article(s) of furniture. Perhaps intended for chairs.

Churn staff: staff within the churn wherewith to agitate the cream till butter is made.

Citterne: a sort of guitar, strung with wire and played with a plectrum.

Cleaver: a short chopper.

Close: an enclosed field.

Close stool: commode.

Cob iron: the rest upon which a spit turns.

Coffer: wooden box with a rounded lid, often covered with leather.

Coif(s): a close cap covering the top, back and sides of the head, worn by women and rarely by men.

Cole rake: a rake to remove ashes.

Comb/Coomb: a measure of grain equal to 4 bushels.

Coper and guild set: an instrument for brewing together with the associated matching equipment required to process a given quantity of liquor in a single operation.

Cord: cord laced across the frame of a bed.

Cordwainer: leather-worker, usually a shoemaker.

Cote: small shed.

Counter (table):
i. a dresser or side-table.
ii. a desk or writing-table for counnting money or doing accounts.

Court cupboard: a two-tiered sideboard, often with drawers to the lower tier.

Coyes: unidentified form of garment. Possible a corruption of coifs.

Cromb:	crome—a wooden handled rake terminating in an iron head consisting of two long, hooked prongs: used to drag manure from a cart.
Crow:	crow-bar.
Cupboard table:	a side table with a shelf or shelves for displaying silver, pewter or earthenware.
Damask:	twilled linen fabric woven with patterns, used for table linen; later a rich silk material.
Danske:	made of spruce imported from Danzig. Danish.
Darneck:	coarse linen fabric used for curtains and hangings.
Diaper:	twilled linen fabric with a small diamond pattern, used for towels, napkins, etc.
Distiller:	apparatus for distilling.
Dole (of herring):	one share of any number of fish divided among fishermen. Much later (18th century) a dole was defined as two nets, each 21 yards in length, and each ship was permitted to carry the number of doles appropriate to its tonnage.
Dornix:	see Darneck.
Drawer (occupation):	a person who draws ale in an inn or alehouse.
Drawing table:	an extending table, the extra leaves sliding under the central portion.
Drift:	a drove-way for the passage of cattle.
Engine:	any mechanical contrivance.
Ewer:	a pitcher with a wide spout.
Falling band:	a pair of strips of thin white material, worn by men around the neck, the ends hanging down in front.
Falling bord:	a board hinged to the wall and supported at the other end by one or two hinged legs. When not in use the board hung flat against the wall.
Far furth:	so long as.
Femble hemp:	hemp from the female plant, considered best for spinning.
Field bedstead:	a collapsible bedstead; a camp bed.
Fillet:	ribbon.

Fire-house:	the kitchen end of a cottage or the dwelling as distinguished from the outbuildings. Probably the only heated room in the house. This term as used in the north of England is equivalent to the East Anglian 'hall'.
Firkin:	a cask holding 9 gallons of liquid or 56 lbs. of butter.
Flewes/flues:	fishing nets.
Flockbed:	mattress stuffed with wool refuse.
Form:	a long seat without a back.
Frise:	thick woollen cloth used for outer garments.
Furrendale (chest):	see Furring deal.
Furring deal:	fixing narrow strips of deal across main spars so as to make a level surface.
Fustian/fuston:	coarse cloth of cotton or hemp or of wool and flax mixed.
Gorgett:	a piece of armour covering the throat.
Graining knife/ board:	used by tanners and skinners for stripping hair from hides.
Gript (kettle):	one with a handle.
Grogan:	coarse fabric of silk and mohair.
Gymmers:	i. hinges. ii. two-year-old ewes.
Hake/Hale:	iron bar over a fire, from which pot hooks hung.
Half-head (bed):	bed with headboard but not tester.
Hayre:	hair cloth; coarse fabric made from horsehair and used for drying malt over a kiln.
Heale (net):	? a net woven in a particular manner.
Heare (cloth):	see Hayre.
Hedgebote:	allowance of planting material for establishing a hedge.
Hempland:	field where hemp is grown, usually of small area.
Hogshead:	a 56 gallon cask.
Holland (sheets):	fine linen cloth; material from Holland being equated with good quality.

Horsemill:	a mill powered by a horse walking in a circle and harnessed to a beam connected to gearing.
Hose:	breeches and stockings treated as a single garment.
Hutch:	a light chest for clothes etc.
Insett (house):	?? occupied houses.
Iron pitch:	a crowbar with a square pointed end, used for making holes in the ground to receive hop-poles.
Jack:	mechanical device for turning the spit when roasting meat before a fire.
Joined (furniture):	with the frame morticed and tennoned.
Keeler/keller:	a shallow pan or tub in which liquids, especially milk, are set to cool.
Keep:	a food-safe or small storage cupboard.
Kercher/kerchief:	a garment worn round the neck or over the head by women.
Kersey:	coarse woolen cloth.
Kettle:	an open cooking pot with a handle to suspend it over a fire.
Kiln:	oven.
Kirtle:	a gown or outer petticoat worn by women, or a jacket by men.
Knop:	a flower bud.
Laten/latine:	an alloy of copper and zinc.
Laun:	fine linen.
Lead:	a vessel made of or lined with lead, used for brewing or pickling.
Leete (four-way):	a cross-roads.
Linbeck:	limbeck, a still for making liquor.
Line:	the cord laced through holes bored horizontally in the frame of a bed, making a network on which to lay a rush mat.
Line boat:	boat used for fishing with a line.
Linsey wolsey:	cloth made from a mixture of linen and wool.

List:	the border or selvedge of cloth; strips of cloth.
Livery bed:	bed for servant.
Livery Cupboard:	cupboard with perforated doors for food storage.
Livery table:	one on which livery (i.e. rations) were placed.
Loom work:	woven material.
Loue (chamber)	unexplained.
Mantle:	loose cloak.
Matts:	rush mats that lay between the cord (q.v.) and the mattress.
Maser/maxer:	a drinking cup without a foot, of hardwood usually mounted in silver.
Messuage:	dwelling house, usually with outbuildings and land assigned to its use.
Miele:	a sandy stretch of land.
Morden:	marten fur.
Moreen:	stout corded stuff, woollen, cotton or both.
Murry:	mulberry or morello coloured.
Napery:	household linen, especially that for the table.
Natt:	a straw mattress.
Neat:	bovine cattle.
Occamy:	an alloy harder than pewter.
Pashel:	beetle, heavy wooden mallet.
Peale/peel:	long-handled implement for passing loaves into or out of an oven.
Pewke:	superior woollen cloth of sombre hue.
Philli and chena:	possible fillet and chenille—ribbon and a soft silk material.
Pickell:	see Pightle.
Pieced (kettle):	patched, mended.
Pightle:	a small field or enclosure.

Pilleon:	Pillion, a pad or small saddle attached to the rear of the saddle proper, to accommodate a second rider, usually a woman.
Pillow bier:	pillow-case.
Platter:	flat dish or plate of earthenware, wood or metal. Porringer: a small dish with upright sides.
Portman (of Ipswich):	There were twelve portmen. After the two Bailiffs they were the most senior members of the borough court.
Posnet:	small metal pot with a long handle and three feet, for boiling.
Press:	large cupboard with doors and usually shelves, for keeping clothes, linen, books etc., sometimes placed in a recess in the wall.
Prick-horned:	erect or pointed horns.
Poke:	sack
Pot-hooks:	hook and chain attached to a bar in the chimney, from which cooking pots were hung.
Powdering tub:	a tub in which meat was salted to preserve it.
Quarte:	skirt.
Quern:	hand-mill for grinding grain.
Remble:	a measure of hemp.
Rost iron:	roasting iron.
Rug:	rough woollen material.
Sack:	a lady's loose gown.
Safe:	a food-cupboard, usually with sides of woven hair for ventilation.
Safeguard:	an outer skirt or petticoat, worn by a woman, over a Kirtle as a protection against dirt while riding.
Saucer:	a dish for holding sauce.
Say(e):	i. serge, a fine twilled fabric made of wool, used for bed-covers, hangings, table-covers etc. ii. a thin kind of silk.
Scuppet:	a broad wooden shovel.

Seaming laces:	laces for joining two edges of cloth.
Sealed/seiled:	ceiled, panelled.
Seeled (bedstead):	bed with a canopy of wood or cloth.
Set net:	fishing net held stationary.
Settle:	long wooden bench, usually with arms and a high back, with a locker underneath.
Shag:	i. Matted wool or hair. ii. Cloth with a long nap.
Shaves:	tools for shaving or scraping wood.
Sheld/shield/(cow)	piebald, particoloured.
Shoat/shote/shott:	a young pig.
Shredding (coverlets):	made from small pieces of cloth; patchwork.
Sillere:	possibly from Sile or Syke, a strainer (usually sile dish).
Singleband:	belt.
Skep:	straw beehive.
Skillet:	cooking vessel with three feet and a long handle.
Skimmer:	utensil for skimming milk, or a cooking ladle.
Skoales:	wooden dishes or basins.
Skors:	scores. As applied to fishing nets, it meant scores of meshes. Herring nets had a one-inch mesh. So a net of 9 scores was 180 inches deep.
Slayes:	the part of a loom through which pass the warp threads.
Slop:	baggy breeches.
Specialty:	a contract for the payent of money.
Spit:	a slender pointed rod of metal or wood, used for thrusting through meat to be roasted as it rotated on the spit before the fire.
Sponge:	i. a long narrow strip of enclosed land. ii. a low bog.
Spurling (net):	sprat net.

Spur(re) r(o)yal:	gold coin worth 15s.; so called because of the device on the obverse which resembled a spur.
Stammel(l):	fine worsted cloth.
Stander:	standish—a metal tray for pens, etc.
Stond:	stand.
Stool work:	chair work.
Stowings:	loppings of a pollard tree.
Stub:	'a load of wood at the stub' was probably coppiced wood.
Stuff:	woollen fabric without pile or nap.
Stythe:	anvil.
Surroyal:	see Spur royal.
Tammy:	worsted cloth worn by working class women, originally made at Tamworth.
Tan vat:	in which hides and skins were tanned.
Tawny:	light yellowish brown.
Tester/Teston:	canopy over a bed, made of wood, often carved, or of fabric.
Tester (of the hour):	perhaps an hour-glass.
Termin:	end.
Thaxter:	thatcher.
Theave:	ewe of the first year.
Tipped (Pot):	? with a lip to aid pouring.
Towcomb:	for separating fibres of tow, hemp etc.
Trammel:	i. net. ii. a bolster.
Travis:	the frame upon which were placed bobbins from which yarn was wound onto a warping mill.
Trencher:	flat wooden dish or plate.
Trivet:	tripod metal stand for a pot or kettle, before or over a fire.
Truckle/trundle (bed):	a low bed on wheels that could be pushed under a high bed when not in use.

Tumbling churn: a revolving barrel containing emery powder, in which castings were cleaned by friction.

Tumbrel buck: the body of a cart or waggon.

Tumbril: a two-wheeled tipping farm cart.

Tun/Tunne(r): large cask.

Tunmere: the processional route in a perambulation of parish boundaries.

Turned (chair): with turned legs and back.

Underbecke: the outshot of a spout.

Uphand hammer: heavy hammer requiring two hands to wield it.

Use: in some contexts means the interest on money.

Valence: border of drapery hanging from the canopy of a bed.

Vantage: profit.

Vanx ruff: vance-roof, garret, attic.

Verges: borders.

Verdners (coverlet): unidentified. Perhaps green baize.

Vialls: a stringed musical instrument, played with a bow.

Virginals: a keyed musical instrument, similar to a spinnet but without legs.

Wainscott: wooden panelling on walls or furniture.

Way: a track as opposed to the king's highway.

Weigh/Wey/Way: a measure of cheese of variable weight, 2 to 3 cwt.

Wheel: spinning wheel.

Wheel-lock: a lock for firing a gun by means of a small steel wheel.

Writings: often means documentary evidence of title to property, both real and personal.

Bibliography

The principal sources consulted when compiling this glossary were:

Antiquary, The, Vol.XXXVI, 1900.

Baker, A., *Glossary of Northamptonshire words and phrases*, 1854.

Buckland, F., *Report on the Fisheries of Norfolk*, 1875.

Clinch, G., *English costume from prehistoric times to the eighteenth century*, 1909.

Cunnington, C.W. and P., *Handbook of English medieval costume*, 1952.

_________, *Handbook of English costume in the 16th century*, 1962.

_________, *Handbook of English costume in the 17th century*, 1966.

Cunnington, C.W. and P. and Beard, C., *A dictionary of English costume 900–1000*, 1960.

Fairholt, F. W., *A glossary of costume in England to the end of the 18th century*, 1970.

Festing, Sally, *Fishermen*, 1977.

Fisher, J. L. *Medieval farming glossary, Latin and English*, 1968.

Halliwell, J.O., *A dictionary of archaic and provincial words*, 4th edition, 1860.

Jenkins, J.T., *The Sea Fisheries*, 1920.

Millward, Rosemary, *A glossary of household, farming and trade terms from probate inventories*. Derbyshire Record Society occasional paper No. 1, 2nd edition, 1982.

Norfolk and Norwich Naturalists' Society, Vol. III containing "Notes on the herring fishery of 1884" by Thomas Southwell.

Norfolk Archaeology—Vol. V, 1859; Vol. XV. 1903; Vol. XX, 1921.

Northeast, Peter, *Boxford Churchwardens' Accounts 1530–1561*, Suffolk Record Society Vol. XXIII, 1982.

Oaks, Alma and Hill, M.H., *Rural costume*, 1970.

Oxford English Dictionary, 1933.

Reed, M., *Ipswich Probate inventories 1583–1631*. Suffolk Record Society Vol. XXII, 1981.

Steer, F.W., *Farm and cottage inventories of mid-Essex 1635–1749*. Essex Record Office publication No. 8, 1969.

Wright, J., *The English dialect dictionary*, 1898.

Yarwood, Doreen, *English costume*, 1972.

Index of Persons

Similar spelling of surnames, e.g. Blomefeild/Blomfeild, Colchester/ Coulchester and Fairewether/Faytherwether have generally been combined, but all spelling variations should be checked. Names are indexed by Will number. The asterisk (*) denotes a testator/testatrix. Abbreviations used in the index: (Wid.), widow; (Gdmn.), goodman; (Gdwf.), goodwife.

Index of Places

This is an index primarily of Suffolk parishes. Names of hamlets, manor-houses, streets, bridges, parsonages, mills, inns, commons, marches and greens are indexed under parishes in which they lie. Parishes not in Suffolk are brought together under their respective counties, e.g. ESSEX.